CW00375542

**introduction to
BUSINESS**

introduction to
BUSINESS

SECOND EDITION

RICHARD D. BROWN   **GEORGE J. PETRELLO**
Northern Illinois University   Wagner College

glencoe publishing company, inc.
Encino, California
Collier Macmillan Publishers
London

Cover photo: Ron Scott

Glencoe Publishing Co., Inc.
17337 Ventura Boulevard
Encino, California 91316
Collier Macmillan Canada, Ltd.

Library of Congress Catalog Card Number: 77-094763

1 2 3 4 5 6 7 8 9 10   83 82 81 80 79

ISBN 0-02-471310-4

BRIEF TABLE OF CONTENTS

DETAILED TABLE OF CONTENTS

9   GETTING THE RIGHT MARKETING MIX   209

PREFACE

APPROACH OF THE BOOK

This text, and the supplementary materials that accompany it, are designed for the introductory business course at the college level. The entire program focuses in general on the functions of business and emphasizes in particular the role of business in the economy and in society.

The aim of this text is to give the student a thorough introduction to the functions of marketing, management, finance, and the forces influencing business decisions in these areas. Special attention is given to the management tools of accounting and information systems. All of these topics are examined within the general theme of the economic and social forces affecting the business environment, forces such as government, international competition, ecological concerns, consumer demands, and labor relations.

With such an array of topics, the approach to the subject of business could take one of numerous forms. Some authors prefer to divide the study of business into very short chapters, each chapter on a separate topic. Others take a systems approach, relating almost every topic to systems analysis. This text takes an eclectic approach, choosing the best characteristics of both these methods.

In any business text, the authors must also decide whether to stress the theoretical or practical approach. Again, we have chosen the best characteristics of both these approaches. Basic theories or principles are set forth for all major topics, and then they are related to real world examples of business implementing these theories in current operations.

It must also be decided how much use to make of charts, graphs, and illustrations. At one extreme is the text with few illustrations, which relies mostly on the written text as the sole instructional tool. At the other extreme is the text that is nothing more than reprinted articles, cartoons, pictures, graphs, and charts, without an integrated set of concepts for the students to learn. Pedagogical aids such as charts, graphs, personality profiles, and business profiles are part of *Introduction to Business*. Their purpose is to attract students' attention and make the book highly readable. More than this, however, these elements are clearly related to the concepts presented. Every one of the illustrations is integrated with the text and highlights a point made in the text.

ORGANIZATION OF THE BOOK

Introduction to Business is divided into seven parts.

Part 1, "The Role of Business," introduces the student to the role of business in the economy and in society. Chapter 1 discusses the role of business in the economy. Chapter 2 explores how business causes and adapts to change in society and the role of profit in the American economy. Chapter 3 explores the relationship between business and society.

Part 2, "Management," takes a look at the management function in business. Chapter 4 focuses on starting a business firm and choosing a form of organization. Chapter 5 emphasizes the principles of management that are important in managing any organization. Chapter 6 summarizes the factors in operating a small business, with a special section on franchising.

Part 3, "Marketing," describes the marketing function. Chapter 7 emphasizes the development of marketing strategies. Chapter 8 discusses consumer behavior and the importance of marketing research. Chapter 9 analyzes the development of the marketing mix. Development, production, and distribution of products and services are surveyed in Chapter 10.

Part 4, "Finance," looks at the sources and uses of funds. Chapter 11 examines the methods for obtaining the funds needed to make profits. Chapter 12 explores the sources of funds, such as the security exchanges.

Part 5, "Information Systems," focuses on quantitative tools used by management in making decisions. Chapter 13 explains why computers and quantitative analysis techniques are used by business managers. Chapter 14 surveys the use and interpretation of accounting and legal data.

Part 6, "Human Relations," discusses the working relations between individuals in organizations. Chapter 15 examines the personnel management function and Chapter 16 looks at labor-management relations.

Part 7, "Business Environment," analyzes the forces affecting the business environment for managers. Chapter 17 explores business and government relations. Chapter 18 looks at international business and economic forces affecting U.S. firms. Insurance needs for business owners are covered in Chapter 19. Chapter 20 projects the future for business and job seekers.

OUTSTANDING FEATURES OF THE BOOK

CONTENT The functional areas of business are explored in depth. Thus the student can build an adequate background for further study in business. Marketing and management as functional areas are covered especially thoroughly. Four chapters are devoted to marketing, a major area in the business world and one in which students show keen interest. A new chapter on marketing strategies highlights this section. In the management segment, there is a unique chapter on operating small businesses and franchises. On other topics, Chapter 2, "Dynamics of Business," examines the general risks and rewards of operating a business. Chapter 18, "International Business," has a timely discussion of increasing competition from foreign firms. The last chapter, "The Future—For Business and Job Seekers," creatively blends future projections for American businesses and industries and the implications for those planning careers in business. The three appendices are on topics not covered in the text, but are nevertheless vital to students studying business. The topics are using the library, finding a job, and understanding metrics.

READABILITY To be valuable as a learning tool, a text must be clear, understandable, and interesting to the student. This edition is all of these things. Its reading level is appropriate for most freshmen and sophomores in college as well as for adult students.

SPECIAL FEATURES At the beginning of each chapter performance objectives capsulize for the student the important topics in the chapter. Chapter previews set the stage for learning. The summaries at chapter end bring major topics together in a brief, precise statement. Testing apparatus for each chapter has been reorganized from the first edition. There are ten review questions, five discussion questions, and three case studies. The first two groups of questions are useful for testing student understanding and retention of concepts. The case studies permit the student to apply the concepts that have been learned to real business problems.

TOTAL LEARNING PACKAGE *Introduction to Business* consists of a textbook, Instructor's Manual, Study Guide, a test bank, and a set of transparencies. Each element of the learning package can be used independently or as part of a total program. The Instructor's Manual contains a substantial amount of information on planning, organizing, and teaching the course. The test bank consists of two forms of 25 questions for each of the 20 chapters and also two forms of mid-term and final exams. The Study Guide, which is sold separately from the text, is a valuable source of self-check questions, discussion questions, and case studies. Answers to chapter questions will be found at the back of the Study Guide.

ACKNOWLEDGMENTS As with most textbooks, this text has been a team effort. There are many individuals who have helped to improve the book. Our thanks go to the following individuals who have reviewed the manuscript or made suggestions for improvement from the first edition of the text: Dr. Robert Listman, Valparaiso University; Dr. Jack Sterrett, Fort Hays (Kansas) State College; Terry Lindenberg, Rock Valley College; Dr. Steve Jennings, Highland Community College; John Manzer, Northern Illinois University; Gene Beckman, Jefferson Community College, University of Kentucky; and Don Busche, Saddleback Community College. We have particularly appreciated the excellent editorial help that we received from Peter O'Brien, the development editor of Glencoe Publishing Co., Inc.

We are grateful to Dr. Louis C. Nanassy, Professor of Business Education, Montclair State College, Montclair, New Jersey, for bringing the authors together as a writing team. We owe a debt of thanks to the many business firms and government agencies that have given permission to reprint cartoons and other illustrations.

Finally, but most importantly, we acknowledge the efforts of our wives and families in the project. We have appreciated their willingness to sacrifice time that we might have spent together but which went instead into the project. To Carol Brown and children, Michele and Michael, and to Barbara Petrello, go our heartfelt thanks and appreciation.

While all of the above persons deserve credit for making the final book better than it would have been without their help, the authors are responsible for any omissions or inaccuracies. If you have suggestions for improvement, we would appreciate a note letting us know your thoughts.

Richard D. Brown
George J. Petrello

part one

THE ROLE OF BUSINESS

Business is an exciting and controversial part of our lives. Most of us eventually work in some form of business since that is where most jobs are. All of us will be critical of it at times because companies are not meeting our needs satisfactorily. We cannot ignore business, for its products and services shape our style of life. In this setting, it is natural to be both critical of and dependent on business. Everyone is.

At the same time, a number of economic and social forces influence what business can do. The auto industry was very profitable until environmental legislation and an oil shortage combined to cut drastically sales and profits. Sugar processing was a fairly low-profit industry until the Arabs and Soviet Union bought record amounts at a time when world supplies were small. The price quickly multiplied and profits soared. These are vivid examples of the effect of economic, social, and political forces on the operation of business.

In Chapter 1, you will examine our economic system to get an understanding of the underlying economic forces at work. This will be helpful to you later as you learn how these forces influence business and the welfare of the consumer and worker. In Chapter 2, you will take a look at why business is dynamic. You will gain insights into the problems of dealing with a business firm or with an industry in which there is a great concentration of firms. There are many controversial issues here for discussion.

In Chapter 3, you will look at society's efforts to reshape business to better serve consumer demands. At the same time, you will gain insight into the problems and rewards business faces in trying to move from purely economic ends to both social and economic goals. This involves many economic and social problems with which you will become involved as citizens.

This section should prepare you for an in-depth study of business and the environment in which it functions. These constraints affect the operations of all business firms that you will study in later chapters.

chapter 1

BUSINESS IN THE ECONOMY

OBJECTIVES

When you have finished reading and studying this chapter, you should be able to:

1. Describe the roles of markets, prices, profits, and competition in the American economy.

2. Name the sectors of the economy and explain their importance, especially the business sector.

3. Contrast and compare our economic system with that of other leading industrialized societies, especially how economic decisions are made and who receives the benefits of production.

CHAPTER PREVIEW

During the early 1970s, the United States and most other industrialized countries suffered unusually high rates of unemployment and inflation. As a result of this double-barreled situation, our economic system came under strong critical attack. Some economists insisted that we needed stronger governmental control over the economy. Others insisted just as firmly that the exact opposite was true: that all economic decisions should be made without governmental interference. Consumers and workers were frustrated because they felt powerless to influence the economy.

The much-talked-about energy crisis has reminded everyone that every country faces the problem of economic scarcity. Every country has unlimited wants and limited resources with which to produce the goods and services demanded by its people. As a result, some type of economic system must be developed to allocate resources efficiently to meet a people's needs.

In the United States, business responds to the demands of consumers by gathering the needed resources and using them to produce goods or services for a profit. If a firm has correctly interpreted consumer wants and been efficient in using the resources, it usually makes a profit. If it misinterprets wants, or is inefficient, the business will probably fail. Adequate competition among businesses is necessary so that firms do not take advantage of consumers. Whether or not adequate competition exists in some industries is a very debatable issue.

Although it is popular to compare economic systems using such categories as capitalism, communism, and socialism, such comparisons are inadequate. A division of economic systems into command and market economies, depending on how their basic decisions are made, is a more effective comparison.

"Well, I don't know how the government's economic indicators are doing, but ours is in a heck of a shape."

Business is central to the American way of life. It employs three out of every four working Americans and serves as the backbone of our economic system. It provides products and services in numbers unequaled in any other country in the world. American business now produces over $2 trillion ($2 thousand billion) worth of products and services a year—a staggering average of almost $10,000 for every American. What is business? How does it function? How does the American economic system differ from other countries' systems? The answers to these questions will be explored in this chapter.

THE ROLE OF BUSINESS

There are about 12 million businesses in the United States. A *business* can be defined as any organized effort to produce products or supply services demanded by people for the purpose of making a profit. Also, business can be used as a general term to refer to all of the businesses that produce products or supply services. General Motors, McDonald's Restaurants, your local dry cleaner, and your family doctor are all in business.

PRODUCING PRODUCTS

Businesses produce products or services. A *product* (or *good*) is any tangible item such as a table, a watch, or an automobile. To produce a product, a business has to use certain resources. These resources are sometimes called the means of production, but are more frequently referred to as the *factors of production*. The factors of production are land, labor, and capital (Figure 1-1).

Land includes all the natural resources used in production. Among these resources are earth, water, coal, oil, metals, and forestry and agricultural products. Many businesses are located where they are because they have easy access to natural resources. For example, to a large extent the American steel industry is located in or near Pittsburgh, Pennsylvania, because it is close to coal and iron ore resources. All steel, aluminum, and glass producers are located near major sources of water because water is used in producing these substances. Locating a firm near energy resources, such as a coal pit or a natural gas well, cuts the costs of production.

In its most general sense, *labor* means all the workers in a country. These include assembly-line workers, electricians, farmers, secretaries, and office man-

FIGURE 1-1 Factors of production

1. Land

2. Labor

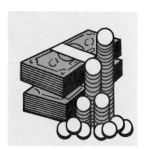

3. Capital: funds and facilities

agers. Businesses usually locate where an appropriate labor force exists. Manufacturing firms frequently locate their plants near cities to be near a large number of potential workers. Electronic firms have found it desirable to locate near major universities specializing in science, such as the Massachusetts Institute of Technology and Stanford University. Some textile manufacturers have moved to the South to be near its lower cost, dependable factory workers.

Capital is the plant and equipment used to produce goods or services. It is also the money with which to buy these items. For many types of new firms, capital expenses are the largest part of the cost necessary to start operations. For a retail store capital would include the premises, cash registers, counters, shelves, and delivery trucks. For a manufacturer, capital would include the plant, trucks, machinery for making items, and the equipment for moving materials.

Consumer and Industrial Products Business produces two types of products: consumer products and industrial products. *Consumer products* are products manufactured for sale to a member of the public. A deck of cards, a bottle of ginger ale, a television set, and a radio are all examples.

Industrial products are items sold to other businesses. Examples would be cash registers, forklift trucks, and canning machines. Industrial products are also items sold to a business for assembling, processing, packaging, or modification. Fresh vegetables bought from farmers by canners would also be an example of an industrial product.

Some products can be consumer products and industrial products, depending on who buys them. A typewriter, for example, can be sold directly to a consumer but it can also be bought by a business. Likewise cars, trucks, cleaning materials, plumbing supplies, or drills can be consumer or industrial products.

PROVIDING SERVICES

A *service* is the performance of work by a business for pay. This work might be done for a consumer or for another business. Cutting hair, cleaning carpets, and repairing automobiles are examples of services performed for a consumer. Processing accounting records, cleaning offices, and renting delivery trucks are examples of services performed for businesses.

THE PROFIT MOTIVE

If the organizer of a business is correct, the business will be meeting a public demand for a product or service and have an opportunity to make a profit. A *profit* is money gained by selling a product or service for more than it cost to produce or supply. Profit provides the incentive for meeting the demand, but there is no guarantee that a new business will ever make a profit. A business may accurately assess that a demand exists but still not make a profit. Producing something that is in sufficient demand contributes toward a profit but effective management is also an important consideration. If costs are too high there won't be any money left

Small appliances, such as these blenders, coffee makers, and irons on display in a department store, are consumer goods.

Monkmeyer Press Photo Service

Aluminum metal is manufactured in large rolls. These rolls are processed into many kinds of products by other manufacturers. In rolled form, the aluminum is an industrial good.

American Iron and Steel Institute

Airplane travel is a service. Here, passengers queue up for baggage check-in at the air terminal.

Camerique

after the costs of production are paid. Thus, no profit. Also important is what competing businesses do. Two businesses could provide an almost identical product at the same price, but if consumers buy from only one company there won't be any profit for the other.

Operating a business always involves financial risk. Money must be spent to hire workers, buy or lease property, acquire equipment and produce something salable. If the firm does not correctly foresee the public's wants or serve them well, there will not be any profit. And, as we shall see, the individuals in the business may lose all of their money. Only if a business wisely anticipates the type of product or service demanded and effectively manages the process of providing it will it ever make a profit.

THE IMPORTANCE OF PROFIT

A business firm hopes to earn a profit by producing products or providing services in response to a demand from buyers.

Profits represent

1. The basic goal of the firm and its means of continued existence.
2. Incentive for efficiency.
3. The standard of comparison with other firms.
4. A source of government revenue.

Usually if a firm's profit declines when compared to the previous year's figures, management will make changes. In most industries, financial data on all firms in the industry is available so that each company can compare its profit with others in the same industry. For example, the supermarket industry normally makes about a 1 percent profit on gross sales. This is meaningful when comparing A&P's profit rate to Safeway's. It is irrelevant to compare A&P's profit rate with that of a manufacturing firm where the gain on sales may average about 5 percent. About 14 percent of the federal government's income comes from corporate income taxes on profit.

RESPONDING TO THE MARKET

Business produces products and services for which there is a consumer demand and sells them in the market to buyers. Demand is created by people who have the means to buy goods and services. There may be millions of people who would like to live in more expensive homes or wear better-made clothing, but unless they can back up their wants with money or credit, business won't respond. Business can meet demand only if it can sell its products or services in a market and make a profit by doing so. A *market* is any place in which buyers and sellers get together. Examples of markets include the New York Stock Exchange, produce markets, farmers' markets, swap meets, and garage sales. Phone calls and letters are also markets. The term *market* is also used to describe all potential buyers of a product or service. Buyers include consumers, government, business, and foreign buyers.

Commodities such as corn, wheat, and lifestock are bought and sold in markets like the Chicago Commodity Exchange.

Becky Roller

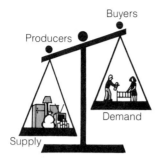 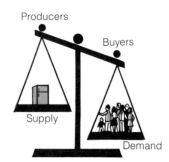

FIGURE 1-2 The price mechanism: supply and demand

DETERMINING PRICES

There's a simple way to explain how prices are determined in our country, though the example is oversimplified. If a great number of homemakers decided to buy chicken and demanded more chicken than was being supplied, the price would rise. If, on the other hand, people got bored with eating chicken and demanded fewer than the supply, the price would drop. If nobody wanted them, their value would be zero. The prices paid for the same chicken reflect the interaction of supply and demand. When there is a great supply of something in demand the price is relatively cheap. Conversely, when there is a short supply of something in demand, the price is relatively expensive. This principle is known as the *price mechanism* (see Figure 1-2).

Prices are signals to business people of a strong or weak demand for a particular product or service. This may alert them to profitable opportunities that normally accompany an increasing demand for a particular product.

THE ROLE OF COMPETITION

Competition is not the same as supply and demand. Supply and demand represents a relationship between buyers and sellers of a product or service. Competition refers to a relationship between sellers *and* between buyers and sellers. Supply and demand operates to the best interests of the buyer when there is competition. We depend on competition to:

1. Keep prices low; people will always prefer to buy the cheaper of two nearly identical items and one will usually be lower.
2. Stimulate firms to provide better service to their customers for fear of losing them to a competitor.
3. Encourage firms to provide new and better goods and services before their competitor does.
4. Eliminate firms that waste the nation's resources by means of loss of business to a more efficient competitor.

COMPETITION IN THE MARKET

At present there is much controversy over whether there is enough competition in some markets to protect the public from price gouging (overpricing). If competition is inadequate, prices do not fully reflect the interaction of supply and demand. They reflect, instead, the degree of control by either buyers or sellers over the market. It has been argued that companies in the breakfast cereal, oil, auto, and computer industries have reaped excessive profits as a result of inadequate competition. Nor is such criticism limited to business. Skilled-craft unions in the construction industry have been accused of controlling the supply of plumbers to keep wages high. And the American Medical Association has been charged with keeping the supply of doctors low so as to maintain high incomes in the profession. Whether or not any of these charges is true is debatable. Without adequate competition, however, the prices of products or services are likely to be higher and the quality of service less.

ECONOMIC SYSTEMS ARE UNIVERSAL

It is not possible for any country to produce all of the products and services that its people desire. There seems to be no end to people's wants, yet the amount of money, skilled labor, precious metal, wood, water, land, and other resources are insufficient to produce all that people want. In every country the main economic problem is scarcity.

As a result, all countries develop an economic system to help them ration their resources yet meet their people's wants. An *economic system* is the organization a country uses to balance unlimited wants and limited resources.

An economic system is the means by which a society provides answers to the following questions (illustrated in Figure 1-3): (1) What shall we produce? (2) How much shall we produce? (3) How shall we produce it? (4) Who'll get what? Business in our society answers the first two questions, although the public can always

FIGURE 1-3 Answers to economic questions

AMTRAK — CAN GOVERNMENT DO IT BETTER?

Economists may make a neat distinction between the market and the command economy, but in the real world such distinctions are increasingly blurred. On the one hand the classic Soviet example of a centrally planned command economy has been experimenting with the free-market model, which encourages market response through the profit motive. On the other hand the traditional free-enterprise economy of the United States is increasingly controlled by government regulations and government agencies.

Antitrust laws heralded this change in America at the turn of the century. By now, government commissions supervise the rates and routes of common carriers such as the railroads, trucks, and airlines; the Securities and Exchange Commission sets disclosure standards for publicly traded securities of corporations; public utilities commissions regulate the rates, the profits, and even the investment decisions of privately owned utilities.

Another sign of the American economy's departure from laissez-faire is the formation of Amtrak, the new national railway passenger system that rides on the tracks of dozens of separate railroad companies. As airline passenger traffic grew and became less expensive, the number of passengers carried by the nation's railways diminished sharply. Profits from these operations turned into heavy losses. The railroads' money-making business, hauling freight, was disrupted by passenger operations. Track had to be maintained at much higher safety levels for the fast-moving passenger trains than would have been required for freight. The railroads, by law, had to keep running these losers, but they didn't have to keep them in tip-top shape. As a result, they neglected what had once been elegant coaches, sleepers, and dining cars and reduced service drastically to cut losses from an operation which they felt could not be turned around.

Finally, the federal government stepped in to ensure that the nation would retain this alternate passenger transportation service and assure that towns not served by the airlines would not be totally isolated. The passenger operations of most of the railroads were consolidated into a single company, Amtrak, whose operations were closely supervised by the government and whose losses were made up by government loans or subsidies.

Some unprofitable routes with low volume have since been discontinued. Other heavy losers have been maintained for the sake of public need and as the result of political pressures. Amtrak was projected to be operating in the black within a few years. Profitability looks more and more distant now, but the user of rail passenger services is being served, at whatever price, after private enterprise wound up unable to do the job. Such intrusions of government into our free-enterprise system seem to be a matter of historical necessity in an increasingly complex and interdependent economy.

veto a product. The third question is answered primarily by business. The fourth is answered by the purchasing power of buyers, as measured by the amount of money or credit they have.

In our country, business provides most of the products and services demanded by the public. In some countries, more of the products and services are provided by the government. In other countries, almost all products and services are provided by the government.

THE AMERICAN ECONOMIC SYSTEM

Among the names commonly given to our economic system are capitalism, free enterprise, and market economy. All of these terms arise from some aspect of our economic system as it developed. Our system has, of course, changed significantly during the past century. The American system is based on four principles that have been modified over the years. They include private property, freedom of choice, free competition in the market, and freedom from government interference.

PRIVATE PROPERTY

The earliest colonists from England insisted on the right of any free white man to own property. They believed that property and the means of production should be owned by individuals rather than by government. They wanted to promote a society in which individuals and not the government would produce the products and services needed. Over the years this has been modified so that anyone, regardless of sex, race, or social class, can own property. The right of private ownership and the use of property is protected by our constitution. Because of the importance of private property, the term *capitalism* came into general use to describe the economic system. It implies that the capital, or means of production, is owned by individuals, not by the government.

FREEDOM OF CHOICE

Freedom of choice refers to economic choices. For producers, this means the freedom to make whatever they want, to buy whatever they want from whomever they want, and to sell to whomever they choose. For consumers, it means the freedom to buy the products and services they desire from whomever they choose. For workers, it means the right to work for whomever they like and in any occupation they select. Freedom of choice gave rise to the term *free enterprise*. Free enterprise implies that each individual has the right to make economic decisions.

FREE COMPETITION IN THE MARKET

In our economic system, all persons make their economic decisions separately. Two centuries ago there was a real question as to whether there would be too much or not enough of something such as food, shoes, medical services, or lumber. A Scottish economic theorist, Adam Smith, saw that competition was the "invisible hand" that would regulate the supply and demand for products and services. His book, *The Wealth of Nations*, published in 1776, influenced the

Economic freedom was as important as political freedom in Revolutionary America. Boston, the center of commerce at the time of the Revolution, was a symbol of the economic freedom sought by the colonists.

economic system that developed in the United States. Smith said that if there were too much of some product or service, the price would drop. Producers would reduce their output to the desired levels so that they could sell what they had made and make a profit. At the same time, the inefficient producers would be forced out of business. This principle of the system gave rise to the term *market economy*. It implies that all major decisions are made in the market through the interaction of supply and demand.

FREEDOM FROM GOVERNMENT INTERFERENCE

The first colonists saw that the economic system would need an occasional referee. However, they did not want the government to interfere with the free market system. All economic decisions would be made by individuals competing with one another in a free market. Any government action that interfered with those private decisions would hinder the decision-making process. The colonists wanted competition, not the government, to regulate the market activities of individuals.

These are the four principles that guide our economic system today, though none of them is strictly applied. Although land is privately owned, various governments—federal, state, local—own millions of acres of land and many of the businesses that compete with privately owned firms. There are a great many restrictions on freedom of choice today. There are restrictions on what producers can make and on the choices of buyers and sellers. Consumers, too, are restricted in their choice of products and services. Entry into many occupations, such as law or real estate, is regulated. There is clearly no longer complete free competition in the market. With the growth of the large corporation has come greater control of all businesses by government. There is no longer freedom from governmental interference. The government has tightened its control over the activities of producers, workers, and consumers in recent years. (Modifications of above-mentioned four principles are discussed in later chapters.)

WHAT DO WE CALL OUR ECONOMIC SYSTEM?

What is the most accurate term to describe our economic system today? It is sometimes called modified capitalism or a mixed economic system (implying a mixture of private and governmental ownership). But perhaps the term *modified market economy* is most applicable. *Modified market economy* implies that most of the economic decisions are reached in the market, but that some are made outside it by the government and other groups. Examples of economic decisions made outside the market would be the establishment of a minimum wage or price-wage guidelines by the federal government.

There are many types of economic systems used by different countries. It has become popular to speak of them as though they fit into three broad categories: capitalism, socialism, and communism. This is an awkward and confusing way to group economic systems, because the terms entail more than just a description of a society's economic organization. They also make assumptions about the political process, social values, and cultural standards of a country. Capitalism, for example, has come to imply not only a market economy, but also a democratic society based on the dignity and worth of the individual. Communism has even more tangled, emotional meanings.

COMMAND AND MODIFIED MARKET ECONOMIES

It is more logical to group economies into two types—modified market and command market—depending on how most of the basic economic decisions are made.

All countries, regardless of wealth or size, have to answer the same basic economic questions. If most of these decisions take place in the market, the country has a modified market economy, described earlier. If most of the decisions originate in a governmental command agency, such as a planning commission or a planning director, then the country has a command economy. The chart in Figure 1-4 shows the characteristics of market and command economies, depending on how the countries answer the basic economic questions.

FIGURE 1-4 Differences in command and market economies

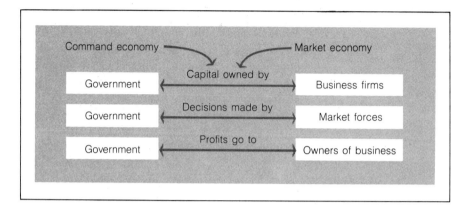

It is clear that the United States, Canada, and West Germany, for example, have market economies, since most decisions are made in the market. The USSR, on the other hand, has a planned or command economy.

USSR'S COMMAND ECONOMY

The Gosplan, or central planning agency of the Soviet government, establishes five-year goals for the kinds and volume of goods and services that it thinks are best for the country. These five-year plans are then further divided into one-year plans that specify the annual output of steel, clothing, and so forth. These are sent to the government ministries responsible for the key industries in the economy. The ministries pass these plans to the heads of large industrial plants, who are told what their total volume and types of products should be. The industrial plant managers then estimate the factors of production needed to produce this volume and in turn give these figures to the ministries, who transmit them to the central planning agency.

The state owns all industries as well as all banks, lending institutions, transportation companies, and retail outlets. This gives the government complete control over the supply and demand of products. The only privately owned businesses are produce stands, where individuals sell the fruits and vegetables they have grown on their small garden plots. (These garden plots, representing about 2 percent of the land used for agriculture, produce about half of the country's fruits and vegetables.)

NO "PURE" ECONOMIC SYSTEM

The United States is considered the best example of the modified market economies and the Soviet Union the best example of the command economies. However, in recent years the United States has taken on many features of a command economy.

In the USSR, stores are government-owned. All goods and services are owned and supplied by the government.

COMMAND DECISION MAKING IN THE UNITED STATES

The U.S. government owns a number of businesses, including the post office, hydroelectric plants, insurance companies, much of the passenger railroad system, and other enterprises. It also engages in some planning activities (see Chapter 3), as it tries to keep the economy growing at a steady rate of 3 to 4 percent a year. In addition, the federal government has appropriated from the market some basic economic decisions. We have minimum-wage laws, price ceilings, and many governmental efforts to regulate the supply and demand of various products. All are features of a command economy. As a result, it is more accurate to describe our system as a modified market economy.

MARKET SYSTEM IN THE USSR

On the other hand, the USSR has taken on some aspects of a modified market economy. As Russia's economic growth began to slow in the 1960s, it became obvious that its bureaucratic planning was inefficient in many respects. While it was possible to get large volumes of goods produced, it became increasingly difficult to produce the kinds and quantities of products that people wanted. As a result of the failure to guide the production of individual factories, there were large inventories of unsold merchandise. If a factory's plan was to produce one million pairs of shoes, it was far easier to produce all of them in black in only a

personality profile:
**RAY MARSHALL—
an economist runs the
labor department**

Management of the U.S. economy is deeply concerned with the management of its labor force, which is one of the factors of production. The Secretary of Labor administers laws and programs that deal with employment standards, job safety and health, employment and training, labor statistics, and labor-management relations. Above and beyond these administrative responsibilities, the Secretary is an economic policymaker charged with carrying out the Labor Department's mission "to foster, promote and develop the welfare of the wage earners of the United States, to improve their working conditions, and to advance their opportunities for profitable employment." More specifically, the Secretary's main job in these times is to reduce unemployment by targeting programs to produce jobs for the young, the old, and the relatively unskilled, who have special difficulties finding employment.

Ray Marshall, who became Secretary of Labor in 1977, has a Ph.D. in economics from the University of California at Berkeley, a school noted for its involvement in social problems, and has been a professor of economics since 1953. His interest in the field of labor history and labor-management relations, his expertise in developing job programs, and his understanding of the role of work force planning in the economy qualified him for his new post. The strong ties he built with labor unions in helping the building trades develop apprenticeship programs for blacks were another qualification.

Marshall's memberships in professional and academic organizations are further evidence of the depth and breadth of his experience and talents. For eight years he directed the Center for the Study of Human Resources at the University of Texas. In addition, he has headed the Industrial Relations Research Association, the National Rural Center, the Federal Committee on Apprenticeship, and the Task Force on Southern Rural Development, and he has served on numerous labor arbitration panels. At the same time he authored or coauthored five books and innumerable articles on such topics as black employment, rural labor development, equal employment opportunity, trade unionism, labor in the South, international labor mobility, and the history of collective bargaining.

His extraordinary capacity for hard work as well as his broad background in labor affairs gave him a national reputation long before he became Labor secretary in the Carter Administration.

few sizes rather than in a variety of colors, styles, and sizes. Most firms achieved their goals by producing what was easiest for them rather than what consumers would buy.

This has given rise to a limited use of the market structure, including a modified profit system. Firms make a profit by selling their output at prices set by the planning agency. If the products do not sell, there will not be a profit. In this sense, profit is an attempt to indicate how well customers' demands are being met. However, in contrast to the way in which profit is used in this country, profits in the Soviet scheme belong not to the factory manager but to the state. (Most top executives in American corporations receive a share of their company's profits.) Also, of course, the plant manager cannot manipulate prices to increase his profits. He must charge the prices set by the planning agency. The communist countries of Eastern Europe, and Yugoslavia in particular, have gone even further in letting the market dictate what is to be produced. As in the USSR, however, the profits usually go to the state, which distributes them as bonuses or for additional investment.

INFLUENCES ON ECONOMIC SYSTEMS

It is clear that economic systems are conditioned by history, culture, political organization, and other social institutions. In India, for example, the strong influence of Hinduism affects attitudes toward material possessions. In Western Europe, on the other hand, the Protestant ethic of hard work, saving, investment, and consumption has led to a drive for material progress. The United States, which was established by people who, besides being driven by the Protestant ethic, were also looking for independence and democracy, has tended to incorporate these principles into its economic system. The USSR, where the Communist party set out to transform an entire society according to collectivist principles in 1917, reflects those principles in a command economy.

COMPARING ECONOMIC SYSTEMS

Which type of system is the most efficient or the best? Comparisons are usually made of a country's total output or the number of vehicles or appliances per person. By this measure, the United States, Canada, and Japan are the most efficient. The best economic system, however, is the one that best meets the goals of a society. In addition to the economic or material standards, it is necessary to measure the quality of life. And, as we shall see later in our discussion of the role of business in improving the quality of life in this country, there is very little agreement on how one measures the quality of life.

BUSINESS AND THE ECONOMY

Let us now take a look at the products and services produced in our country and the groups who buy them.

GROSS NATIONAL PRODUCT

The total value of products and services produced in a country is called the *gross national product* (GNP). The GNP for the United States in 1978 was almost $2 trillion. Most of our products and services are produced by businesses. As we shall

FIGURE 1-5 Purchase of
GNP by sector

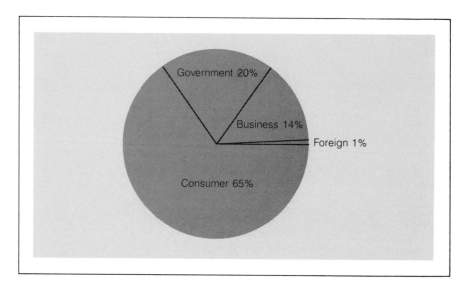

see later, however, government also produces products and services. GNP includes the dollar value of everything—medical services, housing, food, toys, repair work, automobiles, and so forth.

SECTORS OF THE
ECONOMY

Who buys this output? Figure 1-5 indicates that about 65 percent is purchased by
consumers, 20 percent by government, 14 percent by business, and about 1 percent by foreigners. These are considered the main sectors of the economy.

IMPORTANCE OF
BUSINESS

About 85 percent of all workers are employed in producing products and services.
Thus, most of the income in our economy begins in businesses. Since demand for
production and services comes from those who have money, the economy relies
mainly on business for the income with which to purchase products and services.

DEMAND AND INCOME

The flowchart in Figure 1-6 shows the relationship between demand and income
in the American economy. Businesses employ the factors of production in providing products and services. They pay wages and salaries to workers, the cost of
materials and equipment, rent for the use of buildings and equipment, and interest to those who lend to individuals, who then pay businesses from whom they
purchase goods and services. Most individuals also save some of their income and
pay their share of taxes. Thus it is a circular flow. Business responds to effective
demand by paying the factors of production to supply the products and services
needed. These payments then become the money used by consumers, businesses,
and government, in demanding new products and services.

FIGURE 1-6 Circular flow of income and demand

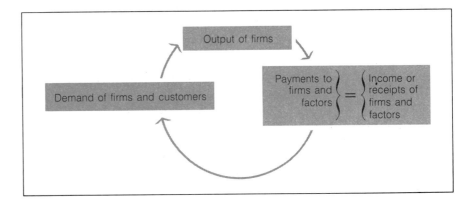

GOVERNMENT AND CONSUMERS IN THE ECONOMY

The economic role of the federal government will be covered in Chapter 17. Basically, however, the federal government has assumed the major responsibility for a healthy economy. It coordinates the efforts of the other three sectors of the economy. The role of the consumer is to purchase goods and services intelligently so that society's resources will be used wisely. If consumers consistently make poor choices, resources are being wasted. This encourages inefficient firms in their use of more resources than are necessary to meet the demands of society.

SUMMARY

Business firms are responsible in our society for supplying products and services that consumers want. They supply most of the consumer products and industrial products. In order to produce anything, firms buy or rent land, labor, and capital to use in production. While the firms have to risk their money to do this, they believe that they can make a profit by doing so. A profit, of course, is the return of an amount greater than the cost of operation.

Business produces those products or services that customers want and are willing and able to pay for. Prices are determined through the interaction of supply and demand in the market. Competition keeps prices down and promotes better products and services.

In the American economy, business firms are mainly responsible for producing products and services. In some countries, government assumes this responsibility. All countries need some type of economic system because there are not enough resources to produce everything that people want. Since most of our economic decisions are made in the market, our economic system is called a modified market economy. The government makes some of the economic decisions and thus modifies the workings of the market.

Some of the pillars on which our economic system is based include: property, freedom of choice, free competition in the market, and freedom from government interference. In command economies, such as that of the Soviet Union, most of the economic decisions are made by the government rather than by business firms and consumers in the market.

The dollar value of the output of an economic system is called gross national product (GNP). In our country, consumers buy about 65 percent of GNP, government about 20 percent, and business about 14 percent. Since most of the jobs originate in business, however, the income to buy the output comes mainly from business.

SUMMARY OF KEY TERMS

Business Any organized effort to produce products or supply services demanded by people for the purpose of making a profit.

Capital Plant and equipment used to produce products and services. Also, the money to buy products and services.

Capitalism An economic system in which the capital, or means of production, is owned by private individuals.

Command Economy An economic system in which most of the economic decisions are made through some command agency, such as a planning commission or a planning director.

Consumer Products Products manufactured for sale to a member of the public.

Economic System The organization that a country uses to balance unlimited wants and limited resources.

Factors of Production The elements essential to the production of products and services: land, labor, and capital.

Free Enterprise An economic system in which individuals are free to go into any type of occupation or business they wish.

Gross National Product (GNP) The total value of products and services produced by an economy in a year.

Industrial Products Products sold to other businesses.

Labor All the workers in a country.

Land All the natural resources used in production.

Market Any place where buyers and sellers get together.

Modified Market Economy An economic system in which most of the major economic decisions are made in the market, but in which some are made outside the market by the government and other groups.

Product Any tangible item.

Profit Money gained by selling a product or service for more than it cost to produce or supply.

Sectors of the Economy Groups which buy the output of the economy, including consumers, government, business, and foreign purchasers.

Service Performance of work by a business for pay.

REVIEW QUESTIONS

1. Name and explain the factors of production.
2. What is the difference between consumer and industrial products?
3. Explain what profits represent for a business firm.
4. Explain how prices are determined.

5. Explain the role of competition.
6. Explain why every country has an economic system.
7. Name the basic economic questions that any economic system has to answer and which groups answer each in our economic system.
8. Identify and explain the four principles of our economic system.

9. Compare and contrast a modified market economy and a command economy in terms of who makes the basic economic decisions.
10. Name and identify the role of each sector of our economy.

DISCUSSION QUESTIONS

1. Explain how it is possible for business to ignore the needs of large numbers of persons who want better housing, clothing, food, or medical care.
2. A modified market economy provides for the distribution of what is produced. Does our type of modified market economy provide for a just and fair distribution of the products and services produced? Why or why not?
3. If the USSR's economy is now incorporating more elements of a market economy and the American system is incorporating more ele-

ments of a command economy, is it not likely that soon the two systems will be very similar? Why or why not?
4. List five firms or industries that you feel are not doing the job they are supposed to do in a market economy in terms of prices or profit.
5. Do you feel that the invisible hand of competition can adequately regulate the American economy today? Give examples to support your answer.

CASES FOR DECISION MAKING

ECONOMIC CHESSBOARD

Upon taking office in 1977, President Carter said that his administration would lower unemployment to 4.75 percent, cut yearly inflation to 4 percent, and balance the budget—all by the end of 1980. These were clearly difficult goals to attain since the unemployment rate was above 7 percent, the inflation rate above 6 percent, and the federal government annual budget deficit about $50 billion.

After a year of pursuing all the goals simultaneously, he announced that the best way to achieve his aims was to push for a GNP growth of about 4.5 to 5 percent a year. With this type of growth rate, the administration hoped to lower unemployment, reduce prices, and control the federal budget deficit.

Considered a gamble by many, the risks involved in this policy are that inflation could be pushed even higher by bottlenecks in production, and a shortage of skilled workers, managers, machine equipment, and even the money supply could develop. Such factors drive up prices and cause inflation.

The president hoped, of course, that with the economy growing steadily business firms would expand their production, leading to new investment in plant and equipment and producing more jobs to cut unemployment. In order to attain the balanced budget by 1980, the president estimated that business would have to increase its investment in new plant and equipment by 10 percent a year. Unfortunately, in 1977 business increased spending for capital goods by only 8 percent and most of that went for new cars and trucks rather than for plant and equipment. Most forecasters were estimating a 5–6 percent increase in capital spending for 1978, far less than the 10 percent figure.

1. What factors do you suppose would have to be present for business firms to increase their spending for capital equipment by a substantial amount?
2. What effect is there on unemployment rates when capital spending is less than estimated?
3. How accurate have President Carter's predictions been on controlling inflation, unemployment, and budget problems?

CLOTHING IS A RISKY BUSINESS

Robert Hall, one of the nation's largest clothing chains, was closed abruptly in 1977, throwing 5,000 employees out of work. Founded in the 1940s, the firm was a profitable operation until 1970. It grew over the years into a nationwide chain of 430 retail stores. However, in its last three years of operation, it recorded almost $100 million in losses.

At one time the chain prospered because it sold attractive clothing for the family at low prices. It was one of the few stores aimed at the low-price market. Based primarily in large cities, its advertising and low prices appealed to many people who wanted stylish, modern clothing at bargain-basement prices. However, its earlier strength turned into a weakness as clothing shoppers increasingly turned to the shopping centers and to discount stores such as K-Mart.

Robert Hall operated most of its stores in urban areas at a time when the population was moving to the suburbs. With only a few of its stores in the large shopping centers, the clothier had difficulty drawing enough customers to its urban stores because of their poor location.

1. When a firm fails to make a profit, is it using the nation's resources in an efficient manner? Why or why not?
2. In your opinion what did the managers of Robert Hall do wrong? Explain your answer fully.
3. If you had been involved in rescuing a company like Robert Hall from going out of business, what plan would you have proposed? Explain your plan as a step-by-step proposal.

POWER TO THE MANAGERS

The Soviet Union has a command economy with decision making centralized in a large committee. Every few years, the government announces that it is loosening controls over the production system. It also indicates that it will give more power to the managers of industrial firms.

A recent announcement from Moscow indicates that, over the next three years, authority will be decentralized in key industries. Decentralization will be accomplished by grouping plants that make related products into "production associations" similar to the large American corporation that makes many products. Top executives of these associations will get more authority to determine production schedules, design products, and develop markets.

The objective of the change is to eliminate much of the inefficiency that comes from the centralized decision making. The power of the *glavki*, or chief supervisors, will be reduced considerably. In future they will concentrate on setting long-term investment and technological policies rather than year-to-year planning of industry.

Central planners in Moscow will continue to make many key decisions on prices, distribution, and allocation of materials. However, leaders see this experiment as a way of reconciling the control that comes from central planning with the efficiency characterizing decentralized industrial decision making.

Answer the following questions:

1. How will these reforms increase the decentralization of decision making in the Soviet economy?
2. What appears to be the roles of the plant managers, the industrial ministries, and the central planners in Moscow in the decision-making process?
3. What do you feel is the best way to combine the benefits of central planning in an economy with the advantages of the decentralization that takes place in a market economy?

RELATED READINGS

Galbraith, John Kenneth. *The Affluent Society*. New York: New American Library, 1968.

Galbraith's best-known book about the economics of opulence. While not easy reading, it is a provocative analysis of the American economy and the values of consumers.

Heilbroner, Robert L. *The Making of Economic Society*. 4th ed. Englewood Cliffs, N.J.: Prentice-Hall, 1972.

Excellent treatment of the emergence of modern economic society and the challenges facing the market economy. Very readable.

———. *Understanding Macro-Economics*. 2nd ed. Englewood Cliffs, N.J.: Prentice-Hall, 1972.

Superb nontechnical analysis of how the American economy works. Unlike most easy-to-read economics books, this one stresses analysis rather than description.

The Incredible Bread Machine. San Diego: World Research, 1975.

Written by six young persons, a very readable book on how capitalism works and why it should be promoted.

Robinson, Marshall, et al. *An Introduction to Economic Reasoning*. 2nd ed. Garden City, N.Y.: Doubleday, 1973.

Excellent book on economic reasoning for the general reader. While a bit more descriptive than Heilbroner's books, it is easy to read and covers all major topics in macroeconomics.

Soble, Ronald. *Whatever Became of Free Enterprise?* New York: New American Library, 1977.

Interesting study of some successful entrepreneurs from all walks of life who have become success stories.

chapter 2

THE DYNAMICS OF BUSINESS

OBJECTIVES

When you have finished reading and studying this chapter, you should be able to:

1. Identify and explain the major changes taking place in the kinds of products and services being produced in this country.

2. Indicate the growth that has taken place in both employment and unemployment patterns in this country.

3. Identify and explain the economic opportunities in owning or operating a business firm and the functions companies perform to earn profits.

4. List the major risks taken by business firms and describe the role of business failure in our economy.

CHAPTER PREVIEW

Nothing stays the same for any length of time, least of all American business. In the past quarter of a century our economy has made some significant gains and undergone some equally remarkable changes. More Americans are at work today than ever before, yet at the same time unemployment continues to rise. As we saw in Chapter 1, we as a nation produce over $2 billion annually in GNP, yet today more than half of that comes from the services we provide for one another, not what we manufacture. This reflects a basic shift in our economy from manufacturing to services. In this chapter we shall examine how these changes occurred and how they affect firms, industries, our total economy, and individuals.

In addition to discussing these changes, we shall also look at their causes. These include the flexibility for growth, profit, and change that is inherent in the American market economy.

Financial risks of operating a business also play an important part in the changing face of American business. Long-term trends, business cycles, and the actions of competitors are factors affecting management decisions and buyer activity. Only the most successful firms are expected to survive because they are the firms that most effectively use the nation's resources.

We begin with a look at the financial opportunities available to business, most notably the incentives for developing and marketing new products and services.

2
THE DYNAMICS OF BUSINESS

In our ever-changing world, America's demands on business—and business' reactions to them—are also ever changing. Through its efforts to make a profit by meeting and creating new demands, business is altering every American's lifestyle. Every year, for example, advertisements tell us that there is a new gadget, say, a new kitchen appliance that no household should be without: the automatic dishwasher, the microwave oven, the garbage compactor. As a result, workers, consumers, and governments must adapt to meet business' new demands. We say, therefore, that American business is dynamic because it is constantly changing to conform to the complex social and economic forces that mold the American way of life.

Perhaps more than any other nation, America has come to symbolize and achieve economic growth and industrial development. As a nation, our people tend to take both almost for granted. Every year Americans expect increased production and a steady stream of new products and services. We expect greater efficiency and productivity. We expect more jobs.

Over the two centuries of our history, business has generally met those expectations and by doing so may have, in fact, reinforced and increased them. During the past 50 years, for example, our GNP has more than tripled. During that period increases in efficiency and productivity have averaged about 3 percent a year. The number of jobs created has grown faster than the population. Today over 94 million Americans have jobs, double the number of 50 years ago. Average personal income has risen about 130 percent during the same period. These statistics testify to a period of remarkable economic growth. And with this growth have come some equally remarkable changes in the makeup of American business.

OPPORTUNITIES IN OPERATING A BUSINESS

American business provides an opportunity for creativity, initiative, and management skills. Unlike a planned economy, discussed in Chapter 1, ours is a market economy geared for change, innovation, and opportunity.

CREATING NEW PRODUCTS AND SERVICES

Our economy remains active and healthy through the introduction of new products and services. It has been estimated that 80 percent of the products now sold in supermarkets did not exist ten years ago. Creativity is essential if an existing business is to remain a viable force in the market.

Not every new item in a supermarket or retail store is a new product. Some may be just a modification or adaptation of an existing product. A new size can of cat food, for example, is not a new product, nor is a different color toothpaste. A *new product or service* is one significantly distinguishable from every other product or service already on the market. Self-developing film, color television sets, and jet aircraft are examples of products people considered new when they were first marketed. Sometimes, however, it is not easy to decide whether or not a product or service is new. Compact cars, touchtone telephones, and self-cleaning ovens all have aspects of new products, yet they can also be considered modifications of existing products.

SEIZING THE INITIATIVE   Many companies have a separate department called Research and Development (R&D) which is responsible for creating new ideas, products, and services.

Many firms succeed or fail depending upon whether or not they have been successful in seizing the initiative and developing new lines of products, thereby adapting themselves to a changing marketplace. One of the most important aspects of our economic system is the potential it allows for increasing profit and expanding a company's activities through marketing initiatives. Frequently this will result in a new product and a greater share of the market.

Several years ago, for example, B. F. Goodrich and Goodyear tire and rubber companies increased their share of the market over the previously dominating Firestone Company when they seized the opportunity of marketing the new steel-belted radial tire. Firestone, complacent with its line of products and share of the market, was slow to move and suffered financially as a result.

EFFECTIVE   In many instances, economic growth through developing and marketing new
MANAGEMENT   products and services is not only beneficial, it may also be essential for carrying on

The touch-tone telephone is a product that was recently introduced to the public. Packaging the phone as Mickey Mouse assures its overwhelming success.

A.T.&T. Photo Center

the business. Only management, through perceptive and often far-sighted decision making, can insure a business' vitality.

A&P food stores, for example, lost its industry leadership position when it failed to detect and protect itself against a mass migration of the middle class from urban areas to the suburbs. Rather than opening new stores in the burgeoning shopping center market, A&P stuck fast with its inner city outlets and consequently suffered a sharp downturn in sales, culminating in several years of losses and the closing of hundreds of its stores. Far-sighted management, flexible and ready for change, could have prevented this outcome by recognizing the opportunities inherent in the development of the shopping center.

THE RISKS OF OPERATING A BUSINESS

No business operates in a vacuum and each firm must be alert to changes in consumer demand, in the business cycle, and in the actions of competitors. There are other, narrower risks, such as fire and theft, which will be discussed in Chapter 19.

CHANGES IN CONSUMER DEMAND

There have been many shifts from some consumer products and services toward others. For example, the demand has gradually decreased for black and white television sets but increased for color; medium- and large-sized cars have decreased in popularity due to the rising cost of gas, while economy cars have grown more salable; certain types of housing, mobile homes among them, are more popular than ever; the services of smaller retailers, especially in urban areas, have grown. In recent years the demand has risen for railroad passenger service, large suburban shopping centers, soybean-based food products (for humans and animals), and many other items.

In addition to these long-term trends, there have been countless short-term or faddish changes in consumer demands for clothing, furniture, housing and household fixtures, food and entertainment. A business must adapt itself quickly to these changes or it will lose its share of the market for a product or service or even go out of business. In the late 1960s the Scott Paper Company was slow to recognize that consumers wanted more colors, patterns, and scents in their paper products. As a result, in many of the paper markets Scott lost its dominance to Procter & Gamble, which foresaw and met the new demands. You can probably think of many examples in your own area where service stations or retail stores have closed or been sold because consumers' demands have changed.

As a result of the consumer movement, in the 1970s consumers began to shop with greater care. For the first time a large number of consumers demanded that quality be consistent with price, whether it be for a $2 frozen dinner or a $2,000 stereo system. Without a clear difference in the quality of items, better educated consumers now buy the cheapest. The higher cost of fuel for homes and transportation and the high rate of inflation have caused another change in consumer demands. Most people now expect to spend less of their income on nonessential items such as luxury goods and leisure activities.

The American economy does not expand at a steady rate. While its annual average growth rate is 3 to 4 percent, this figure varies considerably from year to year. These fluctuations have a great impact on business. They influence the volume of products and services a firm can sell. This directly affects its profits. As a result, business managers keep informed on economic fluctuations and try to anticipate them in their planning. Most large firms have economists on their staff to help them interpret and forecast expected fluctuations.

Three basic types of economic fluctuations that affect business, government, consumers, and workers are: long-term trends, business cycles, and seasonal changes.

The *long-term trend* of the American economy is its expansion or contraction over an extended period of time, such as 50 years. Figure 2-1 shows how our economy

FIGURE 2-1 GNP in current and 1972 dollars and annual growth rate of the real GNP, 1947–1975

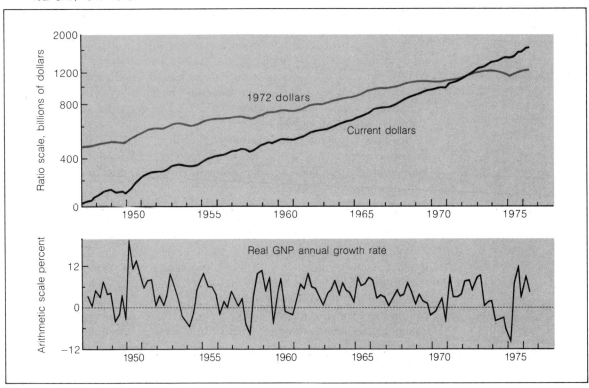

has fared over the past few decades. It reflects the long-term trend of an average rise in the GNP of 3 percent a year. It also shows short-term fluctuations, called business cycles, which are explained in the next section. The trend of the economy is clearly toward growth. Long-term growth rates of individual industries also fluctuate considerably, and it is essential for firms to note the extended trend in the economy and in individual industries. For example, cigarette companies have started to produce other products and services in recent years as a hedge against a forecasted long-term decline in the sale of tobacco products. (In fact, cigarette sales have continued to rise over the course of the past decade but by a smaller rate than before.) The American Tobacco Company has even changed its name to American Brands to describe better its efforts to meet long-term consumer demands.

BUSINESS CYCLES The overall tendency toward expansion in the American economy obscures the fact that there have been many fluctuations in the rate of growth. Fluctuations in economic activity that extend over a period of several years are called *business cycles*. The term implies that the pattern is recurring and predictable, as Figure 2-2 illustrates.

Starting from the low point in economic activity, called the trough or valley, the economy begins to turn upward as businesses hire more workers and expand their operations in anticipation of increasing demand. Output expands steadily until it reaches a peak, which is followed by a decline, called a recession. At the lowest point in the recession, the unemployment rate will be between 8 and 10 percent. Over the course of perhaps six months, the GNP will have declined by about 1 to 3 percent. This contrasts sharply with a depression, which is an even lower level of economic activity.

There has not been an economic depression since the Great Depression of the 1930s, when unemployment rose to 30 percent and the GNP fell by more than 25 percent. Current theory holds that such severe depressions are a thing of the past.

Since the Great Depression many changes have taken place in our economy to reduce the chances for such economic lulls. The government has forged many

FIGURE 2-2 Business cycle

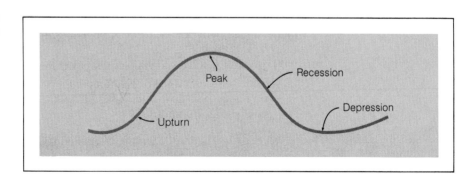

tools to fight these depressions. With broader Social Security and unemployment compensation programs, there is a fairly steady flow of income into the economy. This helps keep demand high enough so that businesses can continue to produce products at a fairly high level. This guarantees that not nearly as many people will be laid off from their jobs. In addition fewer people will be laid off during a recession as a result of these measures. In the 1930s manufacturing, farming, construction, and mining accounted for most of the jobs. When demand fell, workers were quickly fired. Today most employment is in the service industries including government, thereby insuring that severe, abrupt changes in the unemployment rate won't occur. Although some workers may be laid off when demand falls, the number laid off in government service will be much smaller than that in manufacturing, construction, mining, and farming.

Though the extremes in the business cycles appear to have been smoothed out through purposefully preventive measures, business cycles seem to remain a part of every economy, especially economies such as ours in which most of the decisions are made in the market.

REASONS FOR BUSINESS CYCLES

Why has the American economy gone through such a long series of business cycles? Why isn't there a continual gradual increase in economic activity without all of the irregularities demonstrated by troughs and peaks?

Many reasons are given for the existence and duration of business cycles, including the following:

1. The development of new products giving rise to major increases in employment in related areas, such as automobiles, computers, planes, and synthetic fibers.
2. Changes in habits of saving, investing, and consuming.
3. Changes in the amount, cost, and availability of credit.
4. Psychological changes in the outlook of business and consumers.

Changes in the level of economic activity greatly affect individuals, communities, businesses, and governments. The federal government has made tremendous efforts in recent years to eliminate the extremes of the business cycle and thus greatly reduce its harmful effects on all segments of society. These efforts are spelled out in some detail in Chapter 17, in which business and governmental relations are discussed.

It should be pointed out that each industry has its own cycle of ups and downs. For example, the aluminum industry has a history of cycles with a long-term trend of increasing output. The steel industry, too, has a history of cycles, but the long-term trend for output shows only a slight increase.

SEASONAL CHANGES

Seasonal changes are predictable variations in economic activity resulting from the change of seasons. For example, for most retail stores the Christmas and Easter seasons are the high points of the business year. In the summer, greater variety

The arrival of autumn signals the start of the winter buying season. Shopping for warm clothing is an annual event in most of the United States. Seasonal changes directly influence consumer buying habits.

Monkmeyer Press Photo Service

and abundance of products results in lower prices and higher sales' volume. The beginning of school in the fall affects the sale of a large number of items. Winter, spring, summer, and fall each brings with it a demand for a variety of products and services that are not needed at other times of the year. In its planning for the year, a firm will take these seasonal factors into consideration when making decisions about sales, production, and the number of employees that it needs.

ACTIONS OF COMPETITORS

All businesses keep a close watch on their competitors. This is necessary because when a company changes its operations, any changes will almost certainly affect its competitors. Most businesses, in fact, try to anticipate what their major rivals will do and make their own decisions accordingly.

For example, for many years Kodak made self-developing film for the Polaroid Corporation. Then Polaroid began work on new plant and equipment to produce its own self-developing film. In return Kodak planned to market its own self-developing cameras. Polaroid then began developing a line of still cameras. While this is a dramatic and unusual example of competition-watching, the same kind of practice often goes on at the retail level. Gas stations often change their prices within minutes of each other, or a supermarket will extend its hours soon after a competitor does.

business profile: INNOVATION – THE NAME OF THE GAME

There is no question that technological advances make certain goods obsolete. The widespread acceptance of the automobile meant that there was less demand for the horseshoe, for example. But it is also true that general technological advance within a country, which is nearly always accompanied by higher wages, means that the country is less well suited to compete in the manufacture of goods that require a high input of labor, which is expensive. That fact shows up in the changes of goods that the United States imports and exports from decade to decade.

The northeast section of the United States has, almost since the founding of this country, been the center of textile manufacturing. From New England mills, yard goods and made-up clothing were exported to other countries of the world at prices much lower than the cottage industries and primitive weavers of these countries could possible charge. The textile industry in the United States has been declining for quite some time, however. More and more of our shirts and blouses, pants and skirts are now imported from Korea and Hong Kong and Taiwan, to the extent that the garment manufacturing industry is seeking relief in the form of high tariffs and import quotas from the Congress, in order to protect American industry.

The United States has a comparative advantage, however, in goods that require advanced technology in their production. Hong Kong and Taiwan do not have the engineering force to produce their own sophisticated military weapons or their own computers, so they import these items from the United States. To pay for these very expensive products they earn the foreign exchange credits by selling their textiles in the United States.

What the United States winds up selling, therefore, is innovation. As an advanced technological society, it must continue to pursue new ways of applying technology to industry and industrial processes. It must be prepared to abandon enterprises that are no longer profitable or that can no longer compete with the cheaper labor of less-developed nations in favor of those things that it does best. Those things are the manufacturing jobs that require very specialized knowledge, equipment, and skills.

Burroughs, the computer manufacturer, recently moved one of its calculator operations abroad and started production of these mechanical devices there. In the plant which formerly produced calculators it now produces computers. These computers are exported to pay for imported calculators. Thus the course of innovation in industry.

MISCELLANEOUS
EVENTS

There are many other important variables that affect businesses, including such things as changes of governmental policies (tax or environmental controls), misfortunes such as theft, accident, property damage, and the death of a key employee. Protecting people and property against risks is covered in Chapter 19.

CAUSES AND RATES OF
BUSINESS FAILURES

Not every business will make a profit. There are unavoidable pitfalls in starting and operating a business, and many firms will fail. You can probably think of at least one local business that permanently locked its doors because it could not earn a profit, or was making too small a one to justify the owner's expenditure of time and money. The probability is that the firm you thought of was a small one, probably a local retail store.

The failure rate is greater for small businesses and retail stores than it is for large- and medium-sized ones. Most of the businesses that fail have been in operation for less than five years. By far the largest number of failures occurs among retailers not in the manufacturing, construction, service, mining, or wholesale trades.

Dun & Bradstreet, a company that analyzes and rates business credit, has classified the reasons for business failures. About 92 percent of businesses fail as a result of owner inexperience and/or incompetence. Dun & Bradstreet identified some of the areas of incompetence as inadequate sales promotion, heavy operating expenses, difficulties in collecting accounts, unattractive selection of merchandise, too much plant and equipment, poor location, and competitive weaknesses.

Although the failure rate for small firms is higher, large firms also fail. Waltham Watch Company, Penn Central Railroad, Robert Hall clothiers, and W. T. Grant stores are large operations that have recently failed because of financial reasons.

THE ROLE OF
ECONOMIC FAILURE

Our market economy, discussed in Chapter 1, is organized in such a way that it is advantageous for the nation's economy when inefficient firms fail. We depend on business to determine how to produce goods and services and to share with consumers and government the decisions concerning what and how much should be produced. If a business cannot successfully determine and meet customer needs, it is wasting valuable resources and should close its doors. These resources—land, labor, and capital—should then be used by a firm that can use them more efficiently.

This hard but realistic theory has been long recognized as a characteristic of a market economy. It is unquestionably applied when the failing firm is a small one, because there is little economic impact on society. If the neighborhood food store goes out of business because it cannot compete with a local supermarket, only a few people are directly affected and there is little outcry. However, in recent years several large corporations have found themselves on the edge of bankruptcy and appealed to the federal government for help. Their officers have argued that if they were to fail they would have to fire thousands of workers, thereby wreaking havoc on the local and national economies. This fact tests the validity of the theory and stems from the nature of large corporations. Lockheed and Penn Central are examples of industrial giants that have received financial assistance from the federal government when they were about to fail. Whether or not the federal government should bail out troubled businesses remains a controversial issue.

THE DYNAMICS OF MAKING A PROFIT

The purpose of every business is to operate with a profit. No matter what other factors change in American business, profit remains a constant. In general the more successful the enterprise, the greater the profit. The challenge facing business is making the profit as large as possible.

HOW PROFIT IS DETERMINED

Profit does not mean the same thing to the business person as it does to the economist. The business person calculates profit by subtracting all business expenses from all business income. This is called *business profit*. In the case of a retail store this is easy to determine: all expenses are charged to the store and all income is credited to it. For a manufacturer it is more difficult to determine. If a manufacturer produces several products in one plant, the costs and income applicable to each must be separated. Expenses are then divided into fixed and variable.

Fixed costs are the expenses the manufacturer will have regardless of whether or not the plant is in operation. For example, the cost of executive salaries, maintenance help, rent, taxes, interest on loans, and the minimum cost of electricity, water, and other utilities do not change significantly as the volume of production changes. *Variable costs* change with the volume of production. The costs of materials, production employees' wages, and supplies rise and fall with output. The manufacturer will then allocate a percentage of fixed and variable costs to each commodity and also separate the income by commodity. He can then calculate the profit or loss of each product.

The economist, on the other hand, computes the figures a little differently by taking into account the *opportunity cost*, which is the amount of money a firm loses by not using its resources in some other way. If a farmer had invested $50,000 in his farm machinery, for example, the economist would calculate the interest which that money could have earned and consider it an opportunity cost to be added to the other business costs.

WHY DO BUSINESSES RECEIVE A PROFIT?

Successful businesses earn a profit because they efficiently meet customers' demands for goods and services. Profit is really a reward to business for:

1. *Being aware of consumer demands.* The firm that foresees a substantial new demand and moves quickly to meet it is likely to be rewarded with large profits, at least in the short term. Minnesota Mining and Manufacturing (3M)

Britain and France pooled financial resources and engineering talent to produce the Concorde, the world's fastest passenger airliner. It cost millions to build one of these planes.

British Airways

was the first large firm to market "Scratch 'n' Sniff " fragrances. It has profited handsomely as the technique has moved beyond a limited use in magazines to packaging and store display materials.

2. *Taking a risk.* While there are exceptions, generally the greater the risk in a project, the greater the opportunity for profit. After an earlier $100 million flop with the Edsel, Ford Motor Company reportedly staked about $500 million on the Mustang to meet what it thought was a demand for a small, inexpensive American sports car. It was a wise investment. Profits for the Mustang have been enormous and the model has become the industry leader in its category.

3. *Effectively managing resources.* Profit represents a reward for business in managing effectively a nation's resources (the factors of production). Business has the primary reponsibility for deciding how to produce goods and services. As long as it can perform this duty well, it can expect a reward in the form of profit.

PROFIT GOALS   All firms have a profit goal. It may be simple, such as increasing sales and making a higher profit than last year, or very complex, including several profit goals. For some time economic theorists have assumed that all firms want to maximize profits. That is, they try to make as much profit as they can, either in the short run (such as in a year) or in the longer run (as long as the firm is in existence). As your studies progress, you will see that there are many ways of calculating whether or not a company is maximizing profits, but that in reality it is very difficult to do.

Because of the difficulties of using profit maximization as a goal, many other profit goals have been developed, particularly by large firms. Some of these include:

1. *Sales maximization.* A firm tries to reach as much sales as possible, as long as profits reach a satisfactory level.
2. *Share of the market.* A company tries to hold or increase its share of sales in its industry while also maintaining a minimum satisfactory profit level.
3. *Satisfactory profit.* A firm decides on a satisfactory level of profits and strives to achieve it. This might mean a 5 percent increase in profits over last year's or a profit equal to an average of three of its best five years.
4. *Target return.* A firm tries to earn a certain percentage return on income or capital. This percentage is found by dividing total profits by the total sales or by total investment in the firm. For example, General Motors has customarily had as its goal a target return of 20 percent on its invested capital. Another firm may have as a target to earn 5 percent on its total sales.

All of these goals have been documented as major corporate goals in a well-known study by Robert F. Lanzilotti,[1] who found that many large corporations had more than one profit goal. He detected a trend to target return profit goals, particularly by firms that were industry leaders or sold in protected markets, or where goals were set for new products.

PROFITS ACHIEVED BY LARGE CORPORATIONS

Large manufacturing corporations earn an average of about 5 percent a year on their sales. They achieve a return of between 10 and 20 percent on their investment. Profit rates, however, vary greatly by industry and by corporation. While the total profit earned by corporations continues to rise, there are fluctuations in the amount. Judged by some measures, corporate profits are actually falling. As you can see from Figure 2-3, national income has declined while employee compensation as a share of national income has increased.

A LIMIT ON PROFIT?

Are corporate profits too high? According to many public opinion polls, a majority of Americans feel that they are. Many people believe that corporations are entitled to only a "fair" return on their investment, but that what they currently take is more than fair. When people learn that in some years General Motors makes a profit of as much as $3 billion, they believe that all large corporations make just as

1. Robert F. Lanzilotti, "Pricing Objectives in Large Companies," *American Economic Review*, 1958, pp. 921–940.

FIGURE 2-3 Employee compensation and corporate profits after taxes as a percentage of national income. Source: *Statistical Abstract of the United States,* 1977

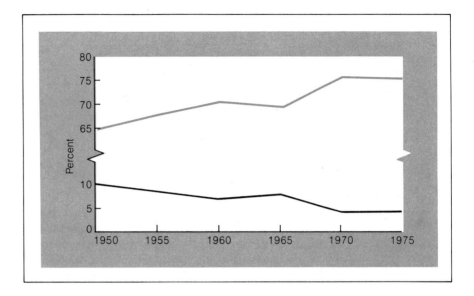

much. Labor leaders, consumer advocates, even some elected officials have called for a limit on corporate profits.

As we saw in the previous section, the typical corporation achieves an annual return of between 10 and 20 percent on its investment. Most of those same corporations could receive about 8 to 10 percent on their money, with little risk, by investing in government bonds.

This means that the typical corporation earns between 2 and 12 percent over what it could get from lending its money with much less risk. As noted earlier, companies get their extra return in our economic system by taking the chances that go with production.

On the other hand, the Federal Trade Commission, in forcing Xerox to share its patents with competitors, noted that Xerox's return on sales was about double the norm. The question that then arises is whether or not the extra profit is for risk taking or for some kind of collusion or monopoly in the market. This has led many critics to argue that a large firm should give away a hefty share of its profits above a fair return—such as 15 percent. Such an arrangement is difficult for many workers, owners, and creditors to accept, however, since they want higher wages, higher profits, and the certainty of the repayment of debts. If profit is limited, a firm is unlikely to pay as high a wage as its employees want; it would certainly not be serving the best interests of the stockholders or creditors.

Of great concern to economists are investors' expectations that future corporate profits are not likely to rise. This keeps stock prices low. Also, many corporations that are in high-profit industries, such as oil, tobacco, and soft drinks, have been investing their profits by buying firms in other industries. They too feel that future profits in their industries will not be as high as those that may be earned in other industries. This was a major reason why Mobil bought Montgomery Ward and Ligget and Meyer bought Alpo.

ECONOMIC POWER AND PROFITS

There is a general feeling on the part of the American public that large firms have the opportunity to make extra profits because they control the market. That is, they have the power to reduce the supply of a product relative to the demand or they can artificially stimulate demand. Either way the price is pushed up, as we learned in Chapter 1, and the large firms make extra profits. This is a serious charge since most of our major industries are dominated by a few corporations.

MARKET POWER

Such a situation—that is, when there are only a few sellers in the market—is called an *oligopoly*. This is contrasted with a *monopoly*, when only one seller or vendor is active in a market, and free competition, where there are lots of sellers and none can affect the market very much. In such key industries as autos, steel, computers, farm machinery, aluminum, rubber, chemicals, oil, and electronics, comparatively few firms dominate the market. These are sometimes called concentrated, or *oligopolistic*, industries. Oligopolies are a special problem because they frequently use their power to keep out other potential competitors. It is also far easier for the member firms to communicate their plans to each other since there are only a few of them.

As a result of this growing national concern, the Federal Trade Commission and the Justice Department have recently brought legal action against several large firms to break them up into smaller ones. They have attacked IBM, AT&T, and the major firms in the auto, rubber, steel, and cereal industries. The motive behind the action is, of course, that through concentration in a market, a few firms will artificially keep the prices high, resist product improvements, and unfairly increase their profit levels.

THE GROWTH OF SERVICES

One of the most significant changes in American business over the past 20 years has been a shift in our GNP from the production of goods toward the providing of services. Today over half of our GNP is composed of services. These vary greatly and are provided by companies ranging from the local dry cleaners to the multibillion dollar operation of AT&T. Advertising, transportation, finance, banking, insurance, building maintenance, data processing, equipment leasing, medical care, and food preparation are only a few of the many services currently provided by American business.

This shift to services has led some experts to say that America now has a postindustrial economy; that is, it has moved beyond the production of products as its major output. In addition about 60 percent of American workers are now employed in service industries. Many reasons are given for this shift. It is partly

White-collar jobs are more plentiful in today's economy than blue-collar jobs. Here, supervisors inspect office calculators.

Sperry Univac

the result of the demands for better education, better health care, better financial and other services. Also, the influx of people to urban areas has brought with it a demand for far more services than were required when most people led self-sufficient lives in rural areas.

PROBLEMS ARISING FROM THE SHIFT TO SERVICES

The shift toward providing services away from producing products has created some widespread problems. Many people's work has changed and this has caused geographical dislocation as people have had to move away from where they had previously worked.

personality profile:
**William Anderson—
entering the computer
age**

William S. Anderson had been with the National Cash Register Co. for 25 years when NCR's board of directors picked him for president of the company in 1972. The decision was surprising to many, for the board passed over dozens of senior executives to choose an auditor born in Hankow, China, who had never served a term at the venerable company headquarters in Dayton, Ohio, where manufacturing and management were centralized.

At the time, NCR was in trouble. Its traditional strengths in the cash register and accounting machine markets were fast being eroded. Its huge and outdated manufacturing plant in Dayton was turning out obsolete mechanical products when the new direction for information handling was clearly toward electronics. NCR's management and marketing organization was fossilized in an out-of-date, inefficient system of doing business. Its international divisions, modeled after the centralized manufacturing and single-product-oriented sales, were in the same shape as the domestic operations. The lone exception to this pattern was the highly profitable Japanese operation, run since 1959 by William Anderson, which had developed and introduced the company's first electronic cash register called a POS or point-of-sale terminal.

Mr. Anderson has almost singlehandedly guided NCR away from its traditional way of doing business into an age of computers and profits. The old Dayton factories have been demolished in an almost symbolic move and the company's headquarters have moved to modern offices in Dayton. Manufacturing has been decentralized so that there are now a large number of smaller plants, each with its own engineering and development group which can quickly improvise product changes. Labor accounted for 75 percent of product cost in the old mechanical fabrication plant; 60 percent to 80 percent of product cost in the new plants is for purchased parts and materials. Sales of mechanical products are less than a quarter what they were in 1972; sales of computer systems and data terminals have more than quadrupled in the same period.

NCR's old marketing organization was organized along political boundary lines, with each salesperson responsible for a particular product. Now each salesperson is responsible for selling all NCR products within a geographical market area.

NCR revenues and profits seem to indicate the Anderson revolution has been a success. The company is now second only to IBM in computer-related business volume.

Another problem has been the difficulty in increasing productivity and efficiency in service businesses. As we shall see in detail in Chapter 7, this arises from the nature of providing services. Most service firms employ more workers than do manufacturing firms of a similar size. Thus although the output of services represents only about 50 percent of the GNP, service activities absorb about 60 percent of the work force.

As a result the prices of most services have risen rapidly, reflecting a combination of increasing demand and rising labor costs, which are not offset by improvements in machines or tools.

Recently, however, it's been shown that effective management can increase productivity in service industries. McDonald's has revolutionized the efficiency and consistency of fast-food operations. Midas Muffler shops, K-Mart discount stores, and Baskin-Robbins ice·cream shops are other examples of effective management that has resulted in greater efficiency in service industries.

On the other hand, however, there could be an advantage to the economy in the expansion of service industries. Although the difficulty of raising productivity may lead to a slower growth rate in the GNP, these industries are not subject to the same ups and downs that afflict manufacturing, agriculture, and mining. As a result, major fluctuations in the economy may be a thing of the past.

There is some evidence of this in the unemployment rates of white-collar workers (people employed in service industries and government) and blue-collar workers (manufacturing, construction, mining, and farming). At present the unemployment rate for white-collar workers is about half what it is for blue-collar workers. Recently, the annual unemployment rate for white-collar workers was 4.3 percent. The unemployment rate for blue-collar workers was 8.1 percent.

THE GROWTH OF
PUBLIC GOODS AND
SERVICES

The two fastest growing categories of employment, as we shall see in the next section, are state and local government and medical services. In addition, all levels of government are spending about 30 percent of the income earned by the labor force. Most of this money comes to various governments in the form of taxes (see in Chapter 17). As a result, in addition to the shift from producing goods to providing services, there is a gradual shift to ever-increasing governmental services. This is consistent with the opinions of economist John Kenneth Galbraith who argues in his book, *The Affluent Society*, that for the public good there should be a reduction in the output of consumer goods and an increase in *public goods and services*: housing, medical care, and education, among others.

EMPLOYMENT AND UNEMPLOYMENT

With the shift from producing products to providing services has come a dramatic alteration in patterns of employment and unemployment.

THE GROWTH OF
EMPLOYMENT

Except for the Depression years of the 1930s and the World War II years of the early 1940s, the growth of employment in the United States has been steady. As the numbers of workers has continued to rise, changes in the makeup of the work

FIGURE 2-4 Labor force participation rates by sex and age, 1950-1976. Source: *Monthly Labor Review*

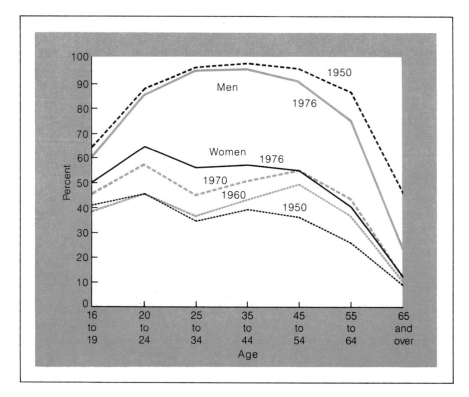

force has taken place. Figure 2-4 shows that women have been increasing their participation in the labor force from 1950 to 1976 while the percentage of men working has declined slightly. The percentage of younger women working shows a particularly rapid increase.

It is expected that the percentage of women in the work force will continue to increase. This is the result of the high cost of living, making it imperative for formerly housebound wives to take jobs, and changing social values, most notably the women's liberation movement of the past decade.

The number of teenagers in the population has begun to decline and teenagers should not grow much as a percentage of total workers. However, since an increasing percentage of teenagers is looking for work, their share of total jobs should remain about the same.

With the growth and changes in employment patterns there have also been significant changes in the types of industries adding workers. Employment in the manufacturing sector has not grown recently. At the same time the number of jobs in other sectors has expanded. Today there are almost as many jobs in the wholesale and retail business as there are in manufacturing. There are only about 4 million more jobs in manufacturing than there are in local, state, and federal governments. This is significant because since the turn of the century manufacturing has provided most jobs in our economy. In the next decade the largest number of new jobs is expected to arise in service industries and in government.

One of the recent oddities in the American economy has been the concurrent rise of employment and unemployment. The labor force grew from 82 million in 1972 to 94 million in 1978. At the same time the number of unemployed rose from 5 million to 8 million. This situation came about because the number of potential workers entering the labor force increased more than the number of new jobs.

Over 11 million new jobs were created from 1972 to 1977. However, it is estimated that over 19 million new jobs will be needed by 1981 if the unemployment rate is to stay at a more acceptable level of about 5 percent. Of the 19 million new jobs, 11 million of them will be needed to find jobs for our growing work force. The remaining 8 million jobs will be needed to offset the number of jobs lost by increases in productivity, including automation. An increase in the productivity rate is necessary if American products are to remain competitively priced with the products of foreign countries.

THE GROWTH OF UNEMPLOYMENT

Unemployment means different things to different people. The department of the federal government responsible for keeping track of unemployment, the Bureau of Labor Statistics, defines an *unemployed person* as someone 16 years of age or older, who is registered with an employment office, but who does not have a job.

Despite many concerted attempts by the government to drive it lower, during the 1970s the percentage of people in the work force who were unemployed never fell much below 7 percent. As Table 2-1 shows, unemployment does not fall as heavily on some groups of people as it does on others. Whites tend to have about half the unemployment rate of blacks; men tend to have a lower rate than women. Older workers have lower unemployment rates than teenagers. The highest unemployment rate for any group is a staggering 36 percent for black teenagers aged

TABLE 2-1 Unemployment rates by group for 1977

Type of Workers	Unemployment Rate
Full-time employees	6.7
Part-time employees	10.2
Whites	6.7
Nonwhites	12.5
Male heads of households	4.7
Female heads of households	7.0
White teenagers	18.1
Nonwhite teenagers	36.1
Married men	3.8
White-collar workers	4.5
Blue-collar workers	8.4

Source: Department of Labor

18 and 19. This is about twice the unemployment rate for whites of the same age. The unemployment rate for white males aged 20 and over, 6.7 percent, has not been a great issue for the nation, though that rate is still much higher than most people would like. Some critics of the present unemployment rate argue that 4 percent, or even 3 percent, is an acceptable level. Others say that no American should voluntarily be without a job and argue for full employment achieved by creating government jobs for the unemployed.

THE PROBLEMS OF
UNEMPLOYMENT

In the mid-1960s, an unemployment rate of 3 percent was considered normal. Today the unemployment rate is up to 7 percent, and many experts doubt that it will ever be significantly lower. Yet it is important that unemployment be lower for it saps the nation of much of its economic and psychological vitality.

Unemployment is an extremely complicated problem and there are many complex reasons for it. Some of them are:

1. The number of inner-city, chronically unemployed people (often referred to as the hard-core unemployed), those who rarely, if ever, work, is growing.
2. Many women and especially teenagers have difficulty finding a job.
3. Widely available unemployment payments make keeping a job seem less attractive than it would be without the opportunity to collect money from the state for not working.
4. An increasing number of businesses prefer to hire part-time employees. In many industries fringe benefits such as paid vacations, free health insurance, and company health services represent about 30 percent of the company's labor costs. A company can avoid paying for the fringe benefits that full-time employees receive by hiring part-time workers.
5. It is increasingly difficult for people to get jobs because many firms have cut their fringe-benefits costs by making do with a smaller number of workers than normal. This means that workers who have jobs receive a great deal of overtime work and pay but those seeking jobs find themselves shut out of factories and offices.

SUMMARY

Over 60 percent of all workers are engaged in producing services rather than products. While the number of jobs has increased steadily, there are still not enough jobs for everyone who wants to work. Women and teenagers have come into the labor market in greater numbers in the past decade. Since they tend to have fewer skills and to change jobs more frequently, their unemployment rates are higher than for older males.

People own or manage business firms because they are rewarded well for success. Besides self-fulfillment, high salaries and fringe benefits await those who are successful either in owning a business or in managing one for others.

The successful business managers or owners are paid from the profits of the firms. Profits are what is left when all expenses are subtracted from all income. Business firms receive a profit in our society for awareness of consumer demand, for risk taking, and for management of resources. Most large firms have very carefully drawn profit goals although smaller firms may not be quite so specific. Successful large firms earn between 10–20 percent return on their investment although some firms earn nothing.

Along with the opportunity for profits, firms face many risks in operating. Changes in consumer demand may reduce profits or even cause a firm to fail. Changes in the economy, including long-run trends, business cycles, and seasonal changes, all affect business operations. The action of competitors also influence the success of any firm. Many firms fail each year. While this seems like a waste, actually failure is a part of our economic system. Only the most successful firms are expected to survive because it is assumed that these are the firms which are using the resources of the country most efficiently.

SUMMARY OF KEY TERMS

Business Cycle   Fluctuations in economic activity which extend over a period of several years.

Business Profit   As the businessperson calculates it: business income minus business expenses.

Fixed Costs   The expenses a business has regardless of whether or not the plant is in operation.

Monopoly   Only one seller in a market.

Oligopoly   Few sellers in a market.

Opportunity Cost   The cost to a firm of not using its resources in some other way.

Public Goods and Services   Goods and services produced by all levels of government.

Seasonal Changes   Predictable variations in economic activity resulting from the changing of seasons.

Unemployed Persons   The number of people 16 years of age or older who are registered with an employment office, but who are without jobs.

Variable Costs   Costs that change with the volume of production.

REVIEW QUESTIONS

1. What is the major change taking place in the kinds of products and services being produced in this country?
2. What are the economic opportunities available in owning or managing a business?
3. Name and explain the functions businesses perform to earn a profit.
4. Differentiate profit-maximization, sales-maximization, share-of-market, satisfactory-profit, and target-return profit goals.
5. What changes are taking place in employment patterns in our country?
6. Define unemployment and explain why unemployment rates are higher today in the United States than they were twenty years ago.
7. Name and explain the major economic risks faced by businesses in this country.
8. Contrast long-term economic trends, business cycles, and seasonal changes as to length and effect on the economy and businesses.

9. Why is it so important that inefficient businesses be allowed to fail in our economic system?

10. What is the difference between a recession and a depression?

DISCUSSION QUESTIONS

1. Is every adult in this country entitled to a job? If so, whose responsibility is it to provide that job?
2. Are profit levels in the auto industry too high? Why or why not?
3. Do you believe that large firms in oligopolistic industries make greater profits than firms in more competitive industries?

4. Should a large firm, such as Lockheed or Penn Central, be allowed to fail and go out of business or should the government attempt to save it?
5. Do you believe that the economic rewards are better in owning your own firm or in managing a business for someone else?

CASES FOR DECISION MAKING

BAILING OUT LARGE CORPORATIONS

Lockheed Corporation developed the L-1011 Tri-Star, a wide-bodied passenger jet, to carry 250 passengers and use medium-sized airports. It had a contract with Rolls-Royce, a British corporation, to produce the engine for the plane. In February, Rolls-Royce management notified Lockheed management that it would be forced into bankruptcy because of large cost overruns on the engine. The British government agreed to take over the management of Rolls-Royce and produce the needed engines if Lockheed could guarantee that production of the plane would continue. The time delay increased costs considerably. As a result, Lockheed's creditors would not advance the additional $250 million needed unless the U.S. government would guarantee the loans. If Lockheed could not get the additional money, it too would go bankrupt. About 31,000 Lockheed workers were employed on production of the plane, as well as another 24,000 workers at Rolls-Royce and other subcontractors. The U.S. government, after considerable debate, agreed to guarantee payment of Lockheed loans on the program if Lockheed did not pay its creditors.

1. Should Lockheed have been permitted to fail and go out of business if it could not successfully produce the TriStar at a profit? Justify your answer.
2. Is there any difference between letting Lockheed fail and letting the corner grocery store fail?
3. Should the federal government help save any large business firms that seem to be failing because the failure might cause hardship to employees, subcontractors, and customers?

HOW MUCH PROFIT IS ENOUGH?

Profit rates for American corporations averaged about 5 percent of sales during 1977. At the same time the return on owner's investment was about 13 percent. That means that for every dollar the owners had invested in the firm, the firm earned 13 cents. At the same time, the government and most economists wanted greater investment in new plant and equipment from the corporations. They saw this as important in creating more jobs and in meeting foreign competition. Yet, American corporations felt the potential profits from such investments were not large enough to take the risk. Even the Chairman of the Federal Reserve Board, which controls the money supply, said "Profits are at an unsatisfactory level." He said this "could well prove an insurmountable barrier to the achievement of full employment in this country."

1. What percentage return do you expect corporations could earn by putting their extra cash in savings accounts or into government bonds, rather than into new plant and equipment?
2. As a percentage return on investment, what level of profits do you feel is fair for most corporations?

HOW SERIOUS IS A HIGHER UNEMPLOYMENT RATE?

Most people agree that everyone who wants a job and is willing to work should have one. While about 2 million jobs are created each year, it appears that our unemployment rate is stuck around 7 percent. A 7 percent unemployment rate means that almost 7 million persons who are looking for work cannot find a job. In addition, there are many others who have become discouraged and quit trying to find a job. There are also many others who would like a better job. Many adults know that only 10 years ago unemployment rates were lower. During good times, we averaged only about 4 percent unemployment. That is about as low as we can get since there is a certain amount of unemployment built into any economy. Industries move, creating temporary unemployment problems. Many persons without skills

to offer want jobs where there are only a few jobs for unskilled persons. Persons voluntarily leave the labor force and then return to work at a later date and have to wait to find a job.

Reasons such as these have prevented us from having less than 4 percent unemployment. However, why can't we get back to that 4 percent figure? It would certainly help a lot of people. Basically, the reason we can't return to a 4 percent unemployment figure is that our unemployment rate is not measuring exactly the same groups which were formerly covered. There is a higher percentage of women and teenagers in the labor market than 10 years ago. These groups have always had higher unemployment rates than males over the age of 19. Females, in particular, are coming into the labor force in greater numbers. Over 50 percent of females age 16 and over are in the work force compared to just over 40 percent in 1970. This compares to about 78 percent of the males in the labor force.

1. Do you think the number of females in the work force will continue to increase? What social and economic forces do you think will contribute to this?
2. Do you feel that the unemployment rate is an indication of economic hardship or a measure of utilization of our human resources potential or both?
3. Should priority in hiring be given to groups where unemployment is particularly high, such as females and members of minority races?

RELATED READINGS

Editors of *Fortune. Challenges for Business in the 1970s.* Boston: Little, Brown, 1972.

Paperback on the uncertainties that face business. It deals with such topics as population changes, changing consumer markets, shifts in the auto in-

dustry, harder times for the arms makers, the increase expected in demand for capital goods, and the mounting bill for pollution control.

Monsen, R. Joseph. *Business and the Changing Environment.* New York: McGraw-Hill, 1973.

Discusses the changing environment for business. Starts with a survey of contemporary social issues, and then looks at capitalism as a business system. Finally, examines tradition and change in American society.

Mintz, Morton, and Cohen, Jerry S. *America, Inc.* New York: Dell, 1971.

A book highly critical of business, depicting big business and big government working together to win protected positions, squeeze out the small firms, exploit the consumers, and administer prices.

Newfield, Jack, and Greenfield, Jeff. *A Populist Manifesto.* New York: Warner Paperback Library, 1972.

An argument for a new majority of Americans to fight the economic privilege of banks, monopolies, labor unions, insurance companies, and other power groups, which results in the exploitation of consumers and workers.

Reich, Charles A. *The Greening of America.* New York: Random House, 1970.

A controversial best-seller that traces the development of values in our society, with our consumption and earning patterns as a central focus. In this book, the younger generation is seen as providing the lasting values that will remake our society.

chapter 3

BUSINESS AND SOCIETY

OBJECTIVES

When you have finished reading and studying this chapter, you should be able to:

1. Recognize the new demands on business for meeting its social responsibilities and the groups making those demands.

2. Identify the major problems in cleaning up the environment and explain the response of government and business to the problems.

3. Define the social responsibilities of business, including why business has been asked to expand its role, and name ways in which business can demonstrate it is meeting its social responsibilities.

CHAPTER PREVIEW

Defective products, dirty air and water, high prices, decaying inner cities, crowded suburbs, and high levels of poverty are all blamed on big business. Is business really to blame for these and other social problems? What responsibilities does business have to the public to improve the quality of American life?

Little more than a decade or so ago, the American people expected business to perform only one major task: produce products and services in sufficient quantities and sell them at reasonable prices. Now, however, the public demands that business be socially responsible. What does that mean? It implies that business, as a social institution, like the government and labor unions, has obligations consistent with its role in society. For example, if business uses streams and rivers in its industrial processes, it has a social obligation to leave those streams and rivers in their original state—or pay the price for cleaning them up; products must be safe and durable, they must be neither dangerous to use nor defective; business must conduct itself in an ethical fashion, rejecting cut-throat practices such as bribery, coercion, and criminal acts.

In many ways these requirements run counter to what many business people see as their major responsibility: making as large a profit as possible. During the past two decades the public's new demands on business and business' resistance to them have been largely reconciled through the intervention of government. Yet even today increasingly heavy demands continue to be made on the business community to meet its social obligations.

In this chapter we shall focus on the many social problems faced by American business today, how they arose, how business and government deal with them, and the reasons why business should meet its social responsibilities. Particular attention is given to the financial aspects of social problems, for it is the apparent conflict between maximizing profits and the costs of social obligations that makes business' social responsibilities such a controversial issue.

THE MILWAUKEE JOURNAL

"We figure that since this place has more air pollution than the national standard, you might as well help us keep it that way."

3

BUSINESS AND SOCIETY

The 1960s and 1970s saw American business criticized by many people for many reasons. The business community seemed to be producing too many unsatisfactory products at too high prices, while sometimes engaging in questionable acts and practices. General Motors' Corvair was a prime example of a giant corporation's producing an unsafe product and engaging in illegal activities to try to protect itself (unsuccessfully, as it turned out). The bribery of overseas officials by American business people became a national scandal, while too few firms took care to hire women, minorities, and the handicapped.

As a result, pressure was brought to bear on American business to rectify its shortcoming. Today, therefore, we see many businesses concerned about ethics, the environment, the less affluent, and the poor. Many firms engage in socially beneficial projects, as business' critics believed it should as a concerned partner in American society. It is expected that business will turn its flexibility, inventiveness, managerial expertise, and resources to social problems and duplicate its financial success story in the area of social improvements.

Among the new demands being placed on American business today are that it protect the environment, be ethical in its relationships with the public and foreign firms and governments, fully meet its responsibilities to the consumer, help create a fairer social structure, and take a creative role in American society.

ENVIRONMENTAL POLLUTION PROBLEMS

Different aspects of *pollution*, the deterioration of the human or natural environment, are many and closely related. They include polluted air and water, solid waste disposal, noise pollution, and land despoliation. Other pollution problems that are important, but perhaps not quite to the same degree, include pesticide control and visual pollution.

AIR POLLUTION

Sources of air pollution are shown in Figure 3-1. As you can see, industry is not the major source of contaminated air, although it is involved in some way with all types of pollution. Transportation is clearly the greatest source of pollutants. It is little wonder, therefore, that the automobile has come under such vigorous criticism since carbon monoxide, mostly from cars, is by far the largest pollutant.

Automobiles aside, the shortage of low-polluting energy sources such as natural gas is an additional problem. This is the result of the rapid rise in prices of oil and natural gas, the drive to reduce pollution, rapid economic growth, and other causes. Figure 3-2 shows the major sources of energy in 1977 compared with the projected percentages in 1985. Note that the Federal Energy Administration is hoping for a big increase in the use of coal and nuclear power and a reduction in the use of oil and natural gas. With imports accounting for 45 percent of our oil supply and a falling supply of natural gas in the United States, we must reduce our reliance on these sources.

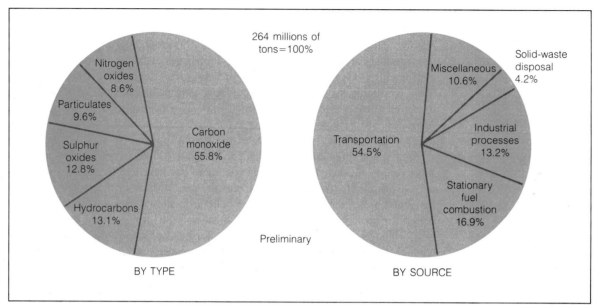

FIGURE 3-1 Air pollution emissions. Source: *Road Maps of Industry,* No. 1700, The Conference Board

At the same time it will not be easy to increase our use of coal and nuclear power. While business is being encouraged to shift to the use of coal, a number of obstacles stand in the way. Ninety percent of our economically recoverable coal is of the high-sulfur variety. As a result, it is difficult to meet existing clean air regulations while burning this fuel. The development of scrubbers, however, which remove sulfur dioxide and particulates from the smoke, may make it possible for public utilities to use more of this type of coal. This is significant because public utilities now burn about two-thirds of the coal the United States uses. Also, the passage of the Strip Mining Act of 1977, which makes it feasible to begin strip mining low-sulfur coal in the Western states, should help develop the production of this type of coal.

Increasing the use of nuclear energy is not going to be easy either. Growing concern over radioactive leaks has led to a number of delays and even cancellations of planned utility plants that were to be nuclear powered. The problem of safely disposing of radioactive nuclear waste material is also an obstacle to the spread of nuclear power plants, as is *thermal pollution,* which increases the temperature of the water that nuclear generators return to lakes and streams. This heated water harms fish and other aquatic life.

NOISE POLLUTION

Another type of air pollution, though not of the chemical or molecular kind, is noise pollution. According to a government study, as many as 40 million people may be headed for—or are already suffering from—various degrees of hearing

The blight of pollution is evident everywhere, even in the remotest regions of the desert country.

EPA-Documerica

FIGURE 3-2 Sources of energy used in the United States today and in 1985. Source: Federal Energy Administration

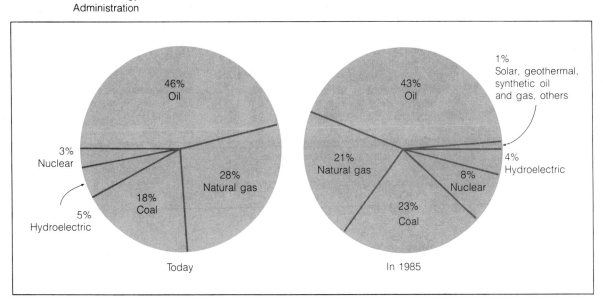

Today

46% Oil
3% Nuclear
5% Hydroelectric
18% Coal
28% Natural gas

In 1985

43% Oil
21% Natural gas
23% Coal
8% Nuclear
4% Hydroelectric
1% Solar, geothermal, synthetic oil and gas, others

impairment. The major noise polluters are factory machinery, cars, trucks, buses, motorcycles; pile-drivers, jackhammers, construction equipment, earth-moving equipment; and incoming and outgoing air traffic at airports. Noise pollution is particularly acute in our cities.

Noise is measured in decibels. Ninety decibels is considered the danger level. Continuous exposure to noise at that level may cause permanent loss of hearing. The Labor Department announced in mid-1975 that it would enforce a limit of 90 decibels averaged over an eight-hour period for all workplaces. Cost to industry for meeting this standard was estimated at $13 billion. Table 3-1 illustrates noise pollution toleration levels.

WATER POLLUTION

Water pollution is a very complex problem today because of the unknown effects of mixing various chemicals in water. The main types of water pollutants are domestic sewage, infectious substances, plant nutrients, organic chemicals, minerals and chemicals, sediments from land erosion, radioactive substances, and heat from power and industrial plants. The government's goal is to have every stream, lake, and river in the United States clean enough for swimming and drinking. A great deal of our water pollution is the result of industrial misuse of natural resources, although many municipalities are guilty of releasing untreated waste into rivers and streams.

TABLE 3-1 Noise pollution tolerance levels in decibels

	140	
		Painfully loud
	130	Limit of range of amplified speed
Jet takeoff at 60 meters (approx. 200 ft.)	120	
Discotheque		Maximum vocal effect
Riveting machine	110	
Jet takeoff at 600 meters (approx. 2,000 ft.)		
Shout at a half foot	100	
New York subway station		Very annoying
Heavy truck at 15 meters (approx. 50 ft.)	90	Hearing damage (8 hours or more)
Pneumatic drill at 15 meters (approx. 50 ft.)		
	80	Annoying
Freight train at 15 meters (approx. 50 ft.)		
Freeway traffic at 15 meters (approx. 50 ft.)		
	70	Telephone use difficult
Air conditioning unit at 6 meters (approx. 20 ft.)		
	60	
Light auto traffic		
	50	Quiet
Living room		
Bedroom	40	
Library		
Soft whisper at 5 meters (approx. 15 ft.)	30	Very quiet

Source: Environmental Protection Agency

Although strip mining costs much less than subsurface mining, its effects on the land are far more visible.

USDA

LAND DESPOLIATION   Land despoliation is perhaps the most recently recognized form of pollution. This includes unplanned urban sprawl, strip mining of coal and metals, and commercial development of national forests, parks, and scenic spots. Unrestricted development of urban areas has contributed to the deterioration of both the inner city and the suburbs. Strip mining, which accounts for half of the coal mined in this country, has left large areas of West Virginia and Kentucky looking like a war zone.

Tied to this is the problem of solid waste pollution. In 1972 some 71 billion cans, 38 billion bottles, 7 million cars, 35 million tons of paper—about 5 billion tons of garbage in all—were discarded by various sources including individuals, businesses, and governments. In addition about 3 billion tons of solid waste dumped by farms, mines, and industries never reached the public collection and disposal systems. The shortage of dumping grounds continues to plague most American cities, and many of them have simply run out of places to discard their trash and other waste materials.

CLEANING UP THE
ENVIRONMENT

Foremost among the new demands placed on American business is that it take measures to protect the quality of the natural environment: the air, water, and land around us. Led by crusaders for this cause, known as environmentalists, the last two decades have seen revolutionary changes in the American attitude about our natural resources.

As too many streams became open sewers, too many cities' air became virtually unbreathable, too much land was ravaged by strip mining, people began to condemn environmental pollution by business. A vigorous lobby known as the conservationist movement gathered momentum. With a history stretching back to the turn of the century and Upton Sinclair's novel, *The Jungle*, only in the past decade or so have environmentalists won widespread public and political support for their ideas.

THE PRICE OF
CONSERVATION

At first the great majority of business people rejected the conservationists' demands for quick and drastic action against the dangers of pollution. Business said that the demands were too costly and that environmental damage was preferable to higher prices and higher unemployment. "There is only one social responsibility for a business," one noted economist has observed. "That is simply to engage in activities designed to increase its profits." Seizing this point of view, industry as a whole lobbied to weaken the main environmental thrust. As a result business weakened its credibility in the area of environmental quality.

In more recent years, however, an increasing number of firms have taken the position that a compromise is needed between a clean environment and efficient production. They realize that if they do not cooperate voluntarily to do what society wants, they will face even stiffer federal and state legislation.

As a result, market forces are today being rearranged to provide the financial incentives for business to cope with pollution, with business and the various levels of government shouldering most of the responsibility. Ultimately, of course, consumers will pay for a cleaner environment—either through higher taxes or through higher prices for products and services. The real issues are finding the economic stimulus that best promotes a purer environment and paying for those benefits to society.

BUSINESS IS CRITICIZED   Business has been severely criticized for its largely uncooperative attitude in promoting a cleaner environment. Many people think business can do more than it has and a number of major criticisms have been voiced.

Lack of Sensitivity   Business is insensitive to the effect of its operations on the environment. It is said that business promotes the convenience or "throwaway" mania of the American people because it results in increased sales. The business response, of course, is that consumers want convenience. Critics claim, however, that business turns out a number of products that threaten the environment when they could be producing less polluting ones. An example frequently given is the great number of plastics that are difficult to recycle and which do not break down chemically for thousands of years, if ever. In addition, the heavy emphasis on packaging strains the environment in that it not only uses great quantities of natural resources but also contributes heavily to the problem of solid waste pollution. About 6 or 7 percent of the energy used by industry goes into packaging, which becomes about 13 percent of our total solid waste.

Pollution Pays   Business has not calculated cleanup costs as a part of the total cost of manufacturing products. As long as business can pass along the costs of pollution, such as dirty air or water, without making the cleanup part of production costs, those costs are not built into the final prices of the products.

Business firms argue, on the other hand, that if they pay all these external costs and some of their competitors do not, they will have to charge higher prices which will result in loss of business. Even if all the firms in an industry agreed to pay the costs of pollution cleanup, their foreign competitors, who would not have to do that, would undersell them in world markets. This illustrates the international scope of the pollution problem. Several world conferences on pollution have been held to try to arrive at some global solutions to the problems. So far, however, each nation prefers to solve the problems in its own way. Eventually, of course, the countries of the world will be forced to work together in establishing pollution standards and regulations, as they do now for world trade and monetary stability.

Because of market forces, business is frequently encouraged to make products that lead to environmental problems. Profits are often greater for industries or products that are greater polluters than for those that are not. Barry Commoner, in his book, *The Closing Circle*, suggests that a type of pollution price tag should be attached to each product, depending on the extent to which it pollutes the environment. Otherwise, as he points out, firms tend to produce the most profitable products, regardless of their effect on the environment. Large cars are more profitable than smaller cars for example. Not until the gasoline shortage developed in 1973 was there a drastic shift to the smaller car. The larger car, of course, besides using more gasoline, causes more pollution and creates more traffic and parking problems. The new farm technology depends heavily on increased fertilizer and pesticides, both of which aggravate water pollution problems. Plastic is more profitable than glass, synthetic fibers more profitable than natural ones, and detergents are more profitable than soaps. But all take a higher toll on the environment. The task is to rearrange market forces so that business is encouraged to put out products that are less polluting.

Slow to Develop Pollution Control Devices Business has been slow to develop and adapt pollution control devices. Again, auto companies are the obvious example, although steel and paper companies have also been cited. Business also claims that in some cases it does not pay to adopt new technology which is unproven, or that constant changes in standards makes investment in new plants an uncertain venture.

Antienvironment Lobbying Business lobbies to weaken antipollution laws. However, other pressure groups are doing the opposite and business recognizes that it must lobby to get across its point of view. Otherwise, it might be impossible for business to operate at a reasonable cost.

Public Relations Instead of Action Businesses cover up their lack of action through intensive public relations and advertising campaigns. There is no doubt that in the last few years large corporations have increased their promotion efforts to show that they are good corporate citizens. Business believes that this is necessary because of the bad publicity it has received.

THE FEDERAL GOVERNMENT'S RESPONSE The federal government assumed the major responsibility for a cleaner environment with the passage of the National Environmental Policy Act of 1969. As part of the act, the Council on Environmental Quality was established to advise the president on environmental matters. It is similar to the Council of Economic Advisors, which counsels him on economy policy. In 1970, the Environmental Protection Agency was created as an independent agency to enforce federal rules involving the environment. It administers all legislation affecting air pollution, solid waste disposal, water pollution, land-use regulation, and most nuclear radiation pollution. There have been many laws subsequently passed to regulate pollution:

The *Clean Air Act* of 1970 directed the setting of national air quality standards to protect the public health. States were ordered to make sure that national standards prevailed in their jurisdictions by 1975. Standards were set for emission levels of a wide variety of pollutants from both installations and transportation vehicles. In addition, in states where the quality of air is higher than the national standards,

business profile: CLEANING UP THE ENVIRONMENT—ARE YOU WILLING TO PAY THE PRICE?

Time was when a company was responsible only to its stockholders. But those good old days when making a profit was a company's only goal now look like the bad old days. The increasing awareness of environmental degradation, of polluted air and water caused by industrial wastes and the noxious products of oil and gasoline combustion, has forced on the business sector a broader sense of its responsibility to the general public and the general welfare. If a manufacturer of chemicals, for instance, dumps wastes into a stream that is used for recreation and drinking water, treating that stream so that such uses can be continued costs money. Americans have decided now that those costs should be borne by the polluter rather than the fisherman or city water user downstream.

This change in attitude will cost business billions, but it will also create new business opportunities for the companies that develop and produce the devices to clean up the environment. Wheelabrator-Frye, for example, has developed and begun to market a new system for city garbage disposal. This system converts the garbage into solid waste that can be used immediately for fill and methane that can be burned instead of natural gas to produce electricity. Other companies are producing scrubbers to filter out impurities before they leave the smokestacks and enter the atmosphere.

The automobile has been the biggest single producer of air pollutants, the major creator of smog. Now that government has called a halt to the production of gas-guzzling, smoke-belching behemoths, automakers, engine-makers, and battery-makers are engaged in a contest to develop a better solution to our transportation needs. A host of electric vehicles are being developed and pressed into use wherever their limited range makes them a practical alternative to the automobile with a combustion engine.

The twin goals of reducing pollution and conserving scarce fuel resources have given enormous new impetus to the development of solar heating systems, and dozens of companies around the country are refining techniques of harnessing the free, clean, inexhaustible power of the sun.

Society's demand for a cleaner environment can be met, and business can be an ally in this effort rather than the enemy.

IN AMERICA'S
GARBAGE HEAP—

Each American gener-
ates from 3 to 4 pounds of
trash per day—or more
than 1,000 pounds every
year. What this country's
trash consists of, as measured by weight:

Paper . . . . .31 percent
Yard wastes . . .19 percent
Food . . . . .18 percent
Glass . . . . .10 percent
Metals . . . . .10 percent
Wood . . . . 4 percent
Plastic . . . . 3 percent
Rubber and
  leather . . . . . . 3 percent
Textiles . . . . 1 percent
Other . . . . 1 percent

All told, the U.S. trash pile
mounted to 130 million tons
in 1973—enough to fill
garbage trucks that, lined
up bumper-to-bumper,
would stretch from New
York to Los Angeles, three
abreast.

FIGURE 3-3 The American
wastebasket. Source:
Reprinted from *U.S. News
& World Report,* May 13,
1974, Copyright 1974 U.S.
News & World Report, Inc.

the air cannot be allowed to deteriorate. The act has great ramifications for industry, shopping centers, cities, and mining and other business firms.

A study by the EPA in 1975 indicated that 156 of 247 regions in the country were not meeting the national standards for at least one pollutant. While the Clean Air Act was modified slightly in 1975, it was not noticeably weakened, even with the economy trying to recover from a recession.

The *Water Quality Act* of 1972 sets stiff guidelines for cleaning the navigable streams and lakes of the country. By 1977, all water treatment plants must have the best feasible technology for cleansing the water returned to a stream or lake; by 1983, they must have the best available technology. The goal is to have all streams and lakes in the country suitable for drinking and swimming by 1985.

The *Resources Recovery Act* of 1970 designed to get firms and cities to recycle the 150 million tons of trash they accumulate annually. Figure 3-3 shows the percentage of each item in the trash, by weight. Notice that some of the waste can be recycled and most can be burned for fuel. The EPA claims that about 75 percent could be burned to generate as much electricity as we get from 150 million barrels of oil.

The *Noise Control Act* of 1972 gives the EPA broad authority to establish noise levels for new motors and engines; for transportation, construction, and electrical equipment; and for aircraft. In addition, while the federal government has most of the control over the manufacturing of products that must meet noise standards, local governments can regulate the use of particular items. For example, a city has the right to ban autos from streets if the noise levels are higher than city minimums.

The EPA has maintained that the Clean Air Act of 1970 is basically a land-use act. It forces states to review the locations of a variety of facilities as to their effect on air quality. Some of these developments are shopping centers, sports complexes, drive-in theaters, recreational areas, as well as industrial plants. In addition, the EPA has the power to regulate strip mining and has a voice in regulating the sale and use of public land. The EPA also regulates coastal zone management by providing 30 states with guidelines on land bordering the oceans. Local and state governments also promulgate zoning laws that affect land use.

ENERGY ALLOCATION

In energy allocation, almost the full responsibility is taken by the federal government. When the Arab nations imposed a boycott of oil to the United States in 1973, the Federal Energy Administration was set up to allocate scarce oil to users. Quotas were established and priorities developed for each group in the country. While state and local governments have some responsibilities, they are minor compared with those of the federal government. In order to give better coordination to energy, the Department of Energy was established in 1977 to coordinate all aspects of the energy program.

THE BUSINESS
RESPONSE

Business' response to environmental lobbying was predictable. Most firms de-nied that their processes cause deterioration of the environment. Others denied that the deterioration was serious. As a result of this response, public criticism in-creased and became even more influential than ever before.

Business Must Pay Current legislation will be expensive for business. An esti-mate of the price tag for pollution control costs during the decade 1973–1983 is expected to be about $284 billion. Approximately half of that amount will come from business, the other half from government or the consumer. Ultimately, of course, much of the costs borne by business will also show up in higher prices. Figure 3-4 shows the estimated costs for cleaning up the environment under legis-lation in force in 1973.

FIGURE 3-4 Price tag for cleaning up the environment. Source: Reprinted from *U.S. News & World Report,* July 30, 1973. Copyright 1973 U.S. News & World Report, Inc.

PRICE TAG
FOR CLEANING UP
THE ENVIRONMENT:
$271 BILLION
Estimates of pollution-control
costs over next 10 years—
To fight air pollution . . . . $143 bil.
Government
spending . . . . $ 6 bil.
Private spending . . . . $ 56 bil.
On auto pollution . . . . $ 56 bil.
Controlling smoke, fumes,
dust from industry . . . . . . $ 81 bil.
and utilities
To fight
water pollution . . . . $116 bil.
Federal government
spending . . . . $ 44 bil.
Private spending
By manufacturing . . . . . . $ 59 bil.
companies . . . . . . $ 13 bil.
By utilities
To fight solid-
waste pollution . . . . $ 8 bil.
To fight noise, radiation, other
forms of pollution . . . . . $ 4 bil.
TOTAL
COST . . . . $271 BIL.

Business Seeks Exemption   Most large firms and some industries have attempted to get exemptions from some of the federal legislation or extensions of the time limit they have to meet the requirements. One of the most hotly contested exemptions was the one year delay in meeting the clean air standards that were supposed to go into effect with the 1978 model year cars. Detroit auto companies said that they could not meet the standards and would have to shut down their assembly lines as a result rather than pay fines of up to $10,000 per car. Congress finally granted the delay, but not without a great controversy. The steel industry has also been pushing for exemptions in the clean water standards, particularly at some of its older plants.

The Environmental Protection Agency did grant an exemption to the eight steel plants operating along the Mahoning River in Ohio. All of the plants were old and the companies argued that they would close them rather than try to install costly pollution controls in the old facilities. Since the firms provided about 15 percent of the jobs directly in the area and indirectly about that many more, the EPA bowed to pressure from the residents of the area, unions, civic and business leaders and gave an exemption.

Are the Benefits Worth the Cost?   The EPA estimated that 300 plants would close in the first five years of the clean air amendments, primarily because firms would not find it economically sound to meet the new requirements. In addition, firms wondered if the devices that are being promoted by the EPA and conservation groups are really worth the cost. In the steel industry, for example, scrubbers must be installed in smokestacks to clean the fumes before they can be emitted into the atmosphere. The results of the tests on the effectiveness and durability of the scrubbers are mixed. Catalytic converters on autos still have to be perfected before they can be fitted on a mass production basis.

One potentially profitable opportunity for business in this area is in "garbage power." At least 11 recovery systems are in operation in the United States with about that many more under construction. The largest garbage burning facility and resource recovery program is in Saugus, Massachusetts. There, in a plant opened in 1975, a private firm burns 1,200 tons of garbage a day. It then sells the steam that is produced to General Electric and the clean ash residue to construction companies for roadbeds and other building purposes. While there is somewhere between $5 and $9 billion in construction of these plants across the country, all has not gone well with them. A $70 million project to convert St. Louis trash into fuel and other recoverable materials was abandoned by the Union Electric Company, as was a demonstration plant in Baltimore, Maryland, built by the Monsanto Corporation.

BUSINESS ETHICS

The question of ethics—the branch of philosophy that deals with the "right" and "wrong" of human behavior—has been connected with business since the beginning of commerce. One of the first issues was interest rates and usury, which is lending money at an exorbitant rate of interest. By the Middle Ages, usury became recognized as an unethical and immoral business practice. Today, most business questions involving ethics are not as clearly defined. Many gray areas are evolving, partially through greater disclosures of hitherto unpublicized business practices, such as the bribery of overseas politicians by American business representatives, and partially through an ever changing view of what Americans regard as ethical and moral activities.

CONTEMPORARY CORRUPTION

The list of possibly unethical business practices would be a long one. It would include using false and misleading advertising, price fixing, conspiring against unions, illegal lobbying, unlawfully influencing government employees, making illegal political contributions, fraud, and selling unsafe products, among others. Today, the American public—and its government—are demanding more honesty from the business community, especially as the list of unethical business practices continues to make headlines. Such is the public's distrust of big business ethics that many people regarded the 1973 energy shortage as a fabrication, contrived by a conspiracy of oil companies in an attempt to boost prices and profits.

MORE ETHICAL CONDUCT

As a result of the public outcry against many of the more notorious business ethics scandals—the milk industry's illegal contributions to Richard Nixon's presidential reelection fund, kickbacks to retailers, fraudulent switching of automobile engines by General Motors—a standard of ethics is slowly evolving that would require corporations (legally considered to be "persons") to conduct themselves according to the same standards applied to individuals. Corporate ethics will continue to be a controversial issue, especially following the new disclosures of conduct that would be considered unethical had a small business person committed them.

SOCIAL RESPONSIBILITIES OF BUSINESS

There is a real question about how business should demonstrate that it is a good citizen and show that it is meeting its social responsibilities.

HOW STRONG A CONCERN?

Peter Drucker, probably the best-known management consultant in the country, has argued for years that the only social responsibility business has is to make as great a profit as possible, assuming that the profit is made legally in an industry where there is adequate competition.

Drucker has said that business cannot behave like anything other than business.[1] He believes that profitability must be the yardstick for business activity in respect to the *quality* of life fully as much as it has been the yardstick for business activity in respect to the quantities of life. Profitability is merely another word for the efficient employment of economic resources.

1. "Business and the Quality of Life," *Sales Management*, March 15, 1969, p. 33.

personality profile:
the Fords and social responsibility

Henry Ford I was a mechanical genius who could read engines the way other people read books. He even approached the making of automobiles as though he were inventing the most efficient engine for their production. Ford introduced interchangeable parts and the first assembly line, both revolutionary techniques in manufacturing. Some of his policies were socially advanced for his time. For example, he hired the handicapped and paid $5 a day in 1914, double the industry wage at that time. The reasons for these policies, however, were that time studies proved the handicapped produced efficiently at their jobs and higher wages meant greater purchasing power to keep factories running. Henry Ford was a great individualist who ran things his way. No union was going to tell him how to run *his* company, so he hired a private army of guards to keep the unions out. For all his inventive genius, Henry Ford I was socially blind, opinionated, and prejudiced.

Henry Ford II, grandson of the founder, took over leadership of the giant auto firm in 1945, when he was only 27. He has been a very different model of Ford, with a better idea of the role of business in society. Indeed, few business leaders today have exercised such leadership in promoting a better society.

On the national level, Henry Ford II helped start the National Urban Coalition, a group of business firms devoted to restoring our decaying urban centers. He was an organizer and leader of the National Alliance of Businessmen, which is devoted to providing jobs for minorities. He heads the National Center for Voluntary Action, a clearinghouse to bring together social agencies and volunteer workers. He also started the Committee for Concerned Consumerism, a business organization which is trying to revitalize the Better Business Bureau and make it more responsive to consumers.

Ford's interests are not just national. Henry Ford II conceived and led the drive to bring downtown Detroit back to life. His company pledged the first $6 million needed for startup costs, and he personally raised the rest of the funds for the $500 million Renaissance Center, completed in 1977. This immense and beautiful complex contains a hotel; residential and office buildings; and restaurant, shopping, and entertainment facilities. This was the first time in decades that business had risked any large investment to halt the downhill slide in Detroit's central district.

One Framework According to this framework, Drucker suggests that responsibility for the quality of life means three kinds of approaches to the problems of the community.

The first and most desirable is an approach in which a problem can be converted into an opportunity for profit. Garbage converters are an example of this approach.

Second, where a problem cannot be converted into a business opportunity, some government regulation may be necessary.

If even the use of regulation does not provide a profitable opportunity for business, then perhaps a third approach of providing a subsidy to business should be considered. Drucker favors grants or subsidies from the government to do a particular job rather than giving a tax break or passing on a hidden charge to the community or consumer.

Other Answers Many other experts have differing opinions on the role of business in improving the quality of life. Some would nationalize key industries, as has been done in a number of countries. *Nationalization* occurs when a national government assumes ownership of a privately owned business. Social responsibilities would then be solely the government's concern. Others would prohibit firms from making a profit above a certain level. In both cases, it is hoped that firms would be encouraged to spend more of their resources in solving social problems as they use solving economic problems. Howsoever firms are involved in social programs, there are restraints on a firm's management in participating in any major social improvement program.

BUSINESS, GOVERNMENT, AND INDIVIDUALS All too often we see business lagging behind some aspects of society's requirements of it. This is perhaps nowhere more obvious than in the way business falls short in dealing equitably with individual members of society. As a result, a number of movements, special interest groups, and laws have brought pressure on business to make certain that it keep pace with changing social realities, especially those involving minorities, consumerism, ageism, and women's rights.

Minorities The National Alliance of Businessmen finds jobs for about 350,000 disadvantaged persons a year, most of them in urban areas. This alliance is an association of about 35,000 companies who agree to hire minority workers. While they can get government subsidies to train the disadvantaged workers, most do not, preferring to go their own way free of governmental involvement.

In 1964 Congress approved and President Johnson signed a significant civil rights act that prohibited discrimination in employment on the basis of race, color, religion, sex, or national origin. This legislation updated the centuries old American credo that "all men are created equal." A five-member Equal Employment Opportunities Commission was also set up by the act. It is the commission's responsibility to investigate charges of discrimination against employers and increase job opportunities for women and minorities.

Ageism   In 1978 Congress approved legislation banning compulsory retirement for most workers before age 70. Though predictions are that not more than about 200,000 Americans eligible for retirement will stay on their jobs as a result of the act, the legislation goes a long way toward "gray liberation." It continues a trend started in 1967 by the passage of the Age Discrimination in Employment Act, which prohibits employers from using age as a factor in the hiring, firing, or promotion of people between the ages of 40 and 65.

As the post-World War II "baby boom" generation grows older, they will no doubt affect and transform the way business reacts to the issue of age in the 1980s and 1990s, as they affected and transformed American society and values in previous decades.

Consumerism   The Consumer Movement of the 1960s and 1970s, spearheaded by consumer activists Ralph Nader and his associates, dubbed "Nader's Raiders" by the press, wrought significant changes on the way business dealt with its customers. A full discussion of consumerism and its impact on business can be found in Chapter 8.

In New York City, the Better Business Bureau sponsors a mobile consumer information center. Consumers are invited to ask questions on how to get the most for their dollars, the legal safeguards available to them, and other consumer-related matters.

Better Business Bureau of Metropolitan New York.

Women's Rights Statistically there are more women than men in the United States at the moment and therefore women cannot technically be labeled a minority. Nevertheless, women faced, and in some instances still do, many of the problems of discrimination that blacks faced in business before the passage of the sweeping civil rights legislation of the 1960s. To combat these limitations, women known as feminists, striving to right society's wrongs against women, lobbied Congress for the passage of the Equal Pay Act of 1963. This legislation made it mandatory for businesses to pay men and women the same salary for the same job. This legislation was supplemented by the Civil Rights Act of 1964, discussed above.

Increasingly today women strive to achieve business equality with men and many have started their own businesses, professional careers, and even banks.

RESTRAINTS ON MANAGEMENT

In smaller firms, there is less restraint on social commitment since the owner may also be the manager, who can commit the firm to social causes as heavily as financially possible. In larger companies, however, managers have a number of groups to which they are accountable for such a decision. Any large corporation can make positive contributions to the quality of life of its employees, consumers, and citizens, as long as those contributions do not detract from its profit goals. If its major economic goals are not met, however, there are a number of related problems.

The Problem of Ultimate Disapproval If profits are lowered significantly customers do not mind in the short run, of course, because they feel that the firm is providing as low a price as possible. But in the long run they may lose because either prices will have to be raised or the firm will not be able to make the same quality product that the customer has come to expect. However, every other group with which the firm deals would find lower profits undesirable.

The board of directors and stockholders would probably demand major changes. Many stockholders might sell their stock, and prospective stockholders would invest their money in other corporations with better earnings prospects. Creditors would be uneasy about a firm's ability to pay its debtors. Workers would be concerned because the lower profit rates might signal a layoff or smaller raises than were expected. Even the government would lose, because the firm will pay less taxes and require more unemployment insurance to pay furloughed workers.

An interesting development of the early 1970s was the emergence of a number of mutual funds that announced they would invest their money only in socially responsible firms. They had a very difficult time attracting stockholders, since very few people are willing to accept a lower rate of return on their money, even for a good cause. While almost all Americans want corporations to be more socially responsible, most of us would prefer that someone else pay for it.

Measuring Social Responsibility   Does that then mean that businesses should not divert resources to improve social conditions? Hardly! Most people believe that a firm's social responsibility is directly proportionate to its resources. The bigger, more successful firms have an obligation to make greater contributions to society than smaller firms. It is ironic that the firms under the greatest attack, such as IBM, General Motors, and the oil companies, are the firms with the greatest resources for contributing to the quality of life in this country.

Most large firms today are concerned about their public image and their impact on the quality of American life. Many have adopted some form of the social audit. A *social audit* is a listing of the social contributions of a firm and their cost to the company. While a number of large firms now use both internal and external authorities to monitor the company's contribution to the quality of life, the social audit is still in its infancy. This is partly because there is no consensus as to what social responsibilities the corporation can be expected to assume. Also there are no guidelines as to how much a corporation should do in any social field. Costs, too, are difficult to measure. However, there is no doubt that corporations will have to do a more effective job of reporting their social contributions.

In the final analysis, businesses will be as socially responsible as the public demands. A business is a creature of society. It will meet the guidelines and behavior that we, collectively, expect and demand. In the short run, it can evade its responsibilities, but in the longer run, it will meet our criteria for socially acceptable behavior. Let us hope that we understand the role of business and its restraints well enough to make intelligent decisions about what is desirable social performance.

SUMMARY

Chapter 3 has focused on the new demands placed on business to meet its social responsibilities. Among these demands are protecting the environment; being ethical with the public, foreign firms, and governments; being responsive to consumers; helping establish a fairer social structure; and taking a creative role in American society. This chapter has also identified some of the groups making those demands. Groups particularly active in making greater demands on business include minorities, older workers, consumers, and women.

The main obstacles for business in cleaning up the environment appear to be measuring the costs that business will have to bear and determining what benefits business will derive from the cost of its efforts. Business is trying to define its social responsibility. However, without a clear understanding by society of the constraints under which business operates, this effort won't be totally effective.

SUMMARY OF KEY TERMS

Clean Air Act Legislation setting national air-quality standards to protect the public health.

Nationalization A national government's assuming ownership of a privately owned business.

Ethics The branch of philosophy that deals with the "right" and "wrong" of human behavior.

Pollution Deterioration of the human or natural environment.

Resources Recovery Act Legislation containing guidelines for solid-waste disposal and encouraging recycling of solid waste.

Social Audit A listing of a firm's social contributions and their cost to the company.

Thermal Pollution Heated water discharged from nuclear generators returned to lakes and streams that harms acquatic life.

Water Quality Act Law establishing guidelines for cleaning the navigable streams and lakes of the country.

REVIEW QUESTIONS

1. What new major demands is society placing on business?
2. What is pollution and how does it relate to business activity?
3. What are the major environmental pollution problems that we face in this country?
4. What is the federal government's role in tackling the pollution problem?
5. What is thermal pollution and why is it a threat to the environment?
6. What is a social audit?
7. What is ethics and what was the first business practice deemed to be unethical?
8. What is nationalization and how does it relate to businesses' social responsibilities?
9. What is ageism and why is it a problem for business?
10. Why is management generally reluctant to take on social programs?

DISCUSSION QUESTIONS

1. What is the role of business in cleaning up the environment?
2. Why should business conduct itself in an ethical way as long as it obeys the law?
3. Why have pressures arisen for business to become more involved in solving social problems?
4. Many people have recommended that business be forced to pay for pollution cleanup without raising prices. Do you believe this is likely to happen? Why or why not?
5. What is your reaction to the statement, "The only responsibility business has to society is to make as large a profit as possible"?

CASES FOR DECISION MAKING

CORPORATIONS MOVE TO THE SUBURBS

DuPage County, Illinois, has the highest growth rate of any county in Illinois, and one of the highest in the country. Almost half a million people live in DuPage, more than three times as many as 25 years ago. There are about 700 manufacturing companies, which provide 45,000 industrial jobs. In addition, several nationally known corporations have their headquarters in the county, and there are large research laboratories and warehouses.

The average price of a home in DuPage County is $35,000, far beyond the reach of factory workers. There are no public housing units. As a result, almost all of the production workers live in Chicago and other towns and commute to the factories. Some companies operate bus service for their workers. The chairman of the county board of supervisors said that it would take $400 million to eliminate the shortcomings of the sewer and drainage systems. Water is also in short supply. All roads are congested, and it is estimated that one in three residents leaves the county each year. Housing costs and taxes have skyrocketed. The head of the recently formed County Planning Commission indicated that the county had lost its enthusiasm for attracting more businesses.[2]

1. If you were a citizen involved in planning a suburban area, what regulations would you want to ensure that firms entering your suburb were socially responsible?
2. At what point do you believe that a community may have all the business that it can accommodate?
3. Should suburban areas be forced to provide some form of low-cost housing (perhaps through one of the government subsidiary plans) so that workers can live near their jobs?

IS G.M. SOCIALLY RESPONSIBLE?

For decades General Motors has been looked on as a great "money machine." It consistently earned 20 percent return on net worth, with annual profits at the $2 billion level in the early 1970s. Suddenly it came under attack from a number of quarters. Its products were called unsafe and the main cause of

2. "Roadblocks Ahead for the Great Corporate Move-Out," *Fortune*, June 1972, pp. 78–172.

air pollution, congestion in the cities, and ugliness in the countryside. It is the symbol of the materialism that is supposed to be degrading American life. It is criticized for being a major polluter and for employing too few blacks.

In 1971, the company spent more than $200 million on pollution controls and $400 million on safety research, plus additional millions on research in new transportation methods. Had they not spent that money, they would again have had a net income of a little above 20 percent on investment. As it was, the return was about 17.5 percent. There is little indication that the company will soon return to the 20 percent return on investment level that it once had. Part of this is caused by the large capital expenditures for pollution and safety controls. The other part is stiffer competition from both domestic and foreign car manufacturers and a switch in American tastes to smaller cars, where profits per car are less.[3]

1. Should the federal government help pay for the additional research needed to develop products that meet federal guidelines for safety or for a cleaner environment? Why or why not?
2. What do you believe has been the effect on General Motors' stockholders since the company's profit rates have begun to decline?
3. Do you believe that General Motors has been socially responsible in the last few years? Why or why not?

ECONOMIC GROWTH VERSUS ECOLOGY

Americans want economic growth so they can have jobs and a variety of low-priced products. They also want a clean environment because they want to be healthy and enjoy the beauty of nature. Sometimes the two goals come into conflict.

A case in point is the controversy involving Reserve Mining Company's activities in northern Min-

3. "G.M.: The Price of Being 'Responsible,'" *Fortune* (January 1972): pp. 99–176.

nesota. The company, a joint venture of Armco Steel Corp. and Republic Steel Corp., was established to extract iron pellets from a hard black rock called taconite. The process involves the heavy use of water so the firm built the plant about 50 miles from the mine on Lake Superior. In the process, it dumped into the lake two tons of waste rock for each ton of pellets it produced. At first this disposal appeared to be no problem, for the lake is 650 to 900 feet deep.

In 1974, however, it was discovered that the rock being dumped into Lake Superior contained asbestoslike particles that cause cancer in humans. As a result the plant was closed for a short time and a bitter court battle produced the decision that Republic Steel could keep operating but would have to build a mammoth waste dump and eliminate the dust particles from the atmosphere.

The total cost of the required pollution control for the plant will be about $370 million, more than the cost of the plant itself. In all American companies spent about $7.5 billion in 1977 for structures and equipment to reduce air and water pollution and to dispose of solid waste.

1. What effect do you suppose the expenditures for pollution control will have on the prices of products?
2. What is the proper balance between economic efficiency and protection of the environment?
3. Is there a need for international controls of pollution as they affect production processes?

RELATED READINGS

Alcaly, Roger E., ed. *The Fiscal Crisis of American Cities*. New York: Vintage, 1977.

Book of essays dealing with the financial problems of large cities, in particular, New York City. The book focuses on the economic, social, and political forces that have combined to bring most large cities to the brink of bankruptcy.

Blair, John M. *The Control of Oil*. New York: Pantheon, 1977.

Well-documented book discusses the relationship between the OPEC countries and the multinational oil companies. The author links the OPEC and the oil companies together in the effort to keep production at the level of world demand instead of running a surplus which would drive the price down.

Jacoby, Neil H. *Corporate Power and Social Responsibility*. New York: Macmillan, 1973.

A careful analysis of the social responsibility of business. The author finds little evidence that the United States is becoming a corporate state. He argues that there is more competition than ever, though the type of competition has changed. He does suggest changes in the social role and control of corporations.

Lindblom, Charles E. *Politics and Markets*. New York: Basic, 1977.

The author, a well-known economist, attempts to place the power of business in society in perspective. He argues that a market economy creates a privileged place for the business enterprise which leads to economic and political clout for large firms.

Perrow, Charles. *The Radical Attack on Business*. New York: Harcourt Brace Jovanovich, 1972.

A paperback selection of readings critical of business and its efforts to meet its social responsibilities. These readings are primarily aimed at showing how large corporations have evaded their social obligations.

part one: **CAREER OPPORTUNITIES**

CAREERS IN ECONOMICS

Of the more than 100,000 full-time economists employed in this country, 75 percent are in business and industry, 10 percent are teaching in colleges and universities, and 15 percent are in government agencies. Economists in business and industry provide management with information for decision making on such matters as markets for, and prices of, company products; the effect of government policies on business or international trade; and the advisability of adding new lines of merchandise, or expanding the company's business. Economists in government provide information used in assessing economic conditions and the need for changes in government policy. Most government economists are in the fields of agriculture, business, finance, labor, or international trade. Economists in universities teach economics and conduct or direct research.

An undergraduate degree with a major in economics is sufficient for many beginning research jobs in government and private industry. Graduate education is very important for individuals planning to become economists. A person considering a career as an economist should be research-oriented, have a good command of mathematics, like detail work, and be able to work as part of a team effort. Oral and written communication skills are required, and economists must be objective in their analysis.

The number of persons graduating with degrees in economics through the mid-1980s will probably exceed available positions. As a result, strong competition can be expected for the moderate increase in jobs. Some persons with economics degrees are likely to take jobs as trainees or management interns in government, industry, or business. The demand for economists is likely to increase fairly rapidly in local and state government, but at a much slower pace in federal government, in industry, and in college teaching. While business firms have a continued need for economic analysis, slower growth rates in many industries make it difficult to hire as many economic analysts as many firms would like.

part two

MANAGEMENT

Being a good leader is what management is all about. To be a good leader one must have a fair amount of natural ability. But as important as natural ability is, there is a need for training and experience in the art of leadership. No matter what the size of the business that one is managing, the major area of responsibility is that of dealing with other people. This is what makes management such a satisfying activity on the one hand, and a source of great frustration on the other when relations with people do not go well.

Before management can function properly, the business must be formed and organized effectively. Organizing a business is discussed in Chapter 4. Since every business is a unique entity, each must be structured on an individual basis. Naturally, a small business requires little formal structure. However, as we shall see in Chapter 6, the manager of a small firm must serve as a jack-of-all-trades. The small business operator has to be the sales, finance, production, and personnel managers. If the small firm is a franchise, the operator must also be able to communicate well with the parent organization.

In larger organizations, the roles of managers become more specialized and the channels for communication are more complex and important. Decision making falls into specific domains. The financial manager must be the ultimate decision maker in financial matters as the marketing manager must be in the area of sales and customer relations. Still, responsibilities overlap and managers must be skillful planners and coordinators to avoid problems and smooth them over if they do occur.

Management can be a satisfying occupation to those who have the talent, education, and training. Besides satisfaction, the salaries and fringe benefits are usually substantial. Many minorities and women are finding entry into management to be easier for them than it has been for others in the past.

chapter 4

ORGANIZING AND MANAGING A BUSINESS

OBJECTIVES

When you finish reading and studying this chapter, you should be able to do the following:

1. Know and describe the three basic forms of business organization responsible for the success of business in the American economy.

2. Know and describe the hybrid business organizations and their reasons for existing.

3. Be aware of the special problems and procedures involved in formulating and organizing a corporation.

4. Be familiar with the special problems and the risks associated with business firms in the United States.

5. Be able to describe the methods used to formulate large business organization, particularly as they have developed in the years since the end of World War II.

CHAPTER PREVIEW

If you have ever helped to plan a school dance or an intramural football league, you probably realize the importance of organization. So too must every business have a structure related to the way it is owned and operated. Usually a business formed by one person and operated by that person is organized as a sole proprietorship. In essence, the owner-operator has complete say in determining policies and making decisions. The owner gets to keep all the profits but, on the other hand, suffers whatever losses there might be.

A slightly more complicated form of business organization is the partnership. In this type of business there is more than one owner and often more than one manager. While a partnership has the advantage of consultation, it also presents a problem: sharing authority and decision making are matters about which people often disagree. Where there is disagreement, important decisions are delayed and the personal relationship between partners can easily deteriorate. This is one of the reasons why the partnership is the least popular of the three major forms of business organizations.

Since the time of the industrial revolution of the late nineteenth century, the corporation has become the dominant form of business organization in the American economy. It is the most popular form because it is organized to facilitate a rapid inflow of capital by selling stock to investors, who then become partial owners of the firm. Because there are often too many stockholders for all of them to have a say in the management of the enterprise, they elect from among themselves a board of directors who determine policy and choose the operating officers for the corporation. Despite some drawbacks from their very large-scale organization, corporations have become the most effective and efficient way to run large and medium-sized businesses in this country.

"And to think that it started out as a little lemonade stand."

4

ORGANIZING AND MANAGING A BUSINESS

Whether we like it or not most of us have a highly organized life-style. We are citizens of a local community that has a distinct governmental organization. We work for companies, belong to unions, or attend schools that are highly organized. We hold memberships in clubs that function independently or as one chapter of a national organization, or we play on teams that are organized individually or in a league. Why so much organization? Because a well-organized activity will run more efficiently and effectively.

Probably more than anything else, the key to the remarkable development and success of business in the United States is oganization. You may recall from your study of American history that the earliest business people functioned independently. That is to say, they supplied their own capital and efforts—both mental and physical—to produce and sell their products. In those days business organization was simple. As production and the market structure became more and more complicated, it became necessary to organize businesses on a more complex and broader scale. An intricate, efficient economic network developed which was a major force in the historical evolution from the individually owned and operated businesses to the huge corporations which dominate American business today.

FORMS OF BUSINESS ORGANIZATION

There are three major forms of business organization: sole proprietorship, partnership, and corporation. Let's briefly look at the important characteristics of each of them.

THE SOLE PROPRIETORSHIP

Bob Musto has worked for six years as a short-order cook in a large downtown lunch shop in Richmond, Virginia. He received some money on his father's death and has decided that he would like to be his own boss. Bob decides to open a small snack shop in a suburban shopping center that will concentrate on the breakfast and lunch trade from stores and offices in the shopping center as well as from three large factories within a two-mile radius. Bob's wife, Evelyn, is willing to help in the store, and Bob figures that only one or two employees will be needed.

In terms of business organization, Musto's needs are relatively simple. His own capital and experience seem sufficient, so his most probable choice of organization would be that of a *sole proprietorship*. By organizing his venture in this manner, Bob will operate his business under the following conditions:

1. He retains all profits for personal use or for reinvestment in the business.
2. He determines the firm's policies.
3. He has full responsibility for management decisions.
4. His operating red tape, such as tax forms and subsequent legal and accounting fees, are held to a minimum.

5. He is literally "his own boss," though he must, of course, continue to satisfy his customers.

6. His income on money invested is unlimited. After paying income taxes, all profits are his and there is no limit on annual earnings.

7. He has unlimited liability. In the event the business fails, creditors can claim all remaining business assets as well as his personal assets to satisfy their claims.

Like all other forms of business organization, there are a number of advantages and disadvantages in being a sole owner. One major problem with sole proprietorship is that of continuity. If Bob became ill and had to enter a hospital, who would take care of his business for him? Another disadvantage is *unlimited liability*. As sole owner, Bob must live with the constant threat of losing, not only his business, but his personal property as well, in the event of a lawsuit. Further, his opportunity for vacation and days off will be severely limited. While being one's own boss sounds attractive, it also entails responsibilities which the average salaried employee or wage earner is usually unwilling to assume. Being a sole owner also limits his opportunity to enlarge his business. He can only borrow a limited amount of money for expansion; since he has no partners or stockholders, he cannot raise needed funds until he decides to reorganize his firm.

Small, single-owner businesses are still the most numerous business form. This kind of business is known as a sole proprietorship.

Robert Rubenstein

PARTNERSHIP

Let us assume that Bob has survived the risks of being in business for himself and that Musto's Sandwich Shop is doing very well. One unexpected result is that many local residents and night workers are coming in at dinner time. Bob sees this as an opportunity to expand, redecorate, and obtain a liquor license to improve his services to the dinner clientele. He has been in business for four years and has done well financially. However, he has three young children and his personal expenses have been high. To expand, Bob will have to borrow or take on a partner. The bank is willing to lend him a considerable amount of money but he still would be in a management bind. His business now demands management 14 hours a day, whereas he was able to get away with 10 when the dinner business was minimal. Furthermore, Bob does not have the time needed to supervise a bar and full-time kitchen staff as well as a crew of waiters and waitresses. He might be able to hire a good manager, but how much could he pay and what fringe benefits and job security could he offer at this stage of the business' development? Bob decides, therefore, to bring in a partner and advertises for one in a financial newspaper. After a series of interviews, he forms a partnership with Paul Volyn, who has been a restaurant manager in Washington, D.C., for many years.

Volyn invests in the business an amount equal to Bob's capital, and both men decide to share profits equally. All other agreements are contained in a formal contract called *articles of partnership*. This contract specifies how profits are

Partnerships have declined in popularity in respect to other forms of business. In some ways, however, they offer advantages not available to the sole proprietor.

Maria Karras

shared, the responsibilities and hours of each partner, their salaries, and the procedures for admitting new partners; it also gives general information about the partners and the business.

The new partnership is to be called the Gaslight Restaurant and Lounge. By setting up a partnership, Musto and Volyn will operate under the following conditions:

1. The partners jointly decide the policy of the firm.
2. Decisions are made by consensus. If more partners are admitted, a majority vote is necessary.
3. Unlimited liability is still present, and both partners' personal assets can be taken by creditors for *all* the debts of the partnership.
4. Each partner can legally bind the partnership by his actions.
5. Each partner may receive a salary as well as a share of profits.
6. The partnership is dissolved upon the death or disability of either partner.

As with sole proprietorships, there are advantages and disadvantages to a partnership. The major advantage seems to be that two heads are better than one. Decision making is joint and therefore problem solving is based on more input. At the same time, if the partners are not compatible this can be a tremendous disadvantage because agreement will be very difficult to reach. Another disadvantage is that any partner can bind all partners if he acts in good faith. Let us assume that Paul Volyn decides to bring in entertainment for the supper crowd and signs a six-month contract with a singing and instrumental group. Musto knew Volyn was negotiating with the group but knew nothing about the six-month contract. Assuming the supper crowd doesn't develop, the group becomes an expensive overhead and a drain on profits. Both partners suffer in this instance for the honest mistake of one. Only general partners—that is, those who have full partnership privileges—can bind all partners. In some partnerships there are limited partners. A limited partner usually has limited liability and limited management voice. He is more or less a part-time associate taken in for the capital that he brings to the business. Even in a limited partnership, there must be at least one general partner. Although a limited partner cannot assume the role of a general partner, there is no reason why he could not work for, or help manage, the firm.

Some partnerships have silent partners or secret partners. A *silent partner* is one who has a share of ownership either as a general partner or, more likely, as a limited partner, but who has no say in the management or operation of the firm. Such a partner is usually someone who has taken a share of ownership for its investment potential only. Obviously, in a partnership with 10 or 50 members, there must be some who are willing to assume the role of silent partners. A *secret partner* is one who has the right to manage and make decisions but whose role as a partner is not known to the public. A physician might choose to be a secret partner in the ownership of a local private country club. There is nothing illegal about one wanting to keep certain business affairs private, and many partnerships have secret partners.

CORPORATION After four years of operating as a partnership, Bob Musto and Paul Volyn have done so well that they decide to build an addition to their restaurant that will contain two banquet rooms, a photography studio, and a cocktail lounge. In this way they will be able to cater extensively to wedding parties and other affairs. Again, there will be a need to raise a large amount of capital, and both men have decided that they want to retain management control as it now exists. Banks are unwilling to lend them all of the funds necessary, so their attorney and accountant have advised them to incorporate and sell shares of stock to relatives, friends, and the general public.

Shares of stock are written evidences of partial ownership in a corporation. Anyone who invests in a corporation must do so by buying shares of the corporation's stock. Such a person is known as a stockholder or shareholder. (See Chapter 12, "Sources of Financing," for more technical information on corporation stock.)

Forming the Corporation The first step that Musto and Volyn must take is to make application to the state in which they live (Virginia in this case) for a *corporate charter*. In most states this application is filed with the office of the secretary of state. There are various legal procedures that must be followed in applying for incorporation, and an experienced attorney is needed to implement the necessary steps. Many states require that there be at least three stockholders at the time of charter and that the corporation have a board of directors and corporate officers including a president, vice president, secretary, and treasurer. In a small corporation, such as that being formed by Musto and Volyn, the principal stockholders, members of the board of directors, and corporate officers are usually the same people. Musto and Volyn, hereafter known as Gaslight, Inc., will have five stockholders: Bob and Evelyn Musto, Paul and Margaret Volyn, and Chester Kraemer, their attorney.

Characteristics of the Corporation By adopting the corporate form, Gaslight, Inc., will operate under the following conditions:

1. Policy is decided by the board of directors, who are elected by the stockholders at an annual meeting. Since a corporation is only a "legal person" and not a living one, it can act only through the directors elected by the stockholders.
2. Each stockholder has as many votes as the number of voting shares of stock owned. These votes are cast to elect members of the board and to reach decisions on other major matters at the annual meeting.
3. Each stockholder has *limited liability*. If the corporation fails financially and its debts are greater than its assets, the corporate debt is limited to the extent

Today, corporations dominate the American business world. One of these corporations is Westinghouse Electric Corporation, a leader in electrical products and heavy generating machinery. National headquarters for Westinghouse is located in Pittsburgh, Pennsylvania.

Westinghouse Electric Corporation

of its assets. Each stockholder, therefore, can only lose the extent of his or her investment in shares of stock in the corporation.

4. Dividends, which must be declared by the board of directors, are paid to stockholders in proportion to the number of shares held by each.
5. Legal problems and red tape must be foreseen in operating the corporation.
6. If a key stockholder, member of the board, or corporate officer dies, the corporation does not cease to exist. Since no one person or persons has sole control, the corporation maintains indefinite continuity.
7. Stock is bought and sold quite easily on a stock exchange as long as there is a demand for it.
8. Income and other taxes will be paid at rates higher than those for proprietorships and partnerships.

There is no doubt that corporations are a very effective method of business organization since they meet the need for bringing great accumulations of capital under a single control. As with all forms of business organizations there are many advantages and disadvantages.

If the principal stockholders of Gaslight, Inc.—Musto and Volyn—were to list the major reasons for forming a corporation their list would include the following advantages.

1. Limited liability. Liability is limited to one's investment in shares of stock.
2. Continuity. The operations of a corporation are not legally interrupted by the death, disability, or disappearance of a stockholder.
3. Ease of raising additional capital. Corporations can always sell more shares of stock or sell bonds to raise additional capital.
4. Ease of transfer of ownership. If an owner wishes to sell his or her share of ownership, the shares are easily transferable.
5. Legal protection for owners. Under law a corporation is considered as a legal person. It is therefore separate and distinct from its owners (stockholders).
6. No managerial responsibilities. Investors in a corporation do not have to partake in the management of the company. Management is delegated to others.
7. Adaptability. The corporation form is adaptable to small-, medium-, and large-sized companies.
8. Flexibility. Corporations can more readily hire managers with specialized skills than other forms of business.

The disadvantages in forming a corporation are as follows:

1. A corporation has more kinds of taxes to file and pay.
2. Organizing a corporation is more difficult and more expensive.
3. Numerous state and federal controls are exercised over a corporation.
4. Corporate activities may possibly be limited by charter restrictions.

5. Relationships between management and employees, as well as between non-managing stockholders and managers, are sometimes difficult to maintain and become fragmented.
6. Special permission must be sought from government agencies to transact business outside of the state of incorporation.

In the case of Gaslight, Inc., the Mustos and the Volyns are on the board of directors and at the time of organization hold a clear majority of stock. By selling nonvoting preferred stock to outsiders, they may be able to raise the capital they need for expansion without losing control of the board. Since they control the board of directors, they will appoint Bob Musto as president of the corporation and Paul Volyn as vice president. Evelyn Musto will serve as treasurer and Margaret Volyn as secretary. Because the firm has been in the community a good number of years, they can borrow from a bank if the necessity exists.

CORPORATIONS AND COMBINATIONS

It was pointed out earlier in this chapter that businesses have grown increasingly larger in the United States. This has meant that many firms have joined together or have been absorbed by larger firms, fostering the growth of giant corporations. Chrysler Corporation is the result of several mergers over the years. Other examples are General Motors, Times-Mirror, and CBS. A *merger* takes place when two or more companies combine to form one. It is the usual practice for the larger, more dominant company to absorb the smaller one, with the smaller firm losing its status as a separate entity. To satisfy the owners (stockholders) of the firm being acquired, they are usually given shares of stock in the dominant corporation at a prearranged rate of exchange. Sometimes the larger firm merges with the smaller firm by buying out its assets. In such cases the owners of the acquired firm do not share in an exchange of stock for shares in the dominant corporation.

Another way that firms may merge is through a method of financing combinations known as a *consolidation*, which is slightly different from a merger. A *con-

TABLE 4-1 A checklist of business organization features

Feature	Sole Proprietorship	Partnership	Corporation
Unlimited liability	strong	strong	none
Limited liability	none	none	strong
Continuity	none	weak	strong
Liquidity	weak	none	strong
Ease of management	strong	strong to weak	strong
Ease of policy setting	strong	strong	strong
Ease of organizing	strong	weak	weak
Ease of financing	strong	weak	weak
Ease of expansion	weak	weak	strong
Ease of termination	strong	strong	weak

☐ = strong   ■ = weak   ☐ = none

business profile: COCA-COLA – FROM ELIXIR TO THE REAL THING

In 1886, Atlanta chemist "Doc" Pemberton developed a reddish-brown syrup with a smidgeon of cocaine (for medicinal purposes) to compete with the many patent medicines and cure-all elixirs of that time. His company recommended it for the relief of hangovers, headaches, menstrual pains, and a host of other problems. One warm summer day Pemberton took some syrup down to Willis Venable at Jacob's Drug Store in Atlanta. An ounce of the mixture was put into a glass, which was then filled with water and ice, creating the first Coca-Cola.

Frank Robinson, the bookkeeper at Pemberton Chemical Company, first suggested the name. He also wrote it out in the style of penmanship popular at the time, creating what is without doubt the most recognized trademark in the world today. People who have never heard of George Washington or Adolf Hitler have no trouble recognizing the name Coca-Cola.

The headquarters of Coca-Cola, now listed by *Fortune* as one of the 50 top corporations in the United States, is still in Atlanta, Georgia. The actual sale and distribution of that magic elixir—which, needless to say, no longer contains cocaine—is handled largely by a number of independent bottlers. These bottlers buy syrup, mix it with carbonated water, and distribute it to retailers in their area. The number of retailers who sell Coke to the public almost exceeds counting. In this way a company with a magic formula but limited capital spread its name around the country and eventually around the globe. That organizational formula for merchandising apparently also had a bit of magic. But, of course, the product was one that people wanted, which is perhaps the first law of success in marketing.

solidation takes place when both firms give up their old identities and structures and form a new entity. In effect, both of the old companies disappear and a new one is formed. United States Steel Company was formed in this way by combining Andrew Carnegie's steel holdings with those of Henry Frick.

A *holding company* is another organizational method used to combine a number of firms under a single control. The advantage of a holding company to its owners is that it allows a relatively small number of owners using a relatively small amount of investment to control a large number of corporations. The holding company is called the *parent*, and the corporations owned by the parent are called *subsidiaries*. The parent is always sure to hold a controlling number of shares of stock in each subsidiary (usually 50 percent or more) and in this way has complete control over policy and functions. As for the parent corporation, the control there sometimes rests in a relatively few hands because, once again, only 50 percent or more ownership of the parent stock is needed to maintain control. Many American corporations operate as holding companies and do so legally. AT&T is the classic example of a holding company. As a matter of fact, AT&T has no manufacturing or installation equipment of its own. All of its operating equipment is in the hands of subsidiaries in which AT&T holds controlling shares of stock. Others are permitted to buy stock in many AT&T subsidiaries, but the controlling amount is always maintained by the parent company.

CONGLOMERATES

The conglomerate is the most recent variation of a holding company, and some experts contend that there is no difference between the two. However, holding companies have tended to form or acquire subsidiaries related in some way to a particular line of business. For example, AT&T has formulated or acquired firms that are involved in the communications field. A conglomerate acquires a hodgepodge of firms for what those firms will contribute to the overall financial growth of the parent. It does not matter to the management in a conglomerate whether the acquired firms have any operating relationship. In fact, many times it is believed that the diversity of operations carried on by the subsidiaries is a good hedge against depression in one or another of the industries they represent.

Gulf and Western Industries is a classic example of a conglomerate. It owns, among other firms, New Jersey Zinc, Brown Shoe Corporation, and Paramount Pictures. It is clear that none of these firms, nor any of the others owned by G&W, have any operating relationship to each other. Subsidiaries of a conglomerate are usually allowed to function with a great deal of autonomy as long as they continue to produce substantial profits for the parent firm.

Every January *Forbes* magazine presents its annual report on American industry. In January 1977 *Forbes* reported that during 1975 and 1976 the United States experienced a new wave of conglomerate growth. Many of the new acquisitions were not by the established conglomerates of the 1960s but by hitherto non-conglomerate firms or by relatively new conglomerates. Of course, the old, well-known conglomerates, such as G&W and Northwest Industries, were very active during this same period. At present G&W owns over 140 companies.

TABLE 4-2 Top 10 conglomerates by gross sales in 1976

Rank	Firm	Approximate Gross Sales (in billions of dollars)
1	ITT	11.7
2	Tenneco	6.3
3	Rockwell	5.2
4	LTV	4.4
5	Gulf and Western	3.39
6	Litton	3.36
7	TRW	2.9
8	Textron	2.6
9	Raytheon	2.46
10	Signal	2.45

Source: *Forbes*, January 1977, and *Fortune*, May 1977.

Table 4-2 shows a list of the top 10 conglomerates in the United States by gross sales for 1976. The list was compiled by the authors with data obtained from *Forbes* and *Fortune* magazines. The number of companies and product lines owned by these top 10 exceeds one thousand. How many of these top 10 conglomerates are you familiar with? Probably not too many. However, you would probably recognize many of their products. For example, Gulf and Western owns Paramount Pictures which produces motion pictures and television series. Tenneco owns Sun Giant which packages fruits and vegetables sold in California and Walker automotive equipment which is sold in the South and in the West.

DOMINANCE OF THE CORPORATION

If farms are counted as business enterprises, there are more than nine million sole proprietorships in the United States. They outnumber corporations, with partnerships ranking third. However, the corporation is by far the dominant form of business organization. It is the corporations, both large and small, that account for the greatest dollar volume of sales and asset ownership in our country. Some of the largest American corporations, such as General Motors, IBM, and Exxon, have annual sales greater than the total of many of the smaller, less developed nations of the world. As for partnership, neither in numbers of firms nor in influence on GNP does it even come close to the sole proprietorship or corporation. In fact, many economists contend that the partnership is a dying form of business organization.

Each year *Fortune* magazine publishes the "Fortune 500." This is a list of the 500 largest corporations in the United States as measured by their gross sales of the previous year. Tables 4-3 and 4-4 show the top 15 corporations on the *Fortune* list for 1976 as well as the top 15 corporations on the *Forbes* "Sales 500" list also based on gross sales. There is, however, a difference between the *Forbes* and

TABLE 4-3 Top 15
companies from the Fortune
500 for 1976
and 1977

Rank		Company	Sales (in billions of dollars)
1977	1976		
1	2	General Motors	54.9
2	1	Exxon	54.1
3	3	Ford	37.8
4	5	Mobil Oil	32.1
5	4	Texaco	27.9
6	6	Standard Oil (California)	20.9
7	8	IBM	18.1
8	7	Gulf Oil	17.8
9	9	General Electric	17.5
10	10	Chrysler	16.7
11	11	ITT	13.1
12	12	Standard Oil (Indiana)	13.0
13	15	Atlantic Richfield	10.9
14	13	Shell Oil	10.1
15	14	U.S. Steel	9.6

Source: *Fortune*, May 1978, p. 240.

Fortune lists. *Fortune* does not include public utility, transportation, banking, or retail companies in its listing. They are excluded because they are not regarded as industrial corporations, companies engaged primarily in manufacturing. The *Forbes* list of 500 includes all corporations, regardless of whether they are industrials or not.

TABLE 4-4 Top 15
companies from the Forbes
Sales 500 for 1976
and 1977

Rank		Company	Sales (in billions of dollars)
1977	1976		
1	2	General Motors	54.9
2	1	Exxon	54.1
3	4	Ford	37.8
4	3	AT&T	36.4
5	6	Mobil Oil	32.1
6	5	Texaco	27.9
7	8	Sears, Roebuck	22.0
8	7	Standard Oil (California)	20.9
9	10	IBM	18.1
10	9	Gulf Oil	17.8
11	11	General Electric	17.5
12	12	Chrysler	16.7
13	13	ITT	16.6
14	14	Standard Oil (Indiana)	13.0
15	15	Safeway	11.2

Source: *Forbes*, May 15, 1978, p. 202.

You'll see from the tables that Exxon, formerly the Standard Oil Company of New Jersey, tops both lists with sales of $48.6 billion for 1976. On both lists, General Motors is second with sales of $47.1 billion. After the top two, the lists vary somewhat because *Fortune* excludes nonindustrials. Undoubtedly most of you will recognize the companies on these tables. You can probably readily identify one or more of their products or services. If you analyze the top 15, it becomes apparent that auto manufacturing, petroleum, and electronic operations tend to dominate.

Fortune reported that out of its 500 top industrials for 1976, 227 had sales of over $1 billion. They refer to these firms as members of their "billion dollar club." *Forbes* reported that all but 43 of the corporations on their 500 sales list showed an increase in sales over the previous year.

These lists point out, in a very dramatic way, how the corporation as a form of business organization dominates the business scene in the modern American economy.

OTHER FORMS OF BUSINESS ORGANIZATION

Not all businesses are organized as sole proprietorships, partnerships, or corporations. Other alternatives for business organization do exist, but most of them are less effective than those cited above. Many are of particular value to firms filling special needs.

COOPERATIVE

Like a corporation, a *cooperative* is a business organization operated as a legal person distinct from its owners and continues to exist notwithstanding their individual deaths or withdrawals. However, a cooperative is created to serve the needs of its respective owners and a person buys shares in it more for the benefits of belonging than for its investment potential.

The classic example of the need for a cooperative is the case of a group of farmers in the Middle Western wheat belt. Each grower must store his wheat and arrange its sales after the harvest. To store the wheat economically and to facilitate selling it, many farmers in local areas have banded together and organized cooperatives. The cooperative is their business association. It usually starts when farmers finance the building of storage facilities. Such a cooperative will probably do more than just store the wheat, corn, or other grain; it will also facilitate the sale of each farmer's crop, pay the expenses of operating the cooperative, and return profits to the farmers. In this way the farmers can stick to the business of farming, which is what they know best, and leave the warehousing and selling functions of their product to agents hired by the cooperative.

JOINT STOCK COMPANIES

You may recall from history that the Plymouth and the London companies were organized as joint stock companies. Joint stock companies are similar to general partnerships because each owner, although not possessing the manage-

personality profile:

James Buchanan Duke — the duke of management

James Buchanan Duke started out as just another North Carolina farm boy whose father grew tobacco. Together, father and son formed W. Duke, Sons & Company and began to actively market their own production. The market for loose tobacco, however, was limited to those who were willing to roll their own cigarettes. Duke recognized early that the market could be greatly expanded by prerolling and prepackaging cigarettes, so he had machines developed that could roll 200 cigarettes a minute.

Seeing the value of product identification in developing consumer loyalty, Duke began to produce tobacco products under many different brand names. This meant that management and marketing had to be organized and refined to meet the challenge of turning a small company into a giant firm. In the course of this growth, Duke eventually joined the five principal cigarette manufacturers into a single combine, the American Tobacco Company, and he became the company's first president.

Next, the red-haired, bull-necked "Buck" Duke turned his attention to plug tobacco, which was at this time a large segment of the market. He squeezed out other producers by reducing the price of one-pound bars from 50¢ to 13¢, instituted a program of free giveaways along with massive advertising, and compelled his cigarette dealers to stock his plug tobacco as well. At its peak, American Tobacco had 90 percent of the market for cigarettes and 80 percent, 62 percent, and 60 percent of the market for snuff, plug, and pipe tobacco, respectively.

The American Tobacco Company succeeded so well as the foremost cigarette manufacturer and so extended its control over the entire tobacco market that the Supreme Court in 1911 declared it an illegal monopoly operating in restraint of trade. The company was broken up into several parts. The segment that retained the name American Tobacco is today a subsidiary of American Brands, Inc.

James Duke himself turned his demonstrated skills as an organizer to other purposes, including the building of water works and hospitals. Before his death in 1925, he established a trust fund of $100 million for the benefit of Trinity College in Durham, North Carolina. Trinity is now known as Duke University.

Cooperatives are popular among farmers and growers. Members of the Sunkist cooperative are shown here at a membership meeting.

Sunkist Growers, Inc.

ment rights of a general partner, does have unlimited liability. The management in a joint stock company is delegated to a board of directors, and ownership is represented by shares of stock similar to those of a corporation. Unlike a partnership, the death of one or more owners does not affect the continuity of the firm. In recent times, almost all joint stock companies have been replaced by the corporate form of business organization.

JOINT VENTURES AND SYNDICATES

A joint venture is similar in organization to a partnership. As with a partnership, each owner has unlimited liability in a joint venture, although management decisions are usually delegated to one individual. Unlike a partnership, a joint venture is set up for an undertaking of relatively short duration. An example would be where 15 or 20 people buy a carload of refrigerators and ship them to South America for sale. Once the enterprise is completed, the joint venture association is dissolved and each owner receives a share of the capital plus or minus profits or losses.

Syndicates are very similar to joint ventures though they are concerned strictly with financial ventures. Syndicates may continue to operate from one venture to another without dissolving and in this way are quite different from other types of joint ventures. One of the most common types of syndication underwrites bond issues.

MUTUAL COMPANIES

A mutual company is similar to a cooperative and a corporation in that the organization is a legal person and its owners have limited liability. It is also a type of organization that fills a personal need for individuals rather than offering investment potential. The classic form of a mutual company is one that sells life insurance. Once someone purchases a policy from a mutual life insurance company, the purchaser automatically becomes a part owner of the firm. At the end of the year, if the insurance company makes a profit on its investments, a portion of this profit (after deducting operating expenses) is returned to policyholders based on the type and amount of their individual policies. These dividends are not taxable by the federal government even though they are income.

Credit unions and savings and loan associations are organized like cooperatives and mutual companies, but there is greater federal and state control of them by law. The idea in both cases is that members are owners and band together for some common reason. Liability is limited and the organization operates as a legal person.

Although organized and operated to make profits for their owners, mutual companies can incur losses. In such situations, the mutual owners may be asked to put up more money or forfeit their share of interest in the venture. This is a rare situation because most of these companies are strictly regulated by government agencies. But the possibility is always present.

SUBCHAPTER S CORPORATION

Many small businesses prefer to organize as corporations to enjoy the protection of limited liability. To them this safety feature is worth the time, effort, and additional expense of forming a corporation. In some cases the federal government gives small corporations a tax break. Under Subchapter S, a provision of the Internal Revenue Service Code of Regulations, a small corporation is allowed to file its federal tax return as a partnership would, even though the business is organized and operated as a corporation. By filing as a partnership, each owner of a small corporation is permitted to include the share of income on the owner's 1040 tax return and pay taxes at individual tax rates rather than at corporation tax rates. In many cases this means a tax savings to the stockholders.

To qualify as a Subchapter S corporation, the firm must be a domestic corporation (that is, organized in the United States) and have no more than 10 stockholders. These stipulations are met by many small corporations.

TREND TOWARD BIGNESS

In the last several decades our economy has seen a shifting away from the prevalence of small businesses to dominance by larger and larger corporations. Yet the small business is far from extinct. In fact, with the advent of consumerism and a rebirth of interest in arts and crafts among the young people in our society, the foundations of small business management have been greatly strengthened.

Nevertheless, bigness has become the trend in most aspects of American life and business has by and large followed this trend. Most corporations are getting larger. Some of this is due to internal growth, while in other cases mergers and consolidations have been the cause.

SUMMARY

All institutions must be carefully organized in order to operate effectively and efficiently. Business firms are no exception to this rule. The three basic forms of business organization are sole proprietorship, partnership, and corporation. Sole proprietorships are the most numerous form, but corporations produce the highest sales dollar volume by far. The corporate organization is usually the most difficult and expensive to form.

There are various hybrid forms of business organization. The most common of these is the cooperative. Cooperatives are a cross between a corporation and a partnership. Mutual banks and mutual insurance companies are examples of businesses organized along the lines of a cooperative.

Mergers and consolidations were common in the 1960s and 1970s. Conglomerates and holding companies are parent corporations that seek subsidiaries through the merger process. Mergers and consolidations enable businesses to expand and diversify operations.

SUMMARY OF KEY TERMS

Articles of Partnership A written contract that specifies the rights, responsibilities, and duties of each member in a partnership. Details concerning sharing of profits and losses, amount of time devoted to the business, and so forth, are carefully spelled out.

Charter A written instrument granted by the proper state authority to those who desire the right to operate a business as a corporation.

Conglomerate A parent corporation with subsidiaries acquired for their investment potential. It gains control of subsidiaries through acquisition of their assets or through exchanges of stock.

Consolidation The process in which two separate

firms abandon their separate identities and organizations and form a new organization and identity. For example, A Corporation and B Corporation merge to form C Corporation.

Forbes Sales 500 List of the top 500 corporations in the United States ranked by gross sales for the operating year.

Fortune 500 List of the top 500 industrial corporations ranked by gross sales for the operating year.

General Partner An owner in a partnership with full rights and responsibilities whose actions are legally binding on all partners.

Holding Company A corporation, referred to as the parent, that owns a controlling number of shares of stock in other corporations, known as subsidiaries.

Joint Stock Company Form of business organization containing certain features of a partnership as well as of a corporation. Ownership is represented by shares of stock, but each owner has unlimited liability.

Joint Venture Similar in organization to a partnership except that management is usually delegated to one individual. A joint venture is established for an undertaking of short duration.

Limited Liability Liability in a firm limited to one's investment in the firm, as is the case with the stockholder in a corporation.

Limited Partner An owner in a partnership who does not have all the rights and powers of a general partner but who enjoys the protection of limited liability.

Liquidity The ease with which an investor can sell his investment (such as stock in a corporation) to another.

Merger When two or more firms join together to form a new firm which is known by the name of one of the old firms. For example, A Corporation (older and larger) and B Corporation merge into A Corporation.

Mutual Company A type of business organization where ownership rests in the hands of the firm's customers or clients. Policyholders in a mutual insurance company are also owners of the company.

Secret Partner A member of a partnership who is not known by the general public to be a partner.

Silent Partner A member of a partnership who does not participate in setting policy or managing the partnership.

Subchapter S Corporation A domestic corporation with 10 or fewer stockholders which files its federal income tax return as a partnership to take advantage of lower tax rates when appropriate.

Syndication Similar to a joint venture organization except it is strictly involved with financial ventures.

Unlimited Liability The legal obligation of investors to use personal assets when necessary to pay off the debt claims of business creditors. All sole proprietors and general partners are subject to unlimited liability.

REVIEW QUESTIONS

1. Assume that you have decided to go into business for yourself. As a sole proprietor, you know that there are advantages and disadvantages in this form of business ownership. Explain what they are in detail.

2. Among the three most common forms of business ownership, partnership ranks third. Why is partnership the least popular form of business organization?

3. What are articles of partnership? What conditions are they likely to contain?

4. All corporations have certain characteristics in common. Name six of them.

5. List five advantages and five disadvantages of

the corporate form of organization.

6. What is the difference between a merger and a consolidation? Between a holding company and a conglomeration?

7. Today American business is dominated by the corporation. Explain why this is so.

8. Refer to Tables 4-3 and 4-4 and then answer the following questions. What corporations appear among the top 15 of the *Forbes* list but not among the top 15 of the *Fortune* list? Why is there a difference between the lists?

9. What is a cooperative? How does it differ from a corporation?

10. In what important way is a mutual company unlike a corporation? How is it similar to a cooperative and a corporation?

DISCUSSION QUESTIONS

1. Outline the steps necessary for forming a corporation. Use sources other than this book and cite them in the bibliography for your report.

2. Try to find at least one example of a merger and one example of a consolidation in back issues of the *Wall Street Journal*, *Business Week*, and other business periodicals.

3. Explain what role each of the following types of business organizations played in the natural gas shortage in the winter of 1976.

Corporations
Sole proprietorships
Partnerships

4. If partnerships play such a minor role in the nation's economic life, why do they still exist?

5. Mergers and consolidations have definitely accelerated the trend toward bigness in business. If this trend continues, it is said that no small businesses will be left in the United States. Comment on this statement.

CASES FOR DECISION MAKING

JOINT VENTURE IN A CAN

Alaska Packers Association, a subsidiary of Del Monte Corporation, specialized in canning Alaskan salmon. In July 1976, the association's cannery was destroyed by fire. Since then, Alaska Packers announced a joint venture to rebuild and operate the cannery. The other partners in the joint venture are Columbia Wards Fisheries, Ward Cove Packing Company, and Chignik Coastal Fisheries, a coalition of five native village corporations located in the area where the cannery is to be rebuilt. Construction of the new unit was to begin in June 1977, with completion by June 1978.

1. Why might a large, prosperous corporation like Del Monte choose a joint-venture arrangement rather than going it alone?

2. Look up Del Monte in *Moody's Industrial Manual* in the library. Use the latest edition you can find. Write a brief report of its history and holdings. What, if anything, does *Moody's* say about Alaska Packers Association under the Del Monte listing?

3. Can you suggest another idea for a joint venture that might be practical in your own area of the country? Be original.

WILL THEY LIVE HAPPILY EVER AFTER?

Several years ago, First National Boston Corporation, a holding company, announced that it had entered into an agreement with Blackstone Valley National Bank of Whitinsville, Massachusetts, to take it over. The price of the acquisition was $2.8 million of the common stock of First Boston. Under the agreement, each shareholder of Blackstone Valley was to get two shares of First National Boston for each share of Blackstone Valley owned by that person. Approximately 102,160 shares of First Boston would be distributed under the arrangement. At the time, First Boston stock was trading on the New York Stock Exchange at $27.375 a share. The acquisition was approved by state and federal agencies, as well as the stockholders of Blackstone Valley National Bank. Plans called for Blackstone Valley to become a national bank subsidiary of First Boston.

1. Why is First Boston considered to be a holding company and not a conglomerate?
2. Why would the acquisition be subject to approval by state and federal regulatory agencies?
3. Approximately how many shares of Blackstone Valley stock were exchanged by its shareholders at the time of acquisition?
4. As a shareholder of Blackstone Valley, what factors might you consider before voting for or against the merger?

TOBACCO PARTNERS

Martin Decat and Barbara Camille each own a tobacco farm in Chesterfield County, Virginia. A third farming neighbor, Fred Kimbel, just built a storage warehouse to dry his tobacco. He had built a very large facility with about 80 percent more capacity than he needs because he planned to rent out the excess space to his farming neighbors. This year Decat and Camille rented from Kimbel. However, Kimbel's latest crop was lost to bad weather and he needs new investment capital. He has invited Decat and Camille to invest in the storage warehouse and become equal partners in its ownership and control. They have the funds and are agreeable to this arrangement since they anticipate needing storage space in the future. (Even with their rental the past year, the facility still had an additional 40 percent excess capacity.)

1. Do you recommend that Decat and Camille go in with Kimbel as equal partners?
2. If not, what other suggestion might you make concerning an ownership plan?
3. Do you think the proposal made by Kimbel to form a partnership is a typical organizational arrangement in the agricultural industry? Explain your answer.

RELATED READINGS

Andrews, Kenneth. *The Concept of Corporate Strategy*. Homewood, Ill.: Dow Jones-Irwin, 1971.

Contains a brief examination of the policies of corporations; and discusses the people who formulate policy as well as the why's and wherefore's of policy formulation.

Bander, Edward J. *The Corporation in a Democratic Society*. New York: Wilson, 1975.

Contains a series of articles on criticism and defense of corporations. There are also articles on corporate responsibility, multinational corporations, and "the coming corporate conscience." Articles are reprinted from the *New York Times*, *Barron's*, *Fortune*, and other sources.

Barmesh, Isodore. *Welcome to Our Conglomerate —You're Fired*. New York: Delacorte, 1971.

Humorous but pointed discussion of the intrigues, deals, and methods used for the acquisition of one firm by another.

Chamberlain, Neil W. *The Limits of Corporate Responsibility*. New York: Basic Books, 1973.

An examination and discussion of the modern corporation and its characteristics as they relate to social responsibility. A bit tough on the role of the corporation but worth the time and trouble to read.

Josephson, Matthew. *The Money Lords*. New York: Weybright and Talley, 1972.

A look at some of the big names in investment banking over the years. Informative and interesting reading about those who control the financial growth of big business.

Kahn, Herman. *The Future of the Corporation*. New York: Mason & Lipscomb, 1974.

Focuses on the changes in our culture and the changes that corporations must make to survive through the 1980s.

McDonald, John. *The Game of Business*. Garden City, N.Y.: Doubleday, 1975.

Describes and discusses the giant corporations and the entrepreneurs who controlled them. It is really an historical perspective of some of the big corporate deals in America.

Sampson, Anthony. *The Sovereign State of ITT*. New York: Stern and Day, 1973.

As the title suggests, this is an exposé of International Telephone and Telegraph Corporation. Although it is probably overly critical, it does give the reader some insights into the unpleasant realities of big business.

Steiner, Peter O. *Mergers*. Ann Arbor: University of Michigan Press, 1975.

Discusses the major conglomerate mergers of the 1960s. Analyzes the effects of mergers on the economy as well as the motivation for such mergers.

chapter 5

MAKING FIRMS SUCCESSFUL

OBJECTIVES

When you have finished reading and studying this chapter, you should be able to:

1. Know and describe the major responsibilities and levels of management in business.

2. Be aware of some of the thinking set forth by past and present leaders in the field of management.

3. Be familiar with some of the major objectives that good managers pursue in running the firm.

4. Describe the various ways in which firms are organized and set out the goals of good management that each method of organization seeks.

CHAPTER PREVIEW

Have you ever tried to plan, organize, and run a party? If you have, you know that it can be a great deal of work. You must compile a guest list, find adequate space, plan a menu, and prepare the food, as well as arrange for games and music or other entertainment. Planning, organizing, and control are prerequisites for a successful party, and the major areas of responsibility for the management of a business.

Managing a firm is much more serious than running a house party, and the stakes are obviously high for those charged with the responsibility. Most firms have three levels of management: the top managers, responsible for major planning and decision making; middle managers, responsible for implementing top management's decisions; and operating managers, who see that the plans are realized in daily operations. Perhaps you aspire to climb the management ladder some day. Do you have what it takes? If you read this chapter carefully, you will begin to get an indication of what it takes to be good at management. Certainly, you will better realize the problems and rewards associated with management.

Every company must rely on the techniques of good managers. In addition, every company must be properly organized to produce its product or service in the most efficient and effective way. Most modern businesses of medium or large size are organized on a line and staff basis. This permits a clear-cut delineation of each manager's responsibility and authority. In a small business firm, the line pattern of organization is usually sufficient since staff managers mostly concern themselves with specialized areas of expertise such as personnel or marketing. These are often not separate responsibilities in the small firm, where the owners must have enough general skill to handle these functions as part of their everyday work.

Every manager must be able to make more right decisions than wrong ones—and must be able to do so quickly. Being able to make the right decision is partly an inborn skill. It is also an ability one can learn or greatly sharpen with instruction and practice. As an example, this chapter discusses the Bayesian technique of improving decision-making skills.

Managers have to know how to handle people in a sensitive way, yet be able to get them to do the job right and on time. Human relations is an important part of the management process, and effective communication is often critical in dealing with people. Read this chapter and then decide whether you would like to work for yourself.

"And here is the top of our executive pyramid."

5
MAKING FIRMS
SUCCESSFUL

Is management an art or a science? To answer this important question, it is necessary to define the term. *Management* is the process by which those in authority plan, organize, and control a business in an effort to make it successful. A firm's success is still primarily measured by its ability to make a large profit. But modern society also measures the success of an enterprise by its ability to satisfy its customers and workers as well as contribute to the social betterment of its community and the nation as a whole. Nevertheless, the goal of maximum profit is still the most important objective.

MANAGEMENT:
ART AND SCIENCE

The answer to the above question is both. The art is the natural talent of the individual—the manager. And the science is what can be learned through formal education and specific job training. The manager is the individual who is active in the management process. Through formal education and on-the-job training courses, managers gain knowledge about laws, agencies, and regulations affecting their industry and employees. They also learn how to communicate and how to calculate. Many skills can be learned that will help a person become successful in management. In fact, a great body of knowledge for formally training future managers has evolved over the last 60 years in the United States. Today, colleges and universities offer undergraduate and graduate programs in management. Many of these programs are so highly specialized that a student often majors in marketing management, financial management, public administration, or some other specialty rather than in the general area of management science. This is especially true if the student intends to go on for a master's degree in management.

Most of today's managers have a college education. As undergraduates many of them majored in business administration, economics, mathematics, or engineering. In many fields, managers are urged to go on for a master of arts degree in business administration or a master of science degree in management. People with law degrees are also frequently found among the ranks of middle and upper management.

TRAINING PEOPLE
FOR
MANAGEMENT

In the first half of 1977, the Conference Board, a private, nonprofit business research group, surveyed a number of business executives and asked what they thought about the success of colleges and universities in training people for management. Forty-one percent thought colleges and universities do only an adequate or poor job; 47 percent thought they did an adequate or fair job; and 12 percent thought they did a good or excellent job. Most executives rated best the schools and colleges that are occupationally oriented. By a ten-to-one margin they thought four-year engineering and science colleges performed particularly well. By a seven-to-one margin they gave high ratings to two-year colleges with vocational training programs.

The Conference Board estimated that the nation's 7,500 largest firms spend more than $2 billion a year on employee education. However, despite all the formal training that managers receive today, most authorities still agree that a natural talent for the job is still the most important attribute. If a man is by nature a hothead, it will be difficult to train him to handle people. If he is not intuitive and lacks common sense, all the formal training in the world will do little to help him overcome obstacles. In essence, a great deal of know-how in management seems to be inborn. Good managers often have a natural ability that makes them' click with other people and helps them reach the right decision more often than not.

MANAGEMENT'S FOUNDING FATHERS

In the nineteenth century, when small corporations began to develop into giants, there was no formal education available in management. Everything had to be learned on the job and one gained entry into management by inheriting a business or by starting one. The only other route was to work your way up the ladder of success from mail boy or blacksmith or whatever low-level job you held in the company. In those days the one criterion for successful management was maintaining the authority to get the job done. This often meant firing people on the spot, cursing and hollering all day, and in some cases physically proving that you were the boss. Fortunately for everyone, we have come a long way since then.

As you go further in your education, you'll hear more and more about two pioneers in the field of management: Peter Drucker and Douglas McGregor. Drucker, author of several books, is one of the outstanding thinkers today in the field of management education. Many people who aspire to be successful managers read Drucker and other thinkers such as McGregor. Don't get the wrong impression. If you read everything Drucker has written, you will not necessarily be a good manager. His ideas are often rather general. Usually he does not get into the specific tools and techniques that all managers must be aware of. And much of what he writes is philosophical rather than "how to." But Drucker and McGregor are not the first to have written about management as a formal discipline to be learned and practiced.

The first great thinker in the field of management was Frederick W. Taylor. Taylor worked in the 1880s at the Midvale Steel Plant, a branch of the Bethlehem Steel Company in Pennsylvania. Taylor had many excellent ideas and took the time to organize and publish them. Some of his ideas are old-fashioned and out of date by today's standards. However, many of them form the foundation for modern theory of management.

Today we take for granted many of Taylor's ideas. For instance, he was the first to maintain that managers as a group had a different economic role from that of the workers whom they directed. Taylor believed that in any business the planning function should be exercised only by managers. The workers' function was to follow the plans and orders developed by managers. In general we still follow this concept today, although the growth of unions has modified it to some extent.

Taylor developed a so-called science of management, which articulated a number of principles, tools, and techniques derived from careful studies of management situations. As was pointed out earlier, most of today's management training stems from the original ideas set forth by Taylor. As with any pioneer in a field, as time went on many of his concepts were challenged and some of them proved unworkable.

LEVELS AND FUNCTIONS OF MANAGEMENT

In a small business, the owner is very often the chief managerial person. Success for such a person is the result of learning from experience and having a special talent for the job. Keep in mind that in the small firm there is less need for complicated organization and far less need to cope with various personnel problems. Nevertheless, it is surprising how many small business owners want to develop their managerial skills further. Great numbers of them enroll in college extension courses in various aspects of management.

LEVELS OF MANAGEMENT

In a small business there is only one level of management—top management. Naturally, in a company such as the restaurant owned by Musto and Volyn (see Chapter 4), top management makes all the more important decisions. In a larger firm, management is usually subdivided into three levels or steps. *Top management* is that level of administration where all the most important decisions are made about planning, organization, and control of the firm. (These terms will be discussed in detail later in this section.) On the next level is *middle management*, those managers who implement the decisions of top management as well as make lower-level decisions regarding operations of the firm. On the lowest level are the operating managers. *Operating management* is responsible for supervising day-to-day operations in some part of the business. People at this level make decisions concerning daily output and personnel under their immediate control. Figure 5-1 summarizes the duties of management at the three levels.

PRIMARY FUNCTIONS OF MANAGEMENT

For managers to know their functions and responsibilities, they must have a clear picture of what the firm wants to achieve. In other words, management's responsibility is to develop and implement the goals of the owners. In a large corporation, these goals are jointly arrived at by the stockholders, the board of directors, and the chief officers of the corporation. Clearly, the board of directors contributes the greatest input in setting goals. Once the major goals have been established, the ways of achieving them can be worked out. In laying plans to meet the major goals, various secondary objectives will become evident and these will have to be dealt with as well. For example, suppose a newly formed corporation determines as its primary goal that it wants to manufacture a light, durable, competitively

FIGURE 5-1 Levels of management

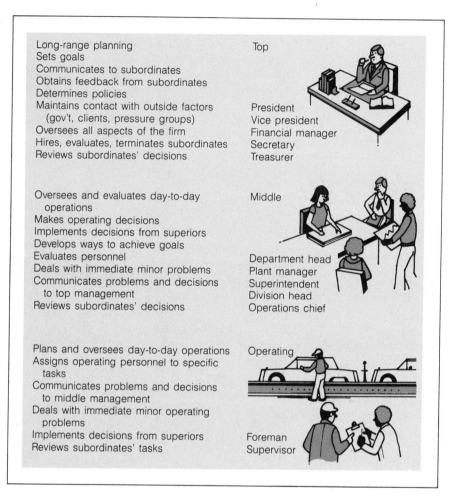

Long-range planning   Top
Sets goals
Communicates to subordinates
Obtains feedback from subordinates
Determines policies
Maintains contact with outside factors   President
   (gov't, clients, pressure groups)   Vice president
Oversees all aspects of the firm   Financial manager
Hires, evaluates, terminates subordinates   Secretary
Reviews subordinates' decisions   Treasurer

Oversees and evaluates day-to-day   Middle
   operations
Makes operating decisions
Implements decisions from superiors
Develops ways to achieve goals
Evaluates personnel   Department head
Deals with immediate minor problems   Plant manager
Communicates problems and decisions   Superintendent
   to top management   Division head
Reviews subordinates' decisions   Operations chief

Plans and oversees day-to-day operations   Operating
Assigns operating personnel to specific
   tasks
Communicates problems and decisions
   to middle management
Deals with immediate minor operating
   problems
Implements decisions from superiors   Foreman
Reviews subordinates' tasks   Supervisor

priced surfboard. Once it has established the specifics of its primary goal, it must decide other questions leading to secondary goals. Such things as quantity to be manufactured, plant location, marketing strategy, and so on are examples of secondary goals. The example could be carried even further by examining tertiary goals. For instance, under marketing strategy, advertising may appear as a tertiary goal.

From the above brief example emerge two of the three most important functions of management. Determining what to produce and deciding how to produce it are integral parts of the planning process of management. *Planning*, therefore, is the first primary function of management. Once the product is decided upon, the second primary responsibility of management, that of *organization*, comes into play. Organization is the roadway along which planning will be carried out. (For a discussion of organization, see "Types of Formal Organizational Structure," p. 122.)

These two functions, planning and organization, are not enough to get the job done. All three levels of management must be sure that all phases of operations are carefully supervised. Employees must have proper incentives if positive results are to be obtained, and management must clearly observe and review each phase of operations. This entire process is known as *control*; it is the third primary function of management. An important part of control is the careful direction of all workers in each step of the operations process.

In the broadest sense, the primary work of managers in any business concerns planning, organization, and control of all functions of the firm to obtain the goals set forth by the owners. The range of activities encompassed in these functions could fill volumes. A few of them will be discussed below to give you some idea of the many secondary functions involved in the management process. Figure 5-2 illustrates many of the various concerns of management.

Planning is the primary function of management. It involves deciding what to produce and how to produce it.

International Business Machines

FIGURE 5-2 The
management
merry-go-round

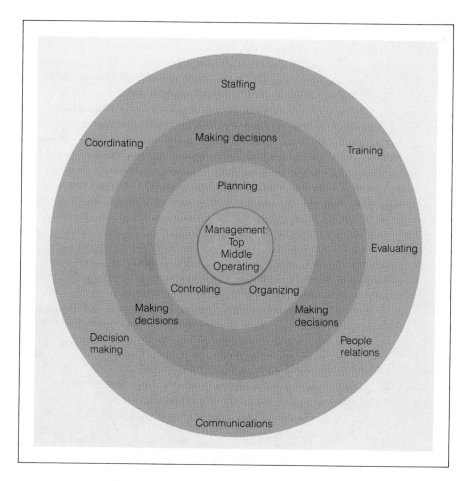

SECONDARY
FUNCTIONS OF
MANAGEMENT While it would be too time-consuming to go into all the secondary or lesser functions of the manager, noting some of them will indicate the scope and challenge of a manager's work.

Coordinating Probably the most important secondary function of a good manager is coordinating programs, whether the manager is top, middle, or operating level. *Coordination* is the know-how to blend the functions of planning, organizing, and control into one smoothly running operation. Successful coordination demands good channels of communication from one level of management to another. Indeed, good communications to and from superiors, as well as to and from subordinates, is another vital secondary function of good management.

Staffing and Training   As management has become increasingly scientific over the last 75 years, it required managers to draw from an ever larger reservoir of basic skills and knowledge. Government pressures combined with those from consumer and labor unions have also made the job of managing far more complicated than it was. Various tests have been devised to help predict a good manager. At present, none of these tests has been consistently successful in determining who are the people best suited for promotion to management. Many firms, however, do use such tests as an aid to their final selections. Management training has become very important in the last two decades for helping both experienced and inexperienced employees gain greater managerial skills. The American Management Association, the major organization in the field, conducts many seminars and workshops for people in business management.

Two-year and four-year colleges and universities have become very active in offering management-training programs. Many of these schools have management centers that specialize in tailor-made training sessions for the community's business and governmental organizations. Some schools have attained national recognition for their outstanding programs.

Human Relations   Managers need to be sensitive to people and at the same time give orders to get a job done. A good manager has to know himself. He must be sure that his values are honest, and he must be self-confident when making decisions. At the same time he must not allow himself to steamroller people who work for him or be deceitful to those he reports to. More often than not, a manager is a man caught in the middle. He is accountable to someone else and has subordinates accountable to him. Human nature being what it is, his subordinates will probably complain to him that there is too much work or too high a goal established for them. From the opposite direction, the manager's superiors will push him to get more work completed and meet greater goals. This is part of the frustration that goes with the job, and the competent manager must be able to cope with it. Every day the good administrator should ask himself: Would I want to work for myself?

Soon after assuming management responsibilities, executives are apt to realize that most of their problems will be human rather than technical. One of the more recent theories involved in human relations is called *transactional analysis* (TA). This method tries to determine how people interact with one another by studying the relationships or transactions between individuals as determined by the particular self-image that each person has. Under the TA theory, all of us relate to others in one of three ways: as a parent, an adult, or a child. If we can determine our relationship to a person with whom we are dealing, the theory states, we will be better able to communicate with, obtain understanding from, and be understanding of the other person.

TA is one approach applicable to the human behavior or behavioral science aspect of management. The *behavioral science* approach to management em-

To manage people effectively, a manager must strive for a good working relationship with the staff.

Michael D. Sullivan

phasizes ways in which the manager can deal with the problems that he faces with people. Behavioral science is strongly tied to human psychology, and many of the eminent behavioral scientists have strong backgrounds in psychology, sociology, and human relations.

Theory X and *Theory Y* is another concept that has gained acceptance in the behavioral science approach to management. Douglas McGregor, a former professor of management at the Massachusetts Institute of Technology, first developed this theory in his book, *The Human Side of Enterprise*, published in 1960. McGregor's theories state that most managers, when dealing with workers, accept Theory X, which is made up of the following elements:

1.　Work is distasteful. People work only for economic survival, not by choice.
2.　The normal individual by nature strongly dislikes work and will avoid it when possible.

business profile: **A PAT ON THE BACK BOOSTS PRODUCTIVITY**

Behavior modification, a behavior technique pioneered by Harvard psychologist B. F. Skinner, is increasingly being used by business managers to increase growth rates, combat slumping productivity, reduce absenteeism and turnover, and improve job satisfaction for employees. The theory is based on the assumption that all behavior can be affected by positive rewards such as praise or recognition.

More than 100 large companies today are using some form of behavior modification. Among them are such well-known firms as 3M Co., Frito-Lay, Addressograph-Multigraph, B. F. Goodrich, Weyerhaeuser, and Warner-Lambert. Many of the programs are being conducted on a trial basis or in selected divisions rather than the whole company. A typical program begins with a series of meetings in which managers and employees discuss mutual needs and problems. Then solutions are proposed. These diagnostic sessions are crucial because through them managers set standards for job performance and determine how the standards will be met. At the same time, employees express their needs and give their managers ideas of the ways in which behavior can be modified. The second step is observing how the worker performs on the job. After that, the manager gives constant feedback, letting employees know right away how their current level of performance compares with the desired level.

Some companies report excellent results. For example, in 1977 3M Co. estimated a cost savings of $3.5 million. Other benefits like increased employee morale are difficult to measure. Most other companies recorded sizable cost savings, along with huge gains in worker productivity. Nearly all have realized a 200-percent return on investment. One California firm, specializing in

aiding firms develop their own versions of the behavior modification system, gives a written guarantee to save companies in one year twice the $15,000 fee the firm charges. One of the factors contributing to the technique's appeal is the growing number of consultants specializing in the field. Some universities have entered the field and conduct reinforcement seminars for executives of corporations.

Despite success, there are still plenty of skeptics. As one director of management development indicated, "Humanists and politicians bridle at the thought of manipulating behavior, and quite frankly, I find myself in the same camp." Because behavior modification has a sinister ring to it, most firms give their programs other names, such as performance improvement or contingency management. Besides the fear of employee manipulation, there are other problems with the behavior modification approach. The system will not work in a firm where the manager has little control over employee reward systems. Neither does the system work well where top management is not committed to the system or where it is difficult to measure performance in jobs. Some critics attribute the success of the Skinnerian principles as just another fad or a gimmick for consultants to use to make a quick fee. Most critics say that the principles are similar to the ones that any good manager has been using for years.

Regardless of the criticisms, the techniques seem sure to be implemented at a growing number of firms in the next few years. There seems to be a major attempt to integrate the principles with the management development programs already in place at most large firms.

3. Most people must be threatened and coerced to get a job done.
4. Average workers crave direction, detest responsibility, and have little ambition. They seek security above all else.

McGregor states that managers could be more successful if they abandoned their traditional concepts (Theory X) and subscribed to what he calls Theory Y. This concept states:

1. Work is as normal to humans as play.
2. Threats and punishment are not the only means to motivate workers. Individuals will respond to challenging objectives and worthwhile commitments.
3. Average workers will accept and even seek responsibility if the rewards and recognitions are clear and worthwhile.
4. Workers are not given enough credit for their willingness to produce and be loyal to the firm. The intellectual potentialities of the average human being are often not utilized to the fullest by management.

TA and Theory X–Theory Y are only two of hundreds, and perhaps even thousands, of behavioral science concepts related to management. Many of these theories have proven relatively successful and have been used for a long time. More and more firms require their personnel to be aware of behavioral science concepts and to be able to apply them in their day-to-day relationships with people.

DECISION MAKING

Whether on the primary or secondary level, decision making is a basic function of management at all times and in all situations. Making the right decision at the right time is one of the tough day-to-day responsibilities of all managers. Some people have a special talent for seeing all sides of an issue and reacting to it quickly with the right solution. Most of us do not possess this special talent and must struggle a bit before making a decision that we hope is the right one. Management educators have attempted to turn decision making into as scientific a process as possible. One of the more recent and popular techniques for aiding management to make the right move is the *Bayesian approach* to decision making. The Bayesian approach recognizes that most managerial decisions must be made under conditions of uncertainty. (*Uncertainty* means that a particular decision may produce a full range of possible outcomes.) Such an outcome could be one that was not anticipated at all at the time the decision was made. The Bayesian approach outlines a process that managers should follow when confronted with important decisions:

1. Recognition of a situation that calls for a decision about what action should be taken.
2. Identification and development of alternative causes of action.

3. Evaluation of the alternatives.
4. Choice of one of the alternatives.
5. Implementation of the selected course of action.
6. Objective evaluation of the course of action.

The Bayesian approach is designed to be a tool for aiding the manager in reaching the right decision. In no way does it guarantee success because the tool, like any tool, is only as good as the hands and mind of the person using it.

Many managers, like many of us in our personal lives, do not recognize a problem or choose not to recognize a problem that needs to be resolved. This is always a case of bad timing, and it usually catches up with the manager later as a much larger problem. It is well to remember the old truism: *Not to decide is to decide.*

MANAGEMENT BY OBJECTIVES

One of the more recent popular behavioral science techniques in management is management by objectives (MBO). Under MBO each business firm's divisions, departments, and managers determine those objectives that they hope to fulfill within the future period under consideration. Such objectives must be consistent with the overall goals of the firm. MBO theory prescribes that objectives must be stated in such a way that the results can be measured. Management by objectives is a technique that invites all qualified personnel to offer input into the establishment of goals and priorities. It then measures the performance of personnel, both individually and collectively, against the stated objectives that they sought to accomplish. At present, MBO is enjoying wide use in both business and public administration. It is still too early to determine the overall effectiveness of this approach.

OBJECTIVES OF EFFECTIVE MANAGEMENT

Over the years many shortcuts have been devised for those who want to meet with some success in managing people and resources. All of the concepts discussed below are based on common sense and the experience of those who have studied and written in the field of management all the way back to the pioneering Frederick Taylor.

DIVISION OF WORK

For any medium or large firm to function efficiently there must be a structural breakdown of work responsibility on all levels. Every employee, from the warehouse janitor to the firm's president, must have a clear picture of where his or her responsibility and authority begin and where they end. At the same time, however, each employee must be allowed sufficient flexibility to get the job done as efficiently and as expertly as possible. Division of work is therefore not an easy

One of the manager's primary responsibilities is to create and maintain an espirit de corps among the members of the staff.

Stock, Boston

concept to follow, but if the manager as well as the firm are to operate effectively, it must be utilized in getting the job done. This management tool will be considered later in this chapter in a discussion on the organization of the firm.

DEVELOPING ESPRIT DE CORPS

If workers are willing and able to accept their responsibility and authority, the natural outcome should be a strong team effort. *Esprit de corps* simply means the pulling together as one unit toward clear objectives and with a common willingness to try as hard as possible to obtain those objectives. Naturally, not every employee in every firm can respond to this spirit. What is important is whether management can gain such support from a large majority of the firm's staff. There is an old saying that nothing succeeds like success. If most employees really believe in what they are doing, they will be successful and this success will serve as fuel to those new people joining the firm.

SUBORDINATING INDIVIDUAL GOALS

Every human being has personal desires and ambitions. This is to be expected and even encouraged by good management. It is when individual goals supersede those of the firm's management that things go wrong. That is not to say that each subordinate should not be allowed to operate as an individual. On the contrary, the good executive who subscribes to McGregor's Theory Y will encourage indi-

personality profile:
ROY ASH —
still in the winner's circle

As president of Litton Industries, Roy Ash was largely responsible for one of the most astounding success stories in American business: the transformation of tiny Litton Industries into the giant firm it still is today. Litton set the pace and served as model for the glamorous conglomerates that sprang up like mushrooms in the 1960s. Taking advantage of the high prices investors were willing to pay for the stock of a company whose management was bringing about such rapid growth, Litton used that high-priced stock to buy up dozens of unrelated businesses. It ran them all under a single system of financial management controls, but with considerable decentralization on the operational level. The company made millionaires out of dozens of its employees and investors. When the stock market collapse of the 1970s brought all the glamor issues and conglomerates tumbling down, Litton fell too, but it never was on the edge of bankruptcy like many others. Today the company remains a giant and profitable enterprise.

In the meanwhile, Roy Ash had departed Litton to serve as director of the Office of Management and Budget under President Nixon. He was no longer with the company when Litton's stock began falling with the market, but some investors blamed him for the company's sharp descent and wrote him off as an empire builder whose ideas had failed.

In 1976, Ash took over as chairman and chief executive officer of Addressograph-Multigraph, an old-line company which had fallen on bad times in the tightly competitive market for duplicators and copiers. Since Ash took over, the company has written off its money-losing product lines and emerged healthy and profitable. A fundamental turnaround has apparently taken place with Ash in the driver's seat, and the reputation of the wizard of the conglomerates is once again secure.

vidual reaction, initiative, and effort. Part of the control and directing responsibility is to foster individualism but dampen it beyond the point at which it overshadows the major goals of the firm.

ENCOURAGING INDIVIDUAL EFFORT

If you read the preceding paragraph carefully, you will probably see that there is no real conflict between subordinating individual goals and encouraging individual effort. Good managers want people to take the initiative, strive for success, and fulfill their potential. All individuals seek recognition and many of them are willing to work for it; those who will strive for it are usually assets to the firm, and their services are generally highly valued.

BALANCING RESPONSIBILITY WITH AUTHORITY

To be responsible for getting a job done efficiently and effectively, one must have a sufficient degree of authority. If people are given tasks, they must understand very clearly the extent of their authority to get the job done. Frequently, subordinates are assigned certain responsibilities without a clear picture of the authority they possess. In such situations relations between people can very quickly become strained, and if this is a predominant malfunction in the firm, team spirit will wither and die. Frequently, granting authority to a subordinate is risky because it is hard to foresee all of the problems, and a written outline of the authority is generally not enough to cover every situation. Those who are charged with responsibility and given authority are in need of intuition and common sense.

INTUITION AND COMMON SENSE

To draw followers, a leader must be fairly intuitive. Intuition goes beyond the ability to analyze data. Frequently the intuitive person can readily second-guess the reactions of others, an obvious advantage when dealing with other people. Like intuition, common sense is a special attribute more evident in some people than in others. Usually it is not something people learn; they are either born with it or not. Common sense is an old expression with a vague meaning. The dictionary describes it as "prudent judgment; realistic and practical understanding."

Intuition and common sense, so essential and so hard to define, are two elements that keep much of the activity of managing within the realm of art. All of us wish we had more of these special abilities. It is probably their lack that makes some people more prone to wrong judgments, and this is a major stumbling block to success in management.

TYPES OF FORMAL ORGANIZATIONAL STRUCTURE

A firm can have a super group of individuals with all kinds of special talents and education. Yet, if the firm is not effectively organized, it will not succeed to its optimum level. Whether we know it or not, we are constantly organizing ourselves as human beings. We organize our time, our written and verbal thoughts, our work, our vacations, and just about everything else that we do. Some of us are better organizers than others and so tend to get more worthwhile things done.

Organization is very important whether on the basketball court, on the campus newspaper, or in the management of a small, medium, or large business. Most business firms are organized in one of three ways: line, line and staff, or functional.

LINE ORGANIZATION

In a small business the manager is usually thought of as a generalist. That is, the manager makes the decisions on all the business's problems. Because of this the *line organization* became the dominant form in the early days of business enterprise. Line organization represents the oldest and simplest type of administrative method of management. In a line organization there are three major principles that almost never vary. They are:

1. Subordinates report to, and receive instructions from, only one immediate supervisor.
2. The line manager has total authority and total decision-making capacity.
3. Instructions and orders flow directly down the line.

LINE-AND-STAFF ORGANIZATION

As a business expands, it becomes increasingly difficult for a line management system to work. Since the line managers are generalists, they often do not possess the special skill and ability needed to handle the specific management chores in a large organization. Personnel recruitment and termination become highly specialized jobs in the large firm, whereas a generalist can easily handle them in a very small firm. As a company grows, various new management positions become increasingly important within the organization. An example would be the personnel manager. It is usually the function of such specialized executives, who are called *staff managers*, to provide the general executives, or *line managers*, with the

FIGURE 5-3 Line organizational structure

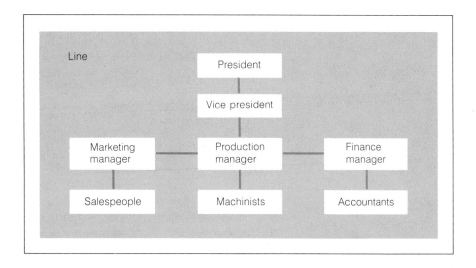

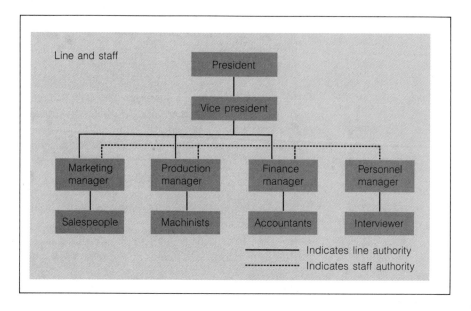

specialized advice, assistance, and services they require to perform their duties properly.

Both line and staff managers have responsibilities; the difference between them is one of authority. Staff managers are only advisors and, as such, do not have the power of a line manager outside their own departments. Staff managers have line authority over those in their own department, but they have only the responsibility to advise and assist line managers. For example, the personnel manager is boss over those who work in the personnel department, but has no authority over the vice president or the manager of marketing. The personnel manager will help the vice president and marketing manager select personnel by keeping personnel records for them and processing their personnel files. In this way the personnel manager assists line managers and all other employees of the firm. Staff managers can be added to the various management levels when and where they are needed as the firm grows and expands.

**FUNCTIONAL
ORGANIZATION**

In some very large firms, staff managers sometimes must extend their authority, on a limited basis, to other departments. Take, for example, personnel management in large companies. The finance, marketing, and similar departments can be big enough to need their own personnel manager. In such cases, the department personnel manager would have to follow instructions from the staff personnel area and would be responsible to the company's personnel manager as well as to the finance or marketing managers. In a sense it becomes necessary for the line man-

FIGURE 5-5 Functional
organizational structure

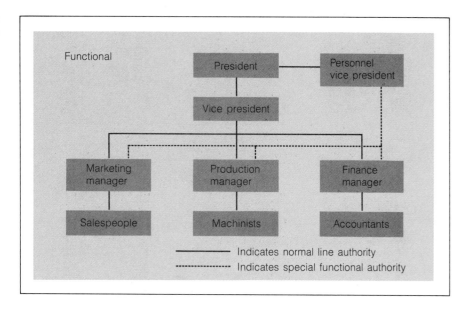

agers to delegate authority to keep specialized functions within their realms working effectively.

Functional organization takes advantage of task specialization while at the same time relieving the line manager of a part of the work load. The problem from the viewpoint of subordinates is that they now have more than one boss, and this can sometimes lead to misunderstandings if lines of authority are not clearly defined. Because of the ever-increasing specialization required in operating a business, functional organization has become more and more important.

No matter what type organization a firm has, there are always exceptions to the system. A strong personality can often seek and gain more authority than he or she is given credit for on the organization chart. The same might hold true in reverse for someone in management with a weak personality. In any case, an organizational pattern is meant to be a guideline without rigid demarcations. In no other way can it serve as an effective instrument of management.

Figures 5-4 and 5-5 show unique diagrams of how two well-known corporations delineate their organizational structure.

SPAN OF CONTROL   In any plan of organization, the duties of each executive and subordinate must be reasonable in scope as well as clearly defined. No person should be given more responsibility than can be handled by a capable, alert, well-trained individual. No person can be expected to oversee operations involving hundreds or thousands of workers unless he or she has enough assistance to do so. The answer to how much

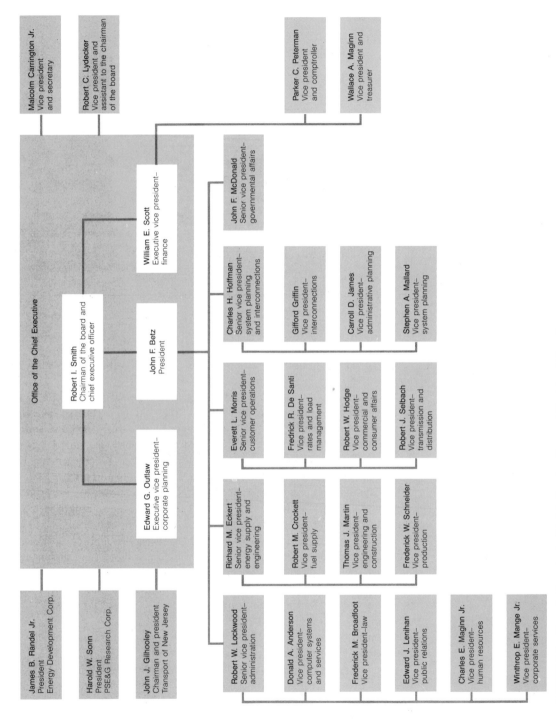

FIGURE 5-6 Organization chart of Public Service Gas and Electric of New Jersey

The span of control extends to two groups: the number of middle managers that a person can direct effectively and the number of workers that the middle manager can oversee properly.

assistance is "enough" is determined by the kind of work and the responsibilities involved.

The concept of span of control is broken down into two distinct aspects: (1) the number of subordinate managers (middle managers) that a person in higher management can effectively direct, which is called the *span of executive control* or *span of management*; (2) the number of workers that an operating manager can effectively direct, which is called the *unit of supervision*. As was stated above, actual numbers vary widely according to the type of goods or service involved as well as the size of the firm and the particular responsibilities of each manager.

For the span of-control concept to work properly within the framework of an organizational pattern, there must be proper delegation of authority. A *delegation of authority* is a granting by a superior to a subordinate the authority needed to complete the assigned tasks. Every manager is responsible to a superior and, in turn, every manager expects subordinates to serve responsibly. Where to draw the line on such authority is always the most difficult problem and one which cannot be entirely defined on an organization chart.

CENTRALIZED OR DECENTRALIZED ORGANIZATION

Should the firm be organized on a centralized or a decentralized basis? This problem is faced by every business that has branch or divisional operations in different parts of the nation or world. Large chain stores are one example of such operations and could be organized either way. Some firms have decided to organize so as to facilitate a pattern of centralized management. *Centralized management* means that the home office makes all pertinent management decisions. Under centralized management, decisions about the hiring and training of career personnel are made and carried out by the home office, and branches receive their key personnel through home-office screening and training. In addition, the home office plans key inventories for stores, production schedules for factories, marketing strategy, and all advertising.

The use of high-speed computers running 24 hours a day has made centralized management a very practical and efficient mode of organization for many firms. In a chain-store operation, for instance, centralized operations utilizing the computer mean that perpetual inventories and automatic reorders are possible. A *perpetual inventory* is a system that keeps track of changes in inventory, whether additions or subtractions, at the moment they occur. With perpetual inventory, a business often employs an automatic reorder system. When inventory dips below a certain level, merchandise is automatically reordered by the company's computer.

In a firm with decentralized management, branch managers are allowed to decide on a number of key plans and decisions concerning branch operations on their own. There must still be some home-office coordination of all operations. Under such an organization, however, branch managers are given more of a span of control in dealing with general problems affecting the local operation. While some efficiency may be lost in a decentralized organization, the added incentive and motivation that go with the opportunity for each branch to innovate and solve its own problems often outweigh the lost efficiency.

OPPORTUNITIES IN MANAGEMENT

Management positions are not as plentiful today as in the past. However, opportunities for job placement in management are still good. The large influx of people into management positions in recent years has diminished the opportunities for advancement and job security that formerly existed.

WOMEN AND MINORITIES IN MANAGEMENT

Do women and members of minority groups now have a greater chance than ever before to break into the world of middle and top management currently dominated by white males? The answer is a resounding yes!

Since the early 1970s, almost all large firms and many of the medium-sized and smaller firms have actively sought more women and minorities for managerial positions. The same is true of government agencies and nonprofit organizations.

This is partly the result of a vigorous "affirmative action" program instituted by the federal government. *Affirmative action* makes all employers accountable for actively seeking qualified minorities and women for vacant positions. Some criticize affirmative action for going too far with the result that many qualified white males are discriminated against. Others praise affirmative action as the major cause of opening doors for those who have been knocking for such a long time.

Regardless of the views on affirmative action, most managers believe it is in the best interest of all to engage minorities and women in managerial jobs. Talent and eagerness to work hard are not limited to white males. For the most part, the old tradition barring women, and the prejudices barring minorities, have been breaking down in the modern corporation's front office.

MANAGERS' SALARIES AND WORKING CONDITIONS

How much money do managers earn? Table 5-1 shows the salaries of the 20 highest paid American executives in 1977 as compiled by *Forbes*. Of course, more than 99 percent of all top-management personnel earn much less. Most top managers earn between $40,000 and $100,000 annually; the figures are $20,000 and $40,000 for middle managers. In addition, most managers receive

TABLE 5-1 Twenty highest-paid American executives in 1977

Rank	Chief Executive	Company	Salary & Bonus*	Total Remuneration	Business Background
			(in thousands)		
1	J. Robert Fluor	Fluor	549	1,121	Finance
2	Donald H. Rumsfeld	G. D. Searle	252	1,113	Administration
3	Steven J. Ross	Warner Communications	905	1,103**	Finance
4	Henry Ford II	Ford	682	1,011	Administration
5	Thomas A. Murphy	General Motors	475	996	Finance
6	Harold S. Geneen†	ITT	986	994	Finance
7	Leonard H. Goldenson	Amer. Broadcasting	750	954	Legal
8	John J. Nevin	Zenith Radio	238	904	Marketing
9	David J. Mahoney	Norton Simon	800	825	Marketing
10	Edward J. Williams	McGraw-Edison	301	817	Finance
11	Charles D. Tandy	Tandy	790	816	Administration
12	Frank T. Cary	IBM	333	807	Marketing
13	Michel C. Bergerac	Revlon	794	797	Administration
14	Wilton E. Scott	Tenneco	496	794	Technical
15	Leslie O. Barnes	Ryder System	452	774	Administration
16	William F. Laporte	Amer. Home Prod.	385	770	Administration
17	Donald M. Kendall	Pepsi Co.	510	750	Marketing
18	Rawleigh Warner Jr.	Mobil	725	745	Administration
19	Clifton C. Garvin Jr.	Exxon	696	724	Technical
20	John D. deButts	AT&T	722	722	Operations

*Includes bonuses paid in cash or in unrestricted shares of company stock.

**Salary, bonus, director's fees and deferred compensation; excludes stock options.

†Excludes amount contingently payable in later years in accordance with long-term incentive program.

Source: *Forbes*, May 28, 1978.

cash bonuses in years when business is good. Fringe benefits and expense allowances are usually quite generous for management personnel.

Don't forget, however, that managers are salaried employees. As such, they cannot expect to be compensated for working extra hours. It is usual for a manager to work evenings or on weekends. Many managers who travel in their work generally leave home on Sunday and travel back on Friday night or Saturday. Management is not a nine-to-five job.

POINT AND COUNTERPOINT: THE IMPORTANCE OF MANAGERS

The idea of being a boss someday is an attractive thought for most people. After all, the manager has a nicer office than most workers and even has a key to the executive washroom! If things go wrong, there are always subordinates to blame. On the other hand, if things go very well, one can stand up and take credit for being the captain of the ship. Management is like coaching. No matter how good or bad a coach you are, the ultimate success or failure of the team will depend on the abilities of the players. Being a good coach is knowing how to orchestrate the talents of the team; and if the team has very little talent, the best coach in the world is not going to emerge with a winning season.

Therefore almost anyone who gets the job can succeed. The trick is to get the position in the first place. Once you obtain a management position, you can lean on everyone around; and if *they* have the ability, you will succeed. The possible exception to this theory would be someone in an area like sales management. In such a field, if sales don't rise, your managerial star begins to fall.

Even if you don't do well as a manager, if you are lucky enough to work for a fairly large firm, they will "kick you upstairs." This usually means that you are placed in a staff position, one in which you can do little harm to the firm's operations. Being kicked upstairs usually means a salary increase and a new, more impressive title, so you are that much better off than before. And now you have a lot less responsibility.

Most experienced managers will say that all of the above is bunk. Take the idea of coaching as an example. It is true that a good coach with a bad team will probably never have a winning season, but such a coach will probably have a much better season than a bad coach with a bad team. A good manager, like a good coach, is someone with the training, experience, and know-how to make the best of whatever combination of resources he has to work with. Because this is the ultimate challenge to managers, being a successful manager is one of the most difficult jobs in any business.

Management certainly appeals to and attracts the nonmanager. However, those in management can tell you that the glamour wears off rapidly under the strain of the responsibilities. Probably the most stressful part of the job is dealing with other people, and there is no rule book to follow in this activity.

SUMMARY

Successful business firms depend on good managers. All businesses are organized in one of three frameworks: line, line-and-staff, or functional structure. Except for very small firms, most businesses have three levels of management. Top management makes the major decisions and helps set forth policy. Middle managers implement the decisions of top management as well as make lower level decisions. Operating managers are responsible for supervising day-to-day operations in some segment of the firm.

The three most important responsibilities of management are planning, organization, and control. Secondary responsibilities include coordinating, staffing, and human relations. Managers must have the ability to get the job done well and yet maintain the respect of those who work for them. The opportunities in management are numerous and the rewards are great for those who can work hard and put in many long hours. In recent years, women and minorities have found more responsible positions in management.

SUMMARY OF KEY TERMS

Affirmative Action Federal program requiring employers to be more responsible in the hiring of minorities and women.

Bayesian Approach A scientific process for aiding managers in their task of making decisions. The Bayesian approach places emphasis on recognizing the alternatives in any given situation, implementing a course of action, and evaluating the course of action by objective means.

Behavioral Science The study of ways to deal with people problems. In recent years the study of human behavior has become a very important aspect of management education.

Centralized Management A way of organizing a firm with many branches so that all important decisions and plans are made by management at the home office. High-speed computers aid greatly in making this type of organization effective.

Channels of Communication The ability to communicate plans, policies, problems, and instructions both up and down the management ladder.

Control A primary function of management involved with observation and direction of the ongoing operations of the firm.

Coordination The know-how to blend the func-

tions of planning, organization, and control into one smoothly running operation.

Decentralized Management A firm organized so that branch managers are allowed to make a number of key plans and decisions about branch operations.

Esprit de Corps A term that means pulling together as one unit toward clear objectives and with a common willingness to try as hard as possible to obtain those objectives.

Functional Organization A pattern of organization where staff managers also have line management responsibilities and authority in certain areas of operations.

Human Relations Managers' ability to combine sensitivity to the needs of workers and customers with firmness in giving orders necessary to get the various jobs done.

Line Organization A pattern of organization in which responsibility and authority clearly flow from the superior to the subordinate all the way down the management ladder.

Line-and-Staff Organization A pattern of organization in which staff managers who are experts in specialized fields work with the line managers to improve the operations of the firm.

Management The process by which those in authority plan, organize, and control a business in an effort to make it successful.

Middle Management Those managers who implement the decisions of top management as well as make lower-level decisions regarding operations of the firm.

Operating Management Those managers on the lowest level who supervise the day-to-day operations in some part of the business.

Organization The roadway along which planning will be carried out.

Planning A primary function of management concerned with determining what to produce and how to produce it.

Span of Control The largest number of workers or subordinate managers that a superior can effectively and efficiently supervise.

Theory X The theory of management that states that work is distasteful and people do it only for economic survival. Therefore, the normal individual must be coerced and threatened to get the job done.

Theory Y The theory of management that states that work is as normal as play. The average worker can learn to accept and even seek responsibility if the rewards and recognitions are clear and worthwhile.

Top Management The level of management that makes or reviews all the most important decisions with regard to planning, organization, and control of the firm.

Transactional Analysis (TA) An approach to understanding human behavior based on how people relate to each other. TA is one area in the behavioral science aspect of management.

REVIEW QUESTIONS

1. What are the levels of management? At what level would an office supervisor normally appear? At what level would a vice president for finance appear? At what level would one of fourteen plant managers appear?

2. List and briefly describe each of the primary functions of management.

3. List and briefly discuss the secondary functions of management.

4. Define MBO and Theory X and Theory Y. In what general category of management study should they be classified?

5. What is the Bayesian approach to decision making?

6. What is meant by balancing authority with responsibility in management?

7. Beside the ability to analyze data, what other characteristics are required of a good manager?

8. What is the oldest form of formal organizational structure? Which is the least popular of the three major forms of formal organizational structure?

9. In what ways is functional organization the same as line-and-staff organization? In what ways do they differ?

10. What is the difference between centralized and decentralized management? Give some examples that you know about.

DISCUSSION QUESTIONS

1. "Equal pay for equal work." How does this slogan apply to the new trend of more women entering middle- and upper-management positions in business?

2. Prepare an organization chart in as much detail as possible for your school, college, or university. Suggestion: Use the school catalog as your data source.

3. Which theory do you think is the more accurate description of the American worker, Theory X or Theory Y? Give reasons for your choice.

4. Comment on the following: It is more important for a manager to be able to get along with subordinates and superiors than it is to make the right decisions.

5. Transactional analysis (TA) and Theories X and Y are only two of many behavioral science approaches to the study of management problems. Look up another behaviorial science approach in the library, write a brief report on it, bring it to class discussion.

CASES FOR DECISION MAKING

RETOOLING THE CORPORATE STRUCTURE

Cleveland Tool Works is a small firm of 600 employees located in three plant and office sites in Cleveland, Columbus, and Dayton, Ohio. Thomas Westerly, president and chairman of the board as well as controlling stockholder, has plans to retire in three years. Since he has no heirs to run the company, but would like to see it continue in future years, he has decided gradually to sell shares to present employees and, if necessary, to the public over the next three years. The present informal structure of the firm appears in Figure 5-7.

The main plant in Cleveland manufactures 40 percent of the firm's total annual output. The Columbus and Dayton plants share the remaining production equally. Each plant maintains its own office but the entire sales force is located in Cleveland. The sales staff travels the entire United States. Each plant hires its own help and does its own payroll. Duplicates of all personnel files are kept at the home office. Westerly owns 95 percent of the firm's common stock. His wife owns 4 percent and the vice president for operations owns 1 percent.

FIGURE 5-7

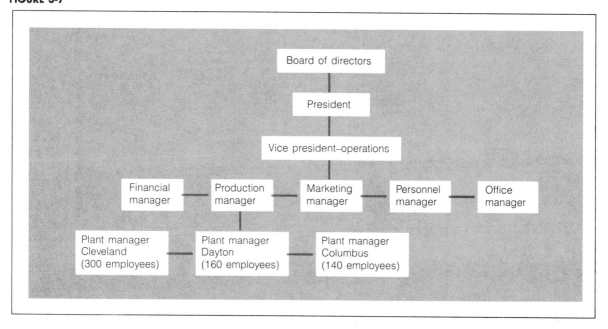

1. Sketch a formal organization structure to serve the needs of the firm after Westerly's retirement.
2. Comment on the present structure in terms of centralization and decentralization and make suggestions for the future under the new plan devised above.
3. How might the sale of common stock help in the future development of good managers?

HELP WANTED

1. List the major characteristics of the type of person who might be interested and qualified for the management position in Figure 5-8.
2. What evidence is there in the ad that the firm is complying with affirmative action?
3. What level of management is the ad related to?

FIGURE 5-8

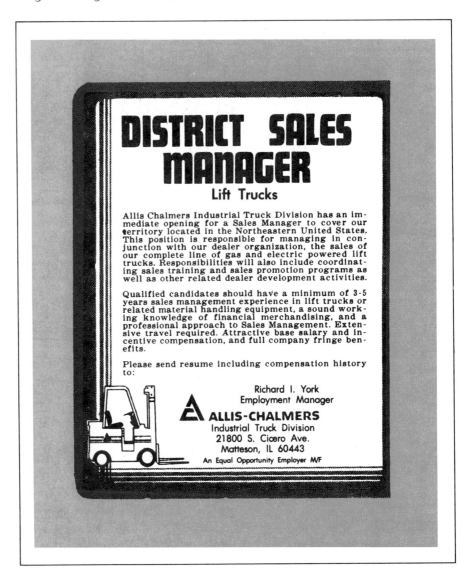

4. How much salary might you suppose such a position would pay?

V.I.P.

In June of 1977, Winston R. Wallin, a career employee, at Pillsbury was named president and chief operating officer. Wallin joined the company in 1948 and started out in the grain department. He held a variety of grain procurement positions until he became vice president of commodity operations in 1970. In 1974 he became vice president of the Agriproducts group and executive vice president of Agriproducts in 1976. Mr. Wallin was highly regarded but his selection as president was something of a surprise. Wallin was 51 years old at the time of his appointment to the presidency. He enjoys playing golf and he came from a farming background. In recent years, Pillsbury has vigorously recruited from outside the firm. Also, the stress has recently been on the company's consumer and restaurant operations.

1. Why did Wallin's appointment come as a surprise?
2. Do you suppose career employees generally make it to the top? Why or why not?
3. At the library check a corporate directory such as the one published by Standard and Poor's to verify whether or not Mr. Wallin still holds the presidency of Pillsbury? If not, who does?
4. What do you suppose are agriproducts?

RELATED READINGS

Appley, Lawrence A. *Formula for Success.* New York: Amacom, 1974.

Written by the chairman of the board of the American Management Association. Discusses planning, objectives, control, standards, rewards, and similar pertinent topics.

Costello, John. "Why Able Executives Reject Jobs." *Nation's Business,* June 1977, pp. 64–66.

A brief summary of the major reasons why executives refuse new positions at higher salaries in a new firm. Sometimes status is the reason. More often it's location, personnel problems, or chain of command.

Drucker, Peter. *Management: Tasks, Responsibilities, Practices.* New York: Harper & Row, 1974.

The latest of Drucker's many books on management philosophy, this book is a very large and comprehensive primer. The student new to the field may want to be selective in reading from this volume.

Hennig, Margaret, and Anne Jardim. *The Managerial Woman.* Garden City, N.Y.: Doubleday, 1977.

Interesting items on management and how they relate to the particular needs of women in the organization.

Jones, Edward H. *Blacks in Business.* New York: Grosset & Dunlop, 1971.

A story of blacks who have made it in management and in business ownership. Interesting reading with some good tips especially suited to minority readers.

Maccoby, Michael. "The Corporate Climber Has to Find His Heart." *Fortune,* December 1976, pp. 98–108.

Comments on the emotional makeup, or lack of same, on the part of the corporate executive. Careerism sometimes produces "flabby-hearted" executives.

McGregor, Douglas. *The Professional Manager.* New York: McGraw-Hill, 1967.

Reflections on the difficult tasks of being an effective manager are presented in this book. McGregor, like Drucker, tends to deal with the philosophical aspects of management. Well written and easy to follow for the serious student of management.

Mandell, Mel. *1001 Ways to Operate Your Business More Profitably.* Homewood, Ill.: Dow Jones-Irwin, 1975.

A basic guide for anyone involved in the operation of a business. Informative for the small, as well as large, business operator.

"T.V. That Competes with the Office Grapevine." *Business Week*, March 14, 1977, pp. 49–54.

Brief article on the use of television as a communications device within an organization.

Townsend, Robert. *Up the Organization.* New York: Knopf, 1970.

An enjoyable, easy-to-read retelling of the author's years of experience in management.

chapter 6

OPERATING SMALL BUSINESSES AND FRANCHISES

OBJECTIVES

When you have finished reading and studying this chapter, you should be able to:

1. Define and distinguish small businesses from large ones.

2. Know the advantages and disadvantages of entering into a small business.

3. Know the essentials of franchising.

4. Describe and discuss the services that the Small Business Administration provides small business operators and prospective operators.

5. Know the advantages and disadvantages associated with buying an existing small business or franchise as well as those associated with starting a new small business or buying into a new franchise.

CHAPTER PREVIEW

Most of us have had the experience of selling greeting cards, candy, or cookies to raise money for a school club or for a service organization such as the Boy Scouts or Girl Scouts. Engaging in this type of activity from time to time can be fun. Many people enjoy it so much that it becomes a motivating factor for them to go into business for themselves.

You have probably also shopped in many small stores and known the owners by name. Perhaps you have worked part-time for a small store or service business. In many different ways, the effects of small businesses on our lives can be as great as the effects of big business and big government. We don't read in the newspaper about policies or price changes by small firms as we would if Ford raised the prices of its cars. Nevertheless, the collective action of small business firms does affect our bank balance and the types of goods and services that we buy.

Being a small business owner can be a very exciting endeavor. One has the opportunity to become financially independent, be creative, and see that creation grow. However, it is not all glamour, and the life of a small business operator must be deeply committed to the development of the firm. To be successful in the small business world requires a great deal of motivation, a tremendous amount of time, lots of money and the ability to borrow, and the stomach to live with a high-risk operation.

6
OPERATING SMALL BUSINESSES AND FRANCHISES

General Motors' annual gross sales exceeds the GNP of many undeveloped nations. Today we tend to think in terms of big business and big government. These institutions are always in the headlines and are often featured in television documentaries. Big businesses and government agencies swamp us with advertising on television, radio, and in newspapers and magazines. For these reasons, and for many more, we tend to forget the importance of small businesses in our daily lives and in the American economy.

If you were to keep a diary of your shopping for one or two weeks, you would probably find that you often patronize a small business or franchise operation. Usually, one buys the daily newspaper at a local store. Your drugstore, dry cleaner, shoe repair shop, hairdresser, and sporting goods store are very often small business operations. As a matter of fact, according to the Small Business Administration (SBA), a federal agency, of the approximately 12 million firms in the United States, about 95 percent are considered to be small businesses.

Nevertheless, in terms of output, the big firms still account for the larger volume of GNP—about 57 percent. But small businesses do generate about 40 percent of the nation's GNP, totaling over $800 billion in goods and services, according to the SBA.

SMALL BUSINESS

How do we distinguish a small business from a big one? Actually, small is a relative term. We have very little difficulty in categorizing IBM and Xerox as big. Common sense also helps us categorize the local plant and flower shop as small. Yet, there are times when we need guidelines and the general rules, from the SBA, cited below may be helpful for identifying a small business.

1. The owner or owners are usually on the premises; so is the manager.
2. The capital is supplied by a very small group, often by only one individual.
3. The firm usually operates on a local basis. There are few, if any, branch operations.
4. The size of the firm is small when compared with the big firms in the industry.
5. For lending purposes the SBA classifies any retailing or service concern as small if annual receipts do not exceed $1 million.
6. The SBA classifies a manufacturing firm as small if its employees do not exceed 250 people.[1]

There are many other sizing criteria developed by the SBA and by the Committee for Economic Development in New York City. But for our purposes the above six guidelines are sufficient.

1. "Meeting the Special Problems of Small Businesses," Committee for Economic Development, New York, 1974.

ACTIVITY AND
ORGANIZATION

Small businesses are found in most areas of economic activity with the exception of capital intensive industries; that is, businesses in which a tremendous amount of capital is needed to provide facilities and equipment. A public utility company is a good example of a capital intensive firm. Naturally, such firms require more investment than one individual or a small group could provide.

However, in the case of service businesses where capital intensity is often low, small businesses predominate. In retailing firms and in some light manufacturing firms, there are many small businesses. A light manufacturing firm is one that requires a small investment in equipment such as would be the case for the manufacturer of a plastic product such as the Frisbee. Farming is often classified as a light manufacturing activity because farming produces products for sale.

Among service firms one must not forget the professionals. Professionals include lawyers, public accountants, dentists, and physicians. In addition to being considered professionals, they are also thought of as being small business operators.

Are all small businesses sole proprietorships? No, although many of them are; many more are partnerships or corporations. In fact, in recent years there has been a trend by small business owners to incorporate. They do this to give themselves protection against liability claims. As you learned in Chapter 4, by being incorpo-

His first shop was so successful that J. C. Penny moved his Golden Rule Store to these larger quarters in Kemmerer, Wyoming, in 1904.

J. C. Penney

rated, the law provides them with limited liability which safeguards their personal, nonbusiness assets.

However, don't think that an incorporated small business is a worry-free operation. First of all, if a small business incorporates, the legal and tax expenses of doing so will be costly. In addition, if a small corporation wants to borrow, lenders will usually require the owner of the firm to cosign the debtor contract. In this way, the unlimited liability feature is set aside, and if the corporation should default on the loan, the creditor would have recourse to the personal, nonbusiness assets of the owner since the owner was the cosigner of the debt contract.

Now you know better than to think that the word *corporation* denotes bigness. In fact, most of the firms that are incorporated are small businesses and the same can be said about sole proprietorships and partnerships. The foundation of business in the United States is still very much composed of small businesses. Franchises, described and discussed later in this section, have made the small business an even more important factor in the business community.

THE CHALLENGE OF SMALL BUSINESS

In recent years many young people have become interested in crafts such as leather work, stained-glass making, plant growing, and the like. They have really become small business operators without realizing it and many of them soon

Most people who are in business for themselves enjoy the independence that comes with ownership.

Maria Karras

found that their skill at the craft was not enough to sustain their effort at making a living. One must know his or her product well. But beyond this, one must be able to cope with money matters, marketing strategies, personnel, advertising, and many other business affairs.

This textbook discusses these functions of modern business in separate chapters, but one must not get the impression that they are not integrated. No one knows this better than the small business owner. The small business owner must be competent in all areas of business management. Even when not on the front line, such as when one hires an accountant or a lawyer, one has to be able to understand what is happening and discuss the subject in an informed way.

In recent years, operating businesses of all sizes has become increasingly complicated. Some of the major reasons for this include:

1. Many new federal and state regulations have come into effect as a result of the consumer movement.
2. New tax laws on the federal, state, and local levels.
3. An increased load of local regulations governing the operations of small businesses.
4. The increasing sophistication of the consumer and the rapid changes in consumer preferences.
5. The larger amounts of capital needed to set up a new business due to inflation and other causes.

ADVANTAGES OF SMALL BUSINESSES

Ask small business owners why they ever entered into the troublesome pursuit of running their own business and you might be surprised at their initial response. Often their primary reason was not the pursuit of a profit at all. Their usual answer is that they enjoy the freedom and satisfaction of working for themselves and the challenges that go with trying to make it on one's own. As a matter of fact, the typical small business person does not earn profits in excess of the salaries paid to middle managers who work for large firms and who do not have to risk capital.

Small business operators are not bogged down by red tape. They enjoy speed of action and flexibility in the management of the firm. For this reason the business can be aggressive and innovative and often can sell at prices below those of larger competitors. Smallness also permits the manager to see the whole operation and thus allows for greater control. This helps determine where problems are developing before they become serious. Good control is also an important element for facilitating correct decision making quickly and easily.

The key advantage of smallness, however, is the ability to get to know your customer. No big business can compete with a conscientious small business owner in personal contact. The degree of trust and satisfaction that is developed between customer and shopkeeper is the fundamental reason why the small business continues to be an important part of the American economy. As a result, the owner of a small business firm is often regarded as an important member of the community and is frequently called upon to serve in community activities.

In recent years, small business owners have become participants in the Social Security program as self-employed taxpayers. In 1962 the Keogh Act was passed by Congress to allow small business owners to participate in a self-employed tax retirement plan. Small business owners can place up to 15 percent of net earnings per year (not to exceed a maximum of $7,500) into a savings account or insurance annuity. The money remains in this account until the person retires (minimum age is 60) and at that point the retired businessperson can collect a pension. Furthermore, during the years that contributions are made, the earnings contributed to the pension plan are free of federal income taxes.

DISADVANTAGES OF SMALL BUSINESSES

While the advantages cited above provide a strong case for going into a small business, the disadvantages of such a move can be as great, if not greater than the advantages. As we discussed earlier, the small business manager must develop integrated skills in production, marketing, finance, and personnel, among other areas. For most people this proves impossible. In addition, most people are not willing to make the sacrifice of time and energy required to get the job done. One cannot expect to work a 40-hour workweek as a small business operator. The day is long, as the following schedule of a husband and wife who operate a small diner in a small town indicates. Their workweek as cook/operator, waitress/operator is as follows (bear in mind that they also employ several waitresses and a dishwasher):

| Monday through Friday | 6 a.m. to 8 p.m. = 70 hours |
| Saturday | 6 a.m. to 6 p.m. = 12 hours |

That's a total of 82 hours a week, a far cry from the usual 9-to-5, 40-hour work week.

Additional disadvantages of smallness were briefly looked at in Chapter 4. There are many other factors too numerous to mention in a brief introduction. Predictably, the rate of failure among small businesses is very high.

FRANCHISING

The conglomerate and other forms of big business organization reached new heights of growth and importance in our economy in the 1960s. Small business also underwent changes during this same period. One of these changes was the growth of franchising, which attracted those interested in small business and became, in a way, a link between small and big business.

A *franchise* is an agreement between an individual and a national company granting the right to market or sell the company's products or services in a particular area. The company is called the *franchisor* and the individual is called the

With a store on nearly every main street in America, McDonald's is the super success story in franchising.

McDonald's Corporation

franchisee. Well-known franchises are McDonald's, Baskin-Robbins, and Goodyear tire stores.

ADVANTAGES AND
DISADVANTAGES

It can be readily seen that franchising overcomes many of the problems that a small business operator faces. Since the franchisor conducts national advertising campaigns, the public can identify with the product or service without the local operator spending years to develop a reputation. Franchisees are also guaranteed location protection and help from the franchisor in solving unforeseen problems in marketing, financing, and other areas.

On the minus side, one must remember that investing in a franchise usually requires a larger amount of capital than would be the case in a similar nonfranchise operation. Also, the local franchisee is vulnerable to changes in the national reputation of the franchise. If the product or service fell out of favor with consumers, the local business operator would suffer.

LEGALITY AND RISKS

Franchise arrangements are drawn up in a legal contract. As with any major contract an attorney should be consulted to review the terms of the agreement. There have been cases where franchisors have very little to offer in the way of a product or service. It is sometimes their main intent to sell franchise rights across the country, to pocket investors' money, and then simply to let the national reputation of the product or service fall flat on its face. A wise investor should very carefully investigate the reputation of the franchisor before signing any agreement.

As with any investment, the element of risk is high for a franchisee. And since the necessary capital is usually more than that usually needed for investing in a small business, the losses can also be greater. On the other hand, if all goes well, the rewards can be much higher and come much sooner than in a nonfranchise small business.

Readers of the *Wall Street Journal* will see many ads for various kinds of franchises. Before one invests, research should be conducted to determine the financial and marketing strength of the franchisor. Libraries, chambers of commerce, and specialized investment information services such as Dun and Bradstreet give information about franchises. The federal Department of Commerce publishes a description of several hundred franchises that operate in the United States. This publication is called *Franchise Company Data Book* and can be obtained from the Government Printing Office in Washington, D.C.

MAJOR TYPES OF FRANCHISES

As with any type of small business, franchising crosses the boundaries of retail outlets, service organizations, light manufacturing firms, and wholesaling houses. An investor who desires a future as a franchisee has a wide variety of business activities to choose from. Since the franchisor will give you the necessary training and some experience, you do not have to be overly concerned about these factors when entering a franchise venture. Naturally, it would be unwise to go into a business that you might not enjoy. For example, it would be foolish to affiliate with a chain of pet shops if you did not like animals.

Of all the types of franchises available, the fast-food chains seem to be the most successful. The fast-food business is one where the customer is waited on quickly and selects from a limited menu of already-prepared items. McDonald's has been the most successful in fast foods, but there are many others that you would recognize and, perhaps, have eaten at. Pizza Hut, Burger King, Taco Bell, and Gino's are just a few of the other successful fast-food franchise operations.

Franchises have also made their mark in the travel and lodging business. Most of the major motel chains, such as Holiday Inns, and Best Western, and Sheraton Inns, are franchises. Franchise outlets are prevalent in the car- and truck-leasing field. National Car Rental and Budget Rent-A-Car are examples. United Campgrounds has become a successful franchise operation catering to those who travel in RVs and trailers.

Franchising has become international in recent years. Many American franchisers have invaded foreign shores. McDonald's can be found in London, Paris, and Amsterdam as well as in many other major cities outside the United States. In addition, many foreign firms have established their own similar franchise chains here in this country.

business profile: A $7.4 BILLION MUSHROOM

Convenience stores stock an average of 3,000 items and emphasize fast-moving "impulse" goods, such as beer, magazines, cigarettes, and snacks. They are rapidly gaining sales from consumers who haven't the time to drive to the supermarket or the patience to wait in long checkout lines.

Much of the industry's growth has been primed by Dallas-based Southland Corp., owner of the 7-Eleven chain. Southland is opening hundreds of new stores annually and supplying about half of their merchandise through distribution centers in Virginia, Florida, and Texas. It is spearheading an industry drive away from slower-moving grocer products to such new categories as gasoline, fast foods, health and beauty aids, magazines, and photo products. Nearly all convenience store operators are adding take-out foods at the same time that service stations are adding such items to the snacks that have always been available from their coin-operated machines. Many believe that

the future of the convenience store industry will be closely tied to gasoline sales.

The average sale at a convenience store is about $1.38. More than half of all sales are to male customers who run in for a pack of cigarettes or beer. These two items account for 30 percent of sales. Another 30 percent of sales are for bakery products and snack foods.

Although Southland owns the real estate, most of its stores are operated by franchisees. They pay $7,000 for a store and contribute 50 percent of Southland's gross sales. For its part, Southland trains two salespersons for the store and handles all merchandising, advertising, and financial statements. Once the three-week training is completed, the franchisees are given a fully stocked store plus $250 in the cash register to begin business. They are expected to make a profit after six months. If there are no profits within a year, the store is closed and sold.

MINORITY-OWNED
FRANCHISES

Many opportunities have opened in recent years for members of minority groups to own and operate franchises that cater to the special wants of ethnic customers. Most of these franchises are in the fast-food trade and some deal with automotive product sales or specialized services such as hairstyling. Figures released by the Department of Commerce for 1974 indicate that there are close to a thousand black-owned franchises in the United States. These same figures indicate 875 franchises owned by Hispanics, 185 owned by Orientals, and 37 owned by Indians. The opportunities in franchising are almost unlimited if one selects the right product or service.

FUTURE OF
FRANCHISING

The 1960s were the golden age of franchising in the United States. Most of the franchisors who successfully established themselves during that period are still going strong. Many of them are now opening new outlets throughout the country and in other parts of the world. So for the prospective franchisee there is still, and probably will continue to be, the opportunity to get into a good thing. However, as franchisors become more successful, the cost of a new franchisee, or the cost of buying an existing franchise, climbs.

As for the growth of new franchises, it is expected to slow down. There will be new franchisors emerging and most of them are expected to enter into the service area. Franchises in janitorial services, home care, security forces, temporary employment agencies, and duplicating and fast-printing services seem to be typical of the direction in which new franchises are being established.

**THE SMALL
BUSINESS
ADMINISTRATION**

During the early 1950s it became clear to many leaders in America that small businesses were being forced out of business by the competition of big business. During the early years of the Eisenhower Administration, Congress therefore established the Small Business Administration (SBA). Since it was established, the SBA has established itself as a friend of small business owners and of people who want to enter into a small business venture. The SBA helps such people in two ways: 1) It provides capital or helps other agencies provide capital for small businesses. It also provides funds for established businesses to get back on their feet after a disaster, such as a flood. 2) It provides management information and training for established business owners as well as prospective owners.

FUNDING FUNCTION

If a small business owner or prospective owner is having trouble borrowing from private sources, the SBA may be able to help. If an applicant cannot get a regular loan, the SBA can lend a small business up to $100,000 if federal funds are available at the time. The SBA also lends funds to private lending institutions so that they have money to lend to small businesses. The most closely related type of lending agency is known as the Small Business Investment Corporation (SBIC). SBICs are *privately* owned lending corporations that are licensed, promoted, and

In disasters such as earthquakes, tornados, and floods, business owners can obtain funds for rebuilding from the Small Business Administration.

U.S. Dept. of the Interior

regulated by the SBA. Part of the SBIC's capital is provided by the SBA and part comes from the investment made by the SBIC owners. There are many SBICs located throughout the country and each is a privately owned company.

Each SBIC takes the funds provided by its investors as well as those provided by the SBA and makes loans to worthy small business firms. The SBICs can also become investors in a small business but may not obtain a controlling interest as a result of the investment. In addition to lending and investing, many SBICs provide management consulting to the business firms to protect their loan or investment.

In order to encourage more minority small business ownership, in 1969 Congress established a special program to set up SBICs that would deal exclusively with minority small business firms. These lending agencies are known as Minority Enterprise Small Business Investment Corporations (MESBICs). They are very similar in operations to the SBICs.

In some cases, the SBA makes direct loans to people who are classified as disadvantaged. These loans are called economic opportunity loans and can be made to those whose total income does not meet the needs of their family and who are unable to get a loan from regular lending agencies at a reasonable rate.

The maximum amount is $25,000, for not more than 15 years. Since no collateral is required, the loan is risky, which is why the SBA lends the money instead of a bank.

The SBA is empowered to make disaster loans to businesses that are damaged in floods, tornadoes, or hurricanes. The loans are made at an exceptionally low rate of interest but are limited to $500,000. The loan may extend for 30 years. In the early 1970s when the downtown shopping area of Wilkes-Barre, Pennsylvania, was ruined by a flood, the SBA was instrumental in the city's recovery with its disaster-relief lending program.

MANAGEMENT ASSISTANCE

There are over 80 field offices of the SBA in the United States, Guam, and Puerto Rico. Although the main function of these offices is in the lending area, an important secondary function is to provide management assistance to small business operators and prospective owners. One of these services involves providing free consultants to help with special problems or to advise on how to expand or get started in a new business.

The Active Corps of Executives (ACE) program is one of the ways the SBA lends assistance. People who serve as consultants in this program are recruited from successful related small businesses or professional fields. Another group of consultants comes from the SBA program called Service Corps of Retired Executives (SCORE). It has established chapters in many cities. SCORE volunteers are retired people who worked as accountants, bankers, economists, retailers, educators, engineers, and the like. When a small business owner asks for help in solving a problem, the local SCORE chapter sends a representative to help. There are over four thousand volunteers in the SCORE program.

The SBA provides management training through a number of programs. They organize and run courses, conferences, problem clinics, and workshops for prospective small business owners. All of these programs can deal with typical problems such as inventory control, budgeting, layout, and advertising.

In addition to courses, conferences, clinics, and workshops, the SBA issues a great number of useful publications. Some of these are free but others are available at a small charge. Two series of publications are "Management Aids" and "Small Marketer's Aids." A large bibliography is also available free from the SBA. Publications are available through the Government Printing Office in Washington, D.C., or through the SBA field offices.

BUYING A FIRM OR STARTING YOUR OWN

Investors have a choice when looking for a small business or franchise to invest in. That choice involves buying a business that is already established or starting a new firm with a brand new identity. There are advantages and disadvantages to each choice.

ADVANTAGES AND
DISADVANTAGES OF
BUYING INTO A
BUSINESS

Buying into a successful existing business has several important advantages. The main problem is to determine the track record of such a firm. Since the prospective buyer is an outsider, it is sometimes difficult to determine whether an owner is selling for the stated reason or whether there is some special reason that is being withheld from a prospective buyer. One should carefully inspect the premises and inventory before making an offer. Of course, the buyer should insist on seeing financial statements certified by an accountant and also speak to the firm's banker and lawyer. The important advantages of buying into an existing business generally include:

1. The goodwill of established customers.
2. A proven relationship with the community and with vendors.
3. Trained employees.
4. Credit with suppliers.
5. A proven location.
6. Physical facilities that are ready-made for the business.
7. The possession of necessary licenses and permits.

There are also disadvantages to buying into an established firm:

1. Changes are sometimes difficult to make without risking the loss of goodwill from established customers.
2. One inherits the previous owner's creditors.
3. The firm's employees may not meet your expectations, or you may not meet theirs.
4. The previous owner may reopen nearby and lure customers from you.
5. The facilities may not be in as good a working order as you had thought nor as well suited to the operation as you had expected.

ADVANTAGES AND
DISADVANTAGES OF
STARTING A NEW
BUSINESS

Some people prefer to buy a franchise or start their own firm. As was mentioned, many people find themselves gradually building a business from a hobby or a part-time job. As is the case in buying into an established firm, there are several important advantages as well as disadvantages to starting a firm:

1. The best-possible location can be selected, based on research.
2. Physical facilities are modeled to the exact needs of the business.
3. Customer goodwill can be developed through one's own policies and relationships.
4. Rapport with suppliers depends on you.
5. Inventories, supplies, and equipment are flexible.
6. The opportunity to make a fresh impact on the community.

CATHY HARDWICK — riches from rags

At the age of eighteen, Cathy Hardwick turned her back on the riches and royalty that were her family's legacy in her native Korea, moved to San Francisco, and opened her own boutique there in 1961. Her own designs eventually attracted the attention of clothing manufacturers on the West and then the East Coast. When they took up her line of women's casual clothes, Cathy Hardwick & Friends, Ltd., grew to an annual gross sales figure of $2 million a year. Hers was no longer a small business.

Ms. Hardwick's creative talent alone might be credit for this achievement. But for the $30 million in licensed designs for products on which the Hardwick design will appear this year—everything from Pepperell sheets to Penney home furnishings to Mikasa bone china—and for the $500,000 which will be her likely share, she thanks her business agent, Mort Kaplan, who used to be president of giant Burlington Industries' home furnishings division. "The licensing is his brainchild. He guided me. We worked for a goal, and it just happened."

Such modesty is an admirable quality, but this kind of success in a small business does not "just happen" except as a result of exceptional talent and considerable business acumen.

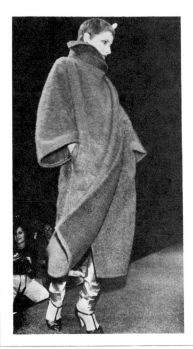

Some of the more important disadvantages to starting a business include:

1. A higher risk in starting a new business than in buying an established one.
2. The demands of capital and time are greater for building customer goodwill.
3. Credit will take time to establish. In the meantime many supplier transactions will have to be paid for in cash.
4. Capital loans are often more difficult to obtain for starting a new firm.
5. It is more difficult to get organized, establish procedures, and develop workable policies.

Whether it is an established business or a new one, operating a small business is not for everyone. It takes a great deal of motivation, a tremendous amount of time, substantial capital and borrowing ability, and the fortitude to live with a high-risk situation.

SUMMARY

Of the 9.3 million businesses in the United States, about 8.8 million, or 95 percent, are considered to be small businesses. Small businesses are defined in many different ways, but the classification by the Small Business Administration seems to be the most accepted (see p. 141). The SBA is an agency of the federal government created in 1953 to help small business firms get started and to help them survive. The SBA helps small business through direct and indirect loan programs, management assistance services, and through the publication of information literature.

Operating a small firm has many advantages and disadvantages. Many people enjoy being their own boss and enjoy the challenge of putting their own ideas to work. On the other hand, the hours are very long and the financial risk is great for a small business owner. Franchising, the process of being a small business owner of an outlet associated with a nationally known firm, is one way to start into a new business quickly. McDonald's and Baskin-Robbins are two examples of the many successful franchise operations. However, it should be pointed out that not all franchise operations are successful.

SUMMARY OF KEY TERMS

Active Corps of Executives Pool of consultants provided for small business operators by the SBA.

Capital Intensive Industry An industry that requires very large amounts of capital to provide facilities and equipment.

Franchise An agreement between an individual and a national company granting the right to market or sell the company's products or services in a particular area.

Franchisee The local small business owner who operates a franchise.

Franchisor The national firm which grants franchise rights to a local small business.

Management Aids A free series of publications of the SBA with tips for managing small firms.

Minority Enterprise Small Business Investment Corporation (MESBIC) Small business lending agency specifically established for the purpose of making loans to minority small business operators.

Service Corps of Retired Executives (SCORE) Retired executives and those in related fields who volunteer through the SBA to help small business operators solve problems.

Small Business Administration (SBA) Agency of the federal government which facilitates lending and gives management assistance to small businesses.

Small Business Investment Corporation (SBIC) Privately owned financial corporations aided by the SBA which makes loans to small business firms.

Small Marketer's Aids A free series of publications of the SBA with tips on marketing for small business.

REVIEW QUESTIONS

1. It is sometimes difficult to say whether a business is large or small. What are six guidelines used by the SMA to determine a *small* business?

2. Comment on this statement. "Small business is important because it accounts for the largest percentage of products and services in the GNP."

3. Why would a small business operator want to incorporate? What are the disadvantages to incorporation?

4. What is the major advantage of a small business over a corporation? In your opinion does this advantage carry weight with the average buyer?

5. What is a franchise? What are the advantages and disadvantages of franchising?

6. Name as many local franchises as you can.

7. How does the Small Business Administration aid small businesses?

8. What is MESBIC? What is its purpose?

9. List the advantages and disadvantages of buying a business.

10. Identify the advantages and disadvantages of starting a new business.

DISCUSSION QUESTIONS

1. Comment on the following: If you have a lot of money to invest, it is better to buy a franchise than to start your own firm.

2. If you were going to start a restaurant, would you look for a franchise to associate with? Would you incorporate your firm? What factors would influence your decision in either case?

3. It has been said that small businesses are a dying part of American business life. Do you think this comment is true or false? Explain your answer.

4. Why should the federal government be helping small businesses through the SBA? (If you believe it should not aid small businesses, state your reasons.)

5. Interview a small business owner in your community and ask that person to give you reasons why he or she enjoys being a small business operator and in what ways he or she does not like being a small business operator. Prepare a report of your findings and bring it to the next class meeting.

CASES FOR DECISION MAKING

TO BE OR NOT TO BE?

Phyllis Uzzolino has been employed as an expert typist-stenographer with a small well-established insurance firm for over 15 years. She is 37 years old and has her own apartment, a new car, and adequate insurance. She has savings accounts totalling $16,000 and $3,000 in mutual funds. Her job seems secure until retirement and her annual salary increases have just about kept up with the cost of living. Her elderly mother lives with her and depends upon her for partial support.

Phyllis just heard about a small steno-duplicating service for sale. The current owner is retiring after 20 years in the business and the remaining 4 employees are older people ranging from five to ten years from retirement age. The firm has a history of being successful, but has not done as well in the past two years as in previous periods. One senior member of the firm is willing to become an equal partner with Phyllis if she is interested. However, this person does not want major management responsibilities. The asking price for the firm is $60,000 and this is considered reasonable for its performance according to an accountant and lawyer that Phyllis has engaged. Phyllis has checked the credit rating of the firm and has asked about its reputation with the local Chamber of Commerce. Both results were mildly favorable.

1. What further information should Phyllis seek?
2. Should she consider going in with the senior member as an equal partner? Why or why not?
3. Should she consider going in on her own and giving up a steady income and job security? Why or why not?
4. What other forms of ownership might she consider?

THE PIZZA DILEMMA

Richard Rich has run a pizza parlor for the past five years. Pizza Place, a new national chain of pizza franchises, has invited Richard to become affiliated. It will cost him $25,000 to buy a Pizza Place franchise and he will have to close his store for two weeks to attend a training class and to refit his present location. Since Richard just finished paying off his business debt of $40,000 on the original store loan, he is reluctant to become involved in financing another $25,000. However, he realizes that Pizza Place is quickly gaining a favorable national reputation through television and newspaper advertising.

1. List the possible advantages and disadvantages of the new venture for Richard. On balance would you recommend or not recommend affiliation with Pizza Place? Why or why not?
2. What other alternative might you suggest for Richard if he is interested in joining Pizza Place?

SMALLNESS IN BANKING[2]

Believe it or not there are still several banks in the United States that are owned by only one person and that are so small they do not come under federal law, the Federal Reserve System, or the insurance protection plan offered by the Federal Deposit Insurance Corporation. According to *Polk's World Bank Directory*, there are only 14 privately owned banks left in this country—4 in Texas, and the other 10 in Pennsylvania, Connecticut, New York, and Iowa. These small business operations do not offer savings accounts, but concentrate on checking accounts and small business loans. One in Texas specializes in lending to cattlemen and has been doing this successfully for many years.

Who would bank with these institutions and why? According to the owners of these banks, many business people who own small businesses in the community deal with them as a matter of first choice. Their customers like their reputation of many years of operation. Furthermore, they believe the reputation of the local bank is more important than insurance on their accounts.

2. Source: *Wall Street Journal*, May 9, 1977.

1. Do you see a future for the expansion of banks in the small business category?

2. Would you deal with a bank similar to those described in this case? Why or why not?

RELATED READINGS

Baumback, Clifford M., et al. *How to Organize and Operate a Small Business*. 5th ed. Englewood Cliffs, N.J.: Prentice-Hall, 1973.

A thorough description of the small business and how it operates. Detailed discussions of policies, management, finance, site location, inventory control, and many other related topics.

Cameron, Jan. *The Franchise Handbook*. New York: Crown, 1970.

Easy-to-understand exploration of the advantages and disadvantages of franchising. Discusses the various types of franchises and ways in which to finance them, among other subjects.

How to Start Your Own Small Business. New York: Drake, 1973.

Describes the various types of businesses most attractive to small investors and gives information on how to analyze the choices of starting a new business or buying into an existing one. Special attention is given to minority-owned business ventures. Softcover.

Mancuso, Joseph. *Fun and Guts*. Reading, Mass.: Addision-Wesley, 1973.

Well-written study of the personal traits needed by the entrepreneur who would be successful.

Payne, Jack. *The New Encyclopedia of Little-Known, Highly Profitable Business Opportunities*. New York: Frederick Tell, 1974.

Examines opportunities in franchising, manufacturers representation, agenting, importing, realty, and the like for the small business investor and operator.

Pickle, Hal B., and Abrahamson, Royce L. *Small Business Management*. Santa Barbara, Calif.: Wiley/Hamilton, 1976.

Well-written and illustrated textbook covering the major aspects of small business management.

The Pitfalls in Managing a Small Business. New York: Dun & Bradstreet, 1971.

Informative look at the most common problems in owning and operating a small business and suggestions for overcoming those pitfalls.

---

part two: **CAREER OPPORTUNITIES**

CAREERS IN MANAGEMENT

Management looks like a glamorous field to the outsider. However, those in management jobs can tell you that the glamour wears thin under the strain of the responsibilities. Probably, the most stressful part of a management job is dealing with other people, and there is no rule book to follow in this phase of managerial responsibilities. The hours are often long and irregular, and travel, while fun at first, can become burdensome in the long run.

Nearly all administrative jobs require a college degree, although the subject area of concentration varies. Some employers seek liberal arts graduates, but most businesses seek people with degrees in business administration or in technical areas such as engineering or chemistry.

There are approximately 10 million people in jobs classified as management positions. The field of management covers just about everything from office and plant managers to bank presidents and city administrators. Management positions in the area of public administration have grown tremendously in the last decade. Public administration managers administer city governments, highway agencies, and similar governmental departments.

Management jobs are expected to increase at a fairly rapid rate in the 1980s. More and more, technical abilities in accounting, computers, engineering, and the like are prerequisites for administrative positions. The entry opportunities for members of minority groups and women are very good in management and will continue to be good for the foreseeable future.

part three

MARKETING

In this section you will look at the exciting field of marketing, the most visible function of business. All of us know about advertising and selling, which are parts of marketing. Some of the other functions of marketing—research, transportation, and information—are less well known. Marketing focuses on the customer and what the customer wants. Those firms that are able to determine what the customer wants and develop the right product or service at the right price in the right place and with the right promotion are the most successful. Those who do not are not successful.

In Chapter 7, you will see how firms develop a marketing strategy for products and services. You will also look at the role of marketing research in gathering the data necessary in formulating a marketing strategy.

In Chapter 8, you will study why consumers buy what they do. Consumer buying habits is a complex subject because it deals with human behavior. You will study the effect of expenditure patterns and psychological and sociological influences on consumer behavior. Lastly, you will study the growing influence of consumerism on buying decisions.

In Chapter 9, you will study the four Ps of the marketing mix—product, place, price, and promotion. You will see how marketing blends these elements in achieving results.

In Chapter 10, you will focus on the development, production, and distribution of products. You will see the stages of new product development, the factors that influence efficiency in production, and the means of distributing the products to customers.

General Foods

chapter 7

MARKETING STRATEGY

OBJECTIVES

When you have finished reading and studying this chapter, you should be able to:

1. Identify the elements of marketing strategy and explain how they relate to each other.

2. Understand the major marketing research areas and the tools that are used to gather data.

3. Name and explain the characteristics of services.

4. Explain the elements of marketing strategy that apply to the marketing of services.

CHAPTER PREVIEW

Nothing is more crucial to the long-term growth and profitability of any business than choosing the right marketing strategy from among the many alternatives that are available. For example, General Motors' decision in the 1920s to pursue a full line of cars with many options contrasted sharply with Ford Motors' decision to produce a one-model, one-color car. GM's decision set the stage for an eventual change in industry leadership. More recently, IBM's strategy of moving into office technology rather than just computer technology clearly places the firm in a different growth path.

Once the basic strategies are chosen, a firm can easily do the planning that accompanies the strategy. The decisions involved in acquiring personnel, land, equipment, and even other companies follows naturally from the long-term plans. Chapter 7 focuses on marketing strategies for both products and services. The section on services is particularly significant because service-related industries are growing more rapidly than are product-related businesses. But the differences in approaches to marketing are less well known. Marketing mix for services and the timing of introducing a service are two aspects of marketing strategies that are examined.

Underlying any change in marketing strategies is the need for accurate and timely data. The major marketing research areas are fully explained, along with the tools that are used in the gathering and analysis of data.

"I've quit trying to make ends meet. I just try to maintain a reasonable gap."

In our society, business's function is to satisfy people's demands for products and services. This implies that business must first determine what products or services consumers want and then create and deliver them. This process is known as marketing.

AN OVERVIEW OF MARKETING

Marketing is the performance of business activities that direct products and services from producer to consumer or user to satisfy customers' demands and accomplish the company's objectives. Marketing, therefore, consists of a large number of business activities: gathering product information, designing and developing, packaging, transporting, advertising, and selling.

These activities help direct the flow of products and services. Thus, business starts with what customers want, rather than what the firm wants customers to have. There are, of course, many people who would argue that it is done the other way around.

It should be noted that the definition includes the marketing of both products and services, not just products. Finally, it is the task of marketing to satisfy customers and, at the same time, meet the company's objectives. As was pointed out in Chapter 1, a business exists to fulfill a want and make a profit. It must do both to stay in business.

THE MARKETING CONCEPT

Marketing considerations are central to business decision making. More and more firms have come to realize the importance of marketing in the last 10 to 15 years. To describe the process of placing the consumer first in all business decision making, the term *marketing concept* was coined. As Figure 7-1 shows, the marketing concept implies that a firm starts by determining what its customers want. Then all production, finance, plant location, and other decisions are made in light of their impact on the customers.

DIFFERENTIATING MARKETS

A sound marketing program should start with a careful analysis of the demand for a product or service. In Chapter 1 we defined demand as people with wants and the money to buy what they want. This is commonly called a *market*. Most marketing people would substitute the word *need* for the word *want*. Marketing personnel tend to use *need* very broadly, referring to the lack of anything that is required, useful, or desired. They see themselves helping customers satisfy physiological and sociological needs. Physiological needs include food, drink, clothing, sex, shelter, and sleep (all required or useful). Sociological needs are those that deal with the way individuals perceive themselves and their fellow human beings. As we shall see later in this chapter, critics of marketing tend to define needs as only physiological. This underlines the criticism that businesses create needs rather than satisfy them.

165

FIGURE 7-1 The marketing concept

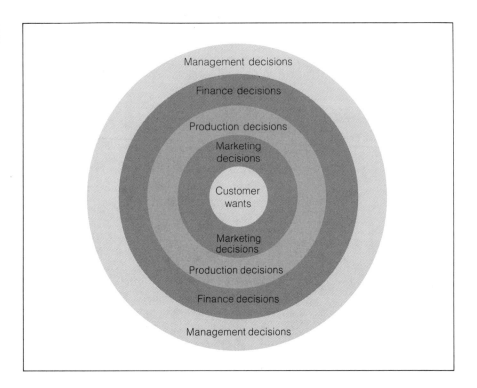

**MARKETING
STRATEGY**

The marketing strategy of a business usually starts with analyzing the opportunities for growth and profits. The firm is likely to move in a direction in which it has an advantage over competitors. IBM, for example, took advantage of its technical expertise and impressive organizational reputation to move into the office copier markets after Xerox and other firms had already established themselves.

SEIZING OPPORTUNITIES

Growth opportunities may be pursued through one of three approaches. The first is to develop new products in an existing market. This is essentially the only approach used by Procter & Gamble, which develops a steady stream of household products. A second approach is for a firm to integrate into retailing (if it's a manufacturer) or into manufacturing (if it's a retailer) or into transportation. Sears has done this by manufacturing some of its products. Pizza Hut also did this when it bought its supplier, Franchise Services, which supplies 95 percent of the chain's food, equipment, and other supplies. A third approach to growth is to diversify into other industries if its own does not show much opportunity for future growth. Mobil Oil took this approach with its purchase of Montgomery Ward and Container Corporation. American Brands, formerly American Tobacco Company, now receives about 40 percent of its sales from nontobacco items. These come

Not every truck buyer is looking for the same size or capacity truck. To meet the needs of the various market segments, Ford Motor Co. produces a complete line of trucks.

Ford Motor Company

from such goods and services as Franklin Life Insurance Company, Jim Beam whiskey, Sunshine biscuits, Master Lock padlocks, and Jergens soaps.

Once the company has determined which opportunities it wants to meet, it can then establish objectives. As we pointed out in Chapter 2, these objectives will be stated as a rate of expected return on investment, or sales or, perhaps, a share of the market.

Once objectives have been determined, a marketing strategy is developed. *Marketing strategy* is the plan of action for accomplishing the objectives of the firm. In a manufacturing firm, this would include elements from the marketing, production, and finance departments. As part of the marketing strategy, the firm must consider market segmentation, target marketing, market entry strategy, the marketing mix, and timing of the strategy.

MARKET SEGMENTATION FOR PRODUCTS

Market segmentation is the division of a large market into several submarkets or market segments, representing the needs and buying habits of a particular group of consumers.

A market can be segmented in several ways. It can be segmented by geography (East, West, urban, suburban, rural, interurban), which is the simplest approach.

This is one of the segmentation patterns used by multinational corporations, such as General Motors, Avon, and Levi's. Products are differentiated in each geographical region with different marketing organizations for each area. Another type of segmentation is by determining end user of the product. For many years, John Deere made machinery only for farmers. It then broadened its line to make a variety of industrial machinery and equipment. More recently, it has concentrated more of its efforts on consumer products, such as bicycles, lawn mowers, and snowmobiles. Figure 7-2 shows the segmentation for cars. A third way of segmenting a market is by customer characteristics. For industrial equipment these would include size; for consumer goods these would include customer class. Customer class might focus on age, buying motives, stage of family life cycle, shopping habits, educational level, and other personal aspects. Segmentation by customer class has become increasingly popular in recent years and is probably the one most frequently used.

TARGET MARKETING FOR PRODUCTS

Once a firm has segmented the market, it must decide which segment it wants to serve. This process is called target marketing. It directs the efforts of the firm to serve the segment of the market in which it would have an advantage over its competitors. These segments must have the following characteristics in order to be attractive to a firm: relatively large present market; potential for future growth; not dominated by a competitor; contains unsatisfied needs that can be served by the firm.

The fast-food industry clearly shows the application of the target marketing concept. McDonald's has grabbed 20 percent of the fast-food business primarily by capturing the under-19 market from which it gets over one third of its revenue. Wendy's, one of the fastest growing fast-food companies, on the other hand, caters to the young adults who want better food. Over 80 percent of Wendy's customers are over 25.

FIGURE 7-2 Market segmentation for automobiles

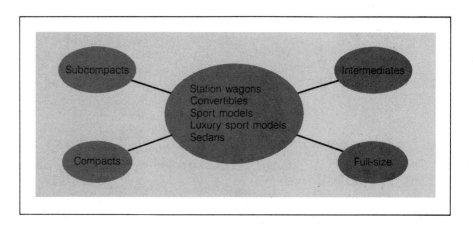

business profile: THE MIDDLETOWNS OF MARKETING

No major company can afford to manufacture a new product unless it is certain that there will be a market for it. One way for a company to determine whether that market exists, whether it should make the enormous investment in a new product, is to give the product a chance in one of the nation's test-marketing cities or towns, which are supposed to represent the national market in microcosm. Consumer reaction in these test towns pretty much determines whether a plant will be built to produce the product in volume and when it should be "rolled-out" regionally or nationally. Market testing of this sort is an important indicator of whether or not a product will make it, and only about 45 percent of new products pass the test and in these sample cities. But even then, there is no guarantee that a product that does well in a test city will fill the till on the national marketplace.

New products can also be marketed regionally, backed with advertising and sales promotion. But it can cost millions of dollars to develop, produce, package, and distribute a product even on the regional level, whereas running it through test cities serves as a kind of scientific straw poll before the election.

Deciding exactly where to test a product can be a difficult decision. Fort Wayne, Indiana, is the only city used by all three of the major test-marketing firms. Erie, Pennsylvania, and South Bend, Indiana, are other popular sites because they come close to the U.S. average in population in age group distribution, effective buying income per capita and per household, and amount spent for merchandise per capita and per household.

There is no such thing as an ideal test market, however, especially one that will serve for all products. "You don't look for a mirror of America as much as a market environment comparable to that in which the product will compete when it is rolled out," says Carl Ravitch, vice president of Audits & Surveys. As the South gains in population, the size of its market, and economic influence, Louisville and Lexington, Kentucky, and Knoxville and Chattanooga, Tennessee, are being used increasingly as test markets.

While this seems simple, many firms have failed in their efforts because they were unrealistic in targeting their segment of the market. Minnie Pearl's fried chicken business was launched with great fanfare only to discover that consumers saw it as a less desirable alternative to Colonel Sanders' Kentucky fried chicken. As a firm learns about what appears to be a potential market, careful analysis may indicate that there is no segment that it can profitably serve. In such an event marketing plans will probably be dropped.

When a firm targets the market it wants to pursue, it may decide to appeal to only one segment of the market or it can try to reach several segments. When Bic entered the razor market, for example, it did so with only a disposable razor, ignoring the rest of the market which accounted for over 80 percent of sales. On the other hand, when Kodak entered the instant camera market to compete with Polaroid it offered customers several models. Kodak thus chose a multiple-segment strategy.

MARKET ENTRY FOR PRODUCTS

The third aspect of market strategy is the market-entry strategy chosen by the business. A firm can enter a market by developing its own products, by acquiring an existing brand, or by collaborating with another firm on a joint venture.

Most of the time a firm enters a new market by developing its own product. Texas Instruments did this by developing its own line of pocket calculators. Philip Morris, the cigarette company, entered the beer market, however, by buying the Miller label. Norton Simon entered the car rental market by purchasing Avis from ITT. The practice of acquiring companies has become increasingly common in the last decade.

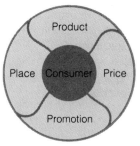

FIGURE 7-3 Shape of the marketing mix

Collaborating with other firms to enter a market is not a strategy available to most American firms because, in general, it is considered a monopolistic practice and is therefore prohibited by law. It is most frequently done in European and Japanese industries where such laws are not as severe. Several electronics companies banded together in Japan, for example, to develop a line of computers. Far from receiving official discouragement, their research and development costs were partially underwritten by the government.

MARKETING MIX

Another important part of the marketing strategy is the development of the marketing mix. The *marketing mix*, as shown in Figure 7-3, is the blending of product, price, promotion, and place. (These will be covered in more detail in Chapter 9.) Through the marketing mix, the firm determines how it will shape its total package of product, price, promotion, and place to the target market. Place indicates the place where the product will be made available to the customer, such as a supermarket, catalog sale, or discount store.

TIMING

The final part of the marketing strategy is the timing of the action to be taken in serving a target market. Up to this point a firm can do everything correctly but be too early or too late into a market to be successful. American Motors sold the right

Whenever a new product is introduced, the marketing mix determines how the product will be handled.

Nabisco

type of small car in the late 1960s and early 1970s but was too early in the market. The energy crisis had not yet been publicized, as it has been recently. Gillette, on the other hand, saw personal-use electric appliances such as hair dryers as the wave of the future. It failed, however, with both its pocket calculator and digital watch partly because it entered the market too late with an imitation product. Successful timing depends on understanding shifts in the economy, the actions of competitors, and the moods of consumers.

THE ROLE OF MARKETING RESEARCH

Determining what types of products and services are demanded, the extent of that demand, and its location are but a few of the functions of marketing research. *Marketing Research* is the search for significant facts helpful in marketing the management of marketing activities. Marketing research is applied to every step of the marketing process.

In 1978 American business spent about $1 billion on marketing research. As an indication of its importance, about 90 percent of medium- and large-sized companies have a marketing research department.

As the American economy becomes more complex, marketing research is increasingly important for business. A recent National Industrial Conference Board study, which has shown that most companies are continuing to broaden their marketing research efforts, bears this out.

Marketing research includes looking into economic facts and patterns of human behavior, since purchasing is rooted in both economic buying motives.

Economic buying motives reflect consumers' concern with the most effective use of their limited resources. They include:

1. Price
2. Durability
3. Dependability
4. Efficiency
5. Convenience
6. Increase in earnings
7. Increase of productivity of property

Emotional buying motives are those concerned with individuals' feelings about themselves or their relationships with others. They include:

1. Self-preservation
2. Fear
3. Pleasure
4. Pride
5. Leisure
6. Ambition
7. Sociability

As shown in Figure 7-4, markets, products or services, sales, promotion, and marketing administration are the first major spheres of marketing research. The first phase of marketing research examines *markets*, that is, the characteristics of potential users of products and services. These might include data on age, sex, income, occupation, geographical location, as well as other facts about users, all of which permit a business to concentrate on a particular aspect of a market.

In the *products* or *services* part of marketing research, desirable features in products, packaging, use of products, rate of consumption, inventory trends, and status of competing products are evaluated. For example, until 10 years ago, turkeys were almost always sold whole. One firm did a study by cutting turkeys into quarters and selling them in selected supermarkets as they would chicken parts.

FIGURE 7-4 Areas of marketing research

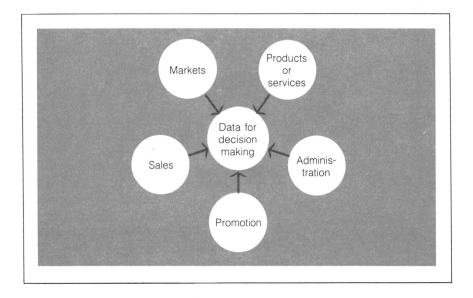

Sales of turkeys increased by 200 percent in one year as a result of selling them in parts.

The *sales* phase analyzes the movement of products according to sizes, styles and customers, sales territory boundaries, and sales quotas. Before Polaroid priced its color Swinger camera for $29.95, it determined that 70 percent of all still cameras sold were priced under $30. In another example, the Gallup organization was commissioned to do a marketing study to determine the favorite foreign food consumed in the American market. Mexican food proved to be the favorite of the 21 to 35 age group. This information was then helpful in selling franchises featuring tacos and enchiladas.

In advertising and sales promotion, marketing research deals with the believ-ability of advertising, motivation research, retention of ideas, effectiveness of various communications media, and the strength of sales promotions. For example, the state of Alaska wanted to know which magazines were most effective in promoting tourism to the state. It ran a series of ads in a number of travel magazines and another series in several popular general magazines. The ads included a coupon that the reader could send to Alaska for more information about visitor attractions. In weighing the pulling power of the ads, state officials found that more requests for tourist literature were received through the general magazines. However, more of the tourists who wrote for literature from the travel magazines actually visited Alaska.

Marketing administration involves a variety of research activities needed to administer the marketing program. Among these activities are investigation of pricing and discounts offered, marketing costs, possible retail outlets, customer credit, and the effect of laws on marketing. A study published in 1967 indicated that the sales of 20 large-volume groups of health and beauty aids had increased about 20 percent in mass merchandising stores (discount stores), but had fallen or stayed about the same in drug and grocery stores.

PRIMARY AND SECONDARY MARKETING DATA

Marketing research is an essential, ongoing activity for any large consumer goods firm, providing a constant stream of marketing data. Data are either primary or secondary. *Primary data*, discussed more fully below, are originated by the researcher to solve a problem under study. Data collected for some other purpose than the one at hand are *secondary data*. Sources of secondary data include internal company records and external sources such as government publications; trade, professional, and business associations; private business firms; advertising media; university research organizations; foundations, and libraries. The major source of secondary data for many firms is the federal government's Bureau of the Census. It generates about 1,200 reports a year, containing about 200,000 pages of statistics, charts, graphs, and other information. Besides measuring the nation's income and population, the bureau produces various special reports on manufacturing, wholesaling, retailing, construction, mining, and service industries. The Pepsi Company, for example, uses the census data for determining if a given area served by its bottlers has enough Spanish-speaking people in it to warrant advertising in Spanish. Normally, it is more difficult to collect secondary data from external sources than from company records, because the external sources are more numerous and the data may appear in a different form from that needed by the researcher.

GATHERING PRIMARY MARKETING DATA

Most marketing research is concerned with either the introduction of new products or services or evaluating proposed marketing methods. As a result, the required information is often not available from secondary sources, and primary data must be collected. There are two basic types of data-gathering devices: the survey and observation.

TEST MARKETING

Much of the data gathered by survey and observation is obtained when a new product is introduced in a test market. A small and clearly defined geographical area in which a company tries out a new product. This is a means to observe consumers' reactions to a new product's appeal, packaging, pricing, and advertising. If the marketing mix seems to be a good one, the firm will begin producing it on a large scale, perhaps nationally. Since millions of dollars are likely to be spent on the new product, the managers want an accurate prediction of how their product will fare. Test marketing helps increase the odds that the product will be a success. About 45 percent of the products test marketed go on to national production and distribution. Most of the large consumer companies, such as Procter and Gamble, General Foods, and Ralston-Purina regularly use test marketing.

personality profile:
MARCEL BICH –
master marketing
strategist

The name of French businessman Marcel Bich is not familiar to many Americans. Anyone who has ever flicked a Bic, however, knows the Bic Pen Corp., the American subsidiary of Société Bic, which is 69 percent owned by the Bich family.

Bich began his business career as an office supply salesman and later began manufacturing ink wells. It was evident to him, however, that the ink well was not a product for the future. In 1953 Bich founded the firm that bears three-quarters of his name. He dropped the final letter because he felt a three-letter word was more attractive and more easily remembered. Bic began producing disposable pens, and over the years it has added disposable lighters, panty hose, and, most recently, disposable razors to its line.

Bich's simple marketing strategy has been extremely successful. He makes only consumer products that can be manufactured cheaply, used briefly, and then thrown away. At the same time he concentrates on improving existing products and marketing them worldwide. This means the company need spend very little money on marketing research or on research and development (R and D) for new products. Funds are needed only to refine existing products and improve their technological capabilities.

In order to make his simple marketing strategy work, he must have a quality product, very low manufacturing costs, and an innovative flair for advertising and packaging to distinguish his product in the public mind. Bich has all of these. Manufacturing plants in the United States, France, Greece, and Italy maintain high standards of quality control. The company is very slow and careful about introducing new products. Bich's philosophy is to avoid marketing a product unless it is at least as good as the best competitor in the market. Intriguing packaging and effective advertising campaigns have given Bic large segments of the market in each of its product lines: one-third of the world market for disposable pens, 20 percent of the disposable pen market, and a large share of the panty hose and stocking market outside the United States.

These markets have been won against very formidable competition. Bich pushed mammoth Gillette right out of the disposable pen market. Even more impressive was the way he edged Gillette out of its leadership in the disposable lighter market. Bich is now challenging Gillette for a share in the disposable razor market.

Product recognition is often directly tied to personality recognition. Hertz and O.J. Simpson have been sprinting along merrily for years.

Hertz System, Inc.

A product is often tested in a few cities over the course of from six months to a year or even more. Procter and Gamble, for example, tested Pringles Newfangled Potato Chips in Evansville, Indiana, for three years before beginning distribution on a wider basis. Although many cities are used for test marketing, Fort Wayne and South Bend, Indiana, Erie, Pennsylvania, and Boston, Massachusetts, are among the favorites. Several factors are considered in choosing cities but one factor is shared by all of them: they must be fairly representative of national buying habits.

DISADVANTAGES OF TEST MARKETING

Test marketing can be helpful in deciding whether or not to begin full production of a product. However, there are disadvantages too. One is the cost. A major test can cost $1 million. Another is the time delay for the additional step. A third problem stemming from the additional time is that the competition is alerted to a firm's marketing strategy. Sometimes a firm will rush through a product without test marketing so that it will be ready when a competitor finishes test marketing its product. The firm can then capitalize on the push being given the competitor's product as it is widely advertised.

Calgon discovered that Procter & Gamble was test marketing Bounce, a new product to eliminate static cling from machine dried fabrics. Calgon was working on a similar product which it called Cling Free. Calgon rushed Cling Free onto the market without testing it so that it could profit from the big advertising push that it knew Procter & Gamble would use for Bounce.

MARKETING SERVICES

Services are also important in our economy. About 45 cents of every dollar we spend as consumers goes for services and more than half of all the purchases of business firms are for services. In addition, 60 percent of all jobs are in the service sector. While services are important to the economy, not much is written about the marketing of services. People tend to think of marketing products not services. There are many marketing experts who believe that the same principles apply to both. There are some major differences, however, as well as some similarities.

CHARACTERISTICS OF SERVICES

Services have some distinctive characteristics which make them different from products. As shown in Figure 7-5, these include intangibility, inseparability, heterogeneity, perishability, and fluctuating demand.

Intangibility Services are, by their nature, *intangible:* incapable of being touched. The customer cannot feel, see, hear, taste, or smell a service. As a result, it is more difficult to communicate to a customer the quality of a service than it is to demonstrate the quality of a product. On the other hand, the business does not have a large inventory to maintain, as is the case for products.

Inseparability The service is usually so closely associated with the seller that the two are *inseparable:* it is difficult to distinguish the seller from the service. This makes services more personal than products and tends to reduce the scale of operation. Some franchising operations have overcome this, however, through emphasis on quality control. Midas Muffler, for example, advertises that it is both a specialist for quality of work and a small, individually owned business with the image of helpful, friendly service.

FIGURE 7-5
Characteristics of services

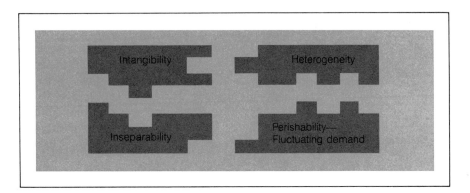

Heterogeneity Unlike the production of products, it is impossible to standardize the production of services and they are therefore called *heterogeneous:* each is unique. While careful training will help overcome this, it is still not possible to have a completely uniform quality of service. It is unlikely, for example, that two Holiday Inns will be the same in the services they offer. Montgomery Ward's or Sears' repair shops differ considerably in quality of work. Probably the best example of efforts to standardize service is McDonald's. It has adopted a factory approach to insure uniform quality of food and services offered.

Perishability and Fluctuating Demand Services are *perishable* in that they cannot be stored, unlike cans of paint, breakfast cereal, garden tools, and many other products. You cannot store seats to a concert, unused hours of computer time, or unused time of a mechanic or a doctor. Also, the market for services is frequently seasonal. Some examples of heavy seasonal demand for services include income tax preparation, cleaning services, recreational facilities, and temporary help.

GROWTH AND CURRENT IMPORTANCE OF SERVICES

Our economy has become the world's first service economy. The greater emphasis on services is due to several factors. First, consumers have had relatively higher incomes in recent years and increased leisure. The result has been that most Americans have about reached the saturation point for consumer products. Consumers began to switch their buying to a range of services that includes education, travel, medical care, personal grooming, and recreation. Business firms, too, have been demanding more services. Business firms have found that their world has become more complex, specialized, and competitive. They need the help of specialists to survive in this climate. They require expert service in such diverse areas as research, taxation, governmental relations, labor relations, advertising, economic forecasting, and information processing.

There is little doubt that services will continue to be important. In addition, new services will develop. However, there are some roadblocks to a very rapid increase in services. Some service industries have limited entry into the field. This is true for a variety of health services, banking, education, communication, and transportation. In other industries, there is a long-term shortage of people with the required specialized skills. This includes a variety of medical occupations, computer processing personnel, and tradesmen, such as brick layers, carpenters, and electricians. Still another roadblock to increased services is the fact that many service firms are very small. They are mainly family operations or small partnerships. This includes such service industries as dry cleaning, shoe repairing, cleaning, auto repair, income tax preparation and travel services. There is, of course, a major effort in some of these industries for larger chain operators and franchisers to achieve greater efficiency with the same techniques that have been used in manufacturing.

In addition to these internal forces, there are some external forces that may slow the development of service industries. One of these is the tendency of some manufacturers of consumer goods to make products that will enable consumers to provide a service for themselves that they had formerly purchased. Examples include the production of low-cost tools that permit people to do much of their own home repairs. Plastic pipe has made it easy to do many of the plumbing jobs that formerly required the services of a plumber. Wash and wear clothes have reduced the need for dry-cleaning services. Specialized tool kits and simplified engines have made it easier for car owners to perform some of their own maintenance work. Related to this is the tendency for more consumers to want to do the jobs themselves. This has led to a boom in products for do-it-yourself builders, fixers, and renovators. This, too, will reduce the demand for services in some areas.

MARKETING STRATEGY FOR SERVICES

The same principles that apply to the marketing strategy of products apply to the marketing strategy of services. Firms must still consider market segmentation, target marketing, market entry strategy, the marketing mix, and the timing of the strategy.

MARKET SEGMENTATION FOR SERVICES

Many of the service industries have carefully segmented the market for their services. Banks, airlines, and insurance companies have identified women as a distinctive part of their markets. Motels and hotels have distinguished families from business travelers in their efforts to carve out segments of the market.

TARGET MARKETING FOR SERVICES

Many firms, after considering the various segments of the market, have chosen their targets carefully. Others have not been able to do that well. Merrill Lynch, the nation's largest stock brokerage firm, has made a major attempt to attract the small investor. They have done this successfully while most other brokerage houses have virtually ignored the small investor. While all life insurance companies have tried to sell to college students, Northwestern Mutual has done more than most large firms to package policies and programs to appeal to college students. In addition, many small service firms have been successful because they were able to identify their target segment of the market and appeal to it successfully.

MARKET ENTRY STRATEGY FOR SERVICES

Market entry strategy is less important in the marketing of services than it is in the marketing of products. However, it still applies for large firms that want to enter a service industry. As an example, Norton Simon wanted to enter the car leasing business. Rather than developing its own business, it bought Avis, the car rental agency. It felt that this was a more effective way to enter the business than developing its own brand name and service facility.

MARKETING MIX
FOR SERVICES
In marketing a service, a firm still has to develop a service, price it, promote it and offer it to consumers in some particular place. Pricing the service may be a little more complicated because it is difficult for consumers to equate price of a service with its quality. Also, development of additional services is somewhat more complicated than developing a further line of products. Also, in many cases it is very difficult to differentiate a product from a service. IBM, for example, sells very few computers. Most are leased. This means IBM provides a service rather than a product, as might at first glance appear to be the case. Fast-food chains are selling a product, but there is a great amount of service involved in the process. Frequently the promotion, for example, makes it seem as though they are basically selling a service. Since services can be sold by themselves or in conjunction with a product, the classification of what is a service often becomes blurred.

TIMING OF THE SERVICE
The same principles apply here as in marketing products. The firm must be in the market at the right time for the service to appeal to consumers. Prior to the energy crunch, firms infusing liquid insulation into buildings had little competition, and little business. With the increase in the cost of fuel, demand soared. Firms that saw this coming and had a marketing mix ready provided a timely service and reaped a healthy profit.

SUMMARY

Marketing is the performance of business activities that direct the flow of products and services from producer to consumer or user to satisfy customers and accomplish the company's objectives. A firm must define its market and tailor its strategies to meeting the demand in the market it chooses. The key elements in marketing strategy are market segmentation, target marketing, market-entry strategy, the marketing mix, and timing of the strategy.

In establishing a strategy, almost all firms do considerable marketing research. Research is done in the following areas: markets or potential markets, products or services, sales, advertising and sales promotion, and marketing administration. Firms gather both primary and secondary data in solving their marketing problems. Much of the primary data is gathered through test marketing. In test marketing a firm introduces a new product and manipulates the product, price, promotion, and place to see what is the optimum marketing mix before going into national distribution.

The marketing of services is important because half of the purchases made today are of services. However, not much is usually written about marketing services. Chief characteristics of services include intangibility, inseparability, heterogeneity, perishability, and fluctuating demand. The same principles of marketing strategy that are used in marketing products can be applied to the marketing of services.

SUMMARY OF KEY TERMS

Economic Buying Motives The most effective use of a consumer's limited resources.

Emotional Buying Motives Those motives that reflect the feelings of individuals about themselves or their relationships with others.

Market People with wants and the money to satisfy them.

Marketing Business activities that direct the flow of goods and services from producer to consumer or user to satisfy customers and accomplish the company's objectives.

Marketing Concept A firm's perception of what its customers want.

Marketing Mix The blending of product, price, promotion, and place.

Marketing Research The search for facts significant in the management of marketing activities.

Market Segmentation Dividing a total, heterogeneous market into several submarkets or segments, each of which tends to be homogeneous in all significant aspects.

Marketing Strategy A plan for accomplishing the growth objectives of a firm.

Need The lack of anything that is required, useful, or desired.

Primary Data Facts originated by the researcher to solve a problem under study.

Secondary Data Data collected for some purpose other than the one at hand.

Target Marketing Directing the efforts of the firm to serving the segment of the market in which it has an advantage over potential competitors.

Test Market A geographical area in which a company introduces a new product.

Want Something desired but less basic than a need to one's existence.

REVIEW QUESTIONS

1. What is the difference between selling and marketing a product?
2. What are the elements of a marketing strategy?
3. What does it mean to segment a market?
4. What are the four Ps of the marketing mix?
5. What is the difference between a rational and an emotional buying motive?
6. What are the major areas in which marketing research is done?
7. What is involved in test marketing a product?
8. What are the characteristics of services that make them different from products?
9. How important are services in the American economy?
10. How does marketing strategy apply to the marketing of services?

DISCUSSION QUESTIONS

1. Can you identify the key elements of a marketing strategy that at least two successful local business firms have used?
2. If you were the manufacturer of a new consumer product, such as a new breakfast cereal, would you test market it before you produced it on a large scale? Explain why you would or would not test market the product.
3. Select a successful local business and identify the target market(s) that it has and is apparently serving well.
4. List and describe as many segments of the mar-

ket as you can for the following consumer goods: washing machines and dryers, breakfast cereals, and beer.

5. Explain why the franchising of service firms is expanding so rapidly.

CASES FOR DECISION MAKING

MARKETING STRATEGY AT MILLER BREWING CO.

Until Philip Morris bought Miller Brewing Co. in 1970, the beer industry thought that it had a homogeneous product. The breweries apparently had the idea that there was one market for beer and one size container that consumers wanted. Then Philip Morris brought in its key marketing personnel and applied the principles of marketing that it had used to move itself up from sixth to second place in the tobacco industry.

The firm segmented the market for beer into demand segments, produced products and packages for those segments, and then heavily promoted the new products. Miller's High Life had been aimed at upper-income consumers and women. Philip Morris aimed it at the consistent beer drinkers, the young men who drank beer after a day of hard work or play. The ads began to feature rugged, handsome young men drinking beer. At the same time, the company reached for the female market with the introduction of a seven ounce bottle. Then the company developed a light beer, but again advertised it for beer drinking young men. With the emphasis on sports heroes, the message was not dieting, but being able to drink great quantities of beer without feeling filled up. Then the company established an agreement with the German Löwenbräu beer company to bottle and sell that product in the United States. Miller saw that the premium beer segment was growing ever faster than the regular beer market. Miller priced its Löwenbräu 25 percent higher than Michelob, the best selling beer in America. The results have been spectacular. By 1977 Miller had moved from seventh place to third in beer sales after only seven years of the new management.

1. Can you identify the elements of the marketing strategy used by Philip Morris to revitalize Miller?
2. What segments of the market did Miller identify and try to develop a marketing mix for?
3. If the principles of marketing strategy are so simple, why do you suppose many firms are unsuccessful in applying them?

MARKETING RESEARCH: A WEAPON AGAINST COMPETITORS

In September 1972, Schick, Inc. began claiming that its Fleximatic electric razor cut "better than the Remington, Norelco, or Sunbeam." This was quite a shock to the electric shaver industry, which was not used to having the products of its firms compared in advertising. This line of advertising was made possible by a new Federal Trade Commission policy that permitted advertisers to name their competition, rather than refer to "Brand X" when tests showed their products to be superior.

Schick maintained that it had done enough marketing research to document its claim. The complaining firms took their case to the National Advertising Review Board and the National Advertising Division of the Council of Better Business Bureaus.

1. Do you think it is fair for firms to claim that their products are better than those of competitors? Why or why not?
2. What kinds of data would be necessary before you could say with certainty that one electric shaver was better than another?
3. Do you believe that the federal government

should establish a consumer testing service which would determine the quality of consumer products and make that information available to consumers? Why or why not?

PIZZA HUT—A STRATEGY FOR FUTURE GROWTH

Pizza Hut, America's largest pizza chain, has come a long way since the first restaurant was opened near the owner's family grocery store in Wichita, Kansas, in 1958. Pizza Huts are primarily centered in the South and Midwest although they are found in all parts of the country. Of the 3,000 restaurants, about half are owned by the parent company. This is unusual in the world of franchising where the parent company usually owns only a small fraction of the total.

Accurate market research has enabled Pizza Hut to surpass Shakey's, the original leader in the field. Pizza Hut has expanded its menu to include sandwiches, salads, and pasta to attract more families and persons who do not like pizza. In addition, the Thick 'n Chewy Pizza was added for persons who do not care for the original thin-crust pizza. Pizza Hut is also testing a new Italian food restaurant with a more elegant surrounding. If that goes well, the firm hopes to franchise these restaurants also.

The success of Pizza Hut has attracted PepsiCo, Inc., which has spent more than $300 million to acquire controlling interest in the pizza chain. PepsiCo saw that the ethnic food market with its 25 percent growth rate is the fastest-growing segment of the market and that Pizza Hut's profits have been growing faster than 40 percent annually. It is a natural acquisition for the firm.

1. Why do you think a firm such as PepsiCo would want to purchase control of a company such as Pizza Hut?
2. What factors do you think were a part of the rapid growth of Pizza Hut?
3. What elements of marketing strategy does it appear that Pizza Hut management applied in achieving industry leadership?

chapter 8

WHY DO CONSUMERS BUY?

OBJECTIVES

When you have finished reading and studying this chapter, you should be able to:

1. Explain the importance of expenditure patterns as a guide to developing the best marketing mix.

2. Identify and explain the psychological influences on consumer behavior.

3. Identify and explain the sociological influences on consumer behavior.

4. Explain consumerism and the response it has aroused from business and government.

CHAPTER PREVIEW

Business firms today are experiencing more difficulty in determining what consumers want to buy than in past years. Shifts in population, higher inflation rates, a flood of quality foreign products, changes in life-styles, and the breakdown of important social institutions have complicated the job of determining why consumers buy what they do.

Besides these forces, there is the feeling that consumers are more cautious and more conscious of where and how they spend their money than they were in past years. Consumers are less willing to buy name brands if the brand names are not noticeably superior in quality to less well-known brands selling at lower prices. Also, there is some doubt that advertising, in particular, television advertising, is as effective a method of persuading consumers as it was thought to be in past years.

With these things in mind, we shall look at the importance of expenditure patterns as a guide in deciding what types of products and services are likely to be in demand. Then we shall study the psychological and sociological forces that appear to influence consumer behavior. Finally, we shall look at the consumer movement and its impact on the buying habits and values of the American consumer.

"I bought a book on consumer protection,
but it fell apart before I could read it."

8

WHY DO CONSUMERS BUY?

Consumers buy the products and services they do for many complex reasons. These reasons are related to (1) the location, age, and income of consumers and (2) the motivation of consumers. For example, how large a group are they, where do they live, what age group do they belong to? Income is also an important factor, as is knowing how consumers spend their money and how they would spend an increase in income. Lastly are the forces that influence consumers' willingness to buy, including the psychological and sociological factors. In this chapter, we will look at all the forces that influence the buying decisions of consumers.

EXPENDITURE PATTERNS AND MARKETING

If a business is to develop a successful marketing strategy, it must determine the segment of the market to which it wants to appeal. Basic to market segmentation is a study of people's expenditure patterns and importance of these patterns to marketing. The expenditure patterns of the American people are so diverse and complex that they must be analyzed in segments to have any meaning. The patterns can be studied by population classification, income distribution, and changes in family life cycles.

CLASSIFYING POPULATION

Populations can be classified in various ways. They can be broken down by (a) regional distribution; (b) urban, rural, suburban, and interurban locations; and (c) age groups.

Regional Distribution It is important to analyze the number of people who live in each geographical region of the United States because there are sectional differences in the demand for many products. Climate, social mores, customs, religion, and other factors shape consumers' habits. People in the West, for example, are less formal than Easterners and spend more time outdoors. As a result, marketing patterns for a variety of recreational and outdoor equipment and services in the two regions are different. Also, of course, regional shifts of population may influence the location of new stores or manufacturing plants.

Local Populations In recent years the migration of people from farms to the cities has slowed noticeably, but the flow from urban areas to suburban and interurban areas has quickened (see Figure 8-1). *Interurban areas* are regions of large population formed when two or more metropolitan areas have grown together, such as the Boston–New York corridor and the Los Angeles–San Diego coastal strip. Many cities are losing population, while suburbs mushroom around them. In addition, the suburbanite is likely to have different wants from a city dweller.

Age Groups The number of people in various age groups and the trends in those numbers are of interest to marketing people. The population is subdivided

FIGURE 8-1 The growth of
suburbs

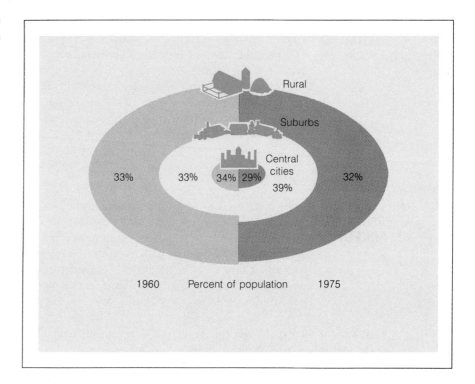

Rural

Suburbs

Central
cities

33%   33%   34% 29%   39%   32%

1960   Percent of population   1975

by age into the following groups: youth, teenage, middle age, and old age. These are frequently further subdivided. For example, the youth age group might be subdivided into infants, juveniles, and pre-teenagers. Business firms try to cater to wants they feel a particular age group has. While this can be helpful in segmenting the market, it sometimes backfires. For example, H. J. Heinz Company discovered that many oldsters were eating the company's baby food, so the company packaged a special line of "senior foods." The product failed, largely because older shoppers, perhaps reluctant to admit to weak digestions, preferred to buy baby food and claim it was for their grandchildren.

INCOME DISTRIBUTION   There is a definite upward shift of incomes in the American economy, with increasing numbers of people in the middle- and upper-income brackets. Table 8-1 shows the median income of families in 1976. It indicates that almost one-third of American families earn $20,000 or more a year and half earn $15,000 or more a year. Since marketing people follow these trends carefully, many business firms improve the quality (and raise the price) of their merchandise to cater to the tastes that increasing income breeds. The market for boats, summer homes, campers, color televisions, and other expensive items expands considerably with rises in income.

TABLE 8-1 Percent of families in each income bracket (based on median family income, 1976)

Median Income	Percent of Population
More than $50,000	2
$25,000–$50,000	16
$20,000–$24,999	13
$15,000–$19,999	19
$12,000–$14,999	12
$10,000–$11,999	8
$ 8,000–$ 9,999	8
$ 6,000–$ 7,999	8
$ 4,000–$ 5,999	7
Less than $ 4,000	7

Source: Census Bureau

Consumer income, which is measured in a variety of ways, provides a lode of data for marketing researchers eager to find out more about their potential markets. The following four measures of consumer income are commonly used:

1. *National income* is the total income that is earned by those who contribute to production, including employee wages and salaries, corporate profits, rental income and interest income. It is the income received by those who supply the factors of production—land, labor, and capital.
2. *Personal income* is all income of individuals, regardless of source. It includes welfare payments, social security payments, and unemployment benefits, as well as income earned from contributing to production.
3. *Disposable personal income* is personal income minus personal income taxes paid to the government.
4. *Discretionary income* is disposable personal income minus fixed commitments such as car payments; house payments; insurance premiums; and essential household needs, such as food, clothing, and utilities. This is a measure of what the consumer has left to spend on discretionary or nonessential items after providing for the necessities.

Consumers, as a whole, are fairly predictable as to what they will do with their increased income. From a number of marketing studies, we know that the following expenditure patterns tend to develop as income rises:

1. A smaller percentage of income goes for food.
2. The percentage of income allocated to clothing increases.
3. Housing and house operation and medical and personal care take about the same percentage of income as before.
4. The percentage of income spent on recreation and education increases.

The family, as the basic unit in society, is the focal point of many marketing approaches.

Barbara Baker

NUMBER, SIZE, AND CHARACTERISTICS OF FAMILIES

Many marketing activities attempt to define and meet the needs of the family, since the family is the basic unit of American society. All families go through a family life cycle, that is, a regular pattern of development. This cycle normally includes: young single adults, newly married couples, young couples with small children, middle-aged couples with teenaged children, older couples without children living at home, older single persons. The family, of course, has different needs at each stage.

There are a number of trends affecting families that relate to market segments. These include: a 50 percent increase since 1970 in the number of unwed couples living together, compared to a 15 percent increase in all households; a dramatically lower birthrate; a two-to-one marriage-divorce ratio compared to a four-to-one ratio in the early 1960s; families with the wife a member of the labor force at 38 percent compared to 25 percent in 1960.

Clearly, the number of families or households directly affects the demand for household items such as appliances and furniture. The size of families or households is also extremely important for marketing. With a reduced birthrate, Gerber Products, for example, has changed its approach considerably. It has begun testing adult foods such as peanut spread, catsup, and even a new line of single-serving foods. Indeed, it has even dropped its famous slogan "Babies are our business . . . our only business."

CONSUMER BEHAVIOR

A great deal of information is available about the characteristics of the population and how much income is available to each group. A great deal is known about how each group spends its money. Considerably less is known about *why* consumers buy the products and services they do. Consumer behavior is shaped by psychological and sociological forces.

PSYCHOLOGICAL INFLUENCES ON CONSUMER BEHAVIOR

From the psychological point of view, consumer behavior is *goal-oriented*. That is, the behavior is motivated by needs that in turn create tensions that influence the consumer to act. In buying, the consumer satisfies needs and thus reduces tensions. Goal-oriented behavior is influenced by how the consumer views the available choices. Figure 8-2 shows the forces affecting consumer behavior. Consumers are selective in the stimuli that they accept, retain, and act upon. What they perceive is, of course, influenced by learning, attitudes, and personality.

Learning *Learning* refers to the changes in behavior resulting from experiences. Our behavior is greatly influenced by our past. This is illustrated by the stimulus-response approach to marketing. The assumption is that learning is what takes place when a link is established between a particular stimulus and a particular response. In its simplest terms, an ad for a "Big Mac" will serve as a stimulus for the consumer to rush out and buy one. Of course, it is not quite that simple. The same ad might serve as a stimulus to go to the refrigerator and have a ham sandwich. It might even convince a dieter to turn off the television or switch channels. The stimulus-response approach is the basis for most of the advertising for national-brand products. Manufacturers assume that if you buy one of their products and like it you merely need the stimulus of an advertisement to buy it again. If the consumer had a satisfying experience, it will probably work. But not all the time. Many consumers are capable of *discrimination*: they can respond selectively to related stimuli. For example, you may plan to make spaghetti for dinner. In the supermarket, you see the Hunt's tomato sauce you want. You've seen it advertised, and the label catches your eye. However, in these days of careful shopping, you note that the local brand is priced four cents less than Hunt's. At this point, the consumer might be motivated by the desire to be economical or the desire to have "the best." There is no way of predicting which

FIGURE 8-2 Goal-oriented behavior

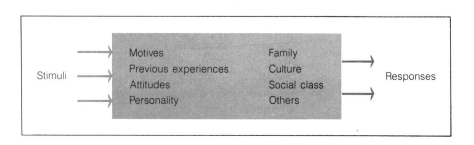

Getting thirsty? Then it works. This ad illustrates the effectiveness of stimulus response advertising.

Sunkist Growers, Inc.

motive is stronger. Much will depend on the degree to which the consumer is conditioned to believe that one brand is better than another.

Attitudes   *Attitudes* stem from our beliefs and our reactions to them. We may believe, for example, that the gasoline sold by major oil companies such as Exxon, Shell, and Texaco is better than that sold by independent oil companies. Reactions to that belief, however, may vary considerably. Some people will not buy gasoline at an independent station because they believe it to be inferior. Many other consumers will buy at a major station rather than at an independent station if the price is about the same. Others may buy at the independent station if the price is lower, but would rather buy at the major station. Attitudes, of course, stem from our experiences. They are learned responses. Our family and our peers are our main sources and teachers of attitudes.

From the standpoint of the marketer, success in marketing a product depends on the ability to understand, predict, and influence consumer attitudes. The marketer will want to confirm or change existing attitudes or create a new attitude toward a new product. Companies with successful products try to help consumers confirm that their product is the best. Coca-Cola, Cheerios, Chevrolet, and Kodak are examples of product lines for which much of the advertising is geared to

business profile: COMPETING WITH MA BELL

Ma Bell is ringing a different tune these days. For one thing, three AT&T operating companies, in New York, New Jersey, and Illinois, have added jokes, horoscopes, and other trimmings to the traditional time and weather services. The reason is that it's paying off nicely, about 28 percent profits on revenues. For another thing, it's growing: revenues are expected to quintuple in the next five years.

Another sign of the changing times is that the giant Bell system now shows signs that it may be entering competition with the novelty phone makers who have been making a killing with everything from French porcelains to Mickey Mouse phones. It used to be that phones were the property of the telephone company, but the FCC changed all that, so now there is a consumer market, and you can buy your own in dozens in styles.

Ma Bell, in other words, is taking on the role of marketer interested in consumer preferences rather than just providing essentially the same service that Alexander Graham Bell introduced a little over a century ago. There are also now appliances that feature automatic answering, automatic dialing, and call-timing, as well as a phone blended with an alarm-clock radio.

Part of the reason for this is that the traditional telephone service is a more or less saturated market in its traditional uses. A more important part is that data processing for business purposes is merging with traditional telephone service, and another giant of American industry, IBM, has become a fierce competitor with Bell in the areas where the two overlap. Communications-based information systems is the fastest growing market segment for both telephone and computer companies. Either could become the dominant force in the evolving hybrid industry, and IBM is used to bold moves while Bell is used to moving slowly under the direction of monopoly powers that have been diluted or taken away from it by the FCC in the telecommunications business.

Ma Bell is going to have to move quickly to keep ahead of IBM. Its entry into consumer marketing and its getting a feel for the market are things it is learning fast. In this new, competitive situation, Ma Bell must attract customers rather than supposing that they have no other choice than the giant.

helping consumers reaffirm the soundness of their buying decisions. It is more difficult to change an existing attitude, of course. Pepsi, for example, tried to change attitudes of Coke drinkers through a series of taste tests. They gave Pepsi and Coke in unmarked cups to a variety of consumers. Then they asked them which tasted better. Since Pepsi was chosen more often in the taste tests, the tests were used in Pepsi advertising. Pepsi tried to change attitudes with this approach and was successful in some markets. In introducing an entirely new product, a firm must create new attitudes about a new product. When trash compactors, microwave ovens, and metal fireplaces were introduced, the producers had to convince consumers that they needed this type of item. It was not so much a matter of selling the firm's product, but of changing the consumer's attitude about the desirability of such a product. Advertising is the most effective means of changing attitudes for producers. However, just how advertising influences the stimuli and responses of consumers is still not well known.

A variety of studies has shown a close relationship between consumer attitudes and their buying decisions. To capitalize on this, a marketer can either change the product to be consistent with consumer attitudes or try to change consumer attitudes toward the product. Since it is extremely difficult to change consumer attitudes toward a product, it is easier to determine what consumer attitudes are toward a type of product and then develop a product that fits those attitudes. That is the approach taken by Procter and Gamble and other successful consumer product firms.

Personality *Personality* is an individual's pattern of inner and outer traits that are a determinant of a behavioral response. There is little question that a consumer's personality will influence his or her perceptions and buying behavior. It is less clear, however, just how personality influences them. Traits include degrees of dominance, sociability, adventuresomeness, and responsibility. Some psychologists believe that these are the dominant forces in determining behavior. Others believe that the situation is the major factor in consumer behavior. In this theory, the individual, through personality, adapts to various situations. While much research in the area still needs to be done, it appears that personality and environment interact to shape behavior.

While this subject appears to have promise for marketers, it is of little help now. Studies have not been consistent in predicting consumer behavior from sets of personality traits. Either the relationship is perfectly obvious or it is difficult to find the relationship. A study of owners of sports-cars and sedans, for example, found that sports-car owners were more active and sociable. Another study that tried to find if the personality traits of Chevrolet and Ford owners were different came to no conclusions.

SOCIOLOGICAL INFLUENCES ON CONSUMER BEHAVIOR   Sociological factors greatly influence how an individual perceives things. Culture, social class, peer group, and family all affect learning, attitudes, and personality. As a result, they greatly influence why consumers buy what they do.

Culture *Culture* is the complex of symbols and artifacts created by people and handed down from generation to generation to determine and regulate human behavior in a given society. A number of cultural changes have recently taken place in our society including:

1. Impulse buying.
2. Desire for conformity.
3. Importance of time.
4. Increased leisure time.
5. Desire for convenience.
6. Upgraded tastes and desire for elegance.

Some people feel, of course, that marketing has caused some of these changes or at least contributed strongly to them. There is little question that marketing has recognized all of them and attempted to translate each into new products or services to meet the changing desires of consumers.

Social Class Social class, too, shapes buying behavior. A *social class* represents a group of people who share similar values and goals based on their income, occupation, housing, and residence area. Marketing experts agree that social classes can be identified, particularly in metropolitan areas. They also agree that there are differences in values and attitudes among classes, and that consumption patterns are symbols of class membership. In many cases, such membership is a more important factor in economic behavior than income level itself. Some of the sociopsychological differences between middle and lower class are listed in Table 8-2.

Keep in mind when considering social classes that no value is placed on being a member of the upper, middle, or lower class. While one's family position is likely to place a person in one of the three classes, that person may later break away from that class to join another. Until about a decade ago, it was assumed that most individuals were trying to move from the lower to the middle to the upper

TABLE 8-2 Sociopsychological differences between social classes	**Middle Class**	**Lower Class**
	1. Directed toward the future	1. Focused on the present and past
	2. Stresses rationality	2. Often emotional rather than rational
	3. Self-confident, willing to take risks	3. Very concerned with security
	4. Interested in world and national events	4. Little interest in events outside the family

personality profile:
**MICHEL BERGERAC –
taking the lead in the
cosmetics business**

The cosmetics industry, unlike steel or copper, depends for its success on mystique and flair. Charles Revson, Elizabeth Arden, Estée Lauder, and Helena Rubinstein created companies whose cornerstones were glamor, not marketing management. Michel Bergerac was named chief executive of Revlon in 1974, however, in order to add marketing-management muscle to the firm. For agreeing to join Revlon, he received $1.5 million, a five-year contract at $325,000 a year, and attractive options to buy 70,000 shares of the company's stock at a low price.

Bergerac's background was unusual for a chief executive in the cosmetics industry. Born in 1932, he had taken a B.A. at the Sorbonne in Paris and had master's degrees in economics and business administration. Prior to joining Revlon he had been director of European operations for IT&T, the giant communications firm. His knowledge of cosmetics and fragrances was negligible, but he knew a great deal about marketing management.

Revlon had always been known for its quality products and its sure instinct for what consumers wanted. However, it had never carefully defined its markets and was not sure which segments of the market it was serving. In addition, planning and basic inventory and financial controls were neglected. Capital investment requirements in the cosmetics industry are low, but inventory and distribution costs are substantial. Bergerac's studies of inventory levels revealed some basic mistakes that were being made in marketing. He stressed the fact that marketing mistakes end up as top-heavy inventories, for retailers can return unsold products to Revlon.

Michel Bergerac has a difficult job: stressing and strengthening marketing-management controls on a firm whose lifeblood is style and flamboyance. This calls for just the right blend of creativity and control.

class. Today, there are many indications that increasing numbers of young people born in the middle class are adopting lower-class values—since they stress the present rather than the future—and are rejecting the usual upward push.

Family and Peer Groups Family and peer groups, such as organized labor unions, churches, or social clubs, have an important influence on the way individuals perceive things. The family is probably the chief influence on what we choose to buy. While women still do a considerable amount of the family buying, the growth of self-service stores as well as night and Sunday shopping have encouraged more men to take part in family buying.

INFLUENCING CONSUMER BEHAVIOR

The area of consumer behavior is a complex one. While the marketing research data in this field is far less precise than for expenditure, it is still important. This is also where critics of advertising and marketing are most concerned with the impact of business firms on our culture, national goals, and individual development. Some critics have charged that large businesses manipulate consumers to buy whatever they want them to. It has been said that consumers no longer exercise a free choice, since business forces them to buy their products through intensive advertising and subtle sales promotion techniques.

Among young people, peer group pressures influence eating habits, clothing styles, and entertainment choices.

McDonald's Corporation

There is no question that business, with an annual advertising budget of $35 billion and a good understanding of how and why people buy, influences consumers. However, a number of factors indicate that, while business can capitalize on changes in consumer wants, it can't sell products consumers don't want. Large cars are more profitable to sell than small cars; yet despite increasing advertising budgets for larger cars in the early 1970s, the large cars accounted for a decreasing percentage of new car sales. The fashion industry, despite great pressure, could not persuade many women to buy its line of midi-length dresses and skirts. There are hundreds of examples of large consumer-oriented companies that have not succeeded with highly touted products, despite the name image the products carried and extensive advertising programs. DuPont reportedly lost about $300 million on its line of Corfam imitation leather products; General Motors discontinued the Corvair, and Ford flopped with the Edsel; Colgate stopped making its Cue toothpaste, and Campbell dropped its Red Kettle soups.

The consumer is neither sovereign nor slave, although many would disagree. The number of consumer products that fail, even after extensive marketing research and advertising, is about 80 percent. The relatively high savings rates of individuals also indicates that, although consumers can be persuaded to buy, they reserve the right to say no. Furthermore, new trends developed during the 1975 recession. Consumers appear to be less prone to fads, less loyal to brand names, and more insistent on quality goods. With the big jump in the cost of necessities, many persons have less money to spend on nonessentials. As a result, they are more concerned with value for the money they spend. More careful shopping and better-informed decisions by consumers are likely to be the result. An unforeseen but beneficial result of these trends will be better use of all resources.

CONSUMERISM

In the last fifteen years or so, the consumer movement has burgeoned, giving birth to the term *consumerism*. This was defined by President Nixon as the adoption of the concept of "buyer's rights." Another way to define consumerism is to say that it is a movement comprised of individuals, business firms, government agencies, and independent organizations that are concerned with consumers' rights. The movement is generally credited to President Kennedy, who, in 1962, formulated a special message to Congress in which he set forth the consumers' bill of rights. (Shown in Figure 8-3.)

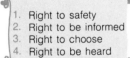

1. Right to safety
2. Right to be informed
3. Right to choose
4. Right to be heard

FIGURE 8-3

MAJOR CONSUMER
COMPLAINTS

Why did the consumer movement begin and why has it grown stronger? There are a number of reasons, but all point to the American consumers' dissatisfaction with the way business has met its obligation to provide the quantity and quality of products and services demanded. Some of the sources of dissatisfaction include:

1. General discontent in society.
2. Unsafe, impure, and defective products.
3. Deceptive promotion.
4. Illusive guarantees.
5. Collusion and price fixing.
6. Sloppy and expensive repair services.
7. No forum or avenue for complaint.
8. Journalistic exposés.

BUSINESS RESPONSE TO COMPLAINTS

With the rise of consumerism, business increasingly felt itself under attack and through trial and error devised ways of dealing with criticism. Consumer complaints have led many individuals and organizations to attack American business for failing to live up to its responsibilities. Business reaction has been predictable. First, business denied that there was a problem or minimized it. Individual firms or an entire industry have placed advertisements in newspapers and on television in which they minimize the problems. A common approach is to blame a few marginal firms which they claim are not representative of American business. However, the consumerism movement is unique in that the largest American firms, such as IBM, General Motors, Procter & Gamble, and AT&T, are singled out as being the cause of most of the complaints.

Another tactic has been to discredit the critics—probably the most infamous example being General Motors' attempt to discredit Ralph Nader by illegally investigating his private life. That resulted in an out-of-court settlement for damages and a public apology to Nader by the president of General Motors.

Another tactic has been the public relations blitz. Many companies have advertised to show their concern for the consumer, as well as for the environment. You have undoubtedly seen many of these. Business firms have also worked quietly to squash proposed consumer legislation or to water it down so that it would have less impact on their industries.

Finally, of course, many executives have come to believe that consumerism is consistent with the best interests of a market economy. As a result, they have made genuine efforts to meet the Kennedy consumer bill of rights. There are many examples. Jewel Food has pioneered with dating of dairy products. Most major appliance manufacturers—Sears Roebuck and Whirlpool, for example—have "translated" the engineering terminology of their warranties into understandable English. Whirlpool has installed a "cool line"—a special phone at the firm's Benton Harbor, Michigan, headquarters so that anyone in the United States can call collect to complain. To give consumers a listening post at Burlington Industries, the giant textile firm has created a special corporate ombudsman (consumer advocate). This keeps company management and technical experts informed on consumer views and complaints.

Consumerism knows no age barriers. The Gray Panthers were organized to protect the rights of older citizens.

Julie Jensen

THE GOVERNMENT RESPONDS

The government's response to consumerism has been swift and dramatic. Congress has passed a flood of legislation to help consumers. More than 90 major consumer-protection proposals became law between 1966 and 1977. Legislation was enacted to protect the consumer in the following areas, among others: credit, meat and poultry inspection, automobile safety, cigarette advertising, fire research and safety, children's clothing, children's nightwear, flammable fabrics, toxic insecticides, and electrical equipment.

Major Federal Laws Some of the major consumer laws passed during this period, often over strong objections from business interests, include:

1. *Fair Packaging and Labeling Act of 1966:* Regulates the packaging and labeling of consumer goods; provides that voluntary uniform packaging standards be established by industry.
2. *National Traffic and Motor Vehicle Safety Act of 1966:* Authorizes the Department of Transportation to establish compulsory safety standards for new and used autos and tires.

3. *Wholesome Meat Act of 1967:* Requires states to upgrade their meat inspection systems to stringent federal standards and to clean up unsanitary meat plants.
4. *Truth-in-Lending Act of 1968:* Requires full disclosure of annual interest rates and other finance charges on consumer loans and credit buying, including revolving charge accounts.
5. *Fraudulent Land Sales Act of 1968:* Requires federal registration of all land offered for sale through the mail to protect consumers against sharp and unscrupulous practices.
6. *Child Protection and Toy Safety Act of 1969:* Amends the Federal Hazardous Substances Act to protect children from toys and other articles that contain thermal, electrical, or mechanical hazards.
7. *Public Health Smoking Act of 1970:* Bans cigarette commercials on radio and television; requires all cigarette packages and published advertising to be labeled: "Warning: The Surgeon General has determined that cigarette smoking is dangerous to your health."
8. *Fair Credit Reporting Act of 1971:* Allows persons to check into and challenge or correct data on their credit at credit bureaus.
9. *Consumer Product Safety Act of 1972:* The Product Safety Commission has authority to set safety standards for products and to ban those presenting a real hazard to consumers.
10. *Magnuson-Moss Warranty Act of 1975:* Requires manufacturers using the term *full warranty* to describe their warranty to correct or replace a defective product within a reasonable period of time. Anything less must be termed a *limited* warranty.

State and City Actions In addition to federal legislation, many states have passed tough laws to protect the consumer. Thirty-four have some form of purchaser protection agency, and have some form of consumer representation at the executive level.

Among cities, New York has been particularly aggressive in safeguarding the purchaser. Its Department of Consumer Affairs has 350 full-time employees. The city also passed the Consumer Protection Act, which gives the city the right to prosecute any business or person victimizing the public through deception.

Executive Action At the same time, the executive branches of the federal and state governments have been busy helping the consumer in the marketplace, President Johnson established the position of Special Assistant to the President for Consumer Affairs in 1964. This office receives about 2,500 letters a month. Complaints about cars are most frequent, followed by charges against mail-order firms. Many are handled by writing to the offending business or by using the "hot line" to the company accused in the complaint. The special assistant also has the responsibility of encouraging and assisting other federal agencies in coordinating consumer activities.

Federal Agencies In addition to the special assistant, a number of federal agencies assist consumers in their relations with businesses. These include the Federal Trade Commission, the Department of Agriculture, the Department of Health, Education and Welfare, the Department of Transportation, the Department of Justice, and the Federal Power Commission. There are numerous divisions and bureaus within these agencies that administer programs to protect consumer rights and consider their problems. Critics point out, however, that frequently the agencies turn out to be controlled by the industries that they are supposed to regulate. Morton Mintz and Jerry S. Cohen, in their best-selling book, *America, Inc.* (1971), claim that since most members of regulatory bodies are from the industry being regulated or leave the agency to work for that industry, it is hard to tell who the regulators are. They charge that the general public is not a party to the deliberations and little attempt is made to protect the public.

Consumer Groups In addition to the executive and legislative branches of government, many groups of consumers are active in supporting the consumer cause. One of the largest and best known of these is the Consumer Federation of America, founded in 1967. It consists of 146 national, state, and local consumer organizations, labor unions, electric cooperatives, and a number of organizations that have consumer interests. The federation claims to speak for 50 million consumers, who belong to such organizations as the National Board of the YWCA, the National Farmers Union, and the National Council of Senior Citizens. From its Washington office, the group promotes consumers' interests by lobbying for legislation, fostering education, and developing programs and activities to make more intelligent customers of the American people.

Two product evaluation organizations, Consumers' Union and Consumer Research, Inc., have long been helpful in developing better-informed consumers. The Consumers' Union, larger and better known, reaches a million consumers in its monthly magazine, *Consumer Reports*, and its yearly *Buying Guide*. It has also recently become active in lobbying for consumer affairs. Consumer Research, Inc., publishes its research findings in *Consumer Bulletin*, with a circulation of about 100,000.

There are, of course, many local groups of consumers who have banded together. When new crises confront the consumers, organizations quickly spring up. Over the years, when meat prices rose dramatically or rents soared almost out of sight, consumers have tended to unite to protect their interests.

BUSINESS AND CONSUMERS WORKING TOGETHER

Many business people have come to recognize that the threat of consumerism also carries opportunities for them. Consumerism is not inconsistent with a market economy, but, indeed, should help strengthen it. To get business and consumerism to work together, business executives may have to rethink their priorities as they affect design, manufacture, and marketing of products. To set the price of an item, for instance, it may be more important to consider product quality and post-sale service than has been the practice. Higher prices may result of course, and they may be difficult to justify to consumers. On the other hand, consumers must also understand and accept their responsibilities if the market economy is to continue working effectively. While in many areas there is no consumer information for effective decision making, in many others the information is available, but consumers typically do not use it. Also, consumer fraud and theft are increasing, representing a serious cost to business. A market economy only works well if both business and the consumer are responsible. Perhaps a dialogue between the two will become more meaningful in future years as both consumers and business concentrate on making the market system work more effectively. Business people have an added incentive to cooperate. They know that if they do not meet the needs of consumers for a responsive and responsible business sector, government will establish new guidelines that will restrict their freedom of enterprise.

SUMMARY

Business firms spend a great deal of money to find out why consumers buy what they do. Firms know that expenditure patterns are fairly predictable when past trends are known. If the number of potential customers and the amount of money they have to spend are known, an analysis can be made of what they will buy. The patterns can be studied by population classification, by income distribution, and by changes in family life cycles.

Much is already known about expenditure patterns. However, much still can be learned about why consumers buy the specific products and services they do. For example, why do they choose brand A over brand B. The reasons are partly psychological and partly sociological. Psychological reasons include previous learning, existing attitudes, and the personality of the consumer. At the same time, sociological forces influence consumers in ways they do not understand or will not admit. Some of these sociological forces include culture, social classes, small reference groups, and family.

Consumerism is a fairly new force. It is a movement of individuals and groups who are concerned with consumers' rights in the market. Consumerism started because consumers felt that they must organize collectively to be heard by business. While some businesses deny that there is need of a consumer movement, most have responded to consumer complaints. The government has moved to help the consumer through a series of laws. The executive branch of the federal and state governments and various consumer groups also are trying to help consumers get a better deal from business.

SUMMARY OF KEY TERMS

Consumerism A movement comprised of individuals, business firms, government agencies, and independent organizations who are concerned with consumers' rights.

Culture The complex of symbols and artifacts created by people and handed down from generation to generation to determine and regulate human behavior in a given society.

Discretionary Income Disposable personal income minus fixed commitments and essential household needs.

Disposable Personal Income Personal income minus personal income taxes paid to the government.

Goal-oriented Behavior Action by consumers which is motivated by needs which create tensions.

Interurban Areas Areas of large population formed when two or more large metropolitan areas grow together.

National Income The total income which is earned by those who contribute to production, including employee wages and salaries, corporate profits, rental income, and interest income.

Personal Income All income of individuals, regardless of source.

Social Class A group of people who have many of the same values and goals based on their income, occupation, housing, and residence area.

REVIEW QUESTIONS

1. How are populations classified by marketers to help them study expenditures patterns? Explain the importance of each of the classifications.

2. Of interest to market analysts are four distinct age groups in the general population. What are these groups? Do you think these age distinctions are too simple? Why or why not?

3. Explain and differentiate personal income, disposable income, and discretionary income.

4. What are some major trends in family life that are having an impact on business and marketing today?

5. What is the stimulus-response theory in terms of consumer behavior? From your own experience, do you think it does or does not work?

6. What are recent cultural changes in our society? Name a product or service that has resulted from each of these changes.

7. Does social class have an effect on consumer habits? Give reasons for your answer.

8. Even with extensive marketing research and costly advertising campaigns, some products never sell. Name 10 products to which this has happened.

9. What is consumerism? Has it had a significant impact on the buying habits of consumers? Why or why not?

10. Name 10 laws that are concerned with protecting consumers. Briefly explain the intent of each of these laws.

DISCUSSION QUESTIONS

1. Many industries affected by shifts in the population, such as the current shift from the North and Midwest to the Sun Belt. Name five industries that are affected by this shift and explain how these industries feel the impact.

2. Changing patterns of family size and life-style affect housing, modes of transportation, and use of leisure time. Discuss the numerous ways in which these changes are evident in the above-mentioned categories.

3. Almost every state, county, and large city in the United States has a consumer affairs office or department like New York City's Department of Consumer Affairs. Write the consumer department nearest you and ask for information describing the local programs conducted by that department. Discuss the findings with your class.

4. Is a strong consumer movement contrary to the interests of business? Why or why not?

5. In addition to the consumer rights already protected by federal laws, there are other consumer areas that need federal legislation. What other areas might these be?

CASES FOR DECISION MAKING

SHIFTING POPULATION TRENDS WORRY THE SOFT-DRINK INDUSTRY

The average American drinks 547 cans of soft drink a year. That seems like a lot until you know that the average consumer between the ages of 13 and 24 drinks 823 cans a year. Clearly this is the group to which all soft-drink producers aim their promotion and products. However, in the next decade this age group will shrink by 10 percent because of the declining birth rate.

The decline in the heavy drinkers of soft drinks worries all makers of soft drinks, but it worries the leader in the field—Coca-Cola—most of all. Coke gets about 95 percent of its income from soft drinks and other beverages. To combat this expected loss in demand from the declining market, Coke plans three basic strategies. It plans to expand overseas sales, to diversify its product line, and to alter its advertising to appeal more to the current 13–24 age groups as it gets older.

1. From what you have seen on television and in magazines, how does Coca-Cola appear to be appealing to older consumers in its advertising, especially those outside the 13–24 age group?

2. What other industries would you expect to be concerned with the drop in the 13–24 age group?

3. How do you suppose the business firms in these industries will adjust to the loss in demand for their products caused by the decrease in the number of young people?

YOGURT, ANYONE?

Sales of yogurt products have shown a steady increase in recent years. Yogurt has been sold as a healthy, low-calorie food appealing to young, upper-middle class consumers. But in general producers seek a broader market, with greater sales potential. Only about 14 percent of the country's households regularly buy the 8-oz. fruit-flavored containers of yogurt. Only about 10 percent of the population eats yogurt once a week and half of the population never eats it.

The growing number of brands on the market testify to the increasing interest of dairy-product companies in the many-sided market that is developing for yogurt. It can be sold as a snack food, a dessert, or a light lunch. It comes in various forms such as soft ice cream, a cottage-cheese base, sour cream, and of course with fruit.

Stricter labeling laws have forced producers to admit that yogurt is not low in calories. However, there is no doubt that it is nutritious. What's more, its taste being so different, it takes clever promotion to get people to try it.

1. To which segment of the market would you expect the makers of soft-frozen yogurt to appeal?
2. What type of appeal would you expect producers to make in attempting to persuade this group to buy the product?
3. Are there any cultural influences that might induce people to include yogurt as part of their diet?

MISLEADING ADVERTISING

The Federal Trade Commission and RJR Foods, Inc., makers of Hawaiian Punch beverage, reached an agreement, called a consent order, that required disclosures about "natural fruit juices" in Hawaiian Punch products.[1] The FTC complaint said that the firm and its advertising agency misrepresented Hawaiian Punch beverages as consisting mostly of natural fruit juices by featuring fresh fruit and fruit trees in commercials and by using the phrase "seven natural fruit juices." In fact, FTC's complaint said, the major ingredients in the products are water and sweeteners, which are added to fruit juices and other ingredients to produce the final product. RJR foods agreed to list the exact juice percentages on its cans. After a year, RJR was permitted to stop the percentage disclosures because it was able to show that the public is generally aware that Hawaiian Punch products contain no more than 20 percent natural fruit juice. Consumer surveys were used to demonstrate public awareness.

1. Do the terms of the agreement seem too severe, too easy, or acceptable to you?
2. Should all food and beverage products carry on the label the exact percentages of each ingredient?
3. Why do you suppose the FTC accepted a consent decree rather than starting a lawsuit against the firm?

RELATED READINGS

Aaker, David A., and Day, George S. *Consumerism.* New York: The Free Press, 1974.

A book of readings about consumerism, dealing with the following topics: perspectives on consumerism, availability and quality of information, postpurchase experiences, and ecology and social issues in advertising.

Key, Wilson Bryan. *Subliminal Seduction.* New York: New American Library, 1973.

Deals with the efforts of advertisers to reach the subconscious mind of consumers and to manipulate consumers by understanding their hidden needs.

Magnuson, Warren G., and Carper, Jean. *The Dark Side of the Marketplace.* Englewood Cliffs, N.J.: Prentice-Hall, 1968.

A very readable little book dealing with the effects on consumers of unscrupulous marketing practices by large firms and the need for stronger consumer legislation.

1. "Disclosures About Hawaiian Punch," *Consumer News,* June 1, 1973.

Nader, Ralph, ed. *The Consumer and Corporate Accountability*. New York: Harcourt Brace Jovanovich, 1973.

Title tells it all.

Why Do We Pay So Much Money? Somerville, Mass.: New American Library, 1975.

Features the most frequently raised questions about why prices are so high and the authors' answers to the questions.

chapter 9

GETTING THE RIGHT MARKETING MIX

OBJECTIVES

When you have finished reading and studying this chapter, you should be able to:

1. **Differentiate consumer and industrial goods, as well as convenience, shopping, and specialty consumer goods.**

2. **Explain the product life cycle and its relationship to product profit rates and obsolescence.**

3. **Explain the role played by middlemen in the major channels of distribution.**

4. **Identify and discuss the major factors that have a bearing on pricing consumer goods and services.**

5. **Differentiate advertising, personal selling, and sales promotion, and contrast the objectives of advertising with criticism of it.**

CHAPTER PREVIEW

When marketing strategies have been chosen and the business firm knows what consumers want, it is time to put together the right marketing mix. The marketing mix is the right combination of product (or service), place, price, and promotion. Successful firms such as Procter & Gamble carefully prepare the marketing mix every time a new product is brought out. Most firms, however, have difficulty in getting all the right elements together. Even Procter & Gamble doesn't always get the right mix, however. Recently, it made an unsuccessful effort to replace General Food's Maxwell House coffee with its Folger's as the leading coffee brand in the East. Amid price discounts and heavy promotion for the product, Procter & Gamble moved into the market before a complete sales force was built up. It had to pull salespeople from other products, which resulted in a sales program that lacked the usual sales push of Procter & Gamble. Folger's share of market did not increase as expected.

In this chapter, you will look at the characteristics of products, including their packaging and the product life cycle. You will look at the channels of distribution and view the role of middlemen, especially retailers. You will look at the factors influencing the pricing decision and some of the pricing strategies used by firms. Finally, you will look at the promotion of products and services, and the important role of advertising.

"Hi! I assemble visual and verbal elements and package and market the result."

9

GETTING THE RIGHT MARKETING MIX

In the previous chapter, we looked at the marketing concept and the marketing mix. In this chapter, we will examine the four elements of the marketing mix—product, place, price, and promotion—in depth. Although it is easier to analyze them separately, no successful firm ever makes a decision about one of the four without considering its effect on the other three.

Marketing is probably the most dynamic function of business. Because it is constantly determining and meeting consumer demands, it must change as consumer demands change. Successful firms determine and meet consumer demands quickly. Unsuccessful firms do not.

Getting the right mix of product, place, price, and promotion is not easy. Sometimes a product sells well for a while if only one or two of the elements of the mix are right. More frequently, however, the product does not sell well or sales are less than they should be if all elements are coordinated. Liggett Group Inc. decided that price was the key to sales for its new high-tar cigarette, Eagle 20. It was sold for five cents less per pack than the traditional brands. What were the results? The new brand did not sell at an acceptable level. Liggett discovered that what the smoking public wanted was a new low-tar cigarette, not a high-tar brand, even though it was cheaper. Hertz, which saw its share of the rent-a-car market falling after Avis' successful promotion using "We're No. 2—we try harder" theme, decided to change promotional strategies. After watching football superstar O. J. Simpson dash through airports with his message that Hertz was the "Superstar of rent-a-cars," the American public responded by increasing Hertz' share of the market over Avis by 14 percent.

PRODUCT

A *product* is anything that satisfies the customer, whether it is tangible like a phonograph record or intangible like a haircut. This definition, which includes both products and services, also includes what the product represents to people as much as its physical appearance. For example, Bayer and Rexall aspirins are quite different products in the minds of many people.

CONSUMER PRODUCTS

There are two basic types of products and they are classed as consumer products and industrial products. *Consumer products* are those which are sold directly to the final consumer. Consumer products can be further divided according to the buying motives of those who buy them. These categories and their characteristics are:

1. *Convenience products.* These are staples, with low unit value, and are frequently purchased in small quantities. Two examples are breakfast cereal and milk.
2. *Shopping products.* These are items that are important enough to warrant comparison shopping for price, fashion, and quality. Examples are a dining room table and a new winter jacket.

Steuben Glass, of New York, is renowned for elegant crystal. This is a trio of porpoise.

Steuben Glass

3. *Specialty products.* These have a distinctive quality and their price is not an important consideration. Fur coats, Gucci luggage, and Lotus automobiles are examples.

It is true that many products could fit into any of the three categories, depending on the buyer's motive. A watch, for instance, may be chosen because it is inexpensive if price is the motive for choice. On the other hand, if price is no object, one could buy a watch costing $100,000. In the first case the watch is a shopping product, and in the second it's a specialty product.

These three categories are a helpful framework for manufacturers and retailers. It permits them to analyze why consumers buy what they buy. With this information they can concentrate on the segment of the market that interests them the most. For example, for a clothing manufacturer, information about buying motives for clothes assists the manufacturer in deciding the quality of the clothes, the most effective price and promotion for them, and the best choice of retail outlets to sell them in.

INDUSTRIAL PRODUCTS

While industrial products do not normally receive great attention in a discussion of the marketing of products and services, they are, nevertheless, a large and vital part of the total output of products and services. *Industrial products* are products that are sold to business for business use or for additional processing before being offered to the final consumer. Approximately 45 percent of all manufactured goods and 80 percent of all farm products are sold on the industrial market. Since most jobs, income, and merchandise are generated by the business sector, the sale of industrial goods is watched carefully as a barometer of how the economy is faring.

Industrial goods can be subdivided into parts, raw material, supplies, partially manufactured goods, and machinery and equipment.

NEW PRODUCT DEVELOPMENT

New product development is essential for the continued growth of a business. Companies risk about $20 billion a year on new consumer products, with approximately 80 percent of the new items failing. Yet, continued profits and increases in sales are dependent on a stream of new products. The shortage of raw materials, inflation, and fear of an energy crunch in the 1970s, however, have resulted in less emphasis recently on new product development. Manufacturers have tended to introduce fewer products, discontinue low-profit items, and modify existing products.

PRODUCT LIFE CYCLE

Products tend to have a life cycle similar to that of a living organism. The stages of the *product life cycle* include introduction (or birth), growth, maturation, saturation, and decline. While products move through the phases of the cycle differently, there is a regular pattern in which sales and profit margin curves slope upward, reach a peak, and then decline. According to one marketing survey, 85 percent of all new consumer brands can expect less than three years of success before their market shares begin to slip. The timing is different for each product, of course. Notice on the graph in Figure 9-1 that the sales curve normally continues to rise for a time after the profit margin curve has already reached its peak.

FIGURE 9-1 Product life cycle

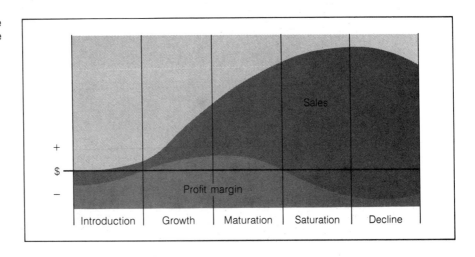

Competition forces prices down, squeezing profit levels. Most durable goods, such as televisions, washers, dryers, and appliances, have declined in price since they were introduced. The price of a small electronic calculator is now about one-fourth what it was when introduced on a large scale about 10 years ago.

INCREASING
PRODUCT LIFE

When the market maturity stage is reached with a product, a firm often tries to increase it through increasing the frequency of product use (for example, eight-packs and twelve-packs of soft drinks), developing varied uses for the product (the effort to make Dr. Pepper a winter drink), and attracting a new user (selling bicycles to adults). When a product's sales begin to decline, a firm must choose among five strategies:

1. Improving or revitalizing the product.
2. Reviewing the factors in the marketing mix.
3. Eliminating the losers in a line of products.
4. Cutting costs to a minimum and selling the remaining supply.
5. Discontinuing the product.

The life of a product depends on reviewing the factors in the marketing mix.

General Foods

Procter & Gamble has the best track record at extending the life of its consumer products. Their tactic is to make major or minor changes in each product twice a year. Coupled with the heaviest advertising expenditure of any company, these modifications have enabled Procter & Gamble to extend the life cycle for most of its products.

The total length of the cycle for a product varies considerably. For example, automobiles in general have been in demand for almost 90 years. However, individual makes of automobiles, such as Packard, Edsel, Hudson, and De Soto, have come and gone. Some items like pet rocks or hula hoops last for just a few months. Some products have long lives. Pears Soap, made from glycerine, has been successfully marketed since 1789. This must be a record of some kind for length of product life cycle.

Product life cycles seem to be shortening in the face of increased competition in almost every category. This is particularly important when you see that the bulk of profits on most commodities is made in the introduction and growth stages of the life cycle, before competition effectively sets in. The so-called lead time that a firm has can be used to cover start-up costs on the product and to make relatively large profits per item. Once there is competition, as shown in the maturation stage of Figure 9-1, the profit level falls as the firm drops its prices to meet the competition. DuPont, for example, made large profits in the first 15 years it marketed nylon since it had no real competition for the fiber. More recently it developed Delrin, which it thought was potentially as profitable as nylon. However, it took only two years for the Celanese Corporation to turn out a product that was very competitive with Delrin.

PLANNED OBSOLESCENCE

The rapid life cycle for products bothers a lot of consumers as well as manufacturers. Many consumers have charged that manufacturers deliberately engage in shortening the product life cycle. This is called *planned obsolescence*; that is, a product is deliberately designed to become unusable after a short period of time. The term is used differently by different people so there is no one generally accepted meaning of the term. There are, however, at least three identifiable types.

1. *Technological obsolescence* occurs when significant technical improvement in a product makes an older model appear less desirable and inadequate, for instance, color television versus black and white. Another example is Gillette's ATRA (automatic tracking razor action) introduced in 1977 to replace Trac II, the first twin-bladed razor. ATRA has a pivotal head and follows the contour of the face.

2. *Intentionally designed physical obsolescence* refers to a product that is manufactured with a shorter life expectancy than it could or should have. Frequently, consumers complain that cars, refrigerators, and washers/dryers could be made to last for 20 years but aren't.

3. *Style obsolescence* is a minor alteration of a superficial characteristic so that

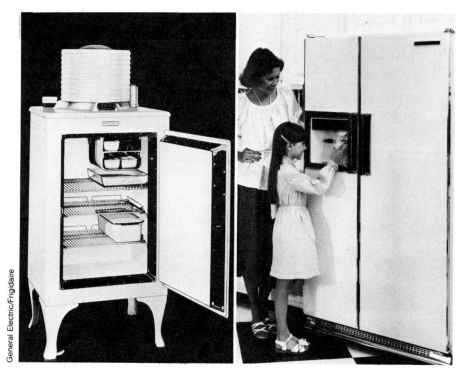

General Electric/Frigidaire

users will feel they are purchasing a product different from the old model. Examples might include changing the item's color or the location of its trim.

STYLE OBSOLESCENCE　While there are complaints about intentionally designed physical obsolescence, particularly as it applies to durable goods, the loudest consumer outcries have been raised against style obsolescence. There is much criticism of the continued drive by American firms to sell a steady stream of mass-produced products through making minor changes in color or design. Vance Packard's *The Waste Makers*, written in 1960, was one of the first of the popular books to attack the efforts of business in encouraging consumer dissatisfaction with the style or color of existing goods. Environmentalists have added fuel to the newest charge by pointing out that the obsession with having products of the newest color and design is resulting in a throw-away society that is harming our environment. Alvin Toffler, in *Future Shock*, painted an even dimmer view of the rapidly changing needs of the consuming public in the following statement:

In a society caught up in complex, high-speed change, the needs of the individual—which arise out of his interaction with the external environment

—also change at relatively high speed. The more rapidly changing the society, the more temporary the needs. Given the general affluence of this new society, he can indulge many of these short-term needs.

Often, without having even a clear idea of what needs he wants served, the consumer has a vague feeling that he wants a change. Advertising encourages and capitalizes on this feeling, but it can hardly be credited with having created it single-handedly. The tendency toward shorter relational durations is thus built more deeply into the social structure than arguments over planned obsolescence or the manipulative effectiveness of Madison Avenue would suggest.[1]

While most companies make every effort to have a continuous stream of new products, there are some exceptions. Until the introduction of its Big Red gum, Wrigley Company, the largest chewing gum maker in the United States, had made no effort to introduce new lines of gum to go with Spearmint and Doublemint. Beechnut, number two in the market, and Chiclet, number three, on the other hand, have aggressively developed new products and launched them with sparkling advertising programs.

NATIONAL AND PRIVATE BRANDS

In building acceptance for a product, a manufacturer normally tries to establish an identity for it in the target market. In doing so, the manufacturer normally makes use of a *brand*, which is a name, term, symbol, or design distinguishing the products of a seller from those of competitors. When the brand is owned by a manufacturer, it is generally called a *national brand*; and when it is owned by a middleman, it is generally called a *private brand*. This is not quite accurate, of course, because many middleman brands—such as those of Ward's, Sears, or Penney's—are better known than many of the so-called national lines.

Who Makes Private Brands?   National brands generally sell for more than comparable private brands because they enjoy consumers' confidence established for them through an extensive promotional campaign. In many cases, the manufacturer may make the national brand and also make the same product under a competing middleman's trademark (see Table 9-1). For example, the Frigidaire division of General Motors makes the Frigidaire refrigerators and also produces refrigerators for Marcor (Montgomery Ward). Most large manufacturers of durable goods also produce private brands. Since these are made according to the specifications of the middlemen, they may be of a higher or lower quality than the line of goods produced by the manufacturers for their own brand.

Why Make Private Brands?   Why do manufacturers make private brands as well as their own national lines? The reason is primarily economic—the increased

1. Alvin Toffler, *Future Shock* (New York: Bantam Books, 1970), p. 67.

TABLE 9-1 Private tire
brands

Who makes the private brands for whom?
Armstrong: Allstate (Sears)*
Dayton (Firestone): Cornell*, Davis (Western Auto)*, Douglas*
Firestone: Amoco*, Atlas*, Getty*, O.K. Tires*, Phillips 66*, Riverside (Montgomery-Ward)*, Shell*, Union 76*
Gates: Davis (Western Auto)*, Riverside (Montgomery-Ward)*
General: Jetzon*
B. F. Goodrich: Atlas*, Co-op*, Fed-Mart, Gulf, Hood, Phillips 66*
Kelly-Springfield (Goodyear): Atlas*, Cordovan, Foremost (J.C. Penney), Mobil, Nation-Wide, O.K. Tires*, Phillips 66*, Shell*, Union 76*, Vanderbilt, Vogue
Lee (Goodyear): Jetzon*, Monarch
Uniroyal: Amoco*, Billups, Co-Op*, Davis (Western Auto)*, Fisk, Getty* Gillette, Guardian, Peerless, Phillips 66*, Shell*

Note: This list is by no means complete. Each major tire manufacturer makes many more private brands than we've listed. We've mentioned only the best known.

*Some lines manufactured by other companies.

Source: From *Popular Mechanics* © 1972 by The Hearst Corporation

sales add to profits and also help the manufacturer reduce unit costs. Since middlemen can find other manufacturers to produce the goods for them if one refuses, there is really no reason not to accept the additional business. Middlemen like to have their own brands, of course, because it builds customer loyalty to their products rather than to those of a manufacturer which customers can buy at other retail stores. Also, there may be a higher gross profit margin for retailers in selling under their own trademark, they may have more freedom and flexibility in pricing their own branded goods, and they may have more control over their supply.

For these reasons, distributors banded together to bring back an appliance brand that had not been sold since the mid-1950s—Crosley. Today only two major manufacturers produce a full line of appliances under their own label— General Electric and the Frigidaire division of General Motors. They sell to large retailers and, therefore, bypass distributors, who felt they had to have their own brand to maintain retail store loyalty to their products. As a result, they reintroduced the Crosley brand.

PLACE

In the marketing mix, *place* refers to the place where products and services are offered to the ultimate consumer or industrial user. The place is more commonly referred to as the *channel of distribution*—a route a product follows as it moves from producer to consumer or industrial user. In between the producer and the consumer, a number of marketing functions must be performed. These include

In today's markets, customers may be hundreds or thousands of miles from the place where the product is made. Quick, dependable distribution is essential to reach the market.

Flying Tigers

buying, selling, transporting, standardizing, grading, pricing, financing, and distributing market information. These functions may be the province of the producer, the consumer, or some middleman.

ROLE OF MIDDLEMEN

A *middleman* is an independent business firm or individual who comes between the producer and the ultimate consumer or industrial user. A middleman buys or sells goods and may also perform other marketing functions. Middlemen either take title to the goods or help negotiate the transfer of title to them. If they actually take title to the products that they direct into the market, they are called merchant middlemen. Wholesalers and retailers are the two main groups in this category. Those who do not take title, but take an active part in the purchase and sales negotiations, are called agent middlemen. Among agent middlemen are brokers, selling agents, and manufacturers' agents. Brokers and agents are useful where market information may not be adequate, as in a situation where large manufacturers reach the consumer through small retailers, or in marketing seasonal items like food.

CHANNELS OF DISTRIBUTION

Several different distribution channels are used to get consumer goods to market (see Figure 9-2). Some of the most common include:

FIGURE 9-2 Channels of
distribution for consumer
goods from manufacturer to
consumer

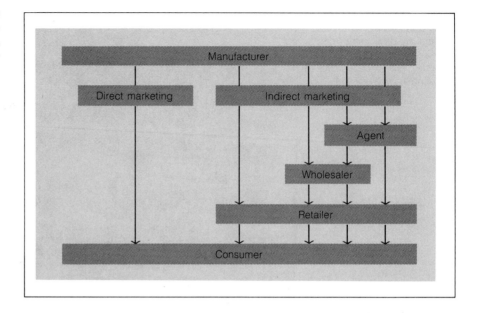

FIGURE 9-2 Channels of distribution for consumer goods from manufacturer to consumer

1. Manufacturer directly to the consumer. Door-to-door selling as conducted by Avon, Beauty Counselor, and Fuller Brush, and most direct-mail efforts are examples of this channel.
2. Manufacturer to retailer to consumer. Most autos are sold this way, as are many types of furniture, appliances, tires, shoes, and paints.
3. Manufacturer to wholesaler to retailer to consumer. This is the most common distribution channel for consumer goods, especially where there is a small manufacturer or a small retailer involved in the flow.
4. Manufacturer to broker to other middlemen to consumer. This pattern is common in the distribution of food and other agricultural products, and when reaching small retailers.

In some ways, channels of distribution for industrial goods and for consumer goods are different. In the industrial channel of distribution, no retailer is normally needed, and indeed, very few middlemen are required. As a result, there is a shorter channel of distribution for industrial goods than for consumer goods. This is also influenced by the expert installation and maintenance service many complex industrial products often require of their manufacturer.

BYPASSING THE MIDDLEMEN Producers often prefer to bypass the middlemen in the channel of distribution. Roadside stands selling fruits and vegetables are familiar examples. Other examples are furniture warehousing, direct mail, door-to-door selling, discount stores,

Two brothers, Ronald & Joseph "Pep" Simek, ran a little tavern called the Tombstone Tap, which shared a common border with a cemetery in Medford, Wisconsin. Struggling to make enough for two families from the tavern, they decided in 1962 that they needed something special to attract customers, far more than an unusual name. It had to be a dish that would be easy to prepare, go well with beer, and draw customers to the Tombstone Tap. Pizza appeared to be the best choice and so Pep spent six months experimenting with ingredients to come up with something unusual. His concoction was a success.

The customers at the Tombstone Tap liked it so well that the brothers decided to expand business. With the help of their wives, they prepared an extra 100 pizzas a week, froze them, and delivered them to taverns in the area. To build a trade, they would walk into a tavern, ask the owner to serve a Tombstone pizza to customers, and then rely on the customers to create a demand for their product. As business increased, the brothers expanded their production facilities, bought more baking equipment, and placed orders for additional delivery trucks.

Tombstone grew by selling first to taverns, then to small grocery stores, and then to supermarkets in a community. Sales are made directly to individual stores, bypassing wholesalers. Tombstone drivers double as salespeople in replenishing a store's freezer cabinet, rotating stock, and taking out old or damaged merchandise. They also ensure favorable shelf space for Tombstone pizza.

As the firm expanded, the Simeks gradually lost their grip on the company. Distribution of the pizzas was the main problem. Distributors were independent businesspeople who used their own capital to establish regional marketing systems for Tombstone. Some were inexperienced and lacked the credit necessary to establish the business. As a result, failure rates among distributors were high. Besides the distribution problem, there were difficulties controlling growth by geographical area. Drivers determined which new accounts were to be started. Since most drivers had all the business they could handle, there was little incentive to go after new business. When the brothers hired a sales manager, he quickly reclaimed troubled distributorships, divided the company's territory into districts, (each of which is headed by a manager who supervises the route salespeople), and compiled sales data for management decisions.

As a result, the distribution problem seems to be solved and sales are again moving strongly. The company is also changing its marketing plan. Whereas in 1973 sales were divided about 75 to taverns and 25 percent to grocery stores, today about 60 percent of sales are to grocery stores. Soon, the firm expects to see sales to grocery stores account for about 70 percent of the company's total volume. In ten years, its market will have been completely reversed.

While large supermarkets offer the fastest and least expensive avenue for growth, Tombstone is following its original unique approach to marketing. It enters a market through tavern sales and sales to small grocery stores. After the product has been available in area taverns and grocery stores for a while, Tombstone then contacts supermarkets, which are more willing to stock the pizzas after demand has been built. So far the strategy appears to be working well.

and mail-order catalogues. While it is possible to bypass all middlemen from the producer to the consumer, it is not possible to bypass their functions. Someone must perform the marketing functions that they would normally perform.

Retailing, the middleman's most recognizable function, has undergone enormous changes in the last decade or so. Some of these trends include:

1. *Crossing-over of functions.* Retailers are getting into manufacturing, while wholesalers and manufacturers are moving into retailing. Most large retailers, such as Sears and Penney's, do at least part of their own manufacturing; and many large manufacturers, such as B. F. Goodrich, Magnavox, and Sherwin-Williams, have opened their own retail stores.

2. *Self-service where possible.* Self-service continues a trend accelerated by the discount stores. Self-service has now spread even to department stores which have in the past prided themselves on the excellent service they gave their consumers.

3. *Handling scrambled lines of merchandise.* Scrambling here refers to the overlapping of merchandise by different types of stores. Supermarkets, for example, now get about 22 percent of their income from nonfood items. Discount stores sell groceries; even department stores are carrying grocery and hardware items.

4. *Greater use of credit.* Virtually all stores push their credit services and encourage customers not to pay cash, but to use credit cards. With the rapid growth of the bank credit card, particularly BankAmericard-Visa and Master Charge, it is easy to charge purchases at many retail stores.

5. *Growth of shopping centers.* Almost all of the new stores opened by such successful retailers as Woolworth, Kresge, Marcor, Penney's, and Sears are in shopping centers. Companies like A&P, with most of their stores concentrated in the old urban areas, suffer a severe disadvantage as the shopping centers pull in more and more customers.

6. *Movement to discount stores.* Discount stores use price as a greater weapon in the marketing mix. Started by the discount stores, which originated in the abandoned warehouses in the New England area, almost every major supermarket, as well as many department stores and drugstores, advertises discount prices today.

7. *The use of electronic data processing for stock control and accounting.* The newest trend in retailing, electronic cash registers provides stores with instant reports on inventory, daily financial status, and sales clerk productivity. No longer needing clerks to process sales tickets, stores are saving $100,000 a year and more according to some accounts. The result has been that fewer personnel are needed, smaller inventories, and savings on equipment and supplies.

8. *Franchising.* Franchising continues to be a fast-expanding form of retailing. With more than 33 percent of retail sales now accounted for by franchisers, it is an exciting blend of large and small businesses.

9. *Increasing use of metric sizes, weights, and measures.* While the United States is slowly switching to metrics, the consumer is seeing a rapid conversion at the retail store. Clothing sizes, food weights, and liquid volumes are marked in both English and metric measure and some cases in metric only. This will be a particular challenge to general merchandise retailers. (For further implications, see Appendix C, "Metrics—Background and Implications for Industry.")

PRICE

Pricing products and services involves a lot of guesswork. Ideally, of course, a firm wants to price its products so that it can make the highest profit possible. If it sets the price too low, it will sell all of its products but not make all the profit it might have with a higher price. If the price is too high, merchandise will pile up on the shelves. The following factors must be considered in setting a price:

1. Consumer demand.
2. Costs.

Prices are determined by many factors, among which are consumer demand and production costs.

Peter O'Brien

3. Stage in the life cycle of the product.
4. Government controls.
5. Importance of nonprice competition.

CONSUMER DEMAND   Consumer demand for a product or service is said to be elastic or inelastic, depending on how consumers react to a change in its price. Figure 9-3 shows how the mechanism works.

Demand is *elastic* if a change in price results in a change in demand for a given product. Demand for the product is *inelastic* if a change in price does not result in a change in demand. Why is this concept of elasticity important? If a firm thinks the demand for its product is inelastic, it will raise the price as high as it thinks the market will bear. It means that while the company may not sell as many at a higher price, its total income will be increased by charging more. If the demand is relatively elastic, the firm will boost its total income by a small price cut since sales will increase substantially.

Salt or hospital services are examples of products or services that are considered relatively inelastic, since an increase in price results in little change in demand. On the other hand, bacon, luxury cars, and household appliances are goods for which demand is considered relatively elastic. The elasticity of demand is normally greater when there are numerous substitutes available, or the product is a luxury item, or when it absorbs a large part of a consumer's total expenditures.

FIGURE 9-3 Elasticity of demand

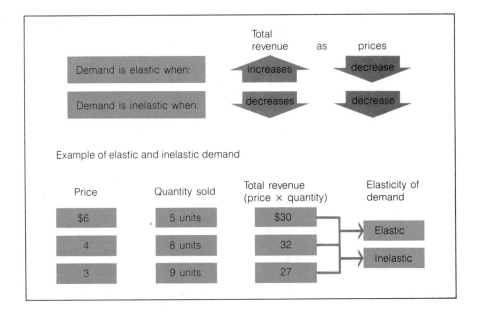

COST INFLUENCES PRICE

Cost is a basic factor in determining the price of any product or service. The cost of making a product is the lowest price level that may be maintained over a long period of time. A company will not ordinarily sell its products under cost for any length of time. It may, however, continue selling some products below cost to stimulate sales of other items in its line or if it needs the unprofitable product to round out the sales line. For example, Gillette has been accused at various times of selling its razors below cost to build up the market for its razor blades. The same charges have been made against Eastman Kodak for the low price of its cameras. Retail grocers sometimes sell a few items below cost to attract more customers so they can sell them other products on which they can make a good profit.

PRICES BASED ON COST

Costs represent a point from which a firm can determine its prices. The market, of course, sets the ceiling on what a firm can charge. Some firms, particularly retail stores, may price their products at cost plus a fixed percentage. This is called a *markup*. Stores with relatively high sales volume, such as supermarkets, take a lower markup percentage than do, say, jewelry stores, which have a lower volume. Table 9-2 provides further examples. While this is an easy way to price, it is not ordinarily the best way for most firms since it ignores the demand in the market. It may result in prices that are too low or too high to yield the firm the highest possible profit from its sales.

PRICING TOO LOW

Most marketing experts agree that a large backlog of unfilled orders for a new product means that the company has underpriced its product. A case in point is the introduction of the first Wilkinson Sword stainless steel razor blade at about 15

TABLE 9-2 Net profit on net sales (median for all retail stores in the industry)

Type of Store	Net Profit (Percent)
Grocery stores	.94
Discount stores	1.17
Department stores	1.61
Gasoline service stations	1.97
Furniture stores	2.00
Hardware stores	3.27
Paint, glass, & wallpaper stores	3.13
Jewelry stores	3.79

Notice that the stores with the lowest net profit on net sales are those with the fastest turnover of merchandise. Those with a higher net profit on net sales, such as jewelry stores, have a slower turnover of merchandise.

Source: Reprinted with the special permission of *Dun's Review,* September 1978. Copyright 1978, Dun & Bradstreet Publications Corporation

cents each. Immediately, there was a heavy backlog of orders caused by the heavy demand. While the firm made money on the blades at the 15-cent price, it would have increased its short-run profits more at first, and then could have broadened sales later by dropping the price.

STAGE IN THE LIFE CYCLE OF THE PRODUCT

Another important variable in pricing a product is the stage in its life cycle. When a product is introduced, the pricing strategy is quite different from that when market saturation has been achieved. When a new product is launched, there are two extremes of pricing strategy—skimming and market penetration pricing.

Skimming means that the producer will sell the product for as high a price as possible to maximize total revenue. This is possible with a distinctive product in the introductory stage of the life cycle or when nonprice competition is used to create an image of distinctiveness. Brand-name products, such as Bayer aspirin, Budweiser beer, or Campbell soups attempt to do this. Of course, some firms then switch fairly quickly to lower prices to discourage competitors. IBM, for example, has traditionally used a skimming pricing strategy in introducing new computer products. After watching smaller firms nibble at their market share, however, IBM (accounting for about two-thirds of this country's computer revenues) switched unexpectedly to a reduction of prices on new products in 1977. With the pricing advantage of smaller, independent firms thus reduced, many customers turned to IBM.

Market penetration pricing implies that the producer will sell the product at a relatively low price to build quickly a wide market for the product. This type of pricing is a good marketing strategy if the demand for the product is highly sensitive to price (elastic demand) and competition is faced immediately. Because most new consumer products can be copied rather quickly by competitors, the pricing strategy adopted by a consumer products firm is more likely to approximate market penetration strategy than skimming. A further advantage of the former strategy, of course, is the increased sales volume, which makes it possible to lower unit costs.

GOVERNMENT CONTROLS

Various government agencies directly influence the pricing strategies that a firm can use. At times, there are outright price freezes or price controls which closely regulate what a firm may charge. Firms in heavily regulated industries, such as transportation, communications, and utilities, have their prices determined by their respective regulatory commissions. The railroads, for example, cannot raise their rates unless given permission by the Interstate Commerce Commission. In addition to such direct controls, the government exercises a number of more subtle restraints over prices charged for consumer items. Interest rates, which are closely influenced by the government, have a strong bearing on the prices of consumer durable goods and housing. When the government negotiates the sale of large amounts of grains to China or the Soviet Union, the price in the American market for these grains and of the products that are made from them is affected. The large sale of wheat to the Soviet Union in 1973 contributed to the jump in the price of bread and other wheat-based goods in the United States.

NONPRICE COMPETITION

Nonprice competition means that one of the other three *P*'s of the marketing mix is emphasized for competitive purposes, rather than price. Large consumer manufacturers, such as General Foods, Hunt-Wesson, and Kellogg, generally keep their prices at about the same level as their competitors. Their rivalry to win additional consumers focuses on new advertising programs, colorful and unique packages, or minor changes in their products. For this reason, many consumer advocates claim that there is not enough competition in the marketplace. The big firms do not compete on the basis of price, they argue, but on gimmicks, without affording the consumer the savings that would come from real competition.

PROMOTION

For many people, promotion and advertising have the same meaning. For marketing people, however, they are not the same thing. To them *promotion* is a much broader term, encompassing all of the personal selling, advertising, sales promotion, and other tools a company uses to persuade a prospective customer to buy a good or service.

Let us first contrast the three major categories of promotion, show their relationship within the promotion mix, and then devote more attention to each one individually. *Personal selling* requires a direct face-to-face relationship between the seller and the potential customer. *Advertising* is any paid form of nonpersonal presentation of ideas, goods, or services by an identified sponsor. *Sales promotion* consists of the related promotional activities that are necessary to supplement personal selling and advertising. Some of these activities include distribution of sample products to customers, exhibits or demonstrations of products at stores or trade shows, preparation of printed material used by salespeople or for point-of-sale displays.

PERSONAL SELLING

With some kinds of products, personal selling is clearly the most important part of the mix, such as in the door-to-door sale of encyclopedias, beauty products, or brushes. With other types of products, such as chewing gum, razor blades, and breakfast cereals, advertising is the key ingredient in the promotion mix. Personal selling is likely to be the major element under the following conditions when:

1. Industrial goods, rather than consumer goods, are being sold.
2. When there is a small company involved—retailer, wholesaler, or manufacturer.
3. The market is concentrated.
4. A salesperson is needed to represent the goods or to fit them to the customer's needs, such as in the sale of building lots, insurance, or stocks and bonds.

Personal selling dominates
some types of selling
situations, for example,
selling automobiles.

Ewing Galloway

ADVERTISING   Advertising, on the other hand, is more likely to be the most important part of the promotion mix when:

1. Consumer, rather than industrial, goods are being sold.
2. The firm is trying to sell to a wide market.

Personal selling, advertising, and sales promotion are used together to accomplish the firm's objectives. While advertising is more visible to most consumers, personal selling is far more important than advertising in selling industrial goods and even considerably more important in most types of consumer sales. The typical large manufacturer of consumer goods spends from 8 to 15 percent of net sales on expenses for personal selling, while spending only about 1 to 3 percent of net sales for advertising expenditures. Producers of industrial products, on the other hand, spend less than 1 percent of sales for advertising, and approximately 10 to 25 percent of net sales for personal selling. There are wide fluctuations, even among producers of consumer products, however. The large firms producing toiletry products devote about 30 percent of sales to advertising, and makers of cosmetics, about 24 percent. Auto manufacturers, on the other hand, spend only about 0.5 percent of sales on advertising. Table 9-3 shows the amounts spent on advertising in a recent year by the country's 10 largest advertisers.

TABLE 9-3 America's 10
largest advertisers, 1976

Company	Amount (millions of dollars)
1. Procter & Gamble	$445.0
2. General Motors	287.0
3. General Foods	275.0
4. Sears, Roebuck	245.0
5. Warner-Lambert	199.0
6. Bristol-Myers	189.0
7. Ford Motor	162.0
8. American Home Products	158.0
9. Philip Morris	149.0
10. Mobil Corp.	146.5

Source: Reprinted with permission from the August 28, 1978, issue of *Advertising Age.*
Copyright 1978 by Crain Communications

MOST MONEY SPENT ON PERSONAL SELLING

It should be remembered that the promotion mix is really a skillful blending of the three techniques. Advertising supports personal selling, making sales people more effective. In fact, it is very difficult for salespeople calling on retail stores to get shelf space for their products unless the products have been heavily advertised so that the retailers are convinced that they will sell.

SALES JOBS

Personal selling is a unique and frequently misunderstood function in the business world. Most people think of a salesperson as either a retail sales clerk or a door-to-door solicitor. Actually, the bulk of the sales jobs in business do not fit either category. Today, more often than not, you'll hear the term "representative" for "salesperson." A manufacturer's representative is a more common title, for example, than manufacturer's salesperson. Sales jobs can be classified as order-getters, order-takers, and supportive sales staff. *Order-getting* is concerned with obtaining new orders for products, and *order-taking* consists of taking repeat orders. *Supporting salespersons* provide merchandising or technical expertise to customers or potential customers.

Rarely does a salesperson perform just one of the above functions; the job is normally a mix of the three. More time may be spent on one of the tasks, though all of them will probably be done. One study of manufacturing salespeople estimates the following breakdown of time spent: traveling and waiting—34 percent; reports, paper work, and attending sales meetings—20 percent; and service calls—5 percent. This leaves only 41 percent of the time available for face-to-face selling. As a result, the cost per salesperson's call can be very high. It ranges from about $50 a call for manufacturer's order-getters selling technical products to about $20 a call for wholesaler and retailer order-takers.

Most of the complaints from consumers about abuses in personal selling deal with the overaggressiveness of some salespeople and firms—particularly in door-to-door selling. As a result, the federal government and most states have passed laws requiring a cooling-off period for sales contracts obtained by door-to-door salespeople to give the consumer an opportunity to cancel. Another complaint is the indifference of retail store clerks, a natural outgrowth of the use of advertising to presell consumer products and the concept of self-service in retail stores.

ORDER-GETTERS All three functions are performed at each level of the distribution channel—manufacturing, wholesaling, and retailing. Order-getters for manufacturers require a high degree of skill since it is their job to locate new customers, convince them to buy the company's products, and help establish and build channel relationships with other manufacturers, wholesalers, and retailers who all may be new customers. If industrial goods are being sold, order-getters must be especially skillful since they must be able to show the customer how they can save money or make additional money. If industrial equipment is being purchased, the salesperson must have technical expertise. In selling other industrial goods, such as supplies, raw materials, and services, order-getters are important but may be required only for the initial contacts.

Order-getters for wholesalers work very closely with retailers in helping them move merchandise from the wholesaler's warehouse to the customer. As a result, these order-getters may become involved in the stocking, inventory control, advertising, store layout, and other operations of the retail store customers. Order-getters for retailers are responsible for selling durable goods and other shopping goods and for the sale of unsought goods, such as encyclopedias, some types of insurance, mutual funds, and new, expensive products. As a group, order-getters normally require a great deal of skill and aggressiveness and, as a result, are well paid. Many manufacturer's order-getters make more than $30,000 a year, with wholesaler's order-getters making slightly less, and retail order-getters the least. Incomes also depend to some extent on the particular industry.

Order-Takers Order-takers for manufacturers follow order-getters to see that adjustments and complaints are handled satisfactorily and that customers are kept informed of new product developments. These salespeople normally have a regular route with a relatively heavy travel schedule and make their calls at fixed times. Besides taking orders for the firm's established products, they occasionally sell new products being developed, help with sales promotion materials, and keep the accounts informed of changes in different aspects of the marketing mix.

Order-takers for wholesalers handle large numbers of items, frequently more than 100,000, and confine their activities primarily to order-taking. The wholesale order-taker keeps in close touch with his accounts to fill any needs that may develop. Since there is not as much emphasis on order-getting as is true for manufacturing order-takers, and since there is considerably less travel, the job is more relaxing but does not pay as well. At the retail level, order-takers are normally the store clerks we encounter at retail stores. Since most convenience goods do not require personal selling and most specialty goods are already presold, usually only shopping goods require aggressive personal selling. As a result, retail store

**personality profile:
JOHN W. HANLEY—
supersalesman for
Monsanto**

John Hanley spent 25 years at Proctor & Gamble, rising from soap salesman to executive vice president by putting in more days and hours than anyone else. In 1971, however, P&G's presidency went to the other executive vice president, Edward Harness, who had risen through the advertising ranks. Hanley lost out most probably on the basis of something other than promise, for his energetic style had given him the reputation of being somewhat brash and insensitive, and Proctor & Gamble did not want a shakeup.

Hanley did not have much time to nurture his disappointment. He was immediately besieged by job offers from other major corporations who appreciated P&G's excellent system for developing managerial talent. Early in the game, Proctor & Gamble gives its brightest and most capable people major responsibilities and turns them loose to demonstrate their managerial abilities. Along the way, they absorb the P&G team approach so that they are able to help each other develop more fully.

Monsanto Chemical's president had resigned suddenly in 1972, and the company was not only leaderless, but had no clear goals and no management development program. For an annual salary of over $400,000 and the understanding that he would have the freedom to be the boss and chief planning officer, Hanley became the first outsider to be Monsanto's president.

Although he had an undergraduate degree in metallurgical engineering from Penn State along with a Harvard M.B.A., Hanley had a lot to learn about the chemical industry from his subordinates. He credits Transcendental Meditation for keeping him collected during the first few hectic years, when he was not only studying petrochemical technology but beginning to restructure the company and steer Monsanto away from commodities to more profitable proprietary products.

Hanley brought to Monsanto many of the management concepts successfully used at P&G. These included delegating authority by pushing responsibility down to the lowest level and improving the work environment so that employees can develop most fully. Decision making has become more structured, and the entire firm is working to develop a team concept of management. In addition, Hanley has introduced an incentive program linking bonuses to individual performance, an idea he could never get P&G to buy.

order-takers frequently spend much of their time arranging and stocking shelves. These jobs require less skill and aggressiveness, so the pay is normally low.

THE LIFE OF A REP The problem of planning, organizing, directing, and controlling the sales operation is a big one. Selecting, training, compensating, and controlling the sales force is the job of sales management. Recruiting good representatives from community and four-year colleges has been increasingly difficult in recent years, despite the potentially high salaries. The unattractive image of a salesperson in our society plus the disruption in normal family life caused by traveling has made it difficult to recruit college graduates into sales except when other opportunities are not available. However, many firms have increased their hiring considerably when they have been able to demonstrate to graduates the excellent career paths available in management for successful salespeople.

Salespeople are paid in one of three ways: straight salary, commission, or a combination of the two. A straight salary offers little incentive and does not relate sales to income. The commission arrangement, on the other hand, encourages the salesperson to ignore the nonselling functions and to be overly aggressive in selling. As a result, a combination of the two is the arrangement that is most frequently used. The wage plan used, whatever it may be, should contain adequate control methods over the sales force, provide reasonable incentive with adequate security for the salesperson, maintain flexibility in meeting sales goals, and be reasonably simple and economical to administer.

TYPES OF ADVERTISING It was mentioned earlier that advertising is any paid form of nonpersonal presentation of ideas, products, or services. Advertising can be divided into product and institution advertising, and each of these can be further divided.

Product advertising consists of informing or stimulating potential customer interest in a firm's products and services. This kind of advertising can be one of three types—primary advertising, competitive advertising, or reminder advertising—depending on the stage of the product life cycle.

Primary advertising attempts to build primary demand for the product category rather than for a specific brand. Product categories would be trash compactors, central air conditioners, diesel-powered cars, and CB radios. First you sell the product category, then you sell your particular brand of the product or service. Trade associations, such as the California Fruit Growers, frequently engage in primary advertising to build demand for their product category.

Competitive advertising tries to convince customers to buy your firm's product rather than a competitor's. It stimulates selective demand. In the market growth stage, and particularly in the market maturity stage of the life cycle, this advertising is useful. Most advertising is of this kind. In recent years naming competitors in advertising has become permissible, a practice in which comparisons of price and quality are compared.

One result has been some nasty charges and lawsuits by firms that have considered the tests or comparisons unfair. Usually, a firm with a smaller share of the market advertises that it is superior to the leading brand in some way. One study indicated that the comparative ads are more confusing and less believable to consumers than other forms of advertising. Obviously some firms, however, feel that it gives them a competitive advantage over the bigger rival.

Reminder advertising is common in the market maturity stage or in the sales decline stage, when a product has achieved a favorable status. Kleenex, Coca-Cola, and Wrigley's Spearmint ads are cast in this mold.

Institutional advertising tries to build prestige or status for a firm or an industry. It does this through seeking to inform the public of services offered, creating a favorable image for the firm or industry, or by promoting some public service, such as the Community Chest or a hospital building program.

THE ADVERTISING CAMPAIGN

Before dollars are committed to advertising, a firm will develop very specific goals. The following is a list of some of the advertising goals that are commonly set by firms for their advertising campaigns.

The ever-versatile VW as advertising medium—the Beetleboard.

Beetleboards of America

1. Support for the personal-selling effort.
2. Introducing a new market.
3. Entering a new market.
4. Increasing the sale of a product.
5. Increasing industry sales.
6. Increasing market share of a product.
7. Reaching people that the salesperson cannot reach.
8. Improving dealer relations.
9. Selling the company brand image.
10. Counteracting prejudice or substitution.

Once a firm has decided on its objectives for a promotional campaign, it decides on a central theme and develops the appeals that it will use, based on the buying motives of its potential market. Management then decides how it wants to allocate its efforts among the three elements of the promotion mix—personal selling, advertising, and sales promotions. In estimating the amount to be spent on advertising, firms use a variety of bases. Some of the more common include: objectives to be accomplished, percentage of sales, amount per unit, and amount spent by competitors.

In developing an advertising campaign, a large firm will call on its advertising manager or someone with a similar title. The manager's task is to plan the campaign within the guidelines already established by top management for the overall marketing mix and the specific promotion mix. The advertising department may plan the campaign, develop the ideas, choose the media to be used, and evaluate the results. This is particularly true among large retailers, whose advertising departments may handle all of the firm's advertising needs.

ADVERTISING AGENCIES Among large manufacturers it is more common for the advertising department of the firm to handle all the firm's direct-mail advertising, dealer displays, and other aspects of its sales promotion. In these companies the advertising department usually acts as a middleman between the firm and an advertising agency for the development of most national advertising campaigns. An *advertising agency* is an independent business that provides specialized advertising and marketing services to other businesses. Since these agencies have considerable technical skills and an objective viewpoint of the client firm, they are an important part of national advertising campaigns.

The arrangements for sharing the work load between the advertising department in a company and an advertising agency vary considerably. Advertising agencies, however, normally are responsible for planning and coordinating the advertising theme, developing the actual advertisements, choosing the advertising medium, and evaluating the results. Agencies are actually paid by the advertising medium that runs the advertisement; the medium bills the firm at its regular rates, less approximately 15 percent commission for the agency. The agency, then, is a middleman, standing between the advertiser and the medium in which the advertising is placed.

Most media charge considerably more for national than for local advertising. The advertising agencies earn their commissions only on national advertising, so that local advertisers, such as retail stores, are discouraged from using advertising agencies, except for minimal services. If advertising agencies are used for local advertising, they are paid a fee by the retail stores for the services they have provided. Many national advertisers, such as General Electric, pass on advertising allowances to retailers, who can buy more advertising space for their money than can national advertisers. The retailer, who is handling the national brand, runs the advertising in a local medium and then is reimbursed for part of the expense by the national manufacturer, such as General Electric. Another method of bypassing the higher national rates is when the national advertiser underwrites the local retailer's ads by matching the advertising funds spent by the retailer for local ads. This is called *cooperative advertising*. In recent years, there has been a trend toward more cooperative advertising. General Motors, for example, has used it heavily in helping its car dealers regain the auto parts business which has been steadily switching to independent distributors.

Advertising agencies represent a powerful force in advertising in this country. They place approximately $15 billion in advertising annually and create and coordinate almost all national advertising. Advertising is a highly competitive business, and firms will frequently change agencies if an advertising campaign is not successful. It is far easier to blame an outside agency than to look closer to home at the total marketing mix put together by the company's top management.

CHOOSING THE MEDIA

In choosing the type of media for an advertising campaign, a number of factors must be considered. First, the firm must decide the type of media it wants—radio, television, newspapers, magazines. Then it must select within each type of media, the classification of media that will effectively convey its message. For example, if it chooses magazines and wants to reach men primarily, it must decide whether or not it wants magazines that emphasize sex, such as *Playboy* and *Oui*, general news magazines, such as *Time* and *Newsweek*, or sports magazines, such as *Field and Stream* and *Sports Illustrated*. Finally, the company must choose the specific medium such as *Reader's Digest*, radio station WLBK, or the *Los Angeles Times*.

In choosing the media, the firm must consider at least the following:

1. Cost of the media.
2. Circulation of the media.
3. Cooperation and promotional aids offered by the media.
4. Requirements of the message.
5. Timing of the advertisement.

TABLE 9-4 Amount of
advertising revenue, 1977
(in millions of dollars)

Media	Percent of Total Revenue	Advertising Revenue
Newspaper	29.2	$1.1
Television	20.1	7.5
Direct Mail	14.8	5.3
Radio	7.1	2.5
Magazine	5.7	2.0
Other	14.8	8.2
Total	100.0	$36.6

Source: Reprinted with permission from the December 12, 1977, issue of *Advertising Age*. Copyright 1977 by Crain Communications.

About $37 billion was spent for advertising in all media in 1977. Table 9-4 shows how this money was divided among the various types of media. As you can see, the most dollars were spent on newspapers. Television, direct mail, and miscellaneous forms ranked next, with radio, business papers, and outdoor advertising trailing. Of the total amount spent on advertising, approximately 60 percent is spent for national advertising and for local coverage. Some media, such as newspapers, rely heavily on local advertising for most of their revenue. Television, on the other hand, gets most of its money from national advertising. The following are the desirable features of each of the major media.

1. *Newspapers.* Flexible, timely, offer market information and promotional assistance, low circulation costs, especially helpful for retailers with a number of items to advertise.
2. *Television.* Versatile, appeals to both sight and sound, great for product demonstrations, flexibility of location and time.
3. *Direct mail.* Personal and selective, flexibility of approach.
4. *Radio.* Versatile, appeals to the ear, flexibility of location and time, reaches potential consumers when they are unable to read or watch television.
5. *Magazines.* Excellent for color pictures, low cost per reader, selective audience, long life of magazine.
6. *Outdoor.* Flexible, low cost, fine for reminder advertising, good use of color, flexibility of geographic coverage.

EVALUATING AND CRITICIZING AN ADVERTISING PROGRAM

It is extremely difficult to evaluate the effectiveness of a particular advertising campaign since the other aspects of the marketing mix have a strong bearing on the results as well. Except for mail-order advertising, it is difficult to attribute a given unit of sales to any specific advertisement or campaign. Also, of course, many advertisements do not attempt to increase present sales, but try to build future sales or goodwill for the firm.

Advertising is increasingly being attacked for its abuses and its distortions of the value structure in this country. The following appear to be the major criticisms directed against advertising.

1. *It is too costly.* In looking at the tremendous amounts spent on advertising, critics point out that firms could lower their prices if they did not spend so much on advertising. However, if the campaign has been effective, it should stimulate sales, which should result in a lower cost of production which normally accompanies an increase in volume. Critics frequently retort, however, that the extra profit from increased sales is kept by the firms, not returned to consumers through lower prices.

2. *It is purely competitive.* It is argued that while advertising might cause consumers to switch from Ford to General Motors, it does not enlarge the market for autos. As a result, advertising really represents an extra cost to producers that prevents them from lowering prices. The assumption is made that advertising does not increase total industry sales, but merely redistributes the income among companies.

3. *It makes people want things they cannot afford.* As was mentioned earlier in the discussion of consumerism, there are many who feel that advertising distorts people's values. That is, people are manipulated to want more material things and to become more materially minded than they would otherwise be. Through advertising people's demands for consumer goods go beyond their present income or that in the immediate future.

4. *It is misleading.* Much of the criticism centers around the charge that most advertising is either misleading at best or false at worst.

5. *It is wasted.* Advertising has been criticized as a waste of company resources because most people are so hardened to it that they ignore the message. There is some support for the point that advertising is becoming less effective for this reason.

6. *It is offensive.* The point is made that most advertising offends because it is geared to third or fourth grade level. While it is true that much mass advertising is simply written, it is also true that mass selling appeal must be simple and basic to be effective for large numbers of people. However, an advertiser should show some respect for the audience no matter how much simplicity is called for in the message.

SUMMARY

A firm will not be successful until it finds the right mix of product, place, price and promotion. Product includes both consumer goods and industrial goods. It also implies more than just the physical product, so that it includes the packaging and container in which the product comes. Firms that understand the stage of the life cycle that their products are in can move successfully to maximize the profit at any given stage through a variety of means.

The place in the marketing mix refers to the channel of distribution. In the channel of distribution for consumer goods and many industrial goods are middlemen, such as retailers, wholesalers, or brokers.

Pricing of products is an inexact procedure. The following factors must be considered in setting a price: consumer demand, importance of nonprice competition, costs, stage of product's life cycle, and government controls. Most firms, in setting a price, follow one of two strategies: pricing at a low price to get a larger share of the market (called market penetration pricing) or pricing at a high price to get as much profit quickly as they can (called skimming-the-cream pricing).

Promotion encompasses all of the personal selling, advertising, and sales promotion for a product or service. Salesmen are either order-getters or order-takers and work for manufacturers or for wholesalers and retailers. Most advertising is either product advertising or institutional advertising, depending on its purpose.

SUMMARY OF KEY TERMS

Advertising Any paid form of nonpersonal presentation of ideas, goods, or services by an identified sponsor.

Advertising Agency An independent business which provides specialized advertising and marketing services to other businesses.

Brand A name, term, symbol, or design distinguishing the products of a seller from those of competitors.

Channel of Distribution The route followed by a product as it moves from producer to consumer.

Competitive Advertising Advertising that convinces customers to buy a firm's product rather than that of a competitor.

Consumer Goods Those goods which are sold directly to the ultimate consumers.

Convenience Goods Staples of low unit value, purchased frequently and in small quantities.

Elastic Demand Demand that changes as the result of a change in price for a given product.

Industrial Goods Those goods sold for business use or for additional processing before being sold to the ultimate consumer.

Inelastic Demand Demand that does not change as the result of a change in price for the product.

Institutional Advertising Advertising that tries to build prestige or status for a firm or an industry.

Market Penetration Pricing Strategy implying that the producer will sell the product at a relatively low price to build quickly a wide market for the product.

Markup Pricing products at cost plus a fixed percentage.

Middleman An independent business firm that stands between the producer and the ultimate consumer or industrial user.

National Brand A brand owned by a manufacturer.

Personal Selling A direct face-to-face relationship between the seller and potential customer.

Planned Obsolescence The deliberate designing of a product so that it will not be usable after a short period of time.

Primary Advertising Advertising that builds primary demand for a product category, rather than a specific brand.

Private Brand A brand owned by a middleman.

Product Whatever satisfies customers whether it has tangible or intangible characteristics or some combination of both.

Product Advertising Informing or stimulating potential customers about a firm's products and services.

Product Life Cycle A cyclical pattern of sales and profit margins for a product.

Promotion All of the personal selling, advertising, sales promotion, and other tools a company uses to persuade a prospective customer to buy a product or service.

Reminder Advertising Advertising that reminds customers that they still like an established product.

Sales Promotion The promotional activities necessary to supplement personal selling and advertising.

Shopping Goods Merchandise whose price, fashion, and quality are important enough to require comparison shopping.

Skimming Pricing Strategy implying that the producer will sell the product for as high a price as he can get to maximize his total revenue.

Specialty Goods Merchandise of a distinctive quality in which price is not an important consideration.

REVIEW QUESTIONS

1. Differentiate convenience, shopping, and specialty consumer products.
2. What are the main differences in marketing consumer and industrial products?
3. Identify the product life cycle and relate it to profitability rates and to product obsolescence.
4. Name the major channels of distribution used in marketing consumer products and indicate the role of middlemen in each channel.
5. Name and discuss five recent trends in retailing.
6. Identify the major factors that must be considered in determining prices of products.
7. Differentiate between elastic and inelastic demand.
8. Contrast and compare advertising, personal selling, and sales promotion as to what is included in each.
9. Contrast and compare the objectives of advertising with the major criticisms of it.
10. What are the major advantages of using each of the media from the standpoint of the advertiser?

DISCUSSION QUESTIONS

1. In weighing the advantages and disadvantages of advertising for society, do you believe that the costs outweigh the benefits to society? Why?
2. Do you believe that makers of consumer goods deliberately try to shorten the useful life of their products? Support your position with examples.
3. Would the final prices of most consumer goods be less if some or all of the middlemen were eliminated from the channel of distribution?
4. What stage of the product life cycle do you believe that the following types of products are in: eight-cylinder family autos? telephones? frozen yogurt? tennis rackets? polyester clothes?
5. If you found two brands of a canned food product, one a national brand and one a private brand of a retailer, with a seven cents a can difference in price favoring the private brand, which brand would you buy? What principles should a consumer follow in choosing between a national and a private brand of anything?

CASES FOR DECISION MAKING

FEWER NEW PRODUCTS?

In the mid-1960s, companies acquired new product lines or entire new companies and put their emphasis on sales rather than profits. By emphasizing sales, they tended to have full lines of products to meet all tastes. Soaring inflation, government controls, environmental pressures, and shortages of raw materials in the 1970s are changing things. Most companies are now concentrating on profits, not on sales. As a result, unsuccessful products are being dropped and profitable products are being promoted. These changes imply that: (1) products will become more functional and have fewer frills, reflecting the narrowing of product lines and conservation of raw materials; (2) product strategies will become more flexible and marketing timetables will be speeded up as supplies and prices of raw materials force a shorter-run perspective; (3) new product development will suffer.[2]

1. Do you think the interests of the American consumer are better served if there are fewer choices of products? Will fewer products mean cheaper products? Explain your answers.
2. If this trend goes on, will it affect the product life cycles of current products? Why or why not?
3. Do you think national manufacturers will be as willing to use part of their production facilities to produce private brands for sale to other manufacturers or middlemen as they have in the past?

DR. PEPPER FINDS A NICHE

The Dr. Pepper Company, founded in 1885, had sales of $28 million and net income of $2.8 million in 1966. By 1973, its sales had topped $100 million,

and net income hovered around $10 million. Meanwhile, the price of its stock rose rapidly, reflecting the swelling sales and profits. It has become one of the glamour or growth stocks in the industry. Chiefly responsible for the growth is President Woodrow Wilson Clements, who has run the company since 1967. On assuming control he quickly decided to keep the same controversial taste formula for the product and to maintain the same price. However, he felt that the promotion and channel of distribution needed changes. He switched the advertising account to Young & Rubicam, which developed the slogan "America's Most Misunderstood Soft Drink." This has become the company's catchword in all its advertising. Besides the fact that it was true, it appealed mainly to young people—who like to think they are misunderstood. They also consume the most soft drinks. Next, he strengthened the bottler network by persuading smaller bottlers to sell their franchises to stronger ones. He also recruited new bottlers. Then he persuaded Coke and Pepsi bottlers to take on Dr. Pepper as well. Since it is officially not a cola, the bottlers could handle Dr. Pepper without violating their franchise agreement with Coca-Cola or Pepsi Cola. The results of both moves have been spectacular.[3]

1. Do the makers of Dr. Pepper have to be concerned with a falling off in sales and profits as the product life cycle reaches the saturation stage?
2. Which of the four Ps do you feel is most important for success in the sale of soft drinks?
3. Do you think the company should consider changing the taste formula for the product since it's achieving greater recognition? Why or why not?

2. "The Squeeze on Product Mix," *Business Week*, January 5, 1974, pp. 50–55.

3. "What Happened When Dr. Pepper Began Thinking Big," *Fortune*, December 1973, pp. 120–128.

PENNEY'S GAMBLES ON FASHION

J. C. Penney Co. is taking a major gamble as it seeks to change its image. For 75 years, Penney's has been identified as a retailer to small-town America, selling private-label softgoods to very price-conscious customers in bargain-basement surroundings. Penney's is trying a complete break from its former image. It wants to be a chain of moderately priced department stores, emphasizing higher-priced fashion in hardgoods, housewares, and especially in somen's apparel. Although Penney's has moved into the big shopping centers with large, attractive stores, it still has the old image and much of the old merchandising and pricing strategy as in previous years. As a result, in 1976, Penney's slid to the third spot in retailing sales, behind Sears and K-Mart.

In 1977 Penney's began to change its image, starting with 24 stores in five major metropolitan areas. It opened what it called its "fashion pilot projects," significantly changing the stores' layouts, merchandise mix, buying and pricing structure, advertising, and personnel. The project was carried to 27 additional cities in 1978 and the entire chain is to be converted by the end of 1979.

1. How difficult do you believe it will be for Penney's to change its image?
2. What aspects of the marketing mix will have to be changed if Penney's is to be successful?
3. What is your impression of Penney's success in their new strategy in your area?

RELATED READINGS

"How A&P Got Creamed." *Fortune*, January 1973, pp. 103–114.

An interesting analysis of A&P's efforts to recapture its former share of supermarket sales. It shows the kinds of actions that were necessary for an old firm to regain its position. By cutting prices, closing unprofitable stores, and heavy advertising, A&P did achieve a significant gain in sales.

Ogilvy, David. *Confessions of an Advertising Man.* New York: Ballantine Books, 1973.

Highly readable insider's look at people in the advertising industry. An excellent summation of the advertising process as practiced by large advertising agencies.

"Pricing Strategy in an Inflation Economy." *Business Week*, April 6, 1974, pp. 43–49.

An informative survey of how firms are pricing to compete in an inflationary economy. Emphasis is on fast and flexible pricing.

"Showing Ad Agencies How to Grow." *Business Week*, June 1, 1974, pp. 50–56.

A look at the advertising agency industry and the largest agency, Young and Rubicam, which now has the greatest volume of billings among all agencies.

"The Squeeze on Product Mix." *Business Week*, January 5, 1974, pp. 50–53.

A stimulating article on the changes in the marketing mix caused by the energy crisis, shortages, and price troubles.

Webster, Frederick E., Jr. *Social Aspects of Marketing.* Englewood Cliffs, N.J.: Prentice-Hall, 1974.

A glance into the dynamic world of marketing as influenced by changing social forces. Examines the marketing mix and how it has been influenced by consumerism, environmentalism, and increasing consumption of services from not-for-profit organizations.

chapter 10

DEVELOPING, PRODUCING, AND DISTRIBUTING PRODUCTS

OBJECTIVES

When you have finished reading and studying this chapter, you should be able to:

1. Identify and explain the steps in product development and explain how firms organize new product development.

2. Distinguish between production and productivity, and describe the characteristics of mass production.

3. Identify the various areas of materials management and relate them to the production process.

4. Identify the parts of the physical distribution process, including the chief characteristics of carriers used in moving products.

CHAPTER PREVIEW

The development of new products in response to the demand of consumers and efficient production and distribution of these products to consumers is the lifeblood of a corporation. The success of a single new product or line of products can make a company's reputation. Xerox's stock was selling for $5 a share before it introduced its first copier. Within five years, the stock increased in price to $250 a share. More recently, IBM introduced a new family of 303X computers. These computers have dramatically changed the price and performance ratios for all firms who make computers.

In this chapter, you will look at the steps in developing new products, including the organizational plans used by firms in the development process. You will also look at the production process and at some of the ways in which firms attempt to increase productivity. You will also look at the relatively unknown, but highly important, area of materials management as it relates to the production function. Finally, you will look at the types of carriers used by producers to get their products into the hands of consumers.

"It's an interesting idea, Ben, but do you really
think the country's ready for it?"

10

DEVELOPING, PRODUCING, AND DISTRIBUTING PRODUCTS

Developing, producing, and distributing products are all closely intertwined and if a new product is to be a success all three must be effectively coordinated. This includes the technical activities of product research, design, and engineering. *Product development* is the process of creating a new product from an idea, and it involves much more than just producing a product.

PRODUCT DEVELOPMENT

In the development of most new products, there is a step-by-step procedure that is followed by most companies. These include: exploration, screening, business analysis, development, testing, and commercialization. (See Figure 10-1.)

STEPS IN PRODUCT DEVELOPMENT

Exploration includes the gathering of ideas for new products. These may come from competitor's products, consumers, scientists, or from sales or marketing people in the company. Monsanto, for example, was in the process of developing a synthetic ribbon. In the process, someone suggested developing a substitute for grass. After the laughter had died down, scientists in the company went to work on the idea. The result was Astroturf, the first synthetic grass, now commonly used on athletic fields.

Screening is the step in which the company reduces the number of ideas to those that seem to have the strongest possibilities. In this stage, ideas may be eliminated because they lack profit potential, involve too much risk, or appear to

FIGURE 10-1 New product development sequence

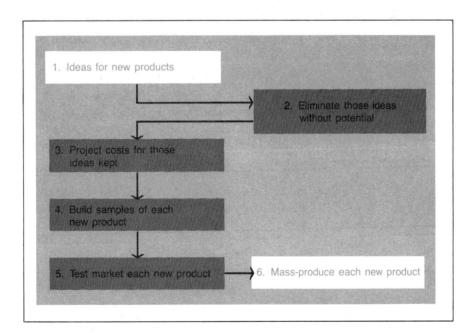

have little consumer interest. Usually, the surviving ideas are ranked according to their potential. Some form of evaluation matrix or chart is used to weigh each of the factors that makes a difference in a product's success.

Business Analysis zeroes in on the expected costs and revenues from each of the products. An estimate is made of the potential market for each product and the estimated sales. The costs of developing, producing, and marketing the product are carefully weighed. Only those products that appear to have good profit potential are retained for the next stage. Of course, business analysis goes on at each stage of a product's development. However, this is the first stage in which formal estimates are made of expected revenues and costs.

Development involves the actual designing and manufacturing of a product or products. This is the first stage in which a large amount of money is spent. If the product is fairly sophisticated, a new watch, truck, or camera, for example, this can be very expensive. For products such as soap, toilet tissue, candy, or soft drink, the investment is not as large. The main objective of this stage is to find out if the product idea is technically possible and attractive to consumers. As a result, packaging is also included in the product development stage.

Testing is the stage in which the product is tested under competitive market conditions. As was spelled out in Chapter 7, this is the stage in which most products drop out. If the product is seen as an imitation, it is likely to be dropped from the line.

Commercialization occurs when the company decides to produce the product on a large scale. If it decides to mass produce the item, the firm may have to invest large sums of money. Kodak, for example, invested $300 million before it ever sold one of its instant cameras. A firm has to invest in new plant and equipment, labor, and all the other factors involved in the process.

ORGANIZING FOR PRODUCT DEVELOPMENT

Most large companies know that new product development is essential for continued growth. In addition, existing products must be modified and improved. All of these things require an organization to achieve these objectives. Whatever pattern is chosen, management must be able to implement creativity, specialization, and coordination. To achieve this, there are four commonly used organizational plans.

The most widely used plan of organization for new-product planning and development is the *product-planning committee*. Usually, it includes representatives from marketing, production, engineering, research, finance, and top management. In most companies, this is an advisory committee to a product manager or a new-product department. In other companies, this committee is responsible for developing the new product through the test-market stage.

The *new-product department* is a small department that usually has responsibility for new product development through the test-marketing stage. This type of structure is an attempt to have persons working full-time on new product development. The head of the department normally reports directly to the president or sometimes to the director of marketing.

The *product manager* is a person responsible for a product or a family of products. Usually his responsibility is not limited to new products. The product manager is sometimes called a brand manager or a merchandise manager and reports to the director of marketing. In some companies, the product manager is responsible only for selling and sales-promotional work for a particular product. Usually, however, the product manager is responsible for the complete marketing program for a product or a group of products. Procter & Gamble and Johnson & Johnson have used the product manager in this way for over 50 years.

A *venture team* is a small group of people selected from several departments with responsibility for managing a product innovation from idea to commercialization. It usually contains representatives from marketing, finance, production, and engineering. The group's goal is to develop a new product that will enter a new market and make a profit. Once the goal is reached, the group is disbanded. If it is not possible to achieve commercial success, the group is also disbanded. When the product has successfully entered the market, it is turned over to other operating executives or even to a new subsidiary company.

PRODUCING THE PRODUCT

Production is the process whereby products and services are produced. Sometimes the term is also used to refer only to the process of converting raw materials into useful products.

Product development can be simple or complex, depending on the product. Westinghouse has designed and built several models of its people mover.

Westinghouse Electric Corp.

Productivity, on the other hand, indicates the efficiency with which products and services are being produced. Most often it is measured by the amount of output that results from a given amount of input (one product per worker per hour, for example). It deals with the efficiency with which a firm uses its factors of production in turning out products and services.

One of the factors contributing to inflation in the 1970s was the small increase in productivity rates each year while wages and salaries rose more rapidly. This, coupled with higher costs for materials and parts, forced prices even higher and added to the inflation problem.

CHARACTERISTICS OF MASS PRODUCTION

American business has tried to increase productivity in the manufacturing of products through mass production. *Mass production* is the large-scale manufacturing of goods using mechanization, specialization of labor, standardization, and automation.

Mechanization   Mechanization is the use of machines to do as much work as possible. As you can see from Figure 10-2, most major industries have a large investment in machines and equipment. The average capital invested per employee in manufacturing is about $30,000. For each employee working strictly in the production process, it is close to $40,000. In other words, it takes about $40,000 invested in machinery and equipment to create one production job in manufacturing.

Throughout its history American business has generally invested large amounts of capital. However, as a nation, we have not invested as high a proportion of our resources in new plants and equipment as have many other countries. These nations have been investing more and consuming less of their output, (GNP) than has the United States. In the long run, this should result in more efficiency or productivity for the firms in these countries, enabling them to sell their products in world markets at lower prices than American firms. This will bring greater sales, more profits, and more jobs to these companies, at the expense of their American competitors.

You can see this in Figure 10-3 which compares annual increases in productivity in the United States and other advanced industrial countries. Between 1966 and 1975, America had smaller increases in output per employee in manufacturing than some other countries. This was caused partly by the fact that during this period, the United States invested only 14.8 percent of its GNP annually in new plant and equipment but during the same period, Japan invested 28.8 percent annually, West Germany 21.8 percent, and France 19.5 percent. The investment in new plant and equipment is a major factor in any increase in productivity. A related problem has been the reduced expenditure for research and development (R&D) of new products by the federal government and about the same level of spending for R&D by private firms. During the same period, all other advanced industrial countries greatly increased their spending on R&D. This

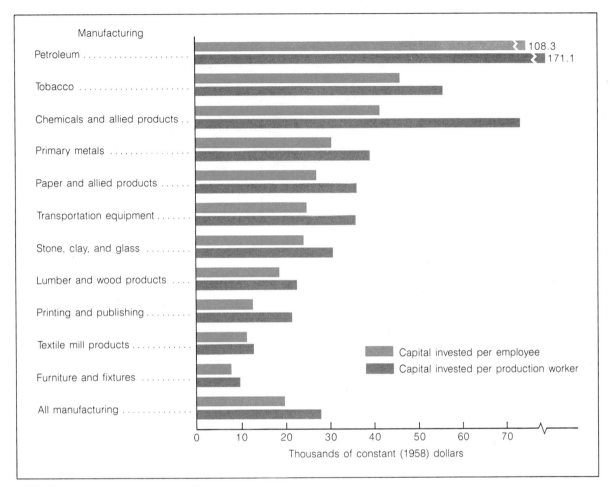

FIGURE 10-2 Capital invested per employee, 1975. Source: *Road Maps of Industry,* No. 1799, The Conference Board

fact was evidenced in the number of patents obtained by foreign inventors in the United States. They more than doubled their American patents from the 1960s to the 1970s.

Specialization of Labor *Specialization of labor* implies that the production process is organized so that each job requires the performance of only a few tasks. This should lower costs in manufacturing. Workers with fewer skills are needed and they can be paid less than skilled craftsmen. Also, less training time is required so workers can help with production more quickly. Greater use of machines is possible. For many industries there does not seem to be a more efficient alternative to the assembly-line. However, today's firms realize that if they

FIGURE 10-3 Average output per employee in manufacturing, 1966–1975

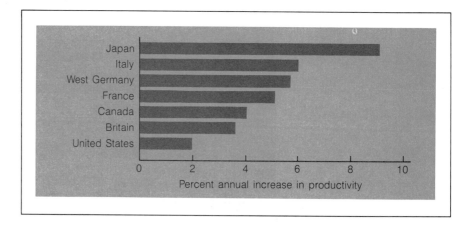

are to achieve their objectives, their employees' jobs must be as interesting and challenging as possible within the limits of the production process.

During the first 50 years of mass production in this country, the emphasis has been on a narrow specialization of labor. Today in many industries this concept is being questioned. Terms such as "blue-collar blues," "job enrichment," "job enlargement," "job rotation," and "democratization of the work place" have come into the business vocabulary. It has become painfully obvious to many people that extreme specialization of labor leads to job boredom and loss of productivity in some cases.

Loss of productivity can be seen in some plants through higher absenteeism, tardyism, and worker turnover. This has been particularly noticeable in assembly-line operations, such as in the auto industry. In the textile industry, the turnover rate for production labor is about 70 percent a year, while for some major industrial companies, it is almost 100 percent annually. In addition to an unstable labor corps, there have been problems with excess scrappage and increasing numbers of unacceptable products.

Many firms are experimenting with ways of making production jobs more interesting and challenging to the worker. Some firms are enlarging their duties or rotating them on specialized tasks. Others are grouping workers into small teams, each of which decides how to get its work done. Still others are shortening the work week.

An example is the so-called "new philosophy" of the Eaton Corp. where blue-collar workers are treated like white-collar workers. Eaton, a diversified manufacturer with sales of about $2 billion a year, pays blue-collar workers weekly salaries instead of hourly wages. The firm also permits them to participate in the corporate pension program and pays for sick absences. Rather than trying to enrich the job or give workers more voice in decisions affecting them, the company chose to

Mass production methods and specialization in labor characterize the work environment in today's large factories.

General Electric/Frigidaire

create an enriched environment for the workers. Output, turnover, and absenteeism have improved with the new system.

Standardization   *Standardization* is the development of uniform methods of operation within a plant. These might include both uniformity of processes or methods and a uniform pattern for operation of machines or equipment. Standardization reduces costs through greater use of machines and through savings in purchasing raw materials, parts, supplies, and equipment.

Through standardization of parts, for example, Ford Motor Company is able to use the same engine and many other parts for its different models of Pinto and Mustang. This results in a lower price per car whether the items are purchased or made by the company. By standardizing purchase orders from all departments, a company reduces the number of workers involved in purchasing. It also should save money through lower shipping fees, volume buying, and better internal control of the process.

One of the major issues concerning American standardization in production is the coming conversion to the metric system, as authorized by Congress in 1975. Most American products are measured in the old English system of weights and

business profile: SMALL IS BETTER — WELL, AT LEAST IT'S MORE EFFICIENT!

The U.S. auto industry is in the midst of the most drastic peacetime changeover in its 80-year history. Under strict government regulations covering safety, emissions control, and fuel economy, the four automakers will have to revamp their products completely not once, but twice, by 1985. By then the big cars that Americans have cherished and demanded for more than 25 years will be replaced by models that are smaller, lighter, and more efficient. They are also likely to be less comfortable and less powerful.

The task will be costly and the outcome uncertain. Capital investment required for the changeover is enormous, probably upward of $50 billion. And this investment must be made with no sure knowledge of how American consumers will accept the change or of whether they will pay the higher prices levied on cars to turn a profit on that huge investment. After all, Detroit has never known how to make money on small cars and has always equated *small* with *cheap*. Consumers who have no alternative may buy, but unless the new cars can be made to appeal to them, sales may not be brisk.

The immediate task of the automakers is to "downsize" their cars to meet federal mileage standards while maintaining market identities for their traditional product lines. Exterior size and weight have already been trimmed, partly through the use of more aluminum and plastics. But these changes in body style and construction were the easy first step.

The second major area of change will be radical engineering redesign of the internal combustion engine. The engines of the future will have to burn more efficiently and completely, deliver more power into vehicle motion rather than overcoming road and air friction, and prevent the emission of pollutants. At the same time they will have to meete the 27.5-mile-per gallon average mandated for all automakers by 1985.

All of the automakers' product development and production skills will be needed to meet these technical challenges. At the same time they will have to change consumer tastes so as to compete with foreign automakers who have until now virtually monopolized the small-car market.

measures, using the pound, the inch, and the pint. All the rest of the industrial world is using or converting to the metric system, using the gram, the centimeter, and the liter. This change will greatly affect manufacturers and consumers and because of its importance, a separate appendix is devoted to it. See Appendix C, "Metrics—Background and Applications for Industry."

Automation   *Automation* implies that machines operate or regulate other machines. It is really an extension of mechanization, where men are replaced by machines. Automation in manufacturing normally includes integrated materials' handling, automatic control systems, and the use of computers. Integrated materials' handling permits raw materials and/or parts to be moved from storage to the assembly line without human handling.

Automatic control systems indicate that the operation of the machines is predetermined and automatically controlled by a computer. A computer is a machine that can perform rapid calculation and make choices from predetermined instructions. For example, a computer might control the adjustment of a carburetor on a car, using computer-driven screwdrivers and wrenches.

Computers have been used extensively in business since 1960. Their use in production, however, was not widespread until the coming of the minicomputer in the early 1970s. Since then, small, low-cost minicomputers have been introduced in many plants. Of the approximate 130,000 minicomputers delivered in 1978, about 40,000 are used in manufacturing. Minicomputers are performing, sometimes in teams, repetitive, specialized jobs. These might include running a single machine tool, keeping tabs on the contents of a warehouse, or testing anything from carburetors to cigarettes. In Polaroid's new operation to make color film, 90 percent of the operations are controlled by minicomputers. The fastest growing use of the minicomputers is in the management of materials, production requirements, and engineering services.

The continued use of mechanization and automation has led to fears that unemployment will increase. However, in the past 10 or 15 years automation has probably increased rather than decreased the number of jobs. Automation does cause some types of jobs to be eliminated but it creates others. This is, of course, a hardship for the worker who is being replaced, as new jobs tend to be more technical and require a higher level of training and education. Business has made efforts to help workers displaced by automation. These include retraining programs, early pensioning of older workers, and extended layoff pay.

A point to remember, though, is that to remain strong in a competitive economy, a company must make use of the latest technology for mechanization and automation. If it does not, its competitors who do will gain an advantage. This will result in more sales and jobs for the rival firms. Even if all American businesses agreed to a technological standstill, their foreign competitors would continue to adopt the latest techniques of production. In that case, sales and jobs would flow overseas to the more efficient firms.

CONTROLLING PRODUCTION

Throughout the production process, a series of controls are necessary. These include control of the production process, of the end products, and of the costs of production. Procedural control is the process of ensuring that production operations are carried out according to schedule. Quality control, on the other hand, includes the establishment of quality standards and the inspections process used in achieving the standards. Cost control includes the determination of what a product should cost to make a comparison with the actual production costs.

FACILITIES FOR PRODUCTION

When a firm decides to produce and market a product, it may take one of three strategies. It may buy a firm which already produces the product, make the product using another firm's technology (called licensing), or develop and produce its own product. Philip Morris could have entered the beer business by producing its own product but instead it chose to buy Miller Brewing Company. Every year hundreds of companies enter new markets this way. The second strategy is used more commonly in international marketing but is also used in marketing in this country. Here a firm agrees to pay a royalty or fee to another firm for the use of its technology to produce a product. A common example is the use of the Ex-Cello Corporation's design for milk containers. Many dairies use the cardboard container with the familiar pouring spout. Since Ex-Cello has a patent on the process, other dairies have to pay to use the process. The third strategy, making the product under one's own patents, is the one that most of us think of. In order to do this, or to make a licensed product, a firm has to use an existing plant or build another plant to make the product. Some times, in fact, products are produced because a firm has unused production capacity and wants to make related products in order to fully utilize the plant. Usually, however, it is necessary to build a new plant.

CHOOSING A PLANT SITE

In choosing a plant location, several factors must be considered. They include: nearness to markets, availability of adequate labor supply, adequate transportation facilities, local and state incentives, nearness to raw materials, availability and cost of utilities, availability of suitable land, and the facilities and attitude of the community. In addition, other newer forces are at work. According to one plant location consultant,

> Transportation, labor, and taxes are still traditional factors in relocating, but the list has been lengthened to include internationalism, foreign competition, changing attitudes toward population expansion, energy shortages, government regulations, the new employment, and a new indifference toward mobility by labor.[1]

In considering all of the above factors, industry as a whole has been moving to the South and West and away from the Northeast as shown in Figure 10-4. More

1. Leonard Yaseen, "New Factors in Plant Siting," *Industry Week*, February 28, 1972, pp. 33–35.

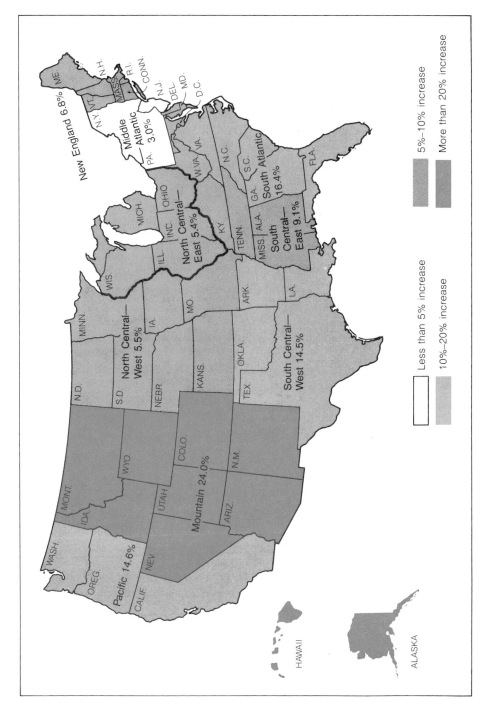

FIGURE 10-4 Expected population growth from 1977—1987. Source: Adapted from *U.S. News & World Report*, May 30, 1977

Less than 5% increase

5%—10% increase

10%—20% increase

More than 20% increase

of the desirable factors are found in these areas than in the more heavily populated Northeast. As a result, the West is expected to add 17 percent more people between 1977 and 1987 while the South is expected to add 14.4 percent. At the same time, the more crowded Northeast is expected to gain only about 4 percent. These basic shifts in population will have a meaningful effect on the location of new plants and on marketing and finance functions. The desire of many business firms to move from the Northeast and North Central areas is partly a reflection of the desire of employees and employers to live in the South and West. It is also a response by businesses to locate near a large pool of relatively low-cost labor and near future markets.

IMPACT OF NEW PLANT ON A COMMUNITY

The location of a production plant has both a positive and a negative impact on a community. A new production plant provides jobs for local workers. The community receives income from the taxes that are paid on the plant and its equipment. The income earned by the workers is spent in the community, generating more business for the retail stores. On the other hand, the plant may cause problems. Extra fire and police services as well as water, sewerage, and school facilities will be needed. There will probably be more traffic congestion. The factory may pollute the water or air or may be noisy or smelly or both. The design of the plant or the type of people who work there may not be compatible with what the majority of the community wants. Production plants do change communities. Before deciding to permit or encourage a production plant to enter a community, civic leaders must weigh these factors carefully.

MATERIALS MANAGEMENT

One of the important considerations in producing products is the purchase, storage, and control of all materials used in production. This is usually called *materials management*.

PURCHASING

In one study of the 100 largest manufacturing corporations in America, it was shown that about half of each sales dollar went for the purchase of materials and services. Because of the importance of purchasing in a firm's operation, most medium- and large-sized firms designate a separate department to carry it out. Requests for all items to be bought by the departments are sent to the purchasing department, which orders them from suppliers.

Purchasing agents are interested in getting the best buy to meet the purchase specifications of each department. This is a difficult decision, with many factors to consider. Some of the decisions faced by purchasing departments include:

1. Whether to buy material or produce it in plant.
2. What quantity to buy. Too large a purchase results in tying up money which is not returning a profit. Too small a purchase could result in paying a higher price. Even worse, the firm could run out of the material during production.

3. Whether to buy from a few suppliers who might give better service or to buy from the supplier who gives the best price for a given specification.
4. Whether to engage in reciprocal buying. This is the purchase of material from a firm that buys your products.

Clearly, purchasing decisions must be coordinated with the operations of the plant. For that reason, purchasing departments are staffed with specialists in production, statistics, and finance. They work closely with production and other managers.

STORAGE   Most firms have a large amount of capital invested in materials and in finished goods kept in storage. One company has estimated that for each $1 in its inventory costs, it pays 20 cents for insurance, storage, obsolescence, and damage to stored material.

WAREHOUSING   An important part of the materials management function is the storing of finished goods, parts, materials, or supplies in a special area. This is called *warehousing*. Almost all finished goods are stored at least once in a warehouse before reaching the final customer. In some industries where production is seasonal, the finished goods must be stored so that they can be sold throughout the year. These might include processed fruits, vegetables, or fish. Other products, such as summer

Warehousing is a vital element in distribution. Most products require storage for some period of time before delivery to the consumer.

American Trucking Association

sporting goods, seasonal clothing, snowmobiles, or lawn supplies are made all year. However, sales for these are heavier in certain months, so goods must be stored for sale during specific seasons.

Warehouse operations may be private or public. *Private warehouses* are those owned by the company storing the goods; public warehouses, found in every medium- and large-sized city, offer storage and handling facilities to any business needing them. They are owned by individuals who offer their warehousing services to the public. There appears to be a trend toward the greater use of public warehouses to reduce overhead, particularly in such industries as food handling. Besides providing storage facilities, they also assemble small shipments and consolidate them into larger ones, saving customers' freight charges. Also, they divide bulk shipments, which may come in rail carload lots, into smaller shipments to customers. A number of food processors have closed their warehouses and now use public warehouses. Their customers, supermarket chains, prefer to have one truck from the public warehouse deliver many product lines to them. Before, food processors sent their goods to the supermarket in their own trucks.

INVENTORY CONTROL   Keeping records of materials on hand and maintaining the appropriate balance of materials is called *inventory control*. This is especially difficult for a large manufacturing firm which may have several thousand different types of materials on hand. Most firms establish minimum and maximum levels of inventory that are acceptable, using one of many sophisticated methods. Another related problem is determining the value of the inventory on hand.

Since the value of inventory is determined in dollars, changes in the value of a dollar affect the worth of inventory. During inflation, the values of both materials and finished goods in inventory rises. This complicates the decision of whether or not to buy more than is presently needed. Deciding to do so can produce a profit on the increase in value of inventory. On the other hand, it creates problems of financing and storage. This has been a particularly difficult decision since the late 1960s when the rate of inflation began to rise rapidly.

DISTRIBUTION   When we think of distribution, we think of getting the products from producer to consumer. While very visible, this is only a part of the entire distribution process. *Distribution* includes the movement of the materials into a plant, their handling within the plant, and the movement of finished products from the plant. A firm tries to coordinate all these movements into a systematic, organized flow. This is difficult because the process cuts across purchasing, production, and marketing. Because it does, it can be difficult to coordinate each of the elements of distribution.

ORGANIZING DISTRIBUTION   There are many different types of organizational structure to accomplish the goal. Some firms put all three aspects under one office, such as a traffic manager, or

personality profile:
**DAVID PACKARD —
product development and
production genius**

When David Packard graduated Phi Beta Kappa from Stanford in 1934, along with William Hewlett, the United States was in the middle of the Great Depression. By 1938 the national economy was still on the skids, but Packard now had an M.B.A., exposure to the excellent management training program at General Electric, and an empty garage. That year he and Hewlett started their own business in the garage, with $500 in capital and one employee, Mr. Packard's wife. Today, the Hewlett-Packard Company is the largest producer of electronic instrumentation in the world, with annual sales of about $1.5 billion. The two co-founders still own over 50 percent of their company's stock.

Packard is an electronic engineer with a flair for management and for making a product that customers need. Although both men are active in the engineering and management areas of the firm, Mr. Packard has tended to concentrate on management and production while Mr. Hewlett sticks more to design engineering.

Almost everything in their product line has been carefully designed to use the strengths of the firm, which include technological expertise and automated production. The founders decided early to limit their scope to electronic instrumentation and data handling. Their early products included a bowling alley signaling device and controls for a telescope. They later expanded into microwave and medical electronic instruments, electronics for analytic chemistry, and computers.

Hewlett-Packard's venture into hand-held calculators, the product for which the company is probably best known, was, however, the result of a fortunate accident. A young man from a major calculator company visited their office to show them a model for an electronic calculator which his firm did not have the electronics capability to build. Hewlett and Packard were interested enough to make the first electronic calculator from the model. Today their complete line of calculators is probably the most sophisticated in the world.

Mr. Packard says his business is developing new products. His business technique stresses growth through internally generated income, management through objectives, and training managers right out of school. Needless to say, the formula has worked well.

Besides his company, Packard has been active in business community affairs as chairman of the Business Council and an active member of Business Roundtable, an organization of businessmen that tries to influence legislation.

even a vice president for distribution. Other firms separate the three functions, with production responsible for the first two and marketing for the third. Still other firms place the entire responsibility in the hands of the marketing manager or the vice president for marketing.

Regardless of how it is organized, there must be close coordination: all of the functions are closely intertwined. There is an intimate relationship between transportation expenses and warehouse expenses, between distribution costs and customer utility, and between packaging and shipping costs.

In many large firms, a traffic manager may be responsible for the aspects of distribution that deal with shipping orders to customers. His office might perform the following duties:

1. Selecting the type of transportation to be used in shipping products and making arrangements with the shippers.
2. Handling all claims against shippers.
3. Consolidating small orders into large ones to save money on shipping.
4. Coordinating use of warehouses for storing finished goods.

TYPES OF CARRIERS   In choosing the most appropriate transportation, the traffic manager must first determine the type of carrier best suited for shipment of a particular product. The choices are common carriers, contract carriers, and private carriers.

A *common carrier* is an independently owned transportation business operating a regular schedule between at least two points. They agree to serve anyone who wants to ship goods over the route. Because this is a service to the public, this service is deemed a public utility and is closely regulated by a governmental agency. All railroads and bus lines, and most airlines, domestic water carriers, and intercity freight motor lines are examples.

A *contract carrier*, too, is an independently owned business. However, contract carriers carry material over routes and schedules that are agreed upon with the shipper. They are much more flexible in their scheduling. Because they enter into private contracts to carry goods, they are not regulated as closely as common carriers. All chartered trucks, buses, airlines, and household moving vans are examples.

Private carriers are owned and operated by the shipper, and the operators of the carriers are the shipper's employees. As you watch trucks go down the road, however, you may not be able to tell whether they are common carriers, contract carriers, or private carriers. Sometimes trucks or other means of transportation are rented or leased on contract to a shipper. They may even have the shipper's name on the vehicle, rather than that of the owner of the carrier. That is another difficult decision for the traffic manager to make. Should the company own its own carriers, contract with a carrier to carry goods, or use the services of a common carrier?

The trucking industry has become this nation's lifeline, carrying every imaginable product from coast to coast. Semitrailers are a familiar sight on any highway.

Stock, Boston, Inc.

CHOOSING A CARRIER

Each of the major types of carriers has advantages and disadvantages for a shipper. The traffic manager must consider these and choose the type of transportation that is most appropriate.

Use of railroads is desirable when goods are to be shipped a long distance, where shipments are in carload lots, and where the size or weight is great. Motor trucks are the most adaptable, flexible method of moving goods. They are the best choice when you want to reach communities lacking rail, air, or water transportation facilities. They are good especially for short hauls and for intracity transportation. Water transportation is good for shipping bulky, heavy goods of low unit value. These might include grain, lumber, minerals, chemicals, or cotton. Rates for water shipping are considerably less than for rail or trucks, although boats generally take longer to move goods. Air transportation is good for moving high-value, lightweight items when speed is important. Packaging can be lighter also since the shocks are not as great as in surface transportation. Pipelines, most of which are owned by oil companies, are excellent for moving petroleum products or liquified products such as liquid coal. Besides low cost, they offer the further advantage of being unaffected by bad weather.

Producers are not limited to only one type of carrier, of course. Frequently, a manufacturer may use several types of carriers in moving one product. Piggybacking, or moving a loaded truck trailer by rail for part of the distance, has been common for many years. In recent years, large metal containers, easily transferred from one type of carrier to another, have been developed to facilitate transportation of goods. In addition, many firms use trucks in combination with barges, trains, and airplanes. Table 10-1 shows the volume of products moved by each type of transportation system.

MANAGEMENT

TABLE 10-1 Volume of
domestic intercity freight
traffic by type of
transport, 1976

Type of Transport	Ton-Mile Volume (in billions)	Percent of Total
Railroad	860.0	38.9
Motor vehilcles	495.0	22.4
Inland waterways	348.0	15.8
Oil pipelines	506.0	22.9
Airways	3.9	.2

Source: *Statistical Abstract.*

SUMMARY

New product development includes the following steps: exploration, screening, business analysis, development, testing, and commercialization. In developing new products, most firms use one of the following organizational plans: product-planning committee, new-product department, product manager, or venture team.

Production is the process whereby products and services are produced. Productivity, on the other hand, indicates the efficiency with which products and services are being produced. In this country, we have tried to increase productivity generally through mass production, which includes the use of mechanization, specialization of labor, standardization, and automation. Tight control must be exercised over the production process, the end products, and the costs of production. In organizing for production, a firm may make a product, buy a firm which is making that product, or borrow some other firm's technology (called licensing). If the firm decides to make its own products, it then has either to make them in an existing plant or to build a new plant. The second choice has an impact on the firm and the community in which the new plant is built.

An important area in producing products is the purchase, storage, and control of all materials used in production. This is generally called materials management and in most large firms is a carefully coordinated effort.

Physical distribution of the products produced includes the movement of materials into a plant, their handling within the plant, and, finally, the movement of finished products from the plant. Since purchasing, production, and marketing are all involved, a variety of organization plans for the process are used by firms. In choosing a type of carrier for transportation, firms must look at the strengths of railroads, motor vehicles, inland waterways, airways, and sometimes oil pipelines.

SUMMARY OF KEY TERMS

Automation Machines operating or regulating other machines.

Common Carrier An independently owned ship-

per operating on a regular schedule between at least two points.

Contract Carrier An independently owned carrier

transporting material over routes and schedules that are agreed upon with the shipper.

Mass Production The large-scale production of goods using mechanization, specialization of labor, standardization, and automation.

Mechanization The use of machines to do as much work as possible.

Private Carriers A means of transportation owned and operated by the shipper.

Private Warehouse A place for storing and handling goods which is owned by the company whose goods are stored.

Product Development The process of developing products that customers desire.

Production The process of converting raw materials into useful goods.

Productivity The efficiency with which goods and services are being produced.

Public Warehouse A place for storing and handling goods that is available to any business which needs it.

Specialization of Labor Concentration by workers on single jobs, each job requiring that only a few tasks be performed.

Standardization The development of uniform methods of operation within a plant.

REVIEW QUESTIONS

1. Name and explain the steps in the development of a new product.
2. Explain the differences in procedure in a firm that places responsibility for new product development in the hands of a committee and one that uses a product manager.
3. Distinguish between production and productivity.
4. Name and describe the characteristics of mass production.
5. Contrast mechanization with automation in production.
6. Explain the difference between specialization of labor and standardization in the production process.
7. Identify and explain the basic factors in choosing a plant location.
8. What are some of the factors that must be considered by a purchasing agent in determining the best buy for the firm?
9. Name and describe the three main areas of materials management.
10. Identify the chief advantages of each type of carrier for business firms.

DISCUSSION QUESTIONS

1. Why do you suppose most large consumer product firms spend so much money on the development of new products prior to the commercialization stage?
2. Can you think of some industries in which it appears that the United States has lower productivity than similar industries in other countries.
3. While automation increases efficiency in production, what possible negative side effects does it have for workers in the firm.
4. Do you believe that business firms should buy parts or supplies in foreign countries for use in manufacturing if the price is lower than they can get in this country? Why or why not?
5. Should common carriers be subsidized by the government?

CASES FOR DECISION MAKING

ASSEMBLY LINE DROPPED BY VOLVO AND SAAB[2]

In Sweden, both the Volvo and Saab auto companies are trying to get away from the traditional assembly line. At Saab, ten-person crews follow a bus down the assembly line for an hour and a half, before turning it over to another group. At Volvo, three-person teams decide how to divide the thirty minutes of work they do in assembling engines. They call for the engines when they are ready for them. If they do three of them in eighty minutes, they can take an extra coffee break.

Both experiments were developed to cut down on high turnover and absenteeism in the factory labor force. Since there is less specialization of labor, the company has perhaps a 10 percent greater investment in tools and training of workers. The results indicate that productivity is about the same, but turnover and absenteeism at both plants are considerably lower.

1. Does this example indicate that specialization and division of labor are no longer basic principles of efficiency for production plants?
2. How much obligation does a manufacturer who uses an assembly line have to design the jobs to be as challenging as possible to the worker?
3. How could a firm determine whether or not an alternative to its present assembly line would result in greater productivity than the assembly-line operation?

MINICOMPUTERS AT PHILIP MORRIS[3]

Philip Morris built a new cigarette plant at Richmond, Virginia, which was completed in 1977. Targeted at $200 million, it should be the most advanced production plant in the United States,

2. "Swedish Auto Makers Test Nonboring Assembly Line," *Chicago Sun Times* (12 November 1973).

3. "Philip Morris: Aiming for a 50 Percent Rise in Productivity," *Business Week*, December 8, 1973, pp. 71–76.

if all plans are carried out. The entire plant is designed around a number of batteries of minicomputers. Originally, two sets of minicomputers were to be used independently. One set was to direct materials handling in the warehouses and another set was to be used in controlling the production process. Since then, the company has decided to integrate all of the production process via the minicomputers. Batteries of minicomputers will keep track of incoming types, weights, and quality of tobacco; determine a production schedule for the plant; blend the tobaccos; instruct the minicomputers in the warehouse to deliver the right amount to the production floor; monitor the production process; control the finished goods warehouse; direct storage and retrieval operations; give directions to the stacker cranes to assemble the order for the trucks which arrive at one of the 20 loader docks. Meanwhile, a separate computer system will have combined the production and labor costs with the overhead costs to determine unit costs and overall costs.

1. Will the use of minicomputers give a great advantage to the larger manufacturers at the expense of smaller manufacturers? Why or why not?
2. In what areas of the entire production and materials management process do you see possible savings for manufacturers who use minicomputers?
3. Do you believe that both department managers and general managers will need to have a background in automation in the future? Why or why not?

BEHAVIOR MODIFICATION INCREASES PRODUCTIVITY

Some years ago, B. F. Skinner, a Harvard psychologist, developed the theories of behavioral modification. As part of the theory system he held that all behavior can be affected by positive rewards such as praise and recognition. The praise and recognition have to follow as rapidly as possible after the behavior has taken place. His ideas were the basis for programmed instruction where the learner receives immediate feedback and reinforcement on the accuracy of a response.

Now the theories are being given a test in industry. Some firms report amazing success. Others see little results and a few firms have had negative results. Some of the major firms which report successful use of the theories include Frito-Lay, B. F. Goodrich, and Warner-Lambert. Most firms that have used the techniques report sizable cost savings and increased worker productivity. While there are many variations, the behavior modification theories are implemented usually in three steps.

First, management and employees get together. Management presents the standards for job perfor-

mance they feel are reasonable and explains how the standards will be met. The employees identify their needs and provide the managers with a list of reinforcers that should "modify" the employees' behavior. Second, worker performance must be observed with a reliable follow-up; third, feedback must be given often to immediately let the employees know how their level of performance compares with the level desired.

1. Does this type of system appear similar to the principles of good management that you would expect any good manager to use?
2. How does this system differ from what is normal in industry?
3. Do you feel the workers are being manipulated in this system?

RELATED READINGS

Ammer, Dean S. *Manufacturing Management and Control*. New York: Appleton-Century-Crofts, 1968.

A paperback primer on manufacturing management for a first course in education or business. It focuses on objectives, organization, optimum use of capital, and management of operations.

Luna, Charles. *The Handbook of Transportation in America*. New York: Popular Library, 1971.

An interesting little book on the history and present status of both freight and passenger transportation in this country. It depicts the historical development of the role of transportation, the major types of transportation, and the government's role in transportation.

Prasad, S. Benjamin. *Modern Industrial Management*. San Francisco: Chandler Publishing Co., 1967.

Book of readings on industrial management. It of-

fers readings in the areas of new concepts in industrial systems and design, application of some analytical methods, and industrial management in global perspective.

"Minicomputers That Run the Factory." *Business Week*, December 8, 1974, pp. 68–78.

A fascinating article about the use of minicomputers in a variety of industrial plants. It focuses on the trends in production and use of minicomputers and contrasts their use with that of electronic calculators and full-sized computers in production and distribution.

"Why Business Ran Out of Capacity." *Fortune*, May 1974, pp. 261–271.

An analysis of the closing of marginal plants by many firms. It traces the impact of environmental legislation and materials shortages as the major cause for closing older plants in some industries.

part three: CAREER OPPORTUNITIES

CAREERS IN MARKETING RESEARCH

About 35,000 people are employed in full-time marketing research jobs according to the latest statistics. Among them are research assistants, specialists in marketing techniques, and supervisory personnel. Employment is likely to be found in large manufacturing companies and independent advertising and marketing research organizations. Other possible choices are major department stores, radio and television stations, newspapers, university research centers, and government agencies. Although marketing research firms tend to concentrate in the largest cities such as New York and Chicago, there are opportunities in many other cities across the country.

An undergraduate degree is usually required for becoming a marketing research trainee. Some firms are even looking for a master's degree in business administration. In preparing for a career in marketing research, the following college-level courses are valuable: marketing, business statistics, English composition, speech, psychology, and economics. With increasing use of computers in sales forecasting, distribution, cost analysis, and other aspects of marketing research, a basic knowledge of data processing is advisable. Job opportunities through the mid-1980s are expected to be good.

CAREERS IN MARKETING: SALES AND ADVERTISING

Approximately 30 percent of the civilian labor force works in some type of marketing activity, if you include those who are employed in retailing,

wholesaling, transportation, communications, and warehousing industries.

SALES   More people are employed in sales-related jobs than in any other category. In 1976, there were 1.3 million salespeople employed in manufacturing and wholesaling, 3.3 million in retail selling, and 1.2 million in other types of sales. In addition, there were 1.9 million retail store managers.

ADVERTISING   About 190,000 people were employed, in 1976, in positions requiring considerable knowledge of advertising. About one-third of them were with advertising agencies, and more than half of the agency personnel worked in New York, Los Angeles, and Chicago. Other jobs in advertising were with manufacturing companies, retail stores, and advertising media. The following are the occupations most commonly found in advertising: artists and layout designers, advertising copywriters, account executives, production managers, advertising managers, and research directors.

Demand for advertising personnel is expected to rise moderately through the mid-1980s. Demand for all categories of salespeople is likewise expected to be favorable during this time.

CAREERS IN PRODUCTION AND MATERIALS MANAGEMENT

There are a number of careers available for college graduates in production and materials management. Among them are traffic managers, purchasing agents, and industrial designers.

TRAFFIC MANAGERS Industrial traffic managers arrange transportation of raw materials and finished products for industrial firms. A college degree in traffic management is usually required. It is offered at large community colleges and universities near major industrial centers. A moderate increase in job openings is expected into the mid-1980s.

PURCHASING AGENTS Purchasing agents buy the materials, supplies, and equipment that are needed in operating the companies they work for. Knowledge of the product and current prices are essential. In hiring purchasing agents, most employers want graduates of schools of business administration or engineering who have taken courses in accounting, economics, and

purchasing. Some prefer to advance people from within the company, whether or not the person has a degree. Job prospects are expected to be good through the mid-1980s.

INDUSTRIAL DESIGNERS Another job category within production is that of industrial designer. Industrial designers combine technical knowledge of materials, machines, and methods of production with their special artistic talent to originate and improve the functional design of machine-made products.

Training for industrial design involves completion of a sequence of courses in this subject at a community college, a technical art school or technical college, or a university. Graduates of engineering and architectural programs may also qualify. Job prospects are expected to be moderately good through the mid-1980s.

part four

FINANCE

Marketing, production, and financing make up the three sides of every business's triangle of existence. Which is the most important? Which comes first in the order of business survival?

Some contend marketing is of first importance to any business. After all, unless you have an idea for a product or service you have no reason to start a business in the first place. And logically, no matter how good a product or service you have to sell, you must be able to produce or provide it for the customer.

However, even if you have a salable product or service and possess the know-how to produce it efficiently and effectively, you must be able to obtain the money necessary for those purposes.

Therefore, side three of any business triangle of existence must be financing. You can't produce or sell anything unless you have the financial resources to do so. Because of this economic fact of life, some experts say that financing comes before marketing and production in the scheme of business operations. It is necessary to attract investors and obtain credit in order to function as a business entity. It is necessary to make profits in order to reward owners, pay creditors, and have funds necessary for expansion of the firm. Raising funds is a constant problem for all businesses of all sizes and of all types and this is the subject of chapters 11 and 12.

chapter 11

OBTAINING FUNDS FOR MAKING PROFITS

OBJECTIVES

When you have finished reading and studying this chapter, you should be able to:

1. Know the difference between the terms *funds* **and** *capital* **and be able to differentiate short-, intermediate-, and long-term funding of business enterprises.**

2. Understand the various ways and means by which funds are generated through the internal operations of the firm.

3. Know and describe the various types of short- and intermediate-term methods of borrowing available to business and be able to identify the different legal instruments that are related to these credit transactions.

4. Be familiar with the meaning of the terms "debt financing" and "equity financing" and understand the reasons why managers may choose one or the other of these methods for raising long-term funds.

5. Know and be able to describe the various features of common and preferred stock as well as bonds.

CHAPTER PREVIEW

Have you ever gone camping and found yourself trying to start a fire by rubbing two sticks together? It's far easier to start a fire with a match. In a way, many businesspeople try to get their businesses started on the same principle as starting a fire by rubbing two sticks together. It can be done, but it's a lot more difficult than using a match. Studies indicate that many businesses do not start with enough capital and, therefore, do not survive the first few difficult years of becoming experienced and established.

All businesses need adequate funds for maintaining operations and growing, as well as for providing bread and butter for their owners. After all is said and done, businesspeople list profit as the primary reason for being in business, and financial resources are necessary for making adequate profits.

Funds are needed for the short-, intermediate-, and long-term survival of all businesses, large and small. Borrowing in various ways is one of the major means by which business operators raise necessary funds for short and intermediate periods of time. This form of generation of funds is known as external financing. Internally, businesses generate short- and intermediate-term funds by retaining a portion of profits in the business, by depreciation write-offs, and by the sale of property and other business rights.

To obtain long-term funds, business can invite additional owners into the business, or they can sell debt obligations, in which case they create a debtor-creditor relationship. The primary way of raising funds through ownership is to sell common or preferred stock to the public. Investors are attracted to this type of venture for two reasons: (1) they hope to see their investment increase in value; and (2) they are likely to receive dividends from the profits of the corporation. A possible objection to this method of raising funds is that with the introduction of new owners, the present owners' share of control over the business can be diminished.

6. Be generally familiar with the responsibilities and activities of people engaged in financial management.

Selling debt obligations to the public is a popular method whereby medium- and large-sized corporations raise long-term funds. Bonds are the most common type of long-term obligation sold to investors and they are usually issued at $1,000 per certificate. Bonds are attractive to investors for a number of reasons. As creditors, bondholders have a prior claim to the assets of a corporation in case it must be dissolved. Bondholders are also guaranteed periodic payments of a specified amount of interest and the return of their investment at the maturity of the bond issue.

As a potential businessperson and as a future investor, you should find this chapter thought provoking.

"I don't see how we can lend you $500.00 'until payday,' Mr. Morris, if you don't have a job."

There are slightly more than nine million privately owned businesses in the United States. All of them were founded by people who thought their products or services would sell and were willing to risk, or invest, savings or borrow the savings of others to get started. *Capital* is the more formal term used to describe an investment by the owners of a business as well as an investment by outside creditors in the form of loans. Of course, the owners expect to make profits as a reward for their risk. Outside creditors usually lend money to businesses in a contractual manner and hope to receive a fixed return of interest at periodic intervals. Naturally, creditors demand safeguards for their investment, such as claims on certain collateral of the business or its owners, if the borrower defaults on the loan. Collateral represents assets owned by the borrower of a loan and pledged to secure the loan. The lender may take title and possession of these assets if the loan is not repaid.

Creditors are not, however, in an absolutely safe position because of their claim on some collateral put up by the business. Sometimes businesses overextend their debt obligations. If a foreclosure and settlement by creditors follows, there might not be enough collateral to satisfy all claims. Even a very large corporation, such as Penn-Central, can go into bankruptcy and not have enough funds to pay all the claims of its creditors. In such cases final settlements of creditors' claims can take many years. Also, it should be remembered that claims of the Internal Revenue Service and state and local taxing authorities take precedent over all other creditor claims.

All businesses need capital to get started. Like young people, businesses have growing pains. They are anxious to extend their markets to new geographical areas or to offer more varied goods and services to the public. This is an ongoing process with all healthy businesses and the need for additional capital occurs many times during the life of the firm. It is not at all unusual to read articles about millions of dollars of new common stock being sold in some of the nation's largest corporations such as Ford Motor Company.

FUNDS FOR
HOW LONG?

While capital is usually thought of as the total amount of money or property that is owned or used by an individual businessowner or corporation, *funds* are usually considered to be a sum of currency plus demand deposits (balances in checking accounts) used or accumulated for a specific purpose. For normal operations as well as for special reasons, all businesses have a need for funds.

Let's examine a small seaside concession located on the New Jersey shore. The concession rents beach towels, chairs, and umbrellas. Around the middle of March, the owner must order his inventory for the new season, which begins around June 1 and runs until Labor Day. However, in March he is probably low on funds because he has had no income from his business since Labor Day of the previous season. For this businessowner it becomes vital to borrow for several months to finance his inventory for the coming season. The loan can be paid back from the income he earns as the season progresses, and his inventory or business equipment can serve as collateral for the loan.

The above situation calls for short-term funding. *Short-term funds* are those needed for a period of one year or less. Fund needs for a period of one to five years are usually classified as *intermediate-term funds*. *Long-term funds* are usually thought of as those needed for a period of five, ten, twenty years, or even longer. A real estate operator who plans to develop a retirement community for residence and recreation would be in need of funds for many years before the complex is completed and sold out and would, therefore, resort to long-term funds.

MONEY AND DEMAND DEPOSITS

Every efficient economy has evolved from a cash basis to a check basis. In the United States most people pay bills by check, while less than 20 percent pay bills by cash. Checks are used so often that they are often thought of as money, and in most business transactions they are treated as such.

Checks and dollars which constitute money in our economy are really no more valuable, in themselves, than a blank sheet of scrap paper. They will burn if you put a match to them or blow away if you throw them to the wind. Naturally, because we know they represent spending power, we would not burn checks or dollars, nor would we throw them to the wind.

Money is a necessity for an efficient economy. It represents a medium of exchange that is generally acceptable. As a medium of exchange, money eliminates the need to barter, exchanging something you have for something I have. Money is also portable; that is, it is very easy to carry around. Imagine using elephants' tusks or bricks of precious metals as money; yet this has been done in the past and is still done in some primitive economies. It certainly would place a damper on business activity in our society. Money is also stable because the government and banking system of the country stand behind it. Thus sellers of products and services do not ordinarily hesitate to accept dollars or checks in payment. Dollars and coins are also durable and are efficiently replaced by banks and the U.S. Treasury when they wear out.

ECONOMIC ACTIVITY AND AVAILABILITY OF FUNDS

Funds in relationship to the needs of business can be compared to water and its relationship to the needs of the community. There is almost always some water available in our reservoirs on which to draw. But in the years when we have heavy rainfall, the reservoir's water level is much higher. The same situation applies to the availability of funds for use by large and small business firms. When the economy is rolling along well and most people are working and earning good salaries and most businesses are earning large profits, both individuals and businesses will have extra income available for investing. The more investment, the greater the level in the nation's reservoir of funds for business financing. Of course in a sluggish economy, people and businesses are usually earning just about enough to survive financially and have little or no excess earnings available for

In seeking a business loan, the small business owner usually borrows from a local source such as a commercial bank.

Ewing Galloway

investment. In this situation the funds available to the business sector of the economy will be minimal.

Economists have observed over the years that in favorable periods of economic activity, when more funds are available and used by businesses, the flame of economic growth is fanned. That is, the more business uses short-, intermediate-, and long-term funds, the more the economic activity of the nation grows. This makes sense if you consider that more money is used to increase inventory, build new buildings, and develop new products and services. All of these activities provide many more jobs, giving spending power to many more people.

OBTAINING SHORT-TERM AND INTERMEDIATE-TERM FUNDS

Where do most businesses obtain the funds that they need for a period of one year or less, or for a period of one to five years? Usually from within the operations of the firm or from outside sources. For purposes of identification, the categories cited above are referred to as internal sources and external sources. Each is discussed in Figure 11-1 in some detail.

INTERNAL SOURCES

For the very smallest businesses—those owned by one or, at most, several individuals—almost all internal funds are obtained by leaving some of the profits earned each year in the business. In the case of our friend who owned the

FIGURE 11-1 Obtaining short- and intermediate-term funds

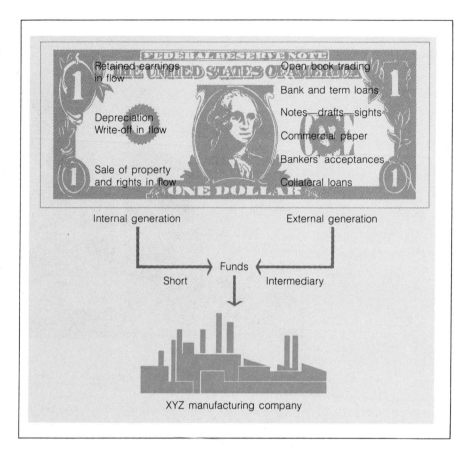

Internal generation   External generation

Funds

Short   Intermediary

XYZ manufacturing company

seashore concession on the New Jersey coast, this method was not entirely satisfactory for getting him through all of his business season and he had to rely on borrowing, which is discussed later in this chapter, as an external source of funds. Even a very small business must from time to time borrow money to survive. Most medium- and large-sized businesses rely on three major sources of internal short- and intermediate-term funds. These sources are retained earnings, depreciation write-off allowances, and sales of business property or rights.

Retained Earnings All businessowners and investors hope that their investments will earn profits. However, it is a rare situation where some of the profits earned are not held in the business for short- or intermediate-term needs. *Retained earnings* are profits kept by the business to serve as a source of funds for future business needs. There is no magic formula for deciding how much of the annual profit should be retained. This varies with the ambitions of the owners and managers and with the degree to which they must rely on business profits for their own personal financial welfare. Even the very largest corporations must be careful when deciding on the level of retained earnings. If the board of directors withholds too much profit from distribution to stockholders in the form of dividends, the resulting dissatisfaction could cause many stockholders to sell their stock, leading to a decline in market value of the corporation's stock.

Depreciation Write-off Allowances   Federal tax law permits every business to estimate the monetary value of wear and tear on its equipment and buildings each year. Such wearing out of these assets is referred to as *depreciation*, a term you have probably heard used in connection with the buying and selling of automobiles. Just a change in model from one year to another causes the current market value of an automobile to decline significantly. Therefore, depreciation takes into consideration the age of the equipment as well as the extent of its use. Because our federal government allows businesses to deduct the estimate of annual depreciation on their equipment as an operating expense along with all other operating expenses, the average-sized business is able to reduce considerably its profits reported for tax purposes. This reduction in reported profits results in a lower amount of taxes due and payable to the Internal Revenue Service, and this savings is considered an additional internal source of funds for the firm. The example below illustrates the effects of the write-off allowance as opposed to a situation where no such allowance is permitted.

Example:

(A) With Write-off		(B) Without Write-off	
Sales Income	$150,000	Sales Income	$150,000
Operating Expense (including $20,000 depreciation write-off)	110,000	Operating Expense (excluding $20,000 write-off)	90,000
Net Income (hypothetical 40% tax rate)	$ 40,000	Net Income (hypothetical 40% tax rate)	$ 60,000
Federal Tax	16,000	Federal Tax	24,000

In case (A), savings in taxes of $8,000 ($24,000 − $16,000) provides internal funds.

Sale of Business Property or Rights   Businesses sometimes find themselves with property or special privileges that they no longer need at the same time that they might be in need of additional funds. In such cases the property or rights, such as patent rights, can be sold for considerable sums of money. The return from such sales provides an instant source of internal funds, although the firm must forego the future utilization of such property or rights. Some years ago, for example, American Motors Corporation sold its Kelvinator Appliance Division as a means of internal funding to help alleviate its financial difficulties.

EXTERNAL SOURCES

Internal sources of funds are not always enough to provide the resources needed for expansion or seasonal demands. Frequently a business looks to outside sources for obtaining needed short-term funds; that is called *external financing*. Usually, external short-term financing means borrowing by the business. In some cases interest is charged for this borrowing, and in some cases it is not. The most popular types of short-term financing are discussed below.

Open Book Trading   Almost every business is given the option to buy on credit from its suppliers. When a firm buys merchandise, supplies, and other items, it is usually billed on the basis of 30- or 60-day periods from the date of invoice. This means that if a firm, such as our merchant at the New Jersey seashore, orders 1,000 beach towels in mid-March at the wholesale price of $2.00 per towel, he will probably receive a statement from the supplier by April 1 requiring him to pay his bill within 30 or 60 days, depending on how lenient his supplier is in such matters. No interest is charged for the credit period involved, but our seashore merchant does have the use of these funds during the credit period. Most businesspeople agree that interest is really charged as a part of the markup in the price of the product, because the supplier must recover his credit cost somewhere. Frequently, suppliers encourage their customers to pay early in the credit period by granting cash discounts.

Bank Loans and Term Loans   "You have a friend at Chase Manhattan" was a popular slogan used by a giant commercial bank in the New York City area. There is no doubt about it, businesspeople must have a friendly banker at hand for borrowing short-term funds. Such loans are granted for up to one year, and the collateral for these loans often consists of the firm's inventory or other specific assets; or it might simply be the general assets of the corporation that are not pledged to other loans. These loans are at prevailing rates of interest, and the interest is generally deducted from the principal at the time the loan is granted. For example, if the New Jersey concessionaire wanted to borrow $10,000 for one year and he was granted a loan by his local commercial bank at 8 percent interest, his proceeds at the time of borrowing would be $9,200 ($10,000−$800 interest). A *discounted loan* is a loan on which the interest is deducted in advance from the amount borrowed at the time the loan is granted as in the example just given.

There is usually one other stipulation attached to borrowing large amounts for a period of one year or less. Many banks require the borrower to keep a compensating balance in the bank during the borrowing period. A *compensating balance* is an amount of deposit that must be kept in the bank until the entire loan is repaid.

This means that if a business desires to borrow $200,000 and the bank requires a 20 percent compensating balance, the firm must borrow $250,000 to get the use of $200,000 (since $50,000, or 20 percent of $250,000, must be kept on deposit as a compensating balance). There is an added interest cost here, because the businessperson must borrow more than is needed to provide funds for the compensating balance.

Term loans are similar to borrowing from the bank on short term, only they are taken for from one to three years. Usually the loan terms provide for payment of the principal in installments over the period for which the loan runs. Interest is usually due with the periodic payments of principal.

Notes and Drafts Frequently, when a firm borrows from a bank, the loan is formalized by the bank's issuing of a note. Another situation, among many, where a note can be used is when one businessperson borrows from another for a short period of time. A *note* is written evidence of a debt prepared by the borrower and held by the lender until paid. It is nothing more than a formal IOU. The person who borrows is the *maker* of the note and the one who lends is the *payee*. The maker prepares the note and gives it to the payee in exchange for the principal. When payment is due to the payee, the maker gives him the principal plus interest (if interest is charged), and the note is returned to the maker. Often a bank serves as safekeeper of the note and handles the collection process for the payee. Figure 11-2 illustrates a note issued between two businesspeople with a bank as collector.

FIGURE 11-2 A promissory note

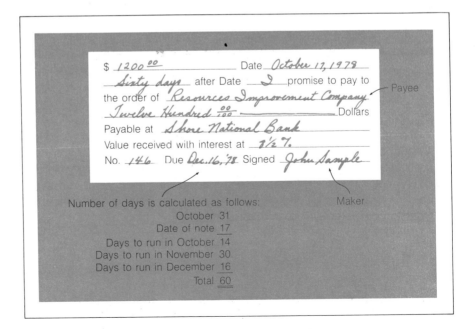

business profile: THE PRICE OF KILOWATTS

Pity the poor public utility. Other American companies can raise their prices to compensate for higher costs without having to answer directly to the government for the fairness of their policies. The market tells them whether price rises are justified by either buying or not buying the higher-priced product or service. Public utilities have no such barometer. They have to justify their price structures to government regulatory commissions that have become increasingly unsympathetic to them in recent years.

Industrial firms sell stock or bonds to raise money for capital improvements. In the past utilities had no problem selling stocks and bonds. Their product, which is a steady supply of energy, is always in demand, and state and federal governments guarantee their market monopoly and financial soundness. Since utilities were a less risky investment than industrial firms, their stock and bonds sold at high prices relative to interest or dividends that they paid to bondholders and stockholders who invested in them.

Recently, environmentalism, inflation, and consumerism have caused the utilities hard times. Concern for the environment has brought legislation that requires utilities to install expensive scrubbers to remove impurities if they burn coal; it has shut off the supply of oil and natural gas because these scarce fuels are needed for gasoline and home heating; it has instituted safety and disposal safeguards that increase construction costs for nuclear plants; it has made compliance with environmental protection laws an enormously complex and expensive process that often delays construction of new generating plants and thereby prevents or delays replacement of obsolete equipment.

Inflation has raised the price of all fuels: uranium, coal, and oil. It has upped the cost of labor and materials for new plant construction. It has also increased the cost of borrowing, because in inflationary times, investors demand higher interest to make up for loss of capital through the declining worth of the dollar.

Consumerism has given the public a greater voice in the running of the economy. Public outcries can keep utility rates down by influencing the politicians who regulate the commissions that regulate the utilities. They can prevent the construction of nuclear plants that produce power more cheaply than conventional facilities.

Today, utilities are starving for and have desperate need of capital—capital to build expensive new plants, to upgrade existing plants to conform to air-quality control laws, and to pay high interest rates on recent borrowings. But investors are not interested in buying the stock of utilities except at bargain-basement prices. The reason is simple. Utilities make less money now and are a less desirable investment because their costs have been increasing rapidly—costs that are a drain on profits—and their profits have been held down by regulatory agencies responding to consumer agitation. Utility bonds cannot be sold unless they guarantee yields so high that payment of high interest from reduced revenues becomes difficult. In other words, both the usual sources of investment capital are drying up for utilities at a time when they desperately need money.

Notes usually carry an interest charge of between 6 and 12 percent of the principal. As for length of time, it is from 30 days to one year. Interest is always stated at an annual rate and is calculated to the specific time in days that the note runs. For example, an $8,000 note for 90 days at 8 percent per year will yield $160 in interest. The interest is calculated as follows:

$$\text{Principal} \times \quad \text{Rate} \quad \times \text{Time}$$

$$\frac{\$8,000}{1} \times \frac{8}{100} \text{ percent } \times \frac{90}{360} \text{ days} = \$160$$

(Note: To simplify computation, the commercial year of 360 days is used.)

Drafts are another way to borrow funds outside the business. Drafts are similar to ordinary notes in appearance and purpose. The major difference is that a draft is prepared by the creditor and presented to the debtor, whereas a note is prepared by the debtor and presented to the creditor. The effects of either are the same. Drafts, like notes, are IOUs payable on demand (a so-called sight instrument) or payable at some future date (a time instrument). Drafts do not usually have an additional charge for interest.

Bankers' Acceptances Bankers' acceptances are really a form of time draft. Assume our New Jersey seashore concessionaire decides to buy some sunglasses from a manufacturer in Italy. As in the case of a time or sight draft, the Italian supplier will present a draft to his New Jersey customer. However, he will prefer that, in addition to the New Jersey merchant's signing the instrument, the merchant's bank also "accepts" the draft. In effect, a banker's acceptance comes about when a bank also signs a note, which means that if the primary creditor (the seashore merchant) fails to pay on the due date, the bank guarantees that it will pay on the note. In this way the Italian merchant has a firm commitment from a bank, a reliable and trustworthy financial agent, in a foreign country thousands of miles away.

COMMERCIAL PAPER The method of borrowing short-term funds known as commercial paper is not available to the small- or medium-sized business. Only large, well-known, credit-worthy corporations can borrow by issuing commercial paper to the public. *Commercial paper* is short-term notes of large denominations—$10,000, $50,000, and $100,000—carrying high rates of interest and with a life of 90 days to a year. They are issued in volume to the investing public and are backed by the general assets of the corporation not already pledged to other loans.

Major corporations such as IBM and General Motors frequently issue commercial paper. Their notes are sold to investors through bond dealers and brokerage houses. Most of the time, commercial paper is bought by large insurance companies, banks, and pension funds. The average individual investor does not usually have the amount of cash required for such an investment.

OBTAINING LONG-TERM FUNDS

Over the course of its history, the American economy has developed from an agricultural to an industrial economy, dominated by massive business, governmental, and labor organizations. Gone are the days when the "mom and pop" type of small business accounted for the major dollar volume of business activity in the United States. Today the business community is typified by large corporations, each employing thousands of people in plants, offices, and stores from coast to coast and, in many cases, in other countries. The long-term funds needed to keep these corporations growing and competitive cannot be raised entirely through profits retained from earnings. Frequently corporations go to the public to raise additional capital for expansion, product development, and many other purposes.

A corporation may choose to borrow the needed funds, in which case it will sell bonds to investors. Raising funds through debt obligations is known as *debt financing*. For other specific reasons a corporation may decide to sell additional portions of ownership in itself to raise needed funds, in which case it would offer shares of stock to the public. Raising funds by selling additional shares of ownership is known as *equity financing*. The reason for equity financing in some cases and debt financing in others is based on many considerations. Such things as the amount of debt the corporation has incurred to date, costs of bond borrowing, and the ease with which stock can be sold are some examples.

STOCKS

Stock is a proportionate share of ownership in a corporation. All buyers of stock become owners, with the right to vote for directors of the corporation and certain other issues affecting the firm. The actual shares are the legal documents proving ownership, and the corporation is obliged to keep the stockholders informed of all important financial and operational matters. It does this through the mailing of quarterly and annual reports as well as by inviting shareholders to the annual meeting of the corporation. When the board of directors declares dividends, stockholders are entitled to receive a proportionate share of them.

Common Stock

Most corporations that sell stock in their company choose to sell *common stock* shares (see Figure 11-3). There are no predetermined dividends paid on common stock and, therefore, the prospect of *capital growth* is usually its main attraction. (Capital growth represents the increase in market value between the cost of buying an investment and its selling price.) Generally, expected capital growth in common stock exceeds that of preferred stock and bonds. By the same token, the risk of losing capital (known as a capital loss) by investing in common stock is greater.

A common stockholder's rights to income distributions, or distributions from the proceeds of the corporation's assets arising from liquidation, are secondary to those of all of the corporation's creditors. In many states, moreover, the rights of common stockholders under these conditions are also secondary to those of preferred stockholders. In short, investing in common stock follows the reasoning that the greater the risk, the greater the return.

FIGURE 11-3   A stock
certificate

Stock certificate. Reverse
side is used in transferring
stock ownership.

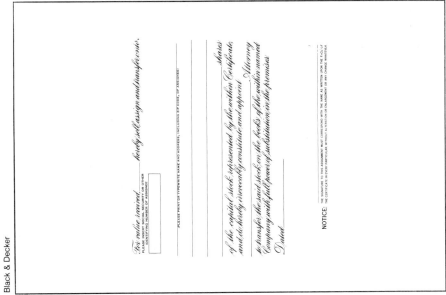

Black & Decker

Preferred Stock   Preferred stock is similar to common stock in most respects, but with some variations. Often, preferred stock is nonvoting stock because the present ownership does not want to lose its decision-making control over the firm. Most preferred stock receives a set dollar percentage of dividends if the board of directors declares one for a particular period of operations. Preferred stockholders always have preference as to their receipt of dividends before common stockholders are paid. Their stock can be *participating* or *nonparticipating*. When it participates it is entitled to share, in some manner prearranged with the common stockholders, in the excess of funds paid as dividends over its contracted rate or dollar amount. For example, assume that a corporation's board of directors declares $40,000 for dividend distribution for the fourth quarter of the year and that preferred is participating. After receiving their regular dividend per share (say $8 per share on 2,000 shares outstanding), $24,000 is left to be shared equally by all classes of stockholders. Each common and preferred stockholder would share in some prearranged manner in the $24,000. For preferred stockholders this represents an additional share of the dividends. This is just one way that preferred stock might participate. Other plans are common.

In some cases preferred stock can also be *cumulative*. This class of stock is entitled to any dividend in arrears at specified dollar amounts or percentage rates per share before any current dividends are distributed to any other class of stockholders. For example, if the owners of cumulative preferred stock are entitled to total dividends of $8 per share for the current period and there are 1,000 shares outstanding, total dividends received for this class of stock for the period would be $8,000. However, if the board of directors concludes that dividends cannot be paid for this period, those having cumulative stocks, as well as all other classes of stockholders, would receive no dividend distribution. If in the following period, $35,000 is declared as dividends by the board of directors, the holders of cumulative preferred stock would receive $8,000 in distribution for the current period as well as $8,000 in dividends in arrears for the previous period before any other class of stockholders receives anything. Preferred stock not entitled to this special arrangement is known as *noncumulative*.

Preferred stock can be both participating and cumulative. Holders of common stock, however, never have the participation or accumulation privileges that are available to preferred stockholders. Nevertheless, the great majority of investors choose common stocks for their possibility of rapid capital growth.

STOCK PRICES AND INFLATION

Over the years, stock prices and the cost of living in the American economy have kept up with each other. Stocks have risen in value an average of more than 4 percent a year and paid an average of about 3½ percent in dividends. But the 1970s have seen some changes. During this decade consumer and wholesale prices have soared while the average value of stocks has remained the same. It is true that some stocks have experienced a tremendous increase in value, while others declined in value over the period. Nevertheless, looking back at the price trend, one realizes that investing in the stock market was not a hedge against inflation during the 1970s.

Forecasters of stock market activity predict that stock prices will revert to their pre-1970s performance and that the prices of stocks will keep up with the rate of

personality profile:
G. WILLIAM MILLER —
new head at the Fed

The chairman of the Federal Reserve Board is just one vote, but when the chairman has the prestige and authority of the venerable Dr. Arthur Burns or his predecessor, William McChesney Martin, that vote can be a veto of administration spending programs. No one was surprised that President Carter, in his drive to place his choices in top government positions, chose to replace Arthur Burns, but no one knew just what to expect of his successor, G. William Miller. *Business Week* warned that the appointment meant a "radically new direction for Federal policy on money supply, interest rates, and the dollar." Yet Dr. Burns himself seemed well pleased with his replacement.

Although Miller had served for some years on the Boston Federal Reserve Board, he was no economist, no specialist in business cycles like Burns. He was a practicing businessman rather than a theoretician and was better known for his social consciousness, public service, and political liberalism than for any ideas on national monetary policy.

He was certainly a fiscal conservative in his private life. He had worked his way through high school during the Depression and although his salary as president and later chairman of Textron grew to $383,000, he always flew tourist class and never used a company limousine. He also pinched pennies in the running of the company: of 64,000 employees, only 170 worked at company headquarters.

Miller had graduated from the U.S. Coast Guard Academy and spent a few years in the Far East before going to law school and joining a prestigious Wall Street firm, one of whose clients was Textron. Royal Little, a legendary conglomerator, had brought together 25 or 30 large companies in very different fields to form Textron. He wanted Miller on his legal staff, but Miller wanted a position in management and got it, winning the presidency of the company at the age of 35. While Little wheeled and dealed as chairman, Miller ran the collection of companies that had been acquired, spending heavily for cost effectiveness and development of new products but managing assets in a manner considered prudently conservative for a conglomerate.

In his new role, Miller's social consciousness has gone hand in hand with fiscal responsibility and the business community has breathed a deep sigh of relief as the new chairman has made it clear that the Federal Reserve Board will keep its independence and integrity.

inflation. Undoubtedly, most of the corporations that are anxious to raise funds are hoping these analysts are correct. When market values of stocks remain high, it is easier and less expensive for corporations to raise needed capital by selling stock.

The following chapter contains a discussion of the institutions and procedures for purchases and sales of common and preferred stock.

BONDS

When a corporation sells common or preferred stock, it is inviting new owners into the business. If it is a small, tightly controlled firm, such a sale will ultimately bring in many more owners and therefore dissolve the control that the original owners maintained. If the original owners want to keep a tight grip on the corporation, and yet raise funds, they will probably sell bonds. Those who buy corporate bonds are in the same position as outside creditors. From a legal point of view, a creditor relationship is a more secure one because the rights of creditors have priority over those of owners. If a corporation finds it necessary to dissolve itself because its assets are not sufficient for continuing operations, the creditors, among them the bondholders, have prior claim to the cash available from the sale of corporate assets.

Another reason owners may choose to sell bonds in preference to stock is that often market conditions favor such a sale. Sometimes bank interest rates are so low that it becomes more practical to offer bonds to the public rather than sell stock.

What is a bond? A *bond* is a written instrument issued by a corporation that promises to pay back the money borrowed after a specific number of years, as well as to pay interest to the holder at set intervals over the life of the debt. The interest due on a bond is usually paid to holders semiannually. Usually after 10 or 20 years, bonds are said to "mature" and the principal amount borrowed (also known as the *face value*) is paid back to the holder. This is not to say that a bondholder must hold the instrument until it matures; if he chooses not to do so, he may sell it to someone else at a market price determined by the forces of supply and demand. Most corporate bonds sell at a face value of $1,000.

THE INDENTURE

Every bond issue must be backed by a written contract known as the *indenture*. This document contains all of the important contract conditions relative to the bond issue involved. The numerous provisions of the indenture are generally outlined in the prospectus that is given to every potential buyer. A *prospectus* is a booklet containing pertinent financial and other information required by law to be given to every potential buyer of new issues of corporate stocks or bonds. The *trustee*, chosen by the issuing corporation, represents the interests of the bondholders.

The indenture generally provides:

1. The name of the debtor
2. The name of the trustee

3. The type of bond being issued
4. The maximum amount of the bond issue in dollars, and the amount of the certificates
5. A description of the collateral
6. A discussion of liens and covenants
7. An *acceleration clause* authorizing the trustee to collect the entire outstanding principal and interest on the issue in the event of default of even one payment of principal or interest by the debtor
8. Details covering provisions for retirement of the issue on the date of maturity
9. The statement of the powers, duties, and responsibilities of the trustee

THE ROLE OF THE TRUSTEE

A trustee versed in legal and financial matters is needed when bonds are sold to a number of individuals. The duties of the trustee are delineated in the provisions of the Trust Indenture Act of 1939. The trustee must be a corporate body, with one specific individual within that corporate body designated to act for the bondholders. Banks frequently serve in this capacity, and you have probably seen many bank names that end in ". . . and trust company." The trustee makes annual reports to the bondholders concerning the property held in trust and is also responsible for notifying the bondholders of any default in the payment of interest and/or principal. In case of default, the trustee represents the bondholders and exercises the power to protect them with the same degree of care and skill as would any prudent individual.

REGISTERED VERSUS BEARER BONDS

In recent years most bond issues have been *registered bonds*, which means the name of the owner (creditor) is on the face of the certificate; such bonds, therefore, cannot be transferred without an endorsement. Interest is automatically paid to the owner whose name appears on the records of the corporate debtor, until it has been officially notified of the transfer of title to a new owner.

Bearer bonds, which are also known as *coupon bonds*, are bonds that do not specify the name of the owner on the face of the certificate. In effect, whoever has possession of the bearer bond receives the interest by clipping the current interest coupon from the bond, filling it out, and mailing it to the corporate debtor. In this way the debtor knows to whom and where to pay the interest.

MAJOR TYPES OF CORPORATE BONDS

An automobile is always an automobile, but there are many different brands and models. The same is true for bonds. The issuing corporation can choose to sell the type of bonds that best suits its needs, and investors can buy the type of bonds that will best satisfy their needs. Some of the major classifications of corporate bonds are discussed below.

Debenture Bonds Somebody once described the debenture bond, illustrated in Figure 11-4, as a giant IOU. It is the most common type of bond issued by large, well-known industrial corporations, such as Chrysler Corporation and U.S. Steel.

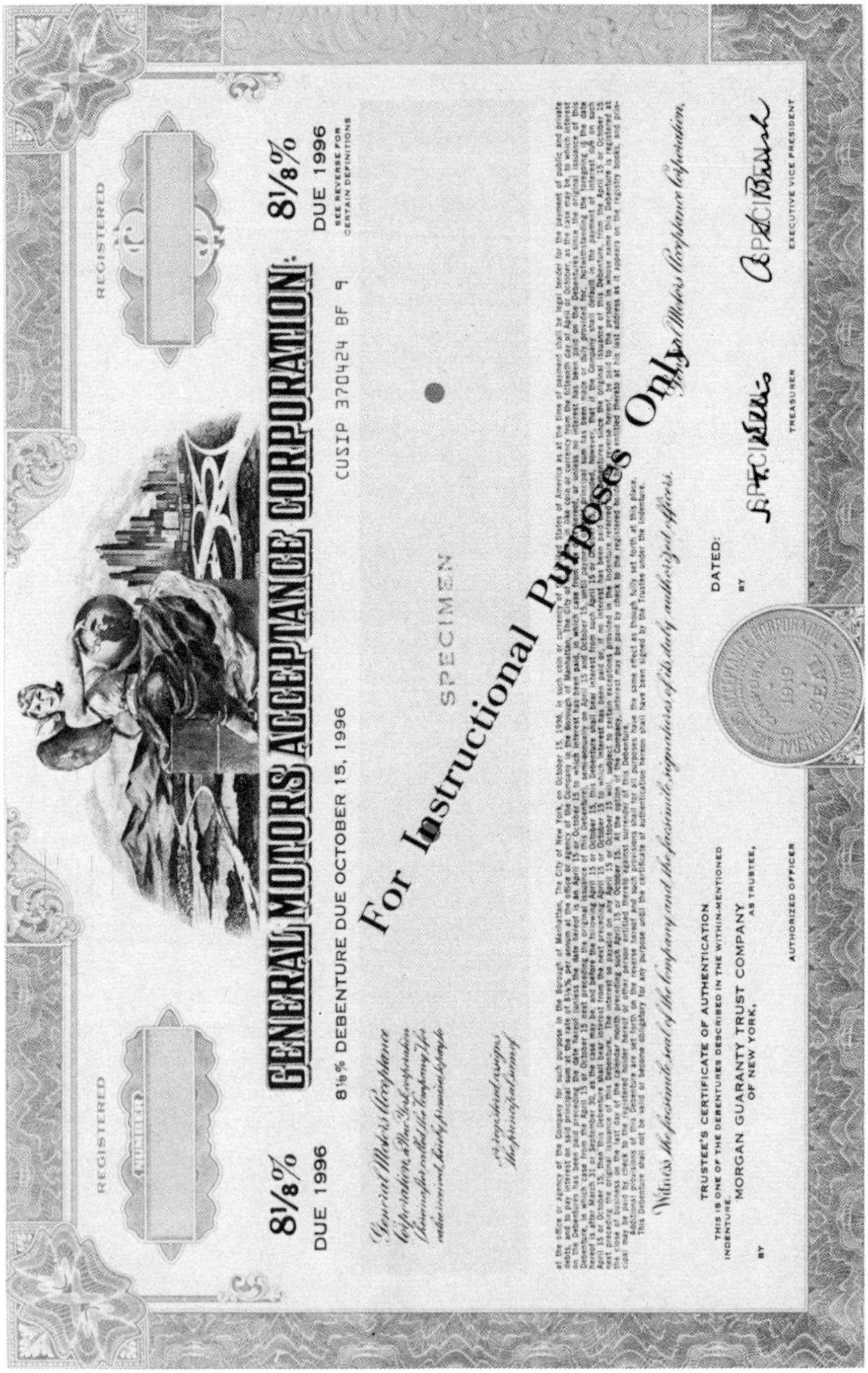

FIGURE 11-4 A bond certificate

Courtesy of General Motors Acceptance Corp.

Debentures have no collateral backing so that the general credit reputation of the corporation is the investor's only source of security. The risk in owning a debenture is not as great as it might first appear, however, since the corporate giants who issue these securities have billions of dollars of unpledged assets against which the bondholders can lay claim should this become necessary.

Convertible Bonds There are many different types of convertible bonds, and their terms, as prescribed in their respective indentures, vary widely. All convertible bonds have one feature in common: They pay a fixed interest rate and if the corporation's growth and profits do poorly over the years, the bondholder is still assured of his return. However, the added feature of these bonds is that they contain a clause that permits the bondholder to convert them in the future into common stock of the corporation at a predetermined rate stated in the bond indenture. This is a valuable feature if the corporation grows rapidly and enjoys large profits as these events usually mean a growth in the market price of its stock.

Usually convertible bonds are also debenture bonds. There is no reason, however, why they could not also be part of any other classification described below.

First Mortgage Bonds This type of bond is secured by a mortgage on some specific property of the corporation, such as a building or the land on which the building is located. This is a very high-grade security because the bondholders have first claim to the property specified in the indenture as security for the bond issues. If the corporation is dissolved, the first mortgage bondholders have first claim to the proceeds from the sale of any assets specified as collateral for their issue. In addition to first mortgage bonds, there sometimes are second and even third mortgage bonds on the same property. In such instances, the first mortgage bonds are the "senior" security and, in the event of a dissolution, have first claim to the property specified as security for the issue. If there are remaining proceeds from the sale of the secured assets involved, the second mortgage bondholders have priority to these. If there are third mortgage bondholders, they get anything remaining after the claims of the second mortgage bondholders have been satisfied.

Collateral Trust Bonds These securities are very similar to first mortgage bonds. However, instead of real estate or equipment serving as collateral for this type of issue, the collateral is usually common or preferred stock or other securities owned by the debtor corporation as an investment in other corporations.

Income Bonds These bonds usually pay a much higher rate of interest than most others because the annual interest payment is subject to a condition. They are unique because the interest on them does not have to be paid unless the corporation has earned it. This means that if the corporation makes no profit in a particular operating year, the interest owed to the income bondholders for that year may be passed and forgotten forever.

Equipment Trust Certificates In this type of long-term note, specific "rolling stock" of the issuing corporation is pledged as collateral for the issue. Title to the equipment is vested in a trustee who holds it for the protection of the certificate holders. When the certificates are fully paid back by the debtor corporation, title goes to the corporation which then owns the equipment. Railroad companies were the first to utilize this type of borrowing to buy new cars. Airlines, steamship companies, and trucking firms now use it to generate funds necessary for the purchase of new equipment. In the event of default, the trustee sells the equipment to pay back the certificate holders.

Sinking and Serial Fund Bonds All of the classifications of bonds discussed above fall into the category of either serial or sinking fund bonds. A *serial bond* issue is periodically retired by the issuing corporation. This permits the corporation to redeem a few of these bonds each year so that the burden of payment on the corporation is not too severe. Each bond is serially numbered and this number indicates when, according to the terms of the bond indenture payment schedule, the bond will be retired.

Sinking fund bonds are all retired on some specified future date, such as 20 years after issue. To guarantee that the corporation will have the necessary funds for retiring the issue, the trustee requires it to set aside a certain amount of money each year for the life of the issue. When the due date arrives, this sinking fund is used to pay off the bonds.

Call Provisions of Bond Issues There are times when a corporation might find it advantageous to pay off a bond issue before maturity. This is particularly so if finance costs drop sharply and the corporation can redeem the old bond issue with its high interest rate for a new one paying a much lower rate. For this reason many bond issues contain a callable provision in the indenture. Such a provision enables the issuing corporation to redeem the bonds before maturity by paying a small premium of from 3 to 10 percent to the bondholders. This premium is based on the face of the bond, and the longer the issue is outstanding before the callable provision is exercised, the smaller the premium will be. The advantage in the call provision is all to the corporation and, except for the premium, the bondholder has little to gain.

FINANCIAL DECISION MAKING The decisions to be made concerning the generation of funds are difficult ones, to say the least. Many a business has gone under because management failed to make the right financial choices. Every business, both large and small, is faced with risks; the reward for taking greater risks can be larger profits, while the punishment is often severe losses. Most businessmen hope to chart the safest course possible leading to reasonably large profits without jeopardizing the firm's financial resources. This is not always possible, and going off course in the direction of too-conservative or too-liberal financing can weaken a business. The business failure rate in the United States is quite high, and many a business fails due to a lack of adequate financial planning and control.

The very large corporations in the United States maintain whole departments to guide management in its financial planning. These departments are staffed with people who have extensive training and experience in accounting and financial analysis. Frequently they rely heavily on quantitative procedures and computer programs to aid them in their financial decision making. *Operations research* is one method of relying on quantitative data and scientific research for rendering decisions. Despite all the sophisticated decision making techniques that have come into play, many correct decisions are still based on the common sense and intuitive abilities of an experienced financial planner.

Of course, small- and medium-sized firms cannot afford the luxury of a financial planning department. In a small firm it is up to the owner-operators to assume the responsibilities and acquire the financial know-how to make the right decisions. Frequently the certified public accountant engaged by such firms helps the managers in this respect. In medium-sized firms the chief accountant, in addition to his accounting duties, is also responsible for joining with top management in making important financial decisions.

COMPETING FOR INVESTMENT DOLLARS

Large and small businesses have to compete for investment dollars just as most people have to compete to earn a living. Whether Chrysler Corporation decides to float a bond issue or sell common stock, it must appeal to an investing public with limited resources.

In the case of large investors such as insurance companies, banks, and pension funds, there is strong competition for their investment funds. Real estate is always an attractive investment. It is a relatively secure type of investment, and often, especially in the 1970s, has proved a better hedge against inflation than corporate stocks and bonds. Large investors are also attracted to government securities. Like corporations, federal, state, and local governments sell debt instruments to the public. Usually they don't pay as high an interest rate as corporate securities, but the security of the invested funds is far greater. There are also certain tax advantages to investing in some types of government securities; deductions are allowed for some types.

As for the small investor, Chrysler Corporation will be competing against the same kinds of investment choices that attract large investors. However, most small investors are limited in the amount they can invest, so they often put money into more modest investment choices such as savings accounts or certificates of deposit. Chrysler and all other large corporations need small investors as well as large ones. To compete they must package their investment opportunities just as they package the goods or services they sell to the public. When Chrysler markets their cars, they produce colorful, well illustrated brochures, showing their cars in attractive settings, surrounded by beautiful models.

To some extent it is the same way with selling stock or bonds to the public. The issue must pay an attractive rate of interest or dividend in accordance with current market conditions. There may need to be added features such as convertible provisions. And, there must be an effective channel of distribution (discussed in the following chapter).

Big business needs the small as well as the large investor if it hopes to maintain fruitful channels for external funds. Likewise, when the deal is right, the small as well as the giant investor will need to invest in corporate securities. In this way, investors are provided with an alternate way of saving money and earning a good return.

SUMMARY

To begin, to grow, to expand, every business needs capital. Capital is usually thought of as the total amount of money or property owned or used by individual business owners or corporations. In addition to capital, businesses need funds for everyday operations as well as for special reasons. Funds are usually considered to be currency on hand plus balances in checking accounts. When businesses need capital or funds for several days to several years they usually raise them through internal or external generation. Retained earnings, depreciation write-offs, and the sale of property and rights are the major internal ways to generate funds. Loans, notes, drafts, and other debt instruments are external ways to generate funds for short or intermediate periods.

Selling equity or debt instruments is one of the most common ways to raise long-term capital and funds (long-term is over five years). Equity instruments include common and preferred stocks. Investors purchasing these securities become part owners of the firm. Debt instruments include bonds and long-term notes. Investors purchasing these securities become creditors of the firm. Most businesses compete against other firms in the money market to attract debt and equity investors.

SUMMARY OF KEY TERMS

Acceleration Clause A clause in an indenture (bond contract) authorizing the trustee to collect the entire outstanding principal and interest on the issue in the event of default of even one payment of principal or interest by the debtor.

Bankers' Acceptance Type of draft endorsed by a commercial bank.

Capital Investment by owners of a business as well as investment by outside creditors in the form of loans. (This term has a more technical meaning in accounting. See Chapter 14.)

Commercial Paper Short-term notes of large denomination and high interest rates issued by well known corporations.

Compensating Balance A requirement imposed on debtors by many banks to keep an amount on deposit in the bank during the period of a loan from the bank.

Demand Deposit A sum of money credited to a checking account.

Depreciation A decrease in the monetary value of a business asset because of deterioration from use and age.

Debt Financing Raising funds for a business through the sale of credit obligations.

Discounted Loan A bank loan on which the interest is deducted by the bank from the amount borrowed at the time the loan is granted.

Equity Financing Raising funds for a business by selling additional shares of ownership.

Funds The sum of currency plus demand deposits (balances in checking accounts) used or accumulated for a specific purpose by a business firm.

Indenture A written contract between the borrowing corporation and the creditors containing all the pertinent conditions relating to a specific bond issue.

Intermediate-term Funds Funds needed by a business for a period of one to five years.

Long-term Funds Funds needed by a business for a term of five years or longer.

Maker A person who borrows by issuing a note to a creditor.

Notes Written evidence of a debt prepared by the borrower and held by the lender until paid.

Open Book Trading Buying on credit from suppliers with 30 to 60 days to pay bills.

Payee The lender in a note transaction and therefore the party to whom a promissory note is made out.

Prospectus A booklet containing pertinent financial and other information required by law to be given to every potential buyer of new issues of corporate stocks or bonds.

Retained Earnings Profits kept in the business to serve as a source of funds for future business needs.

Short-term Funds Funds needed by a business for a term of one year or less.

Trustee A person and corporate body with the legal responsibility to represent the bondholders and enforce their rights under provisions of an indenture.

REVIEW QUESTIONS

1. Define common stock and preferred stock and explain how they differ from each other.
2. Distinguish between debt financing and equity financing and give one example of each.
3. What are the internal sources of short- and intermediate-term funds? Which is likely to be the greatest source of such funds from year to year?
4. Mr. Smith issues a 90-day 8 percent note for $2000 to Mr. Jones dated July 16 of this year.
   a. Who is the payee?
   b. Who is the maker?
   c. How much interest is due at maturity?
   d. How much is due the payee at maturity?
5. Wise Widget, Inc., needs to borrow $120,000 for one year for purchasing a seasonal inventory. It can do so from the Fair Deal Commercial Bank at a rate of 8 percent. One of the provisions of the loan requires Wise Widget to keep a compensating balance of $30,000 in the bank during the period of the loan.
   a. How much must Wise Widget borrow to get the money it needs?
   b. What is the true interest rate on the loan?
6. Define sight drafts and time drafts. In what ways are they different from each other?
7. Using Figure 11-4 on page 288, answer the following:
   a. What is the face value of the bond?
   b. What specific collateral, if any, is pledged to the bondholders?
   c. What is the stated rate of interest on the bond?
   d. What is the name of the trustee?

  e. What is the date of the issue and the date of maturity?

8. What is an equipment trust certificate? How does it differ from an ordinary bond?

9. What is an indenture? What is its importance to the bondholder and to the corporation issuing the bonds?

10. What are retained earnings? How do they accumulate? Why do they sometimes decrease?

DISCUSSION QUESTIONS

1. Although one business person does not charge another a stated fee or interest rate when dealing on open book account, there really is a hidden cost to the purchaser. Explain.

2. How do you explain the fact that many older buildings that have been depreciating for years are worth more today than they were at the time they were built?

3. Fahey Corporation has 10,000 shares of cumulative nonparticipating preferred stock outstanding and 40,000 shares of common stock outstanding. The preferred is entitled to a $60,000 annual dividend and is one year in arrears. This year, $150,000 is available and declared for dividends. How much does each share of preferred stock and each share of common stock deserve in dividends?

4. How do large and small business firms compete for investment dollars?

5. Why is financial decision making so important to both small and large business firms? Why do large firms usually have an advantage in this area of decision making?

CASES FOR DECISION MAKING

HIGH FINANCES

Wagner Corporation, a manufacturer of tennis rackets with plants and offices in Philadelphia, Chicago, and Seattle, has decided to expand its market to the Texas area. It estimates that it will need $20 million to build a new plant and sales office in San Antonio. Ten million dollars will come from the current resources of the firm. The other $10 million will be raised from sales of common or preferred stock and/or bonds. Wagner is owned by about 200 stockholders, six of whom hold 10 percent of the total outstanding shares. The remaining 40 percent of the common stock is owned by the other 194 stockholders. The six major stockholders are the board of directors and they control the firm. There are no preferred stock issues and the only major debt is a 20-year bond issue for $10 million issued in 1974. The present interest rate on bond issues is about 8 percent. Bankers have advised Wagner that investors are available in both the equity and debt markets. Wagner has a good credit rating and is well thought of in financial circles. Its common stock trades in the over-the-counter market.

1. Do you think Wagner should sell stock or bonds to raise the $10 million? Why?

2. If you chose stock, should it be preferred or common? Why?

3. If you had to recommend a combination of stock and bonds how would you divide the sale? Why?

PAYING ITS WAY

The advertisement in Figure 11-5 appeared in the *Wall Street Journal*. Based on the information contained in the ad, answer the following:

FIGURE 11-5

New Issue / March 15, 1978

$11,700,000
(Third and final installment of an issue aggregating $35,100,000)

The Baltimore and Ohio Railroad Company

Second Equipment Trust of 1977

8½% Equipment Trust Certificates
Non-Callable

Dividends to accrue from December 1, 1977. To mature in 15 annual installments of $780,000 on each December 1 from 1978 to 1992.

Issued under the Philadelphia Plan with 20% original cash equity.

MATURITIES AND YIELDS

1978	7.40%	1982	8.15%	1986	8.45%	1990	8.60%
1979	7.70	1983	8.25	1987	8.50	1991	8.60
1980	7.90	1984	8.35	1988	8.50	1992	8.60
1981	8.00	1985	8.40	1989	8.50		

These certificates are offered subject to prior sale, when, as and if issued and received by us, subject to approval of the Interstate Commerce Commission.

Salomon Brothers

Blyth Eastman Dillon & Co.
Incorporated

Drexel Burnham Lambert
Incorporated

1. What kind of debt instrument is being sold?
2. Is the offering being made to the general public? If so, how can you tell? If not, how can you tell?
3. What serves as collateral for the loan?
4. If someone holds a certificate that is to mature in 1987, what is the yield for that certificate?
5. Can you compute the total cost of the equipment (down payment plus borrowed funds)?
6. What happens to the collateral at the end of the lease period?

FIGURE 11-6

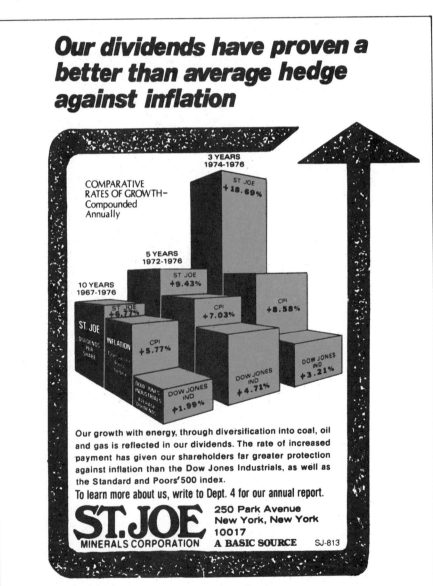

HEDGE CLIPPER

The advertisement in Figure 11-6 appeared in the *Wall Street Journal*. Based on information in the ad, answer the following questions.

1. What type of investor might be attracted to write to the company for a copy of the annual report?
2. Find out what the C.P.I. and the Dow Jones Industrials are. Hint: Check the index of this book under stock indexes. And consult your local library.
3. Find out what the most recent market price is for St. Joe's stock. Use your local newspaper under the listings of the New York Stock Exchange.

RELATED READINGS

Berry, Charles H. *Corporate Growth and Diversification*. Princeton, N.J.: Princeton University Press, 1975.

A sophisticated study of corporate growth, concentration, and diversification.

Kahn, Herman. *The Future of the Corporation*. New York: Mason & Lipscomb, 1974

A forecast of how world economics is affecting and will continue to affect the corporate environment in the 1970s and 1980s. Such problems as pollution and multinational corporations are examined.

Kraus, Albert L. *The New York Times Guide to Business and Finance*. New York: Harper & Row, 1972.

A complete book of information on various types of personal and business investments. Done with the thoroughness associated with N.Y. Times publications, it will be of special interest to someone who wants a detailed introduction.

Nader, Ralph and Green, Mark J. *Corporate Power in America*. New York: Grossman, 1973.

An examination of the economics and political powers of corporations. Although rather negative, it contains some very interesting viewpoints.

Ney, Richard. *Making It in The Market*. New York: McGraw-Hill, 1975.

An interesting presentation of techniques for investing in securities. Among the topics are: selecting your portfolio; the specialist and you; when to buy and sell.

Smith, Adam. *The Money Game*. New York: Random House, 1968.

A humorous account of the various aspects of security trading. Through comical anecdotes it informs and cautions the reader with regard to individual investment strategy.

Smith, Adam. *Super-Money*. New York: Random House, 1972.

Written in the successful style of *The Money Game* cited above. More information on the stock and mutual fund markets in the American economy.

Williams, John M. *Women's Guide to Successful Investing*. Garden City, N.Y.: Doubleday, 1975.

Useful to all investors but primarily aimed at business and professional women, widowed, divorced, or retired.

Zarb, Frank G., et al. *The Stock Market Handbook*. Homewood, Ill.: Dow Jones-Irwin, 1970.

A handbook of terms and procedures used by investors. Well written and written on an elementary level for the novice investor.

New York Stock Exchange

chapter 12

SOURCES OF FINANCING

OBJECTIVES

When you have finished reading and studying this chapter, you should be able to:

1. **Know and describe the essential features and functions of commercial banks, commercial finance companies, and other institutions that deal in short- and intermediate-term funds.**

2. **Be able to define and distinguish between the money market and capital market.**

3. **Know and describe the essential features and functions of commercial banks, insurance companies, and investment banks that deal in long-term funds.**

4. **Be familiar with the role and functions of security exchanges and the over-the-counter market for the selling and buying of stocks and bonds.**

5. **Be knowledgeable about the general principles and terminology associated with investing in stocks and bonds.**

CHAPTER PREVIEW

For a businessperson, obtaining funds should be a shopping venture much like buying a new car or a watch. The shopper must decide what features are essential for his or her needs and then look for the best price and the best service. Commercial banks, commercial finance companies, and insurance companies are the shopping centers that most businesspeople frequent when they need money. Likewise, those who have funds to invest usually put them in these institutions to earn a moderate return on a relatively safe investment.

When corporations issue new stocks or bonds to the public, they generally sell them through an investment banker. Investment bankers, like real estate salespeople, have the necessary know-how for selling their specialty quickly and at the best price. Since most corporations, like most homeowners, don't know the "ins and outs" of the market, as a rule they engage the services of a professional.

Security exchanges are the marketplace for the buying and selling of stock (and some bonds) issued sometime in the past. At one time or another, you or some relative has probably owned shares of stock which were probably purchased through a brokerage house. These firms buy and sell stock for the investing public by becoming members of organized exchanges such as the New York Stock Exchange. Other stocks and bonds are bought in the general market, referred to as the over-the-counter market. The mechanics of buying and selling stock occupy the body of this chapter. You'd be wise to study them well because the chances are you yourself will buy or sell stock during your lifetime.

"And in the event that your corporation repays the full loan of five million in less than ten years, we're prepared to let you have, as a gift from us, two or three small firms."

12

SOURCES OF FINANCING

It is usually not enough for someone who wants to be a good cook to be an expert at the oven. A good cook must also be a clever shopper and find the quality ingredients that are a necessary part of delicious food. The same holds true for the wise borrower and user of funds for business operations. Part of this person's success or failure will lie in the ability to raise funds at a fair cost to suit the particular financing needs of the business. Shopping for funds is not very different from shopping for any other commodity. One has to look around for the best deal at the lowest price.

THE MONEY MARKET

Many of the short-term financing instruments described in Chapter 11, such as commercial paper and bankers' acceptances, are purchased through the money market. The money market is not a specific building on any special street in any certain city. The term refers to those institutions that deal in a general way in the buying and selling of short-term credit obligations (those of one year's duration or less). While the Wall Street area of New York City might be thought of as the hub of the money market in the United States, Chicago, San Francisco, Richmond, Dallas, and many other large cities also carry on an extensive volume of money market transactions.

The brokerage houses, commercial banks, security exchanges, bond dealers, and similar institutions are the individual operators within the money market. It is these institutions which make possible the rapid turnover of millions of dollars of treasury bills, certificates of deposit, commercial paper, bankers' acceptances, notes, and drafts by always being available as buyers or sellers of such instruments. If it weren't for the operations of the money market, borrowers and lenders of short-term obligations would be greatly limited in the volume and sophistication of transactions that they could complete.

PRIMARY AND SECONDARY MARKETS

Financing instruments that are sold for the first time by a borrower to a lender are said to be sold through the *primary* market. Financing instruments that are resold by a lender to another lender are said to be sold through the *secondary* market. It is a procedure similar to that of buying a new automobile from a factory-authorized dealer. The buyer might later decide he no longer wants the car and therefore sells it as a used car. The same holds true in selling financial instruments. A lender might buy a 26 week Treasury Bill directly from the Federal Reserve Bank in his area (the primary market). After holding the bill for 90 days, he may find that he needs cash and therefore decides to sell the bill. He does so by selling it in the resale (used instrument) market, which is referred to as the secondary market. Stock exchanges are prime examples of institutions that carry on most of their transactions in the secondary market. Just as a factory-authorized auto dealer may also have a used car lot, many dealers in primary sales of securities also have a department for making secondary sales.

SHORT- AND INTERMEDIATE-TERM FINANCIAL INSTITUTIONS

There are many different institutions that a businessperson may approach in shopping for funds just as there are many different stores that one can go to for a pair of jeans. Jeans, of course, are sold in clothing stores, but they are also sold in the clothing departments of department stores. Surplus stores and discount stores also carry jeans. Shoppers have a wide selection of merchants to choose from when buying jeans. The same holds true for the borrower of short- and intermediate-term funds. Some of the major lending institutions are described below.

COMMERCIAL BANKS

These should be thought of as the department stores of banking institutions because they offer many different types of services. Commercial banks are the chief sellers of certificates of deposit and commercial paper. They also function as go-betweens in sales of just about any other short- or intermediate-term credit instrument that one can name. Most commercial banks operate with many branch offices throughout their state, a fact that is of great convenience for their customers who borrow or lend by selling or buying financial instruments through the bank. Such banks always maintain relationships with banks in other cities and countries to facilitate transactions outside the state in which they operate. Banks who help each other in transactions across state or national borders are referred to in the banking industry as *correspondent banks*. Commercial banks usually maintain high ethical standards and are strictly regulated by state and federal agencies. For these reasons they are one of the most popular kinds of institutions for handling financial instruments of individuals, businesses, and governments.

COMMERCIAL FINANCING COMPANIES

These are very important institutions for providing the businessperson with funds for periods of up to five years. In some cases they have become so important that major manufacturers have established their own commercial finance companies for the benefit of their authorized dealers. In the auto industry, for instance, General Motors has established General Acceptance Corporation. These are separately managed (and in many cases separately owned) lending institutions that aid authorized dealers in financing their inventories, accounts receivable, and, in some cases, other asset purchases through the buying and selling of the credit instruments involved.

SUPPLIERS AND OTHER SHORT-TERM CREDITORS

Most sales between manufacturers and wholesalers and between wholesalers and retailers are an *open book account*. This means that the purchaser is given a certain period of time after buying the product and receiving delivery for making payment. Thus, a retailer may buy a shipment of goods on June 20 and receive a bill on July 1 with terms of "net 30." This means he must pay the bill by July 31. Under these circumstances, the purchaser really has borrowed funds from the creditor for a period of 30 days or more, depending on when delivery of the merchandise was completed. If the purchaser received the merchandise on the day of sale (June 20 in the example), he would have the merchandise forty days before he had to pay for it and apparently at no interest cost for the period. However, it is probably correct to assume that such merchandise is marked up in price to compensate the seller for the time that the collection is outstanding.

Occasionally merchants can borrow funds from a wholesaler, manufacturer, or fellow merchant who has dealt with them extensively. In such cases a note is usually issued by the borrowing merchant as evidence of the debt. Such notes are generally interest-bearing, although there are situations where non-interest-bearing loans are made to keep the borrower as a customer.

LONG-TERM SUPPLIERS OF FUNDS

Banks will lend money for the long term as well as for the intermediate and short term. Many homeowners and businesses have mortgaged their property by borrowing from a commercial bank. Savings and loan institutions are also active in lending money to homeowners through a mortgage arrangement.

INSURANCE COMPANIES

For a number of years the Prudential Life Insurance Company of America held a mortgage on the Empire State Building, a striking example of the powerful influence of insurance companies in the long-term funding of business in America. Insurance companies are often the firms that will be willing to hold a long-term mortgage on a plant or building. At the end of 1973, life insurance mortgage holdings totaled $81.4 billion, which represented almost one-third of their total assets. At that time, these same companies directly owned almost $8 billion in real estate, including a variety of residential and commercial properties such as shopping centers and high-rise and garden apartments. Figure 12-1 and Table 12-1 give dramatic indication of how investments in mortgages and realty by life insurance companies have progressed over the years.

In addition, insurance companies are ready buyers of corporate bonds and stocks. In some cases, one or several insurance companies might buy the entire bond issue of a corporation, relieving the corporation of selling it in parts to the general investing public. Such transactions are known in the investment industry as *private placements*.

FIGURE 12-1 Distribution of mortgages by type in the United States. Source: *Life Insurance Fact Book*, 1977, American Council of Life Insurance

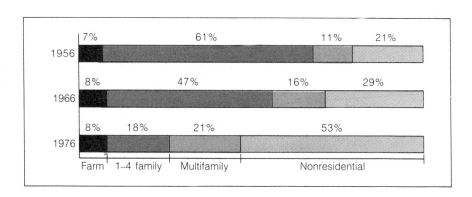

TABLE 12-1 Real estate owned by U.S. life insurance companies (in millions)

Year	Amount	% of Assets	Year	Amount	% of Assets
1890	$ 81	10.5	1962	$ 4,1073	
1895	125	10.8	1963	4,319	3.1
1900	158	9.1	1964	4,528	3.0
1905	171	6.3	1965	4,681	3.0
1910	173	4.5	1966	4,885	2.9
1915	173	3.3	1967	5,187	2.9
1920	172	2.3	1968	5,571	3.0
1925	266	2.3	1969	5,912	3.0
1930	548	2.9	1970	6,320	3.0
1935	1,990	8.6	1971	6,904	3.1
1940	2,065	6.7	1972	7,295	3.0
1945	857	1.9	1973	7,693	3.0
1950	1,445	2.2	1974	8,331	3.2
1955	2,581	2.9	1975	9,621	3.3
1960	3,765	3.1	1976	10,476	3.3
1961	4,007	3.2			

Source: *Life Insurance Fact Book, 1977*, American Council of Life Insurance.

INVESTMENT BANKERS

Ever since the introduction of the corporation, the investment banker has played an important role in long-term financing. The investment banking house is really not a bank in the truest sense of the word, but rather a wholesaler of corporate stocks and bonds. It is the investment banker who brings the corporation's funding product to the general public in the manner illustrated in Figure 12-2.

The investment banker usually serves as an *underwriter* of the corporation's issue. This means that the investment bank buys the entire issue of stock or bonds from the corporation and pays off the corporation immediately. In this way the corporation does not have to wait for its money until each and every stock certificate or bond is sold to the public. Of course, the investment banker buys the issue not at its face value but at some lesser value. The difference between the face value of the issue and the price the investment banker pays for it is known as the *spread*. It is within the spread that the investment banker realizes a profit on the transaction. Such issues are often so large that the investment banker usually resells the issues in parcels to brokerage house associates across the country or around the world, a process known as *syndication*. By doing so, the responsibility

FIGURE 12-2 Issue of corporation stock

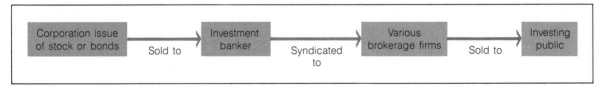

The trading room of Salomon Bros., a major investment banker in New York, is the hub of the firm's worldwide underwriting and market activities.

Salomon Brothers

is broken down regionally, and each brokerage firm then resells its part of the issue to the investing public.

There are two major ways in which a corporation may engage the services of an investment banker. One is to call in an investment banker and describe what the corporation wants to fund and how it expects to go about raising the needed long-term capital. From that point, it is up to the investment banker to set up the details of the security issue and the sale of the securities. The investment banker then buys the entire issue from the corporation and sells it through syndication.

The other method is for the corporation to determine the details of the security issue and how it is to be sold. After this, the corporation presents the details of its plan to a number of investment bankers and invites them to bid on the issue. After the corporation has received all the bids, the firm will sell the entire issue to the highest bidder. From that point the issue is also handled through syndication.

In some rare cases corporations may decide to sell their own issue to the public. This is similar to the situation in which a homeowner decides to sell a house without the services of a real estate agent. Although this can be done successfully, often the process simply does not work out well. Just as real estate firms are experts in the merchandising of homes and land, so investment bankers are experts in the merchandising of stocks and bonds. They have the resources, contacts, and know-how in this area that the corporation lacks.

Trading floor of the New York Stock Exchange on Broad Street in New York City.

New York Stock Exchange

SECONDARY MARKETS AND THEIR ROLE IN FINANCE

Stock exchanges are the best-known market for the resale of securities. Transactions on organized stock exchanges go back many hundreds of years to the establishment of the London Stock Exchange. In the United States, New York City developed as the center for securities transactions; buyers and sellers of securities, or their representatives, would meet beneath a buttonwood tree on Wall Street and carry on their trading. In 1793, they were wise enough to seek shelter in the nearby Tontine Coffee House when the severe winter weather curtailed their street activity. The coffee house, located on the corner of Wall and Williams streets, soon became too small a shelter for the growing securities exchange.

NEW YORK STOCK EXCHANGE

On March 8, 1817, the first formal constitution of the New York Stock and Exchange Board, as it was then known, was adopted. The constitution provided guidelines for listing securities and for membership. A *listed security* is one regularly traded on a stock exchange; a *seat* is the term for membership in the exchange. Having a seat means one has the right to walk onto the floor of the exchange to buy or sell securities.

Minimum Requirements for Original Listing of Common Stocks	American Stock Exchange	New York Stock Exchange
Shares publicly held	400,000, of which 150,000 must be in 100 to 500-share lots	1,000,000
Market value of publicly held shares	$3,000,000	$16,000,000
Number of stockholders	1,200 including 800 holders of round lots, of which 500 must be holders of 100 to 500-share lots	2,000 holders of round lots
Income—net Income—pre-tax	$400,000 last fiscal year $750,000 last fiscal year	— — — $2,500,000 last fiscal year $2,000,000 preceding 2 yrs.
Net tangible assets	$4,000,000	$16,000,000

Source: American Stock Exchange.

In 1863 the name of the exchange was changed to the New York Stock Exchange, and in 1867 the first stock tickers were installed. It is important to note that the New York Stock Exchange also lists and trades a number of corporate bonds. There are many other stock exchanges in the United States patterned after the New York Stock Exchange but operated on a smaller scale. The American Stock Exchange, known as the Amex, is also located in New York City. Others are in Chicago, Washington, D.C., Boston, Philadelphia, Los Angeles, and San Francisco, as well as in many other areas of the country.

Only the largest, best-known American corporations can hope to gain listing on an organized stock exchange. Table 12-2 lists some of the requirements for listing on the New York and American stock exchanges. If successful in being listed, they become part of a vast, efficient, market where individual investors put their savings to work. The exchanges provide investors with a medium in which they may convert their excess savings into securities that they expect will bring income as well as capital gains. Those corporations listed on one or more exchanges are in a far better position to sell new issues of stocks or bonds in the primary market because the investing public knows it can readily resell these securities through an exchange. *Liquidity* is the term used to describe the ease with which an investor may dispose of his investment and receive cash. An organized security exchange is the prime vehicle through which an investor may enjoy liquidity.

WHY BUY STOCK? In recent years the question of why someone should buy stock has seemed an especially good one, because the average prices of stocks listed on the exchanges have fluctuated tremendously. In most cases, stockholders have seen the value of

business profile: HERE COMES THE NEW STOCK MARKET

A new national securities market is beginning to take shape. When established, it will replace the New York Stock Exchange, the American Stock Exchange, and the regional stock exchanges with a single market information system for stocks. Its offices in various cities will be connected by computer lines so that the same market quotations and prices will be available to any purchaser of stock anywhere in the United States. The stock exchanges will be linked electronically with floor brokers at one exchange. These brokers will be able to trade on all markets, permitting them to trade at the best price, wherever it may be. All limit orders—those placed at prices above or below the current level—will go into a central computer file, and will be processed on whichever exchange meets the price of the limit order.

The Securities and Exchange Commission proposed the new system in 1971 and Congress gave its approval in 1975, empowering the SEC to oversee the needed changes. The rationale for the new market is that greater efficiency should result, more information should be available more quickly to investors, and market liquidity should be facilitated. The biggest gainers in the new system should be the individual investors, who for years have been steadily losing ground to the institutions, that had access to information unavailable to the average investor.

Most members of the New York Stock Exchange are opposed to a national market because they feel that the new system will result in a loss of control and business for the New York Stock Exchange. The specialists on the New York Stock Exchange, who are responsible for executing limit orders, are likely to lose much of the $60 million a year they earn in profits.

In order to maintain some degree of control over the growth of a national market, the New York Stock Exchange has piloted its own version of a national securities exchange. Called Intermarket Trading System (ITS), it electronically connects the floors of the New York Stock Exchange, the American Stock Exchange, and four regional exchanges in a test program involving about a dozen stocks. While most of the orders will still come into the New York Stock Exchange, the brokers will have an opportunity to see if there is a better price on another exchange before executing an order. The NYSE maintains control, however, because if a better price is offered elsewhere, the specialist at the NYSE has an opportunity to match the better offer in order to get the business.

The SEC, although studying the ITS experiment, has already indicated that it wants a more competitive system. In the ITS system, the NYSE stock specialists have an advantage because they get to respond to the offers made by specialists at other exchanges. The SEC wants a system in which specialists on all exchanges make their offers at the same time and the customer selects the best one. Such a system would put the individual investors on equal footing with the institutions in terms of available information. While all the exchanges have rules forbidding specialists to disclose the number of shares and the price for limit orders in their books, big institutional block traders have ways of getting a good reading on the situation. This intelligence is extremely valuable in helping the institution decide when to buy, and at what price.

When the national securities market comes, the costs of trading stocks and bonds will go down, increased competition will narrow the gap between the highest and lowest offers, and perhaps the individual investor will once again return to the market in large numbers.

their investments shrink, a very disconcerting experience in an economy in which the prices of most goods and services have risen at a gallop. Historically, people have bought preferred and common stock as a hedge against inflation. In other words, by buying stock and holding it for a year or more, investors hoped to make money on the rise in price between their purchase date and the date of sale. This is referred to as a *capital gain*. Since buying stock requires paying a broker a commission and selling it, the capital gain must be large enough to cover this overhead as well as the transfer taxes that are imposed on the seller, or the investor is not making any real gain on his investment.

HOW AN ORDER IS HANDLED

As was pointed out in a brochure published by the New York Stock Exchange, there are four considerations that should be kept in mind when dealing in stock or bond transactions on an organized exchange:

1. When you buy, you buy from another person.
2. When you sell, you sell to another person.
3. The stock exchange itself neither buys, sells, nor sets prices.
4. The exchange is merely the marketplace.

For purposes of illustrating a transaction, let's assume that Jane Fahey owns 100 shares of U.S. Steel Corporation common stock. Jane lives in DeKalb, Illinois, and has an account with a local brokerage firm that is a member of the New York Stock Exchange. Jane is planning to go to Europe next summer and decides to sell her U.S. Steel stocks to get some money for her trip. Jane calls her broker, also known as an account executive, while on a coffee break at work and asks him for a "quote" on U.S. Steel. The broker has a small quotation machine on his desk that enables him to pushbutton the code symbol for U.S. Steel, and within a second the latest market price for U.S. Steel stock appears on the screen. The price is satisfactory to Jane, so she instructs the account executive to sell her 100 shares of U.S. Steel *at market*. This means that she will sell at whatever the prevailing market price of the stock is when it is sold on the floor of the exchange. The broker calls her order in to the floor representative, who goes to the trading post where U.S. Steel is trading and offers the securities for sale.

In stock trading terminology, sales of stocks in multiples of 100 shares are known as *round lots*. Sales in multiples of 1 to 99 shares are known as *odd lots*. Since Jane is selling 100 shares, she is selling a round lot. The broker will charge Jane a commission to handle this transaction; the purchaser of these stocks will also have to pay a commission to his broker. If this were the sale of an odd lot, there would be a slight additional commission charge because odd-lot transactions are handled in a special way on the floor of the exchange.

Because Jane chose to sell her stock at or about the present market price of the stock, she placed a *market order*. A market order is an order to buy or sell a certain number of shares of a stock at market price. Had Jane decided that she would not sell until the market price of the stock reached a certain price prescribed by her, she would have placed a *limit order*. Limit orders are frequently used by the holder of a stock to prevent future losses or to protect paper profits. For example, an investor may have paid $25 a share for a stock which has risen to $50 per share. He may instruct his broker to sell the stock if it should drop to $40 per share. In this way, he protects for himself a profit of $15 per share.

Let us assume that, in this same day at about the same time, Harry Ratti of Sacramento, California, decides to buy 100 shares of U.S. Steel Corporation after researching for a potentially profitable stock. He calls his local account executive, who is also a member of the New York Stock Exchange, for a quote. The broker dials into his quotation machine and informs Harry of the latest sales price. Harry then instructs the broker to buy 100 shares at market. The broker wires the order to his representative on the floor of the exchange, and the representative goes to the trading post where Jane Fahey's broker is about to sell 100 shares of U.S. Steel. Here is where the *auction market* is in operation. The selling broker tries to get a higher price for his shares than the last best order. The buying broker tries to get his shares at a lower price simply by glancing at the electronic viewer that shows an enlargement of the ticker transactions as they occur during the trading day. If and when both brokers agree on the price, the transaction is completed and the paper work begins.

Buying and selling of stock on the NYSE can be followed on the electronic ticker in brokerage houses across the country.

Dean Witter Reynolds, Inc.

Some interesting terminology has cropped up over the years related to investing in securities. For instance, all of the stocks that an investor possesses is commonly referred to as a *portfolio*. While the market value of stock held in a portfolio can go up on a day-to-day basis, the investor realizes no profits on investments until after selling the stock. *Paper profit* applies to the rise in value of securities while they are held in one's portfolio, since no real profit can be realized until securities are removed from the portfolio and sold. (One could experience a paper loss as well.)

Are you an optimist or a pessimist? There are special terms in stock investing to describe these two attitudes to future events. If you believed that stock prices will rise and, therefore, that it's wise to buy more stock now while prices are still low, you would be known as a *bull* (optimist). If you foresaw stock prices decreasing in the future and feel you'd better sell now while prices are still high, you'd be known as a *bear* (pessimist).

Some people are more conservative in their buying attitudes than others. Such people usually only buy stocks of large, well-known corporations with a record of many years of financial stability and good earnings. These stocks are termed *blue chips*. This term is derived from the blue poker chip, which always has the highest monetary value.

In recent years, average stock prices have not always kept pace with the increase in the prices of goods and services. Therefore, investing in stocks is not always considered a good protection against inflation, especially for a short period of one or two years. At mid-1977, the prices of most common and preferred stocks were lower than they were during their high points in the 1960s. Obviously, making a quick "killing" in the market is not all that easy. In fact, for some people, putting their savings in a lower yielding savings account might have made them financially better off. Despite the occasional gloomy times, however, as the last forty years show, under normal circumstances, an investor can do very well in this investment medium.

THE MECHANICS AND TERMINOLOGY OF BUYING STOCK

From the point of view of the investor, the most convenient way to buy stock is to visit or telephone a stock brokerage firm that is a member of a major exchange such as the New York Stock Exchange. These firms are listed in telephone directories. Some of the largest are names that most people recognize, such as Bache or Merrill Lynch. Of course, a recommendation by a friend or associate who has been satisfied in his dealings with a broker over the years is the ideal way to contact a brokerage house. After finding a broker, the next step is to open an account. The broker (also known as a registered representative or account executive) who is assigned to the investing customer will provide the necessary forms and information to facilitate this procedure. From that point on, it is a case of seeking the right advice and placing orders by telephone or in person. Books have been written on the techniques of investing, and it is beyond the scope of this text to delve into this complicated topic.

Ordinarily, for each stock or bond purchased, the investor is required to remit the cash several business days after the trading date of the purchase. Likewise a seller of a stock or bond must tender the certificate(s) as soon as possible after the date of sale. By doing so he is assured of receiving his payment in a short number of business days.

The two brokers complete their verbal agreement by filling out a slip of paper with each other's firm's name and reporting the transaction back to their phone clerks so that Jane Fahey and Harry Ratti can be informed of the selling and buying prices. In the meantime, an exchange clerk has sent a record of the transaction to the ticker department for transmission over the ticker network.

OVER-THE-COUNTER MARKET

Many corporations do not meet requirements for listing on any organized stock exchange but yet desire the advantages that public trading of their shares can offer. Securities of such corporations are therefore traded in the *over-the-counter market*.

When an investor desires to buy an unlisted stock, or an OTC as it is sometimes known, he simply calls his broker and asks for a quote as he would for a stock sold on security exchanges. The broker has a constant source of quotations for about 5,000 unlisted stocks provided by the communications facilities of the National Association of Securities Dealers Automated Quotations. This name refers to a computerized communications system that collects and stores up-to-the-second quotations on those stocks. Each stock broker associated with the system can get the latest quote on any OTC stock listed by NASDAQ.

For stocks for which no NASDAQ quotes are available, the broker calls several other brokers to determine if they have any of the stock to sell and what price they want. If the broker's customer decides to buy, the broker will buy from the seller who tenders him the lowest quotation.

Many of the lesser known corporations are traded on the OTC. In total number of shares, more are traded over-the-counter than are on the organized exchanges. Many bonds are also traded in the OTC market.

A PROFILE OF AMERICAN SECURITY INVESTORS

It has been calculated that about 20 percent of all sales of securities are to small investors or, as they are also called, odd-lot investors. These are the people who buy stock, often in lots of 99 or less, as a means of earning more on their savings than they would in a savings account. In recent years the plight of the odd-lot investor has been a tough one. Stock prices have fluctuated sharply because of the various domestic and foreign crises our country has had to face. Watergate, the Mideast War, the fuel shortages, all of these have stunted the capital growth of stocks on security exchanges as well as those sold in the over-the-counter market. Not surprisingly, the small investor has not been as active in security trading as he was several years ago.

The bulk of the investors in corporate securities, estimated at 80 percent or more, are the so-called *institutional investors*. An institutional investor is one

TABLE 12-3 Top 25 NYSE companies with the largest number of common stockholders of record, early 1977

Company	Stockholders
American Tel. & Tel.	2,891,000
General Motors	1,254,000
Exxon Corp.	684,000
Int'l Business Machines	577,000
General Electric	555,000
General Tel. & Electronics	509,000
Texaco Inc.	404,000
Gulf Oil	357,000
Ford Motor	334,000
RCA Corp.	295,000
Southern Company	295,000
Consolidated Edison	275,000
Standard Oil of Calif.	271,000
Sears, Roebuck	267,000
American Electric Power	245,000
U.S. Steel	243,000
Eastman Kodak	240,000
Tenneco, Inc.	232,000
Mobil Corp.	229,000
ITT	228,000
Philadelphia Electric	225,000
Chrysler Corp.	218,000
Public Service Elec. & Gas	216,000
Pacific Gas & Electric	214,000
du Pont de Nemours	205,000

Source: *1977 Fact Book*, New York Stock Exchange.
Courtesy of New York Stock Exchange.

which buys stock in large quantities for its portfolio, which represents the savings of many individuals and business people. Pension funds are a prime example of an institutional investor. Workers and their employer contribute regularly to the pension fund on behalf of the employee so that he or she has a retirement income after a certain predetermined age. Pension funds, like insurance companies, take these contributions and invest a portion of them in shares of stocks and bonds. Table 12-3 shows the 25 top companies in terms of numbers of shareholders listed on the New York Stock Exchange.

MUTUAL FUNDS Mutual funds, or investment companies as they are often called, operate in the following manner: Assume that an individual has about $1,000 to invest. He or she could buy common stock directly but, knowing little about security investing, might feel uneasy about doing so. Such a potential investor might decide to buy shares in a mutual fund. Some mutual fund shares can be bought or sold through a broker like shares of stock in any corporation. This type of fund is known as a *closed-end investment company*. Shares of other funds can be bought directly from the investment company itself and will be bought back by that company when and if the holder decides to sell. These funds are known as *open-end investment companies*.

Once one invests in a mutual fund, the managers of the fund commingle the new investor's money with the monies of all other members. Individual investors have no direct control over investment decisions made by fund managers, who aim to make money for their stockholders by buying and selling shares in corporations and by collecting dividends and interest on the corporate securities. Such earnings, after covering operating expenses of the fund, are distributed to the shareholders.

To buy shares in a fund, the investor will often have to pay a commission.

In an *open-end mutual fund*, the value of the holders' shares changes daily according to the asset value of the fund. For example, if on a particular day the stocks and bonds owned by the fund have a value of $20 million and there are one million shares of stock in the fund outstanding, each mutual fund share would have an asset value of $20. In *closed-end mutual funds*, the value is computed in the market by "bid and ask," which depends on supply and demand.

The purchaser of an open-end mutual fund must pay a commission or load charge, in addition to the asset value per share on the day of purchase. Mutual funds that charge commissions are known as *load funds*. Some funds charge no commission because they do not employ direct-selling sales personnel nor indulge in an expensive advertising campaign. These are called *no-load funds*.

Most investment companies give the shareholder the choice of taking income and capital gains distributions in cash or reinvesting them in more shares of the fund. Other plans require periodic investment of set amounts on the part of the investor, with all capital gains distributions automatically reinvested. It is extremely important for the investor to know and understand the details of any investment company plan before making a commitment.

COMMODITY EXCHANGES

Some investors provide funds for businesses by speculating in various forms of business inventory as opposed to buying corporate stocks or bonds. Such investors put their excess savings into the different commodity markets located throughout the United States. Actually, commodity trading is a fairly simple matter. Commodity exchanges are organized markets—similar to the New York Stock Exchange. Instead of selling lots of stocks or bonds, however, they sell lots of wheat, corn, silver, cotton, and other commodities grown or mined. The investor buys a *contract*, which is an agreement to accept delivery on a set lot of some commodity at a future time, usually about six months away. Since most investors really don't want to accept delivery of the commodity when it becomes due, they will sell their contract sometime before the scheduled delivery date. They hope prices for the commodity will go up while they hold their contract, yielding a gain for them on the transaction.

Commodity trading is a very volatile type of investing. One can make large profits or suffer great losses in a very short time. For that reason it is not recommended for the average investor. Sharp price changes often occur in the commodity markets from month to month, week to week, even day to day, depending on the numerous developments that influence market prices.

Businesspeople who produce, market, and process the various commodities are usually the sellers of commodity contracts. They use the markets primarily for hedging of inventories and other forms of hedging. *Hedging* is a protective procedure designed to minimize losses in commodity marketing and processing that arise from adverse price fluctuations. It is a complicated but integral part of the business of every buyer or seller of commodities used in the production of merchandise to be sold to the public. More detailed explanations of commodity trading can be found in various books and pamphlets. Table 12-4 indicates some of the commodities, their sizes and prices quoted on the New York Mercantile Exchange.

TABLE 12-4 New York Mercantile Exchange commodity summary

Commodity	Contract Unit	Minimum Fluctuation		Maximum Fluctuation		Trading Hours	Delivery Months
		Per Unit Quoted	Per Contract Unit	Per Unit Quoted	Per Contract Unit		
Round White Potatoes	50,000 lbs.	1¢ per 100 lb.	$5.00	$.50 per 100 lb.	$250	10:00 a.m.-2:00 p.m.	Nov., Mar., Apr., May
Imported Boneless Beef	36,000 lbs.	2¢ per 100 lb.	$7.20	$1.50 per 100 lb.	$540	10:15 a.m.-1:45 p.m.	Jan., Mar., May, Jul., Sep., Nov.
Platinum	50 troy oz.	10¢ per oz.	$5.00	$10.00 per oz.	$500	9:30 a.m.-2:10 p.m.	Jan., Apr., Jul., Oct.
Palladium	100 troy oz.	5¢ per oz.	$5.00	$4.00 per oz.	$400	10:20 a.m.-1:30 p.m.	Mar., Jun., Sep., Dec.
U.S. Silver Coins	10 bags of $1000 face value each	$1 per bag	$10.00	$150.00 per bag	$1500	9:35 a.m.-2:15 p.m.	Jan., Apr., Jul., Oct.
Gold	1 Kilogram 32.151 troy oz.	20¢ per oz.	$6.40	$10.00 per oz	$320	9:25 a.m.-2:30 p.m.	Jan., Mar., May, Jul., Sep., Dec.,+ 3 current months

Source: Adapted from the *ABC's of Commodities*, New York Mercantile Exchange, 1976.

FINANCIAL NEWS: SOURCES AND INTERPRETATION

Remember when you learned to drive a car? You had to study a manual of rules, regulations, and road sign meanings. To some extent someone learning to invest must do the same thing. There are many rules, regulations, and road signs to become familiar with. One skill that might seem quite elementary at first, but really isn't as easy as it appears, is that of knowing how to read and understand stock quotations in your local newspaper.

STOCK QUOTATIONS

Almost all major newspapers devote several pages to the latest prices of stocks and bonds listed on the New York and other major stock exchanges. Many newspapers also list prices for the over-the-counter market as well. Stocks traded on the New York Stock Exchange are quoted in price variations of ⅛ of $1. If you wanted the current price of a certain security, you would check the listing in your local newspaper by looking for the particular corporate name, which is listed alphabetically. The entry might look very much like this illustration.

52 Weeks				Yld	P-E	Sales				Net
High	Low	Stocks	Div.	%	Ratio	100s	High	Low	Close	Chg.
		— A—A—A —								
53	41⅞	Ace Oil	2	4.95	10	36	49½	49½		.....
21	15⅝	AMF	1.24	6.8	8	367	18⅝	18⅛	18¼	– ⅜
15¾	9⅜	APL	1	7.1	9	100	14¼	14	14	.....
48⅜	32⅜	ARA	1.45	3.1	11	93	46⅝	46⅜	46½	– ½
27⅞	17⅞	ASA	1	3.8	..	646	26½	25	26½	+ ⅝
14⅞	7¾	ATO	.48	3.3	8	227	14⅞	14½	14½	– ¼
40	29	AbbtLb	.72	1.9	17	666	38	37½	37½	.....
21½	11	AcmeC	.80	3.7	8	58	u21¾	21½	21⅝	+ ⅛
5½	2¾	AdmDg	.04	.8	7	60	4¾	4⅝	4¾	+ ⅛

The two figures preceding the name of the company are the highest and lowest prices at which the stock has been traded during the current year. The figure 2 after Ace Oil means that the stock is currently paying total annual dividends of $2 per share. The P-E ratio (price-earnings ratio) of *10* means that the stock is selling at a current market price that is 10 times its last annual earnings amount. Since the stock closed at 49½, and this represents 10 times earnings, earnings must be about $4.95 per share. This means the total earnings for the corporation divided by the total number of shares outstanding equals $4.95. The figure 36 means 3,600 shares were traded on this day. The next four columns indicate the opening, highest, lowest, and last prices of trading in that security for the day; and the net change column indicates the change in price from the closing price of the preceding business day. Note that net change means the change from one day to the next, not the movement during a single day.

personality profile:
DOW Meets JONES

Everybody who knows anything about business and finance is familiar with the name Dow Jones. The Dow Jones Common Stock Index is still the most widely followed index of stock prices. Dow Jones & Company's *Wall Street Journal* is the best-known financial publication in America. Actually, the name Dow Jones is a combination of two last names, Charles Henry Dow and Edward D. Jones.

Charles Dow, born in Stirling, Connecticut, in 1851, on the family farm, took up journalism at the age of 21. After working for the Springfield, Massachusetts, *Daily Republican* and the Providence, Rhode Island, *Journal* for some years, he moved to New York in 1880 and devoted himself to the specialized profession of financial journalism.

Edward Jones, born in Worcester, Massachusetts, in 1856, left Brown University in his third year to become a reporter with the *Providence Press,* where he met Dow and the two became friends. After serving as editor of the Providence *Star* and *Sunday Dispatch,* he moved to New York, where the names Dow and Jones soon became inseparable.

In 1882 Dow and Jones set up their own financial news service in the basement of a soda pop store next to the Stock Exchange. The service thrived so well, partly because of their inventions to get the quotations and news out quickly, that in 1889 they began a financial newspaper, the *Wall Street Journal,* printed daily except Sundays and stock market holidays.

Charles Dow, the *Journal*'s editor, wrote many of the early editorials. Finance was his chief interest, and as journalist, researcher, member of the Exchange, and partner in a brokerage firm, he reached definite conclusions on stock sales and purchases, and on business trends. In an editorial column, Dow explained the short-, medium-, and long-range swings of stocks and related them to business cycles. Later writers assembled the substance of these columns into what came to be known as the "Dow Theory," which holds up in principle even today. No writer has better explained Wall Street's operations to the public.

Jones stayed on till 1899, when he retired. Dow kept working, and writing, until 1902, when the company was sold.

The second line of the illustration shows the preferred stock listing for Ace Oil. Note the pf designation after the company name. P-E ratios are usually not calculated for preferred issues so this column has no number. Note also that the stock price did not change from the previous day's closing so that the net change column has no number.

In the newspaper's over-the-counter listing, names of corporations are also in alphabetical order and bid-and-asked prices are given for each security. Sometimes these listings show the previous bid as well. A buyer will be concerned with the bid price; a seller, with the asked price. *Bid-and-asked* quotations are simply indicators of price ranges and, as such, have their uses for anyone interested in determining the approximate current value of OTC stocks.

The actual trading taking place on the floor of the stock exchange, summarized in the newspapers, is reported by a high-speed electronic ticker tape. Figure 12-3 explains how this ticker tape is read.

STOCK INDEXES

Keeping up with the overall trend of prices on the major stock exchanges can be made easier to some extent by reading or listening to the daily fluctuations in the indexes that measure the movement of stock prices. You have probably noticed more than once that extended radio or television news programs give the latest Dow Jones Industrial Stock Index, as well as one or more other averages, as part of each day's news report.

The *Dow Jones Industrial Stock Index* is the single best-known index of price fluctuations of certain selected securities traded on the New York Stock Exchange. This average of selected common stock prices gives a general, rather than precise, idea of the fluctuations in the securities markets and reflects the historical continuity of security price movements. The index constitutes an average of 30 representative stocks listed on the exchange and is published by the *Wall Street Journal* and hundreds of other daily newspapers throughout the country. In addition to its industrial index, Dow Jones also publishes several other gauges of common-stock prices. These include a transportation index, a public utilities index, and a composite stock average of 65 stocks using prices from all of these indexes. The company also puts out two separate indexes of corporate and municipal bond averages.

Other indexes are available to the public. The *New York Times* publishes its own daily average index of common-stock prices, as do Standard and Poor's Corporation as well as the New York Stock Exchange itself; but the Dow Jones Industrial Stock Index remains the leader because of the historical implications of its price fluctuations. It has been in existence longer than any other index and can, therefore, be utilized to observe and verify the trends in price movement over many years.

INVESTMENT SERVICES

Many firms sell investment advice to the public. Two major publishers of financial information related to corporate securities are Standard and Poor's Corporation and Moody's Investors Service Corporation. These firms sell weekly,

FIGURE 12-3 How to read the ticker tape. Source: Teacher's Manual for *You and the Investment World,* New York Stock Exchange, November 1971, p. 17

The Exchange's ticker is a high speed electronic means of reporting what is happening on the trading floor in New York to brokers and investors throughout this country and in some foreign countries.

Many students are curious about the ticker tape and its symbols. A sample segment of tape is included in the   brief explanation below. In case you visit a brokerage office with a ticker or get questions from your students, a brief summary of the ticker's use and how to read it is given below.

Here is a facsimile of a piece of tape with samples of the common symbols and an explanation of their meanings:

1				5		
ACB	XYZ	DEF	GHIPr	ACB		▪▪
3s28⅛	41½	1100s23⅜	40$_s$94	4s28¹¹³⁄₄₄₈		
2	3	4	6	7		

▪▪▪ AM ▪▪▪ MARKET ▪ UP CENTS ▪▪▪ NYSE ▪▪ INDEX UP▪▪▪▪

11 ▪ 30   3   48 ▪ 14 0 ▪ 03

8

1. ACB—The ticker abbreviation for the name of the company.
2. 3s28⅛—300 shares were traded for 28⅛ ($28.12½) per share. Trades of 200 to 900 shares are abbreviated in this way, e.g., 400 shares—4s; 600 shares—6s, etc.
3. 41½—100 shares were traded at 41½ ($41.50) per share. Trades of 100 shares are reported without a volume indicator, i.e., without the "s" symbol.
4. 1100s23⅜—1100 shares were traded at 23⅜. In trades of 1000 or more shares, the volume is not abbreviated.
5. GHIpr—This is a preferred stock. Stocks without the "pr" symbol are common stocks. Most stock issues are common.
6. 40ss94—40 shares of GHIpr were traded at 94. Preferred stocks and some higher priced common stocks are traded in units of 10 rather than 100 shares. Trades in these stocks are noted in this manner on the ticker, using the actual volume and the double ss.
7. 4s28¼—The first trade indicated here is 400 shares of ACB at $28.25; then a trade of 100 shares at the same price; and finally a transaction of another 100 shares at a fractional price change, $28.37½.
8. The 11:30 a.m. report of the change in the average price of NYSE shares shows it has risen 3 cents. The NYSE Common Stock Index has increased .03 points from the previous day's close.

Courtesy of New York Stock Exchange.

monthly, quarterly, and annual investment analyses to individuals, libraries, and businesses. Their reports include information on particular industries as well as on individual corporations. They provide extensive data as well as an opinion on the future prospects of the firm. Figure 12-4 is an example of one such investment analysis.

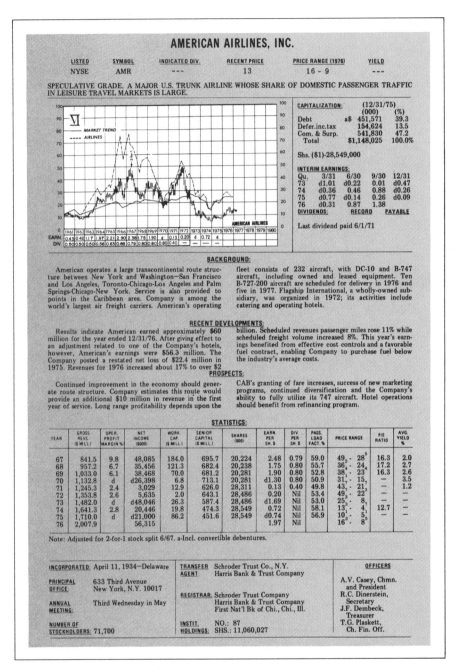

FIGURE 12-4 Investment analysis by Moody's. Source: *Moody's Handbook of Common Stock,* Spring 1977, Moody's Investors Service. Copyright © 1977 by American Airlines.

INVESTMENT
PUBLICATIONS AND
REGULATION

Among the more sophisticated investment publications devoted to the security investor are the *Wall Street Journal*, *Forbes*, *Financial World*, and *Barrons*. The *Wall Street Journal*, published five times a week, is a comprehensive newspaper of financial news, while *Barrons* is a weekly newspaper for the investor. Both these publications are products of the Dow Jones Corporation. *Forbes* and *Financial World* are magazines for security investors. *Forbes* is published every two weeks, while *Financial World* is published fifty weeks a year.

The Securities and Exchange Commission, commonly known as the SEC, was established in 1934 after the Great Depression had devastated the stock market. The SEC is the federal regulatory agency for security trading in the United States. Frequently it publishes bulletins and information brochures about security laws, similar to those provided by some state governments. The commission does not publish investment advice or suggestions.

In addition to publishing information for the investor, the SEC requires that corporations register all new stock and bond issues with it prior to their being offered to the public. This registration statement contains financial and other data about the corporation and about the new issue. Much of this information is included in a brochure called a *prospectus* which is available to anyone interested in the new corporate issue. Under its enabling acts, the Securities and Exchange Commission was established to monitor the activities of corporations, security dealers, and stock exchanges engaged in the interstate sale of securities.

Various states require local corporations to register in a similar manner. State security regulatory powers are known as "*blue sky laws*," probably so named because a state legislator pushing for approval of such legislation once said that security swindlers would try to sell you the blue sky if they could.

One cannot always buy low and sell high in the securities markets. But the more accurately an investor can predict the market, the better his chances of making money. Keeping informed is necessary homework for the security trader. If this seems too complicated or time-consuming, then perhaps mutual funds are the answer. For those who want to do their own investing but cannot afford to subscribe to investment services and publications, a good community or university library should provide the necessary sources.

SUMMARY

Businesses shop around for short- and long-term funds that they need. The marketplace for short-term financing is known as the money market. Shopping for funds in this market involves brokerage houses, commercial banks, bond dealers, security exchanges, and similar institutions. Shopping for funds in the long-term market involves, for the most part, insurance companies and investment bankers.

Selling shares of stock to the public is an important source of funds for corporations. Corporations sell their shares through the open market known as the over-the-counter market or through organized stock exchanges such as the New

York Stock Exchange. The first sale of a new stock issue is known as a sale through the primary market. When stocks are resold by one owner to another, the transaction is known as a sale through the secondary market. *Forbes* magazine and the *Wall Street Journal* are two of many fine sources that give current detailed information about the money market, stocks, stock exchanges, and investment banking.

SUMMARY OF KEY TERMS

Bear An investor who believes stock prices will fall.

Bid-and-asked Price quotations for stocks and bonds traded in the over-the-counter market.

Blue Sky Laws State legislation regulating corporate security sales.

Bull An investor who believes stock prices will rise.

Capital Market Market where securities are bought and sold, representing long-term lending and borrowing of funds.

Closed-end Investment Company A mutual fund whose shares are bought and sold through a broker like shares of stock in any corporation.

Correspondent Banks Commercial banks that are affiliated with commercial banks in other geographical areas and serve as their agent.

Dow Jones Industrial Stock Index Popular daily average of 65 stocks on the New York Stock Exchange published in major newspapers and quoted on radio and television.

Factoring Houses Commercial finance companies that deal in the buying and lending of funds, using as collateral the accounts receivable of the borrowing corporation.

Hedging A protective procedure used in commodity trading designed to minimize losses in commodity marketing and processing that result from adverse price fluctuations.

Institutional Investors Institutions such as mutual funds or pension funds that buy and sell stocks and bonds in large quantities for their portfolios, which represent the savings of many individuals and business firms.

Liquidity The ability to turn an investment or asset into cash quickly.

Listed Security A security that is regularly traded on an organized stock exchange such as the New York Stock Exchange.

Load Fund A mutual fund that charges a selling commission to the purchaser of its shares.

Money Market The marketplace where short-term securities are bought and sold.

No-load Fund A mutual fund that does not charge a selling commission to the purchaser of its shares.

Odd Lot A purchase or sale of 99 shares of stock or less.

Open Book Account Usual billing procedure between wholesalers and retailers, where up to 60 days grace is given between date of billing and date of required payment of bills.

Open-end Investment Company A mutual fund that sells its shares directly to the public and buys them back from holders at current asset value.

Over-the-counter Market The marketplace where stocks and bonds of corporations not listed on organized stock exchanges are traded.

Portfolio All of the stocks that an investor possesses.

Primary Market The market where brand-new issues of stocks and bonds are sold from the issuing corporation to the investing public.

Private Placement The sale of new securities from the issuing corporation to one or several investors.

Round Lot A purchase or sale of shares of stock in multiples of 100.

Seat Membership by a brokerage firm in an organized stock exchange.

Secondary Market Market where issues of stocks

and bonds are resold, such as the New York Stock Exchange.

Securities and Exchange Commission Federal regulating agency for security trading.

Spread Difference between the selling and buying price of a new stock or bond issue handled by an investment banker. The profit comes out of this difference in price.

Underwriter An investment banker who buys a new security issue from a corporation and then sells it through syndication to the investing public.

REVIEW QUESTIONS

1. Define open-end and closed-end mutual funds and explain how they differ.
2. Define load and no-load mutual funds.
3. What is an institutional investor? Name one category of institutional investor.
4. What is NASDAQ? How does it serve the over-the-counter market?
5. What activities occur at a commodity exchange? What is a commodity contract?
6. Explain the syndication function of underwriting.
7. An investment broker buys a new issue of bonds from a corporation for $1.9 million and hopes to sell it to the public for $2.0 million (face value). The process of buying the whole issue is called what? The difference between the $1.9 million and the $2.0 million is called what? Does all of the difference represent profit for the investment bank? Explain.
8. Insurance companies are primarily interested in what kind of funding? Why?
9. What are the major functions of a factor?
10. List the major types of instruments one would observe in money market dealings.

DISCUSSION QUESTIONS

1. In today's newspaper look up the following stocks listed on the New York Stock Exchange and find their P-E ratios and closing prices.
    a. American Brands
    b. General Motors
    c. Ford
    d. Gulf Oil
    e. Exxon
    f. Chrysler
    g. Gulf and Western
    h. IBM
    i. AT&T
    j. INCO
2. Comment on the following statement: "Stocks are one's best investment hedge against inflation."
3. Using the resources of your school or local library, find the following information:
    a. The names and closing prices of the five most actively traded stocks on the New York Stock Exchange for today.
    b. The high, low, closing price, and net change of Armco Steel Corp. common stock listed on the New York Stock Exchange for today.
4. Go through recent back issues of *Forbes* and *Barrons* at your library. Select one article that is of interest to you and make a report to your class on the content of that article. The report may be oral or written.
5. If you wanted to buy 100 shares of common stock, how would you go about buying it?

CASES FOR DECISION MAKING

NOTE PAPER

The notice shown below appeared in an issue of the *Wall Street Journal* (May 31, 1977). Based on it, answer the following questions.

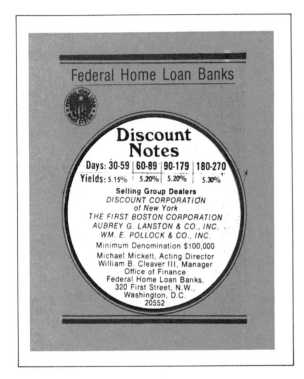

1. Is this a money market or capital market offering?
2. Why do the longer term notes yield higher interest rates?
3. Find out what a "discount note" is.
4. Who are the underwriters?
5. What is the smallest amount of these notes one can buy?

$75,000,000 ACTION

In early 1977, Consolidated Natural Gas Company, a Delaware corporation, ran an advertisement in the financial section of several newspapers inviting the public to bid on the purchase of $75,000,000 principal amount of $x\%$ debenture bonds due June 1, 1997. The bonds were dated June 1, 1977, and the bids must have been sealed and forwarded to the company at its New York office by 11 a.m. on June 7, 1977. Prior to acceptance of any bid, the bidder or bidders would be furnished with copies of the prospectus.

1. Make a list of the types of investors who would be interested in bidding on this issue.
2. What is the collateral for these bonds?
3. What is the time length of the issue?
4. Why was no specific interest rate specified in the ad?
5. Is Consolidated obligated to accept the bids? Why or why not?

TO LIST OR NOT TO LIST, THAT IS THE QUESTION

The Nee Cap Corporation is a national manufacturer of bottle tops and covers for bottles, jars, and cans. The corporation's common stock is traded in the OTC market and there has been quite a bit of investor enthusiasm for this stock over the past year. Nee Cap has 600,000 shares of common stock outstanding, with a current market value of $3,500,000. The 600,000 shares are owned by 4,000 different shareholders, 2,000 of which own at least 100 shares each. Nee Cap has net tangible assets of $6 million and reported net income of $900,000 before taxes and $500,000 after taxes for the last fiscal year. The firm's board of directors would like to have the stock listed on the New York or American Stock Exchange. They believe the prestige and the new market outlet will help increase the growth potential for the market value of each share.

1. Do you agree or disagree with the board of directors reasoning?
2. Can the firm qualify for listing on the NYSE? (See Table 12-2)
3. Can the firm qualify for listing on the AMEX?
4. Do you think the firm should stay in the OTC market? Why or why not?

RELATED READINGS

Brooks, John. *The Go Go Years*. New York: Weybright and Talley, 1973.

Well-written book about investing during the growth years of the 1960s. Contains a series of good stories that should serve as a caution to the inexperienced stock trader.

Commodity Trading Manual. Chicago: Chicago Board of Trade, 1973.

An outstanding textbook giving complete information on commodity trading. Many good charts, graphs, and tables help explain some rather difficult concepts. Serves as an up-to-date, comprehensive guide for the student.

Jensen, Michael C. *The Financiers*. New York: Weybright and Talley, 1976.

Stories about some very successful investment bankers. Interesting accounts of gigantic stocks and bonds deals.

Jessup, Paul F., and Upson, Roger B. *Returns in the Over-the-Counter Market*. Minneapolis: University of Minnesota Press, 1973.

Contains information on the dimensions of the OTC market. Concentrates on investment returns and the impact of portfolio diversification. Somewhat technical but a good source of basic information.

Klein, Roger, and Wolman, William. *The Beat Inflation Strategy*. New York: Simon and Schuster, 1965.

Easy-to-follow guide to investing. Authors point out the economic and financing factors one must observe and act upon in order to invest as a hedge against inflation.

Lawrence, James C. *Your Fortune in Futures*. New York: St. Martin's Press, 1976.

Contains useful information for the prospective commodity investor. Describes how future trading works and what the right mental attitude is.

Malkiel, Burton G. *A Random Walk Down Wall Street*. New York: Norton, 1973.

Points out the frustrations of the average investor. Gives suggestions for overcoming investment frustrations.

Sobel, Robert. *AMEX: A History of the American Stock Exchange 1921–1971*. New York: Weybright and Talley, 1972.

A very interesting description of the roots of the second largest organized stock exchange in America.

———. *A History of the New York Stock Exchange 1935–1975*. New York: Weybright and Talley, 1975.

An interesting history of the New York Stock Exchange over the past 40 years.

part four: **CAREER OPPORTUNITIES**

CAREERS IN FINANCE

The work environment and nature of work in financial institutions have changed drastically in the last 30 years. People who work for banks and similar financial institutions today are encouraged to be oriented to customer service and innovation. Since World War II, many new jobs have been created in banking because of the tremendous increase in the number of banks, savings and loan associations, stock brokerage firms, insurance companies, and the financial planning departments in large corporations. The opportunities are good for those with a college degree and solid basic training in accounting, math, financial management, money and banking, economics, and investment analysis. An interest in working with numbers is essential.

Salaries for banking and financial management personnel are usually very good and the career paths to more responsibility are outstanding. The opportunities for minorities and women are probably at an all-time high. Those who desire opportunities for rapid advancement should not be averse to relocating in large metropolitan cities where most of the nation's financial activities are centered.

BANKING Banks have many levels of job opportunities—presidents, vice presidents, treasurers, operations managers, loan officers, cashiers, and tellers. All of these positions require training beyond secondary school with some background in finance and accounting. Of the more than 250,000 bank officers holding jobs today, women accounted for approximately 20 percent of this amount. Bank officers make

important decisions and must have a broad knowledge of business activity, both on a national level and on a local level.

Through the mid-1980s, employment of bank officers is expected to increase faster than the average for all occupations. The increasing dependence on computers for record keeping and an expansion in banking services means continued demand for more banking officers to provide sound management and effective quality control.

SECURITY BROKERS Selling securities (stocks and bonds) continues to be an attractive job to people who enjoy being in finance. While most jobs are sales jobs, there are some opportunities in management for successful salespeople. About 230,000 people are employed in securities selling. Half work full time in securities firms and in selling mutual funds. Brokerage firms, investment bankers, mutual funds, and insurance companies are the primary employers. While a four-year degree is increasingly important, many of the jobs are open to two-year graduates as well. Moderate growth in the number of positions is expected here.

With the vast number of mergers among brokerage firms in recent years, very few new jobs are expected in the field for the 1980s. Most new positions will be with insurance companies and pension plans where expansion is still taking place.

FINANCIAL ANALYSTS Another large area of employment in the financial field is in financial analysis for industry and business. Individuals in this area are concerned with the best means of securing, using, and maintaining the funds needed by the firm in its operations. They use the data accumulated by accountants. Most of these jobs require a college degree in finance or accounting. More advanced financial analyst positions may require an MBA or other advanced degree.

In recent years many large corporations have set up financial analysis departments to assist top management in making long-range financial decisions.

part five

INFORMATION

Sometimes it seems that numbers are becoming more important in our society than faces or names. Your school issues you a student identification number and your employer does the same. In both cases it is usually your social security number. Your number is a more acceptable form of identification than your name. You are recognized by your credit card numbers, driver's license, and registration numbers, insurance policy numbers, and the number you take in the customer service department of your neighborhood supermarket.

Do we like living within the framework of a number system? Probably not. Yet, we recognize that to run an efficient and effective economy for 220 million Americans, we need effective record keeping and accounting. Since computers are the new efficient and rapid way of accomplishing this goal, we take a look at this key to effective data processing and measurement in Chapter 13.

In fact, accounting and data processing are not as cut-and-dried as the above statement might lead one to believe. There are different ways of analyzing and interpreting data. As we shall see in Chapter 14, there are legal considerations related to information systems and business operations that are of great significance. Accountants, lawyers, computer programmers, and operators are not dull automatons. On the contrary, most of these people find their work exciting, challenging, and important in a society that is so heavily dependent on them. They labor in a dynamic environment and are rewarded with status as well as good incomes.

Whether we like it or not, we live a numerical life. As investors or as managers we learn to read and interpret financial statements as a measurement of success or failure. Even as customers we judge a good buy by the lowest price for the most value.

chapter 13

USING INFORMATION SYSTEMS AND QUANTITATIVE AIDS IN DECISION MAKING

OBJECTIVES

When you have finished reading and studying this chapter, you should:

1. Be aware of the capabilities of an electronic data processing (EDP) system for aiding management in its decision-making role.

2. Know and describe the basic functions of an EDP system.

3. Be familiar with the terminology and special problems associated with computer technology.

4. Be able to describe the methods used for gathering, analyzing, and interpreting data for business use.

5. Be familiar with the terminology associated with statistical methods and procedures.

6. Be aware of some of the contemporary quantitative decision-making methods employed by managers.

CHAPTER PREVIEW

Have you ever gazed up at a corporate skyscraper-headquarters and wondered how one firm could employ so many people and handle so many millions of transactions? Well, it probably couldn't if it weren't for the coming of age of electronic data processing (EDP). Computers and their auxiliary equipment make it possible to process data at a rate never dreamed possible at the time your parents were born. We would not know what to do if all the computers operating in the United States came to a halt, yet the practical computer has only been with us for about 35 years.

Statistics is another story. Ever since humans used their fingers and toes for counting, they have been calculating. Using the computer for statistical calculation and interpretation is infinitely quicker and more accurate than toes and fingers, or even pencil and paper, but statistical concepts must be understood to comprehend the statistical information received from the computer. If a computer prints out that the "mean" of a series of 6,000 numbers is 482, this is of very little value unless it is known what is meant by the term "mean." Both EDP and statistics aid management in the use of quantitative decision-making devices such as the Program Evaluation and Review Technique (PERT) and the Critical Path Method (CPM).

Since statistics can be a very dry subject but a very important one to businesses and their managers, many interesting formats have been devised to make it more palatable to the reader. This chapter will review those presentations, and perhaps statistics won't appear as mysterious and dry as you once thought. Speaking of mystery, most people think computers are mysterious metal monsters. Actually they are not difficult to understand, and we hope this chapter convinces you of that.

The Bionic Man

USING INFORMATION SYSTEMS AND QUANTITATIVE AIDS IN DECISION MAKING

How old are you? Statistics depicting the population of the United States would indicate that if you are a student in a course using this textbook, chances are that you are under 35 years of age. Of course, this is a generalization and there are doubtless many students taking this course who are older than that. Statistics, which can describe many aspects of a person, a place, or an activity, are very useful for businesspeople, and every business student should have some general awareness of how data should be interpreted and presented. The latter part of this chapter delves into the analysis and presentation of data. But the point here is that if you are over 35 years of age, you are older than the age of electronic computers and computer systems. Electronic data processing, or EDP, traces its roots back to 1946, when the first functional electronic computer came into existence. Up to that time there were many early devices that could do calculating, filing, and analyzing of information, but none could work with the lightning speed of the electronic computer.

BACKGROUND OF EDP

Dr. Herman Hollerith, a statistician from Buffalo, New York, invented the first punched card and tabulating machine in the 1880s. The holes in the cards were made by a hand-operated punch and the cards were then placed, one by one, over cups filled with mercury. A device containing rows of protruding pins descended onto the surface of the card and these pins dropped through the holes into the mercury. This action completed an electrical circuit which caused a pointer to move one position on a dial. In this way the difficult and time-consuming job of counting data was automated. Automation, you remember from an earlier chapter, is the process by which machines take over the tasks previously performed by human effort.

One immediate benefit of Hollerith's data processing device was that the 1890 census took only a little over three years to complete because the federal government rented his equipment. In contrast, the 1880 census had taken seven years to execute and this was at a time when population was significantly below that of the 1880–1890 decade.

The IBM corporation, the undisputed world leader in the development, sales, and services of computers, traces its roots back to Dr. Hollerith and his nineteenth-century device that was crude but speedier than human head or hands. By 1914, IBM had four basic business machines in operation.

1. A keypunch machine for punching holes in cards
2. A gang punch machine for punching repetitive data into a large number of cards simultaneously
3. A vertical sorter for arranging cards into selected groups, such as by city or state of addressee
4. A tabulating machine for adding the data punched into cards

The first Hollerith tabulating system resembled a player piano. At the left is the sorter; at the right, the tabulator.

IBM

It would be difficult for us to imagine a computerless society today. In fact, it would be impossible to carry on many of the business and governmental functions affecting the activities of more than 220 million American citizens. Experts contend that the Social Security system, started in the mid-1930s, would have had to be discontinued by the mid-1960s if the electronic computer had not come into existence. This contention is based on the fact that back in the stagnant Depression years no one envisioned the system's growing to cover practically everyone in the country, nor did anyone foresee the huge birthrate increases of the 1940s and 1950s.

In the last 30 years—less than half an average human lifetime—the computer has profoundly affected all of us. Every day we directly experience, read, or hear of new ways in which this marvelous device has changed our habits. In fact, such occurrences usually are so much taken for granted that most of us never notice them. Everytime you step on a self-service elevator, you are being served by an electronic computer system. The same holds true when your automobile driving is regulated by traffic lights, for these, too, are regulated by a computer.

SYSTEMS DESIGN The computer is the heart of any EDP system. *Computers* are electronically powered machines that compute, file, analyze, summarize, and store data. In short, computers store and process data. For business and scientific purposes most data is of a quantitative nature and computers obtain their name from their most important function: computing results and solving problems. Humans can do anything computers can do and a lot more. But, when it comes to storing, processing, and recalling data, computers are far and away the champions. They are far superior to humans in this arena because they store, process, and recall at superspeeds and with tremendous accuracy.

Whether it's a simple computer for figuring a payroll or a very complicated one for guiding a Saturn rocket to outer space, all computers must be designed in a systematic way. Further along in this chapter you will learn that there is more to a computer than just one elaborate machine hissing at you and blinking hundreds of tiny lights. A computer is only one unit in an entire system. Specially trained engineers work with a business to design the system most appropriate to the needs of that particular firm. Such engineers are known as *systems analysts*, and they frequently work closely with the computer salesperson and client to put together the successful design of the system.

The first question for the systems analyst to consider is: Which of the two families of computers will best serve for executing the tasks at hand? Computers are classified as either the digital type or the analog type. *Digital computers* solve problems by counting digits. Therefore, the main work of these machines is computation. An adding machine also counts numbers, but it is not considered a computer. The difference is that computers can automatically, and in an instant, do many problems of all degrees of difficulty, such as finding a square root and adding that result to other computations. A digital computer can also compare two numbers to determine if they are equal or if one is larger.

Analog computers solve problems by measuring one quantity in terms of some other quantity. An analog computer is usually in constant operation, like your speedometer when you drive your car. As you well know, the faster you go, the higher the speed indicated by the needle. The complex analog computers in use today were developed in conjunction with the radar and gunfire control systems devised for aerial surveillance and defense during World War II. Figure 13-1 gives a very simple pictorial presentation of the two basic types of computers.

COMPONENTS AND OPERATIONS OF EDP SYSTEMS

You may have seen the science fiction film *2001: A Space Odyssey*, in which a computer rebels against its human operators and takes control. In real life the computer does not have the capability to initiate action. On the contrary, it is nothing more than large hunks of metal, rubber, glass, and wire. It is up to the human brain to tell the computer what to do, when to do it, and how to do it. The plan for instructing the computer as to what, when, and how to do a task is known as a *program*, and the specially trained individuals who prepare the instructions are called programmers. A program is nothing more than a set of prepared instructions using special symbols and procedures that are fed into the com-

FIGURE 13-1 Types of computers

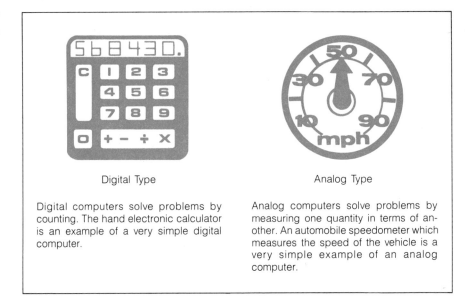

Digital Type

Digital computers solve problems by counting. The hand electronic calculator is an example of a very simple digital computer.

Analog Type

Analog computers solve problems by measuring one quantity in terms of another. An automobile speedometer which measures the speed of the vehicle is a very simple example of an analog computer.

puter through an input device (a term explained later). In effect the program gives the computer the instructions and data it needs to perform a task. For example, if you wanted the computer to prepare the weekly payroll for your firm, you would instruct it to do so and, in addition, give it such needed information as:

1. Hourly rate for each employee
2. Number of dependents for each employee
3. Federal withholding tax table
4. FICA (Social Security) deduction rate
5. Pension deduction rate
6. Rate and hours that constitute your overtime policy

Without specific instructions and without the necessary information affecting payrolls, the machine is not properly programmed for this task. For other chores the computer will need different programs; without a program, the machine is totally helpless. Frequently a new program will contain a number of "bugs." These are flaws in the data that the programmer cannot detect until they are fed into the machine and used by the computer. Such flaws are usually worked out in a very short time with some minor adjustments to the program. In its simplest outline form, an EDP system would look like Figure 13-2.

EDP COMPONENTS   A thorough explanation of the various input devices, functions, and output devices associated with a typical EDP system would take a great deal more than a

FIGURE 13-2 Outline of an EDP system

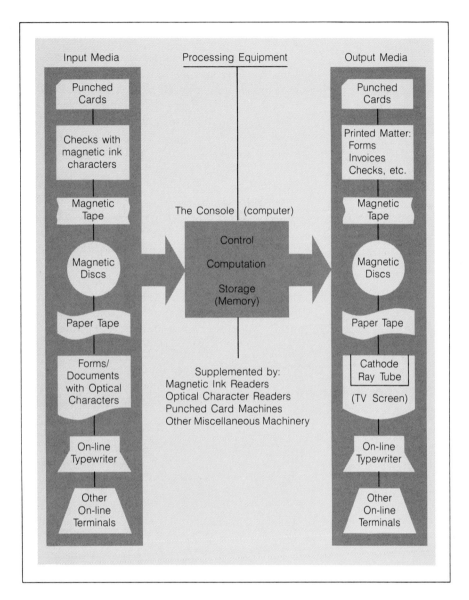

portion of one chapter. However, a brief elaboration of the above outline may help give you a general knowledge of how computers work.

Input Devices To feed programs and data into a computer, one uses an *input device*. Depending on what information is needed and how quickly, the computer operator may use a variety of input devices. One you have all seen (perhaps your class card was one) is the punched card. In the early days of data processing, this was the dominant method for feeding computers, but today it is considered very slow. Magnetic tape and stacks of tape spools in magnetic drums are the fastest way to feed information into the computer. Paper tape is too slow and fragile for most jobs, and the electronic typewriter is so slow it is only used to ask the computer special questions or give the computer special instructions. Remember that the program—that is, the prepared instructions—as well as the data necessary for completing it, must be fed into the computer through one of the input devices.

The Console The large hissing machine with the array of blinking lights is known as the *console*. It is the heart and brain of all EDP systems; here is where all data is processed. Part of the console is taken up by *control equipment* that works from the instructions set forth in the program. The control section gives the mechanical instructions necessary for performing the task at hand. Another area in the computer itself is the *computational section*. This section performs the necessary calculation tasks associated with a particular program. It can perform thousands of multiplication problems in a matter of seconds, and it never has the problems with accuracy that the human brain has. The storage or memory section of the computer is where all the data necessary for performing the program must

IBM's 158 MP virtual storage system.

IBM

be stored. Computers, like closets, come in various sizes; the larger the closet, the more you can store. The same holds true with computers. The larger the computer, the more data can be stored and the greater the task that the computer can perform.

Output Devices   The same devices described as input devices can also serve as *output devices*. The machine can also give output in various forms, the most common being the printout sheet. Once the programmed data is processed by the control unit, the machine's rate of output is extremely rapid. Whole lines of output information are printed in a small fraction of a second, and full sheets of printout paper are turned out so rapidly that operators have a hard time keeping up with stacking them.

In the case of your payroll program, mentioned earlier, the procedures from input through printout would be as follows:

1. The machine is fed the program through one of the input devices.
2. The machine is fed data for storage also through one of the input devices.
3. The control unit in the console will follow the directions specified in the program and take data from storage for processing through the computational section.
4. Processed data will then be channeled by the control units to the selected output device as instructed by the program.
5. The output device selected will print out the completed payroll reports and will probably also print out all payroll checks and check stubs.
6. After completion of the program, the machine will go onto its next program or go back to a previous program it had been working on. If no work is available, the machine will shut down. This, however, would be a very unlikely situation because such costly equipment should never be left idle.

Have you ever visited a large EDP center in a business or governmental agency? You may find that security is very tight. In addition, such facilities are placed in rooms with wiring systems under the floor and above the ceiling to take care of the huge electrical load necessary to keep the computer operating. Such rooms are carefully monitored by special equipment to make sure that the temperature and humidity never vary from certain prescribed levels. Most firms also have their own back-up electric generator to take over should the public utility supply fail. The expense of operating an EDP center is huge, and in most cases the equipment is leased from the manufacturer. In this way the cost is apportioned over a period of time and, more importantly, when the lease expires the firm has the opportunity to change over to newer or different equipment that might better suit its operations.

HARDWARE AND SOFTWARE   Computer *hardware equipment* may be thought of as those individual machines that comprise a particular EDP system. The number of machines will vary with the size of the work load and with the degree of sophistication the particular data processing demands. It is possible to use a separate piece of equipment for each of the five functions in an EDP system: input, control, storage, computation, output. Units which combine control and other functions are also available. One can have 10 or 12 machines if one wants several different types of input or output methods. All hardware is decided upon in consultation with the systems analyst and client. Often some of the hardware, known as peripheral equipment, is many miles from the central processing unit. As an example, a large Chicago insurance company with a central EDP processing unit might have a number of input and output devices located in various branch offices throughout the country. Terminals in the branch office allow them to feed data into the home office and receive processed information back from the Chicago-based control processing unit. All of this can often be done in a matter of minutes. Such a procedure is part of an *on-line* system, meaning that the computer is constantly available to receive, process, and remit information to a number of branches in a matter of moments. It is conceivable that many branches may transmit to the central unit at the same time, causing a jam. Even when this happens, the equipment operates so quickly that the delay may only be a matter of several seconds or minutes.

Examples of computer hardware would be card-reading machines, the console unit, the printout machine, and various other machines such as collators and tabulators. One should read a primer on hardware equipment for a detailed explanation of the operation of hardware equipment. One of the most recent innovations in EDP hardware is the *optical scanning device*, which can read certain types of printed or handwritten matter and convert them into data for the computer. Such a device saves the operators of the system from having to do this themselves before feeding the data into the computer. Many organizations dealing with bulk mailings use optical scanning devices. The United States Postal Service is attempting to perfect an optical scanner that can read the large variety of ways people write numbers. This is one more example of the advance of automation in the data processing field.

Computer *software equipment* is the term applied to the various aids that facilitate the programming of the computer. Paper punched cards, magnetic tape, and even the program itself are examples of computer software. Obviously, the software requirements of the system are planned by the systems analyst while designing the hardware equipment.

Each computer manufactured is designed to respond to certain basic character symbols or combination of characters and/or symbols called a language. Various programming languages have been developed which permit the computer to comprehend the instructions written by the programmer. One such language is known as *COBOL*, an abbreviation that stands for "common business-oriented language." COBOL is the language used by the majority of business firms when programming their computers. Another language is known as *FORTRAN*, and is used more in scientific and mathematical applications than for business purposes.

FORTRAN is the abbreviation for "formula translation." New and easier languages are being developed, and it may not be very long before the computer will be able to take some instructions in everyday English form.

FLOW CHARTS

Computers are able to do much more than keep records of information and calculate payrolls. Many computers are programmed to make decisions and to predict future events. Perhaps you've watched election returns on television and observed the use of a computer to predict the winner of an election based on a very small percentage of the votes counted. Such predictions made by the computer are rarely wrong. To use the computer as a forecaster or decision maker, it is important to outline the logical steps required to solve a problem and make a forecast. Such outlines are usually prepared in diagram form, a procedure referred to as a *flow chart*.

Basically, a flow chart employs symbols such as boxes, arrows, diamond shapes, and oblongs to indicate what is to be done. It serves to break down in a logical way the various steps necessary to solve a problem or reach a decision. In addition, it illustrates how to solve the problem in the least number of steps and, if properly prepared, saves time and labor in programming the computer for the task at hand. A well-prepared flow chart will illustrate in a logical sequence all of the necessary steps for finding the solution to a problem at hand. The example in Figure 13-3, flow charting a student's procedure for getting to school in the morning, illustrates one application of such a device.

BINARY CODE

This is one of the more complicated items of information that relates to EDP and concerns computer arithmetic. The arithmetic of computers is not based on the numbering system that most of us use, namely, the decimal system. All computer operations are in the *binary code*. This system of calculating is based on only two digits, a zero and a one. Using a binary code system, any zero or any one is referred to as a "bit," which is a contraction of the word "binary digit." Computer sensors, having very limited thinking ability, sense zeros or ones as on or off electrical currents. In this very simple fashion, the computer interprets all instructions and numbers through sensing on and off bits.

You do not have to be a math major to understand the binary number system and its relation to the operation of the computer. But you certainly need to read up on the binary code in a text on computers to be thoroughly familiar with the operation of the binary system. However, knowing the binary code system is not necessary to an understanding of the general operations of computers.

MINICOMPUTERS AND MICROPROCESSORS

Thanks to the development of the microprocessor and recent advances in its technology, minicomputers have become an affordable new entry into the world of business data processing. A *microprocessor* is a single integrated circuit that contains much but not all of the ability of a computer. Microprocessors are used

FIGURE 13-3 Program for getting to campus each morning

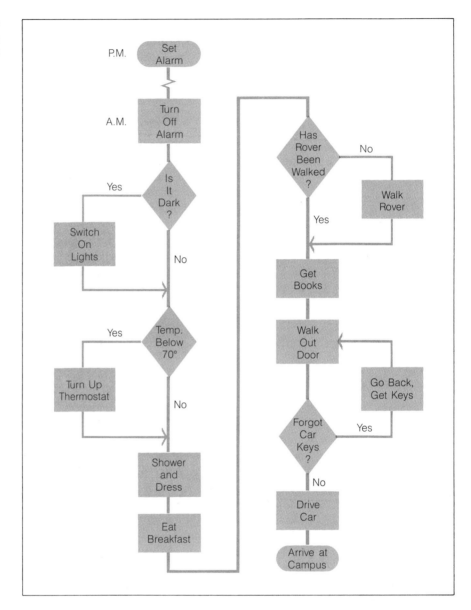

to perform arithmetic logic functions. Its ability to perform is limited and, unlike a computer, it has no memory, or a very limited one at best.

Much more sophisticated microprocessors have been developed that now serve as a basic component for minicomputers. *Minicomputers* are small computers that can perform many of the basic functions that a complete computer can, but they are much less expensive to buy and operate. This innovation gives the business that could not afford a traditional computer the opportunity to have equipment that can perform the same basic functions on a limited scale at a much lower performance cost. Minicomputers are also being utilized by large firms that have complete computers for special functions and by separate operating units of the firm. These minicomputers operate independently but can also share with the firm's large central computer. IBM and Honeywell are two of the major manufacturers of such units. In early 1976, Honeywell marketed a minicomputer priced at about $2,700. This low-priced model can be placed on a table or desk.

The minicomputer field has experienced phenomenal growth during the late 1970s. There are new, even smaller versions called microcomputers, that can be assembled by do-it-yourself hobbyists, and used around the house for domestic data processing needs.

COMPUTER TIME-SHARING

Many firms are too small to be able to afford the high costs of installing and operating a computer. Yet many of these same firms need to use a computer to compete effectively in today's highly competitive markets. For some of these small firms the solution is a minicomputer. Others may solve the problem by affiliating with a computer time-sharing plan. Under such a scheme, the company leases

Most computer manufacturers train and provide technicians for repairing and maintaining their equipment.

IBM

business profile: **THE SCANNER AT THE CHECKOUT COUNTER**

The universal product code on every label of every can or package—that small rectangle with vertical lines—was expected to be the supermarket's instant key to the computer age. So far the lock is turning slowly, but it looks as though the door may be opened soon. Consumers' anger over the removal of individually stamped prices has died down, and the product code is coming nearer to being universal—about 80 percent of packaged items now carry the label. Most shoppers have now seen something of how the system works, and they like it.

At the supermarket checkout counter, a scanner, which uses a laser, passes over the code to identify the item for a computer. The computer then searches its memory for the current price and sends it back to the checkout counter, where it appears on a lighted screen and is printed on a detailed receipt with the name of the item. It works much faster and more accurately than a clerk operating a cash register manually. Shoppers seem delighted with the printout, and markets are gradually leaving off the stamped prices without receiving negative reaction from customers.

By mid-1978, however, only 288 of the nation's 33,120 supermarkets had the devices. Although several hundred more expect to install them within the year, it will still be some time before most stores will put them into use. High cost is less of a factor than it was in the past, however. In fact, the cost of a scanner system is going down as more are sold, technology becomes less esoteric, and other manufacturers enter the market and cut prices to get their equipment in.

Still, a scanner system is a big capital investment that must somehow pay for itself. It does this first of all by cutting labor costs. Second, each item sold is deducted from computerized inventory, so a constant check is automatically kept on stock, making inventory control a day-to-day possibility. Finally, marketing efficiency is greatly improved, for quick tallies can be made of how much of each item is sold in any period of time, how much shelf space is therefore needed, and how long a shelf life the item has. These efficiencies also have an effect on labor costs, for otherwise such inventory and marketing studies use up many hours of time of store managers and stock clerks.

IBM, NCR, and TRW are among the leading suppliers of scanner systems. If market studies indicate that there is a supermarket for scanners somewhere around the corner for you, you can probably expect to see one in your neighborhood in the near future.

time from a computer-leasing firm. The leased time could be on-line or it could be based on a portion of time. For example, if a small clothing outlet wanted to share time on a computer, it might contract to have use of the equipment for three hours on a Friday afternoon. This means that the equipment, which is located on the computer-leasing company's premises, would be reserved for the store at that particular time. By this arrangement the clothing outlet sends data to the leasing center for processing, or the outlet may have its own input terminal on its premises which connects to the leasing company's offices.

In other cases, where the firm needs constant use of a computer, such as bank operations require, then the shared time may be on an on-line basis. In either case, the firm that buys time from the computer-leasing outfit pays for its use of the equipment. This is a much less expensive arrangement than if the clothing outlet and small banking company had to install and operate its own equipment.

THE COMPUTER'S ROLE IN AN AUTOMATED SOCIETY

Today the computer is as necessary to the business firm as inside plumbing is to the homeowner. Twenty-five years ago one of the great debates on college campuses and among labor and management people was the effects of automation on the future need for manpower. At that time many experts in the field contended that automated devices like computers would cause tremendous unemployment problems. Well, here we are with computers far more sophisticated and widespread than anyone imagined they would be 25 years ago. The effect on the labor force seems to be almost opposite from the experts' dire predictions. On the whole, computer technology appears to have opened vast new fields of employment while providing a far more efficient and effective means for recording, analyzing, and controlling the vast flow of data recounting the activities of the more than 220 million people in our country.

As a student you have probably found that your grade reports, class admission cards, transcripts, and other records are now processed by EDP equipment. While we tend to remember the one time the equipment may have fouled up our data, we frequently fail to realize how much quicker and more efficient data retrieval has become. Twenty-five years ago it took as long as two months for college students to receive their grades for completed courses. Today, where EDP equipment is used, the grades are often reported in less than three weeks, and this in institutions with five to 10 times the enrollment they had 25 years ago.

The computer has had a revolutionary effect on all areas of business management. In marketing and production, computers keep perpetual inventories and automatically reorder when necessary. They regulate manufacturing processes, control distribution, bill customers, and keep the financial records up-to-date. In banking the computer lets you make transactions at any branch and allows you withdrawal privileges from machines that remain open after regular banking hours. In all areas of management, the reliance on computer assistance is absolutely essential.

IMPLICATIONS FOR THE
CORPORATION AND ITS
MANAGERS

The computer is about 35 years old, yet modern corporations depend on it so extensively that they could not function adequately without it. Even farmers lease computer time to determine whether buying more acreage or machinery will help them expand and realize greater profits. International Harvester runs "Pro-Ag" seminars for farmers in the grain belt to teach them how to rely on computer help. In less than one minute, the computer projects answers to the farmer's questions about acreage and machinery.

For many years corporations have used this computerized method for predicting the effects of new resources on their growth and survival. The computer has become more than a way of storing and sorting data. It has become a useful tool for aiding management decision making in many areas where quantitative aids are helpful. Later in this chapter, you will read about how computers and statistical analysis fit into the operations research area of management decision making.

The new minicomputers have become valuable portable tools for salespeople, financial executives, and others. Not unlike the handheld calculator you might own, these little machines can be programmed in a similar fashion to the large computers that you have read about earlier. The advantage to the executive is that it can be carried, used on the spot, and there is no delay in getting data processed by the firm's computer department. Often these minimachines use software such as magnetic cards the size of a stick of gum as the program component. The machines can do financial ratios problems, interest discounting problems, and many similar and more sophisticated functions. They now range in price from $250. More and more, nonengineering and nonscientific management personnel are relying on these machines as constant, efficient companions.

RIGHT TO PRIVACY

Perhaps the most telling criticism of our computerized society is aimed at the individual's loss of privacy because of the computer's voracious appetite for data. The memory banks of computers know almost everything about us and, more and more, this information is finding its way into one central storage unit. Our medical records, credit records, tax records, scholastic records, criminal records, and marriage records are all stored in various computer memory banks, and most people dread the thought that someday all of these records might be merged into one vast centralized system.

Can you imagine the dangers in a society where everything recorded about you—voice recordings as well as written records—can be retrieved from one file? Most of us have very little to hide in our personal lives but, on the other hand, who wants every bit of accumulated data available in one central file? Imagine how vulnerable we would be to any governmental agency wanting to pressure us for one reason or another.

Many believe—and rightly so—that businesses and individuals have not been sensitive enough to the inroads made by computers into their private lives. It is important for businesses to have specific and detailed information about credit, financial records, and the like, and only the computer can do this job. But at

Any idea which reel you're on? The record-keeping chores of the Social Security Administration are staggering. For every person issued a Social Security number, a work history is kept on tape.

Social Security Administration

some point in a democratic society, the leaders must draw the line and legislate what should and shouldn't be centralized in data files. The use of our Social Security number for all identifying records seems to embody this trend. Perhaps this is a serious mistake because it facilitates the centralization of all data.

Fortunately, there are some representatives in Congress who are aware of the threat to privacy and freedom presented by computer centralization of data, and they are waging an offensive to enact laws that will prevent this possibility from becoming a reality.

BUSINESS USE OF STATISTICAL DATA

There is no better statistician than a computer. It is faster and more accurate in calculating and analyzing data than any group of human mathematicians could ever hope to be. For this reason, most medium or large-sized firms rely on computers to be their statisticians. This is not to say that humans are not a necessary element in the analysis and interpretation of statistical information. On the contrary, knowledgeable human statisticians must further refine and present data for management's use. Once the data is analyzed and interpreted, it is up to management to use it in making decisions. Figure 13-4 illustrates some of these uses.

FIGURE 13-4 Statistics as a management tool

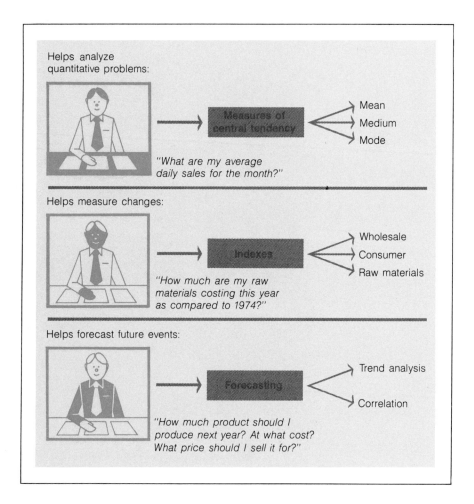

In baseball, a batter's batting average or a pitcher's earned run average or win-loss record are indications of the player's overall performance. It is true that a man may have a poor batting average yet be a great fielder. This situation sometimes happens, so that one can never fully rely on statistics to give a complete indication of a ballplayer's true value. The same type of situation confronts management in a business firm. Statistical information is a very important aid in planning and decision making as well as in summarizing the past record. But statistical information is not the full story, and executives cannot wholly rely on such data.

It is necessary, however, for the alert business manager to know the meaning of certain statistical terms and be able to interpret certain types of noncomplex statistical presentations. Obviously, the more technical treatment of data should be left

personality profile:
PRESTON LOVE—
the lure of the computer

The hottest new device in home entertainment these days seems to be the computer. The swift upsurge of interest in home computers for fun and profit has given birth to a new retail phenomenon: the computer store. There are practical applications that might justify purchasing a computer, like balancing your checkbook, but most people able to operate computers can do such tasks on their own. They want a computer for the sheer entertainment value of owning, programming, and operating their own. Hobby computers may be linked with video games, but they are even more likely to be playthings for people who use computers at work and know some of the more complicated fun things that can be done with them.

The development of the microprocessor, which combines in a tiny package the computing power of thousands of transistors at a price of $12 or so, has reduced the size and price of computers so that they are in reach of more consumers. Computer software or programs, often on tape cassettes, are now available for $10 to $20 each.

Preston Love had worked at IBM for 11 years before setting up a store called Datamart in Atlanta, Georgia, to cater to the tastes of computer hobbyists. He assembles the chips and associated hardware into a customized package for as little as $300 or as much as the customer wants to spend. At that price, it can be cheaper than a color television, and Love believes home computers will some day be just as common as the color television is now. Why buy a computer? One said in 1900, why buy a car?

The first computer store opened in August 1975, but thousands more have sprung up across the country since. A recent Personal Computing Festival, held fittingly enough, in the fantasy atmosphere of the Disneyland Hotel in California, drew tens of thousands of visitors and hundreds of exhibitors.

Mainframe manufacturers like IBM cannot customize for the little guy, but computer retailers like Preston Love can. At his Datamart you can browse just as you would at a stereo shop, trying out various models and hookups to decide on the arrangement and capacity that will best serve your needs and desires. There are attachments to increase memory or information processing capability and even add-ons to synthesize speech sounds so your computer can talk back to you.

to the trained statistician. Like computers, the subject of statistics could be a textbookful of material if one wanted to cover the topics thoroughly. For our purposes of general information the discussion that follows will be as brief but informative as possible.

RESEARCH AND DEVELOPMENT

Almost every business has a department, formal or informal, for carrying on research and development. Obviously, a manufacturer of automobile tires needs a great deal of product research. In addition to exploring the development of new and stronger raw materials, tire manufacturers need to know a great deal about the market makeup for their product. Statistics about such things as the number of automobiles and the sizes of automobiles would be valuable information for a tire manufacturer. Marketing research (see Chapter 6) works very closely with research and development in depicting the statistical personality of a company's market area. The population in a statistical definition, therefore, is the area or total environment of data to be analyzed and interpreted. If the tire manufacturer only sold tires on the Pacific Coast of the United States, his population would be California, Oregon, and Washington. The term *universe* is synonymous with the term population in statistical usage.

COLLECTING, ANALYZING, AND DISPLAYING DATA

In 1936 the *Literary Digest*, a well-known magazine with a national circulation, conducted a poll to determine whether Alfred Landon, the Republican candidate for president, or the incumbent, Franklin D. Roosevelt, would win the upcoming presidential election. Its poll results indicated that Landon would be the next president. The election returns indicated the exact opposite when Roosevelt, in one of the greatest political landslides in history, swept every state but Maine and Vermont. What went wrong? The *Literary Digest* survey was conducted by interviewers who called people whose names were listed in telephone directories. What the pollsters failed to realize was that in 1936 only the most affluent people had home telephones; and since the more affluent in 1936 usually voted Republican, the poll therefore wrongly pointed to a Landon victory.

SURVEYS AND SAMPLING

Obviously, the population asked to respond was the wrong one to choose in polling the 1936 electorate. The survey technique of asking selected people their opinion about something is a good method for gathering data, but the Landon/Roosevelt poll had a serious bias, something statisticians hope to avoid in their surveys. In the 1936 telephone survey, the bias was perhaps so obvious that it was overlooked.

When gathering data, limitations of cost and time make it impossible to survey everyone in a population. Therefore, a survey is usually conducted by sampling. It is hoped that by questioning maybe one out of every 100 people or examining one out of every 100 pineapples, one can draw generalizations that will apply to the whole population. Here is where it becomes necessary to have skilled statisticians and analysts plan and conduct the survey.

There are many different ways to survey a population. One common technique is the mail questionnaire. By sending a question sheet through the mail with a stamped self-addressed return envelope, a large geographical area can be surveyed at low cost and in a reasonable amount of time. Telephone surveys or door-to-door interviews (known as canvassing) are faster than mail questionnaires, but their cost is usually greater. Regardless of the survey method used, there is almost always an attempt to make the survey as random as possible. Random sampling results when each individual in the population has as much chance of being interviewed as any of the others. In the case of the Landon versus Roosevelt survey, this condition did not hold because, although you were part of the universe, you could not be sampled if you did not have a telephone and so were not listed in a telephone directory.

PRIMARY AND SECONDARY DATA

If facts are gathered through a survey technique or through some other method from an original source, such as an interview, the data are known as *primary data*. If data are obtained by reading the resuls of a survey taken by another firm or a governmental agency, the data comes secondhand and is known as *secondary data*. Using secondary data is a far less costly way of obtaining information, but because it comes to the firm indirectly there is more chance for error, and the time between the taking of the survey and its use is likely to be rather long.

A firm in need of information must usually rely on secondary sources for most of its statistical data. For most businesses, the cost factor, as well as a lack of staff trained for the job, makes the gathering of primary data a rare event. Frequently, when firms need a certain bit of statistical information, they hire professional survey and pollster organizations. In this way they get skilled help when they particularly need it.

MEASURES OF CENTRAL TENDENCY

Has anyone ever said that you are an above-average student or that you are of about average height? These terms relate to an area of statistics known as measures of central tendency. *Measures of central tendency* are statistical devices that indicate where one piece of data stands in relationshiop to the whole series of data. The three types of averages or measures of central tendency that are most commonly used are the mean, the median, and the mode.

It would probably be easier to explain these measurements by presenting a meaningful example. Let's assume that we must find the mean, the median, and the mode for a group of scores achieved on a recent Civil Service examination. Nineteen people took the exam and the scores are arranged from highest to lowest, as shown below. An *array* is the term used to describe a list of statistical data arranged as a listing in order of size usually from the highest to the lowest and is usually the first step in processing raw data for further analysis.

1. Array of Civil Service examination scores

96	80	70
94	78	68
90	78	62
86	78	58
84	72	54
84	70	50
83		

The second step is to condense the array by listing the various values and the number of times each value appears in the data. Statisticians call this a *frequency distribution*.

2. Frequency distribution of Civil Service examination scores

Score	Number Attaining It
96	1
94	1
90	1
86	1
84	2
83	1
80	1
78	3
72	1
70	2
68	1
62	1
58	1
54	1
50	1
Total	19

FINDING THE MEAN

The *mean*, or arithmetic average, is probably the most valuable and frequently used measure of central tendency. It is found by dividing the total of a series of numbers by the number of units that make up the series. The number of units that makes up the series is frequently referred to as n in statistical terminology. The calculation of the mean for our Civil Service examination scores would be as follows:

Score	Number Attaining It (n)	Total Points
96	1	96
94	1	94

Score	Number Attaining It	Total Points
90	1	90
86	1	86
84	2	168
83	1	83
80	1	80
78	3	234
72	2	144
70	1	70
68	1	68
62	1	62
58	1	58
54	1	54
50	1	50
Total	19	1437

The mean is found by dividing the total n, which is 19, into the total number of points, which is 1437. The result is $1437 \div 19 = 75.6 =$ mean.

FINDING THE MODE

The mode is very easy to find by inspection. That is to say, the data need not be handled any further. The *mode* is simply the number (or in our case, the score) which occurs most often. If no score appeared more than once, there would be no mode. Looking back to inspect the array we find that this number is 78, which occurs three times. Therefore, the mode is equal to 78. If another set of scores appeared three times, two modes would have to be stated.

FINDING THE MEDIAN

As in finding the mode, we can determine the median by inspecting the array. The *median* is the number (or, in our case, the score) in the array that divides the group in half. Since there were 19 scores in our array, the tenth score would have nine lower than it and nine higher. Counting down from the top of the array to the tenth score gives a median of 78. If an array had an even number of scores such as 20, it would be necessary to average the two middle scores unless they were of identical value.

Note that in our example the median and the mode come out as the same score, 78, while the mean is slightly more than two points lower. Usually all three measurements will vary to some extent. In most cases the mean is the preferred measurement, but there is no reason why the median or mode cannot be used if the data lends itself to their interpretation. In an array where there are extreme variations in values, the usefulness of the median and mode diminishes.

INDEX NUMBERS

No doubt you have heard of the consumer price index which measures the changes in consumer prices since the base year, 1967. In statistics, index numbers such as the consumer price index are important devices. *Index numbers* compare value changes in one period of time to a stable value in a former period of time. The consumer price index is probably the best known of the index series, but government and industry keep indexes of many items affecting the economy or a particular firm. In index statistics there must always be a *base year*, or starting point, with which all future periods are compared. The index number for the future period under analysis is always expressed as a percentage of the base year. So if the consumer price index is at 200 in 1980, this means that consumer prices are 200 percent of what they were in the base year. Since the base year always represents 100 percent, the 200 index indicates prices have risen by 100 percent since the base year.

USING STATISTICAL METHODS FOR FORECASTING

Being able to forecast future trends is vital for most business firms. To remain competitive, a business has to know where its future markets will be and what future consumer needs will be. For such purposes, firms need the ability to estimate accurately their future costs of, and revenues from, their product or service. As consumers, firms must be able to determine future sources of raw materials and estimate what those raw materials will cost.

Nevertheless, despite the sophisticated statistical methods used, forecasts frequently do miss the mark. There are always unforeseen variables that can invalidate the best of forecasts.

A case in point was the unusually severe winter of 1977–78 experienced in most parts of the United States. No one could have forecast that it would be the worst winter in Weather Bureau annals. Who could have forecast its devastating effect on an already bleak energy picture? Who could have estimated the extent of damage to crops in Florida and the South as a result of that winter?

Could coffee roasters have accurately forecast the effect of Brazilian coffee bean price rises on the cost of their product in early 1977? It is doubtful that they, or anyone else, could have known the heights to which the price of coffee beans, the major raw material in their product, would rise.

However unpredictable life may be, there are many statistical applications that aid firms in making forecasts relative to economics, supply, and market conditions. Although a thorough examination and explanation of each method is beyond the scope of this text, several will be briefly considered so you will have a general awareness of why and how they are used.

Trend Analysis If you recall the discussions in earlier chapters, you realize that business is dynamic. Its position in the economy is forever changing. *Trend analysis*, or time series, as it is sometimes called, takes historical data as it relates to identifiable time periods and attempts to forecast shifts in the economy. In other words, historical data about regular periods or events can be drawn on to forecast what will happen. We know, for instance, that in the United States retail store sales are at their highest in November and December. We have historical data collected over many years showing this to be so. We can conclude from such data that, in the future, November and December will be peak months for retail store sales. If we were to plot the future trend on a graph, we would be extrapolating. *Extrapolation* is the process of expanding known past data to infer future events, usually in graphic analysis.

The whole area of statistical forecasting related to changes in the seasons or months is known as seasonal variations. Thus, if you were a motel proprietor in Cocoa Beach, Florida, you would know from past experience that November will be a much slower month for you than March. The same kinds of forecast are made by large corporations, who obviously must rely on statistical experts to make the analysis.

In almost any type of business forecast, population changes as well as seasonal changes must be taken into consideration. The growth or dwindling of a nation's population will always have a major influence on its businesses.

In addition to seasonal variations and population trends, there is a third major area to consider in statistical forecasting—cyclical fluctuations. *Cyclical fluctuations* describe the ups and downs in the economy that occur from time to time seemingly as a result of natural changes in the forces of supply and demand as well as other, unforeseen, influences. Business cycles reflect economic activity, so when the Great Depression struck in the early 1930s, business activity fell sharply and did not recover fully for many years. Statisticians attempt to account for the possibility of cyclical fluctuations in their forecasts, but often they are wrong in their estimates of when these will occur.

Correlation In many instances there is a relationship between two or more sets of data. The extent to which one set of data relates to another is referred to as *correlation*. We know that there is a correlation between fever in the human body and infection. Therefore, since there is a degree of correlation between fever and infection, a doctor can diagnose infection if body temperature exceeds 98.6°. The same kinds of diagnostic forecast can be made by businesses that recognize correlations between two or more sets of variables. For example, as the number of marriages increases in a country, there is bound to be a rise in the number of new housing units required. This is said to be a positive correlation, since the increase in one variable tends to cause an increase in the other. The forecast of increased housing required could be wrong if we introduce a third variable such as one showing that 75 percent of all newlyweds emigrate to a foreign country. Therefore, as emigration of newlyweds rises, the need for new housing falls. This is an example of negative correlation, an increase in one variable causing a decrease in the other.

Although correlation is a valuable statistical technique for forecasting, it is not 100 percent accurate. It does not hold true in all cases that past relationships will continue unaltered in the future. There are always uncertainties, such as the war in the Middle East in October 1973, lurking in the background to thwart the best of forecasts.

OPERATIONS RESEARCH AND QUANTITATIVE TOOLS FOR MANAGEMENT

Management is the art and science of making business decisions. It is an art because in making decisions the manager must rely on human talents and abilities; it is a science because the manager must also rely on quantitative analysis. Since the end of World War II, sophisticated quantitative procedures have been emerging more and more in large firms. *Operations research* (OR) is a type of decision-making procedure using scientific and mathematical techniques for quantitative problem solving. Naturally, the use of the computer and statistical analysis are of major importance.

Operations research is a procedure that contains several essential characteristics:

1. There must be a broad view of the problem to be solved, such as a view giving the perspective of the whole firm.
2. After the problem is identified, personnel with special talents and training are brought together to work on a solution to the problem.
3. These people use physical and social sciences as tools for solving the problem. There is usually an emphasis upon statistical, mathematical, and other techniques including simulation and model building.

SIMULATION AND MODEL BUILDING

Managers use simulation and model building to help them "act out" ways to solve real problems that occur in business. *Simulation* involves constructing a situation that closely resembles actual conditions for the purpose of testing. Usually this is done through the construction of a model. The model is subjected to the same influences and forces that would occur in a real situation. In this way the simulation provides management the opportunity to conduct trials and test runs under conditions that are as close as possible to the real situation. Most of the time the models constructed are mathematical in nature. Often they include physical similarities, behavioral characteristics, and interactions associated with actual conditions.

For example, if you plan to open a record shop you would probably develop a model to determine the kinds of records you would sell, what store layout to use, and how you would categorize and display the records. Cost figures, space dimensions, and similar mathematical information would be an important part of the model. After completing the model you might try it on potential customers to see how practical it is.

PERT and CPM

Program Evaluation and Review Technique (PERT) was a very popular area of OR during the 1960s. The Department of the Army defines it as a "management information and control system used in planning, scheduling, controlling, and evaluating progress on a program." In reality, PERT is actually a network flow chart that estimates the time involved in the completion of various projects that make up a project. It was developed and used successfully by the United States Navy in the late 1950s in completing the Polaris submarine program.

PERT is based on an earlier concept called the Critical Path Method (CPM). CPM was developed by a group of OR specialists at Du Pont together with a team from Remington Rand. The CPM device attempts to trace the time required to complete various "paths" that ultimately lead to the completion of a project. The "critical path" is that phase of the project that is estimated to take the longest to complete. And, since the whole project is not finished until all paths (or parts) are completed, the path that takes the longest to complete is called the critical path.

PERT takes CPM one step further by making three time estimates about each path. These are the optimistic time, the most likely time, and the pessimistic time. PERT expresses these times and the necessary paths to completion of a project in a network diagram similar to the one in Figure 13-5.

Jake Satterfield's network of events and activities for completing college
Jake Satterfield is going to college next fall under one of the following conditions:
Optimistic—Go full time and summers
Most Likely—Go full time during academic year but work full time in summer
Pessimistic—Go full time the first two years and part time thereafter

Event	Completion Time (Years)		
	Optimistic	Most Likely	Pessimistic
A. Freshman year	1	1	1
B. Sophomore year	½	1	1
C. Junior year	1	1	2
D. Senior year	½	1	2
Total years to degree	3	4	5

FIGURE 13-5 Simple network diagram to illustrate network events from above

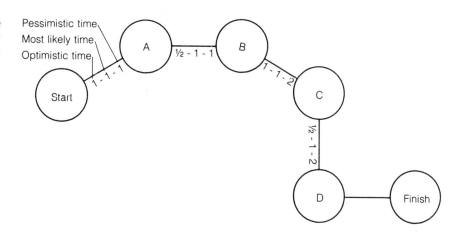

In recent years PERT has lost favor with many OR people. NASA formerly employed it in all space projects costing over $100,000 but now rarely uses it. Many firms have become disenchanted with PERT because they say it is not reliable enough.

Queuing Theory and the Monte Carlo Method

Have you ever suffered the frustration of waiting in line at the supermarket checkout for a long period of time? If so maybe you now avoid the supermarket in which this happens. Businesses want happy customers who will return to buy again, yet they must keep expenses as low as possible by not having too many personnel ready to serve at peak hours but with little to do most of the time. The problem is one of anticipating when customer demand will be greatest and having sufficient personnel available at that time. Queuing theory, sometimes called waiting line theory, attempts to solve this problem through the application of probability theory. Usually past data are utilized to help forecast future demand peaks. Observation and tally keeping are used to note the times when customer load is the greatest and from this information trends are forecasted.

Sometimes, however, it is not practical or possible to spend the time and money to make observations and tallys. Under such circumstances the so-called Monte Carlo method is utilized. Basically the Monte Carlo method uses random numbers from which a selection is made. The problem with ths quantitative tool is that the degree of accuracy in forecasting is not very high.

SUMMARY

Statistical applications can often help managers make better decisions. This is one good reason why it is of value to know about statistical measures such as correlation, index numbers, and measures of central tendency. When confronted with a decision-making problem, a knowledgeable manager relies on an analysis of primary and secondary data to provide statistical information. Obviously, more technical treatment of data should be left to trained specialists in the field.

There is no better statistician than a computer. It is faster and much more accurate in calculating and analyzing data than any human math whiz could ever hope to be. Sophisticated computer systems consist of input and output devices as well as a central console. The console is the brain center of the system and receives its data and instructions through programs fed into it by people known as programmers. Very few businesses could survive without the help of a computer system. Smaller firms can afford minicomputers that offer a full range of services at much lower installation and operating costs than those of full-size computer systems.

SUMMARY OF KEY TERMS

Analog Computer A computer designed to solve problems by measuring one quantity in terms of some other quantity. An analog computer is usually in constant operation.

Array Statistical data arranged as a listing in order of size usually from the highest to the lowest. It is usually the first step in processing raw data for further analysis.

Base Year Used in statistical indexing as the starting point against which all future periods will be computed. The base year index number is always 100.

Binary Code Numbering system based on zero and one used for calculation in the mechanical makeup of any computer.

COBOL (Common Business Oriented Language) A language composed of symbols and/or characters used most often in the programming of computers for business purposes.

Computation Section The section of the console that performs the necessary calculation tasks associated with a particular program.

Computer Electronically powered machine that computes, files, analyzes, summarizes, and stores data.

Console The heart and brain of all EDP systems where all the data is processed.

Control Equipment That part of the console that works from the instructions set forth in the program.

Correlation A relationship that exists between two or more variables in statistical analysis.

Critical Path Method (CPM) An operations research tool used to trace the time required to complete various "paths" that ultimately lead to the completion of a project.

Cyclical Fluctuations Describes the ups and downs in the economy that occur from time to time seemingly as a result of natural changes in the forces of supply and demand as well as other unforeseen influences.

Digital Computer A computer designed to solve problems by counting digits. Therefore, their main work is computation.

Electronic Data Processing (EDP) The field of using sophisticated electronically powered and controlled equipment for the computing and processing of data.

Extrapolation The process of expanding known past data to infer future events; usually used in graphic analysis.

Flow Chart An outline in diagram form of the logical steps required for a computer to solve a problem and make a forecast.

FORTRAN (Formula Translation) A language composed of symbols and/or characters used most often in the solving of scientific and mathematical problems utilizing the computer.

Frequency Distribution A statistical table that is a condensation of an array which lists the various values and the number of times each value appears in the data.

Hardware Equipment The individual machines, such as the keypunch machine and the computer itself, that comprise a particular system.

Index Number A statistical procedure that compares value changes in one period of time to a stable value in a former period of time known as a base period. The consumer price index is the best known of all index numbers.

Input Devices Various materials such as magnetic tape and punched cards that serve to feed data into the processing unit of an EDP system.

Mean A measure of central tendency that represents the arithmetic average of a series of numerical values; used in statistics to determine the average value among a series of data.

Measure of Central Tendency A statistical device that indicates where one piece of data stands in relationship to a whole series of data.

Median A measure of central tendency represented by the number in a series of data which divides the series in half.

Microprocessors A single integrated circuit that contains much but not all of the ability of a computer.

Minicomputers Small computers that can perform many of the basic functions that a complete computer can, but they are much less expensive to buy and operate.

Mode A measure of central tendency represented by the number in a series of data that occurs most often. If no value appears more than once in a series, there is no mode.

On-line A computer that is constantly available to receive, process, and remit information to a number of branches in a matter of moments.

Operations Research (OR) A type of decision making procedure using scientific and mathematical techniques.

Optical Scanning Device A machine that can read certain types of printed or handwritten matter and convert them into data for the computer.

Output Devices Various materials such as magnetic tape and punched cards that receive information processed by the computer.

Program Evaluation and Review Technique (PERT) A network flow chart that estimates the time involved in the completion of various projects that make up a project.

Primary Data Data gathered through an original source such as an interview.

Program Instructions prepared by individuals, known as programmers that tell the computer what to do, when to do it, and how to do it.

Secondary Data Data obtained from reading the results of other surveys, not from a statistical gathering of primary data. Statistics based on data published by the Bureau of the Census would be an example of secondary data.

Simulation Constructing a situation that closely resembles the actual conditions for the purpose of testing.

Software Equipment Aids that facilitate the programming of the computer. Paper punched cards, magnetic tape, and even the program itself are examples of computer software.

Systems Analyst A specially trained engineer who works with a business to design the system most appropriate to the needs of that particular firm.

Time Sharing An arrangement by which a firm may lease time for computer use from a computer leasing company. The leased time could be on-line or be based on a portion of time.

Trend Analysis A statistical device (sometimes referred to as time series analysis) using historical data as it relates to identifiable time periods and attempts to forecast shifts in the economy.

Universe Synonymous with "population." The area or total environment of data to be analyzed and interpreted in a statistical problem. The population for a survey of the Pacific Coast would be California, Oregon, and Washington.

REVIEW QUESTIONS

1. Indicate whether each of the following is an example of hardware or software equipment:
   The punched card
   The key punch machine
   The computer
   The program
   Magnetic tape
   The printout machine
   Paper tape
   The typewriter

2. Name all the input media discussed in this chapter and suggest which are the faster and which the slower sources of input.
3. Name and describe the three basic functions of the computer in an EDP system.
4. What does the program help the computer to do? What can the computer do without a program?
5. What are the essential characteristics of operations research?

6. Describe what PERT and CPM are and how managers utilize these techniques?
7. What is correlation?
8. What are microprocessors and how are they used?
9. What size business firms use minicomputers and for what purposes?
10. What is binary code and what is it used for?

DISCUSSION QUESTIONS

1. You are the administrative director of a bridge authority which charges a 25-cent toll for cars coming into or going out of your city from the south end. Your bridge cuts commuting time into the city by 20 minutes if people choose it over the free route. What quantitative management aids might be of greatest assistance to you for keeping traffic moving smoothly? Suggest ways they might help.
2. Outline a statistical plan for determining the most popular course taken in your school and the major reasons for its being so. Important: You are selecting the most popular course, not the most popular teacher.

3. List four sources of secondary data you might consult if you wanted to determine the number of cigarette smokers in the United States. Use the library for help.
4. Comment on the validity of the following statement: A measure of central tendency tells us what value in a series of data appears more than all other values combined.
5. Prepare a flow chart for the operation of a self-service elevator in a three-story building. Use the flow chart illustrated in this chapter as a model.

CASES FOR DECISION MAKING

SINK OR SWIM

The Aqua Company is a manufacturer of swimming pools and related equipment such as filters, cleaners, and so forth. It employs 1,800 people in three plants located in northwestern California and Seattle, Washington. The company's main plant and office is in Redwood City, California, and it has sales representatives in all parts of the United States. At the present time the company employs an outside firm to do all of its EDP work. The company has never owned or leased its own computer and thinks that this might be a good time to do so.

As a manager trainee working for the firm, you have been asked to suggest ways in which the computer could be used in any or all of the firm's operations.

1. Prepare a list and description of ways that a computer system owned or leased by Aqua could be utilized in its day-to-day operations.
2. Do you think a firm of Aqua's size and extent of operations needs an EDP system? Why or why not?

A WEIGHTY DECISION

The Star Widget Corporation sends out daily shipments with varying weights. They would like to determine the "usual" weight of each shipment and have decided to base this on a typical day when they made 13 shipments with the following weights:

110 lbs.	100 lbs.
120 lbs.	120 lbs.
120 lbs.	130 lbs.
100 lbs.	140 lbs.
130 lbs.	160 lbs.
140 lbs.	180 lbs.
150 lbs.	

You are employed by the Star Widget Corporation as a management trainee and are asked to supply the following, based on the above data:

1. An array in descending order
2. A frequency distribution

3. The mean for the series
4. The median for the series
5. The mode for the series

FUELISH QUESTION

Atlas Fuel Company is a commercial and residential supplier of fuel oil to businesses and homes in the greater Milwaukee, Wisconsin, area. The firm prides itself on its service and has always tried to please its customers. Atlas fills tanks according to their size and the number of degree days since the last fill. Information on degree days is supplied by the weather bureau and is an indication of how cold a particular day has been in the past several years and therefore the relative amount of fuel needed to heat a building. Atlas employed a statistician to keep track of weather information, but this individual will retire in two months. Atlas must decide whether to hire someone else for this job or automate the process. However, Atlas doesn't use any computer facilities for any purpose at the present time. Atlas owns four fuel trucks and two other vehicles and its business has grown at an annual rate of 10 percent.

1. Describe how Atlas could utilize an electronic data processing system for the above process.
2. In what other ways might EDP equipment prove helpful to Atlas?
3. Do you recommend a statistician or EDP System for replacement?

RELATED READINGS

Brown, John A., and Workman, Robert S. *How a Computer System Works*. New York: Arco, 1975.

An introductory yet detailed description of the computer and its hardware and software aids. Lots of good illustrations of equipment and diagrams of procedures. Contains a good chapter on the computer as a tool for managers.

Hawkes, Nigel. *The Computer Revolution*. New York: Dutton, 1972.

A look at computers from their inception into the business and scientific worlds to the present. Very well written with lots of interesting historical information.

Huff, Darrell. *How to Lie with Statistics*. New York: Norton, 1954.

Presents some interesting lessons in basic statistics and demonstrates in a humorous fashion how statistics can be used to deceive as well as inform. Many good cartoons supplement this book.

Kohn, Mervin. *Dynamic Managing*. Menlo Park, Calif.: Cummings, 1977.

Basic introductory textbook in management. Chapters 4, 5, and 6 contain excellent elementary information on decision making and quantitative aids for making decisions.

Langley, Russel. *Practical Statistics for Non-Mathematical People*. New York: Drake, 1972.

More difficult than the title leads one to believe. But a well-written, well-illustrated introductory approach to understanding basic statistics.

Raphael, Bertram. *The Thinking Computer, Mind Inside Matter*. San Francisco: Freeman, 1976.

An interesting book on the computer and how it aids the researcher, the student, and the problem solver.

Reichmann, W. J. *Use and Abuse of Statistics*. New York: Oxford University Press, 1962.

Demonstrates basic statistical applications and how they apply to practical situations; it also deals with the deceptive aspects of statistics. It serves as good supplementary reading in the field of statistics.

Zeisel, Hans. *Say It with Figures*. New York: Harper & Row, 1968.

A practical guide to using figures and statistics. Very useful for anyone in management.

chapter 14

USING AND INTERPRETING ACCOUNTING AND LEGAL DATA

OBJECTIVES

When you have finished reading and studying this chapter, you should be able to:

1. Recognize why the services of accountants and attorneys are essential to business firms.

2. Be familiar with standard forms of financial statements and know why they are important sources of information for the manager.

3. Be able to explain and distinguish between a cash budget and a capital budget.

4. Know some of the major terminology and procedures associated with business law.

5. Be aware of the significant relationship of both law and accounting to the management of business firms.

CHAPTER PREVIEW

If you ever want to own and operate your own business or help manage another business, you will have to know some of the essentials of accounting terminology and business law procedures. It is true that every intelligent businessperson relies on the services of attorneys and accountants hired as employees or engaged as professional practitioners. Nonetheless, the businessperson cannot become totally divorced from some responsibility for understanding the essentials of law and accounting as they relate to particular businesses and industries.

The measurement of a firm's financial success and progress, or lack of them, is best revealed in the periodic presentation and interpretation of financial statements. Financial statements are not unlike box scores of yesterday's baseball game because they too summarize what has taken place. The balance sheet and the income statement are the most important financial statements prepared for every business firm. These statements give details about the various financial resources as well as show whether the firm has made a net profit or had a net loss for the period.

Planning for the financial future of the firm is an important part of the manager's job. The cash budget and the capital budget are two formalized procedures for doing so that draw on the company's accounting data. Some form of budget preparation is essential for the survival of all business firms.

A business firm may complete thousands of contracts in the course of a year. Some of these may be simple oral agreements, while others may involve pages of legal specifications and many signatures. For some contracts, an attorney's services are essential, but for others a knowledge of simple legal business procedures is enough. All firms handle checks, drafts, and other forms of payment, and these instruments are within the bounds of the law of negotiable instruments. Other legal questions and procedures are closely involved with business practices.

Most lawyers who win a case advise their clients that "We have won," and when justice has frowned upon their cause that "You have lost."

Louis Nizer

An accountant is a man hired to explain that you didn't make the money you did.

Evan Esar, 20,000 QUIPS & QUOTES (New York: Doubleday, 1968).

14
USING AND INTERPRETING ACCOUNTING AND LEGAL DATA

Forty or fifty years ago many business people kept only informal financial records. Because government regulations and taxation had little impact on business operations there was no need to keep elaborate balance sheets, hire bookkeepers, and retain tax consultants. Today this type of easy-going financial record keeping is no longer adequate for even the smallest of businesses. Everyone—governments, consumer groups, creditors, stockholders—is now very much interested in the financial goings-on of a firm, and the larger the firm the more pressure it is under to reveal accounting data to outside sources.

ACCOUNTING AND FINANCIAL STATEMENTS

It would not be practical, or even possible, to explain all the major elements that comprise an accounting system. However, every business student, no matter what his or her major area of interest, should become familiar with the accounting terminology discussed in this section. Students often feel that because they are marketing majors, economics majors, or office administration majors, they have no need to learn the basic principles of accounting. Experience has proven time and again that there is nothing further from the truth. Every college student interested in business should take one year of introductory accounting. It will be of immense help in any career.

THE BALANCE SHEET

Parents love to take snapshots of their children at various ages. How often have you looked back at old photographs to see how friends and relatives have changed over the years? A balance sheet is very similar to a snapshot: it gives a picture of a business at one point in its development. A *balance sheet* is a formal statement of all the financial resources owned by the business as well as all its debts. Just about every firm in the United States prepares a balance sheet at least once a year. Many do it quarterly, and some monthly.

Assets   Figure 14-1 is an example of a typical balance sheet. The heading gives the name of the firm, the type of financial statement, and the date of preparation. As you can see, there is a section referred to as "assets." *Assets* are things of value owned by the business. Therefore, such things as cash, office equipment, machinery, and the like are all included. Other types of assets include accounts receivable, patents, and copyrights; although these items are not physical in nature, they have financial value. *Accounts receivable* are the debts owed the company by customers and others; the total value of this debt represents an asset.

Assets listed on balance sheets are frequently separated into categories such as current assets and fixed assets. *Current assets* are those which can be converted into cash fairly quickly; they are said to be liquid. *Fixed assets* are items more difficult to convert into cash. Buildings, land, and machinery are examples of these. Notice that some fixed asset accounts are offset by depreciation.

FIGURE 14-1 Balance sheet

GASLIGHT, INC.
BALANCE SHEET
December 31, 1979

ASSETS

Current Assets:			
Cash		38,500	
Accounts Receivable	20,000		
Less Allowance for			
Bad Debts	1,000	19,000	
Merchandise Inventory		60,000	
Supplies		2,500	
Total Current Assets			120,000
Investments:			
Common Stock		5,000	
Government Bonds		15,000	
Total Investments			20,000
Fixed Assets:			
Building	120,000		
Less Depreciation	20,000	100,000	
Equipment	40,000		
Less Depreciation	5,000	35,000	
Land		25,000	
Total Fixed Assets			160,000
TOTAL ASSETS			300,000

For most firms, current and fixed assets are the most important in terms of dollar value. All firms must rely on cash in hand and on checking accounts to meet day-to-day payments. Likewise, most firms own buildings that contain office equipment or machinery. Thus current and fixed assets are presented at the start of the balance sheet.

Two other categories of assets often appear on balance sheets. One is referred to as *investments*, which includes all of the stocks, corporate bonds, government bonds, and the like owned by the business. Many large firms invest some of their excess cash in stocks or bonds of other corporations or in government securities. They would do so in the same way and for the same reasons as an individual investor would, that is, to put excess money to work to earn interest and dividends.

LIABILITIES		
Current Liabilities:		
Accounts Payable	35,000	
Notes Payable	45,000	
Total Current Liabilities		80,000
Long-term Liabilities:		
Mortgage Payable	40,000	
Bonds Payable	60,000	
Total Long-term Liabilities		100,000
Total Liabilities		180,000
Capital		
Common Stock	90,000	
Retained Earnings	30,000	
Total Stockholders Equity		120,000
TOTAL LIABILITIES AND CAPITAL		300,000

The other category is *deferred expenses* (sometimes called prepaid expenses) and includes those items paid for in advance of use. One example would be insurance, for which premiums are always paid at the beginning of the protection period. In terms of deferred expenses, businesses, like individuals, must purchase insurance protection and pay rent in advance. These two items represent the largest categories of deferred expenses.

Liabilities *Liabilities* represent debts owed to others. Liabilities fall into two categories: current and fixed. *Current liabilities* are those debts that must be paid within one year of the date of the balance sheet. *Long-term liabilities* are those debts due beyond one year from the date of the balance sheet.

Most firms encounter some liabilities. Liabilities are not necessarily bad, however, since borrowing is often the key to expansion and greater profits in the future. There are few businesses, as there are few individuals, who could afford to have built or to buy a building and pay all costs out of pocket. The usual method for financing a building is to borrow.

The final section of the balance sheet is known as the *capital* or proprietorship section. This unit is of most interest to the company's owners since it represents

An accountant is responsible for keeping track of a company's financial condition.

Maria Karras

their financial interest in the firm. Because most firms owe to others, the firm's assets are generally not equal to the capital of the owners. Thus, capital is computed by subtracting liabilities from assets.

Notice that the total assets are equal to, or in balance with, the total of the liabilities plus capital. Thus the name balance sheet. Also notice how compact the entire statement is.

There are two things to remember about balance sheets and all accounting data:

1. All amounts represent the actual cost of the item or debt. There are no adjustments made for inflation or deflation.
2. Only assets and liabilities of the business, not the personal assets and liabilities of the owners, are included. This is so even in the balance sheet of a sole proprietorship.

Remember that the balance sheet is a snapshot of the financial resources of a business on a particular date. On the day after this date, the picture changes; thus, balance sheets must be periodically updated and compared to see the firm's financial program, or lack of it.

THE INCOME
STATEMENT

If the balance sheet is a snapshot of the business' financial resources, the income statement is a motion picture of its operations over a given period of time. All businesses are operating to make profits for the owners. The financial statement known as the income statement lists the revenues, costs, and expenses of the firm and the net profit resulting from operations. Figure 14-2 is a model of a typical income statement (sometimes called an operating statement or statement of operations). Notice that, like the balance sheet, everything is presented in a clear and orderly manner.

The heading of the statement tells the name of the firm, the kind of statement, and the period of time it covers. Unlike the balance sheet, the income statement shows the accumulation of certain financial items over a period of time. A balance sheet would give the amount of cash on hand on a given day, but an income statement would discuss the total revenues earned by the firm for the month or year.

FIGURE 14-2 Income statement

GASLIGHT, INC.
INCOME STATEMENT
FOR YEAR ENDING DECEMBER 31, 1979

REVENUE:

Section 1
Sales	120,000	
Less Returns and Allowances	10,000	
Net Sales		110,000

Section 2
Cost of Merchandise Sold		
Beginning Merchandise Inventory	60,000	
Purchases	30,000	
Total Mdse. Available for Sale	90,000	
Less Ending Mdse. Inventory	10,000	
Cost of Merchandise Sold		80,000

Section 3
Gross Profit on Sales		30,000
Operating Expenses:		
Salaries	7,000	
Power	1,000	
Depreciation	2,000	
Supplies	500	
Insurance	400	
Bad Debts	500	
Miscellaneous	100	
		11,500
Net Profit before Federal Income Taxes		18,500
Federal Income Taxes		8,500
NET PROFIT AFTER TAXES		10,000

As broken down, Section 1 lists sales income less returns and allowances. Sales income represents the total revenue received from the sale of the firm's merchandise to customers. Sales returns and allowances represents refunds to customers for returned merchandise or allowance in the lowering of billed prices of merchandise because of partial damage or spoilage. Therefore, section one, the revenue section, reports all income earned by the firm from operations adjusted for any returns or allowances to customers.

Section 2 shows the cost of merchandise sold and attempts to determine the cost to the firm of the merchandise that is sold at retail price as stated in the revenue section (Section 1). Once the cost of merchandise sold is determined, it is subtracted from net sales and the difference is called gross profit. *Gross profit* is the amount made on sales before subtracting operating expenses.

Section 3 deals with the operating expenses. Every business must advertise, pay rent and salaries, and incur other necessary costs for selling its products and services. Section 3 of the income statement shows these expenses. Notice that the total of the operating expenses is substracted from gross profit to arrive at net profit before federal income taxes. After the taxes are subtracted, the remaining figure is called the *net profit*. This represents the earnings that the owners have made on the investment in the business for the period involved.

As is the case with the balance sheet, two points must be understood:

1. All revenues and expenses are shown at actual cost values, with no adjustments for inflation or deflation.
2. The owners' personal revenues and expenditures from personal sources are not included in the income statement of the business. This is so even for a sole proprietorship.

STATEMENT OF CAPITAL OR RETAINED EARNINGS

Figure 14-3 shows a statement of capital generally used by sole proprietorships and partnerships. Figure 14-4 shows the statement of retained earnings used by corporations. In either case, the purpose of these statements is to show changes in the business's capital investments over the period of time under consideration. These statements start with the investment by the owner or stockholders at the beginning of the period and show how this is modified by increased investments or profits earned from operations. If the owners withdraw more than the amount of profit earned, it naturally follows that the investment from the beginning to the end of the period will decrease. If, however, profits remain after some withdrawals are made by the owners, then the investment will increase over the period. In most firms, it is necessary for the owners to withdraw some profits for their families' living expenses. If a firm is to grow, however, some profits must be retained to help finance this growth.

THE ACCOUNT

Hundreds of transactions occur daily in the life of the average business. *Transactions* are financial events such as the sale of merchandise for cash or the payment

FIGURE 14-3 Statement of capital

MUSTO AND VOLYN PARTNERSHIP
STATEMENT OF CAPITAL
For Year Ended December 31, 1979

Capital, January 1, 1979		60,000
Additional Investments		5,000
Total Investments		65,000
Net Income	20,000	
Less Withdrawals	15,000	
Increase in Capital		5,000
Capital, December 31, 1979		70,000

FIGURE 14-4 Statement of Retained earnings

GASLIGHT, INC.
STATEMENT OF RETAINED EARNINGS
For Year Ended December 31, 1979

Retained Earnings, January 1, 1979		15,000
Plus Premium from Sale of Common Stock		10,000
Total Retained Earnings		25,000
Net Income	10,000	
Less Dividends Paid	5,000	5,000
Total Retained Earnings, December 31, 1979		30,000

of the electricity bill. Accounting personnel must insert each of these transactions into the records of the firm. The key tool that they use for doing this is known as an *account*, a record of debit and credit entries. An account is kept for each major category of asset, liability, capital, revenue, cost, or expense encountered by the firm. Since every business keeps cash on hand or in a checking account, every firm would set up an account for cash. The same would be true for other items such as equipment, accounts payable, capital, etc.

All of the firm's accounts are recorded on pages in a book, or on cards in a file, or as storage in a computer. The system depends on the business' needs. Naturally, the larger the firm is, the more it will rely on a computerized system. Regardless of the physical arrangement, the entire book, file, or storage unit of accounts is referred to as a *ledger*.

A typical account appearing as a page in a ledger book might look as follows:

FIGURE 14-5

Cash   Page 1

DEBITS AND CREDITS The left side of an account is known as the *debit* side. If one debits an account, it means information, including a dollar amount, is being inserted on the left side of the account. The right side of an account is known as the *credit* side. If one credits an account, it means information is being inserted on the right side.

It is important to remember that debit and credit only mean the left side or right side of an account. The effect of debiting or crediting an account, however, is the same as adding to or subtracting from the account. For example, assume a firm deposited $25,000 cash into its checking account. The firm's ledger at this point would require two accounts: one for cash, and one for owner's capital.

FIGURE 14-6

Cash   Owner's Capital

Cash is an asset account. The rules of debits and credits as they apply to assets state that a debit to any asset increases the balance of the account and a credit decreases the balance. Since the owner just completed a transaction inserting $25,000 into a checking account, cash has been clearly increased to $25,000. This will require a debit to the cash account as follows:

FIGURE 14-7

Cash

Aug. 1 $25,000

Owner's capital is a capital account. The rules of debits and credits as they apply to capital state that a debit to a capital account decreases the balance of the account whereas a credit increases its balance. (Note this is just the opposite of the asset debit and credit rule.) Since the owner just deposited $25,000 cash into a new business, owner's capital has clearly increased to $25,000. This will require a credit to the owner's capital account as follows:

FIGURE 14-8

Owner's Capital

Aug. 1 $25,000

In summary, the transaction recorded into the accounts required a debit to cash of $25,000 and a credit to owner's capital for $25,000. This increased the balances of both the cash and capital accounts. One can see that the debit to cash was offset by a credit to capital. In every transaction recorded into the accounts debits must be equal to credits. This procedure is popularly known as double entry accounting. After the above entry is made, the companies records would indicate:

$$\text{Assets } \$25,000 = \text{Capital } \$25,000$$

From the above, a very simple balance sheet could be prepared.

The effects of debits or credits on account balances varies with the family of accounts involved. In our example above, cash in the asset family was increased by debiting, whereas owner's capital in the capital family is increased by crediting. The rules for debits and credits for each family appear as follows:

Assets   Increase on debit side and decrease on credit side.

Liabilities   Increase on credit side and decrease on debit side.

Capital   Increase on credit side and decrease on debit side.

Revenue   Increase on credit side and decrease on debit side.

Cost   Increase on debit side and decrease on credit side.

Expense   Increase on debit side and decrease on credit side.

You will learn a great deal more about these rules in an accounting course. The above is only meant to serve as a brief introduction.

FINANCIAL RATIO ANALYSIS

Alert managers must know how to read and understand basic financial statements, and they must also know how to understand basic interpretations made from the data in these statements. Some of these interpretations of data are reached by working very simple formulas, a technique known as a *financial ratio*. Financial ratio analysis guides the businessperson in determining what is right or wrong with the financial aspects of the firm. Managers also find such analysis useful in planning for the future. When a physician checks your blood pressure or takes your temperature, it is to gather data that will prove helpful in making a decision concerning your health. Usually a temperature or blood pressure reading is helpful to the doctor, but sometimes such information is of little value. The same holds true for financial ratio analysis results; often they are helpful to the manager but sometimes they are not. Never can they take the place of sound judgment based on solid business experience.

CURRENT RATIO

The current ratio is the best known and most used of all financial ratios. To find the current ratio, one must extract two total figures from the balance sheet: the total of current assets and the total of current liabilities. After these figures are ascertained, a formula is constructed as follows:

$$\text{Current Ratio} = \frac{\text{Current Assets}}{\text{Current Liabilities}}$$

business profile: COMPETITION COMES TO ACCOUNTING

The public accounting profession has long been dominated by the eight largest firms, known as the Big Eight. Competition among these firms has always been handled very discreetly, the individual companies preferring their clients to seek them out when they needed accounting services. Governed by a code of professional ethics that banned advertising until 1978 and still prohibits uninvited direct solicitation of new accounts, the accounting profession has maintained a low-key approach to marketing its services.

That has clearly changed in recent years, however, and the Big Eight firms are pursuing potential clients in a whole new world of competition. Three firms claim to be No. 1 in the industry—Peat, Marwick, Mitchell on the basis of revenues; Arthur Anderson on the basis of more clients on the New York and American Stock Exchanges; and Price Waterhouse on the basis of client sales, client net income, client employees, and client total assets. Since only these three firms of the Big Eight publish financial statements, it is a little difficult to see how the Big Eight as a whole are doing. To most outsiders, it appears that the Big Eight firms are not only engaged in a variety of marketing strategies and fierce competition, but are just about keeping their total share of the market.

The marketing strategies among the eight companies vary considerably. All are publishing pamphlets and sponsoring seminars on the important accounting issues of the day. There is also far more intense bidding for new business than before. Whereas in the past a simple letter and an interview with top management were all that was required for bidding on a new major account, now there are several "elimination" rounds, featuring comprehensive proposals outlining how the firm would handle an auditing job. A campaign might cost between $10,000 to $50,000. While accounting firms are prohibited from directly soliciting business, they make major efforts to develop contacts at all large firms so that they can be invited to bid on jobs. This process is known as practice development, or PD for short, among the professional members. All the large firms require their partners to join community and social clubs and even to pay a percentage of their salaries to nonreligious charitable organizations.

Some Big Eight firms, and perhaps all of them, also develop lists of companies that may be considering changing auditors. They point out the advantage of their services so that potential customers will believe that their audit techniques are superior. Big Eight members are acquiring knowledge of specializations within industries so that they can be particularly helpful in auditing firms in those industries. In addition to auditing services, some of the Big Eight have gone heavily into tax services, management consulting, and feasibility studies. International markets are objects of increased attention as well as the smaller firms in this country. Many of the firms have even expanded their government auditing services although the profit rates are very low on government auditing jobs because competitive bidding is usually required.

A question has arisen about the increased emphasis on marketing. It is whether the efforts have affected service to customers. A barrage of lawsuits against public accounting firms in the past few years would indicate that perhaps the professional standards have slipped a little under the competitive pressure. However, the industry spokesmen deny any erosion of standards and point out that the threat of lawsuits ensures that the work will be done thoroughly and cautiously no matter how severe the time pressure.

Based on the balance sheet of Gaslight, Inc. the restaurant formed by Musto and Volyn in Chapter 10 (see Figure 14-1), the formula would be worked as follows:

$$CR = \frac{120,000}{80,000} = 1.5\!:\!1 \text{ or } 1.5$$

How meaningful is the number 1.5? Is this a good reading or a poor reading? It all depends on what other firms in the same business and of about the same size are doing. What is normal or healthy for one firm in one industry might not be healthy for another firm of a different size in a different industry. Most accountants would say, as a very general rule of thumb for most businesses, that a current ratio of 3:1 is healthy. This means that there are three times as many dollars of current assets as there are dollars of current liabilities. That is to say, if all current liabilities should become due immediately, the company could raise three times as much in dollars by selling the current assets. This assumes that current assets could be sold at the value indicated on the balance sheet. In our example above, we have only $1.50 for every $1 of current liability. Some managers would interpret this as an indication to cease borrowing until the firm's current ratio position becomes firmer.

QUICK ASSET RATIO OR ACID TEST RATIO

The quick asset ratio, like the current ratio, measures the liquidity of the firm. That is to say, it attempts to determine the cash available to meet debt obligations. It is more critical than the current ratio because it leaves out certain current asset amounts when measuring the current assets against the current liabilities. Referring again to the balance sheet illustrated, we extract only cash and accounts receivable (net) to ascertain the numerator of our formula. After doing this, we proceed as we did in finding the current ratio. The formula is as follows:

$$\text{Quick Asset Ratio} = \frac{\text{Cash} + \text{Accounts Receivable}}{\text{Current Liabilities}}$$

In the case of the Gaslight, Inc., balance sheet, the formula would be worked as follows:

$$QA = \frac{57,500}{80,000} = .794$$

This means there is 79.4 cents of quick assets available for every $1 of current liability. By most standards this would not be a very healthy ratio, although checking it against industry norms might indicate otherwise.

This ratio is truly an acid test of how well a firm can pay all its current debts by selling its accounts receivable and combining it with its cash balance. Often the quick asset ratio is referred to as the acid test ratio. The current ratio and quick asset ratio are known as *liquidity ratios* because they measure a firm's ability to raise cash to meet its current outstanding debts.

PROFITABILITY RATIOS

Profitability ratios measure the profits earned by the firm (usually after taxes) on investments, assets, or sales. These ratios give an indication of how successful the firm is as a profit maker, but again, as with the liquidity ratios, the result must be compared with that of other firms of comparable size in similar lines of business.

The formula for the ratio of net profit to sales is:

$$\frac{NP}{S} = \frac{\text{Net Profit after Taxes}}{\text{Sales}}$$

The income statement will serve as the source of information for the formula. In the case of Gaslight, Inc., the formula would be as follows:

$$\frac{NP}{S} = \frac{10,000}{110,000} = 9.1$$

This means that for every $1 of sales for the year, the owners realized profits of 9.1 cents after taxes. This would probably be a very good return on sales since the national average for corporations in the United States varies from 5 to 7 percent on a year-to-year basis.

The formula for the net profit to net worth ratio is:

$$\frac{NP}{NW} = \frac{\text{Net Profit after Taxes}}{\text{Capital}}$$

The income statement and the balance sheet serve as the sources of information for this formula. In the case of Gaslight, Inc., the formula would be as follows:

$$\frac{NP}{NW} = \frac{10,000}{120,000} = 8.33$$

This means that the return to owners on their capital, which represents their investment in the business, is 8.3 cents for every $1 of capital invested. This would be below the national average for corporations, which is usually between 11 and 12 percent.

MEASURES OF SOLVENCY

Finding out whether a firm is solvent means finding out whether the firm has more assets than liabilities. Remember that the *realized value of assets* is the determining factor, not the amounts as stated on the balance sheet. It is one thing for Gaslight, Inc., to show assets totaling $300,000, with this figure being a fair and accurate cost of the assets. But if these assets are sold today, will they bring $300,000 cash to pay off creditors? They may very well, particularly if the economy has experienced inflation over the life of the business. Two of the most important ratios for measuring solvency are discussed below.

DEBT TO EQUITY RATIO

The figures needed to compute the debt-to-equity formula are found on the balance sheet. The formula is constructed as follows:

$$\frac{L}{NW} = \frac{\text{Liabilities}}{\text{Net Worth}}$$

Using the data from Gaslight, Inc., for this formula, the following would result:

$$\frac{L}{NW} = \frac{180,000}{120,000} = 1.5:1$$

This means that there is $1.50 of debt owed by the corporation for every $1 of investment made by the owners. Again, data of this type are of little value unless they can be compared with averages for firms of similar size and business.

LONG-TERM DEBT TO TOTAL ASSETS RATIO This ratio reveals what percentage of the firm's assets is absorbed by long-term debt. Remember that long-term debt is owed for a period of more than one year and could run for as long as 30 or 40 years. Such debts are usually paid back in monthly, semiannual, or annual installments of interest plus principal. The formula involves data from the Gaslight, Inc., balance sheet and appears as follows:

$$\frac{FL}{A} = \frac{\text{Fixed Liabilities}}{\text{Total Assets}}$$

For Gaslight, Inc., the formula will appear as follows:

$$\frac{FL}{A} = \frac{100,000}{300,000} = 33.3$$

This indicates that of every $1 of assets owned by the firm, 33.3 cents of it is pledged to the payment of long-term liabilities. The remaining 66.6 cents is available to meet short-term debt (current liabilities) and the claims of the stockholders against the firm. All creditors have preference claims on the assets of the firm. This means that all creditor claims must be satisfied before the stockholders receive any return on their capital in case the business is discontinued.

BUDGETS FOR MANAGEMENT GUIDANCE Every situation in life requires some plan for action. Individuals buy insurance to help protect themselves against the economic losses of fire, theft, and accident. Businesspeople also buy insurance as protection against economic losses that may occur. However, the successful business must do more than plan to cope with traumatic events like fire and theft; it must plan as well to meet everyday financial situations that are bound to arise.

Budgets are nothing more than plans to cope with the future economic problems of the firm. They are not concerned with how things will be done but rather with the dollars needed to get them done.

CASH BUDGETS Cash flows in and out of a business at a constant rate. However, the inflows of cash derived from revenues and other sources are not always adequate at any given moment to meet the outflows. It is similar to a situation where an individual gets paid once a month. On payday he has lots of money, but if he doesn't budget that money it will not last the month. To complicate the situation, in some months, expenditures of individuals and businesses are greater than in other months. Therefore, budgeting also requires that at certain times adequate cash be set aside to meet heavy future demands on cash.

In preparing a cash budget, a firm always starts with an estimate of what the cash receipts will be for a stated period of time, usually one week or one month. The same type of estimate is made of expenditures for the period. If receipts exceed expenditures, the balance is applied to future requirements or channeled into an investment. If receipts are not adequate for meeting expenditures, surplus funds must be used. If these are not available, investments must be sold to raise cash or the firm must borrow it.

The most common sources of cash receipts include the following:

1. Receipts from cash sales

2. Receipts from collections on accounts and notes receivable.

3. Receipts from the sale of assets

4. The most common expenditures of cash include:

5. Payments to creditors

6. Payments for the purchase of assets (including merchandise)

7. Payments for operating expenses such as salaries

8. Payments to the owners as a return on their investment

In no case can a firm estimate exactly what its receipts or expenditures will be for any given period of time. At best, management uses data accumulated from past operations as a guide for planning its cash budgets. Sometimes unexpected situations cause the budget estimate to be wide of the target. This is to be expected on rare occasions, and the firm's executives must have an emergency plan for such a situation. In many large corporations, several employees spend all of their time working on cash budgets. Such personnel have extensive training in accounting and financial management.

CAPITAL BUDGETS   *Cash budgets* are prepared for weekly or monthly periods. Usually cash budgets are not drawn up for longer than three to six months into the future. *Capital budgets*, on the other hand, are long-range plans for the plant asset needs of the firm. Because of this, capital budgets are prepared for periods extending up to 10 years and even longer in some cases. All firms require cash budgets, but only those firms using substantial quantities of heavy equipment have need of capital budgets.

personality profile:
BROCK ADAMS –
politics and the business
of law

When Brockman Adams resigned from Congress to become Secretary of Transportation, the House lost a man whom *New Times* magazine numbered among the "Ten Brightest Congressmen." Like Jimmy Carter, Adams was born in Georgia, but he was transplanted to Seattle, where he graduated *summa cum laude* in economics from the University of Washington. After Harvard Law School, he joined a Seattle law firm and eventually formed his own law partnership with two colleagues.

Like many other lawyers who see the natural connection between the "business" of law and that of government, Adams embarked on a political career, challenging the incumbent for Congress in 1964. He easily won the election and subsequent elections in a district whose constituency suffered high unemployment because of aerospace industry layoffs. Congressman Adams occasionally voted against his personal beliefs to save or provide jobs for his constituents, but he opposed continued production of the antiballistic missile and the B-1 bomber.

In addition to achieving the hitherto impossible task of getting through Congress a bill granting home rule to Washington, D.C., Adams became a Congressional expert on transportation: "I view transportation more as a necessary public utility than a purely free-enterprise business." He was instrumental in setting up Amtrak for passenger rail operations and Conrail as a successor to seven bankrupt Northeastern and Midwestern railroads, including the Penn Central.

Adams brought to his new position as Secretary of Transportation the conviction that the United States must convert its "every-industry-for-itself transportation system" into an efficient "interlocking network." This view reflects the melding of his background as economist, lawyer, and politician.

A capital budget is a formal plan for replacing obsolete equipment or buildings as well as acquiring equipment or facilities for expansion, besides specifying when these changes will occur. The plan also outlines methods for raising the cash and credit needed for buying the new equipment; this is referred to as the "capital." If a firm had no such plan, it could easily find itself in financial difficulties the next time it needed funds to replace some aging, worn-out equipment. As you probably realize, manufacturing equipment, buildings, and computers cost many thousands of dollars and in some cases millions.

In recent years public utilities companies have been some of the hardest pressed to replace equipment. Many of their earlier capital budgets had not sufficiently taken into account the need for better environmental devices to keep the air and water clean. As a result, many public utility companies found themselves very short of funds for buying the sophisticated equipment needed.

BASIC LEGAL CONCEPTS

As well as serving as their own accountants, many businesspeople were their own lawyers 30 or 40 years ago. As was the case with accounting problems, legal problems have become more and more complicated since the Great Depression. Today practically no businessperson would think of doing legal work. The following discussion of several major legal topics is only intended to familiarize the potential manager with some of the terminology and procedures related to business law. In no way could such a discussion give the reader sufficient information to handle any legal problems.

CONTRACTS

Almost every day managers make agreements with suppliers, customers, advertising agencies, and countless other people and firms. Some of these agreements are made over the telephone and others through the mail or in person. Sometimes a handshake seals the bargain or sometimes there is a formal signing of legal documents. A *contract* is the term applied to an exchange of promises that constitute an agreement binding on all parties. The courts will enforce a contract if it was made for a legal purpose and properly executed. Proper execution does not necessarily include the signing of an agreement. In some cases, courts will enforce an oral agreement as long as the facts can be ascertained.

For a contract to be enforceable, certain elements must be present. These include:

1. *Mutual assent:* The minds of the parties to a contract must meet. That is to say that all parties must be talking about the same subject matter and not be confused about the terms of the subject agreed upon.
2. *Competent parties:* Certain people cannot ordinarily enter into business contracts by law. Minors and people certified insane, are examples of those who are not considered competent parties.

3. *Legal purpose:* An agreement of a business nature that is harmful to society is not legally enforceable. For example, one cannot enter into an agreement with another to burn down a third party's factory and expect the terms to be legally enforceable.

4. *Consideration:* In the eyes of the law an exchange of something for nothing is not legally enforceable. Therefore, something of material value must be exchanged by both parties for a contract to be legally enforceable. However, the court will not weigh how fair the exchange of values is. If one wants to sell a 1979 Ford Mustang for $500 cash to an interested buyer, this would be considered adequate consideration; and if all other contractual elements are satisfied, it would be a legally enforceable contract.

5. *Written form:* Certain contracts must be stated in written form to be legally binding. In the case of sales of land or realty, the agreement must always be in writing; otherwise the courts will not enforce it.

A contract which contains all of the above essentials is referred to in legal terminology as *valid*. This means that it is enforceable in a court of law.

PERSONALTY VERSUS REALTY

At one time or another every businessperson buys or sells land, equipment, or other forms of property for use in his business. Legal terminology breaks all property down into two general categories, and the legal treatment of transactions involving property varies depending upon the category under which the property falls.

Land and buildings are known as real estate or *realty*. The law is very specific and rigid with regard to realty transactions. The legal procedures required to transfer realty from one party to another can sometimes require several weeks or even months to complete. A search must be conducted through the old records of ownership of the property to assure the new owner that no back taxes or other creditor claims are outstanding against the holding. The law states that any new purchasers of property are liable for the unsatisfied claims against the property incurred by any of its former owners. In addition to the search, there are usually legal procedures required to set up the financing of the property, since most realty is purchased with a combination of a cash down payment and a mortgage for the balance. Tax problems can also complicate the legal steps in realty transactions.

Personalty includes all other forms of business property. The term is derived from the phrase "personal property." Such things as store equipment, merchandise inventory, and office supplies would be examples of personalty. The legal concepts and measures associated with personal property are not nearly as rigid or specific as those connected with realty. Still, if the personalty entails a large expenditure of money, the steps for executing the contract can be quite complicated.

AGENCY

Agency is a legal relationship resulting from an agreement between two parties that one of them, designated the agent, shall act on behalf of the other, designated the principal, subject to the principal's control, in transactions with third parties. Power of attorney, one popular form of agency, is a relationship in which someone, usually an attorney, is authorized to act on someone else's behalf. In granting a power of attorney, one might give a lawyer the right to execute a land purchase contract in South America. The one granting the right is the principal and the attorney is the agent. As long as the attorney acts in good faith, all actions in executing the contract in South America bind the principal. It is as if the principal acted at the closing of the agreement in South America.

As businesses have expanded, it has become more and more common for them to engage agents to help complete agreements. Usually an agent has an expertise for certain business affairs exceeding that of the principal, an added advantage to a business engaging an agent. One disadvantage of using an agent is the possibility of losing control in key decisions affecting transactions. Often the demands for completing many kinds of transactions in scattered geographical locations leave the firm little choice.

NEGOTIABLE INSTRUMENTS

Negotiable instruments are credit instruments that not only serve as evidence of indebtedness but are also widely used as substitutes for money. Promissory notes, checks, certificates of deposit, and drafts are examples of negotiable instruments. Being negotiable, they can be endorsed and passed on to another holder. Because negotiable instruments circulate freely, their use is strictly regulated by the Uniform Negotiable Instruments Law and the Uniform Commercial Code, adopted by most states as part of their business law regulations.

To be negotiable an instrument must comply with five specific requirements of the Uniform Negotiable Instruments Law and the Uniform Commercial Code. These requirements specify that:

1. A particular written form and signature be used
2. Unconditional promise or order to pay be stated
3. Payment to order or bearer be stated
4. Payment of a sum in money be certain
5. Payment on demand or at a specified time be stated

Remember that the major advantages of a negotiable instrument are: (1) that it can be passed to another as a substitute for cash on endorsement and; (2) that it serves as written evidence of a debt. *Endorsement* is the act of signing a negotiable instrument to signify that one will fulfill the terms of an instrument in case of default by the original maker. To be valid, the signature must be in the appropriate place on the form. Another name for a negotiable instrument is commercial paper. All of the instruments cited earlier in this discussion are explained in other chapters.

PATENTS AND COPYRIGHTS

Patent and copyright laws are federal legislation intended to protect inventors and writers from having their work used by, and for the profit of, others. A grant of a

The Hoe printing press was the marvel of its age. For each technical advance in its design, a new patent was issued.

patent entitles the holder to prevent other parties from making, selling, or using the inventor's particular invention for profit-making purposes for a period of 17 years. An infringement exists, even though all the parts or features of a particular invention are not copied, if there is a substantial duplication of the original invention. The purpose of a patent is to give the inventor the exclusive right to profit from his invention. It is hoped that such a right will encourage innovation in technology, thus helping to serve society. After 17 years, a patent is no longer in effect and others may use the invention.

A copyright is the right given by law to prevent others from printing, copying, or publishing a work resulting from creative effort and intellectual labor. Such a right was granted for a period of 28 years and could be renewed for an additional 28 year period. In 1976, a new copyright law was passed by Congress and signed by the president. The new law grants an author a copyright that extends over his or her lifetime plus fifty years beyond the date of death. The new law also states that all copyrights in existence at the time the new law was enacted were extended for a period of 75 years. Infringement of copyright in general consists of copying the form of expression of ideas or conceptions without written permission. A person guilty of infringement of a copyright or of a patent is liable to the owner for financial damages as determined by the courts. The owner is also entitled to an injunction to restrain further infringement.

Many firms engaging scientists, engineers, writers, composers require them to sign contracts forfeiting all patent and copyright privileges to the firm for certain financial considerations.

Law and accounting are established professions, but laws are always changing and accounting rules are often revised. Management must keep up with the general trend of change so it is not relying on outdated laws or procedures. Some recent developments include the following items.

For years the accountant has valued the assets of the firm at cost value with no regard to increases in value due to inflation. This has been sharply criticized by economists and others as an unrealistic approach to keeping financial data. For example, if a firm purchased a building in a downtown area in 1960 for $100,000, that building would be shown on the financial statement at $100,000 less accumulated depreciation to date. In fact, due to real estate price inflation, the same building might be salable at a value of $200,000 in 1979. The economist contends this is its true carrying value. The accountant claims to be dealing with "historical cost" and the fact is the building was purchased for $100,000. Furthermore, when it is sold, and only then, will its selling price be recognized and a gain shown on the sale. Many accountants have compromised to some extent by showing current values in footnotes or in parentheses next to the historical cost data.

Auditing is the term given to the process by which independent public accounting firms are engaged by a client to check the accounting work of the accountants employed by the client. All medium and large firms engage outside independent CPA firms to come in and make annual audits. After completion of the audit, the independent CPA issues a written opinion on the accuracy and uniformity of the statements in compliance with basic accounting principles. Figure 14-9 shows a sample of such an opinion known as an unqualified opinion because there are no exceptions noted by the auditing firm in terms of accuracy or compliance with accounting principles.

In recent years, many unqualified opinions by CPAs were later proven wrong when firms were sometimes proven guilty of fraud, tax evasion, or other financial misdeeds. Many injured parties sued the independent auditors for damages because they contended they were negligent or too superficial in their audit. As a result, in recent years independent CPAs have tightened up and refined audit procedures. They have also increased their coverage of malpractice insurance. (See Chapter 19.)

Attorneys frequently handle cases involving suits on a percentage-of-damages fee basis. This means they charge the client a percentage of the damages won in court as their fee. In suits involving small amounts, the settlement often doesn't benefit the client because after paying the attorney's fees, there is little left. In recent years, some states have established small claims courts where procedures are informal and clients can plead their own cases without the need for an attorney. However, these courts only exist in certain areas and are only for small claims, usually under $1,000.

FIGURE 14-9

SMITH, JONES, AND DOE
CERTIFIED PUBLIC ACCOUNTANTS
Anytown, U.S.A.

OPINION OF INDEPENDENT ACCOUNTS

To the Board of Directors and Share Owners of Gaslight, Inc.

In our opinion, the accompanying financial statements present fairly the
financial position of Gaslight, Inc., at December 31, 1979, and the
results of their operations and the changes in financial position for
the year ended in conformity with generally accepted accounting principles consistently applied. Our examination of these statements were
made in accordance with generally accepted auditing standards and
accordingly included such tests of the accounting records and such other
auditing procedures as we considered necessary in the circumstances.

SMITH, JONES, AND DOE

Smith, Jones, and Doe
January 31, 1980

SUMMARY

Every firm must regularly keep adequate financial records and must occasionally
deal with legal problems. Financial statements are the annual summaries of how the
firm did with respect to profits and resources for the past year. The major financial
statements are the balance sheet and the income statement. The balance sheet
lists the assets, liabilities, and net worth of the firm while the income statement
shows the revenue, cost of merchandise sold, and the operating expenses as well
as the net income. Accounts kept in a ledger file facilitate the presentation of the
annual financial statements. Certified public accountants are engaged by most
firms to conduct periodic audits of their books and records.

All firms enter into legal agreements related to various business transactions,
such as the purchase or sale of realty or personalty. These agreements are called
contracts and are enforceable in a court of law. Businesses also deal with checks,
notes, drafts, and other similar documents known as negotiable instruments.

Patents and copyrights are also sought by businesses to protect inventions or other types of creative works. Lawyers are engaged or retained to help with legal problems and to help prevent such problems.

SUMMARY OF KEY TERMS

Accounts Receivable Debts owed the company by customers and others.

Acid Test Ratio A liquidity ratio used to measure the extent of cash available to meet current debts. It is determined by dividing cash and receivables by current liabilities.

Agency A legal relationship resulting from an agreement that someone, an agent, shall act in a legal capacity on behalf of another, the principal.

Assets Things of value owned by a business.

Auditing Procedure of verification whereby an independent Certified Public Accountant checks the accuracy and conformity of accounting records of clients.

Balance Sheet A formal statement of all the financial resources owned by a business as well as its debts.

Capital The value or equity of the owners (stockholders) in the financial resources of their business. It can be found in dollars by subtracting the firm's total liabilities from total assets.

Capital Budget Long-range financial plans for the plant asset needs of a firm.

Cash Budget Short-range financial plan of the cash needs and revenue expectations of a firm; usually prepared for several future weekly or monthly periods.

Contracts An agreement of a legal nature that binds the parties. It can sometimes be executed orally as well as in written form.

Copyright A right given and protected by law to prevent others from printing, copying or publishing a work resulting from creative effort and intellectual labor.

C.P.A. Abbreviation for Certified Public Accountant, an individual who is licensed by the state to prepare audits, appear in court, and certify the financial statements of firms that are audited.

Current Assets Assets that can be converted into cash fairly quickly.

Current Liabilities Debts owed by a business that are payable in one year or less.

Current Ratio A liquidity ratio that measures the availability of current assets for paying off current debt. It is found by dividing current assets by current liabilities.

Endorsement The act of signing a negotiable instrument to signify that one will fulfill the terms of an instrument in case of default by the original maker.

Fixed Assets Capital items owned by a business such as land, buildings, and equipment. Ordinarily it takes some time to convert these items into cash.

Gross Profit The difference between revenues and the cost of the merchandise sold. Represents the dollar markup on merchandise sold by the business.

Income Statement A financial statement that lists the revenues, costs, and expenses of the firm and the net profit resulting from operations.

Investments Those assets owned by the firm in the form of stocks and bonds of other corporations or government units.

Ledger A book or file of the firm's accounts.

Liabilities Debts owed to others by the business.

Long-term Liabilities Debts owed by a business that are payable in a period of time exceeding one year.

Negotiable Instruments Credit instruments that not only serve as evidence of indebtedness but are also widely used as substitutes for money. Checks and notes are examples of negotiable instruments.

Net Worth Another accounting term for capital (see above).

Operating Expenses Costs incurred in running a business.

Patent A legal grant entitling the holder to prevent others from making, selling, or using a particular invention for profit-making purposes for a period of years.

Personalty A legal term meaning all forms of property except real estate owned by a business or individual.

Plant Assets Another accounting term for fixed assets (see above).

Power of Attorney A form of agency in which an agent is empowered to act on a principal's behalf in executing a legal transaction.

Proprietorship Another accounting term for capital (see above).

Quick Asset Ratio Another accounting term for acid test ratio (see above).

Realty A legal term meaning all forms of land and buildings.

Statement of Capital or Retained Earnings A financial statement to show changes in capital investments over a designated period of time. If the statement relates to a sole proprietorship or partnership, it is known as a statement of capital. If it relates to a corporation, it is known as a statement of retained earnings.

REVIEW QUESTIONS

1. Is a firm more likely to have an accountant or a lawyer as a full-time employee? Why?
2. What are the five elements essential for a legally binding contract?
3. How do the purpose and format of a copyright differ from those of a patent?
4. Distinguish between *personalty* and *realty*. Which requires greater attention to legal detail and why?
5. If assets are $20,000 and liabilities are $16,000, how much is capital? If assets are $60,000 and capital is $20,000, how much are liabilities?
6. Define liquidity and explain how it relates to the classification of assets on the balance sheet.
7. How do the purpose and format of a cash budget differ from those of a capital budget?
8. What are fixed assets? How is depreciation related to fixed assets?
9. Define agency. What are the advantages and disadvantages in hiring an agent?
10. What five conditions are necessary for a negotiable instrument to comply with the Uniform Negotiable Instruments Act?

DISCUSSION QUESTIONS

1. How is auditing different from write-up work in accounting? Which must be performed by an independent Certified Public Accountant?
2. Comment on the validity of the following: The most important type of financial statement is the income statement.
3. If you completed an oral contract with someone, and no one other than the parties to the

agreement was present, would the contract be legally binding if it was proper in all other respects? Why or why not?

4. Comment on the following: The advent of sophisticated electronic data processing systems has reduced the need of most firms to hire accounting personnel.

5. List as many reasons as you can why a business should hire an attorney.

CASES FOR DECISION MAKING

GIANTS COLLIDE

In June 1977, International Telephone and Telegraph Company (ITT), one of the nation's largest corporations, filed a suit in federal court against another industrial giant, American Telephone and Telegraph Company (AT&T). The suit alleges that AT&T violates antitrust laws by refusing to purchase telephone equipment from companies it does not own. Currently, AT&T purchases all of its equipment from Western Electric, a wholly owned subsidiary. IT&T further claims that tests indicate the equipment it sells is superior. Therefore, quality should not be a defense in the case. At the time of this writing the suit has still not been settled.

1. Do you believe one company should be able to sue another for loss of profits? Why or why not?

2. How does this case relate to the current suit of the federal government against AT&T? (Hint: See Chapter 17, "Business and Government Relations.")

3. What is the total amount of damages ITT is seeking in this suit?

AUDIT ANGLES

In a *Wall Street Journal* (June 13, 1977) article it was reported that Peat Marwick, Mitchell & Co. is attempting to catch more fraud in its auditing procedures. (Peat Marwick is the largest of the large public accounting firms in the United States.) The accounting firm wants to detect the increasing number of corporate frauds and needs suggestions for doing so that extend beyond the realm of normal accounting procedures. Therefore, it has announced that it will award grants to the academic community for research in this area. The firm believes that an interdisciplinary approach, perhaps using psychologists and sociologists might extend the horizons of the auditing process. Peat Marwick reports that most corporate frauds are exposed through tips, anonymous letters, or a change of heart by a participant other than through an audit.

1. Define *fraud*. Refer to either an English language or a law dictionary.

2. Why do you think most frauds are not discovered during audits?

3. Why are large accounting firms so interested in lessening the opportunity for fraud among their client firms?

NEWTON'S LAW OF EQUITY

One year ago, Carmine Newton opened a men's clothing store in Sacramento, California. At the end of the year he had $65,000 invested in inventory and $6,000 was owed to him by customers on account. He had $3,000 cash in the firm's checking account and $1,000 in supplies on hand. He owed $8,000 to the bank on a one-year note and owed $2,000 to his landlord on the lease for the store. Store equipment owned totaled $10,000 and the first year's depreciation on equipment was $1,000. Newton's sales for the year totaled $80,000 and his net income was $20,000. His firm was organized as a sole proprietorship.

1. What was the value of his fixed assets at year end?
2. What was his net worth at the end of the year? (Note: Use only balance sheet items to determine this figure.)
3. What was his current ratio for the firm?

4. What was the net profit to sales ratio for the firm?
5. What was the net profit to net worth ratio for the firm? (Note: Use amount ascertained in part 2 above for net worth.)
6. What were his costs and expenses for the year?

RELATED READINGS

Accounting: A Career for Women Too. Chicago: American Women's Society of Certified Public Accountants, 1974.

Describes the opportunities for women in the field of public accounting and contains the answers to many questions asked by women aspiring to a field that has been the exclusive domain of men for many years.

Fenten, D. X. *Ms. —Attorney.* Philadelphia: Westminster Press, 1974.

Points out the difficulties of a woman toward becoming successful in a law career. Attempts to explore the prejudices and distresses faced by women who enter the legal profession. Written by a man.

Green, Mark J. *The Other Government.* New York: Grossman, 1975.

Stories of Washington lawyers and how they protect their clients. Many of these accounts deal with business and how it is involved.

Information for CPA Candidates. New York: American Institute of Certified Public Accountants, 1970.

Good information for students who want to go into certified public accounting. Tells what professional training is required and what work experience and examination procedures have to be met.

Kirk, Russel. *The Roots of American Order.* LaSalle, Ill.: Open Court, 1974.

A history and criticism of the law and its effects on human behavior.

MacKenzie, John. *The Appearance of Justice.* New York: Scribner's, 1974.

Provides a discussion of our courts and system of justice as well as some excellent food for thought in the area of justice and society.

McNeill, I. Eugene. *Financial Accounting—A Decision Information System,* 2nd ed. Santa Monica, Calif.: Goodyear, 1974.

Good basic text on introductory accounting. Especially good for management candidates who want an introduction to the field.

Tracy, John A. *Understanding Accounting.* Englewood Cliffs, N.J.: Prentice-Hall, 1971.

A primer in the area of basic accounting. Easy-to-follow guide for the nonaccounting student. It covers the major topics in sole proprietorship, partnership, and corporation accounting.

part five: CAREER OPPORTUNITIES

CAREERS IN COMPUTERS/STATISTICS/ACCOUNTING/LEGAL

All computer-related jobs require specialized training. There are clerical and nontechnical positions such as keypunching, data library management, and computer installation management. However, community college and four-year college graduates are primarily interested in programming and systems analysis. Both areas have great growth potential and the numbers of employees in each are expected to be among the fastest growing of any field.

PROGRAMMERS Programmers prepare step-by-step instructions for the computer to follow. Computer programming can range from very simple tasks to highly complex programs requiring applied mathematics. Programmers usually work in large firms that need and can afford extensive computer systems.

Training requirements for programmers vary from employer to employer. Some programmers are college graduates and others take special courses to supplement their experience in fields such as accounting. Job openings in the field are expected to be good through the mid-1980s.

SYSTEMS ANALYST A systems analyst plans the activities involved in processing data to solve a specific business, scientific, or engineering problem. Business organizations usually look for people with experience in accounting, business, or economics, and, of course, people with science background are preferred for work in scientifically oriented organizations.

Employment of systems analysts is expected to grow faster than the average for all occupations through the mid-1980s. The best chances for

employment will be in large organizations in major cities and the federal government.

STATISTICIANS A field closely related to computer programming is statistics. Statisticians collect, develop, analyze, and interpret data. Often they are involved in planning surveys and designing experiments as well. A bachelor's degree with a major in math or statistics is the minimal educational requirement. For some positions, a bachelor's degree in economics or some other business field, with a minor in statistics, is the best educational mix.

CAREERS IN LAW AND ACCOUNTING

In 1978, there were about 400,000 lawyers in the United States. Of this number roughly 25,000 were in federal government positions and another 20,000 were employed by state and local governments. Law school is usually a three-year program undertaken after completing studies for an undergraduate degree, usually in political science, history, or business administration. The first two years of law school are generally devoted to basic courses in legal contracts, property law, and courtroom procedures. In the third and final year, the student may take specialized courses such as tax, corporate, or labor law. To be admitted to practice, one must pass the bar examinations administered by the individual state in which one lives.

According to the *Occupational Outlook Handbook,* there are many law school graduates coming into the job market and competition for good jobs is expected to be keen. The employment of lawyers will probably grow moderately through the middle of the 1980s, and there should be good opportunities for the well qualified. Law serves as a good background for many business occupations, and many attorneys often take management and finance positions with companies.

PARALEGAL CAREERS   In addition to highly trained professional lawyers, there are many so-called paralegal occupations. These are positions for people who are educated in some of the general principles and procedures of law but not trained or expected to function as lawyers. They do some of the supportive jobs in law firms that used to be done by the lawyers, thus freeing attorneys to concentrate on the more complex aspects of their work. A paralegal position is analogous to the relationship between a nurse and doctor.

Paralegal personnel are expected to be more than legal secretaries. To some extent the job is considered professional, and the person aspiring to fill such a post must take an intensive program of very specific training. Many private business schools, community colleges, and universities now offer two- and four-year undergraduate paralegal programs. Graduates are finding it rather easy to obtain jobs with larger law firms, and it may soon be that the medium-sized and smaller firms will also be looking for paralegal employees. Training for paralegal work requires intensive study in various areas of law, including estates and trusts, real estate, litigation, employee benefit plans, general practice law, and criminal law. The patience, ability, and willingness to do extensive research work and write extensive reports are requirements.

ACCOUNTING CAREERS   Some people confuse bookkeeping with accounting. A bookkeeper is one who inserts financial information about the business into the accounting system. However, because of a lack of experience or education, the bookkeeper does not have responsibility for interpreting financial data or for advising on or making financial decisions. Every accountant must know bookkeeping well, but responsibilities go far beyond those of a bookkeeper.

In 1978, there were more than 800,000 accountants in the United States, and about 20 percent of these were Certified Public Accountants. Only about 3 percent of all CPAs and only 22 percent of all accountants are women, so the field is wide open for women. About 20 percent of all accountants are engaged in public accounting, while about 60 percent work in private firms or what is sometimes referred to as industrial accounting.

Most firms expect their accountants to have an undergraduate degree in the field. For beginning accounting positions, the federal government requires four years of college training with at least twenty-four semester hours of credit in accounting and related subjects. Work experience in the field is usually thought of as essential to completing a master's program.

The need for accountants is expected to be very substantial right through 1985. Thousands of additional openings are resulting from expansion of firms in the field as well as from retirements, deaths, and people leaving accounting jobs. Data processing has eliminated many of the lower level jobs in the field, but has balanced that with many new opportunities for highly trained accountants to prepare, administer, and analyze the data made available by these systems.

Because the work requires the accountant to deal constantly with numbers, a good accountant must be a logical thinker, have an extensive knowledge of basic accounting principles, and possess an aptitude for math.

part six

HUMAN RELATIONS

In this section we will focus on the human factor in business—the employees.

In Chapter 15, you will look at the efforts of personnel departments to bring together the goals of employees and the goals of the firms for which they work. You will look at the process whereby employees are brought into a firm and provided with services and compensation. In addition, you will look at some of the forces that affect the morale and productivity of employees.

In Chapter 16, you will look at the collective bargaining process and examine the influence of organized labor unions on business and on our society. In doing so, you will learn about the tools that both labor and management use in trying to get an edge in the bargaining process.

Part Six deals with an area that will be of great interest to all readers because most individuals are likely to be employed by an organization or to be employing other persons in their own business. The principles of human relations are vital to an understanding of people in a work environment. Hopefully, you will gain insights into the frustrations and expectations of employees.

chapter 15

PERSONNEL MANAGEMENT

OBJECTIVES

When you have finished reading and studying this chapter, you should be able to:

1. Define the scope and organization of personnel management departments in large firms.

2. Identify and explain the major functions of personnel management.

3. Name the major elements of employee morale and describe the effect of high or low morale on the productivity of a work force.

4. Explain why there are increasing difficulties in matching the needs of employees with the objectives of a business.

5. List and briefly explain the major legislation promoting affirmative action programs in companies and explain their effects on the personnel policies of firms.

CHAPTER PREVIEW

There has been a great deal of debate in recent years about whether American workers are happy and productive. In popular magazines and newspapers, they are frequently pictured as dissatisfied with their jobs. A number of management consultants have indicated that workers must have more interesting tasks and be treated as individuals, not as parts of a machine; otherwise business as well as the whole economy will suffer.

At the center of this controversy stands the personnel department in large firms. The personnel department has the major responsibility for matching the needs of the employees with the goals of the firm. Personnel management is concerned with attracting, developing, utilizing, and maintaining a work force. This is a large task, starting with an analysis of the jobs in the firm and of the manpower required to fill them. Then, the right number of workers with the appropriate qualifications must be recruited and hired. Besides orienting new workers to their jobs, the department is likely to be responsible for the training and education programs for all workers.

All employees should be evaluated regularly. The personnel staff has a role to play here, along with the employee's department. The personnel department also administers the compensation program, with all its record-keeping activities. Packages of direct payments and fringe benefits must be put together. These must be satisfactory to the employees, yet economically feasible for the firm. Ordinarily, health and safety programs, which are growing in number and complexity, are also a part of the personnel department's responsibilities.

In doing its job, the personnel department must constantly monitor the morale of the work force. If morale seems low, the personnel people must work with top management and the line managers to rebuild it. Low morale normally is accompanied by low productivity.

To make the personnel management function even more difficult these days, affirmative action programs must be carefully developed. Because of the historical discrimination against women and blacks and other minorities in business and other organizations, there are now a number of federal and state guidelines that must be followed in employment practices.

"Yes. But can you type?"

15
PERSONNEL MANAGEMENT

There is a growing recognition that employees may be the most valuable asset of any business. In the last 25 years, we have seen the economic rebirth of Japan and West Germany. At the beginning of this period, their businesses were still rebuilding after the destruction of World War II, but by 1978, many of their industries were the most efficient in the world. While many factors have contributed, this high performance has been attributed mainly to the quality and motivation of their employees.

Enlightened management recognizes the importance of its personnel in increasing the economic efficiency of the firm. It makes every effort to attract and reward the employees who can make the most significant contributions to the company's goals. At the same time, it knows that it must help the workers meet their individual goals. This is where personnel management comes in.

SCOPE OF PERSONNEL MANAGEMENT

Personnel management is concerned with attracting, developing, utilizing, and maintaining a work force. All levels of management in a firm have a part to play in performing the function.

PERSONNEL FUNCTION INVOLVES EVERYONE

Top management determines the overall goals of the firm. The implementation of these goals affects the number and quality of the workers whom the firm can attract, the amount of authority and responsibility that will be given to employees, the ways in which the work force will be utilized, the reward system, and the number of employees who will be maintained.

The employees' immediate supervisors also play an important role in the personnel management function. They either recommend, or have the final authority for, hiring the employees who work in their departments. They also influence the perception the employees have of the job and of the company.

In small firms, the personnel management function may be performed by someone who also has other duties. In larger firms, however, the major responsibility is the province of a separate department, which may be called by one of several names, including personnel department, personnel management department, industrial relations department, or personnel administration department. It is the job of this department to plan, organize, direct, and control the activities connected with securing and maintaining the work force a firm needs.

ORGANIZATIONAL PATTERNS

To carry out these activities, a variety of departmental organizational plans may be used. A typical organizational plan for a personnel department in a large industrial corporation is shown in Figure 15-1.

As you can see, the manager of the department has line authority over the divisions of the department. He has the power to command. But he has staff authority with other operating departments. He can advise the line departments in the areas of personnel, but he does not have the power to command. He is more

FIGURE 15-1 Personnel
                    manager

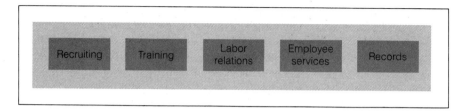

Recruiting | Training | Labor relations | Employee services | Records

of a facilitator and a coordinator of personnel activities for the firm. The divisions on the chart indicate the areas in which he performs these functions.

FUNCTIONS OF PERSONNEL MANAGEMENT

Securing and maintaining adequate personnel starts with an analysis of the tasks to be done on a job. When this is known, the department can determine the characteristics a worker needs to be successful in an assignment. Workers who fit the description can then be hired. For all large firms, job analysis has already been done on existing jobs. As new jobs are created or as old ones are changed, a new job analysis must be written.

ANALYZING PERSONNEL NEEDS

A *job analysis* is a study of the specific tasks in a job and the environment in which the work is performed. It examines such things as the location of the job, duties and responsibilities, equipment used, and working conditions. From this analysis, a *job description* is written. This is a statement of the duties, responsibilities, and conditions of a specific job and is the basis for selecting and training workers. Since it is also used for promoting and transferring employees, it must be done carefully and concisely. Some job descriptions even indicate the importance of, and future changes in, the job. When this is included, it indicates that a firm is using job analysis as part of a long-range projection of its personnel needs.

HOW ARE JOBS ANALYZED?

A person who writes job analyses is called a *job analyst*. The job analyst gathers data in several ways: by observation of the worker, by a questionnaire filled out by the employee and/or by a supervisor, or by interview. It is possible to get many versions of what a worker actually does, depending on who provides the information. The final job description is likely to be a mix of what a worker actually does and what the company would like the worker to do.

After jobs have been analyzed, they must be classified. *Job classification* is the process of rating the value of jobs to a firm. This enables a concern to set the rate of pay for each job performed and to group similarly rated jobs. It is also helpful in transferring and promoting employees.

PERSONNEL PLANNING When this preliminary and vital work has been completed, the personnel department is ready to fill job vacancies as they occur. Determining the number of new employees to be hired depends on needs. Personnel planning is concerned with bringing employees into the company, their employment there, and their termination. It is a continuous process so that the number of qualified workers needed will always be available.

For small firms, it may be a matter of finding a replacement when an employee quits or is fired. For most larger firms, however, careful projections are made of the number of new employees needed for a given period. Large firms know from past records what their demand for new employees will be. They can project the number of people who will quit, die, or retire. They also know of seasonal or other changes in their labor force needs. They can accurately predict what effect a technological change will have on the number of workers needed. Also, they can determine how the firm's growth will affect its need to recruit employees.

All of this implies that the personnel department works closely with other departments. For example, it is in constant touch with the production department in a manufacturing plant so that it knows the types of jobs being created, the number of employees needed, and the date they will be needed. It has the same relationship with the marketing, finance, accounting, and other departments. This is another application of the systems concept in business. The quality and quantity of outputs are first determined, then the quality and quantity of inputs are established. In this case, the personnel department is concerned with the quality and quantity of the labor force input.

In most large firms, finding new employees is a continuous activity. Because it is working with long-term personnel needs, a personnel department must constantly seek new people and replace those who resign or retire.

RECRUITMENT OF WORKERS The important sources for locating potential employees are likely to include the following: advertising, public employment agencies, private employment agencies, colleges and university placement offices, public and private vocational schools, labor unions, and friends of workers.

Public and Private Employment Agencies Employment agencies provide services to both employers and prospective employees. Every state has a number of branches of the state employment agency which keep lists of workers who register for employment. They make these lists available to firms and other possible employers. Applicants may be tested to determine their level of skill. Public employment agencies provide these services at no cost to the workers or employers. Private employment agencies, on the other hand, are independent businesses. They provide many of the same services as public employment agencies. Because they want to make a profit, however, they are more aggressive at recruiting prospective workers and at finding jobs for their registrants. They earn most of their income by placing workers in jobs, for which they receive a percen-

These students are members of the MESA program (Mathematics, Engineering, Science Achievement) at a Los Angeles school. They are visiting the Aerospace Corp. to discuss careers in aeronautics and space engineering.

Aerospace Corp.

tage of the first month's pay or of the first year's salary. This fee may be paid either by the firm or by the worker.

Recruitment Sources   Once employee needs are known, recruitment of workers begins. The recruitment process varies considerably, depending on the company and the type of workers needed. Assembly-line workers might be found through advertising, public employment agencies, or through friends of workers. Accounting positions might be filled through advertising, private employment agencies, or college and university placement offices. Top management may also be recruited through advertising or through private employment agencies.

In all three of these instances, advertising is a means of recruiting applicants. However, the advertising may be placed in quite different types of media. For a vice president of marketing or another top position, a firm might advertise in the *Wall Street Journal* or some other specialized publication which is read by experienced executives who might be considering a move. Figure 15-2 shows such an ad for an executive position. It is typical of those placed by firms looking for experienced executives. In recruiting assembly-line workers, on the other hand, the classified section in the daily newspaper will probably be used. Both private and public employment agencies may be good sources for clerical, technical, and sales help. In addition, managerial positions are often filled through private employment agencies.

FIGURE 15-2 McDonald's
recruiting advertisement.

McDonald's BUYER

A career opportunity exists within the highly visible environment of our Corporate Headquarters. Our unparalleled success in the restaurant business requires us to seek an experienced Buyer for kitchen equipment.

The ideal candidate for this challenging position must be a self-starter and will have three to five years of successful, relevant experience, preferably in the restaurant, metal fabrication, or refrigeration industries. Academic credentials should be in English or Business. Good analytical and communication skills are required. This position entails some travel.

For immediate consideration, forward your record of accomplishments, including salary history, in confidence, to:

Deirdre Burton

Personnel Supervisor

McDONALD'S CORPORATION

McDonald's Plaza

Oak Brook, Illinois 60521

McDonald's Is An Equal Opportunity Employer M/F

McDonald's Corporation

Of particular interest to college students are the recruitment programs. Most major corporations send a representative to various campuses, where interviews are usually scheduled through the college's placement office. The recruiter normally screens for those applicants who can best meet the needs of the company. These are then invited to the company for further interviews and testing. All companies have guidelines for college recruitment. Some only visit colleges and universities in certain geographical areas; others may prefer employees from only a few selected schools. Still others may want only graduates who have a MBA degree (Master of Business Administration). More details about how to find a job appear in Appendix B.

THE SELECTION
PROCESS

The selection process varies widely, also, depending upon the company and the type of employee being selected. The personnel department may play only a small role in the selection of executives or salesmen but probably will be more actively involved in the selection of production or office personnel. In large companies, there are several steps in the selection process.

Preliminary Screening Some applicants may be rejected because they do not fit the requirements specified on the job description. If the job description calls for typing at 60 words per minute but the applicant cannot type, there is no point in considering the worker for that job. If a person with a speech problem is applying for a telephone operator's job, it is clear that he or she cannot handle that assignment. Sometimes these applicants are eliminated in a preliminary interview. At other times, they are eliminated when someone compares their qualifications with the job description.

Application Form An applicant who successfully completes the preliminary screening has met the minimum qualifications called for in the job description. He or she is then asked to complete a written application, a form that serves several purposes in the firm. It provides a record of the applicant's background that can be matched against the job description, and it also serves as a guide for the interview that may follow. If the candidate is hired, the application is useful in evaluating the person's qualifications for other spots in the firm. Also, if there are no immediate openings, the application form can be a basis for contacting the applicant for employment later.

Testing Applicants for some types of jobs may also be asked to take tests to determine if they will be productive employees. There are many types of tests. They may evaluate skills, general intelligence, interests, or aptitude for the kind of work. Some firms place great faith in the ability of tests to help select the most effective employees. Most firms, however, use them only to filter obviously unfit applicants.

The Interview Interviews with company representatives may, in many cases, be the most important tool in employee selection. There may be only one interview, or many. For college graduates, there are generally at least two and sometimes more than that. There may be a preliminary screening with the person who visits college campuses. There may be a second meeting with representatives from the personnel department and the department in which the applicant will work. If the

In a job interivew, it is important to make a good impression on the person who is interviewing job applicants.

Maria Karras

company interviews more applicants than they can hire for positions, there may be a third interview after the employee has been selected. At this time, the person is offered the job and his orientation begins.

References   As part of the information on the application form, a firm normally requests references of the applicant, who is asked to list individuals who can attest to character and ability. Most applicants name former employers, credit references, personal acquaintances, or teachers. It is unlikely that an applicant would willingly use a reference who would give a bad recommendation. However, the firm hopes to find additional information that would throw more light on the applicant's suitability for employment. This process might foreshadow possible future personnel problems.

ORIENTATION   After an employee is hired, an orientation or induction process begins. By this means the new employee becomes familiar with the work place, fellow employees, and the supervisor. It can be a very formal, organized process, or an informal, unstructured one. In small firms, it is likely to be very short and informal. An employee may be introduced to his supervisor and fellow employees and told of company policies. The worker may also get some printed materials about the company. Following this, work begins.

In many large companies, on the other hand, the process is more complex. Because the company is much larger, there is a need for more orientation. As a

business profile: NINE TO FIVE IS NOT THE ONLY WAY

Bit by bit, American workers are freeing themselves from the tyranny of the clock on the office wall. After decades of eight-hour days and five-day weeks, a small but growing cadre of workers and their bosses are experimenting with such concepts as "flexitime," job-sharing, compressed workweeks, and permanent part-time jobs.

While the movement is very strong in Western Europe, only about a million of the 95 million persons in the work force in the United States have truly flexible working hours in offices and factories. The most popular of the plans is the "flexitime" arrangement. Under flexitime, workers arrive any time between 6:30 and 9:00 A.M. and leave when their eight hours are completed—just so long as they are on the job during certain "core" times, such as 9 to 11 A.M. and 2 to 4 P.M. There are many variations of working hours. One of the benefits of flexitime is that it eliminates the double standard for executives and staff—each can come

and go on a less rigid time schedule. Executives and managers have always had flexible hours. Now all employees have them

Job sharing, where two workers share one full-time job, is growing in popularity, as is the trend to open up more permanent part-time jobs. While employers are excited about permanent part-time positions, some critics argue that this is a device for employers to pay lower wages and grant few, if any, fringe benefits. The compressed workweek in which employees work four ten-hour days or three twelve-hour days has not caught on. While it has been successful in some firms, it has been dropped in others because of excessive worker fatigue and higher absenteeism among the workers.

Some labor experts do not believe that these flexible working arrangements will ever become widespread. They point out that what is more likely to develop is a five-day, thirty-five hour workweek or longer vacations and more holidays.

result, there may be a number of orientation sessions detailing company rules and policies and the employee's rights and responsibilities—probably conducted by a personnel representative. The part of the orientation program concerned with the actual adjustments to the job might then be handled by the department supervisor with whom the employee will be working.

TRAINING AND
EDUCATION
PROGRAMS

Various training and education programs are necessary in business: very few new employees can work satisfactorily without some preparation. In addition, further training is needed when new jobs are created or when workers must be retrained to perform other jobs. Also there are times when the company wants to educate all employees about such issues as safety, economic problems facing the firm, or the dangers of drug use on the job. In small firms, all of these can take place informally without interrupting work—during breaks, at lunch, or while the work is being performed. In larger firms, however, more planning and organization are necessary. The overall responsibility for training and education is likely to be centered in a division of the personnel department. Motorola Corporation, for example, like most large firms, has a director of education and training.

A variety of training methods might be used. In most large manufacturing and retail companies, a combination of on-the-job training and vestibule training are likely to be used, both of which are explained below.

On-the-Job Training *On-the-job training* means that the worker learns the details of the job while actually working. This procedure is most effective when the person already has the necessary basic job skills or when the job calls for only minimum skills. A secretary or an assembly line worker might be trained in this way. In either of these cases, a supervisor or fellow employee can help the new employee make the small, necessary adjustments.

Vestibule Training When there are a great many skills that must be developed, however, an on-the-job training program is not effective. An entire assembly line cannot wait for one worker to learn how to weld a part on a machine. A cashier cannot learn to operate a complex cash register while customers wait. For these reasons, *vestibule training* may be needed. In this training, the workers learn the job in a special type of classroom, or vestibule, which duplicates the job environment. That is, all the equipment and tools needed to do the job are in the classroom, and the worker is trained until he or she has the necessary skills to be effective in the assignment. Then the person is transferred "on line," where the actual job is to be performed. Vestibule training, which permits the use of skilled instructors, is particularly effective when large numbers of workers need a few days or weeks of special instruction.

Management Education In addition to training and retraining programs for skilled workers, most large firms have education programs for the development of supervisory personnel and executives. These may include in-company development courses taught by company supervisors and executives or by university professors. In addition, most large firms will reimburse supervisors and executives for additional college work that will be of help in their jobs. Many large companies send their top managers to executive development programs at universities through the country.

The personnel department is responsible for training and education. It may employ teachers for some of the classes or conduct training on the job or in vestibule. However, it ordinarily concentrates on planning and organizing the training and education. The department develops the objectives for the program; secures staff, materials, and facilities for the task; and handles all the related paper work.

EMPLOYEE EVALUATION

Following training or retraining, an employee is placed on the job. Soon it is necessary to evaluate performance with what is sometimes called employee appraisal. *Employee appraisal* is necessary for determining the value of an employee in his present job. It is the basis for increases in pay and also for determining whether the employee should be transferred, promoted, or discharged.

Employee Appraisal   At the end of a period of time, say three or six months, each new employee is evaluated. This may be done informally in smaller firms. In larger concerns standardized procedures are usually followed which include an employee appraisal form to be filled out by at least one supervisor. The results are then usually communicated to the worker in a conference. Figure 15-3 is an example of a performance planning and evaluation form used by Motorola. Notice on the top of the form the emphasis on the responsibilities and performance factors and/or results to be achieved. On the bottom, the actual achievements and the level of achievement are evaluated.

If the employee's work is unsatisfactory, discharge or transfer to another job may be required. If performance is satisfactory probably no change will follow. On the other hand, transfer or promotion may follow. In making this decision, the manager is guided not only by the employee appraisal forms, but also by the person's work record.

Transfer, Promotion, and Discharge   A *transfer* is a shift from one position to another without an increase in duties, responsibilities, or pay. Transfers are made for many reasons. There may be a personality problem with one supervisor, an older employee may need to be moved to an easier job, one section may have a heavier work load. A *promotion* is a shift with an increase in duties and responsibilities and probably an increase in pay. Promotions are given, however, because the individual has demonstrated the ambition and ability to handle more challenging tasks. Where the workers belong to a labor union, however, promotion in most cases may be made on the basis of seniority. *Seniority* indicates length of

FIGURE 15-3 Performance review form used by Motorola Inc.

MOTOROLA INC.

NON-EXEMPT PERFORMANCE REVIEW PROGRAM

EMPLOYEE DATA

NAME	SOC. SEC. NO.	DEPT.	DATE OF LAST REVIEW	SERVICE DATE	REVIEW DATE
SUSAN M. WHITE	123-45-6789	AB125	11/77	3/74	11/78

JOB TITLE	TIME IN POSITION		TIME WITH SUPERVISOR	
SECRETARY II	YRS. 0	MOS. 4	YRS. 1	MOS. 2

DESCRIPTION OF DUTIES AND RESPONSIBILITIES

BRIEFLY LIST AND DESCRIBE MAIN DUTIES AND REQUIREMENTS OF THE JOB PERFORMS SECRETARIAL DUTIES FOR COST ACCOUNTING DEPARTMENT. COMPILES MONTHLY REPORTS AS REQUIRED USING JOURNALS, LEDGERS, AND OTHER HISTORICAL ACCOUNTING DATA. PROVIDES DIRECTION TO THREE DEPARTMENTAL ACCOUNTING CLERKS.

LIST SPECIFIC WORK TASKS ACCOMPLISHED SINCE HIRE OR LAST REVIEW. LIST SKILLS AND STRENGTHS OF EMPLOYEE. SUSAN WAS PROMOTED TO THE POSITION OF SECRETARY II AFTER SERVING AS AN ACCOUNTING CLERK. SUSAN HAS BEEN QUICK TO LEARN HER NEW RESPONSIBILITIES. THE REQUIRED FINANCIAL REPORTS ARE GENERATED WITH A MINIMUM OF DIRECTION. SUSAN HAS EFFECTIVELY PROVIDED DIRECTION AND ASSISTANCE TO THE THREE ACCOUNTING CLERKS REPORTING TO HER. SUSAN CONSISTENTLY HANDLES HERSELF IN A PROFESSIONAL MANNER, COMMUNICATES EFFECTIVELY, AND EXHIBITS A SINCERE ENTHUSIASM TO DO THE BEST JOB POSSIBLE.

DEVELOPMENT / IMPROVEMENT FACTORS

LIST SPECIFIC WORK TASKS OR DEVELOPMENT FACTORS TO BE ACCOMPLISHED. LIST ANY SPECIFIC SKILLS AND/OR TRAINING REQUIRED TO ACHIEVE THE GOAL.
SUSAN NEEDS TO BECOME FAMILIAR WITH A BROADER CONCEPT OF ACCOUNTING PRINCIPLES. I HAVE ENCOURAGED SUSAN TO PURSUE A PART-TIME EDUCATION IN ACCOUNTING. THIS WILL ENABLE SUSAN TO BE GIVEN ADDITIONAL ASSIGNMENTS AND INCREASE HER EXPOSURE TO OTHERS IN THE ACCOUNTING FUNCTION. SUSAN'S JOB KNOWLEDGE RATING REFLECTS HER SHORT TENURE IN HER NEW ASSIGNMENT. HER QUALITY RATING SHOULD IMPROVE WITH THE ADDITIONAL EXPERIENCE AND EDUCATION WE DISCUSSED.

FACTORS	RATING
Job Knowledge	2
Quantity of Work	3
Quality of Work	2
Work with Others	3

PUNCTUALITY   Acceptable ☒   Not Acceptable ☐
ATTENDANCE   Acceptable ☒   Not Acceptable ☐

Summary Rating
0 ___ 1 ___ 2 ___ X ___ 3 ___ 4

DEFINITION
0 — Does not meet requirements
1 — Meets minimum requirements; needs improvement
2 — Meets requirements
3 — Exceeds requirements
4 — Superior Performance

SUMMARY (THE CONCLUSIONS REACHED BY THE EMPLOYEE AND SUPERVISOR AFTER ABOVE ITEMS ARE DISCUSSED.)
SUSAN IS IN AGREEMENT WITH THE COMMENTS SHOWN ABOVE. SUSAN HAS EXPRESSED AN INTEREST IN AN ACCOUNTING CAREER AND WILL BE GIVEN ASSIGNMENTS AND COUNSELING TO ALLOW HER TO ACHIEVE HER CAREER GOALS

SIGNATURES

EMPLOYEE SIGNATURE	DATE	INTERVIEWING SUPERVISOR	DATE	INTERVIEWER'S SUPERVISOR	DATE
Susan M. White	11/9/78	John P. Jones	11/9/78	Frank S. Smith	11/11/78

MOTOROLA FORM NO. 3447-43R2 →   PERSONNEL FILE COPY

time on the job. It may mean time with the company, on the job, or in a department.

A *discharge* occurs when an employee is permanently dismissed by the company. In small companies the worker may simply be told that his services are no longer needed. In larger companies there will be an established procedure for handling separations. This is particularly true where workers are unionized and the conditions under which a discharge can take place will be spelled out in the union contract.

METHODS OF PAYING EMPLOYEES

One of the most important functions of the personnel department is the administration of employee compensation programs. This is frequently called wage and salary administration. Blue-collar and nonsupervisory workers, as well as many white-collar workers, are generally paid hourly wages. Administrative, professional, and executive employees normally receive monthly salaries.

From the employees' point of view, pay is more than the measure of the standard of living he can afford. It is also a status symbol, a measure of his economic value to society. His pay is compared with that of his friends, and he may associate his personal worth with the income he earns. For that reason, a raise of a nickel an hour may take on far greater personal meaning than the money involved. From the company's point of view, labor costs are probably the main determinant of the prices of its product. They greatly affect the competitive position of a firm. Also, the level of pay and the fairness of a wage structure are important in maintaining a motivated, productive work force. This, too, goes beyond the pay itself and affects the morale of the work force.

Employees' pay consists of direct and indirect payments. *Direct payments* are cash wages paid to the employees at the end of a work period. Indirect payments, more commonly called *fringe benefits*, are deferred payments employees receive at a later date. Let us look first at direct payments.

Direct payments are determined by the type of work performed or by the quality of an individual's performance on a job. Almost everyone agrees that the rate of pay should vary with the performance of the individual. In many jobs, however, it is difficult to measure accurately the individual's performance or output. As a result there are a variety of pay plans, some stressing the job performed, others emphasizing the output of the individual, and some combining both aspects.

Time Payments Some employees are paid on the basis of the time they spend on the job. These include many production and office employees and skilled craftsmen who are paid an hourly rate. If they work more hours than a normal week, which is 40 hours, they may be paid time-and-a-half or double time. This extra rate is paid for working weekends, holidays, or longer hours during the week.

Salary Payments Most white-collar workers and executives are paid a salary which is based on work performed for a period of time. Unlike time payments,

Employees can receive wages one of three ways: time payments, salary payments, or piece-rate payments. A time clock keeps track of hours worked for those on time payments.

D. Stevens

salaries are based on work performed for a week, month, or year. Workers paid by salary do not receive extra compensation when their hours extend over the 40-hour-week norm. Nor do they receive extra pay for high productivity.

Piece-Rate Payments   In a *piece-rate system*, the employee receives a certain amount per hour plus a bonus for producing more than a certain number of items. For example, an employee may earn $3.50 per hour for producing eight items or less in that time. If the worker produces more than eight, an extra 10 cents per item for the increased production will be paid. This system can be used where the output per worker is easily measurable.

Other Bonus Systems In addition to piece-rate systems, there are other forms of compensation that reward workers for job performance. One is to distribute a share of the company's profits to the employees. This *profit-sharing* gives each employee an incentive to be more productive so that the total company's profits are higher. Some firms tie these bonuses to decreases in scrappage or rejected products; others link them to lowering unit labor costs. If labor costs are reduced by 3 percent, this can be paid to workers as a bonus.

One of the difficulties with all of these systems is that many employees have difficulty in relating their current efforts to the overall increase in profits or productivity. They see themselves as only one small part of the many forces that influence profits or productivity. For that reason, many companies regularly conduct education programs to help employees better understand the relationship between their efforts and the rewards that come through higher company profits and productivity.

Special Compensation The most popular form of extra compensation, other than cash bonuses, is some form of stock option. In a stock option, the executive is given the option of buying at a later date company stock at its current market price. The assumption is that the value of a share of stock will rise. The executive then can later purchase the stock at the lower price of the option date and can either sell it at a profit or keep it for additional increases in its value. An executive may also get extra compensation based on the performance of the company. This could take the form of a cash bonus or shares of stock in the corporation.

For salespeople, a commission, which is normally part of the total compensation package is an important motivation to increase sales. Most salespeople are paid a base salary as well as an expense account to cover out-of-pocket travel expenses. The salary is important for the beginning salesperson and also to ensure that the salesperson provides the basic services to customers that the company thinks are important.

EMPLOYEE SERVICES AND BENEFITS Direct payments are only a part of the total package of compensation for employees. The percentage of payroll costs going into fringe benefits is almost 40 percent. Fringe benefits are the extra benefits and services that are paid to employees as part of their total compensation. Table 15-1 shows the proportion of total fringe benefits that is spent for each item.

The proportion of compensation paid for fringe benefits has risen rapidly during the past 20 years. Organized labor, knowing that these fringe benefits add to a worker's security, has made it a point to stress them in bargaining. Union leaders know that frequently firms are more willing to increase their future expenses for fringe benefits than they are their current payroll costs. Whether the extra com-

TABLE 15-1 Percent of
fringe benefits spent on
each type of fringe benefit

Type of Fringe Benefit	Percent of Fringe Benefit Total Costs
Social Security (employer's share)	15.9%
Pension plans	15.6%
Insurance	14.6%
Paid vacations	14.6%
Paid rest, lunch periods	10.2%
Paid holidays	9.4%
Workmen's compensation	3.5%
Paid sick leave	3.4%
Profit sharing	3.1%
Unemployment compensation	2.9%
Other benefits	6.8%

Source: U.S. Chamber of Commerce.

pensation is in the form of direct payments or fringe benefits, it is a cost to business. As the percentage of fringe benefits increases, companies find it less expensive to pay overtime to a few workers or to hire part-time workers than to hire additional full-time workers—each of whom will receive a large package of fringe benefits.

HEALTH AND SAFETY PROGRAMS

Attention to the health and safety of employees is good business. Increased medical and insurance costs and decreased productivity are expensive by-products of a poor health and safety system. According to the National Safety Council, there are about 2.2 million work-related injuries and about 14,000 work-related deaths a year. These cost about $9 billion in lost wages, insurance, medical costs, and lowered productivity. Work-related alcoholism costs about $4 billion; mental illness, $3 billion; and drug abuse even more. A rule of thumb is that when an experienced employee is incapacitated, it costs the company about one-and-a-half times the employee's wages.

Because of the increasing concern for the health and safety of employees, the controversial Occupational Safety and Health Act (OSHA) was passed in 1970. Its purpose is to ensure safe and healthful working conditions for employees. About 5 million business firms, employing approximately 65 million people, are covered under the act. An OSHA inspector visits any of the businesses covered by the act to check on the health and safety features of the work place. OSHA makes over 100,000 visits a year. In the last couple of years, OSHA has devoted more of its resources to job-related illnesses and diseases rather than to accidents which was its main focus in the beginning.

As a result of the passage of the OSHA and the increased awareness of the economic and social effects of safety and health, most large firms have given increased attention to these matters. Most industries are opposed to the act because its guidelines are too technical and lengthy and its standards too expensive to

Employees of Xerox Corp. are encouraged to take part in company-sponsored exercise programs. Here, women employees are doing a warm-up exercise.

Xerox Corp.

meet. Because small firms had difficulty in even deciphering the 325 pages of standards, Congress later amended the law to limit inspection to firms with more than 25 employees. The noise-control guidelines alone are estimated to cost business between $13 and $31 billion. Organized labor, on the other hand, has called for stronger standards and control of the work place.

MORALE AND PRODUCTIVITY

The feeling that employees have toward their jobs, their co-workers, and the company is called *morale*. It is a measure of how individual needs are matched with the demands and rewards of the job. Much has been written in the past 20 years about the relationship between morale and productivity. Many people believe that when morale is high, productivity is high, and that the reverse is also true. Many companies, aiming to have happy, productive workers, have tried a variety of ways to increase morale. Recent studies are contradictory, however. It is generally agreed that when a labor force is low-spirited, it is not likely to be very productive. However, some studies have shown that groups with high morale are not always productive. Part of the problem is in the measurement of morale.

MEASURING MORALE

The following indicators of morale are usually examined: cooperation, loyalty, pride, and discipline. They are measured indirectly through data on absenteeism,

**personality profile:
ROBERT TOWNSEND —
management by
revolution**

Robert Townsend's *Up the Organization* is no standard guide to management, but a call to revolution: "Start dismantling our organizations where we're serving them, leaving only the parts where they're serving us." Such unorthodox teaching, backed up by a hard-headed practicality, seemed to work for Townsend, however. During his three years as president of Avis, profits grew from zero to $5 million, boosted largely by an advertising campaign organized after Townsend followed another of his maxims: "Fire the whole advertising department and your old agency."

Perhaps innovation came naturally to Townsend, whose father was an inventor. In any case, after his graduation from Princeton, he threw away management practices which had become a virtual religion at the "monster corporations and agencies" and let in a lot of fresh air, showing himself to be one of the most original top executives of the past decade.

Townsend believes the main point in revivifying a stodgy corporation filled with deadwood is "to get you and the people you work with fired up to achieve whatever goals you select." In other words, the secret for breathing new life into an organization that is being choked by its own weight is to become people-oriented, to manage and motivate personnel, to pay attention to the human element in business rather than just balancing the books.

For a generation of Americans increasingly worried about the inefficiency and impersonality of its growing bureaucracies, government and corporate, Townsend proposes a brand new model: a loosely structured but highly principled organization led in person by a decisive executive toward a common goal that transcends mere personal gain. It may not sound easy, but look what happened to Avis when it tried harder.

labor turnover, number and type of complaints filed against management, and employee participation in decision-making. The difficulty lies in that morale is multidimensional. It includes group cohesiveness, supportive behavior, job attitudes, and job satisfaction. In addition, it is possible for a group of workers to enjoy the company of their fellow workers but to dislike the tasks they perform together. In this situation there may or may not be high productivity.

Until fairly recently, most companies have assumed that higher pay would lead to greater motivation and morale of employees. Frederick Herzberg, an expert in industrial psychology, has shown that this is not only a false assumption but a damaging one as well.[1] He indicates that there are two dimensions to movitation and morale. One dimension, called the *hygiene factors*, includes such things as wages, fringe benefits, and physical working conditions. If these are not considered adequate, dissatisfaction will arise. However, even if they are sufficient, no positive attitudes and motivation result. Like preventive medicine (hence their name), they avert dissatisfaction but do not promote satisfaction or high morale.

The other dimension of morale is the *motivational factors*, which actually lead to positive attitudes, job satisfaction, and high morale. They include recognition, responsibility, opportunities for advancement and personal growth, feelings of accomplishment and achievement, and a sense of individual and job importance. These motivational needs of employees are more difficult to meet than the first group of hygiene or economic needs. As a result, the task of the personnel department has become even more challenging during the last few years.

FLEXIBLE WORK WEEK

Most of the efforts of the personnel department in meeting employees' needs are still concentrated on the economic and physical aspects. A shorter work week, more flexible work hours, earlier retirement plans, more pleasant working conditions, and better fringe benefits are some of these. A number of surveys indicate that the efforts work in some companies but not in others. As an example, many companies have established a four-day work week, in which the employees work nine or ten hours a day. Some have abandoned the plans after a trial because either the employees did not like them or management found them unworkable. Several life insurance companies have gone to a three-day, 36-hour week for their computer operators. Work performance appears to equal that of the five-day 40-hour week schedule. The key appears to lie in developing the work week that both employees and company want. As a result, a variety of plans will probably continue to be used.

WHAT DO EMPLOYEES WANT?

One of the difficulties in developing higher morale in a company is the differing perceptions of what employees really want. Management tends to believe employees want their economic needs filled as their main priority. Employees, on the other hand, expect to have social and emotional needs satisfied on the job as well.

1. Frederick Herzberg, "The Motivation-Hygiene Concept and Problems of Manpower," *Personnel Administration* (January-February 1964): 3–7.

The seemingly widening gap between what workers expect from their jobs and what they actually receive is a disturbing development. Rising educational levels have led many young people to expect more from work than their parents and grandparents did. Work was probably just as monotonous for their parents. However, according to Herzberg, the personal and social needs of workers were satisifed by activities connected with social, ethnic, religious, and family traditions. As a result, work was expected to provide only for economic needs. With most of these traditions breaking down for many workers, however, there is widespread discontent with life and, therefore, with jobs.

WORK AND LIFE-STYLE

A changing life-style for workers may be part of the reason increasing numbers are refusing to put in overtime. Workers have begun to take new views of the place of work in their lives, with the result that the traditional work ethic of the United States is deteriorating. There are probably two main factors for it: (1) a younger, better-educated work force, and (2) the changing nature of work in a highly industrialized society. In most companies, it is very difficult for the worker to identify his contribution to the final product. He is likely to have performed a very small part of the total job and probably can't even see his part or service in what is sold. As a result, he is not as concerned with product quality or production costs.

INCREASING JOB SATISFACTION

There is much disagreement about the nature of job dissatisfaction, its extent, and its causes and solutions. There is little doubt, however, that personnel departments believe that they have to take some new steps to increase job satisfaction. Most of the measures have to do with increasing worker-involvement in decisions, workers' responsibilities, and management's recognition of employee efforts.

Corning Glass Works, in producing hotplates at their Medfield, Massachusetts, plant, used an assembly-line operation with employee specialization and a supervisor to check the quality. In 1965–66, they changed their process so that each worker assembled a hotplate by herself. She then plugged it in, checked it without additional supervision, and initialled her final product. Each group scheduled its work and decided on refinements in the work process. After six months, rejects dropped from 23 percent to 1 percent, absenteeism from 8 percent to 1 percent, and productivity rose. General Electric, at its plant near Columbia, Maryland, is using employee recognition and participation in reducing apathy, frustration, and absenteeism among blue-collar workers. From the employer's point of view, the efforts are deemed successful. In three separate elections the employees have voted not to be represented by unions, an indication of job satisfaction.

AFFIRMATIVE ACTION PROGRAMS

A personnel department has a number of guidelines that it must follow in employing and maintaining a work force. Besides extensive company regulations, there are many government requirements designed to eliminate employment discrimination according to race, color, and sex. The Equal Pay Act of 1963 and the Civil

Rights Act of 1964 have had dramatic effects on personnel policies. Their full effects are still emerging as new court rulings continue to clarify what must be done.

FEDERAL LAWS   The Equal Pay Act was passed to correct "the existence in industries engaged in commerce, or in the production of goods for commerce, of wage differentials based on sex." The Civil Rights Act has 11 sections, with Title VII most relevant to business. Title VII prohibits employment on the basis of race, color, religion, sex, or national origin. It specifically forbids employers to discriminate in hiring, training, compensating, promoting, or discharging workers. Unions also are prohibited from segregating, expelling, excluding, or classifying workers. The Equal Employment Opportunity Commission (EEOC) was established under the Civil Rights Act. Its members are appointed by the president with the approval of the Senate to see that the provisions of this act are carried out. It has become very controversial. Critics charge it with inefficiency because its backlog of cases reached 135,000 by the end of 1977. Even the General Accounting Office, another government agency, says that the EEOC has had little impact on race discrimination or sex bias in the job market.

These laws were necessary because minorities and women have historically been discriminated against by most organizations, including business. Only in federal government jobs do minorities have an employment rate equal to their percentage of the total population. However, the average income of black workers is about 44 percent below that of white workers. This is an improvement over the

FIGURE 15-4 Complaints of job bias filed with the Equal Employment Opportunity Commission. Source: Reprinted from *U.S. News & World Report.* Copyright 1977 U.S. News & World Report, Inc.

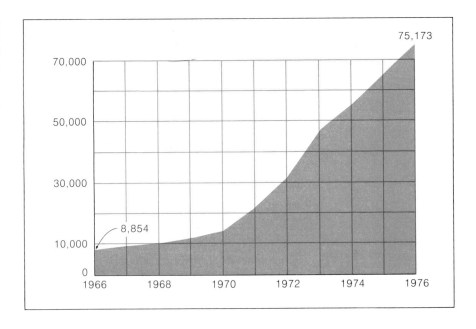

last couple of decades, but still not acceptable to most people. Working women, on the other hand, earn only about 60 percent of the income of their white, male counterparts, with the gap apparently widening.

EFFECT ON PERSONNEL
POLICIES

With the enactment of effective legislation, many businesses have established affirmative action programs in their personnel departments. A number of lawsuits have been instituted by minorities and women to relieve the effects of discrimination. Such key industries as construction and skilled crafts are required to fill controversial job quotas set for minority workers. Many companies have changed their employment tests considerably to eliminate advantages for white persons with better reading skills. In a study of 42 large firms in the South, 64 percent had done away with written tests for applicants. Most of the firms also had modified their interview procedures and application forms to eliminate discrimination. Training programs have also been revamped—particularly where a company has undertaken programs to prepare unemployed, unskilled ghetto workers for employment in firms.

All this has added a challenging dimension to personnel work, forcing personnel departments to change many procedures. It is no longer enough for a firm to show that it is not discriminating against women and minorities. It must prove that it gives an equal opportunity to everyone in recruiting, hiring, training, placement on the job, compensation, promotional opportunities, and discharge. This has necessitated more extensive record-keeping and a far more careful accounting of the procedures followed. It has given firms less flexibility in hiring and extended the length of time needed to hire and integrate employees. Besides pressure to hire more women and minorities, firms are also increasingly being urged to move minorities and women into professional and management positions.

The recent high rates of unemployment, which started in 1974, have made it difficult for firms to determine which workers should be laid off. Corporations are caught between two conflicting pressures: from the unions for layoffs based on seniority on the one hand and on the other hand from the Equal Employment Opportunity Commission for layoffs based partly on seniority, but also on race and sex. The Supreme Court settled part of the issue in 1977 with its landmark decision that seniority systems that do not have racial underpinnings are not unlawful. In effect, the court said that seniority takes precedence over antidiscrimination goals such as a percentage of workers which must be from minority races.

SUMMARY

Personnel management is concerned with attracting, developing, utilizing, and maintaining a work force. While all levels of management have a role to play, the personnel department is the central focus.

The personnel department is responsible for recruiting, training, evaluation and compensation and services for all employees. The processes start with job analysis and include constant manpower planning.

Recruiting is an on-going process in large firms. Important sources for locating potential employees are likely to include the following: advertising, public employment agencies, private employment agencies, colleges and universities, public and private vocational schools, labor unions, and friends of workers.

The recruitment process is likely to include application forms and interviews and perhaps some testing as well. Following hiring, an orientation program is usually held. Personnel departments conduct a variety of training and education programs including on-the-job training, vestibule training, and management education programs. Constant evaluation is necessary to determine promotional paths and compensation. There are a variety of compensation packages depending on the type of job, but most include salary or wages and some kind of fringe benefits, which can run as high as 40 percent of total compensation.

The personnel department administers a variety of employee services, and keeps almost all records for employees. In addition, the department monitors the morale and productivity of the labor force and tries to keep both as high as possible. This has become increasingly difficult with new values and goals of many employees in which work is becoming less important.

Affirmative action programs mandated by such federal acts as the Equal Pay Act and the Civil Rights Act have made the personnel management process more complex. This pressure for equality has caused all companies to alter their personnel process and policies considerably and to keep far more detailed records than they did.

SUMMARY OF KEY TERMS

Direct Payment Cash wages paid to an employee at the end of a work period.

Discharge Permanent dismissal by the company.

Fringe Benefits Extra benefits and services that are not part of direct payments.

Job Analysis Study of the specific tasks in a job and the environment in which they are performed.

Job Classification The process of rating the value of jobs to a firm.

Job Description The written report of the job analysis.

Morale The feeling employees have toward their jobs, their fellow workers, and the company.

On-the-job Training Learning the details of a trade while actually doing the job at the work station.

Personnel Management Concerned with attracting, developing, utilizing, and maintaining a work force.

Piece-rate System A certain amount of pay per hour plus a bonus for producing more than a certain number of items.

Profit-sharing A share of the company's profits distributed to the employees.

Promotion Job change with an increase in duties and responsibilities, and a probable increase in pay.

Seniority Length of time on the job.

Transfer A shift from one position to another without an increase in duties, responsibilities, or pay.

Vestibule Training Learning a job in a special type of classroom or vestibule which duplicates the work environment.

REVIEW QUESTIONS

1. Identify the roles played by top management, foremen, and fellow employees in the personnel management process.
2. Contrast job analysis, job description, and job classification as to the procedure and the use made of each.
3. Contrast the major sources in recruiting employees for a top management job and for assembly-line jobs.
4. Indicate how vestibule training and on-the-job training might be used in a large firm.
5. Compare the effect of piece-rate payments, time payments, and profit-sharing on hourly production employees.
6. Name the basic indicators of employee morale and explain how they are measured.
7. What is the effect of morale on the productivity of workers?
8. Explain the effects of the major federal legislation promoting affirmative action programs on the personnel policies of business firms.
9. What needs do employees expect to have filled from their jobs.?
10. Are seniority systems unlawful if they tend to make it more difficult for women and minorities to get and keep a job?

DISCUSSION QUESTIONS

1. Do you think that community college graduates and senior college graduates should interview for the *same* jobs in management-training programs in large firms? Why or why not?
2. For what types of jobs should college graduates expect some sort of testing?
3. Do you think assembly-line workers should be paid a straight hourly wage rate or participate in some form of incentive system for higher production or lower costs? Explain your answer.
4. If your employer offered you a 10 percent salary increase or a 5 percent salary increase and 5 percent in fringe benefits, which would you choose? Why?
5. Should quotas be established in the major classification of jobs in firms for women, blacks, and other minorities?

CASES FOR DECISION MAKING

CATCHING THE NEW MANAGERS[1]

The attitudes of college graduates toward their jobs with large firms is changing personnel policies for a

1. "Young Managers Less Eager to Adapt So Firms Alter Policies," *Wall Street Journal* (February 18, 1974): 1.

number of companies. Most large firms are making fewer transfers of executives from one location to another. If they do encourage a transfer, the company is paying more of the expenses of the move. Since college graduates want to be doing productive work as soon as possible, training programs in many cases have been shortened. Many junior management jobs have been enriched. A survey of Eastern Michigan University business administration graduates showed that "interesting varied work" was given highest rating in evaluating prospective jobs. Another area of personnel policy influenced by college graduates is the decreased emphasis on personnel tests and psychological tests for management trainee applicants.

1. Do you believe that personnel policies such as those mentioned above may lead to greater job satisfaction for college graduates in larger firms?
2. What is the responsibility of personnel administration departments in matching the goals of the firm with those of potential managers?
3. How far should a corporation go in trying to fit the job to the personal values and goals of individuals in management positions with the firm?

LAST IN, FIRST OUT[2]

The slowdown in big car sales in late 1973 resulted in substantial layoffs of auto assembly workers in many plants. Particularly hard hit were women workers. In 1972, all firms having government contracts of any kind were directed by the federal government to recruit women for production jobs. Many were hired. However, in the layoffs, workers with the least seniority were laid off first, including almost all of the women. Black workers fared somewhat better as many had held their jobs longer as a result of the movement to hire blacks in the middle 1960s.

1. Does the seniority system discriminate against women, blacks, and other minority groups in hiring and promotion policies?
2. Should quotas be established for hiring and

2. "Woman: Last In, First Out in Detroit," *Business Week* (February 16, 1974): 51.

promoting women, blacks, and other minorities in major job categories?
3. To protect women, blacks, and other minorities, should all large layoffs of workers have to be approved by a government agency, as is true in France and some other countries?

PRODUCTIVITY COULD INCREASE, IF . . .

Almost everyone is for greater increases in productivity or efficiency. Greater productivity means greater output, more jobs, stable prices, higher profits, and steady wage and salary gains. Unfortunately, American productivity has declined and has not risen much even during economic recovery periods. Why?

The reasons are diverse, but include the following: fewer workers are moving off the farms and into commercial and industrial jobs; more teenagers and women are entering the labor market and they tend to lack skills and change jobs frequently; service industries account for 70 percent of all nonfarm jobs now and productivity is less in these industries; employees tend to place work as less important in their priorities; outmoded business practices and work rules by unimaginative management and shortsighted labor; research and development are getting a smaller share of the nation's income than they did before.

1. If productivity seems to be so important for everyone's benefit, why do you suppose there is not a national effort to achieve it?
2. What do you believe can be done to improve productivity in an organization that you are familiar with?
3. How can we change attitudes toward work so that all workers can feel that the quality of work they do is important to their self-image?

RELATED READINGS

Lorsch, Jay W., and Lawrence, Paul R., eds. *Managing Group and Intergroup Relations.* Homewood, Ill.: Irwin, 1972.

A paperback of readings on problems of managing groups within organizations and managing relations among groups in an organization. It contains cases and conceptual readings on leadership, social change, interpersonal relations, and conflict management.

Matteson, Michael, et al. *Contemporary Personnel Management.* San Francisco: Canfield Press, 1972.

A paperback of readings on changes taking place in the areas of human resources and problems, manpower, and environmental quality. The articles point out the application of new techniques, theories, and approaches to the major areas of personnel administration.

Nash, Allen N., and Miner, John B. *Personnel and Labor Relations.* 2nd ed. New York: Macmillan Co., 1973.

A paperback emphasizing strategies for solving personnel problems. It stresses recent research findings, managerial problem-solving, and strategies to achieve a more effective organization. Cultural, geographical, industrial, and individual differences are considered and constraints on personnel decisions are discussed. This is heavier reading than the others in this section.

Patchen, Martin. *Participation, Achievement, and Involvement on the Job.* Englewood Cliffs, N.J.: Prentice-Hall, 1970.

A look at the questions of when an individual is only putting in time to make a living and when he has a feeling of achievement and a sense of solidarity with the work organization. An analysis of motivation and identification with the work organization.

Pigors, Paul; Myers, Charles A.; and Malm, F. T., eds. *Management of Human Resources.* 3rd ed. New York: McGraw-Hill, 1973.

A paperback of readings on the management of human resources. It focuses on the contributions of the behavioral sciences and the administrative problems that must be faced by management in developing and using human resources.

chapter 16

LABOR-MANAGEMENT RELATIONS

OBJECTIVES

When you have finished reading and studying this chapter, you should be able to:

1. Trace the growth of organized labor in the United States.

2. Identify basic trends in labor growth and strength today.

3. Identify and explain the areas of management decision making affected by organized labor.

4. List and explain the steps in the collective bargaining process.

5. Identify the tools used by labor and management in promoting their respective points of view.

CHAPTER PREVIEW

Labor-management relations have a powerful effect not only on the two parties involved, but on society as well. Their interaction greatly influences the price and quality of products and services available to all of us. In addition, they affect everyone's wage and salary rates.

We tend to think of these relations in dramatic terms, such as the strike by workers to protest speeding up of assembly lines in the General Motors assembly plant in Lordstown, Ohio, or the 109-day coal miners' strike of 1978. However, very few bargaining efforts result in strikes; most of the negotiations go on continually without much fanfare. While labor and management use a variety of techniques to gain an advantage, both realize that there is a limit to benefits they can achieve.

Large labor unions developed in response to the large industrial corporations formed after the Civil War. Many industrial plants maintained unsafe working conditions, while providing little pay and almost no job security. Unions were formed to give the individual workers a collective voice in bargaining with management.

Organized labor grew most rapidly in the 1940s and 1950s. The rate of growth slackened considerably in the 1960s as the number of blue-collar jobs declined and white-collar jobs increased. However, in the 1970s, white-collar workers have been joining unions in increasing numbers, adding noticeably to union strength.

Unions influence all areas of management's decision making. Everything from plant location decisions to personnel policies are affected by unions. Job security has been added to the original union goals of higher wages, better working conditions, and shorter hours. Virtually any decision made in a business organization affects some of these four main objectives of unions.

The collective bargaining process remains a mystery to most people. It is difficult to see how two sides can agree privately on a contract when publicly they seem to be so far apart. Both sides have a variety of tools which they use in trying to assert their point of view. Eventually, of course, agreement is reached, although the process may be a long, uncertain one.

Collective bargaining seems to work well, although there is much criticism of it. There are those who believe that either or both parties have too much power. Both sides have been criticized for very large wage increases which are merely passed on to the consumer in the form of higher prices. They also have been charged with not working together enough for greater productivity to help this country compete more effectively with foreign firms. Whether these criticisms are valid, you will have to decide for yourself as you read the chapter.

Doing his own hangup

16
LABOR-MANAGEMENT RELATIONS

Organized labor and management are two of the strongest forces in our society. Their interaction and the extent of their willingness to work together greatly influence the kind of society that is emerging in the United States. There are those who argue that organized labor has too much power. They claim that unions can force their will on management, resulting in higher prices for all Americans. Members of labor unions, on the other hand, feel that a strong union is necessary in bargaining with large firms. How did organized labor get its power? What are the relative bargaining strengths of labor and management? What effect does the power of labor unions have on firms and the economy? These are questions that we shall try to answer in this chapter.

A BRIEF HISTORY OF ORGANIZED LABOR

Workers have organized themselves into bargaining groups for thousands of years. Modern labor unions in the United States, however, date from about 1800. At that time, workers in the skilled trades—printers, shipbuilders, carpenters, and shoemakers—banded together to bargain with employers. They realized that they would have more influence as a group than they would as individuals, but their associations were considered illegal and they had no right to strike. Since the firms for which they worked were small, large-scale organization was not necessary. Also, if a skilled worker was unhappy with his employer, he merely changed employers or went into business for himself. By the 1820s, organized labor had defined its major goals—higher wages, better working conditions, and shorter hours.

ORIGINS OF LARGE UNIONS

The coming of the big industrial firms in the Northeast by the time of the Civil War gave rise to the large-scale organization of labor. The large corporation gave management far greater power over individual employees, who were forced in many cases to work long hours with little pay. Working conditions were often hazardous, and women and children workers were frequently exploited, particularly in the textile industry. As a result, larger union organization became necessary. While there had been a number of efforts at forming national labor organizations, the Knights of Labor became the first truly national union. Beginning as a local garment workers' union, it claimed more than 700,000 members by 1885. It began to fade, however, when its members could not agree on its goals. One group wanted to emphasize *collective bargaining*: negotiations between labor and management. The other wanted to use political action to bring about social change.

Meanwhile, a new labor group was organizing—one which was to be dominant up to the present time. Several craft unions joined together into an association of unions which was later to become the American Federation of Labor (AFL). This organization united *craft unions*, an association of workers skilled in a craft or trade. It was firmly committed to the concept of achieving its goals through collec-

The Haymarket Riot in Chicago followed a sudden bomb explosion during a labor rally. The year was 1886.

Library of Congress

tive bargaining, not through political or social change. Under the leadership of Samuel Gompers, the union followed a policy of neutrality in political elections, preferring to spend its energies on bargaining with employers for better pay and working conditions and for shorter hours.

Organized labor maintained a gradual growth in membership, gaining in good times, losing in recessions. Labor unions were still illegal, however. Strikes, when they came, were frequently marked by violence between workers and strikebreakers (scabs) hired by management. Employers also could get a court injunction prohibiting strikes, and labor leaders were frequently jailed for strike activity. The Norris-LaGuardia Act of 1932 recognized workers' rights to organize into unions and it restricted the use of the court injunction in work stoppages. It also outlawed the "yellow dog" contract, a practice whereby employees were forced, as a condition of employment, to agree not to join a union.

NATIONAL LABOR RELATIONS ACT

With the election of Franklin Roosevelt and a Democratic majority in Congress in 1932, great changes took place in the labor movement. Roosevelt was attuned to the union movement and encouraged a flurry of legislation to help organized labor. The National Labor Relations Act of 1935 was the turning point for the unions. Better known as the Wagner Act after its sponsor, it was called the Magna Carta of organized labor. It declared the following employer practices illegal:

1. Restraining employees from joining a union
2. Interfering with the organization of a union
3. Discriminating against employees who had testified under the law
4. Discriminating among employees to discourage union membership
5. Refusing to bargain collectively with the chosen union

In addition, the act established the National Labor Relations Board. This federal agency administers the provisions of the Wagner Act in settling disputes and in determining unfair labor practices. Until recent years, businesspeople have felt the board favored labor in its rulings. The act also authorized the *closed shop*, where only union members are hired by a firm. This gave organized labor control over the employees who could be hired. Naturally businesspeople denounced the Wagner Act and predicted chaos for society. Already suspicious of Roosevelt and the Democratic party, the business community became even more hostile to both.

Organized labor grew rapidly in this environment, although it split its ranks in 1936. The AFL was organized along craft lines. With the coming of large industries, such as auto, steel, and rubber, some unions leaders wanted to organize these workers by industry. An *industrial union* is an association within one union of all the workers in an industry, regardless of the type of work they do. A split developed and the Congress of Industrial Organizations (CIO) was formed in

The AFL-CIO holds regular conventions at which the aims and policy of organized labor are discussed and planned by the leadership of the affiliated unions.

AFL-CIO

1938. By organizing workers in many fields who were not eligible for craft union membership, the CIO soon rivaled the larger AFL in membership. In 1955 the two associations merged to form the AFL-CIO, with George Meany as president.

Today, the organization chart of the AFL-CIO looks much like that of the federal government. Local unions are banded together into state and district union organizations, which in turn are combined into about 125 national and international unions, such as the International Ladies Garment Workers Union. At each level, unions from various industries form councils to promote organized labor's point of view in public opinion and legislation. In addition, about 200 local unions are directly affiliated with the AFL-CIO. The national and international unions have a great deal of autonomy as long as they do not violate the rules of the AFL-CIO. As an example, the Teamsters Union continued to support President Nixon long after the official AFL-CIO policy was to oppose him. An organizational chart for the AFL-CIO is shown in Figure 16-1.

LABOR-MANAGEMENT RELATIONS ACT

Organized labor continued its rapid growth until after World War II, when a series of disastrous strikes was climaxed by a nationwide railroad strike in 1946. The American people were outraged by the unions' naked use of power, and public pressure brought forth the Labor-Management Relations Act of 1947. This was designed to curb the rising power of labor unions and bring a better balance to labor-management relations. The act is more popularly known as the Taft-Hartley Act, after its chief sponsors. A series of unfair practices by labor unions was listed, and organized labor was forbidden to:

1. Coerce employees to join a union
2. Make employers discriminate against employees to get them to join the union
3. Refuse to bargain collectively
4. Strike to force an employer to bargain with a union or to get him to recognize a union different from the one certified by the National Labor Relations Board
5. Charge excessive initiation fees where it had a union shop contract
6. Practice *featherbedding* (forcing employers to continue jobs that are no longer necessary in the firm, such as firemen's jobs on diesel trains)

The act also outlawed the closed shop and restricted the use of the union shop. In a *union shop*, the employee does not have to be a member of the recognized union, but must either join it after a period of time on the job or pay union dues. Through Amendment 14B, the act granted the states the right to outlaw the union shop through a statewide election. This is called the *right-to-work* clause by many people. To this date, 19 states still have right-to-work laws; they are mostly agricultural states and in the Midwest, West, and South. The act also has a provision to protect the public against strikes in key industries. If the president feels that a strike will imperil the national health or safety, he can secure a court injunction forbid-

FIGURE 16-1
Organizational chart
of the AFL-CIO.
Reproduced with
permission from *Labor Law
Course,* 21st ed., copyright
1972. Published and
copyrighted by Commerce
Clearing House, Inc.,
Chicago, Ill.

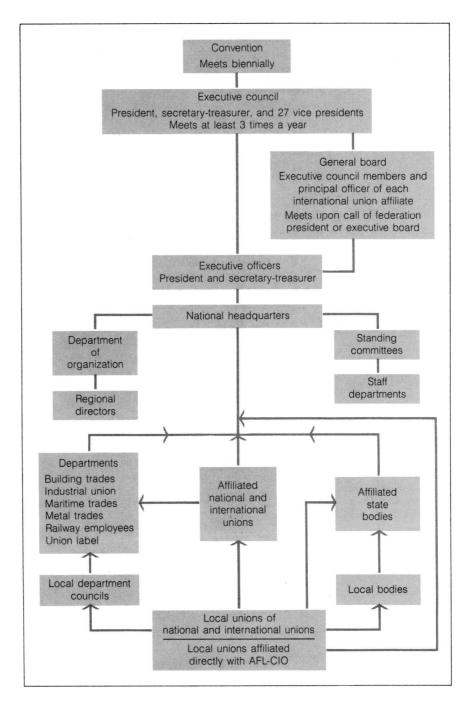

ding a work stoppage for 80 days. During this cooling-off period, further efforts are to be made to reach an agreement. If no agreement is reached, however, the injunction is dissolved and the work stoppage can continue. The coal miners' strike of 1978 is an example. Miners stayed away from the pits despite a back-to-work injunction.

Organized labor, on the other hand, has resented the Taft-Hartley Act as unfair and unnecessary. Management hailed it as essential to redress the power balance. Since 1947, no major legislation has been passed to change the balance of power between the two. However, the Labor Management Reporting and Disclosure Act of 1959 (Landrum-Griffin Act) was designed to require both labor and management to make reports to the Secretary of Labor on union activities. It was aimed primarily at the corruption and racketeering prevalent in some labor unions at that time.

TRENDS IN LABOR GROWTH TODAY

After 15 years of growth, membership in labor unions dropped 3.8 percent from 1974 to 1976. This left total union membership at about 19.4 million members. These union members represent about 20 percent of the total American labor force, or about 25 percent of the total nonfarm force.

As you can see from Figure 16-2, however, the percentage has fallen from a high of 33.2 percent of all nonfarm employees in 1955. About 79 percent of union members belong to the AFL-CIO. Of those union members not belonging to the AFL-CIO, about two-thirds belong to either the Teamsters Union or the United Auto Workers Union. Both unions were expelled from the AFL-CIO for violations of union policy.

UNION GROWTH SLOWS IN THE 1960s

Growth in union membership began to slow in the 1960s, a slowing that was reflected in the percentage of elections won by unions and in the size of bargaining units organized. In elections to determine whether workers wanted unions to

FIGURE 16-2 The percentage of unionized workers in the total work force has been declining since 1955. Source: Bureau of Labor Statistics

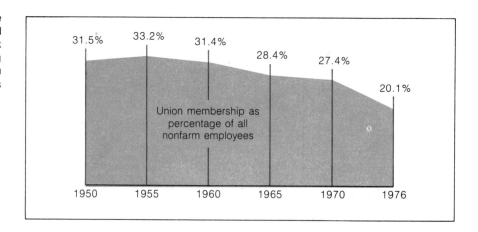

31.5% 33.2% 31.4% 28.4% 27.4% 20.1%

Union membership as percentage of all nonfarm employees

1950   1955   1960   1965   1970   1976

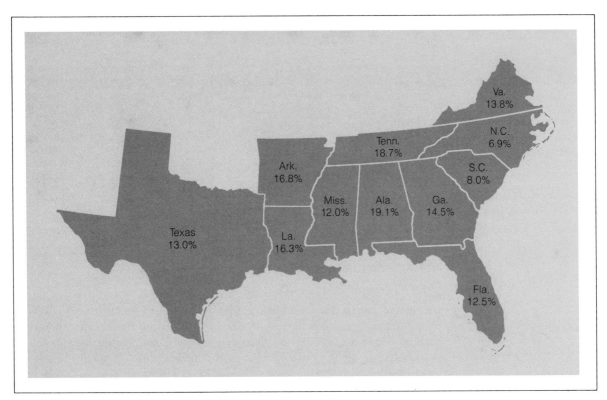

FIGURE 16-3 Percentage of nonfarm workers belonging to organized labor unions in the South. The national average is about 20 percent. Source: Bureau of Labor Statistics

represent them, workers voted against union representation in 52 percent of the elections in 1975–76. These years were the first ones since 1935 that unions lost more elections than they won. In addition, the size of the new work groups that unions were able to organize was smaller. There were several reasons for the slackening growth. Technology, foreign competition, changing consumer demands, and rising labor productivity helped reduce the demand for blue-collar workers, a group that has historically been the backbone of the labor movement. At the same time, the number of white-collar workers who have traditionally resisted union efforts to organize them rose. Also, large manufacturers began to move their operations to the South and Southwest and to smaller communities, where organized labor was not as strong and could not count on as much support from other unions. This is shown in Figure 16-3.

UNIONS AND WHITE-COLLAR WORKERS

In the late 1960s and early 1970s the number of white-collar workers belonging to unions began to rise rapidly.

The largest labor unions are shown in Table 16-1. Notice that most of these are either industrial or craft unions. On the other hand, when you look at where the growth is taking place, you get a different picture. Table 16-1 shows the gain in

TABLE 16-1 America's largest labor unions

	1960 membership	1974 membership	Change (in percent)
Teamsters	1,484,400	1,973,000	Up 33
Auto workers	1,136,100	1,545,000	Up 36
Steelworkers	1,152,000	1,300,000	Up 13
Brotherhood of Electrical Workers	771,000	991,000	Up 28
Machinists	898,100	943,000	Up 5
Carpenters	800,000	820,000	Up 2
Retail clerks	342,000	651,000	Up 90
Laborers	442,500	650,000	Up 47
State, county, municipal employees	210,000	648,000	Up 208
Service employees	272,000	585,000	Up 115
Meat cutters	436,000	525,000	Up 20
Communications workers	259,900	499,000	Up 93
Hotel, restaurant employees	443,000	452,000	Up .02
Teachers	68,000	444,000	Up 552
Operating engineers	291,000	415,000	Up 43

Source: *Statistical Abstract of the United States, 1977.*

percentage among unions attracting 100,000 or more members from 1960 to 1970. You can see that the fastest growing unions are those with white-collar workers, illustrating one of the dynamic aspects of union membership. Figure 16-4 shows the rapid growth in white-collar membership.

From 1960 to 1976, while other union memberships grew by only 8 percent, white-collar membership grew by 56 percent. The threat of inflation and the spreading militancy of white-collar workers apparently were the spurs to their

FIGURE 16-4 Number of white-collar workers in labor unions. Source: Bureau of Labor Statistics

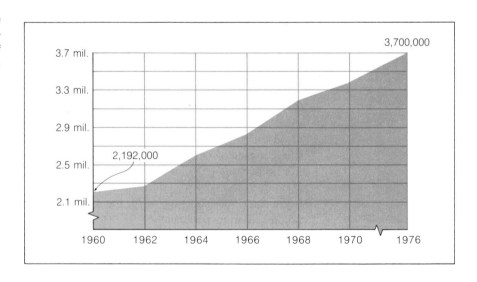

greater union membership. Professional people like teachers, engineers, lawyers, doctors, and dentists began to join the movement in growing numbers. One labor official credited strikes called by teacher groups with the rise in the new respectability of unions for white-collar workers. He indicated that when teachers join unions and strike for their rights, it breaks down the attitude that a union card demeans a salaried person. About half a million teachers belong to the AFL-CIO. Another 1.5 million belong to the National Education Association, which has taken on many of the characteristics of a labor union.

PUBLIC-EMPLOYEE UNIONS

About 14 million workers are employed by local, state, and federal government, and about 5 million of these are members of public-employee unions. Collective bargaining groups are illegal in most types of public employment. For all federal workers, except United States Postal Service employees, Congress determines compensation. However, through executive order federal employees have the right to bargain in a number of nonpay areas. Only 12 states grant broad bargaining rights to both state and local workers and only four permit a limited right to strike.

State and local government employment soared from 6 million in 1960 to almost 12 million in 1975, while federal government employment remained steady at a little less than 3 million. To reach this large potential membership, the AFL-CIO has established what could eventually be the largest single division in

Leaders of the 19,500-member United Teachers of Los Angeles receive training on the union's collective bargaining contract with Los Angeles Unified School District. Collective bargaining between teachers and local school boards was made possible by passage of a California state law in 1975.

business profile: **UNIONS' MUSCLE FLEXES FAR BEYOND NUMBERS**

While the percentage of American workers belonging to unions has been slowly declining in the past couple of decades, unions continue to exercise a strong influence in the economy in a variety of ways not understood by many people. When unionized blue-collar workers in a plant get a wage increase, for example, the company usually grants identical new benefits to their nonunion white-collar workers. In most communities, nonunion plants often raise the wages of their workers in line with rising union scales.

The influence of the unions goes far beyond the bargaining table, of course. They help elect and defeat politicians at election time. Labor representatives can be found in the halls of Congress and in every state legislature. Presidents, governors, and special interest groups call on unions for advice and support.

However, the central role of organized labor remains collective bargaining. Almost 200,000 agreements are in force between management and unions. Contrary to the image conveyed by national coal or steel negotiations, most bargaining is decentralized and covers workers for single companies or single plants. Also, the day when a union leader could tell his members to take a contract whether they like it or not is over. Members have the right to ratify contracts and usually that is done by democratic vote.

Every union negotiator faces constraints when confronting management. At one extreme, the union may be weakly organized at the plant or office, permitting management to bargain from strength. Or the union may be strong at one plant, but the employer can switch production to another plant. At the other extreme is a situation in which the union is so strong that it can virtually write its own contract. The ultimate irony for the union

leader is that if he succeeds too well at bargaining, the union's future becomes clouded. This happened to construction unions in the early 1970s when wages and work rules became so restrictive that nonunion building construction firms won an increasing share of construction contracts, leading to high unemployment among union craftsmen.

There is no escape for unions or employers from rules of the market-oriented economic system. The settlement must not be so expensive as to place the firm in an uncompetitive position in the market. It must be high enough to keep the workers abreast of inflation and provide some gains in income. Because they understand what is economically possible, experienced labor and management negotiators sometimes can guess the final per-hour cost of an agreement even before they start bargaining. The job thus becomes one of arriving at that figure without loss of face and deciding how to distribute it—how much for higher wages, how much for improved medical benefits, and so on.

A major criticism of unions is that they foster inflation, particularly in such highly organized fields as coal and steel, where contracts are negotiated on an industry-wide basis. To make a case for this criticism, it would be necessary to show that unions are stronger in these industries than they were in the late 1950s and early 1960s when the inflation rate was comparatively small. In fact, their strength, in terms of numbers, is less. A far greater cause of inflation, say most economists, is the government's management of the budget and money supply.

Organized labor, although it spends most of its time on collective bargaining, is also active in the political process. The No. 1 job of the AFL-CIO is to foster a healthy political climate for unions.

the federation: a public-employee department. One of the fastest growing unions in the AFL-CIO is the American Federation of State, County, and Municipal Employees, with almost a million members.

Public employees do frequently strike now, although in most cases it is illegal. Union leaders indicate that strikes will continue to occur because in contrast with the private sector, there is no formal legal machinery to resolve labor disputes in the public sector. Labor leaders see this area as potentially the greatest source of new members for the association.

WOMEN AND BLACKS IN UNIONS

Another dramatic development in the growth of organized labor has been the increase in the number of its women and black members. About 20 percent of the membership of the AFL-CIO are women. At the same time, only about 4 million of the 34 million working women in the United States belong to unions. About 3 million blacks, one-third of all black workers, belong to unions.

The women's liberation movement of the late 1960s and early 1970s has had an impact on the organized labor movement in several ways. First, more women are entering blue-collar jobs. The Coalition of Labor Union Women, an alliance of blue-collar working women, was formed in 1974 to help end sex discrimination in wages, hiring, and job classifications. It also hopes to elect more female union officials, since less than 5 percent of AFL-CIO officials are women. Women in the white-collar labor force are also becoming more militant, an aggressiveness showing up in the increasing numbers of women teachers, secretaries, nurses, and office workers who are joining unions.

Black workers, too, have formed their own coalition within the AFL-CIO. Called the Coalition of Black Trade Unionists, it seeks to get more representation for blacks in the AFL-CIO. While blacks represent about 15 percent of the membership of American unions, they have only token representation on executive councils. In addition, several unions have been found guilty of discriminating against blacks. In a trend expected to accelerate, both blacks and women have become more militant in demanding a greater voice in union affairs in recent years.

AREAS OF MANAGEMENT DECISION MAKING AFFECTED BY ORGANIZED LABOR

During the past 40 years, organized labor has assumed many of the powers that were once the sole domain of management. It has forced management in many types of business and government operations to permit workers a greater voice in decisions affecting them. Workers have felt that almost every major decision touches them and that they should be consulted before decisions are made. Some of the basic areas of decision making that are now influenced by organized labor are discussed below.

Location or Relocation of a Plant   If a union can convince the National Labor Relations Board that the reason for a plant relocation is to escape a strong local union, the move can be prevented. For example, when the Schlitz Brewing

Company wanted to close its Brooklyn brewery, the National Labor Relations Board ruled that it could not close for at least 17 months, by which time the company's contract with the Teamsters Union would have expired.

Introduction of Labor-Saving Equipment   In strongly unionized industries, the introduction of equipment that might displace workers is subject to careful negotiation. The International Typographical Union dropped its opposition to computer-set type only after securing an agreement that no present workers would be laid off as a result of the innovation.

Promotions   As we saw in the section on personnel management, seniority is the normal basis for promotion among organized workers. Management may wish to promote a person who it feels is more qualified to do the job, but it can do that only within the context of the seniority system. The seniority system has come under attack in recent years, however, because its critics say it discriminates against minorities. Groups of both blacks and women have challenged its use when it has favored white males. As a result, some changes in the application of seniority are likely to take place.

Wage Scales and Levels of Wages   While management may set the wage scales initially, they are frequently changed through negotiation with representatives of organized labor. Wage levels are always determined through collective bargaining between management and labor.

One of the areas of wage levels that labor and business constantly disagree about is the level of the minimum-wage law. The *minimum wage* law defines the lowest wage that may be paid for employees who work for firms covered by the legislation. All but about 10 million workers are covered by this law. Labor unions want it pushed higher to provide more purchasing power in the economy and thus provide more jobs. Management, on the other hand, argues that a higher minimum wage will force employers to do away with unskilled or low-skilled jobs, thus contributing to higher unemployment rates, particularly among teenagers.

Work Processes   How work is to be performed and under what conditions is always subject to negotiation. Most unions will resist efforts to change a job that results in their union members losing work as compared with other unions. For example, the sheet metal workers have resisted efforts for years to permit craftworkers in other unions who are making repairs to a machine to remove anything in the machine to get to the defect. In another instance, a clause in the contract between the United Auto Workers (UAW) and Chrysler Corporation gives the union an equal voice in experiments to improve the work environment.

There are many other areas of decision making where unions demand a voice with management. In education, for example, teachers' unions have demanded reduced class loads, greater say in curriculum development, fewer extra class activities, and even greater police protection. The manager, no matter whether in a public or private organization, is increasingly having to account to the employees for the decisions that he wants to make.

THE COLLECTIVE BARGAINING PROCESS

Over the years, unions have tended to strive for higher income, better working conditions, and shorter work hours for their members. These have remained constant goals since the formation of the AFL. However, several subtle changes have taken place in achieving these goals.

GOALS OF UNIONS

Originally, the main focus in wage negotiations was on higher pay. In more recent years, unions have bargained harder for deferred income for their members. The current UAW-Chrysler pact, for example, provides for a maximum pension for retired workers of $700 a month. Better pensions and a variety of other fringe benefits make it difficult to compute what the total income for each worker really is. In addition, there has been a major push by most unions for cost-of-living clauses in contracts. These so-called *escalator clauses* are designed to protect members from inflation, a phenomenon aggravated in the late 1960s and early 1970s. Over 5 million workers are covered by escalator clauses in their contracts, providing extra raises as the consumer price index rises.

In addition to the three main goals, most unions have also demanded a larger voice in management decision making. They feel that the workers are entitled to help make decisions that affect their jobs. The major issue in the 1973 auto strike, for example, was not more money, but the right of workers to refuse to work overtime. It also must be kept in mind that union leaders may have goals independent of those of their members, such as advantages for themselves or more power for the union organization. A shocking example was Tony Boyle, head of the United Mine Workers, who was convicted in 1974 of ordering the murder of a union rival and also of hiring friends and relatives for nonessential jobs at very high salaries.

GOALS OF BUSINESS

The goals of business were described in Chapter 1. Essentially, business firms offer products or services to the public to make a profit for themselves. The owners risk their money to bring together the productive resources that can be developed into products or services. The owners feel that since it is their money at stake, they should make all the decisions or delegate them to managers. They do not feel that employees should make the decisions since they are not risking their money.

Since labor can be thought of as a factor of production, similar to raw materials, parts, supplies, and capital, some employers feel it should be bought and sold on the market just as any other factor is. While this is an extreme point of view, it is sometimes the impression that employers present to employees and their union. Most employers see organized labor as a factor that must be considered when making decisions regarding the firm. They build plants with the workers' feelings in mind and develop supervisory policies that are compatible with the worker's interests. If all firms felt this way and communicated it to workers, unions would probably be less militant.

Collective bargaining is the process through which management and representatives of organized labor unions reach agreement on working conditions in a business. Workers in a firm choose a union to represent them by secret vote in an election usually supervised by the National Labor Relations Board, with a majority necessary to certify a union. The election may cover all workers in a plant or business or it may cover several branches owned by a firm.

Representatives of the union and of management then meet to develop a labor contract. The first meeting is mainly a procedural one, with the ground rules developed for future meetings. In subsequent sessions, the union will present its list of demands. Management will counter with its offers. The meetings are a series of negotiations with both sides bringing in detailed facts to support their bargaining positions. Usually, the two sides have similar data, but draw different conclusions from them. When the labor agreement has been reached by negotiators, it is then submitted to the union membership for a vote. If the terms are totally unacceptable, the workers may vote to strike to enforce their demands.

Collective bargaining is the process by which labor and management discuss their differences on such subjects as wages, work schedules, and productivity.

personality profile:
DOUGLAS A. FRASER — steering the United Auto Workers

In 1977 Doug Fraser was elected president of the United Auto Workers. He was a popular choice among the rank and file, with whom he feels at home, so he had little opposition. That was partly because of his demonstrated ability and warm personality. It was also partly because he was, like his predecessor, Leonard Woodcock, a firm disciple of Walter Reuther, the legendary leader of the UAW for 24 years until his death in a plane crash in 1970.

The United Auto Workers, under Reuther's leadership, have been heavily committed to social as well as collective bargaining goals. "The labor movement is about changing society," Fraser says. As a liberal-progressive labor organization closely aligned with the Democratic Party, it has pushed hard for national health insurance and for ending racial discrimination in employment. "A person who doesn't get angry with injustice should retire," is Fraser's view. In addition, the UAW is strongly in favor of a four-day workweek, reducing unemployment, and a guaranty of job security.

Fraser faces several problems. For one thing, the changeover from big to smaller cars will mean more automation and fewer auto workers. There is increasing indifference and alienation among younger workers, who refuse to get involved in active unionism. Attendance at local meetings is down to 2 percent of membership rather than the 20 to 80 percent who used to show up. The union's top leadership is still mostly aging Reutherites, and no group of young leaders seems to be emerging to take their place. In addition to winning concessions at the bargaining table, Fraser must pacify the 125,000 skilled tradesmen in the auto industry who feel that they are getting less than their fair share of contract settlements in comparison to the relatively unskilled auto workers. Lastly, the UAW's rift with George Meany's AFL/CIO remains to be healed. Their recombination could do much to stem the labor movement's decline in recent years by giving unionism a united front.

If the job can be done, Fraser appears to be the one to do it. He's been in the auto industry all his life, starting out as a metal finisher in a DeSoto plant and then working for the UAW as a local union president, staff member, assistnat to Reuther, and union vice president in 1970. Although he is a self-proclaimed ultra-liberal and a formidable bargainer, he understands economic realities. He disapproved of wildcat strikes in 1973 and was willing to concentrate on nonwage issues during that period of wage-price controls. Because of such flexibility, he is well liked and respected by the auto industry.

If the contract does not quite meet the expectation of the members, they may instruct their negotiators to continue bargaining to gain additional concessions in the contract. More likely, however, the majority of the members will vote to accept the pact. The contract then goes into effect for one to three years, the typical length for labor agreements. Ordinarily, a labor contract continues in effect if neither party amends or terminates it. Collective bargaining begins months or even a year or two before the effective contract expires.

THE LABOR CONTRACT

The written labor contract can be as brief as 10 or 15 pages or as long as a telephone directory, like the contract typically used in the auto industry. Almost all have the same basic features. They include the classifications of workers to be covered by the contract; the rights and duties of management and labor in regard to compensation, work procedures, and personnel policies; procedures for handling grievances; and procedures for renewing the contract. Grievances are complaints—usually by workers, but sometimes by management.

The contract spells out the rights and responsibilities of management and labor. It is a binding agreement. However, as in most contracts, there is room for disagreement about how its provisions are to be implemented. This may result in a grievance. When these disagreements or grievances arise, it may be necessary for a third party to mediate or arbitrate the dispute.

Mediation is an attempt to settle a labor dispute or grievance through the assistance of a neutral third person. The mediator listens to both sides and attempts to help them reach agreement. Although without power to enforce any decision on the participants, the neutral person serves to improve communication. The mediator may be a local civic leader, such as a mayor or a university professor. For assistance in settling disputes in industries engaged in interstate commerce, the Federal Mediation and Conciliation Service may provide mediators. This federal agency has a staff of several hundred mediators who are available to help prevent loss of production in key industries.

Arbitration is a stronger action than mediation. Again, a neutral third party helps bring about agreement, but with the power to enforce whatever decision is reached. When arbitration is to be used, both parties must agree to the process and decide in advance who the third party will be. The arbitrator is much like a judge in a court of law. The American Arbitration Association, an independent agency for settling labor disputes, is normally named in labor contracts as the arbitrator. The questions that are to be submitted to arbitration are listed in the contract. They normally do not include such basic issues as pay, hours of work, or working conditions, but usually deal with work procedures or policies.

LABOR-
MANAGEMENT
INTERACTION

After nearly 40 years of interaction between strong unions and strong management, the relationship between these two forces now shows a certain maturity. Most companies feel that labor unions have a definite role to play in the business world and accept that role. Most unions recognize that they will not represent their members well if they make it difficult for the firm to make a profit. Yet both sides realize that they must use every weapon at their command to gain a competitive bargaining advantage. Both possess a variety of bargaining tools, some subtle, others strong and direct.

MANAGEMENT'S BARGAINING TOOLS

There are various employers' associations in which firms band together in dealing with labor unions. Probably the best known is the National Association of Manufacturers. These groups help disseminate information to member firms, engage in public relations, and assist in lobbying. *Lobbying* is the effort to influence federal, state, and local government legislation by pressuring elected representatives in a variety of ways. Management also brings in strikebreakers to do the work normally performed by striking employees. This can be a successful technique if it is relatively easy to get replacements. If the work is highly specialized, however, or large numbers of workers are involved, it is not a very effective device. Sometimes the supervisors and managers are able to keep a business or service open by taking over the workers' jobs themselves for a short time.

Another bargaining tool is the *lockout*. The *lockout* is the refusal of an employer to permit employees to work and is used occasionally when workers deliberately slow production. It also occurs when a contract has expired and an industrywide union strikes only one firm in the industry. The other firms may then close, too, to prevent the union from playing one firm against another. An *injunction* is another tool for management bringing pressure on organized labor. This is a court order forbidding members of organized labor from engaging in some action against the employer—that is, illegal picketing or threatening workers or management. It is seldom used these days, however, except in the cases of violence or fraud on the part of the union. There are other, illegal tools that can be used, such as blacklists of employees, but these are seldom brought into play.

LABOR UNION'S BARGAINING TOOLS

Labor, too, engages in lobbying efforts to bring pressure on elected representatives. In addition, unions use picketing and boycotts as major weapons. *Pickets* are persons carrying signs at the entrance to a business preventing people from entering the premises or informing the public about the strike. A *boycott* takes place when workers refuse to purchase goods or services from companies whose employees are on strike. A union will often try to enlist public support by asking people to boycott products involved in a dispute. This is one of the tactics used by the United Farm Workers in trying to get the makers of Gallo wines to recognize them rather than the Teamsters Union as the official bargaining agent of the workers. Another type of boycott, the *secondary boycott*, goes even further. This occurs when members of a union refuse to handle the goods of another company whose employees are on strike. Secondary boycotts are illegal but are still used occasionally.

The strike, or the threat of a strike, is still the strongest weapon labor unions have. Strikes are most often called when they place management at the greatest disadvantage. For example, if demand is high for a company's products, a strike is

The strike is the labor union's strongest weapon. Because it is often extremely costly to both labor and management, the strike is being used less frequently than in the past.

particularly effective. If inventory levels of its product are low or if a competitor may gain at the firm's expense, a strike also is a potent weapon. In the auto industry, for example, the United Auto Workers Union normally calls a walkout against only one company. It hopes the loss of sales and profits to the other auto makers will force the company being struck to yield substantial benefits to get production started again.

Unions strike to achieve a number of purposes. In a *walkout strike*, workers stay off their jobs to enforce their collective bargaining demands. A *wildcat strike* is one in which workers walk off their jobs without the sanction of their union representatives. Sometimes, unions call for a *slowdown strike*, in which the workers stay on their jobs but work at a slower pace than normal. Occasionally, union leaders call a strike to demonstrate the strength of a union or to achieve worker unity.

There is some indication that organized labor will use the strike, or threat of a strike, less often in the future. The United Steel Workers and the steel industry signed a contract in 1973 that barred a steel strike. The contract indicated that if negotiations failed to settle all issues when the contract was negotiated, all those unresolved would go to arbitration. Also, in some other key industries, agreements have been reached faster and without strikes than in previous years. As Figure 16-5 shows, strike activity in the United States has declined dramatically in recent years, after peaking in 1970. Neither labor nor management, however, expects organized labor to give up the strike as a potential weapon.

FIGURE 16-5 Dollar loss from work stoppages. Source: *Monthly Labor Review*

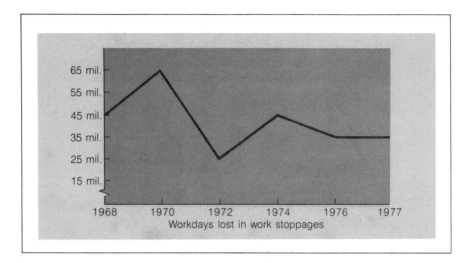

Workdays lost in work stoppages

POLITICAL ACTIVITY OF LABOR AND MANAGEMENT

In addition to lobbying, both labor and management are active in other aspects of politics in pursuing their goals. Since Roosevelt's New Deal of 1933, organized labor has generally supported the Democratic Party, while most businesspeople have tended to favor the Republicans. As a result, the American public tends to view big business as being in close partnership with the Republican Party. It is true, however, that labor unions frequently support Republican candidates for office at all levels, and management frequently supports Democrats. At the national level, for example, the AFL-CIO was officially neutral for the 1972 election, and numerous businesspeople supported Lyndon Johnson, the Democratic candidate, in the 1964 election. Organized labor's political muscle has come mainly from voter registration, ringing doorbells, driving voters to the polls, and other jobs requiring manpower. They have also given considerable money to finance individual campaigns. Management, on the other hand, mainly provides only financial support for election campaigns. Some businesses or trade associations do, however, make specialists in various areas available to the Republican campaigns without cost. These might include speech writers, fund raisers, or advisors on governmental policy. Critics have said that big business also exerts great influence over the government agencies that are supposed to regulate it. Most of the top-level executives in the government agencies come from business or get jobs in business when they leave government service. Mintz and Cohen, in their book, *America, Inc.*,[1] claim that big business "controls" all the major federal government regulatory agencies.

1. Morton Minz and Jerry S. Cohen, *America, Inc.: Who Owns and Operates the United States?* (New York: Dial Press, 1971).

DOES COLLECTIVE BARGAINING WORK?

Many people question the effectiveness and fairness of collective bargaining. There are those who think that labor has most of the clout and can force management to do what it wants. There are others, by contrast, who feel that big business merely passes on to the consumers whatever costs they incur through collective bargaining. They feel that the firms have little incentive to resist labor's demands. As a result, both big business and big labor are blamed for rising prices brought on by wage increases that are greater than might be the case in industries where unions are not strong.

PUBLIC CONFIDENCE IN MANAGEMENT AND LABOR

In a Roper Organization national poll in 1977, only 48 percent of Americans expressed "some confidence" in labor leaders; in 1975 the figure was 50 percent. Among union members, 51 percent said they have confidence in the system of organized labor. In the same poll, public confidence in business leaders had risen 10 percentage points, from 62 to 72 percent from 1975 to 1977. Critics of the organized labor system wonder why business, labor, and the government cannot work together more effectively. They look at West Germany, Japan, and the Scandinavian countries where there seems to be a close working relationship among the three groups. In the United States, government, business, and labor frequently seem to regard each other as enemies. It would seem more profitable for all to identify with their common concern: greater productivity resulting in better products, more jobs, and higher pay as well as other benefits.

THE FUTURE OF COLLECTIVE BARGAINING

When you consider all of the criticism of the process, it seems logical to wonder why collective bargaining survives. Actually, there are counter arguments to all the points raised above. Congress feels the relative bargaining strength of labor and management is fairly equal, for no new legislation has been seriously considered to change the balance of power since 1947, when the Taft-Hartley Act weakened the unions' bargaining position. While both labor and management bargain furiously, ordinarily a work stoppage does not take place. It is true that businesses can pass on some of the higher labor costs that are won by labor unions, but there is a limit to that. At times, management must absorb the greater labor costs through lower profits. At other times, the higher price for their products may reduce demand considerably. A case in point is the coal industry. Until oil prices began their rapid rise, the coal industry was a declining industry. At least part of the decline was due to higher prices, the result primarily of relatively high wages paid to workers.

Then, too, there are increasing numbers of examples of management and labor working together for the good of the firm. The United Rubber Workers Union and the big tire-making companies joined efforts to increase productivity and keep plants in Akron, Ohio, operating. The United Steel Workers Union and the steel companies have developed a close working relationship to increase productivity and reduce time lost to strikes to their mutual benefit. The Amalgamated Clothing Workers and the International Ladies Garment Workers have played major roles in stabilizing the once erratic clothing industry. Collective bargaining plays a key role in our market economy. As long as it is, this dynamic, changing process will continue.

SUMMARY

Large labor unions began to develop after the Civil War in response to the increased power of big business. Growth of unions was slow, however, until the 1930s when organized labor was supported by the Roosevelt administration. From that point, organized labor grew rapidly until it was necessary to curb its power somewhat with the Taft-Hartley Act of 1947.

In the past decade, the percentage of nonfarm workers belonging to unions has declined slightly. The increase in the number of white-collar jobs and the movement of industry to the South and Southwest have made it difficult for unions to add new members as fast as the labor force expands. However, the fastest growing areas of unionization are those in government, and in white-collar jobs.

Most areas of management decision making have been influenced by labor unions, including location or relocation of a plant, introduction of labor-saving equipment, promotions, wage scales and levels of wages, and work processes.

The collective bargaining process involves a meshing of the goals of business and unions. Unions tend to strive for higher income, better working conditions, and shorter working hours for their members. In the bargaining process, both sides start with a position and interact until they can agree on a written labor contract. The contract includes all of the issues that have been bargained for, including pay, promotion, working conditions, equipment used, management processes, and other items. Sometimes it is necessary to use the services of a mediator or an arbitrator to reach agreement.

In the bargaining process, management has a number of tools to use, including employers' associations, lobbying, strikebreakers, lockouts and injunctions. Labor unions have the strike as their main weapon, but also use lobbying, boycotts, and picketing. Both groups are active politically in achieving their goals. The effectiveness of the collective bargaining process in this country is always open to question. However, it seems to be the best process given the other values that we have.

SUMMARY OF KEY TERMS

Arbitration Help in reaching agreement by a neutral third party with the power to enforce whatever decision is reached.

Boycott Refusal by workers or consumers to purchase products or services from companies whose employees are on strike.

Closed Shop Only union members are hired by a firm.

Collective Bargaining Negotiations between labor and management.

Craft Union An association of workers skilled in a craft or trade.

Featherbedding Forcing employers to continue jobs that are no longer necessary.

Escalator Clause A cost-of-living clause in a

labor contract designed to protect workers from inflation.

Industrial Union Association in one union of all the workers in an industry, regardless of the type of work they do.

Injunction A court order forbidding members of organized labor from engaging in some action against the employer.

Lobbying The effort to influence federal, state, and local government legislation.

Lockout Refusal of an employer to permit employees to work.

Mediation An attempt to settle a labor dispute or grievance through the assistance of a neutral third person.

Minimum Wage The lowest hourly wage that can be paid to an employee who is covered by federal minimum wage legislation.

National Labor Relations Board Federal agency that administers the provisions of the Wagner Act in settling disputes and in determining unfair practices.

Picket A union member demonstrating against an employer during a strike action. Pickets usually carry signs explaining why they are on strike. Members of other unions generally do not cross picket lines.

Right-to-work Clause A state law that prevents union shops.

Secondary Boycott Refusal by union members to handle the products of another company whose employees are on strike.

Slowdown Strike Workers staying on the job, but working at a slower pace than normal.

Union Shop Place of employment in which an employee does not have to be a member of the recognized union, but must either join it after a period of time on the job or pay union dues.

Walkout Strike Workers staying off the job to enforce their collective bargaining demands.

Wildcat Strike Workers walking off the job without the sanction of their union leaders.

REVIEW QUESTIONS

1. During which period of time did organized labor make its greatest gains?
2. Contrast the purposes and provisions of the Wagner and Taft-Hartley acts.
3. Identify two basic trends in union membership today.
4. How successful have unions been in recent years in attracting white-collar workers?
5. Name and explain four major areas of management decision making affected by organized labor.
6. What are the major goals of labor unions?
7. Identify the provisions that are normally included in a labor contract.
8. Explain the role of mediation and arbitration in the collective bargaining process.
9. List and explain two major tools used by management and two used by unions in their efforts to promote their respective points of view.
10. How are union and management active in achieving their political goals?

DISCUSSION QUESTIONS

1. Should all government employees have the right to belong to a collective bargaining unit?
2. Would a higher minimum wage reduce the job opportunities in your community for persons under 21?
3. Do you believe that the right to strike should be eliminated in key industries in this country? Why or why not?
4. Should there be a limit to the participation of unions in management decision making?
5. How effective do you feel the collective bargaining process has worked in this country?

CASES FOR DECISION MAKING

THE OPEN SHOP CUTS COSTS IN CONSTRUCTION

The construction industry has long been dominated by the building trades unions. A large construction firm has had little choice but to go to union hiring halls for carpenters, electricians, plumbers, pipe fitters and others. Until 1970, construction workers' wage increases were the largest in the country and their weekly wages were higher than those of manufacturing workers.

From that high point in 1970, however, the wage gains have moderated. Much of the moderation is due to the rapid rise of the open shop. With the high wages of union construction workers contributing significantly to excessive costs in construction, activity fell rapidly. As a result, unemployment rates in the construction industry rose to 15 percent and even higher in some areas. Nonunion contractors could then hire the unemployed construction workers at lower rates than the union demanded and bid less than contractors who were using union labor. As a result, the jobs began to flow to nonunion contractors and today about a third of all nonresidential construction is performed by nonunion contractors. Some large contractors have maintained the union shop, however, because of a shortage of good nonunion labor and because the unions maintained fairly high quality through apprenticeship programs.

1. Would an open shop in all construction lead to lower prices in construction and better quality jobs?
2. Would you expect to find an increase in the number of open shops in the construction industry?
3. Should the union shop be banned because it increases labor costs?

LABOR VICTORY WITHOUT A STRIKE[2]

Costly strikes have been frequent in the steel industry. To avoid these, the industry and the United Steel Workers agreed to a radical new approach to collective bargaining. In March 1973, the union agreed not to strike in exchange for a $150 one-time payment for each employee covered, a guarantee of at least a 3 percent a year wage increase, and full cost-of-living protection. Then the two sides sat down to hammer out a new labor contract that would prevent strikes. If they could not come to terms on any issue, they both agreed to submit the issue to binding arbitration. They finally agreed on a three-year contract in April 1974, which both sides publicly stated was a fair one. While wage increases were to average only about 4 percent a year for the contract, fringe benefits were considerable. In addition to a cost-of-living provision of a penny an hour raise for every three-tenths of a point increase in the Consumer Price Index, pension benefits were improved substantially.

1. Do you believe that strikes should be forbidden in such major industries as steel, autos, rubber, and trucking?
2. Should all occupations have provisions for cost-of-living increases based on the Consumer Price Index? What effects would this have on prices?
3. Should compulsory arbitration always be used to settle differences of opinion between management and labor, rather than permitting either side to shut down production?

AUTOMATION VERSUS PEOPLE[3]

The International Typographers Union and many daily newspapers have not been able to reach agreement on the use of automated typesetting machines for over 10 years. A costly strike in New York City resulted in four daily newspapers closing. Under the contract which the papers had with the unions, management could not introduce computer-set type into its composing rooms. The two sides continued to operate without a contract since they could not

2. "The USW's No-Strike Victory," *Business Week*, April 20, 1964, p. 62.

3. "Heating Up: The Battle over Automation in Printing," *U.S. News & World Report*, May 6, 1974.

agree on how to handle the automation issue. On nearby Long Island, *Newsday* newspaper and the local ITU union agreed on a three-year contract, by contrast giving management complete freedom to utilize automation as it sees fit. In exchange, management guaranteed lifetime positions for 262 of 274 persons working in the composing room. Similar contracts were signed for the Augusta, Georgia, *Herald* and Davenport, Iowa, *Times-Democrat*, permitting extensive use of automation to cut costs.

1. Should a labor union have the right to prohibit or slow the introduction of labor-saving technology into a plant? Why or why not?

2. What responsibility does management have for providing for workers who lose their jobs because of mechanization and automation?

3. The Director of the Federal Mediation and Conciliation Services suggested that a newspaper council composed of representatives of management and labor should work together to improve the industry. Do you believe that labor has the right to be a part of decision making in all aspects of a company's operations?

RELATED READINGS

Hall, Burton H., ed. *Autocracy and Insurgency in Organized Labor.* New Brunswick, N.J.: Transaction Books, 1972.

A collection of essays about members of unions who are attempting to achieve membership participation and control of their unions. It is a guideline to the aspirations and activities of rank and file labor members who want a greater voice in their unions. A number of unions are examined.

Jenkins, David. *Job Power.* Baltimore: Penguin Books, 1974.

A dynamic little book about industrial democracy and the abolition of autocratic forms of organization in favor of decision-making power for employees. The author analyzes labor organization in a number of countries besides the United States and looks at efforts to improve productivity and morale through worker participation.

Nierenberg, Gerald I. *The Art of Negotiating.* New York: Cornerstone Library, 1968.

An interesting little book on the psychological strategies for gaining an advantage in negotiating. While it has primary application for labor-management negotiations, its principles of understanding human motivation are applicable to any negotiated arrangement.

Schoen, Sterling H., and Hilgert, Raymond L. *Cases in Collective Bargaining and Industrial Relations.* Rev. ed. Homewood, Ill.: Richard D. Irwin, 1974.

A casebook paperback containing a variety of union-management problem situations, in which the student can apply principles learned in the preceding writings. They are real-life cases of the kind that managers are likely to encounter in situations involving labor unions.

part six: CAREER OPPORTUNITIES

CAREERS IN PERSONNEL ADMINISTRATION

Of the more than 300,000 people employed in personnel administration jobs last year, about 75 percent worked in private businesses and industry. Government agencies were the second largest employer, and a small number of personnel people were in business for themselves as management consultants and as experts in employee-management relations.

A college education is becoming a prerequisite in the personnel field. Many private business firms hire recent college graduates for junior personnel positions and then train them for their own particular needs. Other firms prefer to transfer present employees, with the proper credentials, from one department to another. In the latter case, the employee is thoroughly familiar with the kinds of skills and talents to look for in potential employees.

To be successful in personnel management one must be able to speak and write effectively and have an aptitude for working with people of all levels of intelligence and experience. A liking for detail, a high degree of persuasiveness, and a pleasing personality also are important.

Employment prospects are likely to be best for college graduates with specialized training in personnel administration, although graduates with other backgrounds will be considered. Opportunities in personnel work are expected to expand very rapidly as total employment rises in the next decade.

part seven

BUSINESS ENVIRONMENT

This section deals with the external forces affecting the operation of a business firm. Over the past century, we have moved further and further from the principles of free enterprise. In addition, today American business is influenced to a far greater extent by foreign competitors than it was even a decade ago.

In Chapter 17, you will examine business and governmental relations. You will study the various ways that government interacts with business. You will also look at some of the important federal legislation that affects. business. The role of important federal agencies will be stressed along with how taxes affect business.

In Chapter 18, you will look at the international business environment. You will study the effects of world trade on American business and the economic and political forces affecting trade. You will look at the

principal competitors for our business firms and how the balance of trade and balance of payments affects business. Also, you will take a look at the role of multinational firms.

In Chapter 19, you will study ways in which business protects itself from risks. You will look at the process of risk management and then focus on the role of insurance companies in the business world. You will look at the various types of insurance protection with a particularly close look at life insurance.

In Chapter 20, you will peer into the future as it is likely to influence business and workers. You will look at the major changes that are developing and that will have a great impact on firms and on the types and numbers of jobs available. The last part of the chapter focuses on employment in a changing world.

chapter 17

BUSINESS AND GOVERNMENT RELATIONS

OBJECTIVES

When you have finished reading and studying this chapter, you should be able to:

1. Describe the various government roles in commerce and industry.

2. Demonstrate familiarity with the general purpose of each of the major acts of legislation intended to prevent restraint of trade in the United States.

3. Distinguish and differentiate among executive, administrative, and judicial influence in the operation of our federal government and recognize their relationships to the business community.

4. Explain how fiscal and monetary influences affect our economy.

5. Recognize the availability of subsidies to businesses and the general sectors of business that can qualify for government assistance.

CHAPTER PREVIEW

Just as an automobile's internal combustion engine needs enough oil to help it run smoothly, so every community and every nation needs some governing by a central authority to help it run effectively. In the early days of the United States, the general attitude toward government was that it should have as little power as possible; consequently government existed almost wholly to protect its citizens. Later government took on a stronger role when it became a regulator. Various agencies were established by the executive branch to regulate international trade, domestic transportation, and the like, implementing acts of protection and regulation passed by Congress. As the nation grew and became more complex, so the executive and judicial branches of our government also became larger, more powerful, and more complicated. Not surprisingly, government became much more expensive.

During the Great Depression of the 1930s, the federal budget totaled 9 billion dollars; today it is well over 25 times that amount. It wasn't until the twentieth century that the federal government became a competitor to business in some areas and a subsidizer in others. The massive Tennessee Valley Authority is the classic example of how our federal government has become a property owner and competitor to private business. The Small Business Administration currently serves as a good illustration of how the federal government helps businesspeople through advice and low-interest, or no interest, business loans.

You may remember President Carter's much publicized energy package as originally proposed in 1977. Or, perhaps, you recall his proposal to regulate price rises in the health field. Carter pushed these programs because of his concern with solving our energy problems and slowing the stubbornly high growth rate of inflation. Congress was reluctant to go along with the Carter program, but President Carter was not the first president who has attempted to influence economic activity through government policy. Fiscal policy has become an established procedure for every administration since the time of Franklin D. Roosevelt. The Federal Reserve System and its board of governors also attempts to influence the economic policy in the United States through monetary controls. You will learn more about these very important topics, fiscal and monetary policy, as you read on.

17
BUSINESS AND GOVERNMENT RELATIONS

Have you ever noticed how different your brother or sister's behavior is with friends than when he or she is with your family? Have you ever noticed the same thing about yourself? Honestly, isn't your behavior different in school than it is at home or on the job? All of us have different sides, so to speak. It is no different with federal, state and local governments. In recent years, especially on the federal level, government has become more and more diversified. To put it another way, our government wears many different "hats"; Figure 17-1 categorizes these roles.

THE MANY HATS THAT GOVERNMENT WEARS

If you ask local businesspeople what they think of the government's roles in regard to commerce and industry, their responses are likely to be negative. Most businesspeople resent some of the influences that government has had on the business sector of our economy, and they see this influence as having increased rapidly in recent years. Yet if you probed further, you would probably find that most businesspeople recognize the need for some government regulation and protection. Delve a bit deeper and you'll find that they are happy to have government as a consumer and in some cases as a subsidizer. Few businesspeople welcome government as a competitor, however; fortunately, government is weakest in this area, although its competitive force is increasing from year to year.

In the early days of our country, the only roles granted to government were protector and regulator. Even in these roles, the government had little power because people were suspicious of any violations of their constitutional rights. Probably our government first became a consumer, subsidizer, and competitor when it invested in the building of canals, such as the Erie Canal in the early nineteenth century, for the long-distance transportation of freight and passengers. It has only really been in the last 45 years that the federal government has become deeply involved in the functions of regulation, consumption, subsidization, and competition. Perhaps your conception of these terms and how they relate to government and business in our economy is rather vague. If so, the discussion below should help clarify your thinking.

A DEFINITION OF GOVERNMENT

"Government" is a very broad term. It includes the federal government and its multitude of departments and agencies whose administrators are appointed by the

FIGURE 17-1 The many hats of government

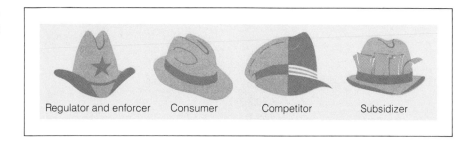

Regulator and enforcer   Consumer   Competitor   Subsidizer

president, some of them requiring the approval of the Senate. The diagram in Figure 17-2 gives a reminder of the broad scope of the federal government in the United States.

There are, of course, governments for each of the 50 states as well as thousands of county and local governments. In addition there are many authorities that are government initiated and controlled (to a degree), such as the New York Port Authority which operates the bridges and tunnels in the New York metropolitan area.

GOVERNMENT AS REGULATOR AND ENFORCER

Every sport has its rules and uses referees, judges, and umpires to enforce them. The same holds true in the world of commerce but in a far more complicated way. There is the obvious police and fire protection provided to businesses by government on all levels, as well as protection against credit defaults or failure to carry out contracted obligations. There are many laws and agencies that protect the public and the business community against *monopoly*, the takeover of a market for a particular product or service by one supplier. This legislation against monopoly, has evolved to provide a much greater range and degree of protection than the first law in this area, which was enacted more than 90 years ago.

The first major efforts of the federal government to regulate business came in the late 1800s, with the development of big business on a massive scale and im-

In its role as regulator, the federal government controls interstate commerce. In addition, each state requires interstate shippers be licensed to transport cargo within that state.

Stock, Boston, Inc.

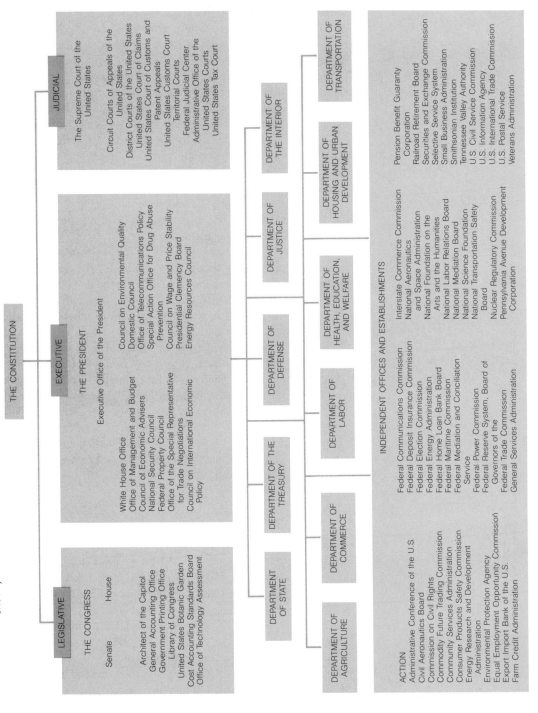

FIGURE 17-2 Structure of the federal government (only the major agencies as shown). Source: *Statistical Abstract of the United States,* 1978

provements in transportation and communication. One of the first important acts was the Interstate Commerce Commission Act of 1887, passed to curb the growth of trusts and monopolies which were threatening free competition. Marked by such dynamic leaders as Rockefeller in oil, Carnegie in steel, Vanderbilt in railroads, the era of the "robber barons," as they have been called, was alive with efforts to stifle competition and increase control of the markets.

The Sherman Act, discussed below in detail, was the first law with any significant clout in prohibiting some restraint-of-trade activities. Many years later, a special antitrust division was set up in the Department of Justice. There are now about 300 attorneys and thirty economists working in that division alone.

Industrialists continued to find new ways to get around the law after the Sherman Act was placed on the statute books. The Clayton Act of 1914, also detailed below, was passed to close some of these loopholes.

With these two major acts, it became difficult for firms to monopolize the market, although there are charges that it is still being done in a few markets. There have been numerous attempts in the 1960s by firms to grow while avoiding the violation of these and other pieces of antitrust legislation. The conglomerate, which has apparently not stepped over the bounds of antitrust laws, has grown rapidly. Conglomerates, you will remember, are large corporations, such as Gulf and Western Industries, that grow by buying firms in other industries besides their own.

Gulf and Western started as a manufacturer of auto parts. Later, it bought a zinc mine, a shoe factory, and even went into the film industry by buying Paramount Studios. It also owns many other totally unrelated corporations.

Recently, the Justice Department has taken the position that any move by one of the 200 largest industrial corporations to acquire another large firm in any industry is also a violation of the antitrust laws. This has yet to be established in court, but you might want to watch for future developments in this area. Some of the major legislation preventing restraint of trade, all of it enforced on the federal level, is discussed later in this chapter.

The Sherman Act Our government was almost 125 years old before it took a hand in making it illegal for a company or group of companies to take over the market supply for a particular product or service. The Sherman Act declared illegal "every contract, combination in the form of a trust or otherwise, or conspiracy, in restraint of trade or commerce among the several states, or with foreign nations. . . ." It further stated that "every person who shall monopolize or attempt to monopolize or combine or conspire with any other person or persons, to monopolize any part of the trade or commerce among the several states, or with foreign nations, shall be deemed guilty [of a crime]. . . ."

In effect the act took restrictions in the common law (unwritten law in England dating back to the Middle Ages) and made them part of the federal law of the United States. The intent of the Sherman Act was to prevent one individual or group of individuals from gaining exclusive control over the supply of any goods or services in the marketplace. By preventing such control, the act protected the citizenry because it helped maintain competition for goods and services, keeping their prices in line with supply and demand.

Think of the consequences of only having one baker of sliced bread for all of California. Such a business could charge almost whatever it pleased for a loaf of bread and if California's consumers wanted sliced bread badly enough they would have to pay the asking price. Under competition, the various bakers in a marketplace must compete on the basis of price, among other factors. If one baker decides to charge a great deal more than the others, the public will not buy this bread and soon the operation will be out of business. However, if all the California bakers got together and collectively decided to raise the price of bread by 50 cents a loaf, then consumers are right back where they would be if there were only one baker in the marketplace. Such an act by the bakers of combining forces to stifle price competition is an example of a restraint of trade.

The purpose of the Sherman Act was to prevent such practices. Notable exceptions to regulation by the act, however, were labor unions and government agencies.

Nevertheless, large businesses were able to avoid the act by forming huge business corporations owned and controlled by a few powerful people and known by the term "trusts." It wasn't until 1913 that two other major pieces of legislation were formulated and enacted as a result of the efforts of the Theodore Roosevelt and Woodrow Wilson administrations.

The Clayton Act Passed in 1914, the Clayton Act attempted to plug some of the loopholes left after the passage of the Sherman Act, as well as strengthen the enforcement powers of the Justice Department. Furthermore, the Clayton Act settled the controversial question whether or not labor unions were subject to antitrust regulation. After this law was passed, labor unions were held to be excluded from the provisions of this and the Sherman acts.

The Clayton Act not only dealt with the size of business as a possible characteristic indicating monopoly, but also with business practices. In effect, it was more specific than the Sherman Act. Some of the major provisions of the Clayton Act are:

1. To prohibit *price discrimination* by making it illegal to charge different prices to different purchasers for the same goods. (Sellers would sometimes charge one buyer much more for the same goods than they would charge another buyer. This was done in an attempt to force a buyer out of business, perhaps because the seller owned a share of a competing firm.)
2. *Tying contracts* were declared illegal. This occurs when the vendor required the buyer of a certain commodity to agree to buy other goods from the same vendor as a condition of the sale of the needed commodity.

Until 1890, the year in which
the Sherman Antitrust Act
became law, trusts
exercised so much control
over the Congress that
political cartoonists satirized
the dangerous extent of
their power.

Library of Congress

3. *Community of interests* were made illegal. This practice arises when a few
   stockholders maintain control of competing corporations and, therefore,
   dominate the boards of directors and coordinate activities of competitors, so as
   to control the market.
4. Also declared illegal were *interlocking directorates*. The same people forming
   a majority of two or more corporations' board of directors and being able to
   harmonize efforts of each corporation for purposes of restraining trade. In this
   situation, corporations who competed in interstate commerce could not have
   the same individual on their board of directors thus eliminating individuals
   manipulating competing firms' operations.

The Federal Trade Commission Act A special federal administrative agency
was established in 1914 to strengthen compliance and enforcement of the antitrust
laws created by the Sherman and Clayton acts. The Federal Trade Commission
Act also gave the government, through the Department of Justice, the right to
initiate actions against those who engage in illegal monopolistic practices. Prior to
this act, such legislation had to be initiated by individuals or businesses.

The Robinson-Patman Act The Robinson-Patman Act, passed in 1936, was
designed to protect the small business from large firms which could sell goods at

unreasonably low prices for periods of time to force it out of business. The act specifically forbids setting low prices for the purpose of destroying competition or eliminating a competitor.

The Great Atlantic and Pacific Tea Company was found guilty of violating this act in 1947. A subsidiary of A&P charged its parent firm (A&P) less than it charged other customers, and the company was found to be in violation of the act. The courts ruled that such a practice unfairly strengthened A&P's position in the market.

The Celler-Kefauver Act In 1950, Congress, in an effort to strengthen the Clayton Act, passed this legislation, also known as the Antimerger Act. It not only stated that the purchase of a competing corporation's stock for control was a violation of antitrust law, but it also made the purchase of the assets of a competing firm a violation. In effect, this legislation stated that all kinds of mergers were prohibited that substantially lessened competition, provided the Federal Trade Commission could prove such a consequence.

Figure 17-3 demonstrates the inroads of the federal legislation on business activity in restraint of trade. Notice how much broader the scope of federal law deterring restraint of trade has become over the years. Human nature being what it is, once a rule or law is effected, there are always some individuals who find a loophole allowing them to do as they please. This is what happened after the

FIGURE 17-3 Increasing scope of government regulation over restraint of trade

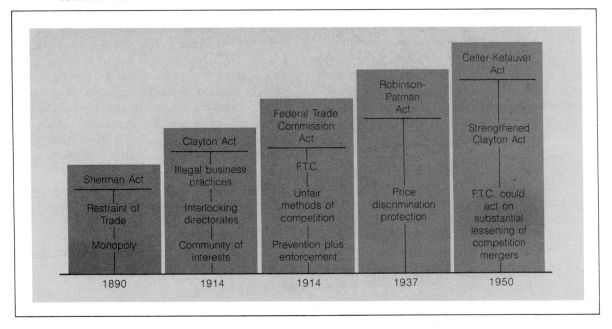

business profile: ENVIRONMENTAL LAWS CAN AID BUSINESSES

Business and government relations took a new turn when the National Environmental Protection Act (NEPA) became law in 1970. The act gave the federal government the major responsibility for determining the standards for a clean environment. Shortly thereafter, the Environmental Protection Agency was formed to enforce the provisions of NEPA. From that date until very recently, business has been on the defensive.

Environmentalists were quick to see that the act could be used to dispute to death any project they opposed. The reason is that NEPA requires an environmental impact statement for any project requiring federal agency approval or participation, such as for a dam or power plant. An impact statement, showing the impact on air, water, and wildlife caused by the project, may take years to develop. Even then it can be challenged in court for several more years. Utility companies, seeking to build a giant coal-fired power plant on the Kaiparowits Plateau in southern Utah, gave up after environmentalists delayed their project for five years while the costs rose from $500 million to $3.76 billion. Environmentalists have won in many other cases, particularly since 25 states also have passed laws similar to NEPA, which are designed to protect air and water quality and wildlife in the states. Throughout all the litigation, big business has been portrayed as the force opposed to the environment, and the environmentalist groups have been depicted as the "good guys."

Now, however, there appears to be a change in business-government relationships in regard to the environment. By 1975 judges began broadening their view of the environment to include more than air, water, and wildlife. The social and economic impact of decisions on projects is beginning to be interpreted as environmental as well. As a result, businesses are beginning to win cases in court in which they show that the social or economic impact of environmental decisions may be more damaging than the impact on nature. For example, the EPA refused to issue a permit for the use of DDT against the tussock moth in the Pacific Northwest, fearing a detrimental effect on other wildlife in the area. The Pacific Legal Foundation, a business-backed law firm, convinced the court that the risks involved in using the insecticide were negligible compared to the environmental damage done by the moth larvae, which destroyed 700-million board feet of timber last year. The case was settled out of court when the agency dropped its opposition and granted a DDT permit.

By showing that the "environment" means the overall social and economic impact on people living in the area, business firms frequently succeed in convincing judges that federal and state environmental laws or EPA decisions are more harmful because they ignore other needs. Even when the firms do not win lawsuits, they are able to use the same tactics of the original environmentalists by asking for an environmental impact statement, which may block or modify a wide range of government regulations that are disliked by business. As a result, businesspeople are finding that federal and state environmental laws need not be the bane of their lives. They are able to work within the law to show that the environmental impact of legislation or projects must consider the effect on jobs, on working conditions, and on other economic and social conditions as well as the impact on wildlife and quality of the air and water.

Sherman Act was passed. Businesspeople found ways around its broad, rather general edicts. The courts decided that such loopholes were legal, showing the need to reinforce the Sherman Act, and thus setting the stage for the Clayton Act. Historically, the same pattern has created the need for more specific and more encompassing legislation over the years. In addition, as the economy and the business sector have changed, the laws have had to be altered or updated to meet new situations.

EXECUTIVE INFLUENCE AND ADMINISTRATIVE LAW

Up to the time of the Great Depression the executive branch of the federal government almost always exercised a hands-off policy with regard to business and the economy. During the administrations of Franklin Roosevelt, this changed as the need for more government intervention and direction became obvious.

Administrative Law　　If you look at Figure 17-2 you will observe a host of federal agencies, almost all of which have a profound effect on the operations of large and small firms in the United States. Many times these agencies set forth administrative decrees to settle disputes or situations that have no precedent for settlement. For example, where there are no court decisions or legislation governing a situation before an administrative body, the agency may choose to pronounce a ruling and require a business to obey it. In such cases, the decision of the agency is called *administrative law* and it becomes binding on the individual or business involved unless an expensive, time-consuming lawsuit overrules the agency's decree.

Influence of the President　　President Calvin Coolidge said "the business of America is business" and proceeded to let affairs take their course. In recent times presidents have been more active in attempting to influence the climate of business in America. President Kennedy, in an effort to stem inflation, challenged a price increase by the steel industry through private ultimatums and public statements. He was successful in his efforts but shook the confidence of the business community. Presidents Johnson, Nixon, Ford, and Carter effectively used the press and the prestige of their office to influence business activities, and they met with a fair degree of success in these efforts. As can be noted from Figure 17-2, the president has many cabinet-level advisors who must be in touch with the business community on a day-to-day basis. Often they function as go-betweens for the president on the one hand, and business firms and associations, labor unions, farm groups, and the like on the other. The president also has a *Council of Economic Advisors*, economists with outstanding qualifications and reputations who advise him on matters of economic significance.

In recent years, presidents have taken increasingly bold action in an effort to direct the economy on what they perceive to be a more favorable course. Sometimes they have succeeded; at other times they have flopped.

Employment Act of 1946 The federal government attempts to regulate the economy so that the nation can enjoy relatively stable prices, low unemployment, and a high level of production. The power to do this was given to the federal government by the Employment Act of 1946. The act stated that as national policy the government was to assist the private sector of the American economy by promoting maximum employment, production, and purchasing power. It also created the Council of Economic Advisors appointed by the president to analyze and interpret economic developments and recommend national economic policy to him. Harry S Truman was the first president to put the provisions of the act into effect.

This legislation merely formalized what had happened under the administration of Franklin Roosevelt. In the midst of a paralyzing depression, President Roosevelt turned to the economic ideas of John Maynard Keynes, who was developing his revolutionary theories in England at that time: government should be willing to increase employment by instituting monetary and fiscal programs.

JUDICIAL INFLUENCE   The courts have always had tremendous impact on business and commerce in our country's 200-year history. If you ask businesspeople, they can probably tell you of at least one instance where it was necessary to go to court to win a point or defend a position. In recent years, IBM has been sued by competitors and the Justice Department. The corporation has a very busy legal department defending it from allegations of restraint of trade, and the court battles will probably continue for years to come. The courts are supposed to serve as the impartial arbitrators of all business disputes, and their interpretations in certain situations can result in settlements worth millions of dollars for or against certain firms. In recent years, consumers and consumer organizations have resorted to court action to obtain product satisfaction. This kind of action, combined with the increase in cases of tax disputes and challenges to the rulings of administrative agencies, have tremendously increased the work load of the courts.

Although court decisions serve as precedents, it should be pointed out that judges are not completely rigid in their interpretations. There is always a certain amount of flexibility in interpreting law, because over a period of time the needs and wants of business and society as a whole change. With the role of our federal government so markedly increased in the last several years, the legal constructions of the courts have gone along more and more favorably with the increased federal influence.

FISCAL AND MONETARY INFLUENCE ON THE ECONOMY   The federal government has two major sets of tools that it uses to regulate the economy. These are generally called fiscal policy and monetary policy. Each type of policy has particular mechanisms that are used to accomplish its purpose. *Fiscal policy* deals with the use of the federal Treasury through the federal budget and tax collections to regulate the economy. *Monetary policy* is concerned with regulating the supply of money and credit outstanding. Most economists define the *money supply* as currency plus demand deposits (balances in checking accounts) outstanding in the economy. The nation's supply of money and credit is regulated by the Federal Reserve System.

Fiscal Policy   John Maynard Keynes, the influential economic thinker, mentioned previously, devised a theory of economics that held that government could stimulate greater economic activity when necessary by spending more money than it takes in. Such a procedure is known as deficit spending and means that government through the Treasury must borrow the money that it spends over and above its receipts from tax collections and other sources. The federal government borrows money by selling treasury notes, bonds, and bills to individuals, corporations, and fiduciary institutions. The *Keynesian theory* also states that if the economy is fully expanded, meaning there are no more goods and services available to meet demand, the government should spend less money than it takes in. In this way demand will diminish and the economy will cool off a bit. Why would anyone want to diminish an economy operating at full capacity? The reason is that full capacity gives a constant rise in the prices of goods and services, leading to serious inflation.

Since the days of Franklin Roosevelt's administration, economic administrators in Washington have utilized the Keynesian theory of economics in an effort to expand or contract economic activity. In some cases it has worked out as theorized; at other times it has not. Nevertheless the federal budget, to some degree, is planned with the concepts of Keynes in mind. (In recent years many experts in the field have become disillusioned with Keynesian theories because many of his concepts have not worked as well as expected.)

Another fiscal tool of the federal government for stimulating a lagging economy or cooling an overheated one is federal tax policy. As can be observed from Figure 17-4, most of the revenues of our federal government are derived from individual and corporate income taxes. Therefore, if the administration wants to stimulate economic activity it might lower income tax rates. Individuals and corporations will probably spend the balance, thereby increasing demand.

If the economy is running at full capacity and the administration chooses to cool it down, one way of doing so would be to increase income taxes. With fewer dollars in their pockets, individuals and corporations have less to spend, demand for products and services dwindles, and the economy cools down. The ways in which budgeting and tax policy influence economic growth or contraction can be summarized as:

	Inputs	Budget Spending	Income Tax Collections
TABLE 17-1	To increase economic growth	+	−
	To cool economic growth	−	+

FIGURE 17-4 Budget
receipts from 1967 to 1977.
Source: *United States
Budget in Brief*, 1977

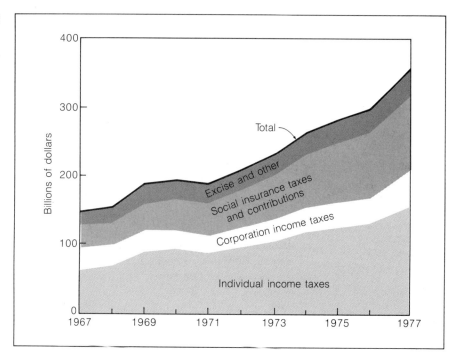

President Kennedy was the first to use tax policy effectively for increasing economic activity after the recession in the early sixties. Presidents Johnson through Carter also subscribed to this policy; so both budget and tax policy changes have deep political significance, and frequently the political considerations carry more weight than the economic ones.

Monetary Policy   The Federal Reserve System and its board of governors are the principal directors of monetary policy for stimulating or contracting economic activity in the United States. The members of the board of governors are appointed by the president and approved by the Senate. However, their terms run for 14 years and they cannot be replaced by a new administration, or a president that they have displeased, before that time. Therefore, the board has a great deal of independence in deciding what monetary courses of action to pursue. This is not to say that they do not wish to cooperate with the administration in power, but there are times when they disagree on the course or degree of action to be chosen. In such cases they are free to go their own way in initiating monetary policy. Figure 17-5 illustrates, in simplified terms, how the Federal Reserve Board works.

The fact that the Federal Reserve System is independent of the Treasury Department, which of course is under the direction of the president, often results in a lack of coordination of fiscal and monetary policy. As an example, sometimes the Federal Reserve System is concerned about inflation and makes borrowing more

The Federal Reserve System and its board of governors are the principal directors in setting monetary policy to stimulate or restrict nationwide economic activity.

Federal Reserve Bank of Cleveland

expensive by raising the interest rate. At this same time, a president who must seek reelection may want to keep unemployment low, and therefore take action opposite to that of the Federal Reserve. The Federal Reserve is more oriented to economic activity, while the president is usually politically sensitive.

The Federal Reserve uses a variety of instruments to regulate the supply of money and credit in the economy. These instruments are more difficult to understand than the tools of fiscal policy and are beyond the scope of this book. If you are interested, however, you can read the publication by the Federal Reserve System listed in the selected readings at the end of this chapter.

In addition to these methods of controlling the availability of money and credit in the economy, the Federal Reserve has the weapon of moral suasion on its side. Moral suasion is simply the ability to influence public opinion through press releases, talks before bankers and businesspeople, literature issued to businesses and the public, and other similar actions. If the Federal Reserve believes there is too much money and credit in the economy driving it to full capacity, it will vent this opinion to the banking and business communities. If that doesn't help, it will also bring one or more of its other methods into play.

GOVERNMENT TAXES AND BUSINESS

Government has become a very expensive operation in our society. The federal government currently operates on a budget far in excess of $400 billion, a budget climbing to where it soon will be many billions more. Several years ago, the Nixon administration formulated, and obtained congressional approval of, a tax-sharing plan. This plan, called *revenue sharing*, called for some of the taxes collected by the federal government to be turned over to the state governments as a supplement to the latter's budgets. Obviously, such a plan implies that Uncle Sam has done very well in collecting taxes over the years.

The major federal tax on businesses is the corporate income tax, which accounts for about 13 cents of every tax dollar collected by the Treasury. Those

FIGURE 17-5 The Federal Reserve and its monetary tools. Source: Federal Reserve Bank of New York

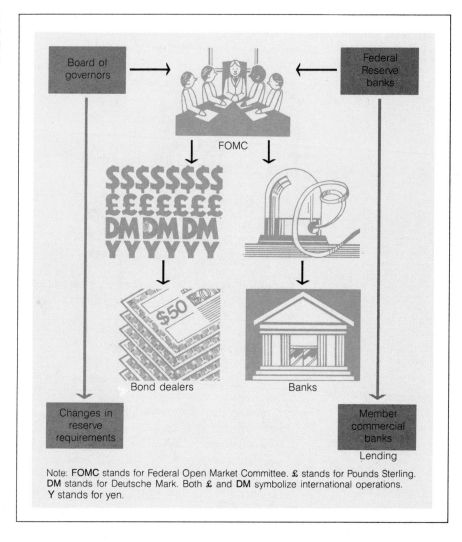

Note: **FOMC** stands for Federal Open Market Committee. **£** stands for Pounds Sterling. **DM** stands for Deutsche Mark. Both **£** and **DM** symbolize international operations. **Y** stands for yen.

businesspeople who are not operating in a corporate form of organization pay taxes on their profits by filing an ordinary 1040 tax return just as an individual wage earner would. Businesspeople also contribute toward each of their employees' social security tax as well as paying a federal and state levy for unemployment. Federal excise taxes, which are really sales taxes on certain items, are paid by the businessperson but passed on to the consumer as part of the cost of the item sold.

Businesses also pay state and sometimes city income taxes as well. Often they must pay highway use taxes or fees for various licenses. State and local governments also exact large real estate and property taxes from businesses.

personality profile:
**JUANITA KREPS —
first woman Secretary of
Commerce**

When Juanita Kreps was appointed the 25th Secretary of Commerce in December, 1976, she had had 30 years of experience in the academic world as a teacher and administrator. She had also served on numerous governmental advisory committees and on the boards of directors of the New York Stock Exchange and a number of major corporations.

Born and raised in the coal-mining community of Lynch, Kentucky, she developed a keen interest in economics during the Depression years and earned a Ph.D. in economics at Duke University in 1948. During her academic career at Duke as professor of economics, dean, and eventually university vice president, she specialized in labor force demographics and working women and wrote or coauthored a number of books: *Sex in the Marketplace; American Women at Work; Lifetime Allocation of Work and Income; Sex, Age, and Work; Changing Composition of the Labor Force; Contemporary Labor Economics;* and *Principles of Economics.*

Naturally enough, her labor background has encouraged Secretary Kreps to see business problems in human terms. She has attempted to expand the role of the Commerce Department beyond mere boosterism to "encourage business to perform well all tasks that improve human welfare." She doesn't promise pie in the sky, however, but recognizes, for instance, that the way the economy is structured today, not even a business boom will of itself reduce unemployment in the United States to the much-heralded but rarely attained 4 to 5 percent level of the total work force.

Annually, Americans submit themselves to the rigors of making out their federal income tax return. Even the IRS lends a hand.

United Press International

Many of the large corporations maintain entire departments of trained personnel who spend all of their time 12 months a year filing federal, state, and local tax returns. Most states require special income tax returns from corporations doing any business at all within their borders. The Ralston Purina Corporation, for example, claims to file more than 3,000 tax reports every year with the federal government as well as with various foreign, state, and local governments.

Taxes are a tremendous burden for individuals as well as businesses, but they are important for a variety of reasons. They are the way the government raises most of its revenue, the means by which society pays for the tasks it wants the government to do, one of the costs of doing business, a redistribution of income, and a method of regulating various segments of society.

There is today a great hue and cry for tax reform, probably stronger than it has been for some time. Many people feel that the rich and the corporations are not paying their fair share and that the average worker is being taxed too heavily. Almost everyone wants a better tax system.

GOVERNMENT AS CONSUMER

Since 1973, budgets for the state of New York have exceeded the total budget of the federal government of 50 years ago. It is obvious that government on all levels has become an avid consumer. Of course, government has always been a major purchaser of fire trucks, post offices, military uniforms, and the like. However, as in all other areas within its scope of influence, in the past 40 years government has become a major consumer. Atomic energy for peacetime use is just one dramatic example. In the case of atomic power plants, only the federal government can own the nuclear core of the plant, even though the rest of the plant's facilities belong to the public utility firm involved. As the core's owner, therefore, the government is the major purchaser of radium and components necessary in nuclear core construction. Another striking instance of the government as a powerful consumer is in the amount of its spending on various space explorations. Not only were steel, plastics, wire, electrical components, and other similar products purchased for these projects, but pharmaceuticals, dehydrated foods, special clothing, and many, many more items were supplied by large and small businesses.

On a smaller scale, city and county governments have moved into providing more new services than were ever thought of 50 years ago. Perhaps, your city or town has tennis courts, swimming pools, and other free or low-cost recreational facilities. Taking labor as a purchasable item, imagine all the attendants, instructors, maintenance workers, and the like that are needed to operate these facilities. Also remember that government is constantly buying supplies and equipment to keep up these facilities.

In one of his last speeches as president of the United States, Dwight Eisenhower warned of the growing threat of the *military-industrial complex.* Eisenhower believed, and many agreed, that too much of our nation's wealth was being pumped into military spending and that a special closeness between the military and big business was mutually cultivated. The military gained because it had more of the weapons and personnel that it believed it needed; business gained because it had more contracts and made more profits. Therefore, when we think of the federal government as a consumer, we usually think of the vast sums spent on military items and foreign aid. Although paying for military equipment and personnel is still a major part of the federal budget, Uncle Sam has expanded his spending into many other areas.

Figure 17-6 shows that 55 cents of every dollar spent by our federal government goes toward improving our human resources. Such programs as education, medical research, welfare, and various social and scientific projects all benefit from substantial federal outlays. Note that only 26 cents of each dollar is now allocated toward defense spending. If you were to compare this pie diagram to one of, say, 1965 (at the height of the Vietnam War), you would see that defense spending then would account for a much greater proportion.

In all areas, the federal government has become a huge enterprise. Congress alone employs about 38,000 people as staff members for congressional offices and related agencies, such as the General Accounting Office, the Government Printing Office, the Congressional Budget Office, and the Library of Congress.

The executive branch of government, which is responsible to the president, employs over 2.7 million workers. This includes those who serve in all cabinet departments, special agencies, the Postal Service, and the Federal Reserve System. The judicial branch of the federal government employs about 12,200 judges and supporting staff.

Truly, we are living in the age of big government as well as big business. Also keep in mind that state and local governments employ many hundreds of thousands of workers not included in the above figures.

GOVERNMENT AS COMPETITOR

Few people think of the United States Post Office as an on-going business; nevertheless, the post office was recently reorganized to operate in a more busi-

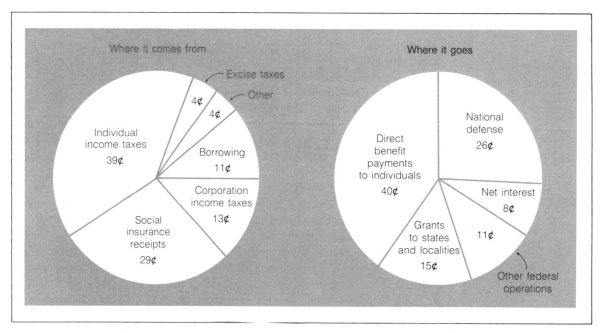

FIGURE 17-6 The budget dollar for 1977 (estimate). Source: *United States Budget in Brief,* 1977

nesslike way. To some extent postal service does compete with private businesses such as package delivery services, the telephone companies, and telegraph services, although the services of the private businesses are usually much more expensive. The post office also sells money orders and this, in a very small way, competes with the same service provided by banks, savings and loans associations, and other financial agencies.

Other examples of federal ownership can be cited as competitors of private business, and the list has been growing in recent years. Amtrak is the familiar name for the National Railroad Passenger Corporation that now runs the railroad passenger service in the United States through contractual arrangements with private railroads. Most of us would agree that private rail passenger service needed help to survive and that Amtrak may be the answer. However, the airlines and long-distance bus companies will eventually feel the competition when and if Amtrak becomes successful. Many times an immediate, recognized need brings the federal government into an ownership role, and the consequences of competing with business do not become apparent until a later date.

For years the federal government has competed with private insurance companies by providing very low-cost insurance for veterans, government employees, and the like. For years the federal government has competed with private producers of electricity through its massive Tennessee Valley Authority (TVA) project in the Tennessee River basin. In both these instances the institutions established by the federal government were filling needs that private enterprise had not been able to meet. Federal life insurance was provided for American soldiers whose lives were too uncertain for private companies to insure. And inexpensive life insurance minimized employee turnover in the days when federal salaries were considerably lower than what industry offered for comparable work. Because private enterprise failed to supply adequate power to the region, TVA came into being during the presidency of Franklin Roosevelt. Today it is a very large producer of hydroelectric power.

In another sense the federal government has become a keen competitor. Businesspeople compete with each other to find the best possible employees for the fairest wage they can afford to pay. Such federal agencies as the Internal Revenue Service and the Department of Defense, to name just two, have become very aggressive recruiters of top-notch personnel in the last decade. Perhaps a few of you can remember when working for a government agency didn't pay much but did offer job security. Today the situation is much different; working for Uncle Sam pays very well, offers many fringe benefits, and still provides the security that it did in the past. Obviously businesses, especially the smaller ones, are hard pressed to compete with the recruiting techniques and resources of the federal government.

There is also growing competition between business and government on the state and local level. Some states operate liquor stores for regulatory purposes. In many states private authorities have been instituted for specific purposes such as building and operating highways. Often these authorities branch out and compete with private enterprise by building and operating entertainment facilities and restaurants along the roadway. Many municipalities operate their own water and gas distribution systems in direct competition with private utility suppliers.

One of the major questions for Americans to decide in the future is how much more ownership and competition do we want our governments on the various levels to get into? Do we want broad government health care insurance for all citizens rather than just Medicare for the aged? Do we want government ownership of the railroads? Do we want government ownership of telephone and telegraph services? These and many other questions will arise again and again in the future, and public pressure will ultimately decide them.

GOVERNMENT AS SUBSIDIZER

Funk and Wagnall's *Standard College Dictionary* defines a subsidy as "pecuniary aid directly granted by government to an individual or private commercial enterprise deemed beneficial to the public." In a broader sense, however, we might think of a subsidy to business from the government as a much more subtle device. For example, a particular community wanting to attract a large firm might grant that firm a designated amount of tax forgiveness for a certain number of years. In other words, it might lessen the tax burden on that company's proposed properties or, in a sense, subsidize its entry into that community. This forgiveness could last for perhaps 10 years, maybe even 99 years, depending on how much the community wants the firm. Remember new firms in an area generate employment, housing demands, and other spending for government and business services.

Price supports for farmers are one of the many subsidy programs run by the federal government.

Harold M. Lambert

An even more subtle example of a subsidy by our federal government is the protection it affords to inventors of new products and creators of new works of art. If one invents a new product, the inventor may apply for a patent from the Patent Office. If granted, the patent allows no other firm to duplicate the product for 17 years. After this time, however, any firm may duplicate the process. In this way, the federal government encourages businesses to innovate and subsidizes this innovation by protecting the firm's right to be the only supplier of its new invention for its first 17 years of life. The same type of subsidy applies to a written work, a print, a piece of music. A new copyright law passed by Congress and signed by President Ford in 1976 protects an author for his or her lifetime and 50 years beyond. It also extended all copyrights in existence at the time the new law was enacted for a period of 75 years. Once a copyright is granted, no one may use the author's copyrighted material for economic gain or mass distribution without the permission of the author.

Specific industries have enjoyed federal subsidies for a number of years. Reductions in federal income taxes are available to those firms engaged in drilling for oil or mining operations to encourage continued exploration and development of the nation's natural resources. American farmers have received federal subsidies for many years. These include commodity price supports, measures to curb the production of surplus crops, programs promoting soil conservation, research and technical assistance on farming problems as well as schemes granting credit to the farmers. Some contend that our recent food and grain shortages can be traced back to an overly vigorous program of surplus control by the Department of Agriculture. It is probably too soon to know the validity of such charges.

One of the special tasks essential to a firm's success is to know what subsidies are available for which it might qualify. After this, management must develop the know-how to obtain the needed assistance. This often requires filing complicated applications, attending hearings, and adhering to legal restrictions and obligations.

Most people are aware that the trend in American business over the past 75 years has been toward bigness. More and more of the smaller firms have grown larger or have become part of a larger firm. To help preserve the competitive position of the smaller business in the marketplace, the federal government subsidizes small businesses both with money and information. During President Eisenhower's term of office, the Small Business Administration (SBA) was founded. One of the major functions of this branch of the Department of Commerce is to lend small businesses money at generally lower rates of interest than might be available through ordinary sources. For details on the organization and functions of the Small Business Administration refer to Chapter 6, "Operating Small Businesses and Franchises."

SUMMARY

In every respect the four "hats" of government have increased in size tremendously from the day you were born to the present time. Has government intervention been a plus factor for the nation? The answer must be a resounding "plus" if we use our increased standard of living and social well-being as a measure. The growth of business profits, the growth of personal income, the growth of individual and business assets have all been concurrent with the growth of government influence.

Although some say we still have a long road to travel, it has been through government intervention and coercion that the poor and minorities have come to enjoy a more generous share in the harvest of American economic growth. Opportunities for women and minorities in business have opened up because government has paved the way and not because of individual initiative on the part of people in firms. If it weren't for government pressures, it would still be 1954 for minorities and 1933 for the poor. If it weren't for government spending and taxes, the phenomenal growth of the American economy would only have been an unrealized possibility.

Is it time for a change? Perhaps government has gone one step too far, particularly in the area of taxing and spending. Government is a great culprit in the vicious inflation draining our economic strength. It tells people not to spend so prices will stabilize, yet it spends more and more each year, forcing prices even higher. Government officials talk about the evils of rising prices, yet do nothing but talk, while the huge profits of petroleum companies and other firms spiral upward at an alarming rate.

Government agencies compete unfairly with private business. They use public funds to provide services that put private firms out of business.

SUMMARY OF KEY TERMS

Administrative Law   Decisions from governmental agencies, with no specific legislative approval or judicial precedent, that become binding on businesses or individuals unless challenged and overruled in court.

Community of Interest   A few stockholders maintaining control of competing corporations and, therefore, dominating the boards of directors of these companies and controlling the market.

Copyright   Recognition by the federal government of the right of ownership to some written work.

Council of Economic Advisors   Economists with outstanding qualifications and reputations who advise the president on matters of economic significance.

Fiscal Policy   Manipulation by the Treasury Department of the federal budget and tax collections to influence the economy.

Government   The federal government and its many departments and agencies, as well as all state and local governments.

Interlocking Directorate   The same people who form a majority of the board of directors of two or more corporations and who direct the policy of each corporation for purposes of restraint of trade.

Keynesian Theory   Concept devised by economist John Maynard Keynes that government should be involved in increasing employment by monetary and fiscal methods at its disposal.

Military-industrial Complex   Threat that too much of the country's wealth would be spent on military programs.

Monetary Policy   Regulating the supply of money and credit outstanding to influence the economy.

Money Supply   Cash and demand deposits (balances in checking accounts) outstanding in the economy.

Monopoly   The takeover of a market for a particular product or service by one supplier.

Patent   A grant by the federal government of an exclusive right to some invention.

Price Discrimination   A supplier's charging different prices to different purchasers for the same products.

Restraint of Trade   Illegal takeover of the market for a particular product or service by one supplier.

Revenue Sharing   Turning over some federal tax revenues as supplements to the budgets of the states.

Trusts   A combination of businesses controlled by one major firm and its board of directors.

Tying Contracts   An agreement stating that the vendor requires the buyer of a certain commodity to agree to buy other products from the same vendor as a condition of the sale.

REVIEW QUESTIONS

1. Explain the following terms.
   a. Interlocking directorates
   b. Price discrimination
   c. Moral suasion
   d. Income tax
   e. Deficit spending
   f. Discount rate

2. Identify each of the major roles that the federal government fulfills.

3. List the major features of the Clayton Act of 1914.

4. Why did Congress pass the Celler-Kefauver Act of 1950?

5. How does the Federal Trade Commission assist in antitrust enforcement?
6. What are the two most important tools used by the federal government to help regulate the economy?
7. Describe the makeup of the Federal Reserve Board of Governors.
8. What is revenue sharing? How does it operate?
9. Describe the makeup and functions of the Executive Branch of the government.
10. What are patents and copyrights? How do they offer protection to inventors and artists?

DISCUSSION QUESTIONS

1. Assume you were in a decision-making capacity in the U.S. Department of Energy. Would you recommend increased or decreased participation by the government in the regulation of energy usage? Cite several examples of how you would increase or decrease government's role.
2. If you were a member of the Federal Reserve Board of Governors and the economy had a large percentage of unemployed people, huge inventories held by business, and lack of demand for products and services, what fiscal and monetary policies would you suggest for getting the nation started on solving the problem?
3. Scan your local newspapers and find an article citing a current event involving government and business. It can be specifically between one government agency and one business firm or between the government and an industry as a whole. Clip the article and briefly summarize it in writing.
4. List the advantages and disadvantages of having the federal government compete with big business.
5. Should government increase its role as a regulator of business activity? If so, in what specific areas?

CASES FOR DECISION MAKING

BITTER SWEET![1]

In May 1977, the U.S. District Court in Brooklyn, New York, found four Northeastern refined sugar manufacturers guilty of a conspiracy to fix prices of cane sugar sold for industrial purposes. The companies involved were PepsiCo, SuCrest Corp., RSN Projects, Inc., and CPC International, Inc. Each of the companies was given the maximum fine for such an offense, $50,000. A federal grand jury indicted

the companies in March 1977, and the case dates back to an incident in August 1972, when Amstar Corporation, the country's largest refiner of sugar, announced a new pricing policy. The indictment alleged that the four Northeastern refiners got together and discussed Amstar's new policy and agreed to mutually start similar policies.

1. Do you recognize the names of any of the indicted companies? If so, can you name any of the types of products that they manufacture?

1. *Wall Street Journal*, May 20, 1977, p. 2.

2. From the time of the incident through the completion of the case took how many years? Is such a lengthy period fair to the indicted firms? Is it fair to the public?

3. Do you think the fine imposed on each company was fair?

4. Can you cite some harmful effects of price fixing to the consumer and society?

ANOTHER FISHY STORY[2]

People in Suffolk County, New York, a fishing area on Long Island, are alarmed at a recent move by the Food and Drug Administration. This agency has proposed that PCB (polychlorinated biphenols) pollutants in fish standards be raised from the present standard of five parts per million to two parts per million. Tests indicate that most fish (mainly bluefish and striped bass) taken from the waters off Suffolk County contain an average of 2.57 to 3.89 parts per million. Therefore, the county is afraid the new standards would ruin its fishing industry. They further maintain that since Suffolk County accounts for 80 percent of the commercial catches in the state of New York the consumer would suffer as a result of this change in standards for PCB pollutants.

1. What would be the consequences for consumers if the PCB level is lowered?

2. What suggestion would you make for helping to solve the problem?

IN THE WORKS

Wagner Works, Inc., is one of only three manufacturers of homework machines in the United States. It accounts for about 20 percent of the domestic market. The two other firms in the industry are Zero Corp. and Homework Unlimited, which supply 30 and 20 percent of the market respectively. The remainder of homework machines sold in the United States come from Japan and West Germany, and represents 30 percent of the market. Each year the foreign manufacturers have increased their share of the U.S. market slightly. Wagner Works and Homework Unlimited have been holding merger talks for some time, and they propose to reorganize under the Wagner Works name and trademark. Each of these companies makes a similar machine, and they believe that by joining together they can lessen costs and sell the same basic machine to the public at a cheaper price. You have been asked to study the proposed merger in light of the various laws regarding restraint of trade.

1. Do you believe the proposed merger might be in violation of any such law?

2. If so, what law or laws and what section or sections of the law(s)?

3. In view of your findings, suggest whether the merger should continue, stop, or be modified?

4. What defense might Wagner Works make to support a proposed merger?

RELATED READINGS

"Arming for the 21st Century." *Time*, May 23, 1977, pp. 14–23.

An extensive article on the cost of maintaining and updating military facilities.

Federal Reserve System. *The Federal Reserve System, Purposes and Functions.* Washington, D.C.: Board of Governors of the Federal Reserve System, 1963.

Describes the way the Federal Reserve System operates. Clearly written and very easy for the novice to understand.

2. *New York Times*, May 22, 1977, p. 34.

"How Government Works." *U.S. News & World Report*, May 9, 1977, pp. 44–66.

A comprehensive review of the structure of the U.S. government. Includes descriptions of the executive, judicial, and legislative branches.

"How to Halt Excessive Government Regulation." *Nation's Business*, March 1976, pp. 20–24.

Talks about the problems of management in relationship to government. Attitudes, communication, ethics, are highlighted in this excellent overview article.

Martin, M. A. "Should the Government Rescue Companies?" *Dun's Review*, September 1971, pp. 43–44.

A discussion of whether or not the federal government should come to the aid of financially troubled firms.

"A Report Card on the Supreme Court." *U.S. News & World Report*, March 7, 1977, pp. 60–64.

Interesting and informative article on the performance of the Supreme Court. Article is based on a survey of 508 replies from federal and state judges as well as from distinguished lawyers.

Rosen, Gerald R. "The State Takes on the Public Interest." *Dun's Review*, April 1977, pp. 48–50, 113.

Business people in California feel that they are being harassed by public interest groups such as the Sierra Club. They are striking back against such groups with lawsuits.

"The Voice of Business Grows Stronger in Washington." *Nation's Business*, March 1977, pp. 20–36.

A very complete article highlighting the activities of the United States Chamber of Commerce in its role as communicator for business. The article cites some of the gains the organization has scored for business.

Wagner, Susan. *The Federal Trade Commission.* New York: Praeger, 1971.

Traces the history of the Federal Trade Commission and discusses and describes its organization and effectiveness.

chapter 18

INTERNATIONAL BUSINESS

OBJECTIVES

When you have finished reading and studying this chapter, you should be able to:

1. Contrast the effects of world trade on business, consumers, workers, and the federal government.

2. Explain what is included in the balance of trade and balance of payments and indicate why a favorable balance in both is important to this country.

3. Identify and explain the economic and political forces affecting international business.

4. List our major trading partners and describe the trade relations that we have established with each.

5. Identify a multinational corporation and explain the effects of multinational firms on world trade.

6. Describe the organizational patterns used by American firms in selling in foreign markets.

CHAPTER PREVIEW

When you think of the products you use every day that came from foreign countries, it can stagger your imagination. The coffee you drank this morning came from Brazil, the sugar from Central America, the shoes you have on may have been made in Italy, and you may drive a Japanese Toyota or a German Volkswagen. You may drink tea processed by Nestlé, a Swiss company, or shave with a Norelco razor, made by a Dutch company. The possibilities are endless.

The point is that international trade is important to us as consumers, workers, and citizens. The more efficiently American businesses compete with their counterparts from other countries, the more jobs are created here. If this country sells more products and services abroad than it buys there, we have a favorable balance of trade. This is a measure of our businesses' success in competing for markets here and abroad, since they originate nearly all our exports. Many factors have a bearing on how successful businesses can be in world markets. Wage and inflation rates in this country compared with those in other countries have an impact, as do taxes on imported products and limits on the number of products sent into our country and other countries.

While our businesses trade in almost every country, our main trading partners are Canada, Western Europe, and Japan. This is chiefly because they are advanced industrial economies such as ours. They have the means to pay for our products and the technical expertise to make the products we need. Although other countries would like to buy more from us, they lack the funds to do so.

Selling in foreign markets is not like selling in the United States. Foreign countries have different cultural and social patterns. Even within a country, tastes and values are varied. As a result, American businesses have had to change many of their ideas about doing business. New organizational patterns have also had to be developed to make the most effective use of management and workers in foreign countries.

Finally, we need to look at the role of the multinational corporation in international business. There is a good deal of concern about these large firms. Most governments in the world keep a close eye on the multinational companies in their countries. At the same time, the multinational firm is welcomed into most countries because of the capital, technology, and management expertise that it brings.

"Remember when 'Made in Japan' meant shoddy goods?"

INTERNATIONAL BUSINESS

At first glance, international trade would not seem to be of major importance to the United States. We sell only about 6 percent of our total output abroad, as compared with 25 to 30 percent for most other industrialized countries. International trade is important to us, however, for many reasons. It has a dramatic effect on business, consumers, workers, and the government. Let us take a closer look at some of the ways our commerce with other nations affects our lives.

EFFECTS OF INTERNATIONAL TRADE

International trade affects almost every business in this country. Most very large firms produce and sell merchandise for overseas buyers.

EFFECTS ON BUSINESS

Products and services sold to other countries are called *exports*. Almost all of America's 50 largest industrial corporations have plants in foreign countries, while even our smaller firms are now selling more abroad. Many retail stores and wholesalers sell some products that are made overseas, and manufacturers very frequently use parts, raw materials, or supplies that were bought from foreign firms. Products and services bought from other countries are called *imports*. Almost all the platinum, nickel, magnesium, and bauxite we use are mined abroad. About 45 percent of our oil comes from other countries, as was made painfully clear during the 1974 oil embargo. Some manufacturers buy all or most of their parts abroad and assemble them in this country, and most of them face some competition from products made by foreign firms.

A number of large American firms depend on foreign markets for a substantial percentage of their sales and profits. As a matter of fact, about a third of our agricultural products go to other countries as well as a third of our mining construction equipment and tractors. In addition, about a fourth of our electrical equipment, machine tools, computers, and planes normally reach foreign markets. For some firms, over half of sales and/or profits come from overseas customers. Table 18-1 shows the percentage of their total sales which are earned abroad by some large firms.

EFFECTS ON CONSUMERS

Consumers are affected by international trade in two ways. First, they are able to buy a greater variety of merchandise than if we had no foreign trade. There are a number of consumer products that cannot be made in this country or can be

TABLE 18-1 Percent of sales abroad

Massey-Ferguson	90%
Exxon	68%
Colgate-Palmolive	55%
Singer	50%
ITT	50%
H. J. Heinz	47%
National Cash Register	44%

Sales of foreign-made cars account for 20 percent of the auto sales in the United States. In recent years, the prices of these cars have increased in view of the falling value of the dollar.

Auto-Expo

made only at very great cost. As an example, all pimientos, vanilla, and coffee as well as 90 percent of all wigs, umbrellas, radios, and portable tape recorders come from other countries.

International trade benefits consumers in another way. It provides an additional source of competition for American firms. It was said earlier that adequate competition is needed if the consumer is to get the best product at the lowest price. Foreign auto manufacturers were much more responsive to the American consumer's demands for a high quality, low-priced small car than were the Detroit manufacturers. Radial tires, which are safer and increase gas mileage, were pioneered in France. Particularly in industries in which a few large firms dominate the market, such as auto, steel, rubber, and aluminum, foreign products provide the consumer with desirable alternatives.

EFFECTS ON WORKERS   Workers are affected by international trade because their jobs are affected. Sales of American-made products abroad create jobs for American workers. According to the Department of Commerce, over 3 million American workers owe their jobs to foreign sales. The Department of Commerce estimates that one new job is created for each $15,000 of foreign sales by an American manufacturer. When products made overseas and sold here replace domestic goods, the number of jobs may be reduced in this country. This is a complex subject and will be explored fully later in the chapter when multinational firms are discussed.

EFFECTS ON GOVERNMENT

International trade also affects the federal government. In addition to negotiating constantly with other governments concerning trade regulations and taxes on trade, the government must provide support services to American business firms. These are available through the Bureau of International Commerce of the Department of Commerce, which has offices in major American cities. Our foreign commerce also draws on the services of commercial and economic officers in American embassies and consulates in foreign countries. Great masses of marketing and economic data are made available to American corporations about doing business in every country in the world. International trade is also important to the government because payment for products by some countries helps provide the money for government economic and military aid to underdeveloped countries.

BALANCE OF TRADE

Almost all American products and services sent abroad are sold by business firms, but foreign products and services are bought by business, government, and consumers. The difference between the money Americans pay for imports and the money foreigners pay for American exports is called *balance of trade*. A *favorable balance of trade* means that the United States sold more products and services abroad than it bought from foreign countries. An *unfavorable balance of trade* indicates that more was bought from foreign countries than sold to them.

RECENT TRENDS

All countries want to have a favorable balance of trade. This means that there will be more money flowing into a country than flowing out. It also indicates that the businesses of the fortunate country are efficient in comparison with those of other nations. We must keep in mind, however, that other forces besides efficiency of business are involved in a nation's trade balance. These will be explored later in this chapter.

The United States, which had a favorable balance of trade every year from 1888 to 1971, experienced its first *unfavorable* balance in 1971. Figure 18-1 shows the unfavorable balance of $25 billion in 1977. After favorable trade balances all those years, why did things change in the early 1970s? Part of the reason, of course, is that many foreign firms simply became more efficient. In such basic industries as steel, shipbuilding, textiles, cameras, as well as in some areas of electronics, automobiles, and small household appliances, foreign firms outperformed their American competition. In part this was caused by lower unit labor costs, but just as important was the greater speed with which foreign firms applied new technology in some of these areas. In many cases, overseas companies have newer plants and equipment. Ironically, West Germany and Japan, our World War II enemies, had to build new plants since many of the older ones were destroyed during that war. In some American industries, such as steel and textiles, pre-World War II plants are still being used.

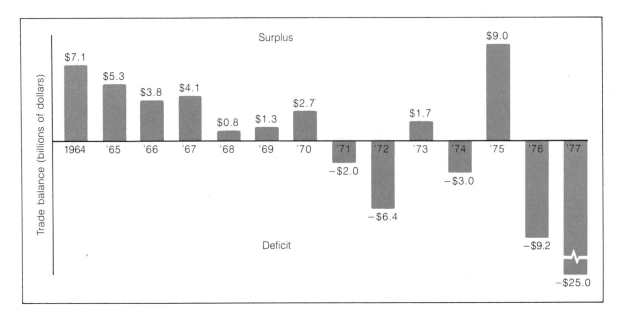

FIGURE 18-1 U.S. balance of trade

Until recently, taxes on imports were higher in the United States than in other industrialized countries. At present, as shown in Table 18-2, taxes on imports into the United States are still higher than those in some European countries, but lower than in Japan. On the other hand, in Japan especially, but also in Europe, the governments tends to help business more than in the United States. There are government subsidies for research and development in most advanced industrialized countries. In addition, the government permits large corporations to work together on developing new products, a practice outlawed in the United States. In addition, there are far more governmental regulations required for introducing foreign products into Japan than is the case in the United States.

Compounding the balance of trade problem has been the threefold increase in oil prices on world markets since 1971. Because the United States imports about 45 percent of its oil, the cost of these imports has risen sharply. In 1977, for example, the United States had a record unfavorable balance of trade which was partially caused by the $40 billion spent for oil imports.

TABLE 18-2 Tariff rates on goods coming into the United States, Japan, and European countries (in percentages)

Country	Type of Goods Imported		
	Industrial Supplies	Semifinished Products	Manufactured Products
United States	2.5	5.6	8.8
Japan	3.4	6.3	12.7
European countries	0.4	4.8	8.2

Source: Ministry of International Trade and Industry.

ECONOMIC AND POLITICAL FORCES AFFECTING TRADE

There are a number of forces that tend to stimulate or dampen trade between countries. These can be categorized as *economic* or *political*.

ECONOMIC FORCES

In considering the economic forces of international trade, it is important to examine the relative strengths and weaknesses of each country's economy.

DOMESTIC AND INTERNATIONAL ECONOMY

The level of economic activity in a country has an effect on its ability to buy and sell in world markets. If the economy is operating at a high level of capacity, incomes will be high so that consumers will probably buy foreign products. If there is a recession, however, consumers will not have much extra money and will buy few foreign products. The United States, for example, had a strongly favorable balance of trade in the recession year of 1975, but an unfavorable balance of trade in 1977 when its level of economic activity was far higher than in other industrialized countries. Another example of the link between domestic and foreign economies is the effect of a country's rate of inflation on its ability to compete in world markets. Sometimes the United States' inflation rate is higher than that in other advanced industrialized countries, indicating that the costs of operating business firms are rising faster here than abroad. Their resulting higher prices make their products less competitive in world markets.

Absolute Advantage Another economic influence on international trade is the quantity and quality of the factors of production available to businesspeople in producing products for world markets. Businesspeople in the United States are fortunate because they have at hand large amounts of capital, most natural resources, land, both skilled and unskilled labor, and management talent. Consequently, it is possible to produce almost anything efficiently. In other countries, businesspeople are not as fortunate. Japan has very few natural resources, Pakistan very little skilled labor, and Peru lacks capital. Good management personnel and

The U.S. balance of trade has taken an unfavorable course ever since the price of oil was quadrupled in the early seventies.

business profile: AMERICA AS AN INVESTMENT OPPORTUNITY

The image of the ugly American grew up at a time when American companies were investing heavily abroad to expand markets and increase profits. Domestic markets were close to being saturated, and domestic supplies of raw materials were shrinking or becoming expensive. The marketing know-how of American oil companies made them the masters of worldwide oil production. Superior technology gave American computer and chemical firms an edge over foreign producers. And foreign markets had vast pools of cheap labor that meant lower production costs on items manufactured or assembled there.

The tables have not yet entirely turned, but foreign investment is at least becoming a two-way street. Foreigners now have a big stake in this country, and that investment is rising. To the extent that foreign investment provides new facilities, the trend creates new jobs for Americans, even if the owners are Japanese. At least a fraction of the profits, however, are sent abroad. This, plus the very idea of foreign ownership of key industries, seems to create some uneasiness among Americans. Thus far, however, foreign investment has not gone beyond 10 percent of total investment, and it is dwarfed by the still rising tide of American investment abroad.

The overriding reason for foreign investment in our country seems to be faith in the fundamental economic strength of the United States and in its political stability, plus a desire to penetrate the huge U.S. market. It seems to have little to do in the long run with the balance of trade or fluctuations in the worth of the American dollar. However, one exception exists. The influx of foreign investment is influenced to some extent by the huge number of dollars in the hands of foreign nationals. American oil purchases from countries whose domestic investment chances are exceedingly limited have caused a flood of American dollars in these countries.

Another consideration is fear of future U.S. protectionism. If firms enter the U.S. market now, they are guarded against denial of access to the market later by high tariffs or other such measures that are being discussed.

Coldwell Banker & Co., the nationwide real estate broker, reports a strong interest in income-producing properties by Germans, Britons, and Far Easterners who are buying future rents at today's prices. Even farmland is being bought up by Europeans who expect its value to increase.

For the major auto importers, building assembly plants in the United States seems to be the wave of the present. The recent completion of a Volkswagen assembly plant in Pennsylvania is one example. The lower value of the dollar in relation to the German mark and the Japanese yen has meant that prices of autos made in these countries have risen sharply. Assembling cars here is one way of keeping imports' prices competitive with the prices of domestic autos. And staying competitive in the American market is crucial to the large foreign automakers because they sell so much of their product here.

The United States was almost the only source of capital at the end of World War II, when the other industrialized nations were financially exhausted. But now there are other rich countries in the world, the industrialized European countries and the oil-rich Arab countries in particular. There are also wealthy individuals in undeveloped lands who find the United States the best place to stash away some money. For all these reasons, we can look forward, whether we like it or not, to buying German or buying Japanese in the future when we buy "American."

practices exist in only a few countries. When a country has a unique mixture of the factors of production that permits it to produce a product at less cost than other countries, that country is said to have an *absolute advantage*. Saudi Arabia and Libya can produce oil at lower cost than the United States. Taiwan can produce radios and Japan can produce ships less expensively than the United States. On the other hand, the United States can produce soybeans, computers, and airplanes at lower cost than any other country. In all of these cases, a country has an absolute advantage over another country because its costs are lower for producing the item. This is the primary reason that business firms in the country with the advantage tend to put their money into producing those products. They know they will be able to sell them because of the absolute advantage in costs.

Comparative Advantage On the other hand, countries which are fortunate in having large amounts of the factors of production may be able to produce most products and services at lower costs than most other countries. They have to decide, then, in which industries to concentrate their efforts. It is to the advantage of the country for the firms to concentrate their efforts (and capital) in products in which the country has a comparative advantage. Where a country concentrates its production in the areas in which it has the greatest advantage over other countries, it is applying the principle of *comparative advantage*. As an example, the United States could become one of the world's biggest producers of rice, olives, or wood carvings if it chose. However, since we can produce other things even more efficiently, concentrating on rice, olives, or wood carvings would not be a wise use of resources. Our comparative advantage is greater in other products.

POLITICAL FORCES A number of political forces have an effect on international trade. In many cases, these may be more important than economic forces in a business firm's abilities to compete in world markets.

Quotas *Quotas* are limits on the amount or volume of products that can be imported. Quotas are used for both economic and political purposes. They may be used for political purposes when the intent is to discourage imports from a country for political purposes. Many countries in the world, including the United States, used either very strict quotas or a complete boycott of Rhodesian products when that country's racial policies were unacceptable to most countries. The United States has used quotas for economic purposes when it wants to provide protection to specific industries. For example, for many years the United States has limited the number of tons of steel that can be imported. Quotas also have been used for textiles, oil, and meat.

Tariffs A *tariff* is a tax on imports. All countries have a schedule of tariffs, differing for each commodity. In general, if a country wants to encourage the importation of a product, it charges no tariff, or a very low one; if it wants to bar a foreign product, it erects a high tariff. For example, the United States has no tariff on coffee, since we do not produce it and want to encourage its importation. Margarine, on the other hand, is taxed at 15 cents a pound, which protects domestic producers against low-cost imported margarine. Usually, if a country wants to protect a particular industry, it raises the tariffs for competing products from foreign countries. Representatives from most of the noncommunist industrialized countries meet annually to review tariff schedules and procedures. While authority for trade tariffs and regulations is given to Congress, much of it has been delegated to the president. Trade tariffs are mainly regulatory devices, but they also bring in a small amount of revenue—about 2 percent of the federal government's income. As can be seen from Figure 18-2, American tariff barriers have fallen during the past 60 years.

LOWER OR HIGHER TARIFFS

The question of using tariffs as an economic weapon is more complex than it would at first appear. Tariffs can be used to protect industry but they can also harm it.

Lower Tariffs It might seem at first glance that a country should have high tariff barriers on everything that it produces. While most imports can be kept out through higher tariffs, it can be done only at a very great cost. Raising tariffs on most imported products would prompt other countries to raise their tariffs in re-

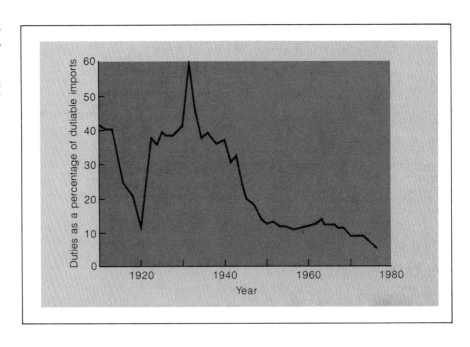

FIGURE 18-2 Import duty rates on goods shipped into the United States, 1920–1977. Source: Citibank Monthly Economic Letter, March 1977

taliation, making it more difficult for a country's businesses to compete in foreign markets. Also, higher tariffs may be bad for consumers. If consumers can buy a better radio at a cheaper price from an importer than from a domestic manufacturer, they will do so. This added competition forces companies to remain efficient. If poorly run business firms are protected from more competent foreign competitors by tariffs, resources which should go into efficient industries are wasted. Finally, and most importantly, nations should concentrate on producing the products in which they have the most advantage in the factors of production. In this way, the world's factors of production are used most efficiently.

Higher Tariffs If these points are valid, why is there such great pressure for higher protective tariffs? Some people argue that any industry necessary for national defense must be kept strong through higher tariffs or subsidies, if necessary. As an extreme example, not many people believe that the United States should buy its tanks from West Germany, even if they can be produced there at a lower cost. The shipbuilding industry has been heavily subsidized by the federal government to enable American firms to compete with shipbuilders from Japan and some other countries.

Another argument advanced for higher tariffs is the infant industry argument. The line of reasoning is that new industries should be protected by tariffs until they have grown and matured. This was probably a valid argument 150 years ago, when American business was just getting started, but it is hardly valid today.

A final argument for higher tariffs comes from those who believe American workers are protected by higher tariffs. Their theory is that higher tariffs keep out foreign products made with cheaper labor. Doing this creates more jobs for Americans, usually at higher wages. While this has great appeal to some workers, there is little logic to recommend it. First of all, these workers are also consumers who will have to pay higher prices on the products protected by higher tariffs. The worker as consumer will therefore have less money left to buy other things. Also, the countries whose products we are blocking will then raise their tariffs, making it difficult for our firms in other industries to sell abroad. This will cut the number of jobs available in those industries.

It is interesting to note, however, that management and unions in such industries as steel and textiles, have banded together to promote higher tariffs in these industries. They have been motivated by statistics showing that foreign shoe manufacturers have increased their share of the American market from 22 percent in 1968 to 46 percent in 1977, while 300 American shoe factories have closed, with the loss of 70,000 jobs. With those figures in mind, the International Trade Commission, a government agency established to recommend relief for industries threatened by imports, has recommended a limit on imports of shoes and a higher tariff for shoes imported above the limit. The shoe retailers association, opposing the measures, estimates this would cost American consumers at least $500 million a year. Clearly, it is not an easy problem to solve.

AMERICA'S TRADING PARTNERS

U.S. business firms trade with businesses, consumers, and government of almost every country. As Figure 18-3 shows, however, the areas with which we do most of our trading include Japan, Canada, and Western Europe (particularly the members of the European Economic Community—EEC), as well as the oil-producing countries. There is a logical reason. These countries have the money to buy our products and the economic efficiency to make and sell products that

FIGURE 18-3 U.S. balance of trade with main trading partners. Source: Department of Commerce

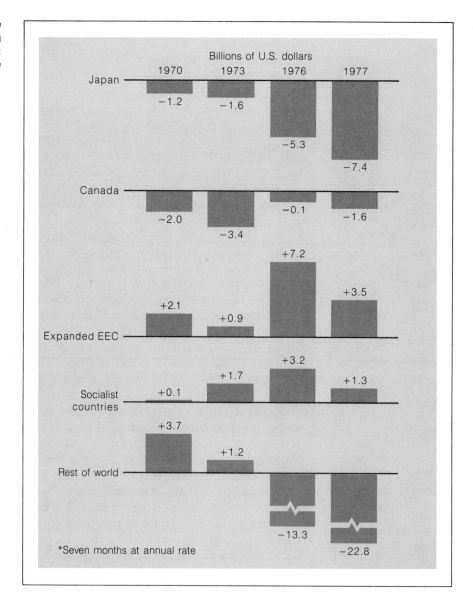

American consumers want. Notice in the chart that there was a favorable balance of trade with Western Europe and the socialist countries in 1977, but an unfavorable balance with Japan, Canada, and the rest of the world. Most of the unfavorable balance with the rest of the world was accounted for by oil imports exceeding our exports. The bill for imported oil in 1977 was $45 billion. The net effect was an overall unfavorable balance of trade of about $27 billion.

COMMON MARKET Let us take a closer look at the complexities of doing business with our main trading partners. Most of the Western European countries belong to the European Economic Community, or, as it is more popularly called, the *Common Market*. It was formed in 1958 by the Treaty of Rome with West Germany, France, Belgium, Luxembourg, the Netherlands, and Italy as members. In 1973, the United Kingdom, Ireland, and Denmark joined the association. The intention was to create an economic unit in which the countries would have a common external tariff and no internal tariffs. In this respect, it would resemble the United States. Florida and Arizona, for example, have the same tariff schedule for products coming into either state from another country but none for products moving between them.

Common Market Principles While a common tariff barrier has not yet been completed for all products, much progress has been made. No tariffs are charged on products moving between the countries. This gives Common Market businesses a big advantage over firms from other countries trying to sell to a Common Market member. Some American companies anticipated this factor from the beginning and built plants in EEC countries. In this way, they are treated as business firms of the country. For example, the IBM typewriters made in the Netherlands are not subject to tariffs when sold in West Germany. If the IBM typewriters were made in the United States, however, the purchasers would have to pay tariffs if the machines were sold in one of the Common Market countries.

The United States and the Common Market Direct American investment in Common Market countries is over $40 billion, about 30 percent of all our investments abroad. This statistic gives some indication of the importance that American firms have placed on having ready access to Common Market countries. There is good reason for their doing so. The Common Market, as an economic unit, is larger than the United States in population and in gross national product.

One of the most industrialized and technically advanced areas of the world, the EEC countries produce more steel and automobiles than the United States. Wary of American domination of key industries, many Common Market countries are concerned about the large American investment in Western Europe. This has prompted many mergers of firms in several countries to compete more effectively with the larger American firms. In addition, the Common Market has been discouraging big firms from dominating important industries. It began an investigation of the economic power of IBM, for example, when that company had 60 percent of the market for computers.

CANADA As you may recall from the chart of the countries with which we trade, we do a great deal of business with Canada. In addition to importing such greatly needed raw materials as oil, timber, iron ore, bauxite, and copper, the United States buys a great many sophisticated industrial products from our northern neighbor. In part, this is due to the large number of firms owned or controlled by American companies operating in Canada. American interests own 45 percent of Canada's manufacturing operations, 56 percent of its mining and smelting, and 60 percent of its petroleum and natural gas. To a large extent, the Canadian firms owe their capital and management efficiency to parent American firms. The influx of American capital and management has helped economic growth in Canada, but it has also created fears among Canadian citizens of American domination of their economic life. As a result, the Canadian government periodically asserts greater control over new investment by American firms. In almost every national election, American domination of Canadian industries is a political issue.

JAPAN The third large area with which we do a great deal of trading is Asia and, in particular, Japan. That country is one of the greatest economic success stories in history. From an economy badly shattered by World War II, Japan has emerged as the second largest economic power in the world, with a GNP of over $1 trillion. Japanese businesses are competitive in a wide range of products, ranging from shipbuilding to electronics. A combination of factors enable them to undersell their chief rivals, the United States and the Common Market countries, in many product lines. Their firms normally have low unit labor costs because of somewhat lower wages, efficient use of the newest technology, and a dedicated work force. The government also helps through stimulation of exports and heavy restriction on competing products coming into the country. In addition, since Japanese consumers are not as materialistic as those in Western Europe or the United States, they consume less. This makes more of the output available for new plants and equipment, rather than for consumer goods.

Heavily stressing exports, the Japanese have had a strongly favorable balance of trade with the United States and Common Market countries in the past few years. Because of the low prices of Japanese exports, both the Common Market countries and the United States have set quotas on a variety of products. The Japanese success in exporting autos, steel, ships, televisions, cameras and other goods has alarmed other advanced industrialized countries. Japan's competitors charge unfair competition since it is claimed that the Japanese discourage imports in their country through a variety of subtle but illegal government restrictions. In addition, it is charged that the Japanese government illegally subsidizes firms and that Japanese firms sell many products at lower prices abroad than they do at home. This is possible, critics charge, because imports are kept out by high tariffs and government restrictions. The controversial issue of Japanese exports—and Japanese restrictions on imports—is certain to continue in Japan, at home, and abroad.

BALANCE OF PAYMENTS

Closely related to the matter of balance of trade is the balance of payments. Countries receive money by selling products and services abroad and spend money when they buy products and services from abroad. There are other transactions in which money is received or spent. For example, when our government maintains troops abroad or when American tourists spend dollars overseas, money is leaving this country.

FAVORABLE AND UNFAVORABLE BALANCE OF PAYMENTS

The difference between all the money received from abroad and all the money spent abroad by a country in a year is called the *balance of payments*. If receipts are larger than expenditures, there is a *favorable balance of payments*. If the reverse is true, there is an *unfavorable balance of payments*. The main categories of items for which the United States has receipts and expenditures are trade, travel and transportation, military, investment, and government grants and aids. Table 18-3 shows the receipts and payments for each category in 1977. As you can see, a favorable balance in military and investment income were not enough to offset a huge deficit in merchandise and other categories. The result was a $17.4 billion deficit in our balance of payments with other countries.

EFFECT OF UNFAVORABLE BALANCE OF PAYMENTS

Who really cares or is affected by the balance of payments? The answer, of course, is that all of us are affected in our roles as consumers, workers, businesspeople, and taxpayers. Why is this? The balance of payments reflects whether or not a country is paying its way in the world. No country today can keep paying out more than it takes in for a very long time. If it does, it indicates that it is not able to pay its bills. Such insolvency can be cured by various means. A country may take steps to reduce inflation or unemployment so as to increase its real output. It may reduce its overseas investments, its military commitments to other countries, its foreign aid program, or the foreign travel of its citizens. In short, it must reduce the unfavorable balances in the items that make up the balance of payments. As you can see, any of these measures would have a great effect on American citizens because our national spending on all these items is high.

TABLE 18-3 U.S. balance of payments, 1977

(in billions of dollars)	
Merchandise	−27.0
Military	+ 1.8
Investment income	+12.8
Direct investment	− 2.7
Purchase of securities	+ .8
Other (including foreign aid)	− 3.1
BALANCE	−17.4

Source: U.S. Department of Commerce.

Another possible measure to correct a continuous deficit in a country's balance of payments is a devaluation of its currency. *Devaluation* means that the value of a country's currency is reduced as compared with that of another country. What a currency is worth is determined by what individuals are willing to pay for it on world markets and is expressed in terms of a relationship to other currencies. For example, the American dollar is equal to approximately 2.4 German marks. If the American dollar were to be devalued, you would get fewer marks per dollar. Currency values are said to be floating; that is, currencies do not have any fixed value, but float (or change) in response to supply and demand.

Until 1971, the American dollar was tied to gold and other currencies were tied to the dollar. The United States promised to buy gold from or sell gold to central banks of foreign countries at $35 an ounce. When it was clear that we no longer had enough gold to meet our debts to other countries, we could no longer honor the promise. At that time, we had about $10 billion in gold and about $80 billion in debt, or claims against the dollar by other countries.

The American dollar was devalued by about 8 percent in 1971 and about 10 percent in 1972.

American Business Helped   Devaluation helped American businesses in two ways. First, it made their costs of production and marketing less than those of foreign producers, since the dollar was worth less than most foreign currencies. Businesspeople could pay their costs with dollars that were worth less than before devaluation. Also, foreign competitors had to price their products higher for the American market than they did before devaluation, or take less profit per sale. Since it took more dollars to pay for foreign goods than it did before devaluation, imports were slowed. Businesspeople facing keen foreign competition benefited from devaluation. As a result, there was a strong favorable balance of trade in 1973 as compared with unfavorable balances in 1971 and 1972.

Consumers Hurt   Devaluation hurts consumers in some cases. Devaluation of the dollar had little effect on prices of products made and consumed in the United States; however, imports became more expensive. A Toyota Corona, for example, that sold for $2,500 in 1972 cost $3,500 by 1974, mostly due to the two devaluations plus rapid inflation in Japan. When the Ford Pinto and Chevrolet Vega were first introduced they sold for about $150 to $200 more than the Volkswagen Beetle. While all increased in price, the Beetle leaped to about $200 more than the Pinto and Vega in 1974. Consumers were hurt in another, less noticeable, way. Many "American-made" products contain foreign parts. These increased substantially in price with devaluation, making American-made products more expensive as well. And American travelers also had problems because devaluation meant that the dollar would not buy as much as before devaluation in other countries.

SELLING IN FOREIGN COUNTRIES

When an American firm decides to sell in foreign markets, it has many adjustments to make. In addition to economic factors, such as trade barriers, differences in currencies, and laws, there are social and cultural elements to consider.

CULTURAL AND SOCIAL INFLUENCES

The negotiation process in closing a business deal is far more subtle and complex in Japan than in England or West Germany. Deodorants do not sell well in the Mediterranean countries where men and women believe that a certain amount of body odor is natural if not even desirable. In the Netherlands, blue is considered feminine and warm, while Swedes associate it with masculinity and coldness. An American company developed a corn-processing plant in Italy, only to see it fail because Italians think of corn as "pig food." All of these are examples of cultural and social differences. They could be supplemented by thousands of examples from the files of American firms who have learned too late that there is no such thing as a European or a world market for a product. Social and cultural tastes vary from one country to another and even from one region of a country to another, just as they do in the United States.

ORGANIZING FOR OVERSEAS SALES

When a business wants to sell its products abroad, it has a number of approaches it can use. If a firm is small or wants to sell only a small part of its production abroad, it may operate through an export agent.

Export Agents   An *export agent* is an independent business that represents a number of noncompeting American firms abroad. It has contacts with customers or sales prospects, many of whom may be foreign import agents who will resell the goods to merchants from their countries. After securing a firm position in the foreign market, the American manufacturer could eliminate the export agent and sell directly to the foreign import agent. This is not a major step, but should be taken with care because it may make it difficult to establish a good working relationship with the foreign import agents.

Sales Branch   If sales continue to grow, a firm may decide to set up its own sales organization in the country in which it wants to sell. This is called a *sales branch* and is a sign that the firm is making a large commitment to overseas sales. Foreign sales are no longer considered supplementary to the domestic market. By opening a sales branch, the company acquires the tool for making its own sales contacts in the foreign country. As a result, however, it may come under pressure from the government of the host country, which may want it to manufacture—or at least assemble—its product in the host country so that the production jobs will be held by its citizens. This has happened in auto production in South America. It has been less expensive for years to produce automobiles in Detroit than in Argentina or Brazil. However, these governments have pressured the auto manufacturers to serve those markets by locating plants there, rather than by importing from the United States.

General Motors owns this Opel plant in Russelheim, West Germany. The factory is a GM branch subsidiary.

General Motors Corporation

Branch Subsidiaries   Larger firms generally sell to foreign firms by setting up foreign branches or foreign subsidiaries. A *foreign branch* is a division of a company located in a foreign country. It could be a sales or warehouse operation or an assembly or manufacturing plant. More likely, however, the parent company develops a separate subsidiary company to make the product in the foreign country. The subsidiary, though owned and controlled by the parent company, is then a separate cost center, with control of both costs and profits.

MULTINATIONAL FIRMS

Most large manufacturing firms in the United States today are no longer national firms. Their interests and production are worldwide in scope and seldom do they sell only in the American market. As a result, they are called multinational firms.

There are many definitions of a multinational firm. Some people believe that any firm that sells in more than one country is multinational. An increasingly popular definition of a multinational firm is more restrictive, and probably more accurate: To be classified as a *multinational firm*, a company has to have sales above $100 million, operations in at least six countries, and overseas subsidiaries accounting for at least 20 percent of its assets. By this definition, only about 4,000

personality profile:
**ARMAND HAMMER —
art and oil mix**

Armand Hammer started out following in his father's footsteps by becoming a physician. But so many other projects intervened that the only time he practiced medicine was when he revived a woman stockholder who had fainted at an annual meeting of Occidental Petroleum, the company of which he has been chairman for more than 20 years.

On a vacation trip to Russia after completing his medical studies, he became acquainted with Lenin and other leaders of the Revolution. He stayed on for nine years, till 1930, setting up business deals, including the sale of Russian art pieces, to raise hard capital for a country that was in economic ruins as the result of war and internal dissensions. As a result of his contacts with these revered figures, he probably has more influence in the Soviet Union than any other U.S. capitalist.

In the 1950s, Hammer took control of the modest U.S. based oil driller, Occidental Petroleum. When Occidental embarked on two major oil concessions in Libya, major oil companies were surprised and the business community regarded the venture as very risky. Occidental made a big find, developed it in record time, and produced at one point a quarter of all Libya's crude. Even nationalization, in which Libya gained 51 percent of Occidental's operations, did not stop the company's expansion. Hammer stayed in Libya, entered the North Sea oil fields, and reestablished relations with the Soviet Union, organizing a giant ($20 billion) chemicals exchange.

At the same time, Hammer arranged for a cultural exchange, the important 1973 exhibit of Russian art in the United States. By then Dr. Hammer had parlayed the artistic interest awakened by his early Russian experiences into one of the most extensive private collections in the world. Russia was willing to deal with this oil broker, who was an old friend of Lenin's and who was enhancing its image abroad by displaying its artistic heritage.

Lately, Hammer has been traveling south of the border a great deal, exhibiting his personal art collection and arranging for a showing of Mexican art in the United States while talking enthusiastically about Mexico's great oil potential—possibly as big as Saudi Arabia's. Having ousted the multinational oil companies in the 1930s, the Mexicans aren't likely to invite an outsider to develop their oil fields, but joint ventures in chemicals and fertilizers and arrangements to market Mexican oil in the United States are distinct possibilities.

companies qualify, accounting for about 15 percent of gross world output. The 20 largest industrial firms are shown in Table 18-4.

Contributions and Criticisms   There are many people who maintain that the multinational firms promote economic development, international prosperity, and even world peace. They transfer technology and new production processes to all countries. In 1972, for example, American firms transferred about $2.5 billion in technology to other countries in the form of licenses and patents. A *license* is the right to make a product over which a company has exclusive control in its home country. For example, Xerox licenses its processes for making its copiers to firms in other countries. Since the multinationals are outside of national politics in countries other than their home base, they tend to help each country get the most from its economic resources. On the other hand, many critics assert that they exercise undue influence on their own government's foreign policy decisions, that they dislocate national economies, and that they make it difficult for countries to determine their own destinies.

Effects on Jobs   As a result of these criticisms, organized labor and some members of Congress have made serious attempts to reduce the incentive for American firms to invest abroad. An AFL-CIO study showed that 500,000 jobs had been exported by the multinational corporations in the late 1960s—mostly to low-wage

TABLE 18-4 20 largest industrial companies in the world, 1977 (sales in billions of dollars)

Company	Country	World Sales
Exxon	U.S.	48.6
General Motors	U.S.	47.1
Royal Dutch/Shell Group	U.K.-Netherlands	36.0
Ford Motor	U.S.	28.8
Texaco	U.S.	26.4
Mobil	U.S.	26.0
National Iranian Oil	Iran	19.6
Standard Oil of Calif.	U.S.	19.4
British Petroleum	U.K.	19.1
Gulf Oil	U.S.	16.4
IBM	U.S.	16.3
Unilever	U.K.-Netherlands	15.7
General Electric	U.S.	15.6
Chrysler	U.S.	15.5
IT&T	U.S.	11.7
Standard Oil (Ind.)	U.S.	11.5
Philips	Netherlands	11.5
ENI	Italy	9.9
Francaise des Petroles	France	9.9
Renault	France	9.3

Source: *Fortune Magazine*, August 1977.

areas such as Taiwan and Hong Kong. Multinationals countered with their own figures. They cited a Department of Commerce study indicating that employment rose two-and-a-half times faster for 125 major multinational firms than it did in the average domestic company. Another study showed that only about 8 percent of the output of foreign affiliates of American multinationals came back into the United States. Most of these were from Canada and other areas with wage rates comparable to ours. To help check the power of multinational firms, however, some labor unions are trying to deal with them on an international basis. Companies that have had talks with international labor unions include Nestlé; Dunlop-Pirelli, a rubber manufacturer; and Philips, the Dutch electrical and electronics manufacturer.

Tax Incentives In addition, the government is under pressure to make it less attractive to invest overseas. One way to do that is to remove some of the tax incentives for foreign investment. Currently, American corporations do not pay American income taxes on the profits of their foreign subsidiaries until the profits are returned to the parent company and declared as income. Moreover, the income tax owed on these profits can be reduced dollar for dollar by income taxes paid in the foreign country where the profits were earned. Critics are bringing pressure to have both of these tax incentives rescinded.

Foreign Country Control Another major effort to reduce the power of multinational firms is the greater control many foreign countries now exert over them. The classic case is the successful move by the Arab countries to force multina-

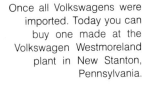

Once all Volkswagens were imported. Today you can buy one made at the Volkswagen Westmoreland plant in New Stanton, Pennsylvania.

Volkswagen Westmoreland

tional oil companies to pay higher prices for oil and to sell a controlling interest to the host countries. Brazil requires that two-thirds of the employees of multinational firms be Brazilian and almost all countries have pressured for similar treatment. In addition, most foreign countries routinely limit the percentage of foreign ownership permitted in firms in their key industries.

Decreasing Advantage in Producing Overseas   There is evidence that the tremendous export of capital from the United States into foreign countries may begin to slow. For about 25 years, multinational firms have expanded their overseas investments at about 10 percent a year. This was primarily in response to two pressures: (1) In the 1950s, it was necessary because of the foreign restrictions on American exports; (2) In the 1960s, the foreign investment continued because there were significant cost advantages in foreign countries. Neither of these reasons seems to be as important in the 1970s. Among industrialized countries at least, the trade barriers have been greatly reduced in recent years. Also, labor costs and inflation rates have risen much more rapidly in most other industrialized countries in recent years than in the United States, giving a cost advantage to the American firms. Wage rates are now about the same in Japan and West Germany, our two strongest competitors, as they are in the United States.

It would appear then, that while multinational firms will continue to invest overseas, the rate of capital flow may slow appreciably. The major incentives for overseas investment in the 1970s seem to be to: (1) conform to investment and trade restrictions of underdeveloped countries; (2) take advantage of special pools of raw materials in some countries; (3) lower transportation costs for bulky items; (4) take advantage of special tariff considerations, such as those that prevail in the Common Market.

GROWING FOREIGN INVESTMENT IN THE UNITED STATES

Another trend that is expected to continue is the growing number of foreign firms assuming multinational characteristics. The list of the largest multinational firms is now dominated by American companies. In years to come, more foreign firms will appear on the list, and more of these are likely to establish plants and subsidiaries in this country. Prior to 1970, there was only a slow increase in the amount of investment by foreign firms in the United States. However, with the devaluation of the dollar, foreign manufacturers can get more for their money by investing here. Volkswagen has become the fifth auto manufacturing firm in the United States because it can lower unit labor costs by producing the Rabbit here rather than in West Germany. Starting with a Sony plant built in San Diego in 1972 to produce television sets, many Japanese firms have begun building large plants in America. Since 1966 there has been a fourfold increase—to about $35 billion—in direct foreign investment in the United States. Still, that amount is only about a fifth of the total of direct investment that American firms have in other countries. It does appear, however, that many foreign firms see the American economy as more stable than their own countries. Also, unit labor costs in the United States are now lower than in the Scandinavian countries and some other advanced industrialized countries. In addition, it is easier to provide better services to customers by having production and parts available in the United States.

SUMMARY

International trade is important for business, consumers, workers and the government. We hope for a favorable balance of trade, selling more products and services abroad than we buy from foreign countries. Unfortunately, in recent years this has not happened to the United States for a variety of reasons, primarily because of higher bills for imported oil.

A number of economic and political forces influence the level and pattern of international trade. The economic forces include the strength of the domestic economy, the advantage in production costs a country has over world competitors, and the types of products in which countries can specialize to use their resources most efficiently.

The political forces include the establishment of quotas and tariffs, usually to protect a domestic industry. Lower tariffs by all nations promote free trade which should promote economic efficiency for all. However, when an industry has trouble competing with industries from other countries, it lobbies for higher import tariffs to help keep out foreign products. Higher tariffs mean higher prices for consumers, of course. This is a complicated matter since it is hard to know whether foreign firms that sell for lower prices are more efficient, willing to take a loss to establish a market, or are being subsidized by their government.

American businesses trade primarily with the Western European countries, Japan, and Canada since these countries have higher incomes and also produce a wide variety of products for export.

The balance of payments is the difference between all the money received from abroad and all the money spent abroad by a country in a year. We hope to have a favorable balance of payments, but usually do not. This is one of the major factors that has led to a gradual reduction or devaluation of the dollar.

American firms selling in foreign countries use a variety of plans. They may use export agents, establish their own sales branch, purchase a subsidiary or simply build a plant and sell the product abroad. The multinational firms, those which have sales above $100 million, operate in at least six countries, and have 20 percent of their assets overseas, are very influential in international trade. The multinational firms are criticized for exploiting some countries and for not being loyal to any country. However, they have become an important influence on all international trade among countries.

SUMMARY OF KEY TERMS

Absolute Advantage   A unique mixture of the factors of production that permits a country to produce a product at less cost than other countries.

Balance of Payments   The difference between all the money received from abroad and the money spent abroad by a country in a year.

Balance of Trade   The difference between the money a country pays for imports and the money foreigners pay for exports.

Common Market   Economic unit composed of West Germany, France, Belgium, Luxembourg, the Netherlands, Italy, the United Kingdom, Ireland, and Denmark.

Comparative Advantage   A country's concentrating its production in the areas in which it has the greatest advantage over other countries.

Devaluation   Reduction in the value of a country's currency as compared with that of another country.

Export Agent   Independent firm that represents several noncompeting firms abroad.

Exports   Goods and services sold to another country.

Favorable Balance of Payments   Receipts from foreign countries greater than payments to foreign countries.

Favorable Balance of Trade   Selling more goods and services abroad than a country buys from foreign countries.

Foreign Branch   A division of a company located in a foreign country.

Imports   Goods and services bought from other countries.

License   The right to make a product over which a company has exclusive control in its own country.

Multinational Firm   A company with sales over $100 million, operations in at least six countries, and overseas subsidiaries accounting for at least 20 percent of its assets.

Quotas   Limits on the amount or volume of products than can be imported.

Sales Branch   A separate sales organization of a company in a foreign country.

Tariff   A tax on imports.

Unfavorable Balance of Payments   Payments to foreign countries greater than receipts from foreign countries.

Unfavorable Balance of Trade   Buying more from foreign countries than a country sells to them.

REVIEW QUESTIONS

1. Contrast the effects of world trade on business and consumers as to prices paid and products available to consumers.
2. Explain what is meant by balance of trade and balance of payments.
3. Explain the reason why it is important to the United States to have a favorable balance of payments.
4. Give at least two illustrations of how the level of a country's economic activity can influence international trade.
5. Indicate the purpose of the Common Market and explain how large American corporations have acted to gain maximum benefit from it.
6. Describe the characteristics of a multinational corporation.
7. List the organizational patterns used by American firms to sell in foreign markets.
8. What is the difference between comparative and absolute advantage in producing for world markets?

9. Explain the difference between quotas and tariffs.

10. With which countries do we have the greatest dollar volume of trade?

DISCUSSION QUESTIONS

1. Which groups in this country are helped by devaluation of the dollar and which groups are hurt?

2. Do you feel that multinational firms based in the United States should be forced to produce most of their products for export in this country?

3. Do you feel that it is fair for a foreign corporation to own more than a half interest in a business firm in an important industry of a country? Why or why not?

4. If we are interested in protecting the jobs of American workers, why is it not the best policy to raise tariff barriers so that it will be more difficult for foreign firms to compete with American firms in the United States?

5. Now that some of the Arab countries are running large balance-of-payments surpluses, do you think it is fair for them to use that extra money to buy up American firms in this country? Why or why not?

CASES FOR DECISION MAKING

AMERICAN-STYLE LAYOFF IS UN-FRENCH

Because of slumping auto sales, Chrysler France decided to lay off 684 of the 23,000 workers at its plant just west of Paris. Other automakers in France faced a similar problem, but chose to slow production without laying off workers. The Chrysler layoff was the largest furloughing of French workers in years. One industrial official commented, "We don't have the kind of job mobility you have in the United States. This kind of thing is just not done." A government official indicated that the real problem is that "we are dealing with a multinational company whose top decision makers are in Detroit, not Paris." An increasingly militant union is pushing for reductions in the labor force through early retirement and reduced work hours, not layoffs. The Labor Ministry, which had to approve the layoff, indicated that it would not let the situation get out of hand.[1]

1. "France: Chrysler Tangles with the Establishment," *Business Week* (June 8, 1974): pp. 38–39.

1. Should a company have the right to lay off workers when it no longer needs them for current production?

2. What is the obligation of a multinational firm to adjust its operations to the social and economic values of a country in which it operates?

3. Is this an illustration of the power of a multinational firm over a country or over an area in which it operates? Why or why not?

A YEN FOR DOLLARS

Direct foreign investment in the United States by foreign firms is increasing rapidly. Foreign-owned business assets are about $35 billion compared to about $170 billion of American investment abroad. The Japanese, in particular, are building production plants in the United States. The Japanese government is encouraging this with a 30 percent tax write-off on investment in American plants. European firms also are building more production plants. They like the abundant supply of skilled labor and the lower inflation rate than Western Europe has. Some foreign firms which have used American firms to do their marketing have now taken over this function themselves. For example, Canon Inc., a Japanese maker of cameras and office equipment, has taken over the marketing of its products in the United States, after distributing through Bell and Howell for a decade.

1. What effect will the foreign investment in the United States have on our balance of trade and balance of payments?
2. Do you think it is desirable for foreign-owned companies to have plants in our country? In what ways are we helped and in what ways are we hurt by the move?

RADIO SHACK FINDS TOUGHER SLEDDING IN EUROPE

Radio Shack is the leading merchandiser of amateur electronic gear in the United States. The success of the discount-merchandiser specializing in private-label electronic equipment is based on strategically located stores, a wide product mix sold at discount prices, and heavy advertising.

When Radio Shack opened its first European store in 1973, the firm believed that its American marketing strategy would be successful in Europe also. So far, that has not been the case. There are some subtle differences in marketing products to European enthusiasts and American enthusiasts. First of all, far more Europeans are brand-name conscious and are willing to pay a premium for name brands. That places the private-brand name "Radio Shack" at a disadvantage. Second, the company had difficulty finding good locations for their stores. As a result, they chose sites in poor locations. Accustomed to giving away items such as flashlights to attract customers in the United States, Radio Shack found that the practice was illegal in Germany and resulted in an injunction to stop the practice. Belatedly, the firm discovered that its hottest selling item in the United States, the CB radio, is banned in Britain, Belgium, and Holland.

1. Before an American consumer products firm begins to market in a foreign country, what factors does it have to understand about the market?
2. Can you think of any type of consumer products that can be marketed in a foreign country just as they are in the United States?
3. How can firms eliminate the problems involved in adapting their marketing processes to other countries?

RELATED READINGS

Henley, Donald S. *International Business, 1977: A Selection of Current Readings.* East Lansing, Mich.: Michigan State University, 1977.

Readings dealing primarily with international marketing. Contains a variety of levels and types of readings with selections taken primarily from business magazines.

Said, Abdul, and Simmons, Luiz, eds. *The New Sovereigns—Multi-National Corporations as World Powers.* Englewood Cliffs, N.J.: Prentice-Hall, 1975.

An interesting paperback on the influence that multinational firms have on the countries of the world.

Thorelli, H. B., ed. *International Marketing Strategy.* Baltimore: Penguin, 1973.

Paperback of readings in international marketing. Contains articles on general principles of international marketing and individual case studies of industries, and looks at international marketing efforts of both large and small firms.

Zenoff, David. *International Business Management.* New York: Macmillan, 1971.

Well-known textbook in the field of international business which looks at the entire process of managing the international operations of various firms.

chapter 19

PROTECTING PEOPLE AND PROPERTY AGAINST RISKS

OBJECTIVES

When you have finished reading and studying this chapter, you should be able to:

1. Recognize the significance of risk management to the firm and know the difference between pure risk and speculative risk.

2. Discuss the major types of property and liability insurance protection needed by firms and individuals.

3. Know the major features of life insurance protection as it relates to the family breadwinner and to key executives in the business.

4. Identify the problems of risk associated with doing business on credit and be familiar with insurance protection available for minimizing these problems.

5. Understand the role of state and federal governments as insurers of individuals and businesses.

CHAPTER PREVIEW

If you have ever visited Las Vegas, Nevada, or San Juan, Puerto Rico, you know the excitement generated by the gambling environment. Everyone is anxious to take a chance at blackjack or with the mechanical one-armed bandits. Gambling can be fun and relaxation, especially when it is not carried to excess. In a more general way, however, every day of our lives we are thrust into risk situations, although not with the drama or excitement we find at a casino. Buying a new home or entering into a business contract involves substantial economic risk. No matter how careful we may be, almost every business transaction exposes us to some degree of risk that can lead to economic loss.

Fortunately, insurance protection is available to businesses and individuals for taking some of the financial loss out of risk situations. In most cases, insurance cannot reduce the degree of risk, but it can replace all or at least some of the money lost in a mishap. No business can insure its ability to make profits for its owners, but all businesses can protect themselves against losses from fires, thefts, accidental damage to their motor vehicles, and a similar variety of hazards. The various state governments as well as the federal government have set up some insurance programs in areas where the welfare of American society is at stake. Most insurance protection, however, is contracted for with private companies who have earned reputations for integrity in the field.

Protection against financial losses to property or bodily injury to other people is known as property damage and liability insurance. This type of insurance coverage is essential for anyone who owns a business, a home, or a motor vehicle. Many state laws require owners of motor vehicles to have such protection before they can receive a valid registration for their vehicle. In all cases a wise businessperson or homeowner will be sure to have adequate property damage and liability insurance. The courts have been very generous in recent years in making awards to individuals whose property or persons were damaged by another's property.

Life insurance benefits provide the insured's dependents against the loss of earning power through the difficult and often long period of financial and emotional adjustment. In some cases the insured may take out a policy containing an element of savings in it and, after reaching a certain age, can cash in this policy and receive its full value. Most people who buy life insurance, however, do so for the financial protection that it affords their survivors.

Below is a list of some of the major risks for which insurance protection is available.

Health	Disability	Dog bite
Fire	Burglary	Comprehensive
Life	Bad debt	Kidnap/ransom
Theft	Collision	Bank failure
Product liability	Bodily injury	Malpractice

For full details be sure to read and study this chapter very carefully.

Definitions of Insurance:

A guarantee that, no matter how many necessities a person had to forego all through life, death was something to which he could look forward.

Fred Allen

Paying for catastrophe on the installment plan.

Anonymous

Eugene E. Brussell, DICTIONARY OF QUOTABLE DEFINITIONS (Englewood Cliffs, N.J.: Prentice-Hall, 1970).

19

PROTECTING PEOPLE AND PROPERTY AGAINST RISKS

You probably know a relative, friend, or co-worker who has had a car broken into or stolen. You may have heard of someone whose house, office, or store was damaged by fire. It is to be hoped that people who are victims of such calamities have insurance protection to help pay for the financial losses resulting from their misfortune. But even insurance protection cannot prevent one's car from being stolen or one's house from burning down. The sole benefit of an insurance policy is that the insured receives new funds to replace the stolen car or to rebuild the damaged house.

The mishaps cited above are obvious examples of losses that can be covered by insurance. It is a rare, and perhaps a very foolish, individual who does not have automobile insurance or fire insurance protection for home and personal property. Most people realize that misfortunes of this type occur often enough to justify the expense of carrying insurance protection.

Premium is the cost of purchasing an insurance policy. Premiums may be paid monthly, quarterly, or annually, depending on the type of policy. The insurance company is called the *insurer*; the person or business whose life, health, or property is financially protected by insurance is called the *insured*. Another name for the insured is *policyholder*; the policy is the written contract between the insurance company and the insured specifying the type and extent of coverage. A basic principle underlying all insurance policies is that the policyholder have an insurable interest in the life, health, or property being covered by the terms of the policy. In other words, the insured must show that a financial loss would occur from a misfortune that is covered by the insurance contract. In cases of life insurance, an insurable interest always exists if one takes out life insurance on his or her own life.

GENERAL FEATURES OF INSURANCE

Not every insurance company will insure you against every kind of loss. A wide variety of insurance companies protect against potential disasters.

RISKS

Every time you cross the street, you run the risk of being run over by a car. Every time someone opens a store for the day there is the risk of being robbed or of having someone suffer injury on the property. *Risk* is the exposure to financial losses or injuries. It can sometimes be minimized by careful, deliberate precautions. A sprinkler system in a department store can prevent fire from spreading, and periodic medical checkups can reduce the chances of premature death from a sudden heart attack or cancer. But no amount of precaution can totally eliminate risks from our business or private lives. About the best we can do is inform ourselves of the various ways to minimize hazards and to act according to this information. The next best step is buying adequate insurance protection to cover financial losses resulting from business or personal misfortunes.

Unfortunately, not all risks can be covered by insurance protection. This is especially true for businesspeople, many of whom have been wiped out by one

The business owner should be fully insured against liability claims.

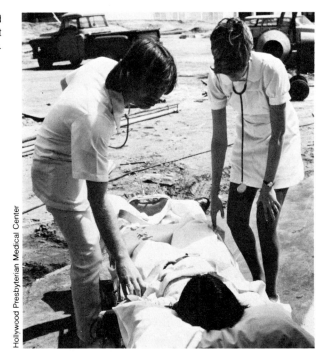

Hollywood Presbyterian Medical Center

major tragedy or another. In recent years flooding, especially as a result of hurricanes, has caused major devastation to businesses as well as homes. A case in point occurred in the summer of 1977 when the downtown area of Johnstown, Pennsylvania, was engulfed by flooding. Insurance policies do not ordinarily cover flood damage, and many businesspeople suffered tremendous financial losses as a result of this act of nature. You might wonder why one cannot buy flood insurance from private insurance companies. It is because the risk in one concentrated area would be so high that the cost of premiums to cover it would be prohibitive for an insured party to pay. Recent federal legislation has made some forms of limited flood insurance available to individuals and businesses.

Businesspeople cannot obtain insurance for loss of profits. Even a successful business that has been operating at a profit for decades is not an exception. The recent natural gas shortages forced many businesses that were formerly successful to cut back on production and suffer financial losses. Table 19-1 shows some of the types of major risks encountered by businesses and individuals and indicates whether they can be cushioned by insurance.

There is an old expression, "You can't learn to swim unless you get into the water." The same holds true for the relationship of risks to profits. Businesspeople cannot realize substantial profits unless they are willing to take some chances. Knowing this, they sometimes deliberately take risks. Such is the case when a

TABLE 19-1 Types of risks

Insurable	Uninsurable
Theft	Flood
Fire	Loss of Profits
Bad Debts	Crop Failure
Disability	Price Fluctuation
Life	Business Failure
Collision	Strikes
Vandalism	Competitive
Unemployment	Innovation
Retirement	War
Business Interruptions	Expropriation
Employee Dishonesty	Riot
Water Damage	Technological
Product Liability	Changes
Health	Government
Legal Expenses	Changes

businessperson decides to stock a new and different product never before accepted in a marketing area. In a sense this is gambling, a situation thought of as a *speculative risk. Pure risk*, on the other hand, results from everyday events rather than from taking a chance on a new product. It is the pure risk that exposes the firm to the greatest possibility of financial loss, since the speculative risk can be controlled to some extent through wise decision making.

There is very little a businessperson can do about insuring against the lack of sales for a new product. Speculative risks can only be controlled by wise management based on broad experience in the business community. Many of the pure risks that businesspeople face are also uninsurable. You can't get insurance against a new competitor's opening on your block and taking away half your sales. You can't obtain insurance against an expressway's being built parallel to the road where your business is located. You can't buy insurance against the possibility that the major corporate employer in your town will close its plant, forcing half of your customers to leave the community. These are just a few of the many situations that make risk a way of life for every business. Obviously, no insurance company could afford to protect against such risks at any reasonable premium cost. Businesspeople must learn to live with chance and be alert to indications of increases in the possibility of economic losses from risk.

Wise Risk Management By installing burglar alarms, sprinkler systems, safety valves and the like, management can help cut a company's losses from perils. Almost all plants conduct safety campaigns and many award prizes to employees who practice safe working habits. Insurance companies encourage this type of risk management; indeed, they are often reluctant to issue an insurance policy to a firm unwilling to participate in such programs.

Wise management is also a requisite for preventing a firm from suffering net losses and going out of business. This is one of the major purposes for studying a textbook of this type. Managers of households as well as businesses must develop techniques for recognizing the changes in economic conditions, changes in market conditions, and changes in all other significant factors that affect their enterprise. Failure to do so quickly enough could mean financial disaster.

Self-Insurance   *Self-insurance* is a technique by which a business periodically sets aside cash reserves to be drawn upon only in the event of a financial loss resulting from a misfortune of the pure risk type. In a sense the business is serving as its own insurance company, a practice most firms cannot afford. Only a very large concern, such as one with a number of stores or offices spread over a wide geographical area, can afford to be self-insured. In the event of the loss of one of the stores from fire or other hazard, the cash reserve would be drawn upon to cover the loss. The reserve in such a situation would be built up by assessing each store or office in the chain for periodic payments (premiums) to the fund. In a sense it is very much like the procedure used by insurance companies for insuring a number of different firms throughout a geographical area.

Self-insurance management eliminates the insurance company and therefore saves the chain a great deal of the expense. However, if the firm suffers a major financial loss in the early years of the self-insurance program before adequate cash reserves can be built up, it could mean a great economic setback. In addition, the self-insured firm invests the reserve cash and earns interest, rather than paying the premiums that enable the insurance company to do so.

Hedging   One economic loss that cannot be minimized through insurance can be reduced or eliminated through a management technique known as *hedging*. Many firms buy raw materials that go into the production of the final product they sell to the public. Thus a manufacturer of chocolate candy needs to buy large quantities of cocoa as the main ingredient in its finished merchandise. It usually buys its cocoa through importers who deal with African and South American cocoa growers. What happens if the candy firm places an order for cocoa and the price of the delivery is higher than expected because of shortages arising from a poor growing season? Should it raise the price of candy and risk driving away its customers? If the price problem is a relatively short-term one, this would not be a wise course of action. The alternative is to place "sell" orders for cocoa with the New York Cocoa Exchange at the same time as the firm places its "buy" order with the cocoa importer. In this way any change in buying price will be offset by the change in selling price, since the chocolate manufacturer has become both a buyer and a seller. The procedure is diagrammed in Figure 19-1.

The process of hedging is a very complicated one and requires a good deal more explanation and discussion than we have space for in this introductory text. If you have ever visited New York City or Chicago, be sure to tour one of the

FIGURE 19-1 Hedging as a form of business insurance protection

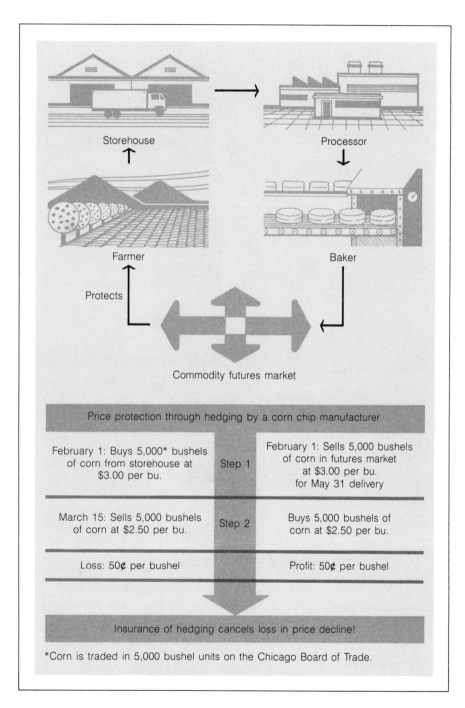

commodity exchanges such as the Cocoa Exchange on John Street in New York City or the Chicago Mercantile Exchange on North Franklin Street. These exchanges welcome visitors and give tours as well as brochures that explain hedging as one of the many features of commodity trading.

INSURANCE COMPANIES

Some insurance companies specialize in a particular type of insurance. Some sell only life insurance while others, such as the Blue Cross and Blue Shield companies, sell only health insurance. Recently, most insurance companies have diversified their types of policies, and many of them now sell several kinds of protection. Some of the larger firms in the field sell almost all forms of insurance including life, health, auto, fire, theft, and others. Since insurance firms are regulated by state law, all of them must comply with the marketing policy set forth under those laws. As with any other service they buy, businesspeople will be better able to make the most advantageous purchase if they understand the kinds of policies available as well as how the insurance companies set their prices.

MUTUAL COMPANIES

Some insurance companies are owned by the policyholders they protect. These are called *mutual* companies. Although only about 10 percent of all insurance firms are mutuals, this small minority controls over 50 percent of all investments made by insurance carriers. This imbalance is accounted for by the fact that the large life insurance companies, such as the Prudential Life Insurance Company and Metropolitan Life Insurance Company, are of the mutual type.

In a mutual company the policyholder's premium includes an amount necessary to operate the insurance company. If, at the end of the year, this premium exceeds the actual cost of operation, a portion—known as the dividend—is returned to the insured. In effect the term *dividend* is a misnomer since the policyholder is actually only receiving a rebate on part of the premium. This is one way to know whether or not your insurance carrier is a mutual company because companies organized in the other major form do not pay dividends to policyholders.

There are times when insurance companies do not have a good financial year. If the insurance company finds that it requires additional funds to remain solvent, mutual policyholders can be required by state regulation to pay additional premiums over and above the contracted rate. Fortunately, this situation rarely comes about thanks to strict state insurance laws and regulations.

STOCK COMPANIES

Insurance firms owned and operated as stock companies are similar in organization to any other corporation: To become an owner one must buy stock in the firm. Those who seek insurance protection and become policyholders are customers, not owners. As in any other corporation, dividends are paid to stockholders and not to customers. In the case of mutual insurance companies, should losses be greater than premiums paid, the company has the right to assess policyholders an additional amount to cover their share of the losses. In a stock company, by contrast, the stockholders must bear the burden of such losses. It should be clear that in a stock company, a stockholder need not be a policyholder nor does a policyholder need to be a stockholder.

SPREAD OF PROTECTION

If a firm can't afford to cover its own financial risks, how can an insurance company afford to do so? The answer can best be understood through use of a practical example. Let us assume there are 30 students in your English literature class and that the course textbook costs $10. Let us further assume that statistics gathered by your professor over the last 10 years indicate that every semester at least one student out of a class of 30 loses the book. You might devise an insurance plan for the class by assessing each student a 35-cent premium. This leaves a fund of $10.50 available in the event of loss. (The extra 50 cents could be for a receipt book or sales tax.) If no one loses the book, the premiums could be returned to the class at the end of the semester. Will this insurance program work? It depends on whether all 30 of the students want to join. It may be that only 20 want to participate. Still, at a cost of a 50-cent premium the idea might still be feasible. If, however, only five wanted to participate, a $2 premium per student might be too much for protection against a possible $10 loss, especially as the odds of losing your book are only one out of 30 if past statistics serve as a reliable predictor of future losses.

Two important mathematical concepts are brought out in this example:

1. The law of averages
2. The law of large numbers

The *law of averages* states that if your computation is based on a very large number of similar risks, a certain number of predictable losses will occur. The important consideration in predicting losses through the law of averages is that there must be a large number of cases.

The *law of large numbers* states that the larger the number of cases used to compute the data, the closer the actual experience will approximate the predicted outcome. The law of large numbers, therefore, applies probability to past experience to predict future outcomes. Life insurance companies employ mathematical specialists called *actuaries* who use the laws of averages and large numbers to predict life expectancies and construct mortality tables to show results. Life insurance companies charge premiums based on *mortality tables*, and their degree of accuracy is amazingly precise.

PRINCIPLE OF INDEMNITY

Can someone insure the same piece of property for its full value with several different insurance companies? The answer is no, because of the *principle of indemnity*, which states that a person or business may not collect more than any actual cash loss in the event of damage caused by an insured hazard. In the same vein, insurance contracts specify that misrepresentation or fraud will void an in-

business profile: THE HIGH COST OF MALPRACTICE

Americans are a litigious people. The consumerism of the 1970s awakened them to their right to seek damages through the courts if they don't get their money's worth when they pay for services. Juries composed of other consumers awakened to their rights and also to the duties of professionals providing a service have been awarding large damages in such suits. This matter assumed crisis proportions during the mid-1970s when ballooning medical malpractice awards sent doctors' insurance premiums skyhigh and forced some insurers to drop this coverage altogether so that doctors in some localities couldn't find malpractice insurance at any price. Many M.D.s gave up their practice or moved; others took the risk of continuing to practice without coverage.

By the late 1970s medical malpractice rates were holding steady and even declining in some cases. Doctors had made great efforts to inform patients of the hazards of surgery, and the public had become better educated and more sympathetic to the problems and uncertainties doctors face. But now huge malpractice premiums are besetting all sorts of other professionals. Whether it's called malpractice, errors-and-omissions, or professional liability insurance, it points to a single trend, that providers of services are increasingly being made to answer for alleged mistakes that cause some real or imagined suffering, whether they are architects, real estate agents, corporate officers and directors, travel agents, or, ironically, other lawyers. As the liability of other professionals becomes define by suits, malpractice insurance is being set up for other groups such as insurance agents to protect them, for instance, against mistakes made in buying insurance—forgetting to renew a policy or not filing a claim on time.

In 1977 a woman and her daughter who had been kidnapped, robbed, and beaten in a shopping center sued the architect, Skidmore, Owings, & Merrill, among others. A Skidmore partner explains, "Basically, they sued us for designing a shopping center that was conducive to kidnaping." The court dismissed the suit, but malpractice premiums for architects and engineers jumped about 45 percent the next year.

Naturally, the higher premiums are a burden to the professional, but in the long run these costs are passed on to the innocent ordinary consumer in the form of higher fees. The consumer pays not only when large damages are awarded, but even when such suits are dismissed, because the large legal costs of defendant insurance companies are also passed on in the form of higher premiums.

The insurance industry itself gains little from the burgeoning malpractice practice. Only 5 percent to 10 percent of insurers even write such policies, and revenue from them constitutes no more than 5 percent or 10 percent of income for any of these companies. Lawyers' malpractice premiums about doubled between 1976 and 1978, but the legal profession is the only beneficiary of this trend toward litigation other than the consumer who wins a suit. For every lawyer or other professional sued for a mistake there is a lawyer representing the plaintiff. What they pay to protect against their own malpractice is a drop in the bucket compared to all the new business some of them are getting.

A society interested in protecting the average John or Jane Doe from the incompetence of an unscrupulous or careless provider of professional services is to be applauded, but no claim is awarded that is not paid for, and the million-dollar damages assessed against an attorney is not covered by his premium, but by the premiums assessed on all members of that profession, charges that are passed on to all consumers.

surance contract. Failure to reveal material information to the insurer at the time of application will likewise void the contract.

INVESTING INSURANCE FUNDS

What does the insurance company do with the money collected from premiums? Obviously, this money must be readily available to pay benefits, but in the interim insurance companies may invest these funds, subject to state regulation. Such funds are frequently invested in government bonds and other types of relatively safe liquid assets. Life insurance companies often invest in long-term opportunities such as real estate and corporate securities. Table 19-2 shows the percentages of life insurance investments of various types for 1975.

Insurance companies are among the largest investors in real estate in the United States. Many of them have invested in land and built housing projects, shopping centers, and industrial parks—undertakings that have been financially successful over the years. As the value of real estate has increased in this country, the insurance companies as landlords have prospered tremendously. Insurance companies invest much of their premium money in loans to businesses and individuals in the form of mortgages. Many of the largest buildings in the United States are financed by investment money supplied by insurance companies.

BASIC TYPES OF INSURANCE PROTECTION

There are several hundred types of insurance policies when one considers all the types and combinations of protection that can be found in one policy. Buying insurance protection is like buying a sandwich. With a choice of bread, cold cuts, dressing, lettuce, and fixings, it's not uncommon for one person to order ham and Swiss cheese on rye bread with mayonnaise while another wants salami with onion on white bread with lots of butter. The same holds true for insurance. A businessperson might buy a basic protection policy which includes insurance against fire and water damage, insurance against theft, and on-premises liability protection. The combinations may vary greatly and, as was stated above, if one shops around, chances are that choices of coverage could be in the hundreds.

Choosing a good insurance carrier and local agent is an important decision. Most businesspeople rely on advice from other business associates before making this decision. Some insurance agents are designated as Chartered Property and

TABLE 19-2 Distribution of acquisitions of investments by U.S. life insurance companies, 1975

Type of Investment	Percentage
Corporate Bonds	73
Government Securities	10
Stocks	5
Mortgages	7
Real Estate	2
Policy Loans	3

Source: *Life Insurance Fact Book, 1976*, American Council of Life Insurance.

Liability Underwriters (CPLU). The *CPLU* designation is earned by agents who take courses and pass examinations in property and liability protection.

Since it is not possible to cover all personal and business insurance needs in one chapter, we will limit our discussion to the most important forms of coverage for businesses and businesspeople. Let's relate our discussion to Gaslight, Inc., the successful restaurant and catering house (see Chapter 4), owned by a small group of stockholders headed by Bob Musto and Paul Volyn, who also operate the business.

PROPERTY AND LIABILITY INSURANCE

One of the most common ways to buy insurance in combination is to buy a property and liability insurance policy. Under this plan, the business obtains financial protection against a number of hazards which always includes fire, burglary, public liability, product liability, and, often, business interruption. Such a policy is usually less expensive than if each type of protection were purchased under separate policies. Figure 19-2 demonstrates the variety of protection available under a blanket policy for homeowners.

FIRE PROTECTION

Fire protection is fairly inexpensive but rates depend on a number of factors related to the business. These include:

1. Type of business
2. Location of business
3. Type of structure housing the business
4. Efficiency of the local fire department

Premium rates for Gaslight, Inc., will probably be higher than for most other firms because the frequency of fires in restaurants is higher than in most other types of retail outlets. If the firm is located near a hazardous area, such as a military munitions depot, the premium rates will be higher than average. A firm whose plant is constructed of brick will often pay a lower premium than one occupying a wooden building. Naturally, the more fireproofing used in construction, the lower the premium will be.

Fire departments are rated and graded by insurance companies just as you are evaluated by your professors. The more efficient the fire department, the lower the fire insurance premium is likely to be in the area it serves. Volunteer fire departments usually receive lower ratings than full-time professional fire departments. Not surprisingly, extensive records are kept by insurance companies on the performance records of fire-fighting companies.

Fire rarely completely destroys a building. If an insured could, he might very well buy insurance for only one-half or two-thirds the value of his building. In this way, he would force the insurance company to bear the full extent of damages (assuming damages are fractional) while paying a lower premium for partial pro-

PART 1
FIGURE 19-2 Typical property and liability protection for homeowners. Source: *INA Homeowners Insurance Brochure,* Insurance Company of North America

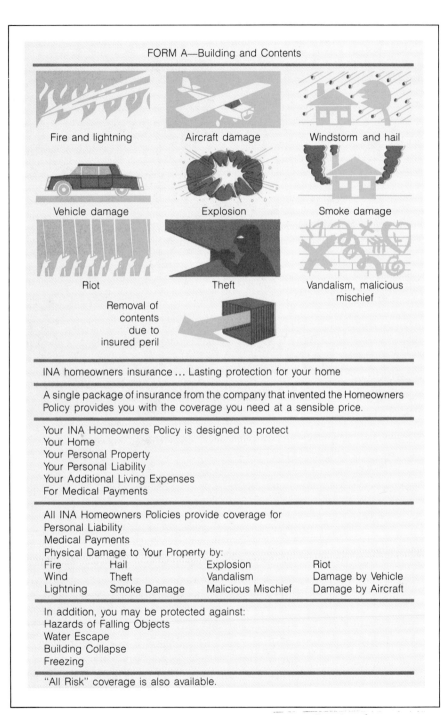

Continued on next page

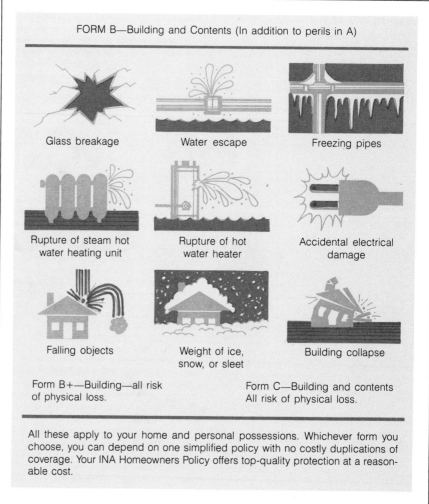

FORM B—Building and Contents (In addition to perils in A)

Glass breakage

Water escape

Freezing pipes

Rupture of steam hot water heating unit

Rupture of hot water heater

Accidental electrical damage

Falling objects

Weight of ice, snow, or sleet

Building collapse

Form B+—Building—all risk of physical loss.

Form C—Building and contents All risk of physical loss.

All these apply to your home and personal possessions. Whichever form you choose, you can depend on one simplified policy with no costly duplications of coverage. Your INA Homeowners Policy offers top-quality protection at a reasonable cost.

tection. To prevent this, insurance companies instituted a *coinsurance clause* in all fire coverage, requiring that the insured buy coverage up to a stipulated percentage of the value of the property, usually 80 percent. If they fail to do so, they must bear a proportion of each fire loss equal to the amount of coverage they lack. For example, if Gaslight, Incorporated, property is valued at $100,000 but is insured against fire losses for only $40,000, the risk is only partially covered because they have not insured for 80 percent or $80,000. This means that if a fire occurs and damages are $10,000, the insurance company will only pay $5,000. The calculation would be:

$$\tfrac{1}{2} = \frac{40,000 \text{ actual coverage}}{80,000 \text{ required coverage for coinsurance}}$$

$\tfrac{1}{2}$ or 50% of $10,000 actual loss $=$ \$5,000

BURGLARY AND THEFT INSURANCE

Burglary and theft insurance protects the business against break-ins after hours, and an additional clause can protect against "theft," which generally refers to holdups during business hours. Rates vary according to the crime history of the neighborhood as well as the protection record of the local police department. Sophisticated burglar alarm systems also help to lower premiums for this kind of insurance.

PUBLIC LIABILITY INSURANCE

If anyone is injured on your premises and sues your firm for negligence, public liability insurance helps pay for any court awards to the person hurt. If an employee of the firm is injured, his recourse is usually employees' disability insurance, and all employers in all states are responsible for belonging to some kind of insurance protection plan for this purpose. Workmen's compensation insurance is a monopoly of the state guaranteeing medical expenses and salary payments to workers injured on the job. In case of the subsequent death of the employee, payments are made to the dependents of the deceased for a specified period of time. Private disability covers risks not covered by workmen's compensation or extends protection against risks it covers.

PRODUCT LIABILITY INSURANCE

Let us suppose that one of the customers at the Gaslight Restaurant eats a sandwich containing a piece of bone. As a result, two teeth are chipped resulting in $600 worth of dental work. This dental work means two days loss of work, so the customer sues Gaslight for $1,200 total damages. Product liability insurance pays damages arising from customers' suits because of harm caused by the use and consumption of a company's product. Unfortunately, no matter how careful a firm is, such insurance is still essential.

MALPRACTICE INSURANCE

Malpractice insurance is a form of service liability insurance in the same general category as product liability. In recent years, doctors have found themselves subjected to huge increases in suits by dissatisfied patients who believe that the physician erred in the treatment or surgical procedure. As a result, the premiums for malpractice protection have gone up several hundred percent in the last several years.

AUTOMOBILE INSURANCE

Every individual and every business firm owning and operating a motor vehicle should have basic automobile insurance protection. The essential protection is against bodily injury and property damage. These are liability safeguards that pay the damages awarded in suits by injured parties who have incurred medical expenses, lost a loved one, or suffered damage to their property as a result of the policyholder's automobile. Bodily injury liability insurance will pay the policyhold-

Collision insurance covers the cost of repairs resulting from the fender-bender you knew would never happen.

American Stock Photo

er's legal liability for injury to any number of people hurt. However, the amount of coverage is limited by the terms of the insurance contract. The same stipulation in the contract holds true for property damage. This type of policy is frequently sold in combination with other forms of automobile protection cited below.

Liability for bodily injury and property damage is the most important basic coverage that a driver must have. If one is sued as a result of negligence, the award to the injured party or deceased individual's survivors can be a great sum of money. Young people found negligent by the courts can be indebted for the rest of their lives if they don't have adequate insurance protection against these risks. Court awards in such cases have run into several hundreds of thousands of dollars; while the defendant may have insurance protection, often it is not enough to cover the judgment completely. Fortunately, such situations are rare, but they do serve as a warning to get as much bodily injury and property damage protection as possible.

Collision Insurance   If an automobile or truck owned by an individual or business is damaged in an accident, collision insurance will pay the cost of repairs. Such insurance is very useful when the owner of the damaged vehicle cannot collect from the other party to the accident because it was the fault of the damaged vehicle's owner. Collision insurance is also useful when a vehicle hits a pole or some other object where no other driver is at fault. Even when another driver is at fault, people may still collect collision insurance from their own insurance company and have their company sue for damages from the other party's insurance carrier under property liability laws. Almost every collision coverage features a $100 or more deductible clause, which excludes from coverage the first $100 of damage to the insured vehicle. By requiring the owner of the vehicle to pay this amount, the clause keeps small claims to a minimum and lowers the cost of premiums—or at least so insurance companies maintain.

Medical Insurance Medical payments insurance will pay hospital and doctor bills up to a specified amount for the insured and occupants of the car who are in an accident. Usually a $500 limit is placed on the total of such bills per occupant. Medical costs beyond this amount often have to be paid out of the insured party's pocket, although in some cases they are covered by liability for bodily injury.

Comprehensive Insurance There are other hazards in owning an automobile. Car thefts, for instance, are far from uncommon these days. Comprehensive insurance pays financial losses resulting from theft as well as damage to the insured vehicle from causes other than collisions. Assume you are driving along a highway and a dump truck loaded with rocks whizzes by. Often rocks fall from these trucks like tiny meteors bouncing along the road. Suppose one of them hits your windshield; replacement is very expensive. If you have comprehensive coverage, the insurance carrier will pay the cost of the new windshield. Comprehensive coverage also pays financial losses resulting from fires to a vehicle; again the cause cannot stem from an accident. As with collision coverage, some comprehensive coverages contain a $50 or $100 deductible provision.

Towing Expenses For an additional small premium, one may obtain towing coverage for cars or trucks. This means the insurance carrier will pay up to a specified maximum each time it is necessary to tow a vehicle as a result of an accident or breakdown.

Financial Responsibility and No-Fault Many states will not issue a motor vehicle registration unless applicants can prove that they have bodily injury and property damage insurance. If they do not, a large fee in addition to auto registration costs is usually required. This fee is put into a fund to pay bodily injury or property damage claims against such people. However, it is not an insurance fund and does not protect the uninsured driver against judgments. The fund merely compensates the injured party or survivors for emergency expenses. The negligent driver must still stand the financial losses as an uninsured motorist.

Some states have adopted varying forms of *no-fault* auto insurance. Under no-fault insurance, certain court procedures are eliminated because bodily injury and property damage claims up to a specified amount are settled with one's own insurance carrier. There is no effort to determine who is at fault and who must pay, since the insured parties are compensated by their own insurance carrier. Unfortunately, no-fault insurance, where adopted, has only been in token form, and the significance of such adoption has been more in public relations than in practical insurance protection for the driving public.

LIFE INSURANCE

The idea behind life insurance is to pay death benefits to those who have an insurable interest in the deceased. In most cases this would be a spouse and children, but in some cases it could also be the firm that the deceased owned or in whose management he took an active part.

No one can predict when or how a particular individual will die, but the skill and know-how of insurance company actuaries enable them to calculate with great accuracy the total number of deaths in a year expected among their policyholders. As with all types of insurance premiums, those for life insurance are based on historical data and future predictions of death rates.

Many people subscribe to life insurance plans on an individual basis. Some people buy life insurance protection as part of the pension plan where they work. Others buy life insurance as part of mutual fund plans. *Group plans*—those which are a part of a pension, mutual fund programs, and the like—ordinarily do

Life insurance provides an income for the family or beneficiary of the life policy in the event of the insured's death.

American Stock Photo

not require the insured to have a physical examination before being admitted. Usually individual life insurance plans do require a physical examination before final acceptance.

As with property and liability insurance, choosing a life insurance agent and company is a difficult task. Television advertising has become an important and effective medium for helping insurance companies recruit new customers, but the agent is still the person who has to close the sale. A good agent must be sincere in his choice of insurance plans for the client as well as possess technical competence. A Chartered Life Underwriter (CLU) is a special designation attesting to the technical competency of the agent. The *CLU* is earned by taking courses and passing rigorous examinations in the area of life insurance protection and related fields.

There are many different forms and combinations of life insurance protection available. In a general sense they can be broken down into several major categories.

Straight Life Insurance   Probably more people are covered by straight life insurance protection than any other kind. The insured pays a monthly, quarterly, semiannual, or annual premium of a set amount over the life of the policy and for this receives protection for the rest of the insured's life. In some cases premiums must be paid for as long as the insured lives; but under certain policies, premiums are no longer required after age 65. One added feature of straight life insurance is that the policy accumulates a *cash surrender value*. This means that the policy contains an element of savings that the policyholders can withdraw if they decide to cancel the protection. It should be understood, however, that although the cash surrender value increases as the policy becomes older, it never equals the total premiums paid on the policy.

The major advantages of a straight life policy are that it can be purchased at relatively low cost and that it does have a cash surrender value. The major disadvantage is that full payment on the policy can only be received upon the death of the policyholder.

Term Life Insurance   Term life insurance is known as a pure insurance protection because, unlike straight life, it does not develop cash surrender values. Term life insurance is for the person who wants the most life protection at the lowest possible cost. Usually term policies run for five-year periods with the option of renewal for an additional five years without another medical examination. For a new homeowner or new businessperson who is heavily in debt, the term policy represents the lowest-cost protection. If the insured should die, debts will fall to the family, and the death benefits from the term policy could ease the burden of debt payments.

The chief advantage of term insurance is that one can get the greatest amount of protection for the lowest cost. The chief disadvantage is that term life insurance is strictly a gamble with death. If the insured outlives the life of the term policy (and this is very likely), then there are no savings or other benefits derived from this type of protection.

Limited Payment Life Insurance   Limited payment protection is identical to straight life insurance protection. It also contains the cash surrender feature of straight life. It differs from straight life in that premiums on limited payment life policies are due for only a stated number of years, usually 20 years from date of issue. Since the protection is comparable to straight life, each premium on a limited payment policy must be quite large for the policy to be paid up in 20 years.

Those who would benefit from such a policy are people who make large incomes in the early years with the expectation that their earnings will diminish as they get older. This might be the case with a model or dancer. Limited payment life policies allow such people to pay for their insurance protection while their incomes are high without having to worry about premiums later in life when income might fall off. As in the case of straight life, the insurance carrier only pays the face value of the policy upon the death of the insured.

Endowment Life Insurance   In one way an endowment policy is similar to a limited payment one because premiums are paid for a limited number of years. The unique feature of this type of policy is that at the end of the payment period, the insured, if still alive, collects the full value of the policy. As with straight and limited life insurance, the endowment life does have a cash surrender value. But since it pays off to the insured on an expiration date (unlike straight or limited payment life), it is the most expensive form of insurance protection. Some people prefer it, however, because they feel it is a forced savings plan and the only way they can be sure of saving money for their later years. Of course, if they should die before the endowment is paid up, the death benefit will be available to those who need it.

General Life Insurance Features   Under all of the above types of protection, the insured has the right to designate who is to receive the proceeds of the policy. This recipient is referred to as the *beneficiary*. In some cases, an alternate recipient is designated in case the beneficiary and the insured die at the same time. This person is referred to as the *contingent beneficiary*.

Many life insurance policies have a suicide clause. This usually states that if the insured takes his or her own life, the insurance company is released from paying any death benefits to beneficiaries. In addition, most life insurance policies contain a *double indemnity clause* specifying that in case the insured suffers an accidental death, the policy pays twice its face value to the beneficiary.

With the exception of term life insurance, most life policies allow the insured to borrow against the cash surrender value of the policy. This is a very inexpensive

personality profile:
**RALPH SAUL —
new policies in insurance**

For years, INA, the nation's oldest common stock and seventh-largest property and casualty insurer, had been limping along under the direction of insurance executives. A few years ago the company took a new direction by bringing in as chairman Ralph S. Saul, who knew nothing about the insurance business, and assigning him the task of smoothing out some of the deep dips in its cyclical earnings pattern.

INA had tried diversifying by making acquisitions of companies whose earnings were more steady, but some mistakes were made. Saul has sold off the losers and made new acquisitions whose growth rate is higher than that of INA's basic business. As a former chairman of the Management Committee of the First Boston Corporation, former director of the Division of Trading and Markets of the American Stock Exchange, and former president of the American Stock Exchange, Saul knows a great deal about a lot of companies and should be a good judge in their worth.

INA's original property and casualty business is, nonetheless, still the main problem. To solve it, Saul has hired an innovative insurance insider, veteran executive John Cox, who is stressing the risky but high-premium casualty business that other companies are afraid of because of the huge losses it may entail, but demanding also to write the client's less risky property policy as a kind of insurance on its insurance. Cox is also increasing INA's international strength, recruiting foreign nationals to run foreign operations and giving them greater control.

In the meanwhile, INA has had a few years of excellent earnings, but Ralph Saul concedes that much of the improvement is just the result of lower inflation and higher rates throughout the industry. The real test of Saul and Cox's innovations will come when this still-cyclical business turns down again. "Come back in five years," says Saul. "It'll be that long before the results of our strategies are visible."

way to obtain a loan, but a perilous one in that the life protection on the borrowed portion of the policy ceases until the loan and interest are paid back.

KEY PERSONNEL AND PARTNERSHIP PROTECTION

Many firms, especially small- and medium-sized ones, are quite dependent on one or two key personnel for making the important decisions or providing specialized skills that keep the firm afloat. Often, a sales manager has a unique talent for the job and has spent many years cultivating excellent customer relations. The death of a key individual, such as the sales manager cited above, could mean a substantial loss of revenues for the firm, particularly in the short run. For this reason, many firms take out key personnel insurance. This protection is often term life insurance with the business as beneficiary.

The key personnel policy might also contain additional clauses to meet special needs. Such a clause would provide disability benefits in case the key person is disabled and can no longer perform for the firm in a productive manner. The premiums on key personnel policies are paid by the firm and are a legitimate operating expense. The firm is, of course, the beneficiary if the insured dies or becomes disabled. Because the company is the beneficiary, key personnel should have their own life policies to protect their relatives.

Partnership insurance works in a fashion similar to key personnel insurance. This is logical since a partner in a firm is usually a key part of management. However, there are sometimes clauses in partnership protection policies that are not found in key personnel policies. One such clause provides funds for the surviving partner to buy out the share of the deceased partner from the deceased's estate. Again, as in the case of key personnel policies, each partner should have his or her own basic insurance protection for the sake of dependents.

PREPAID LEGAL INSURANCE

More and more, employers of unionized employees are being asked to include prepaid legal insurance in the package of employee fringe benefits. These plans are similar to health insurance plans such as Blue Cross and Blue Shield. Prepaid legal insurance is written on a group basis with premiums paid by the employer and employee or wholly by the employer or employee. When the insured has a legal problem he or she consults a lawyer who is a member of the plan. Plans allow claims up to a certain number of hours of legal help, usually 30 to 80, or up to an annual maximum amount such as $1,000. Such plans are being provided by more employers, and employees like the idea of being able to consult an attorney without major cost.

CREDIT AS A SPECIAL RISK

Years ago most business transactions were on a cash-and-carry basis. Today, the situation is the reverse; most business transactions are on a credit-and-carry basis. Even the very small business must resort to granting credit to survive the competitive battle for getting and keeping customers. Many businesses now subscribe to national credit card plans such as Visa or Master Charge. These plans handle the paperwork and credit searches, and the business subscribing to the plan pays a small percentage of sales as the fee.

Firms dealing with accounts receivable generally subscribe to the services of a local credit agency to give them historical information on the credit reputation of potential open book customers. The best known of the national credit information organizations is Dun and Bradstreet. Businesspeople who subscribe to the Dun and Bradstreet service receive at their request reports on any other firms who subscribe. Each subscriber also receives the Dun and Bradstreet Reference Book, a page of which is shown in Figure 19-3. This publication is designed for use as a ready reference by sales, purchasing, and credit departments of businesses. There is a detailed credit report on file for every firm listed in the Reference Book. The Reference Book is published every two months and lists the firms in alphabetical order by city or town within their particular state or province.

CREDIT INSURANCE

No matter how careful a firm is in checking credit prospects, there will always be some bad debts incurred for one reason or another. Wholesale insurance protection against bad debts is not available, but there are some types of credit insurance that managers may consider. The two areas of credit insurance are credit life insurance and bad debt insurance.

Credit life insurance reimburses the creditor for financial loss resulting from the death of the debtor. This frees the creditor from the need to collect from the estate of the deceased debtor, saving a great deal of time and money. Practically all credit life insurance is written on a group plan, although individual policies are available. This type of protection is most often sought by mortgage lenders, banks, credit unions, retail establishments, and other firms who handle many credit transactions.

Bad debt insurance is not to be confused with credit life insurance. Bad debt insurance, sometimes known as credit insurance, is a type of protection for the insured firm against unusually high losses resulting from the granting of credit to accounts receivable customers. This type of insurance requires the policyholder to bear a part of each loss on accounts receivable, thus forcing the insured to exercise care in the granting of credit on account.

KIDNAP/RANSOM INSURANCE

Kidnap/ransom insurance is a new type of protection of some interest. Lloyd's of London, a very famous British insurance association, offers protection to those who might be kidnapped and held for ransom. To receive benefits from the policy, the kidnapped person's relatives must determine positively that a kidnapping of the insured has actually taken place. In addition, they must call in the proper law enforcement authorities and cooperate with them in their efforts. The insurance is available to citizens of the United States, and Lloyd's claims that many

Name of city, town, or village.

Directly under each town are the bank listings for that town, with names of principal bank officers.

Standard industrial classification code for line of business. For explanation of the code, see pages XI, XII, XIII, XIV, and XV.

"A" indicates an *additional* name and "C" a *change in rating* since the previous revision. The Reference Book is revised every two months. The "A" and "C" in this position are not to be confused with the Estimated Financial Strength symbols in the rating column to the right of the listing.

Branch listing. Where the branch and headquarters are in the *same* state, no rating is given for the branch. In these listings the legend "Br of" is shown directly below the listing with the headquarters town where rating will be found, i.e., "Br of" Johnstown."

Where the branch and headquarters are in *different* states, a rating is shown at the branch. Because closing dates for the staes are not all the same, subscribers should take into consideration that a branch rating may not always correspond with its headquarters rating.

When the symbol * follows a name, it indicates that the business is a corporation and "Corporation", "Corp.", "Incorporated", "Inc.", "Limited", or "Ltd." has been omitted.

Population. These are the official statistics of the 1960 census issued by the United States Government. Absence of a number in this position indicates that according to the 1960 U.S. census either the town or village had less than 1,000 inhabitants, or it is an unincorporated community, without natural or defined boundaries, that merges into other unincorporated communities and in these instances "census" takes the position that no fair division of the combined population can be determined.

Heading used for all non-post office towns. Businesses in a non-post office town are listed under the post office which serves it—in this case under Carterville.

Canadian population statistics are the latest available but vary as to year in the different provinces. Those for incorporated towns are government statistics; for other towns local estimates are used, generally for the same year as the latest census.

Name of County or Parish, if any.

Code number of Dun & Bradstreet reporting office. See page headings in Reference Book for corresponding names of offices.

Numbers in the rating column following the bank name indicate approximately, in thousands, the combined totals of Capital Stock, Capital Debentures, Capital Reserves, Surplus and Undivided Profits. On Canadian banks these numbers are omitted.

Business name used for buying.

Ratings always appear at the extreme right end of the line. In this example, B + 1 means Estimated Financial Strength $300,000 to $500,000; Composite Credit Appraisal, High. The full Rating Key appears on front and back inside covers.

A numeral immediately preceding the rating marks the year when the business was established or came under present control or management. Thus, 3 means 1963, 5 means 1965. Absence of a numeral in this position indicates that the business was established prior to ten years ago. This feature is not used in listings of branch locations.

Line of Business. See Abbreviations, pages V, VI, and VII.

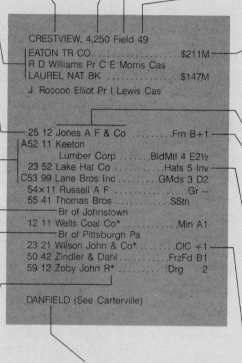

CRESTVIEW, 4,250 Field 49
EATON TR CO. $211M
R D Williams Pr C E Morris Cas
LAUREL NAT BK $147M
J. Roscoe Elliot Pr I Lewis Cas

25 12 Jones A F & Co ....Frn B+1
A52 11 Keeton
    Lumber Corp ......BldMtl 4 E2½
23 52 Lake Hat Co ....Hats 5 Inv
C53 99 Lane Bros Inc ....GMds 3 D2
54x11 Russell A F ....Gr --
55 41 Thomas Bros ....SStn
   Br of Johnstown
12 11 Wells Coal Co* ....Min A1
   Br of Pittsburgh Pa
23 21 Wilson John & Co* ....CIC +1
50 42 Zindler & Dahl ....FrzFd B1
59 12 Zoby John R* ....Drg   2

DANFIELD (See Carterville)

FIGURE 19-3 Explanation and use of listings. Source: Used with special permission of *Dun's Review*, July 1968. Copyright 1968, Dun & Bradstreet Publication Corp.

wealthy American families have purchased policies through the Lloyd's association. Many firms fear the kidnapping of key personnel serving in foreign countries. Kidnap/ransom protection can serve as an aid for the safe return of such personnel in the event of kidnapping.

GOVERNMENT AS AN INSURER

It was mentioned earlier that state governments serve as insurers for workmen's compensation in all 50 states. The federal government, in turn, serves as an insurer for the *Federal Insurance Contribution Act* (*FICA*). You probably feel more comfortable with the term "Social Security," the common name applied to the act. Most people don't realize that besides being a pension insurance plan, social security pays death benefits to spouses and dependent children. In recent years social security has been expanded to cover sole proprietors and partners. Therefore, private businesspeople must pay social security taxes, known as *self-employment taxes*, when they file their federal income tax returns. The result is that they are as protected as employees of any firm would be.

FEDERAL DEPOSIT INSURANCE CORPORATION

An agency of the federal government known as the Federal Deposit Insurance Corporation (*FDIC*) insures savings accounts up to $40,000. If a banking institution should fail, no matter what the reason, any depositor who has lost funds would be compensated by the FDIC, usually within a matter of a few days. It is important to note that protection is only guaranteed up to $40,000 per account in any one bank. This will not prevent someone from being protected above $40,000 as long as he has accounts in several different banking institutions. The Federal Savings and Loan Insurance Corporation is a similar government insurer for funds of depositors in savings and loan institutions. The protection limit is also $40,000 per account.

SECURITIES PROTECTION INSURANCE CORPORATION

Like the FDIC discussed above, the Securities Protection Insurance Corporation (*SPIC*) is quasi-governmental and provides insurance protection to investors in common and preferred stock. As with FDIC, premiums are paid by member institutions, which in the case of the SPIC would be brokerage firms. Each investor who leaves securities and/or cash with a brokerage house which is a member of SPIC is protected up to $50,000 if the house should become insolvent due to fraud or any other reason. If only cash is left with the brokerage house, protection can only be up to a maximum of $20,000. As with FDIC coverage, the $50,000 limit applies to each individual account with each brokerage house. This means an investor can be fully insured by having several stock/cash accounts with different brokers if no one account exceeds $50,000.

Member banks of the Federal Deposit Insurance Corporation (FDIC) display this sign on their premises, usually near the teller's cage or the bank's exterior window.

SMALL BUSINESS ADMINISTRATION

In recent years the Small Business Administration (SBA) has taken a more active part in the insurance aspect of business management. The SBA, although not an insurer in the traditional sense, does provide funds to alleviate financial losses occurring from natural disasters. Thus, when floods hit the business section of Johnstown, Pennsylvania, several years ago, the SBA provided funds for rebuilding at no interest or very low interest to those businesses that qualified. For a more detailed discussion of the SBA, refer back to the chapter on small business management.

SUMMARY

Everyone should have protection against financial loss. Insurance is the method most people use. Business operators are especially vulnerable to financial loss; therefore they insure themselves against a variety of risks. In addition to personal insurance needs such as health and life protection, business operators need insurance to protect against defects in product or malpractice. They also need protection on business property in case of fire, theft, or water damage. Also, many firms take out life insurance on key managers in the firm to compensate the firm in the event of the death of an important, effective leader. Credit life insurance and bad debt insurance are two other forms of coverage necessary to the effective management of many firms.

SUMMARY OF KEY TERMS

Actuaries Mathematical specialists who use the laws of averages and large numbers to predict life expectancies and construct mortality tables to show results.

Beneficiary The person who is to receive the proceeds of a life insurance policy upon the death of the insured.

Cash Surrender Value An element of savings that accumulates in certain types of life insurance policies that the insured may withdraw upon canceling the protection.

Coinsurance Clause Provision in fire insurance policies that require that the insured buy coverage up to a stipulated percentage of the value of the property, usually 80 percent. This clause prevents the insured from underinsuring in the expectation that financial losses on partially damaged property will be borne in total by the insurance company.

CLU Abbreviation for Chartered Life Underwriter, which is a designation that can be earned by agents who take courses and pass a rigorous examination in the area of life insurance protection.

CPLU Abbreviation for Chapter Property and Liability Underwriter, a designation earned by agents who take courses and pass rigorous examinations in the area of life insurance protection.

Contingent Beneficiary An alternate beneficiary to a life insurance policy in the event the beneficiary

and the insured die at the same time.

FDIC Abbreviation for Federal Deposit Insurance Corporation, which is the agency of the federal government that insures savings accounts up to $40,000.

FICA Abbreviation for Federal Insurance Contributions Act, the official name of the Social Security old age and life insurance program.

Group Insurance Plan Insurance policies that are a part of pension, mutual fund programs, and the like.

Hedging A management technique protecting a firm against uninsurable economic loss whereby a firm simultaneously places buy and sell orders for its raw materials, thus offsetting any increase in the purchase price.

Insured The person or business whose life, health, or property is financially protected by insurance.

Insurer The insurance company that provides protection to the individual or business.

Key Personnel Insurance Insurance on the life of a key employee of a firm stating that the firm is the beneficiary of the policy.

Law of Averages Mathematical concept stating that if your computation is based on a very large number of similar risks, a certain number of predictable losses will occur.

Law of Large Numbers   Mathematical concept stating that the larger the number of cases used to compute the data, the closer will the actual experience approximate the predicted outcome.

No-fault Auto Insurance   Insurance that eliminates certain court procedures because bodily injury and property damage claims up to a specified amount are settled with one's own insurance carrier.

Policyholder   The insured individual or business.

Premium   The cost of purchasing an insurance policy.

Principle of Indemnity   The principle that states that a person or business may not collect more than any actual cash loss in the event of damage caused by an insured hazard.

Pure Risk   Risk that results from everyday events rather than from taking a chance on a new product.

Speculative Risk   Gambling.

Self-insurance   A technique by which a business periodically sets aside cash reserves to be drawn upon only in the event of a financial loss resulting from a misfortune of the pure risk type.

SPIC   Abbreviation for Securities Protection Insurance Corporation which insures a customer's cash or securities left with a brokerage firm up to $50,000.

REVIEW QUESTIONS

1. How do speculative risks differ from pure risks?
2. What factors determine the premium n a fire insurance policy?
3. What are the major forms of investments made by insurance companies? In which of these did they invest the majority of their funds in 1975?
4. Name and briefly describe three economic risks for which government provides insurance protection.
5. How does credit insurance differ from credit life insurance?
6. What is prepaid legal insurance and how does it work?
7. Why is term life insurance called "pure insurance protection?"
8. What is the most popular form of life insurance protection? What is the most expensive form?
9. What is no fault insurance? What type of property coverage does it usually apply to?
10. What do insurance companies do with the premiums they collect?

DISCUSSION QUESTIONS

1. Comment on this statement: Everyone should have as much life insurance protection as financially possible since we are all going to die sooner or later.
2. Comment on the validity of the following: Every firm should carry key personnel insurance on certain employees of the firm.
3. Assume you are a single proprietor of a small cash-and-carry dry cleaning establishment that does retail work from a store as well as pickup

and delivery work with a small van. The business has assets of $75,000 and liabilities of $45,000. List and discuss your insurance needs for the firm in their order of priority.

4. Comment on the validity of the following

statement: Since a barber and dentist are in service-type businesses, they have no need for product liability insurance.

5. How do the laws of large numbers and of averages relate to automobile insurance?

CASES FOR DECISION MAKING

PROFITABLE INSURANCE[1]

Aetna Life and Casualty Company reported second quarter profits for 1977 to be almost double what they were for the same quarter in 1976. John H. Filer, chairman of the board, issued a statement from the firm's headquarters saying that the increased profits were part of a trend that has developed over the past several years. He also stated that all major segments of the insurance carrier's business contributed to the improved results. This included the casualty and property companies, auto, and homeowners insurance. First half results for 1977 were a net income of $188 million or $3.50 per share which is 119 percent greater than for the first half of 1976.

1. Go to your library or local insurance agent that represents Aetna and obtain information about Aetna Life and Casualty Company. Find out its relative size in the industry and how it invests its money. Also obtain the names of its president and several of the other officers as well as the location of the company's headquarters.

2. Hypothesize on what types of insurance coverage might be provided by Aetna's casualty and property companies.

3. Based on the financial data given above, calculate Aetna's profit for the first *half* of 1976.

1. *Wall Street Journal,* August 1, 1977, p. 9.

PRODUCT LIABILITY HEADACHE[2]

Product liability suits have become one of the greatest problems for insurance companies and businesses who sell products to the public. The Department of Commerce reported that suits in this area have increased at an explosive rate and loss per claim has outpaced the rate of inflation. Settlement per claim in 1965 was $11,644 and this average rose to $79,943 in 1973. Courts are ruling more strictly for the injured party. In recent years most states have moved away from a strict doctrine of negligence which means that the plaintiff no longer has to prove that the manufacturer was negligent in any way. All that has to be proven is that the manufacturer made the product involved in the injury and that it was somehow defective. The cost of product liability insurance has skyrocketed. Sporting goods, drugs, chemicals, and power mowers are big areas of claim losses. No end to the dilemma appears in sight.

1. List as many reasons as you can for product liability claims to rise so rapidly. (Omit those suggested above.)

2. Comment on the following: No matter who pays the liability claim, ultimately it is the consumers who will pay.

3. Do you agree with the liberal interpretation moving away from the strict doctrine of negligence? Why or why not?

2. *Dun's Review,* January, 1977, pp. 48–50, 76.

SWANK CLOTHES

Milton Swank is majority stockholder and president of Swank Clothes, Inc., a chain of six medium-sized men's clothing stores located in the greater San Francisco Bay area. None of the stores is closer than two miles to any of the other stores. Swank's insurance premiums for property and liability protection on the stores has doubled since 1970 and he and his board of directors are very concerned. The current insurance premium is $26,000 annually and the trend of increased premiums appears to be continuing. Total claims against insurance coverage have been $18,000 since 1970. Asset value of inventory, equipment, and building for each store averages about $220,000. Swank and his board are considering self-insurance in lieu of their present policy.

1. List the factors that should be considered in a decision to self-insure.
2. Do you think the firm should use self-insurance or continue with an insurance company? Why or why not?
3. List some probable reasons why Swank's insurance premiums have doubled since 1970.

RELATED READINGS

Gillespie, Paul, and Klipper, Miriam. *No-Fault: What You Save, Gain, and Lose with the New Auto Insurance.* New York: Praeger, 1972.

Discusses the strengths and weaknesses of no-fault auto insurance. Also suggests some alternatives to no-fault plans.

Gregg, Davis, and Lucas, Vane B. *Life and Health Insurance Handbook.* Homewood, Ill.: Irwin, 1973.

A very complete reference source on all of the major phases of health and life insurance. Such things as probability, reserves, and legal considerations are also discussed.

Gregg, John E. *The Health Insurance Racket and How to Beat It.* Chicago: Regnery, 1973.

A rather strong indictment of some insurance companies, hospitals, and physicians. Rather negative in approach but contains some positive suggestions.

Healy, John J. *A Game of Wits.* New York: McKay, 1975.

Stories from the files of a top insurance investigator. Recalls his most fascinating cases of insurance fraud claims and deceptions.

Life Insurance Fact Book, 1978. New York: American Council of Life Insurance, 1978.

This softcover book published annually by the American Council of Life Insurance contains many valuable facts concerning all phases of the life insurance industry. Recommended for research purposes.

Magnusen, Warren, and Segal, Elliot. *How Much for Health?* Washington, D.C.: Luce, 1974.

A book advocating health insurance protection for everyone through a national insurance program.

Shore, Warren. *Social Security: The Fraud in Your Future.* New York: Macmillan, 1975.

Warns about the financial crises faced by the Social Security Administration. Will the money you pay into Social Security be there when you retire? This book suggests "not likely."

chapter 20

THE FUTURE—FOR BUSINESS AND JOB SEEKERS

OBJECTIVES

When you have finished reading and studying this chapter, you should be able to:

1. Identify and explain the major changes that are likely to influence the future growth of business and industries.

2. Relate the changes taking place in society with their effects on job opportunities in the future.

CHAPTER PREVIEW

Growth of the business community and job opportunities is greatly influenced by changes in our society. A well-managed company anticipates these changes and produces products and services that meet the needs created by change. Job seekers can also benefit from considering changes likely to take place in our society. Today, for example, there is a definite shift in the country's population toward the South and West—the so-called Sun Belt. In addition, population expansion is greater in nonmetropolitan areas while the urban areas are losing population, reversing a long-term trend. The most important population shift, however, is in the size of age groups.

In the next decade, there will be fewer people entering the work force. As a result, the unemployment rate should drop. Slower economic growth will be caused in part by higher energy energy costs, in part by a slowdown in the application of new technology, and in part by a drop in investment in new plant and equipment.

Foreign trade will become stiffer for American firms because world technology has now caught up with and surpassed in some areas American technological superiority.

The American life-style will change too, with less emphasis on materialism and more on personal fulfillment.

Changes in employment patterns are expected. Service-related businesses will assume a larger share of the job market. The most rapid growth will be among clerical, professional, and technical workers.

Getting back in shape

20
THE FUTURE — FOR BUSINESS AND JOB SEEKERS

All well-managed businesses plan for the future. Continued growth and profitability for a firm are based on anticipating new opportunities. Successful firms correctly anticipate business opportunities and develop strategies to meet them. There are numerous examples. It is no accident that Michelin has recently built several new plants in the South for production of radial tires. Ten years ago the firm correctly saw that radials were the tire of the future. Michelin also saw that American labor costs were rising more slowly than those in Europe. The firm also understood that its costs could be lowered by locating its plants in the South. It is now ready to be a powerful competitor in the domestic passenger tire market, loosening the grip of American firms.

It is also no accident that Xerox and IBM are becoming strong competitors in the information processing industry. A decade ago, Xerox was the glamour company in the office copier business. IBM was known for its leadership in computers. Both correctly saw, however, that an integrated information processing, or word processing, industry would develop and both started working toward that end. Xerox started with its copiers and later developed an automatic typewriter, computers, and other office hardware. IBM started with its computers, developed an office copier, and then developed its memory typewriter and other hardware. As a result, both have now developed sophisticated information processing systems which are in great demand. Both are able to help business reduce the cost of office communication while improving its effectiveness.

The farther into the future one tries to predict, the less accurate are the forecasts. There are a number of factors, however, that can be identified now and which will influence future developments for firms. In this chapter, we shall look at some of these developments and try to relate them to the changes that are likely to take place in the job market. Within this broad framework, of course, there will be other smaller changes that will affect particular industries and particular jobs. The major forces affecting the future of business, however, appear to be: changes in population, changes in the labor force, changes in the economy, changes affected by energy, changes in technology, changes in international trade, and changes in life-styles.

CHANGES IN POPULATION

Probably no other factor will have stronger impact on business in the next decade than changes in population. These changes include both shifts in population location and the sizes of age groups.

SHIFT TO THE SUN BELT

The dramatic shift in population from the Northeast and North Central states to the South and Southwest was described in Chapter 8. People are increasingly migrating to warmer parts of the country, believing that these areas offer more of what they want in a life-style.

The population of the Sun Belt region, the South and Southwest, is growing at a faster rate than any other region in the United States.

ERDA

TREND AWAY FROM CITIES

In addition to shifts of population to the South and Southwest, there appears to be a trend away from cities and even metropolitan areas. Of the top 20 cities in size, 14 lost population from 1970 to 1975. The six cities that are still growing are in the Sun Belt. In the 1970s, nonmetropolitan areas grew at the fastest rate—not the cities or the suburbs. For the first time in the nation's history, the population shift was away from the cities. Some of the growth in nonmetropolitan areas has come from people who have moved beyond the urban sprawl. They may commute 50 to 100 miles to work each day. This trend is bound to slow down, however, with the rapid increase in the cost of commuting. The main group moving from metropolitan to nonmetropolitan areas, however, may continue to grow. They are the people who are moving to different, less populated sections of the country. Growth of nonmetropolitan areas is expected to continue for at least the next 10 years. More and more people are trying to escape from the pollution, high taxes, crime, job shortages, and pressures of giant metropolitan areas. In the process, they are indicating that their expectations of the quality of life have changed. The same factors that have led them to leave metropolitan areas are also encouraging manufacturers to move to nonmetropolitan areas also. Many firms have set up factories in smaller communities where they face fewer of the problems of the metropolitan areas.

Despite these shifts, however, most jobs and people are still located in major metropolitan areas. Nearly 75 percent of the American populace is still jammed into the 23 urban regions that together cover only about 16 percent of the nation's total land area. The largest of these strip cities or megalopolises is the Boswash area. It stretches over many states from Boston to Washington, D.C. About 20 percent of the nation's population is contained in this area. Despite shifts in population, it is clear that most of the population will live in urban areas for the foreseeable future. It is likely, though, that the percentage of persons living in metropolitan areas is not likely to grow much in the next decade, and may even decline.

CHANGES IN AGE CATEGORIES

Changes in the size of age groups within the general population will have the strongest impact on business. These changes are the result of wide variations in the birthrate during the last 40 years. As Figure 20-1 shows, the number of children under 13 years will increase about 10 percent over the next decade. The number of teenagers, however, will decline 17 percent during this period. Young adults will be up 13 percent and young middle-aged people up a whopping 31 percent. There will be fewer older middle-aged people (down 1 percent) while the number of elderly people will be up 19 percent. All these changes will occur within an anticipated population increase of only 9 to 10 percent for the decade.

These population shifts directly affect the demand for various products and services, causing it to expand or shrink. With the increase in the number of babies, the demand for baby food, clothes, toys, and services for infants will go up. At the same time the teenage market will shrink, resulting in a lessening of the demand for records, jeans, high schools, and soft drinks. The large increase in young adults will bring about greater demand for apartments, fast-food restaurants, convenience foods, and inexpensive recreation. Most of this group cannot afford

FIGURE 20-1 Changes in age groups from 1977 to 1987. Source: Bureau of the Census

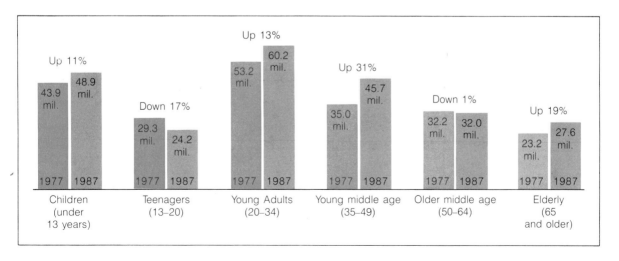

houses, so most will live in apartments. Moreover, they will increasingly choose to eat out or prepare quick meals at home, because both husbands and wives will be working.

The great growth in young middle-aged persons should translate into a greater demand for single-family houses. They will also demand consumer durables such as appliances on a greater scale, travel, and more extensive leisure activities. The elderly will become much more important to business than before. This is particularly true for firms who produce products and services in the following categories: travel, entertainment, apartment buildings, nursing homes, and health care.

CHANGES IN THE LABOR FORCE

Population shifts will affect the makeup of the labor force in the near future. The sharp drop in the birthrate in the 1960s will mean a drop in the number of new workers seeking jobs in the 1980s. Figure 20-2 shows the size of that drop. According to the Labor Department, the size of the total work force will increase by only 15 percent from 1977 to 1987. This is considerably less than the 24 percent growth from 1967 to 1977. (The labor force is comprised of persons aged 16 and over who have jobs or who are seeking them.) One immediate benefit from a decline in the number of new job seekers will be a decrease in the unemployment rate. The Labor Department expects that the unemployment rate will fall to 4 percent in the early 1980s.

One of the major factors behind the large number of new job seekers has been the increase in the number of women looking for work. This trend is likely to continue, and the Labor Department estimates that half of all women aged 16 and over will be in the labor force by the mid-1980s. Women now make up about 40 percent of the labor force. By 1987, the figure will be 42 percent.

FIGURE 20-2 Increase in the number of job seekers from 1947 to 1987. Source: Department of Labor

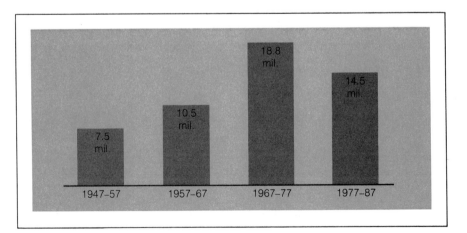

CHANGES IN THE ECONOMY

The American economy will change slowly over the next 10 years. The Bureau of Labor Statistics projects that real GNP should rise about 3.6 percent a year from 1980 to 1985, compared to an average annual rate of 6.2 percent from 1975 to 1980. The slower growth rate will be caused by the continued shift from the production of products to the providing of services, higher energy costs (discussed later in this chapter), a drop in increases in productivity, and the continued shift from private to public employment. Productivity rates will slow down because of the growth of service industries and government, both of which are less productive than manufacturing. At present, about one-third of American workers are in manufacturing jobs. By 1987 only about one-fourth will be in manufacturing. In 1972, government employed about 15 percent of the work force. By 1985, it will employ about 18 percent.

Productivity rate increases are vitally important to economic growth rates. According to the Bureau of Labor Statistics, productivity increases will average only 2.2 percent annually from 1972 to 1980 and will average 2.6 percent annually from 1981 to 1985. If these statistics are proven correct, the nation is in for trouble in its battle to add jobs and reduce inflation. Furthermore, if productivity is not higher, American manufacturers will lose their competitive edge with foreign firms.

This situation will be further complicated if the slowdown in new plant and equipment investment is not reversed. Lower hopes of future profits have kept stock prices depressed and made the raising of capital for expansion difficult. Without higher return on capital investment, business firms will be unwilling to modernize their plant and equipment and thus productivity will fall for yet another reason.

CHANGES AFFECTED BY ENERGY

Rising energy costs are already affecting American life-styles and American industry. America depends heavily on oil and gas to keep running. Domestic supplies of both these resources are dwindling. Although many average citizens seem to think that oil and gas producers are deliberately misleading the public when they warn of coming shortages, experts agree with the producers. Huge payments for imported gas and oil have wrecked the balance of trade for this country in recent years. Yet progress on energy legislation in Congress moves at a snail's pace.

Furthermore, the price of gas and oil from domestic sources is below its costs on the international market. Therefore, Americans are paying less than the true cost of producing the oil and gas they use. The result is a devaluation of the dollar and a growing dependence on foreign oil.

When oil prices tripled in 1973, coal seemed to be the answer to America's energy needs. Or so everyone thought. However, the shift hasn't happened. From filling 17 percent of the nation's energy needs in 1973, coal now fills only 19 percent of those needs. Neither has nuclear power bridged the gap. At one time, it

Electrical generators of the future may cause you to stop and stare. This seven-story-high, vertical-axis wind turbine generator is being tested by the Department of Energy. It develops 30 kilowatts of power at 25 mph.

ERDA

was thought that nuclear power would supply half of America's energy needs by 1990. That is no longer possible because of the rising costs of building nuclear plants and because of intensified pressure from the public which is concerned about operating safety and waste disposal at nuclear facilities.

Obviously, energy will cost more in the future. Besides adding to inflationary pressures and causing trade imbalances, the high cost of energy will slow economic growth. In addition, continued high cost will force changes in consumer life-styles and buying habits. In buying durable products such as household appliances and autos, consumers will now look for energy-efficient products at reasonable prices.

CHANGES IN TECHNOLOGY

Technology, or applied science, is crucial in economic growth for any country. It is said that technology and the increase in capital expense per worker are the main forces behind economic growth. Since most people still expect economic growth to act as a means of solving society's problems, increased use of technology in industry is vital. Most of the world's technology has come from research and development, a joint effort of private business, government, and universities.

Technology creates jobs, raises productivity, reduces inflationary pressures, and improves living standards. In the last few years, American technology has focused on miniaturization in electronics, use of the computer, health care, the development of new materials, and the development of energy-efficient durable goods.

Much of the technology of the future will be focused on using computers and on solving the twin problems of pollution and cheap energy. New investment in power plants, mines, pollution controls, and other products needed to solve environmental and energy problems will also stimulate growth among technology-oriented companies and the industries that supply them such as steel and aluminum. New applications of computers for offices, homes, factories, and consumer items will be expected.

More money will be spent for research and development in the coming years. In the 1960s and early 1970s, investment in research and development by American industry declined dramatically. American companies sold or licensed their technology to other countries on a wide scale. Japan alone bought almost a billion dollars worth of American technology, some of which it has improved. As a result, there were fewer inventions and technological breakthroughs in this country. American industry began to look to other industrialized countries for new technological applications. Disc brakes and radial tires, for example, were pioneered abroad. So were high-speed trains, stretch fabrics, soft contact lenses, and the X-ray body scanner. Today the situation is changing. Both the government and business have begun to realize that the key to growth and to competing with foreign firms is to continue to research and to use technology here.

CHANGES IN INTERNATIONAL TRADE

Dramatic changes are expected in international trade for the United States in the years to come. Some of these changes are already evident. Prior to 1970, the United States had a powerful, largely self-contained economy. American firms built factories all over the world and set up mining companies to send the raw materials, such as bauxite and copper, back to this country. These firms provided their own financing for almost everything. Although a variety of products and services were imported the U.S. balance of trade was favorable every year for about a century. Our dollar was the most stable, powerful currency in the world. Since we exported only about 6 percent of our output, overseas trade was important but not vital for most industries. Since then some major changes have occurred.

Two things have changed the picture: the tripling of oil prices in 1973 and increasing reliance on foreign oil. The result has been that there is a deficit in our balance of trade. The imbalance in trade has led to a steady erosion in the value of the dollar. At the same time, developing countries have raised the price of raw materials such as tin, coffee, and bauxite. With a huge domestic appetite for products, the United States is running out of many vital materials. It is estimated that by the turn of the century, the United States will import over half of its basic industrial minerals. These include iron, copper, and aluminum.

Obviously, the volume of imports will continue to increase, but the volume of exports should expand also. About 6 percent of the GNP was exported in 1977. By 1985, 12 percent of the GNP will be exported. Foremost among exports will be technically sophisticated products such as airplanes, military weapons, computers, and electronic equipment. More foreign firms will build factories here in the United States. A larger number of our basic industries will be dominated by foreign-owned firms, just as American-owned subsidiaries dominated foreign markets in the past. Multinational firms, based in Japan and Western Europe, will join the ranks of the American giants. The 20 largest foreign-owned firms operating in the United States are listed in Table 20-1.

CHANGES IN LIFE-STYLES

A change that will affect everyone directly will be the new outlook on life values and personal goals. It is predicted that Americans will be less interested in material possessions and more interested in self-fulfillment. Also, there will be less emphasis on overcoming nature and more on living in harmony with it. Tastes in clothing, shelter, recreation, transportation and food are expected to show marked change.

TABLE 20-1 The 20 largest foreign-owned firms in the United States

U.S. Company	Ownership	Percentage of Foreign Ownership
Shell Oil	Netherlands-Britain	69
Brown & Williamson Tobacco	Britain	more than 90
Joseph E. Seagram & Sons	Canada	more than 90
Grand Union	Britain	82
National Tea	Canada	84
North American Philips	Netherlands	60
International Nickel	Canada	more than 90
American Petrofina	Belgium	72
Ciba-Geigy	Switzerland	more than 90
Nestlé	Switzerland	more than 90
Lever Brothers	Netherlands-Britain	more than 90
Akzona	Netherlands	65
Alcan Aluminum	Canada	more than 90
American Hoechst	West Germany	more than 90
Moore Business Forms/F. N. Burt	Canada	more than 90
Hoffmann-LaRoche	Switzerland	more than 90
BASF Wyandotte	West Germany	more than 90
Massey-Ferguson	Canada	more than 90
Hanson Industries	Britain	more than 90
Certain-Teed Products	Britain-France	51

Source: The Conference Board

Among the many recreational sports Americans will pursue in their leisure time will be skiing.

American Stock Photo

Leisure time and flexible working hours will give Americans more time in which to pursue their nonwork interests. The boom in leisure products and services has already started and will continue to expand. Today, supplying the needs of campers, hikers, tennis players, and joggers has become big business. Likewise, do-it-yourself industries, such as remodeling, refinishing, and hobbies, are experiencing major growth.

Other predicted trends include less emphasis on the home as a center of activities. Outdoor recreational pursuits and eating more meals outside the home will contribute to this trend. A swing to apartment living is already underway, caused partly by the rising cost of home ownership and partly by the mobility of apartment living. In addition, participation in religious and cultural activities is expected to increase through the nation. Church attendance is already moving toward record figures. The visual and performing arts are flourishing. Live theater, for example, appears to be established in every major metropolitan area and in smaller communities as well. All these things appear to mean that the American public is seeking a higher quality of life than it has in past decades. The emphasis is on doing things to develop one's body and mind and in building meaningful relationships with others.

personality profile:
**GEORGE SZEGO —
taming the sun god**

What's up for the future? The sun is, for certain. The rising costs of conventional fuels such as oil, not to mention less conventional ones such as uranium, have spurred the investigation of substitute sources of energy. At the same time, environmental concern over smog and radioactive wastes have given particular importance to the development of "clean" energy sources, the most obviously abundant of which is the sun.

What's been wrong with solar energy so far is that technology to utilize the sun's energy has not advanced enough to make it cheap. Major solar research and experimental programs have been funded so far by the government. Many of these programs are now winding up, however, and it is thought that the solar energy industry may finally be ready to turn to the commercial market. George Szego, who operates InterTechnology Corp. from a converted Safeway store, is well poised to take advantage of the situation.

Szego, who has a Ph.D. in chemical engineering, is recognized as a pioneer in the field by people in the Department of Energy and the giant energy companies. He has worked on power projects for TRW and General Electric, and his InterTechnology Corp. has competed successfully with such giants for government money to fund solar energy projects which had little likelihood of payoff. Within the next few years, Uncle Sam is expected to withdraw its financial resources from the infant industry and push it to try its own wings. This will leave ITC and other small companies, which have considerable debt and no profits so far, on the spot.

Szego's big asset is his experience in the field, which gives him a chance to compete successfully in solar collectors while developing his exclusive rights on a system to generate electrical power from the sun's rays by osmotic pressure, created by liquid diffusion through a membrane. Once this process is in place there are no irreplaceable fuels, no pollution-control costs, and no reprocessing and storage costs. However, it will take money to make the transition from science to business. "As this industry grows," says Szego, "it'll be a lousy job just to run a think tank." With his exclusive rights and specialized knowledge of solar technology, George Szego looks like a good investment for a company that has the capital to invest in him and ITC.

EMPLOYMENT IN A CHANGING FUTURE

Some aspects of the future, such as the population increases or decreases, can be predicted with remarkable accuracy. Others, such as the growth of specific industries, are less easy to predict. Nevertheless, on a broad scale, it is possible to predict with some accuracy where industrial growth will take place. It is also possible to pinpoint some of the occupational areas that are the most promising. For example, the service area is likely to grow in importance for job seekers.

SERVICE WORKERS

Two-thirds of the American work force is employed in service industries today. By 1985, the percentage is likely to be three-quarters. However, the growth rate within service industries varies by category. Health care and business services, such as accounting, data processing, maintenance, and advertising, are expected to grow especially rapidly. The second fastest growth area—government—will primarily expand at the state and local government levels. New jobs in government will be in the areas of health, sanitation, welfare, and police and fire protection. Employment in the finance, insurance, and real estate sector will increase most rapidly in banks, credit agencies, and among security and commodity brokers, dealers, exchanges, and services. Jobs will be created at a fairly rapid rate in contract construction as a result of the continued need for homes, apartments, offices, stores, highways, and other physical facilities.

Retail trade, which is the largest division within the service industries, has expanded sharply since 1960. Its growth will be slower in percentage terms but still will be a major source of job opportunities. The use of electronic data processing equipment in sales and automated warehousing equipment as well as the increase in the number in self-service stores and vending machines will negatively affect employment. Manufacturing jobs involved with producing consumer durable goods are likely to grow more rapidly than those producing nondurable goods. Employment in transportation and public utilities will jump slightly. More jobs will be available in air and water transportation and fewer in railroad transportation.

FIGURE 20-3 Projected employment growth by industry, 1975–1985. Source: Bureau of Labor Statistics

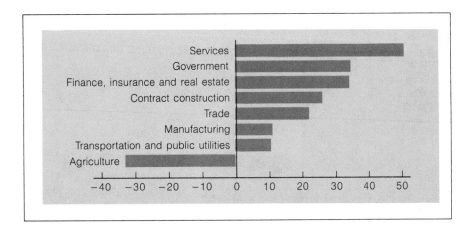

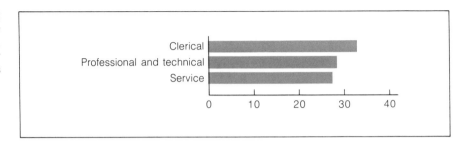

CLERICAL AND PROFESSIONAL WORKERS

Clerical workers will be the most in demand in the near future (see Figure 20-4). Clerical workers include those who operate computers and office machines, keep records, take dictation, and type. The demand will be strong for those qualified to perform jobs involved with electronic data processing operations.

Professional and technical people will continue in high demand. Among them are dentists, scientists, accountants, attorneys, architects, doctors, and nurses. A re-emphasis on scientific and technical knowledge seems likely and so people with scientific and technical specialties will be needed.

Service workers include those who maintain law and order, assist professional nurses in hospitals, give haircuts and beauty treatments, and home maintenance. This group will grow rapidly with rising demand for hospital and other medical care. There will be a greater need for protective services as urbanization continues. There will also be more frequent use of restaurants, beauty salons, and other services as income levels rise and an increasing number of housewives take jobs outside the home.

EDUCATION AND TRAINING

In considering a career, one should not eliminate an occupation because it is not among the fastest growing. Figure 20-5 shows that more jobs will be created from deaths, retirements, and other separations than from growth in industries. It is important, however, to realize that sufficient skill and education are prerequisites

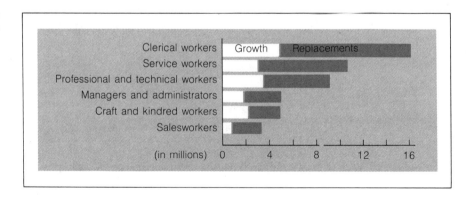

Foremost in growth areas in employment in the near future will be technology and the applications of technology to business. Industry will seek highly trained technicians and scientists for years to come.

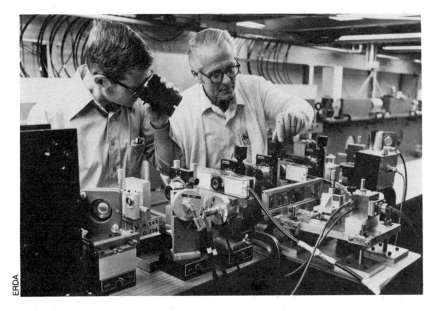

to employment. By and large, employment will be most readily available in those occupations requiring the most education and training. For example, employment in clerical and professional and technical jobs will grow faster than in all other occupational groups.

Also, unemployment rates tend to be higher among persons of lesser education and training attainments. Education beyond high school has been standard for many professional occupations for a long time. Other areas of work increasingly require more than just a high school education. As new, automated equipment is introduced on a wider scale in offices, banks, insurance companies, and government operations, skill requirements are rising for clerical and other jobs. Employers are increasingly seeking better trained workers to run complicated technical machinery.

It would appear that communication and quantitative skills are more important than ever and will increase in importance for all workers. Mathematics, statistics, and a working knowledge of data processing are going to be increasingly important to many workers. The ability to communicate both in writing and orally will also take on increasing importance. In many clerical, technical, and managerial jobs, particularly those involving the use of the computer, both communications and technical skills will be needed.

LEVEL OF EDUCATION AND INCOME

Besides giving one an edge in competing for jobs, advanced education makes a difference in lifetime income. As Figure 20-6 shows, people with some college education tend to make more money than those with only a high school education. In turn, those who have completed at least a college degree tend to make more than those with only some college. However, the difference will vary widely

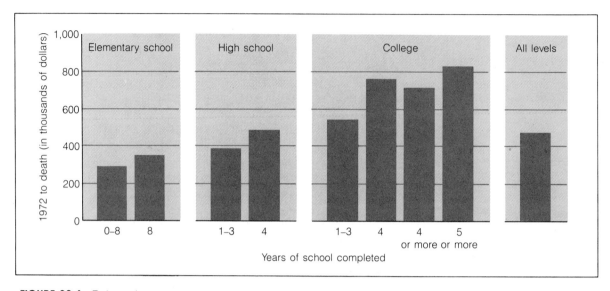

FIGURE 20-6 Estimated lifetime earnings by length of education. Source: Bureau of the Census

by type of occupation. A further complicating factor is that the number of jobs that require a college education is expected to be less than the number of applicants by 1985. This means that the people with college degrees will be taking jobs that formerly were held by those with less than a college education. As a result, it will be increasingly difficult to compete in many occupations without some college work. A spillover of college graduates into nontraditional fields is already evident. The proportion of workers with four or more years of college education has increased by more than 60 percent in clerical, service, and blue-collar jobs from 1970 to 1975. These are areas that have traditionally had very few college graduates. Community college and four-year college graduates will be increasingly competitive in the same job markets. Community colleges have shown that they can train students for many occupations in two years or even less, and that the number of students completing career education programs in these institutions is increasing rapidly. Community college graduates may find that while they are very employable, they may need to go back to school at a later date for additional skills and education.

SUMMARY

Although the future is always uncertain, all well-managed firms plan for it. Successful firms anticipate changes in our society and move to take advantage of them. Some of the changes that are anticipated in the future include: changes in population, changes in the labor force, changes in the economy, changes affected by energy, changes in technology, changes in international trade, and changes in life-styles in society.

The population will shift to nonmetropolitan areas and to the warmer areas of the country. The number of persons in the young middle-aged and elderly groups will rise considerably while the number of teenagers will fall. The labor force will grow at a slower pace than it has in the past decade, and the economy should also grow at a slightly slower rate. This should result in a lower unemployment rate.

Energy will cost more and will affect the life-styles of all Americans. Much of the technological applications in the years just ahead will focus on the use of computers and on solving the problems of pollution and low-cost energy. On the international scene, the American economy will be affected more than it has been by fluctuations in international prices and in the economies of foreign countries. As America imports more of its raw material and oil needs at higher prices, it will be more difficult to maintain a favorable balance of trade and payments. The dollar may continue to decrease in value.

The life-styles of the American people will be altered. There will be less emphasis on material things and more emphasis on recreation, leisure activities, and the development of the total personality.

The employment picture will undergo considerable change. There will be an increase in the number of service workers and an increase in the number of clerical and professional workers. Education and training will be even more important than they are today because a greater level of skill and knowledge will be needed than in the past. The return on investment in education and additional training will continue to be much higher than on any other type of investment.

REVIEW QUESTIONS

1. Name and explain some of the major population shifts that will affect business and employment in the next 10 years.

2. What changes taking place in the economy are likely to influence the number of jobs available in 10 years?

3. What role does technology play in the creation of economic growth and the number of new jobs?

4. What changes are likely to take place in international trade that will affect businesses in this country?

5. In which industries would you expect the most rapid growth to take place in the next 10 years?

6. Do you believe the following generalization is true: "The more education you have, the easier it is to find a job."

7. Do you see the increasing costs and shortages of energy as slowing economic growth, speeding it up, or both?

8. In planning for the future, what types of occupations offer the best possibilities for long-term employment?

9. What changes in technology are likely to influence the number and types of jobs available in the future?

10. What changes in life-styles appear to have an impact on the types of products and services that will be produced in the future?

DISCUSSION QUESTIONS

1. How would you react to this statement: "Since it appears that there will be fewer jobs requiring a college education than the number of graduates in the next 10 years, it is clear that a college education is not very important in today's working world."

2. In addition to the examples in the chapter, name some industries or firms that can expect to benefit by changes taking place in the age distribution of Americans.

3. Of the possible future trends mentioned in the chapter, which ones are related to the kind of career path that you expect to follow?

4. Which industries appear to you to have the best growth potential for the next 10 to 20 years based on the projections of this chapter?

5. Which industries appear to have the least growth potential for the next 15 years based on the projections of this chapter and other information that you may have?

CASES FOR DECISION MAKING

A NEW LIFE-STYLE IMPACTS FIRMS AND FAMILIES

A government sponsored report on the quality of life in the United States, published in December, 1977, shows a picture of steady improvements, and, for some, dramatic changes in life-styles in the past 25 years.

As compared to 1960, the following patterns have emerged: less time spent on family care and more on leisure activities; decreased time spent on being home with the family and visiting friends and more time spent watching television, reading and going to movies and the theater; fewer first marriages but more divorces and remarriages; fewer deaths from heart disease, strokes, and tuberculosis but more deaths from cancer, suicides, cirrhosis of the liver, and homicide.

In addition to these patterns, other trends have emerged: housing is larger and more comfortable; the average size of families is shrinking and is expected to be three by 1990; life expectancy is longer; median income of families is double what it was in 1947 even adjusting for inflation; an increasing number of families now receive income from sources other than their jobs.

1. From these patterns, which industries have the most favorable future judging by the trends that are developing?

2. If you were interested in your own business that could take advantage of one or more of these trends, what would it be and why?

3. What are some other trends that affect life-styles that are not mentioned in this study?

MASS PRODUCTION TECHNIQUES FOR HOSPITAL SERVICES.

Hospital costs have skyrocketed in recent years as part of the overall increase in health care costs. One way to reduce hospital costs is to divide the cost of technology and specialization among many hospitals. The new nonprofit hospital chains that own, lease, or manage their affiliates are an attempt to do that.

So far there are 31 major hospital chains with about 400 member hospitals. Chain hospitals gain from mass purchasing of supplies and medicines. A chain may also help balance out occupancy rates so that hospitals that are overbooked can refer patients to other hospitals. Hospitals in the chain can specialize in certain areas such as cancer therapy or open-heart surgery, which will eliminate expensive duplication of equipment. In addition, the chain process could result in better financial management and auditing of physician and hospital services.

While there are some disadvantages, such as increased paper work and loss of decision making by individual hospitals, the benefits appear to far outweigh the problems. So far, the chains are based mainly in medium-sized cities in the Midwest and West. National expansion is expected soon.

1. From the patient's point of view, does this trend appear to be a good one?

2. What problems can you see in adapting the chain hospital system to large city hospitals?

3. What business and career opportunities do you see if this trend continues?

part seven: CAREER OPPORTUNITIES

CAREERS IN GOVERNMENT

There is no doubt about it—a government job for a college graduate means security and good fringe benefits. However, with government salaries becoming much more competitive with those paid by business firms, the number of applicants for government jobs far exceeds the available openings. Nevertheless, there are opportunities in federal agencies and departments.

FEDERAL GOVERNMENT: THE LARGEST EMPLOYER The federal government is the largest employer in the nation; hence jobs will be available for graduates of community/junior colleges and four-year colleges. There are about 2 million white-collar jobs in the federal government, including budget analyst, claims examiner, purchasing officer, administrative assistant, and personnel officer. In addition, college graduates may enter technical, clerical, and aide-assistant positions at higher levels than persons with a high school education.

While employment in the federal government is expected to grow only moderately in the coming decade, continued population expansion will create more jobs for social security claims examiners, accounting and budget workers, and business and industry specialists.

STATE AND LOCAL GOVERNMENT JOBS In state and local governments, growth in jobs should be faster than at the federal government level. Over half of these jobs are in education. While many jobs are in specialized fields such as teaching, health services, highway work, and fire and safety control, there are a number of opportunities for clerks, administrators, fiscal and budget administrators, bookkeepers, and accountants.

CAREERS IN THE INSURANCE INDUSTRY

From clerical to executive level, there are many job opportunities in the insurance industry. For clerical jobs, skills in typing, filing, business math, and in some cases stenography are essential. Executive positions usually require people with college degrees in business administration finance, economics, or, in some cases, the liberal arts.

Because of its stability and strength, the insurance industry provides a relatively high degree of job security. Recessions appear to affect employment here less than in many other industries.

CLAIMS EXAMINERS AND UNDERWRITERS Two types of jobs in insurance are claim examiners and underwriters. Claim examiners, or claim representatives, investigate the details of a claim involving large amounts of money, particularly when there is question about the size of the settlement, when a false claim may have been made, or when a claim exceeds a specified amount. Some college experience is preferred for applicants. About 35,000 persons are employed as claim examiners. Growth is expected to be small to the mid-1980s.

Insurance underwriters appraise and select the

risks their company will insure. They approve applications for life, property, liability, and health insurance. Because the success of the insurance company depends on the effectiveness of its underwriters in choosing good risks, underwriters hold responsible positions and are selected carefully. A college degree is usually required.

CLAIMS ADJUSTERS   There are over 150,000 claims adjusters in the insurance industry. These are the people who settle claims made against an insurance company. The adjuster, as agent for the firm, attempts to establish the validity of the claim and to reach a fair monetary settlement with the concerned parties. While a college degree is not usually required for employment, it is helpful in advancing to senior or supervisory positions.

AGENTS AND BROKERS   Insurance agents and brokers are the middlemen of the insurance industry. These are the people who sell the policies to individuals or businesses. Part of the service that they should provide is informative; they are supposed to assess the insurance needs of their

potential customers. An insurance agent acts as an employee of one insurance company or as an independent agent who sells for several different insurance companies. A broker, on the other hand, is not under contract to, or affiliated with, any insurance company. Instead, brokers assess and meet the insurance needs of their clients through the various companies for which they act as broker.

Agents and brokers can take formal courses to update and broaden the scope of their professional knowledge. As for undergraduate education, a bachelor's degree in the liberal arts, economics, or business administration is usually adequate. Certification as a Chartered Life Underwriter (CLU) or Chartered Property or Liability Underwriter (CPLU) can be earned by taking courses and passing a series of examinations. Many agents and brokers pursue these certifications because it indicates their expert knowledge of the insurance field. There are about 450,000 agents and brokers in the insurance field. Since an overwhelming percentage are men, the opportunities for women should be good.

appendices

A
TRACKING YOUR FIRST JOB

Throughout this book, we have pointed out some of the career opportunities available in business, government, and other sectors of our economy. In this section, we will look at some of the factors you should consider in finding and applying for a job.

You must keep in mind, of course, that work is only one aspect of your life. If you are to choose the type of career that you want, you will have to know where work fits into your other values. It is important that you have a pretty good idea about the kind of life-style that goes along with the job you select. Besides shaping your life at work, your career also influences the type of people with whom you will mingle, the entertainment and recreation you will enjoy, the social groups you are likely to join, and even the location of your housing and shopping. For this reason, a job is more than a means of earning income. It shapes and influences you and your values. As you seek that first job leading down a career path, keep that in mind. Now, let's look at what is involved in the job-hunting process.

To make this section as accurate as possible, it has been adapted from material actually used by business and colleges. The material on job-hunting was adapted from *Job-Hunting (and Job-Switching) Takes Planning*, a publication of the Recruiting and College Relations Department of DOW Chemical U.S.A. The sections on interviewing and job resumes were adapted from NIU *Job Hunter's Guide*, written by Dr. Charles A. Harkness, Assistant Director of the Placement Bureau, Northern Illinois University.

JOB-HUNTING

During your college years, you've met your academic tests by preparing yourself through study. With job-hunting, too, careful step-by-step preparation is important, since it leads to one of the most important decisions you will make in your lifetime.

CAREER COUNSELING

If you haven't already sought the counsel of others in helping you decide which industry is best for you, we urge you to do so now. Then you should decide which companies within that industry are the most interesting and attractive. Your faculty and your campus placement director or career counselor can be of invaluable assistance in this regard. Your college placement office or career counselor will also have publications that will help you analyze careers that might suit you. Some of these publications include:

College Placement Annual. Published annually by College Placement Council, Inc., P.O. Box 2263, Bethlehem, Pa. 18001. This provides information on the types of jobs that specific firms have open for the year for college graduates. It gives information about the firms as well as helpful hints on applying for a job.

Occupational Outlook Handbook. Published annually by the U.S. Department of Labor, U.S. Government Printing Office, Washington, D.C. This is a comprehensive listing of all major occupations with a description of duties, opportunities, requirements, and future outlook for those jobs.

Occupational Outlook for College Graduates. Published annually by the U.S. Department of Labor, U.S. Government Printing Office, Washington, D.C. This is a listing of all major occupations for college graduates and has a description of the duties, opportunities, requirements, and future outlook for those jobs.

Talk to your friends who are employed in jobs you're interested in to determine what their work involves. If you are married and want a kindly but really knowledgeable assessment of your strong and weak points, your spouse is by far the best equipped to give it to you.

If there's a psychological testing service at your school, take advantage of whatever facilities it offers to appraise and analyze your strengths and weaknesses. Once this is done, a counselor can suggest certain kinds of work in which you should find both success and enjoyment. Follow this with an interview and a counseling session in the student placement bureau or career counseling office. You will find that the placement director and your teachers are just as interested in your success as you are. Their reputations—the respect in which they and their profession are held—depend in good measure on their ability to help you become a productive citizen.

CULLING THE COMPANIES Since the number of companies you can interview is limited by the time you have available, you'll need to be selective. Some questions you might wish to ask yourself in scaling down the list are:

1. Does the company offer the type of work I want?
2. What is the company's growth rate relative to that of its industry?
3. What are the product or service fields of special interest to the company? Do I have any particular interest or background in these fields?
4. Do the geographical locations of the company's operations appeal to me?

A little research will provide the answers to most of these questions. Publications (to be found in your college placement office or library) containing this information include: *The College Placement Annual, Thomas' Register of American Manufacturing, Moody's Industrial Manual, Standard & Poor's Corporation Records, Dun & Bradstreet's Reference Book of Manufacturers, Fitch's Corporation Manual,* and company annual reports. The employment columns and career-opportunities issues of business and technical publications are other mines of information. Most detailed of all are the recruiting literature and annual reports of specific companies. Again, seek counsel from your placement director and your faculty; chances are good that they have actually visited the companies in which you are interested.

Although the campus interview may not be as promising a job source as it once was, companies still send out recruiters each year looking for talent to strengthen their organizations and keep them vital. The competition has intensified, but meeting and talking with a recruiter is still worthwhile. Help in preparing for interviews with recruiters can be found on pages 573–577.

HELP IS CLOSE BY While checking out opportunities described by the campus recruiters, you'd be wise to look for other possibilities nearby.

Acquire as much knowledge as you can about the city or area you live in or want to live in and the businesses located there. A knowledge of the products and services provided by various firms will tell you where to go to apply for a position. Familiarity with the street layout will save you time and money. Knowing who the prominent people in the business world are will enable you to talk intelligently about them with a prospective employer.

In addition to the help available to you in the college placement office, there are two very valuable aids that are probably in your home at this moment: the daily newspaper and the telephone directory. Many a promising opportunity has been uncovered by the intelligent use of these publications.

Newspapers A careful scanning of the classified ads is a must in the routine of anyone looking for work, and an early answer to the most promising ones can be very advantageous. Your friends may tell you not to bother with the "blind" ads (those giving a box number for receiving replies), but don't ignore them—they sometimes hold hidden treasure.

Don't neglect the rest of the newspaper. You do not have to read every word in it; if you did, you might not have time to look for a job. But at least glance over every page and read the items that may be of help to you. News items may give you clues as to where work is or will soon be available and also where it is useless to look. Read all items with headings similar to these:

Air Base to Phase Out

New Plant for Area

Layoff at Acme Announced

Million Dollar Expansion Planned

Bids Let for School Construction

Think, and use your imagination. If an air base is to be phased out, it is pointless to apply there for work even if it does employ 6,000 people. If the phasing out is to be rapid, competition for other available jobs in the area may be very keen. Would this be a good time to move? Or to take a job temporarily for less money than you had hoped to get?

If there is to be a new plant in the area, this means not only new jobs in that particular industry but also an increase in construction work, clerical jobs, and a general upswing of the economy.

The Telephone Directory   Use the telephone directory. Notice that we said use the directory—not the telephone. In general, it is far better to make a visit than to call, whether you are trying to find out if the company is accepting applications or contacting a company to which you have already applied. Go, because even though the company may not be accepting applications, it may take one from a person as nice-looking and well-qualified as you! Go, because if you are already there, the employer just might have time to interview you briefly.

Why go if there are no jobs open? Because there may be one open tomorrow or next week.

The telephone directory can be useful for finding the addresses of companies to which you wish to apply, and the yellow pages can give you the names of businesses you do not know. For instance, if you are looking for a job in air conditioning, the yellow pages will have a list of the companies that do this kind of work. Go to each of those places.

THE MAIL CAMPAIGN

You may need to initiate a mail campaign as part of your employment search. A summary of your qualifications, called a *resume*, and a personal letter expressing employment interest are essential in such a strategy.

PREPARING AND USING A RESUME

A resume is nothing more than a "free form" application blank. It is one of the best tools available for your employment search. Prepare it carefully and well.

But in spite of its resemblance to an application blank, the resume is different. Most application blanks (and most resumes) tend to be obituaries. They tell about what you *have done*. What you want to tell is what it is that you *can do*. A typical example of the "obituary" entry might be:

Sep 1976–   Assistant Night Manager, McDonald's, in
May 1976   DeKalb, Illinois
              Had full responsibility for restaurant
              two nights each week.

Now, let's rewrite this item so that it shows what you can do for the firm to which you are applying:

I am a responsible individual who can maintain careful and accurate records, both in inventory and cash control. During my senior year in college, I was assistant night manager for the McDonald's franchise in DeKalb, Illinois. We had neither cash nor inventory shortages during the period for the nights that I worked.

Doesn't that tell more about you than the "obituary" entry? Think through some of the other things that you might want to include in your resume. To what extent can they be reworked to tell more about your capabilities?

The "free form" aspect of the resume allows you to do with it as you please. Possibly your grade point average isn't the world's best; you wish it could be ignored. Here's your chance; don't put it in your resume. If it isn't there, you don't run the risk of being screened out because it's low. Don't mention the subject until you're asked about it—and if you're never asked about it. . . . The same thing goes for any other potentially derogatory or damaging information. Don't put it in the resume; you've just improved your chances of getting an interview, and that's what the resume is all about. On the other hand, don't lie. A lie will ultimately be found out, and very possibly not until after you have been employed. When it is, you may be fired. Again, the reaction might also be, "If he'll lie about that, what else will he lie about?" and there could go the chances for promotion.

It may be best to write a different resume for each employer to whom you apply so that you can tailor it to fit that particular business or position. But even if you use the same resume hundreds of times (as you may if you are seeking a hard-to-find job or fishing for the best possible opening), you will want to make the employer realize that you have spent some time considering his particular company. For that reason, *do not send mimeographed resumes or carbon copies.* If you have to type a hundred copies, grit your teeth and do it. It will pay off.

A printed resume is an entirely different matter. The very fact that you have gone to the trouble and expense of having it printed marks you as a person of resource and imagination. A couple of rules to follow in resume preparation:

1. Keep it short. The fewer words you use to tell your story, the more likely it will be read. Hold it to one page; there is little excuse for exceeding one page—and the more you put down, the less likely it is that it will be read.
2. Keep it attractive. No—that doesn't mean having it printed in four colors. That means neat, concise, clean, readable. A buff-colored paper might make it stand out a bit in a pile; don't use your favorite lavender stationery. And a best-foot-forward photograph of yourself will fix you more firmly in an employer's mind.

After the Writing: Have it reproduced. Multilith is fine. Offset press is better, but it isn't absolutely necessary. Probably you should make 100 copies.

Some sample resumes follow. Look them over; what format seems to fit you? How could you tell your story best? Remember, you are involved in a sales job; you are the "product" for sale. Make yourself as attractive to the "customer" as you possibly can.

Now: The time has come when you must "market" yourself. You have a resume that you've spent considerable time preparing; it must be used effectively. Remember, you have just enough money left to get you through the first month after you graduate; you can't spend time trying to use an ineffective marketing program. Don't get in your car and drive around dropping off resumes at random, unannounced. Gas is too expensive for that (and your time is too valuable). Plan ahead and pick your targets carefully.

You've probably selected the geographic area in which you would like to work. Research it thoroughly, finding the companies or agencies you'd like to work for. Develop a list of about 20.

Begin some research into each of those 20 firms. What is it that each does? What office or division or department within each one does the sort of work that you want to do? What can you do for them? (What they can do for you is give you a paycheck. What the firm wants to know, however, is what you can do for it that will earn that paycheck.) Is the person who supervises that department the individual who can say "You're hired"? If he is, get his name. If he isn't, who is?

Now that you have the name of the individual who can hire you, you are ready to go looking for the job. Go directly to that individual either by mail or in person and present your case. Let him know exactly what it is you have to sell that you think this particular company should buy. What you have to sell, of course, is you. What is it about you—your ideas, your approach, your grades, whatever— that you think is sufficiently distinctive to make the individual you are talking to say "You're hired"? Of course, a copy of your resume accompanies the letter when you make your first contact, or else it goes with you when you make your first direct personal contact.

Or: You can attempt to "mass market" yourself. For this, you will need a copy of the telephone directory's yellow pages for a given community. Better yet, write the Chamber of Commerce and get a copy of the industrial directory. That is going to cost you anywhere from $3.00 to $15.00. For this approach you should probably double the number of resumes that you will have printed—200 instead of 100. Start sending resumes, with a good cover letter, to all those firms that interest you.

Generally, you can expect a 25 percent response to letters sent out under the "shotgun" technique. What about the other 75 percent? After about two weeks, get on the phone and start calling. Your conversation might start with a statement like: "You have received my resume. I hope you have had a chance to review it. When may I come for an interview?"

This is a procedure that will work well in a metropolitan area. If you are trying to locate outside a metropolitan area, the shotgun approach is more difficult to use because of the greater distances between employers. If you feel you need help in putting your resume together or have a special problem in job location (geographic, industrial, social), you should seek help from your college placement bureau or career counseling center.

RESUME FOR: LOIS M. SCHULTZ

2000 Suburban Estates   After June 1, 1980:
DeKalb, Illinois 60115   2026 Keeney St.
815-758-5215   River Grove, Illinois
                                   60171
                                   312-864-6430

PERSONAL   Single   Age: 22
INFORMATION: Height: 5'5"   Weight: 115

                A beginning position as a personnel management
                trainee. I hope to specialize ultimately in
                wage and salary administration at the corporate
                level.

EDUCATION: 1976-80   Northern Illinois University, DeKalb
                           B.S. in Business Administration
                           Major: Management. This is a
                             comprehensive major. However, within
                             the limits allowed, I placed emphasis
                             on personnel management.

EXPERIENCE: Summers   National Car Rental, Chicago
                1975-77   General office clerical work. Worked
                             as summer relief in personnel department,
                             general accounting, and reservations.

                Summers   Sears, Roebuck & Co., Chicago
                1978-79   Worked as assistant data processing
                             librarian in the Sears Corporate
                             Headquarters.

                Sept-May   History Department, Northern Illinois
                1977-80   University
                             Clerical Assistant to the departmental
                             secretary for three years while a
                             student.

                In addition, I worked as a waitress and cashier
                while earning 75 percent of my college expenses.

INTERESTS   President, Beta Lambda Sigma Honorary Society
                Member, Society for Advance of Management
                Enjoy skiing, reading
                Worked as a volunteer one night weekly at Illinois
                  State Training School for Girls, Geneva, for
                  four years.

REFERENCES   Available upon request.

RESUME FOR

> MARK L. WOODFORD
> 1339 Dorchester Road
> DeKalb, Illinois 60115
> 815–753–5432

PERSONAL: Married, no children
               Height: 5'10"
               Weight: 165
               Age: 22

JOB   Customer sales with agriculturally oriented business.
OBJECTIVE: Ultimately I would like to be a regional sales manager.

EDUCATION: 1978–80   Kishwaukee Community College, Malta, Illinois
                         Associate in Arts Degree Major: Business
                         Administration

EXPERIENCE: Summers   DeKalb Agresearch, Inc., DeKalb, Ill.
               1978–79   Initially rogued hybrid seed corn fields. Served
                         as roguing crew supervisor for two summers and
                         as crew scheduler and time keeper for two
                         summers.

               1979–80   DeKalb Fertilizer Co., DeKalb, Ill.
                         Worked part–time during school year in both
                         inside and outside sales.

               Have also worked as bus boy, carryout boy, and
               undergraduate research assistant. These jobs have
               provided 90 percent of my college and living expenses.

               INTERESTS
                AND ACTIVITIES:
                         President, NIU Young Republicans
                         Treasurer, American Marketing Association
                         Enjoy skiing, hunting, camping, chess.

               REFERENCES: Available upon request.

LETTERS TO ACCOMPANY RESUMES

Probably the single most important document that you can use in your job search is the letter that goes with the resume. Remember, you are selling yourself; the letter is the first impression that you will make on the prospective buyer. It has to be a sales type letter.

It also must reflect your abilities and personality. If you come across in the letter as a "sharp" person, and thus get an interview, you must be able to carry that "sharpness" through the interview and ultimately into the job.

The important quality is: What is it about the letter that makes you different? What is it, after the employer has read the letter, that will make reading the resume irresistible?

The letter should be concise and short. You should be able to tell your story in 200 to 250 words. Don't get involved in long explanations of why you contacted the firm, or why your grade point average is what it is, or anything else. What you want is an interview; you can go into the details at that point.

Get some "feel" for the firm that you are writing to. Is it a conservative firm? Then don't write a flashy letter. Are you seeking a laboratory or design or research position? Then don't write a letter that is "hard sell." Are you looking for a public relations or personnel type of position? Then be creative in your letter. Give the reader some idea that you are a person who is different, who does not deal with stereotypes. If you are seeking a production position, then have some feeling for people and person-to-person contact in your letter. And if you are looking for sales—THEN SELL. Regardless of the type of letter, it must be free of grammatical, spelling, and typing errors.

Each letter should be individually prepared (another good reason for keeping them short). Before you write, do some investigating of the particular firm or even of the particular job for which you are applying. Make your letter as personal as you possibly can.

If your mail campaign has been carefully planned and carried out, you can expect a few of the companies you've contacted to ask you to come for an interview. Knowing in general how interviewers conduct meetings and what they will look for in your conduct will make the experience less nerve-wracking for you. You might even enjoy it!

WHAT IS AN INTERVIEW?

An interview is a conversation with a purpose.

The whole idea of the interview is to try to determine how well you fit the *personnel* needs of the business. You will seldom be asked technical questions; any interest that anyone has in your technical qualifications can be evaluated by looking at your application, your transcript, talking to your faculty, etc. Your face-to-face time with the interviewer need not be taken up with things that can be found elsewhere. Probably the basic question that the interviewer is trying to answer is one that runs along these lines: How would I like to have this person sitting at the desk next to mine?

You should be asking yourself the same question during the interview. How would I like to be associated with people like this interviewer? (No, you won't be sitting at the next desk, but people throughout the company are going to have many qualities in common with the interviewer. While you talk with the interviewer, consider that you are talking with most of the people in the firm.)

QUESTIONS AND ANSWERS

What kinds of questions are asked in an interview and what kinds of answers are sought? Here are a few samples of questions you may be asked and answers you may want to give.

TELL ME ABOUT YOURSELF

Now, *that* is an open-ended question. What kind of answer fits it? No, you don't begin with "I was born in Chicago, May 26, 1951." The interviewer knows that; it is on your application or your resume. What the interviewer wants to know is what is it that makes you tick; what is it that sets you apart? How well can you express yourself? A much more fitting beginning for an answer might be: "I'm a person who tries to enjoy life . . ." or "I'm an analytical person . . ." or some such beginning.

WHAT WOULD YOU LIKE TO BE DOING FIVE YEARS FROM NOW?

This is a difficult question to answer. Probably, if you pinned the interviewer down, the person probably couldn't tell you his or her plans five years in advance. You need to come up with an answer that shows you as you would like to be: "In five years I think I could be a responsible assistant district sales manager." "I should be in a position to manage one of your company's smaller stores; possibly I could be the assistant manager in a medium-sized unit." "In five years, I hope to be back in school full-time working on my doctorate in _____ ." (With an answer like the last one, you probably shouldn't have bothered taking the interview in the first place.)

DO YOU HAVE ANY QUESTIONS ABOUT THE COMPANY?

"What is it that you make?" is not a proper question at this point. You should already know; in fact, you should already know almost as much about the firm as the interviewer knows—in a general way, of course. You must be well acquainted with the firm.

WHAT KIND OF POSITION DO YOU WANT WITH _____ ?

Be sure that you have a definite type of position in mind. In today's job market, you cannot say "I'm really not certain; what kinds of positions do you have available?" If it is obvious that the only thing the particular representative is looking for is salespersons, then you must want to be a salesperson; otherwise you wouldn't be interviewing with them. If the company is looking for a wider variety, then an answer might be: "I want to be involved in the public relations aspects of your firm. I am especially interested in working with your house organ, _____ . Will you have an opening on the staff of _____ available this spring?"

For a more thorough analysis of what to expect in an interview, get a free copy of *Making the Most of Your Job Interview* from your local New York Life Insurance Company representative. It outlines in depth how to prepare for an interview and how to conduct yourself during the interview.

WHO WILL INTERVIEW YOU?

Companies select interviewers who have a broad knowledge of company functions, jobs, and operations. The interviewer generally will not know every detail about each specific job opening but should be prepared to talk about most aspects of his company. You may be talking with a line technical executive, a personnel director, or a production manager. No matter what department the person represents, you may be confident that the interviewer's job is to get to know you as a potential colleague, not to trip you up. The interviewer will have been briefed with approximately the same type of information previously suggested for you. For example, recruiters representing Dow Chemical Company are told:

> There is no one best way of interviewing students on campus. Interviewing is a highly individualized process and each interviewer should establish his own technique, rather than copying the methods used by others. Adopt a style that will be comfortable for you and for the interviewee.
>
> Objectives of the interview are to evaluate, to give information, to sell the qualified applicant, and to make a friend for Dow.

Dow Chemical interviewers are also given the following information on making the best use of the twenty- or thirty-minute interviewing time:

> Review the student's resume in advance of the interview if possible. Put the applicant at ease. Appraise the applicant during the interview. Even the applicant's questions can tell you something about him. Use open-end questions that cannot be answered by a single "yes" or "no." Answer the applicant's questions. Don't do all the talking. If you find yourself talking more than 50 percent of the time, you're probably talking too much. Use the deliberate pause to test the conversational skill of the applicant. Do not use stress-interviewing techniques on campus. Communicate openly. Any question asked by an applicant deserves an honest and frank answer. Ascertain, and come to some conclusion about, the applicant's interests, his ability in line with his interests, his personality, and his motivation and effectiveness. Do not make copious notes during the interview. Stay on schedule. Advise the applicant what will happen next and approximately when this will happen.

The interviewer is required to write an evaluation for each interviewee. This evaluation will generally cover appearance and mannerisms, communication and verbalization skills, social ability, adaptability, sensitivity to the needs of others, maturity, willingness to work, geographic flexibility, willingness to travel, willingness to follow through, and soundness of goals.

VISITING THE COMPANY

Following your on-campus interview or interview-by-mail campaign, you may receive a letter from the company's home base advising you it doesn't have a job for which to consider you at the present time. Some companies may indicate they would like to keep your name on file for future reference. If they say this, they generally mean it. Most companies continually review their current application files over and over again in an attempt to match applicant with job opportunity.

Or you may be invited next to visit the company's home base, its laboratories, stores, or plants. Generally, you will receive a letter of invitation asking you to specify the date when you can come. You should accept such an invitation only when you are sincerely interested in exploring employment with that company. If you want to accept, do so by letter, wire, or phone. Most companies are very happy to have you call collect to arrange the date, especially if time is important.

Do not set such an immediate date that the company has no time to plan and prepare for your visit. There will be people they will specifically want you to see; laboratories, offices, or production facilities they want you to visit. It is important that the right people be there to greet you and show you the facility when you arrive.

Your first contact at the offices of the potential employer will probably be with the technical and professional placement, personnel, or employment department. In some instances it may be the recruiter you met on campus. All are there to help you put your best foot forward and to enable you to make the best possible impression on any and all people with whom you may have discussions.

GETTING READY FOR THE COMPANY VISIT

You should approach the company visit in the same manner as the campus interview or interview-by-mail campaign. However, you will have far more time and it will be proper to ask much more specific questions concerning conditions of employment, salary, fringe benefits, job duties, career progress, and the like.

Any company that invites you to visit expects to pay your expenses. When you are traveling by air at company expense, you are usually expected to travel tourist class. Most companies expect you to fly, stay in a moderately priced hotel room, and eat good meals. Your judgment in handling expenses is one of the more objective factors whereby a company can evaluate you.

THE WAITING GAME – THE COMPANY'S DECISION AND YOURS

Most companies will be in a position to let you know their final decision within a week or 10 days after your visit. If, after receiving an offer, you still have questions about the job, location, or other details, feel free to make a collect call to the personnel department that handled your schedule. They will appreciate it. If you told the company you would give them a decision by a certain date following receipt of their offer, do so. In your letter of acceptance try to give the personnel manager an approximate date when he might expect you to report to work. If you live in a different city, the company will then make arrangements so that you will not be coming into the city at a loose end.

THE FOLLOW-UP

The most important personality trait in the job-hunting process is persistence. Persistence has often got jobs for people when all else failed. It has often landed jobs for people who were not as attractive, personable, or even as well qualified as others who waited passively for the employer to call them.

So to the question of whether to go back after the first interview, the answer is yes. Go back and keep going back—not often enough to annoy the employer, but often enough to demonstrate your sincere desire to work for the company. If you go too often, you may make a nuisance of yourself. If you do not go at all, it will be interpreted as meaning that you either weren't eager to work or have already found a job.

Going back makes the employer recognize your name and remember it. Employers are well meaning about keeping applications and calling for people who have filled them out. But frequently when hiring times comes, they remember the person who showed the most interest in working for the company by coming back a second or third time, and they pull that person's application out of the file without looking at the others. This is one of the facts of life that nobody tells you. Employers and personnel people are quite aware that it is true, but they will not tell you. Why? Because they do not want to be bothered with people applying for work except when they have jobs open. But when a job opening occurs they remember the person who kept coming back without being told. This cannot be stressed too strongly. *The one personality trait that is most likely to get you a job is persistence.*

How often should you make these follow-up visits? It's hard to say. At some companies where the turnover rate is high, once a week might not be too often. At others, with hard-to-fill professional positions, once a month is often enough.

JOB ALTERNATIVES IN A BUSINESS SLUMP

To be realistic, today's job seeker must plan alternative courses of action on the assumption that it may be months, or even years, before the most appropriate job becomes available. While still pursuing your best opportunity, you may find others, equally promising, in the courses of action suggested here.

LOWER-LEVEL ENTRY JOBS

Apart from paying the rent and buying the groceries (no mean matter in a recession), entry-level positions can serve as a good launchpad for more interesting career positions.

LABOR CONTRACTORS

Temporary jobs found through labor contractors can also sustain you. They can add to your background of skills and give you some good insights into business operations. Occasionally, they lead to offers of permanent, higher-level spots.

RELATED AREAS

Jobs in fields close to the one you most prefer can also support you, while providing you with a good observation post for openings in your main field. You may also have the advantage of using some of your special talents while finding others you weren't aware of.

CONSIDER A COUPLE OF YEARS IN THE MILITARY

The pay and fringe benefits in the military are excellent now. The military offers an opportunity to learn skills that will be helpful in getting a civilian job later if you choose. There is far more flexibility than there was only a few years ago.

STAY IN SCHOOL

If you are finishing a degree at a community or junior college and cannot find a permanent job, give serious thought to going on for a college degree. With additional specialized training and a four-year degree, you may be able to qualify for many jobs for which there is a shortage of workers. If you are finishing at a four-year school, it is probably *not* a good idea to stay on for a master's degree. Most employers would prefer to hire employees with not more than a bachelor's degree, unless the person has extensive experience also.

CAREER INFORMATION SOURCES

The following organizations publish materials concerning career opportunities in specialized areas of business for college graduates:

ACCOUNTING OCCUPATIONS

American Institute of Certified Public Accountants
666 Fifth Avenue
New York, N.Y. 10019

National Association of Accountants
505 Park Avenue
New York, N.Y. 10022

National Society of Public Accountants
1717 Pennsylvania Avenue, N.W.
Washington, D.C. 20006

ADVERTISING, MARKETING, AND SALES OCCUPATIONS

American Advertising Federation
1225 Connecticut Avenue, N.W.
Washington, D.C. 20036

American Association of Advertising Agencies
200 Park Avenue
New York, N.Y. 10017

American Marketing Association
230 North Michigan Avenue
Chicago, Ill. 60601

Direct Mail Advertising Association
230 Park Avenue
New York, N.Y. 10017

Industrial Marketing Associates
530 Pleasant Street
St. Joseph, Mich. 49085

Marketing Research Association, Inc.
P.O. Box 1415
Grand Central Station
New York, N.Y. 10017

National Association of Wholesale Distributors
1725 K Street, N.W.
Washington, D.C. 20006

Sales and Marketing Executives International
Student Education Division
630 Third Avenue
New York, N.Y. 10017

ECONOMICS OCCUPATIONS

American Bankers Association
1700 Pennsylvania Avenue
Washington, D.C. 20006

American Economics Association
1313 21st Avenue South
Nashville, Tenn. 37312

FINANCIAL ANALYSTS OCCUPATIONS

Financial Analysts Federation
219 East 42nd Street
New York, N.Y. 10017

Financial Executives Institute
50 West 44th Street
New York, N.Y. 10036

Financial Executives Research Foundation
50 West 44th Street
New York, N.Y. 10036

FINANCIAL INSTITUTION OCCUPATIONS

American Bankers Association
Personnel Administration and Development Committee
1120 Connecticut Avenue, N.W.
Washington, D.C. 20036

American Savings and Loan Institute
111 East Wacker Drive
Chicago, Ill. 60601

Mortgage Bankers Association of America
1125 15th Street, N.W.
Washington, D.C. 20005

National Association of Bank Women, Inc.
111 East Wacker Drive
Chicago, Ill. 60601

INFORMATION SYSTEMS
AND STATISTICS
OCCUPATIONS

American Federation of Information Processing Societies
210 Summit Avenue
Montvale, N.J. 07645

American Statistical Associations
810 18th Street, N.W.
Washington, D.C. 20006

Association for Computing Machinery
1133 Avenue of the Americas
New York, N.Y. 10036

Data Processing Management Associations
505 Busse Highway
Oak Ridge, Ill. 60068

INSURANCE
OCCUPATIONS

American College of Life Underwriters
270 Bryn Mawr Avenue
Bryn Mawr, Pa. 19010

American Institute for Property and Liability Underwriters
Providence and Sugartown Roads
Malvern, Pa. 19355

Health Insurance Association of America
1701 K Street, N.W.
Washington, D.C. 20006

Institute of Life Insurance
277 Park Avenue
New York, N.Y. 10017

Insurance Information Institute
110 Williams Street
New York, N.Y. 10038

INTERNATIONAL
BUSINESS
OCCUPATIONS

National Foreign Trade Council
10 Rockefeller Plaza
New York, N.Y. 10020

Trade Relations Council of the United States
122 East 42nd Street
New York, N.Y. 10017

LABOR-MANAGEMENT RELATIONS

American Federation of Labor and Congress of Industrial Organizations
815 16th Street, N.W.
Washington, D.C. 20006

International Brotherhood of Teamsters, Chauffeurs, Warehousemen, and
Helpers of America
25 Louisiana Avenue, N.W.
Washington, D.C. 20001

National Federation of Independent Unions
910 17th Street, N.W., Ste. 553
Washington, D.C. 20006

National Labor-Management Foundation
1629 K Street, N.W., Ste. 553
Washington, D.C. 20006

United Automobile, Aerospace, and Agricultural Implement Workers: International Union
8000 East Jefferson Avenue
Detroit, Mich. 48214

MANAGERIAL OCCUPATIONS

Administrative Management Society, World Headquarters
Maryland Road
Willow Grove, Pa. 19090

American Institute of Management
125 East 38th Street
New York, N.Y. 10016

The American Management Association
135 West 50th Street
New York, N.Y. 10020

Society for the Advancement of Management
1412 Broadway
New York, N.Y. 10036

Society of Professional Management Consultants
150 Broadway
New York, N.Y. 10038

PERSONNEL MANAGEMENT OCCUPATIONS

American Society for Personnel Administration
19 Church Street
Berea, Ohio 44017

The Information Center
Public Relations Society of America, Inc.
845 Third Avenue
New York, N.Y. 10022

International Personnel Management Association
1313 East 60th Street
Chicago, Ill. 60637

National Employment Counselors Associations
1607 New Hampshire Avenue, N.W.
Washington, D.C. 20009

Public Personnel Association
1313 East 60th Street
Chicago, Ill. 60637

PRODUCTION
MANAGEMENT
OCCUPATIONS

American Apparel Manufacturers Association
16111 North Kent Street
Arlington, Va. 22209

American Iron and Steel Institute
150 East 42nd Street
New York, N.Y. 10017

American Society for Quality Control
161 West Wisconsin Avenue
Milwaukee, Wisc. 53203

American Society of Traffic and Transportation, Inc.
22 West Madison Street
Chicago, Ill. 60602

Grocery Manufacturers of America
1425 K Street, N.W.
Washington, D.C. 20005

Motor Vehicle Manufacturers Association of the United States, Inc.
320 New Center Bldg.
Detroit, Mich. 48202

National Association of Manufacturers
277 Park Avenue
New York, N.Y. 10017

National Association of Purchasing Agents
11 Park Place
New York, N.Y. 10007

B

Do you have a case to solve for this course? Or a term paper to write on some assigned topic? Or some question to be answered on government regulation or taxes? All of these tasks can be accomplished by consulting the proper library and the information sources it contains. The following are the most important types of libraries for finding business and economic information:

WHERE TO FIND INFORMATION

Public libraries of cities and towns

University and college libraries

State and federal government libraries and archives

Corporation libraries

Law firm libraries

HOW LIBRARIES WORK

Every library has a card catalog located near the entrance to the building. These catalogs list each book held by the library on a small file card, and these are arranged in alphabetical order. Each book is actually listed on three separate file cards: one indexed by author, another by title, and a third by subject. For example, if you wanted to find the book, *The Enterprising Americans* by John Chamberlain, you could look under *Chamberlain, John, (The) Enterprising Americans,* or under *Business History.* In this way one can locate a book by knowing only its author, its title, or its subject.

After locating a desired book in the card catalog, note its call number. Then go to that number in the "stacks," which are shelves where the books are located, arranged numerically. Reference books will have the prefix "Ref" in front of their call number. This indicates that this book can be found only in the reference section of the library. Practically all libraries catalog their books under one of two numbering systems: either the Dewey Decimal System or the Library of Congress System. Both of these appear on page 584.

Magazines and newspapers are usually found in a special section of the library known as the "periodical room." Such publications are arranged in alphabetical order by title and, often, issues one year or older are bound in large volumes or stored on microfilm stored in filing cabinets. Usually, libraries do not allow users to take magazines or newspapers off the premises, which means that information must be copied or photostated.

Other reference sources such as dictionaries, encyclopedias, handbooks, almanacs, and directories are also to be used only in the library. They are shelved in a special section of the library known as the "reference area." Usually a reference librarian is available to help users of such sources find materials that they need. For a discussion of some of these materials, see "How to Use Your Library" at the end of this appendix.

LIBRARY CLASSIFICATION SYSTEMS

The major groups of the Dewey System are the following:

000—General Works
100—Philosophy
200—Religion
300—Social Sciences–Sociology
400—Philology
500—Pure Science
600—Useful Arts
700—Fine Arts–Recreation
800—Literature
900—History
600—Useful Arts
610—Medicine
620—Engineering
630—Agriculture–Agronomy
640—Home Economics–
       Domestic Science
650—Communications, Business
660—Chemical Technology
670—Mechanical Trades
690—Building

The 650 group is subdivided as follows:

650—Communications, Business
651—Office Economy
652—Writing: Materials, Typewriters,
       Ciphers
653—Abbreviations, Shorthand
654—Telegraph, Cables, Signals
655—Printing, Publishing, Copyright
656—Transportation, Railroading, etc.
657—Bookkeeping, Accounts
658—Business Methods–Industrial
       Management
659—Other Topics

The 651 group is subdivided as follows:

651   —Office Economy

651.1—Office Buildings and Rooms
651.2—Equipment
651.3—Organization
651.4—Administration
651.5—Records, Files and Filing
651.6—Special Material
651.7—Correspondence, Reports, etc.

The major groupings of the Library of Congress System are the following:

A   General Works
B   Philosophy and Religion
C   Auxiliary Sciences of History
D   Universal and Old World History
E–F   America
G   Geography, Anthropology,
       Folklore, Manners and Customs,
       Sports and Games
H   Social Sciences
J   Political Science
K   Law
L   Education
M   Music
N   Fine Arts
P   Language and Literature
Q   Science
R   Medicine
S   Agriculture
T   Technology
U   Military Science
V   Naval Science
Z   Bibliography and Library Science
HA   Statistics
HB   Economic Theory
HC   Economic History and Conditions
HD   Economic Industrial
HE   Transportation and Commerce
HF   Commerce
HG   Finance
HJ   Public Finance

INDEXES	Indexes guide researchers to sources of information about any topic listed in books, magazines, or newspapers. By looking under the topic of interest listed in alphabetical order, you will be directed to a number of books or articles relative to that subject. Frequently cross-references are made to other topics listed in the index that are similar in nature to the one being researched. Indexes usually break down into two major categories: those dealing with books, and those dealing with newspapers and periodicals. The following indexes are listed according to that breakdown.

PERIODICAL INDEXES	*Accountants' Index and Supplements.* Published by the American Institute of Certified Public Accountants about once every two years. The various supplements are indexed by author, subject, and title, and there are appropriate cross-references.

Agricultural Index. This guide is published on an annual basis by the H. W. Wilson Company.

Business Education Index. Published annually by the McGraw-Hill Book Company for the Delta Pi Epsilon national fraternity in Business Education.

Business Periodicals Index. This is an annual publication but is always up-to-date with monthly supplements. It indexes over 150 periodicals in the areas of finance, business, labor relations, management, insurance, banking, advertising, economics, and other related fields. It is the most important index of periodicals for business researchers.

Cumulative Index of the National Industrial Conference Board Publications. This guide has been published by the National Industrial Conference Board from 1962 through the present time. It indexes many NICB publications of interest to the business and economics researcher.

Engineering Index. Published every year by the Engineering Index Service located in New York City. There are almost 300 subject areas of information indexed.

Funk and Scott Index of Corporations and Industries. A publication of the Funk and Scott Publishing Company of Detroit for the past 15 years. These volumes are published weekly and monthly and are bound once a year. This guide indexes and describes articles and speeches from publications of investment houses and brokerage firms, as well as financial publications, document services, and the like.

Index of Economic Journals. Published by Richard D. Irwin, Inc., since 1965. This guide indexes articles from American and foreign economic periodicals and is arranged so that one may obtain information by name of the author or by subject areas. All entries in this index list the author, title of the article, and the journal, plus page number within that journal.

Index to Labor Union Periodicals. An annual guide with monthly supplements published by the University of Michigan School of Business Administration.

This index lists citations for articles from about 50 major labor union publications.

New York Times Index. Issued twice a month by the *New York Times*, and cumulated annually. All articles appearing in the *Times* are indexed by heading of subject, person, and organization name.

Social Sciences and Humanities Index. Published annually since 1966 by the H. W. Wilson Company. Indexes articles of interest printed in journals dealing with the social sciences and humanities.

Poole's Index to Periodical Literature. Of value to those who want to research topics printed in periodicals from 1888 to 1908. This guide lists items by subject only. The work is published by the Houghton Mifflin Company.

The Readers' Guide to Periodical Literature. Published on an annual basis by the H. W. Wilson Company with monthly supplements. This is probably the best-known and most important index of periodical literature. Every researcher should be familiar with it.

Ulrich's International Periodicals Directory. Published by the R. R. Bowker Company of New York. It is an international guide to many thousands of periodicals.

Union List of Serials in Libraries of the United States and Canada, 3rd ed. This index lists magazines and the libraries in which they can be found.

Wall Street Journal Index. Published by the Dow Jones Company on a monthly basis. All articles appearing in the *Journal* are indexed.

NEWSPAPERS, BULLETINS, AND BROCHURES INDEXES

Directory of Newspapers and Periodicals. Published yearly by N. W. Ayer, Philadelphia. It contains various items of information—such as circulation statistics, subscription rates, name of publisher, page sizes—about newspapers and periodicals published in the United States and Canada.

Vertical File Index. Published monthly by the H. W. Wilson Company since 1932. Lists subjects found in free or inexpensive pamphlets and brochures. It also includes government documents and some mimeographed material.

How to Use the Business Library. By H. Webster Johnson and published by the South-Western Publishing Company. A good general source of additional indexes and guides to specialized periodicals for business and economic researchers.

BOOK INDEXES

American Statistics Index. Published annually by the Congressional Information Service, Washington, D.C. Probably is the most comprehensive guide to statistical publications of the United States government.

Book Review Digest. Published by the H. W. Wilson Company on a monthly basis, with an annual bound volume. This guide lists books reviewed in more than 75 periodicals and usually contains quotations from a few reviewers as well as citations of other reviews. Items are indexed by book and author.

Books in Print. Published by the R. R. Bowker Company from 1948 to the present. This guide is a listing of books currently in print in the United States. Each item lists the author, title, and publisher of the book as well as the price. Certain categories of books, such as those on poetry and drama, are not listed.

Cumulative Book Index: A World List of Books in the English Language. Published monthly by the H. W. Wilson Company. Lists books published in English in all parts of the world but does not list government documents. Each item is indexed by author, title, and subject.

National-Union Catalog. Published by the United States Library of Congress Card Division. Indexes works catalogued by the Library of Congress and by hundreds of other libraries throughout the United States. Items are indexed by author, and there is an annual edition, with monthly and quarterly supplements.

BUSINESS PERIODICALS

The following selected periodicals deal with general information about business and the economy. Get into the habit of reading several of them regularly. If you do, you will develop a breadth of understanding about events, problems, and issues that are important to businesspeople and consumers. All of these publications are available at local libraries as well as at university and college libraries.

Business Week. Weekly magazine of business, economics, and management news. Also has statistical indexes of economic activity.

Changing Times. Monthly magazine of items pertinent to the field of personal finance and consumerism. Lots of tips on how to save money as a wise buyer.

Dun's. Monthly magazine of business news and techniques of most interest to business scholars and those in management.

Forbes. Bimonthly magazine of investment news and investment advice. Very heavy on information about the stock, commodity, and bond markets.

Fortune. Bimonthly magazine with business news and feature articles on people and businesses in the economy.

Financial World. Monthly magazine of investment news and information of greatest interest to financial managers.

Harvard Business Review. Scholarly articles on various subjects in business and economics.

The Journal of Accountancy. Monthly journal of news, articles, reports on meetings, and other items of interest to accountants and managers.

Journal of Business. Quarterly journal devoted to the technical aspects of business and economics.

Journal of Marketing. Monthly magazine concerned with marketing studies and research.

Nation's Business. Interpretive articles on the latest developments in management, labor, economics, and government relationships to business.

Printers Ink. Weekly magazine of articles and news related to the areas of management, sales, and advertising.

Survey of Current Business. A monthly compendium of statistical indexes related to industrial production, commodity prices, domestic trade, and many similar topics.

The Wall Street Journal. Daily (weekdays only) newspaper of current national, international, and business news as well as feature articles on business and economic topics.

GOVERNMENT PUBLICATIONS

There are a tremendous number of publications issued by departments, agencies, divisions, and bureaus of the federal government, as well as many published by various state governments. Some of these publications are free, others are sold. The following list is a small cross section of some of the more popular government publications.

Business Cycle Developments. Issued monthly by the U.S. Department of Commerce. It gives about 70 principal economic indicators and over 300 components used for different economic measurements. Information of this type is of most value to someone interested in economic projections.

The Congressional Record. Published daily by the U.S. Government Printing Office when Congress is in session. Gives the complete proceedings and debates of the U.S. Senate and House of Representatives.

The Federal Register. Published by the Division of the Federal Register of the National Archives on each weekday in the year. It gives details of all regulatory matters issued by various agencies and bodies of the national government.

Foreign Commerce Weekly. Published by the U.S. Department of Commerce, it gives up-to-date information on foreign countries and their production and trade in various commodities. This publication also reviews laws, regulations, and industrial progress of foreign nations.

The Monthly Catalog of U.S. Government Publications. Available from the U.S. Superintendent of Documents, this is a monthly listing of all publications issued by the various departments and agencies of the U.S. government.

Monthly Labor Review. Published monthly by the U.S. Department of Labor Bureau of Labor Statistics. Articles and information in the field of labor of general and specific interest.

Municipal Year Book. Published by the International City Managers Association, Chicago, Illinois. It gives information on current problems of cities, statistics of cities, and population trends. The directory contains five parts, each concerned with a different area of municipal information.

Occupational Outlook Handbook. Published annually by the U.S. Department of Labor Bureau of Labor Statistics. Gives up-to-date projections for the future of various occupations and professions. Also gives descriptions of current conditions in each field.

Official Gazette. A weekly publication of the U.S. Patent Office, it gives information pertaining to patents and trademarks. Various lawsuits as well as pending litigation in the area of patents and trademarks are reviewed. This publication also contains specifications and drawings for patents issued each week as well as other relevant information.

Statistical Abstract of the United States. Published yearly by the U.S. Government Printing Office. It presents summary statistics on all phases of the social, political, economic, and industrial aspects of the United States. This is the most important single reference source for statistics on just about every pertinent area of activity.

Survey of Current Business. Published monthly by the U.S. Department of Commerce. It contains charts, articles, maps, and statistics on all phases of the U.S. economy. The latest statistics and discussions of business activity are presented in detail.

United States Government Manual. Published annually by the U.S. Government Printing Office. Purposes and programs of government agencies are described.

ALMANACS, HANDBOOKS, ENCYCLOPEDIAS, DICTIONARIES

The Accountant's Encyclopedia. Published by Prentice-Hall, Englewood Cliffs, N.J. Four volumes of information on various aspects of accounting—such as systems, procedures, audits, practices, and administration—of interest to accountants, lawyers, engineers, financial managers, and students in the field.

Accountants' Handbook. Published by Ronald Press, New York. Gives a general survey of the information covered in the field of accounting such as theory of accounts, essentials of financial statements, principles of auditing, features of federal taxation.

Business Executives' Handbook. Published by Prentice-Hall, Englewood Cliffs, N.J. A general manual of topics related to management of business firms. Such things as credit, advertising, and legal procedures are given general coverage in this publication.

Consumer Reports Buying Guide Issue. Published annually by Consumer Union of United States Inc., Mt. Vernon, New York. Contains information and test results on product and services that consumers are most interested in purchasing.

The Dictionary of Foreign Trade. Written by Frank Henius for Prentice-Hall, Englewood Cliffs, N.J. Defines pertinent terms and techniques used in the study of foreign commerce.

Dictionary of Modern Economics. By Douglas Greenwald and others, 2nd ed., McGraw-Hill Book Co., New York, 1973. Defines terms, in nontechnical language, related to the field of economic study. Serves well as a scholarly introduction to the field of economics.

Dictionary of Occupational Titles. Published by the U.S. Department of Labor. Contains a long list of job titles and descriptions for both career and noncareer types of jobs. Describes the current status of each occupation and gives future projections for the occupation and industry. This volume also goes into the average salary expectations and numbers of people employed in each occupation.

The Economic Almanac. Published by the National Industrial Conference Board of New York City. Contains detailed statistical information about the United States economy, business, labor, and government. Serves as a useful guide to students and business managers who seek brief descriptions and statistical profiles on a variety of economic topics.

The Encyclopedia of U.S. Government Benefits. Published periodically by Wm. M. Wise & Co. A very extensive guide to government service organizations and agencies and the types of services that they perform.

Financial Handbook. Ronald Press Co., New York. A general information volume on banking, money, and corporation finance. Banking procedures, investment trading, credit, working capital, and financial agencies are just several of the many topics covered in this publication.

Marketing Handbook. Published by Ronald Press Co., New York. A series of topics dealing with various phases of marketing management comprise this work. Advertising, sales promotion, research, and other related topics are included.

Readers Digest Almanac and Yearbook. Published by W. W. Norton & Co., Inc. Contains over 1,000 pages of current and historical information on all phases of American and international life.

Toll-Free Digest. A directory of almost 15,000 toll-free telephone listings. Includes airline, hotel, business service organization telephone numbers.

The World Almanac. Published by the New York World-Telegram, New York. An annual, soft-cover volume of facts, tables, and information about all aspects of the economic, social, political, and educational environment of the world. This almanac originated in 1885.

BUSINESS DIRECTORIES

Business directories are sometimes referred to as trade directories. These volumes provide data about manufacturing and distribution trades. Such information is of particular value to firms in the field covered by the directory as well as to those in allied industries.

Dun & Bradstreet Middle Market Directory. Listing of manufacturers, retailers, and service organizations giving their major business activities, annual sales revenues, number of employees, office address, etc.

Automotive Industries, Products Guide. Provides detailed data on various significant statistics relative to the automobile industry. Such items as passenger car sales, truck sales, employment, earnings, and strikes are included in this directory.

Ayer Directory of Newspapers and Periodicals. Lists the circulation, publishers, and editors of all newspapers and magazines printed in the United States, Canada, Bermuda, and Newfoundland.

The Congressional Directory. Provides lists and information reports on U.S. senators and congressmen as well as congressional committees, special agencies, and other major departments of the federal government.

Directory of House Organs. A list of internal and external magazines, their editors, and the companies that publish them. These are not to be confused with magazines for sales to the public for profit.

Marquis Who's Who in America. A directory of individuals distinguished for their achievements and position. A brief biography of each person listed is given.

Moody's Manual of Industrials. A directory consisting of separate volumes that provide information about corporations and their stock issues. History of the firm, lists of officers and directories, descriptions of business activity, and listing of long-term debt are some of the items of information presented about each firm listed. The separate volumes include: Industrials, Public Utilities, Transportation Companies, and Financial Companies, as well as various government agencies.

Poor's Register of Directors and Executives. Lists the names of officers and directors of over 90,000 manufacturing, public utility, transportation, financial, legal, and mining firms.

Standard Corporation Records. Contains historical and current financial data on companies and organizations offering investment opportunities. Published by Standard and Poor's.

Thomas' Register of American Manufacturers. A register of products, manufacturers, trade names, trade organizations listed alphabetically. Useful for one who knows a trade name for a product but wishes to locate the manufacturer, or vice versa.

C

METRICS — BACKGROUND AND IMPLICATIONS FOR INDUSTRY

Businesses in the United States are quietly making the move to metrics as a system of measurement. After two centuries of inches, pounds, quarts, acres, and other assorted unrelated measures, the United States is joining most of the world in measuring in metric terms. (Besides the United States, only Brunei, Burma, Liberia, and Yemen are not on the metric system.) A United States Metric Board, authorized by legislation in 1975, will coordinate the gradual change to the metric system.

The implications of the metric system are great for all Americans. All of us will have to learn a new system of measurement. Business, on the other hand, will have to produce goods and services based on the metric system. Besides trying to educate all employees to the new system, the firms will have to carry dual inventories of goods and services to meet the old standards and the new ones. The conversion will be very expensive and very confusing. That is why the United States has put it off as long as possible. Now there is no choice. American exporters are handicapped because they have to produce products of different measurement for the domestic and world markets. Importers have the same problem. Retail stores carrying imported products have difficulty explaining metric sizes to consumers. The United States, isolated in world markets as the only nonmetric industrial nation, has finally decided to join the rest of the metric world.

How did we come to this isolated position? Why didn't we go metric earlier? What is different about the metric system? What are the implications of a conversion to metrics?

HISTORY OF METRIC MOVEMENT[1]

On December 23, 1975, President Ford signed into law the Metric Conversion Act of 1975. The law declares that ". . . the policy in the United States shall be to coordinate and plan the increasing use of the metric system in the United States and to establish a United Metric Board to coordinate the voluntary conversion to the metric system." This law thus lays the foundation for the present change from the English System of Weights and Measures to the International System of Units, which is better known as the Modernized Metric System. While the International System of Units (SI) will be new to many Americans, it holds the promise of solving many educational problems dealing with measurement and at the same time providing our nation with a clear and concise system of measures compatible with those used in the remainder of the world.

This system of measures grew out of the system of measures known as the Metric System, which was developed in France in the late 1790s. It is based on a group of units, to be described later in this article, and a set of prefixes, which affixed to the name of one of these units indicates the amount of that unit used as a standard of measurement. Its strong point is that all of the measures are based on

1. From *Metrics: Introduction and Overview*, a monograph by John A. Dossey, published by Illinois State University.

groupings of tens, like our numeration system. This system has undergone many revisions since its inception and adoption by almost all of the countries in the world. At the Eleventh General Conference on Weights and Measures in Paris in 1961, the system was brought up to date with many of the standards being redefined in terms of modern physical quantities. The name of the system was changed to *Systeme International d'Unites*, International System of Units. This modernization, coupled with a push from large United States corporate concerns doing significant trade overseas, brought pressure on the United States Government to enact legislation such as that finally signed into law on December 23, 1975.

THE SI SYSTEM

BASIC UNITS

The SI System of measures is quite easy to learn and many say that there are only about seven things one needs to know in order to survive in everyday living. Let us begin our trip through the system by first looking at the basic units of measure in the system. The basic standards of measure, their symbols, and their uses are as follows:

Type of Measure	Standard	Symbol
Length	meter	m
Mass	kilogram	kg
Time	second	s
Temperature	degree Kelvin	°K
Electric Current	Ampere	A
Luminous Intensity	candela	cd
Amount of Substance	mole	mol

Multiples of these basic units of measure are indicated by a set of prefixes. These prefixes, when added to the basic units given above, indicate the amount of one of the basic units being used in a given measurement situation as the standard of measure. These prefixes and their numerical values are as follows:

Prefix	Numerical Value	Symbol
kilo-	1000 × base unit	k
hecto-	100 × base unit	h
deka-	10 × base unit	da
———	1 × base unit	———
deci-	0.1 × base unit	d
centi-	0.01 × base unit	c
milli-	0.001 × base unit	m

BASIC NEEDED FACTS

USE OF UNITS AND PREFIXES

An example of the use of these basic units with the prefixes would be a linear measurement. Suppose one was measuring the distance from his home town to Chicago. The appropriate metric unit of measure would be the one which corresponds to the English unit of miles. This is the kilometer, or 1000 meter, unit. An analysis of the word "kilometer" shows the root of "meter" and the prefix of "kilo-." The meter is the basic unit of length and the prefix of "kilo-" indicates 1000 of these meters. A decimeter, on the other hand, is a unit 0.1 of a meter in length. These multiples, and submultiples, of a meter might be shown on a place value chart something like this:

1000 m	100 m	10 m	1 m	0.1 m	0.01 m	0.001 m
km	hm	dam	m	dm	cm	mm

The symbols beneath each of the values are a combination of the symbols for the unit meter and the proper symbol for the prefix needed.

This small set of units and prefixes decreased the number of units that one must memorize, to say nothing of the ways in which the various units are related to one another. This system, based on ten, is easy for a student to associate with our numeration system or with our decimal system of coinage. Furthermore, the fact that the system employs the decimal notation simplifies calculations, especially for the student who is weak in mathematics.

For ordinary usage, the SI system of measures is even more economical. Not all of the basic units mentioned earlier come to play in everyday settings. The important units for common usage are the meter, the kilogram, and two other units derived from those mentioned earlier, the liter—for volume and capacity, and the degree Celsius—for everyday temperatures.

The liter, 1, is the basic measure for volume and capacity. Sizewise, it is the metric equivalent of our present quart and the liter is legally defined as a cubic decimeter. The degree Celsius, °C, is the unit of temperature employed in nonscientific settings. The Celsius scale corresponds to the Centigrade scale with which you may already be familiar. In the SI system, the scale is called the Celsius scale in honor of its inventor, Anders Celsius. The scale runs from 0°C at the freezing point of water to 100°C at the boiling point of water. Negative temperatures are recorded for temperatures below the freezing point of water down to −273°C, the absolute zero, and above 100°C for very intense temperature situations.

ECONOMY OF FACTS

While the number of basic units one must know for immediate recall is four, the number of prefixes needed in the same manner is three, giving us the seven facts mentioned earlier. The three essential prefixes are the kilo-, center-, and milli-.

EASE OF
CALCULATIONS

In addition to the smaller number of units required for measurement, the calculative skills required are much simpler. No longer will involved fraction problems stand as a hurdle in the slow student's path. The SI measurements, being expressed in decimals, require only that the student be conversant with the basic operations for whole numbers and the rules for the placement of the decimal points in decimal calculations. This is assuming the student has an understanding of the decimal place values discussed earlier. These skills are much easier to acquire than those associated with the operations on fractions resulting from English measurements. In addition, the speed with which a decimal calculation can be completed is far greater than the speed for a rational number calculation. They also fit the input of a hand calculator quite well.

Basic metric conversions

Linear Measure	
1 inch	= 2.54 centimeters
0.3937 inch	= 1 centimeter
1 mile	= 1.609 kilometers
0.621 mile	= 1 kilometer
Cubic Measure	
1 cubic inch	= 16.39 cubic centimeters
0.06 cubic inch	= 1 cubic centimeter
1 cubic yard	= 0.7646 cubic meter
1.308 cubic yards	= 1 cubic meter
Liquid Measure	
1 fluid ounce	= 2.957 centiliters
.0338 ounce	= 1 centiliter
1 (U.S.) fluid quart	= 0.946 liter
1.057 (U.S.) quarts	= 1 liter
1 (U.S.) gallon	= 3.785 liters
0.264 (U.S.) gallon	= 1 liter
Square Measure	
1 square inch	= 6.452 square centimeters
0.155 square inch	= 1 square centimeter
1 acre	= 0.4047 hectare
2.471 acres	= 1 hectare
1 square mile	= 2.590 square kilometers
0.386 square mile	= 1 square kilometer
Weights	
1 ounce (avoirdupois)	= 28.35 grams
0.035 ounces (avoirdupois)	= 1 gram
1 pound (avoirdupois)	= 0.4536 kilogram
2.2046 pounds (avoirdupois)	= 1 kilogram
1 short ton	= 0.9072 (metric) ton
1.1023 (short) tons	= 1 (metric) ton

IMPLICATIONS FOR INDUSTRY

Industry in the United States would appear to have the most to gain from a conversion to the metric system. About half of the 1,000 largest companies have begun converting their manufacturing specifications to the metric system. Others are waiting to see how serious the country appears to be about conversion to metrics. They know that while metrification is a national policy, the Metric Conversion Act sets no deadlines and calls for voluntary conversion. Many will not change unless it is in their immediate economic interest. The steel industry, for example, said as late as 1973 that the conversion costs for the steel industry would be too much for it to be feasible. However, when General Motors, a key consumer for steel, became the first important manufacturer to launch a conversion program later in that year, the steel industry moved quickly to implement a metric system.

For manufacturers, one tough question is whether to make a "soft" or "hard" conversion to metrics. A soft conversion means that the company simply changes numbers on its products, but not the dimensions. A food processor can convert the ounces in a can of peaches to grams, for example. A hard conversion is far more expensive. It involves making products to metric specifications, which involves retooling, new machinery, and double inventories for a number of years. This can be done successfully, however, as was the case for the industrial fasteners industry. The Industrial Fasteners Institute, working closely with the International Organization for Standards, coordinated an effort by member firms to develop a series of metric screw-thread dimensions and nut-bolt sizes. This resulted in a single world system of metric fasteners. In the process, it considerably reduced the number of sizes previously manufactured, thereby lowering costs and broadening the market for fasteners.

The conversion to metrics in manufacturing, however, may come slowly. Orders for metric machine tools, used in making industrial machinery, have not increased very much in the last couple of years. Also, the fact that many manufacturers have decided to continue producing products in the old measurements as well as in metrics will slow the conversion. Few firms are switching directly to metrics and discontinuing their old product sizes and weights.

On the other hand, there is some indication that the conversion may come more rapidly than appears to be the case now. Sears, for example, has said that it plans to convert all its products to metric sizes by 1985. The switch will put great pressure on its suppliers and other large retailers to convert to metrics also. Also, there is a great emphasis on metrics in the educational system, from elementary school through college, which should help smooth the transition for many persons. Finally, the federal government is encouraging "thinking metric" through the use of highway signs showing distances in kilometers as well as miles. Auto manufacturers, as a result, are now producing cars with speedometers showing distances in both miles and kilometers.

GLOSSARY

Absolute Advantage A unique mixture of the factors of production that permits a country to produce a product at less cost than other countries.

Acceleration Clause A clause in an indenture (bond contract) authorizing the trustee to collect the entire outstanding principal and interest on the issue in the event of default of even one payment of principal or interest by the debtor.

Accounts Receivable Debts owed the company by customers and others.

Acid Test Ratio A liquidity ratio used to measure the extent of cash available to meet current debts. It is determined by dividing cash and receivables by current liabilities.

Active Corps of Executives Pool of consultants provided for small business operators by the SBA.

Actuaries Mathematical specialists who use the laws of averages and large numbers to predict life expectancies and construct mortality tables to show results.

Administrative Law Decisions from governmental agencies, with no specific legislative approval or judicial precedent, that become binding on businesses or individuals unless challenged and overruled in court.

Advertising Any paid form of nonpersonal presentation of ideas, goods, or services by an identified sponsor.

Advertising Agency An independent business which provides specialized advertising and marketing services to other businesses.

Affirmative Action Federal program requiring employers to be more responsible in the hiring of minorities and women.

Agency A legal relationship resulting from an agreement that someone, an agent, shall act in a legal capacity on behalf of another, the principal.

Analog Computer A computer designed to solve problems by measuring one quantity in terms of some other quantity. An analog computer is usually in constant operation.

Arbitration Help in reaching agreement by a neutral third party with the power to enforce whatever decision is reached.

Array Statistical data arranged as a listing in order of size usually from the highest to the lowest. It is usually the first step in processing raw data for further analysis.

Articles of Partnership A written contract that specifies the rights, responsibilities, and duties of each member in a partnership. Details concerning sharing of profits and losses, amount of time devoted to the business, and so forth, are carefully spelled out.

Assets Things of value owned by a business.

Auditing Procedure of verification whereby an independent Certified Public Accountant checks the accuracy and conformity of accounting records of clients.

Automation Machines operating or regulating other machines.

Balance of Payments The difference between all the money received from abroad and the money spent abroad by a country in a year.

Balance Sheet A formal statement of all the financial resources owned by a business as well as its debts.

Balance of Trade The difference between the money a country pays for imports and the money foreigners pay for exports.

Bankers' Acceptance Type of draft endorsed by a commercial bank.

Base Year Used in statistical indexing as the starting point against which all future periods will be computed. The base year index number is always 100.

Bayesian Approach A scientific process for aiding managers in their task of making decisions. The Bayesian approach places emphasis on recognizing the alternatives in any given situation, implementing a course of action, and evaluating the course of action by objective means.

Bear An investor who believes stock prices will fall.

Behavioral Science The study of ways to deal with people problems. In recent years the study of human behavior has become a very important aspect of management education.

Beneficiary The person who is to receive the proceeds of a life insurance policy upon the death of the insured.

Bid-and-asked Price quotations for stocks and bonds traded in the over-the-counter market.

Binary Code Numbering system based on zero and one used for calculation in the mechanical makeup of any computer.

Blue Sky Laws State legislation regulating corporate security sales.

Boycott Refusal by workers or consumers to purchase products or services from companies whose employees are on strike.

Brand A name, term, symbol, or design distinguishing the products of a seller from those of competitors.

Bull An investor who believes stock prices will rise.

Business Any organized effort to produce products or supply services demanded by people for the purpose of making a profit.

Business Cycle Fluctuations in economic activity which extend over a period of several years.

Business Profit As the businessperson calculates it: business income minus business expenses.

Capital Plant and equipment used to produce products and services. Also, the money to buy products and services. Also, the value of equity of the owners (stockholders) in the financial resources of their business. It can be found in dollars by subtracting the firm's total liabilities from total assets.

Capital Budget Long-range financial plans for the plant asset needs of a firm.

Capital Intensive Industry An industry that requires very large amounts of capital to provide facilities and equipment.

Capitalism An economic system in which the capital, or means of production, is owned by private individuals.

Capital Market Market where securities are bought and sold, representing long-term lending and borrowing of funds.

Cash Budget Short-range financial plan of the cash needs and revenue expectations of a firm; usually prepared for several future weekly or monthly periods.

Cash Surrender Value An element of savings that accumulates in certain types of life insurance policies that the insured may withdraw upon cancelling the protection.

Centralized Management A way of organizing a firm with many branches so that all important decisions and plans are made by management at the home office. High-speed computers aid greatly in making this type of organization effective.

Channel of Distribution The route followed by a product as it moves from producer to consumer.

Channels of Communication The ability to communicate plans, policies, problems, and instructions both up and down the management ladder.

Charter A written instrument granted by the proper state authority to those who desire the right to operate a business as a corporation.

Clean Air Act Legislation setting national air-quality standards to protect the public health.

Closed-end Investment Company A mutual fund whose shares are bought and sold through a broker like shares of stock in any corporation.

Closed Shop Only union members are hired by a firm.

CLU Abbreviation for Chartered Life Underwriter, which is a designation that can be earned by agents who take courses and pass rigorous examination in the area of life insurance protection.

COBOL (Common Business Oriented Language) A language composed of symbols and/or characters used most often in the programming of computers for business purposes.

Coinsurance Clause Provision in fire insurance policies that requires that the insured buy coverage up to a stipulated percentage of the value of the property, usually 80 percent. This clause prevents the insured from underinsuring in the expectation that financial losses on partially damaged property will be borne in total by the insurance company.

Collective Bargaining Negotiations between labor and management.

Command Economy An economic system in which most of the economic decisions are made through some command agency, such as a planning commission or a planning director.

Commercial Paper Short-term notes of large denomination and high interest rates issued by well-known corporations.

Common Carrier An independently owned shipper operating on a regular schedule between at least two points.

Common Market Economic unit composed of West Germany, France, Belgium, Luxembourg, the Netherlands, Italy, the United Kingdom, Ireland, and Denmark.

Community of Interest A few stockholders maintaining

control of competing corporations and, therefore, dominating the boards of directors of these companies and controlling the market.

Comparative Advantage A country's concentrating its production in the areas in which it has the greatest advantage over other countries.

Compensating Balance A requirement imposed on debtors by many banks to keep an amount on deposit in the bank during the period of a loan from the bank.

Competitive Advertising Advertising that convinces customers to buy a firm's product rather than that of a competitor.

Computation Section The section of the console that performs the necessary calculation tasks associated with a particular program.

Computer Electronically powered machine that computes, files, analyzes, summarizes, and stores data.

Conglomerate A parent corporation with subsidiaries acquired for their investment potential. It gains control of subsidiaries through acquisition of their assets or through exchanges of stock.

Console The heart and brain of all EDP systems where all the data is processed.

Consolidation The process in which two separate firms abandon their separate identities and organizations and form a new organization and identity. For example, A Corporation and B Corporation merge to form C Corporation.

Consumer Goods Those goods which are sold directly to the ultimate consumers.

Consumer Products Products manufactured for sale to a member of the public.

Consumerism A movement comprised of individuals, business firms, government agencies, and independent organizations who are concerned with consumers' rights.

Contingent Beneficiary An alternate beneficiary to a life insurance policy in the event the beneficiary and the insured die at the same time.

Contract Carrier An independently owned carrier transporting material over routes and schedules that are agreed upon with the shipper.

Contracts An agreement of a legal nature that binds the parties. It can sometimes be executed orally as well as in written form.

Control A primary function of management involved with observation and direction of the ongoing operations of the firm.

Control Equipment That part of the console that works from the instructions set forth in the program.

Convenience Goods Staples of low unit value, purchased frequently and in small quantities.

Coordination The know-how to blend the functions of planning, organization, and control into one smoothly running operation.

Copyright A right given and protected by law to prevent others from printing, copying or publishing a work resulting from creative effort and intellectual labor. Also, recognition by the federal government of the right of ownership to some written work.

Correlation A relationship that exists between two or more variables in statistical analysis.

Correspondent Banks Commercial banks that are affiliated with commercial banks in other geographical areas and serve as their agent.

Council of Economic Advisors Economists with outstanding qualifications and reputations who advise the president on matters of economic significance.

CPA Abbreviation for Certified Public Accountant, an individual who is licensed by the state to prepare audits, appear in court, and certify the financial statements of firms that are audited.

CPLU Abbreviation for Chapter Property and Liability Underwriter, a designation earned by agents who take courses and pass a rigorous examination in the area of life insurance protection.

Craft Union An association of workers skilled in a craft or trade.

Critical Path Method (CPM) An operations research tool used to trace the time required to complete various "paths" that ultimately lead to the completion of a project.

Culture The complex of symbols and artifacts created by people and handed down from generation to generation to determine and regulate human behavior in a given society.

Current Assets Assets that can be converted into cash fairly quickly.

Current Liabilities Debts owed by a business that are payable in one year or less.

Current Ratio A liquidity ratio that measures the availability of current assets for paying off current debt. It is found by dividing current assets by current liabilities.

Cyclical Fluctuations Describes the ups and downs in the economy that occur from time to time seemingly as a result of natural changes in the forces of supply and demand as well as other unforeseen influences.

Debt Financing Raising funds for a business through the sale of credit obligations.

Decentralized Management A firm organized so that branch managers are allowed to make a number of key plans and decisions about branch operations.

Demand Deposit A sum of money credited to a checking account.

Depreciation A decrease in the monetary value of a business asset because of deterioration from use and age.

Devaluation Reduction in the value of a country's currency as compared with that of another country.

Digital Computer A computer designed to solve problems by counting digits. Therefore, its main work is computation.

Direct Payment Cash wages paid to an employee at the end of a work period.

Discharge Permanent dismissal by the company.

Discounted Loan A bank loan on which the interest is deducted by the bank from the amount borrowed at the time the loan is granted.

Discretionary Income Disposable personal income minus fixed commitments and essential household needs.

Disposable Personal Income Personal income minus personal income taxes paid to the government.

Dow Jones Industrial Stock Index Popular daily average of 65 stocks on the New York Stock Exchange published in major newspapers and quoted on radio and television.

Economic Buying Motives The most effective use of a consumer's limited resources.

Economic System The organization that a country uses to balance unlimited wants and limited resources.

Elastic Demand Demand that changes as the result of a change in price for a given product.

Electronic Data Processing (EDP) The field of using sophisticated electronically powered and controlled equipment for the computing and processing of data.

Emotional Buying Motives Those motives that reflect the feelings of individuals about themselves or their relationships with others.

Endorsement The act of signing a negotiable instrument to signify that one will fulfill the terms of an instrument in case of default by the original maker.

Equity Financing Raising funds for a business by selling additional shares of ownership.

Escalator Clause A cost-of-living clause in a labor contract designed to protect workers from inflation.

Esprit de Corps A term that means pulling together as one unit toward clear objectives and with a common willingness to try as hard as possible to obtain those objectives.

Ethics The branch of philosophy that deals with the "right" and "wrong" of human behavior.

Export Agent Independent firm that represents several noncompeting firms abroad.

Exports Goods and services sold to another country.

Extrapolation The process of expanding known past data to infer future events; usually used in graphic analysis.

Factoring Houses Commercial finance companies that deal in the buying and lending of funds, using as collateral the accounts receivable of the borrowing corporation.

Factors of Production The elements essential to the production of products and services: land, labor, and capital.

Favorable Balance of Payments Receipts from foreign countries greater than payments to foreign countries.

Favorable Balance of Trade Selling more goods and services abroad than a country buys from foreign countries.

FDIC Abbreviation for Federal Deposit Insurance Corporation, which is the agency of the federal government that insures savings accounts up to $40,000.

Featherbedding Forcing employers to continue jobs that are no longer necessary.

FICA Abbreviation for Federal Insurance Contributions Act, the official name of the Social Security old age and life insurance program.

Fiscal Policy Manipulation by the Treasury Department of the federal budget and tax collections to influence the economy.

Fixed Assets Capital items owned by a business such as land, buildings, and equipment. Ordinarily it takes some time to convert these items into cash.

Fixed Costs The expenses a business has regardless of whether or not the plant is in operation.

Flow Chart An outline in diagram form of the logical

steps required for a computer to solve a problem and make a forecast.

Forbes Sales 500   List of the top 500 corporations in the United States ranked by gross sales for the operating year.

Foreign Branch   A division of a company located in a foreign country.

FORTRAN (Formula Translation)   A language composed of symbols and/or characters used most often in the solving of scientific and mathematical problems utilizing the computer.

Fortune 500   List of the top 500 industrial corporations ranked by gross sales for the operating year.

Franchise   An agreement between an individual and a national company granting the right to market or sell the company's products or services in a particular area.

Franchisee   The local small business owner who operates a franchise.

Franchisor   The national firm which grants franchise rights to a local small business.

Free Enterprise   An economic system in which individuals are free to go into any type of occupation or business they wish.

Frequency Distribution   A statistical table that is a condensation of an array which lists the various values and the number of times each value appears in the data.

Fringe Benefits   Extra benefits and services that are not part of direct payments.

Functional Organization   A pattern of organization where staff managers also have line management responsibilities and authority in certain areas of operations.

Funds   The sum of currency plus demand deposits (balances in checking accounts) used or accumulated for a specific purpose by a business firm.

General Partner   An owner in a partnership with full rights and responsibilities whose actions are legally binding on all partners.

Goal-oriented Behavior   Action by consumers which is motivated by needs which create tensions.

Government   The federal government and its many departments and agencies, as well as all state and local governments.

Gross National Product (GNP)   The total value of products and services produced by an economy in a year.

Gross Profit   The difference between revenues and the cost of the merchandise sold. Represents the dollar markup on merchandise sold by the business.

Group Insurance Plan   Insurance policies that are a part of pension, mutual fund programs, and the like.

Hardware Equipment   The individual machines, such as the keypunch machine and the computer itself, that comprise a particular system.

Hedging   A protective procedure used in commodity trading designed to minimize losses in commodity marketing and processing that result from adverse price fluctuations. Also, a management technique protecting a firm against uninsurable economic loss whereby a firm simultaneously places buy and sell orders for its raw materials, thus offsetting any increase in the purchase price.

Holding Company   A corporation, referred to as the parent, that owns a controlling number of shares of stock in other corporations, known as subsidiaries.

Human Relations   Managers' ability to combine sensitivity to the needs of workers and customers with firmness in giving orders necessary to get the various jobs done.

Imports   Goods and services bought from other countries.

Income Statement   A financial statement that lists the revenues, costs, and expenses of the firm and the net profit resulting from operations.

Indenture   A written contract between the borrowing corporation and the creditors containing all the pertinent conditions relating to a specific bond issue.

Index Number   A statistical procedure that compares value changes in one period of time to a stable value in a former period of time known as a base period. The consumer price index is the best known of all index numbers.

Industrial Goods   Those goods sold for business use or for additional processing before being sold to the ultimate consumer.

Industrial Products   Products sold to other businesses.

Industrial Union   Association in one union of all the workers in an industry, regardless of the type of work they do.

Inelastic Demand   Demand that does not change as the result of a change in price for the product.

Injunction   A court order forbidding members of organized labor from engaging in some action against the employer.

Input Devices   Various materials such as magnetic tape

and punched cards that serve to feed data into the processing unit of an EDP system.

Institutional Advertising Advertising that tries to build prestige or status for a firm or an industry.

Institutional Investors Institutions such as mutual funds or pension funds that buy and sell stocks and bonds in large quantities for their portfolios, which represent the savings of many individuals and business firms.

Insured The person or business whose life, health, or property is financially protected by insurance.

Insurer The insurance company that provides protection to the individual or business.

Interlocking Directorate The same people who form a majority of the board of directors of two or more corporations and who direct the policy of each corporation for purposes of restraint of trade.

Intermediate-term Funds Funds needed by a business for a period of one to five years.

Interurban Areas Areas of large population formed when two or more large metropolitan areas grow together.

Investments Those assets owned by the firm in the form of stocks and bonds of other corporations or government units.

Job Analysis Study of the specific tasks in a job and the environment in which they are performed.

Job Classification The process of rating the value of jobs to a firm.

Job Description The written report of the job analysis.

Joint Stock Company Form of business organization containing certain features of a partnership as well as of a corporation. Ownership is represented by shares of stock, but each owner has unlimited liability.

Joint Venture Similar in organization to a partnership except that management is usually delegated to one individual. A joint venture is established for an undertaking of short duration.

Key Personnel Insurance Insurance on the life of a key employee of a firm stating that the firm is the beneficiary of the policy.

Keynesian Theory Concept devised by economist John Maynard Keynes that government should be involved in increasing employment by monetary and fiscal methods at its disposal.

Labor All the workers in a country.

Land All the natural resources used in production.

Law of Averages Mathematical concept stating that if your computation is based on a very large number of similar risks, a certain number of predictable losses will occur.

Law of Large Numbers Mathematical concept stating that the larger the number of cases used to compute the data, the closer will the actual experience approximate the predicted outcome.

Ledger A book or file of the firm's accounts.

Liabilities Debts owed to others by the business.

License The right to make a product over which a company has exclusive control in its own country.

Limited Liability Liability in a firm limited to one's investment in the firm, as is the case with the stockholder in a corporation.

Limited Partner An owner in a partnership who does not have all the rights and powers of a general partner but who enjoys the protection of limited liability.

Line Organization A pattern of organization in which responsibility and authority clearly flow from the superior to the subordinate all the way down the management ladder.

Line-and-Staff Organization A pattern of organization in which staff managers who are experts in specialized fields work with the line managers to improve the operations of the firm.

Liquidity The ability to turn an investment or asset into cash quickly. Also, the case with which an investor can sell his investment (such as stock in a corporation) to another.

Listed Security A security that is regularly traded on an organized stock exchange such as the New York Stock Exchange.

Load Fund A mutual fund that charges a selling commission to the purchaser of its shares.

Lobbying The effort to influence federal, state, and local government legislation.

Lockout Refusal of an employer to permit employees to work.

Long-term Funds Funds needed by a business for a term of five years or longer.

Long-term Liabilities Debts owed by a business that are payable in a period of time exceeding one year.

Maker A person who borrows by issuing a note to a creditor.

Management The process by which those in authority plan, organize, and control a business in an effort to make it successful.

Management Aids A free series of publications of the SBA with tips for managing small firms.

Market People with wants and the money to satisfy them. Also, any place where buyers and sellers get together.

Market Penetration Pricing Strategy implying that the producer will sell the product at a relatively low price to build quickly a wide market for the product.

Market Segmentation Dividing a total, heterogeneous market into several submarkets or segments, each of which tends to be homogeneous in all significant aspects.

Marketing Business activities that direct the flow of goods and services from producer to consumer or user to satisfy customers and accomplish the company's objectives.

Marketing Concept A firm's perception of what its customers want.

Marketing Mix The blending of product, price, promotion, and place.

Marketing Research The search for facts significant in the management of marketing activities.

Marketing Strategy A plan for accomplishing the growth objectives of a firm.

Markup Pricing products at cost plus a fixed percentage.

Mass Production The large-scale production of goods using mechanization, specialization of labor, standardization, and automation.

Mean A measure of central tendency that represents the arithmetic average of a series of numerical values; used in statistics to determine the average value among a series of data.

Measure of Central Tendency A statistical device that indicates where one piece of data stands in relationship to a whole series of data.

Mechanization The use of machines to do as much work as possible.

Median A measure of central tendency represented by the number in a series of data which divides the series in half.

Mediation An attempt to settle a labor dispute or grievance through the assistance of a neutral third person.

Merger When two or more firms join together to form a new firm which is known by the name of one of the old firms. For example, A Corporation (older and larger) and B Corporation merge into A Corporation.

Microprocessors A single integrated circuit that contains much but not all of the ability of a computer.

Middleman An independent business firm that stands between the producer and the ultimate consumer or industrial user.

Middle Management Those managers who implement the decisions of top management as well as make lower-level decisions regarding operations of the firm.

Military-industrial Complex Threat that too much of the country's wealth would be spent on military programs.

Minicomputers Small computers that can perform many of the basic functions that a complete computer can. but they are much less expensive to buy and operate.

Minimum Wage The lowest hourly wage that can be paid to an employee who is covered by federal minimum wage legislation.

Minority Enterprise Small Business Investment Corporation (MESBIC) Small business lending agency specifically established for the purpose of making loans to minority small business operators.

Mode A measure of central tendency represented by the number in a series of data that occurs most often. If no value appears more than once in a series, there is no mode.

Modified Market Economy An economic system in which most of the major economic decisions are made in the market, but in which some are made outside the market by the government and other groups.

Monetary Policy Regulating the supply of money and credit outstanding to influence the economy.

Money Market The marketplace where short-term securities are bought and sold.

Money Supply Cash and demand deposits (balances in checking accounts) outstanding in the economy.

Monopoly The takeover of a market for a particular product or service by one supplier. Also, only one seller in a market.

Morale The feeling employees have toward their jobs, their fellow workers, and the company.

Multinational Firm A company with sales over $100 million, operations in at least six countries, and overseas subsidiaries accounting for at least 20 percent of its assets.

Mutual Company A type of business organization where ownership rests in the hands of the firm's customers or clients. Policyholders in a mutual insurance company are also owners of the company.

National Brand A brand owned by a manufacturer.

National Income The total income which is earned by

those who contribute to production, including employee wages and salaries, corporate profits, rental income, and interest income.

National Labor Relations Board Federal agency that administers the provisions of the Wagner Act in settling disputes and in determining unfair practices.

Nationalization A national government's assuming ownership of a privately owned business.

Need The lack of anything that is required, useful, or desired.

Negotiable Instruments Credit instruments that not only serve as evidence of indebtedness but are also widely used as substitutes for money. Checks and notes are examples of negotiable instruments.

Net Worth An accounting term for capital. See definition under Capital.

No-fault Auto Insurance Insurance that eliminates certain court procedures because bodily injury and property damage claims up to a specified amount are settled with one's own insurance carrier.

No-load Fund A mutual fund that does not charge a selling commission to the purchaser of its shares.

Notes Written evidence of a debt prepared by the borrower and held by the lender until paid.

Odd Lot A purchase or sale of 99 shares of stock or less.

Oligopoly Few sellers in a market.

On-line A computer that is constantly available to receive, process, and remit information to a number of branches in a matter of moments.

On-the-job Training Learning the details of a trade while actually doing the job at the work station.

Open Book Trading Buying on credit from suppliers with 30 to 60 days to pay bills.

Open Book Account Usual billing procedure between wholesalers and retailers, where up to 60 days grace is given between date of billing and date of required payment of bills.

Open-end Investment Company A mutual fund that sells its shares directly to the public and buys them back from holders at current asset value.

Operating Expenses Costs incurred in running a business.

Operating Management Those managers on the lowest level who supervise the day-to-day operations in some part of the business.

Operations Research (OR) A type of decision-making procedure using scientific and mathematical techniques.

Opportunity Cost The cost to a firm of not using its resources in some other way.

Optical Scanning Device A machine that can read certain types of printed or handwritten matter and convert them into data for the computer.

Organization The roadway along which planning will be carried out.

Output Devices Various materials such as magnetic tape and punched cards that receive information processed by the computer.

Over-the-counter Market The marketplace where stocks and bonds of corporations not listed on organized stock exchanges are traded.

Patent A legal grant entitling the holder to prevent others from making, selling, or using a particular invention for profit-making purposes for a period of years. Also, a grant by the federal government of an exclusive right to some invention.

Payee The lender in a note transaction and therefore the party to whom a promissory note is made out.

Personal Income All income of individuals, regardless of source.

Personal Selling A direct face-to-face relationship between the seller and potential customer.

Personnel Management Concerned with attracting, developing, utilizing, and maintaining a work force.

Personalty A legal term meaning all forms of property except real estate owned by a business or individual.

Picket A union member demonstrating against an employer during a strike action. Pickets usually carry signs explaining why they are on strike. Members of other unions generally do not cross picket lines.

Piece-rate System A certain amount of pay per hour plus a bonus for producing more than a certain number of items.

Planned Obsolescence The deliberate designing of a product so that it will not be usable after a short period of time.

Planning A primary function of management concerned with determining what to produce and how to produce it.

Plant Assets An accounting term for fixed assets. See definition of Fixed Assets.

Policyholder The insured individual or business.

Pollution Deterioration of the human or natural environment.

Portfolio All of the stocks that an investor possesses.

Power of attorney A form of agency in which an agent is empowered to act on a principal's behalf in executing a legal transaction.

Premium The cost of purchasing an insurance policy.

Price Discrimination A supplier's charging different prices to different purchasers for the same products.

Primary Advertising Advertising that builds primary demand for a product category, rather than a specific brand.

Primary Data Facts originated by the researcher to solve a problem under study. Also, data gathered through an original source such as an interview.

Primary Market The market where brand-new issues of stocks and bonds are sold from the issuing corporation to the investing public.

Principle of Indemnity The principle that states that a person or business may not collect more than any actual cash loss in the event of damage caused by an insured hazard.

Private Brand A brand owned by a middleman.

Private Carriers A means of transportation owned and operated by the shipper.

Private Placement The sale of new securities from the issuing corporation to one or several investors.

Private Warehouse A place for storing and handling goods which is owned by the company whose goods are stored.

Product Any tangible item. Also, whatever satisfies customers whether it has tangible or intangible characteristics or some combination of both.

Product Advertising Informing or stimulating potential customers about a firm's products and services.

Product Development The process of developing products that customers desire.

Product Life Cycle A cyclical pattern of sales and profit margins for a product.

Production The process of converting raw materials into useful goods.

Productivity The efficiency with which goods and services are being produced.

Profit Money gained by selling a product or service for more than it cost to produce or supply.

Profit-sharing A share of the company's profits distributed to the employees.

Program Instructions prepared by individuals, known as programmers that tell the computer what to do, when to do it, and how to do it.

Program Evaluation and Review Technique (PERT) A network flow chart that estimates the time involved in the completion of various projects that make up a project.

Promotion Job change with an increase in duties and responsibilities, and a probable increase in pay. Also, all of the personal selling, advertising, sales promotion, and other tools a company uses to persuade a prospective customer to buy a product or service.

Proprietorship An accounting term for capital. See definition of Capital.

Prospectus A booklet containing pertinent financial and other information required by law to be given to every potential buyer of new issues of corporate stocks or bonds.

Public Goods and Services Goods and services produced by all levels of government.

Public Warehouse A place for storing and handling goods that is available to any business which needs it.

Pure Risk Risk that results from everyday events rather than from taking a chance on a new product.

Quick Asset Ratio An accounting term for acid test ratio. See Acid Test Ratio.

Quotas Limits on the amount or volume of products that can be imported.

Realty A legal term meaning all forms of land and buildings.

Reminder Advertising Advertising that reminds customers that they still like an established product.

Resources Recovery Act Legislation containing guidelines for solid-waste disposal and encouraging recycling of solid waste.

Restraint of Trade Illegal takeover of the market for a particular product or service by one supplier.

Retained Earnings Profits kept in the business to serve as a source of funds for future business needs.

Revenue Sharing Turning over some federal tax revenues as supplements to the budgets of the states.

Right-to-work Clause A state law that prevents union shops.

Round Lot A purchase or sale of shares of stock in multiples of 100.

Sales Branch A separate sales organization of a company in a foreign country.

Sales Promotion The promotional activities necessary to supplement personal selling and advertising.

Seasonal Changes Predictable variations in economic activity resulting from the changing of seasons.

Seat Membership by a brokerage firm in an organized stock exchange.

Secondary Boycott Refusal by union members to handle the products of another company whose employees are on strike.

Secondary Data Data obtained from reading the results of other surveys, not from a statistical gathering of primary data. Statistics based on data published by the Bureau of the Census would be an example of secondary data. Also, data collected for some purpose other than the one at hand.

Secondary Market Market where issues of stocks and bonds are resold, such as the New York Stock Exchange.

Secret Partner A member of a partnership who is not known by the general public to be a partner.

Sectors of the Economy Groups which buy the output of the economy, including consumers, government, business, and foreign purchasers.

Securities and Exchange Commission Federal regulating agency for security trading.

Self-insurance A technique by which a business periodically sets aside cash reserves to be drawn upon only in the event of a financial loss resulting from a misfortune of the pure risk type.

Seniority Length of time on the job.

Service Performance of work by a business for pay.

Service Corps of Retired Executives (SCORE) Retired executives and those in related fields who volunteer through the SBA to help small business operators solve problems.

Shopping Goods Merchandise whose price, fashion, and quality are important enough to require comparison shopping.

Short-term Funds Funds needed by a business for a term of one year or less.

Silent Partner A member of a partnership who does not participate in setting policy or managing the partnership.

Simulation Constructing a situation that closely resembles the actual conditions for the purpose of testing.

Skimming Pricing Strategy implying that the producer will sell the product for as high a price as he can get to maximize his total revenue.

Slowdown Strike Workers staying on the job, but working at a slower pace than normal.

Small Business Administration (SBA) Agency of the federal government which facilitates lending and gives management assistance to small businesses.

Small Business Investment Corporation (SBIC) Privately owned financial corporations aided by the SBA which makes loans to small business firms.

Small Marketer's Aids A free series of publications of the SBA with tips on marketing for small business.

Social Audit A listing of a firm's social contributions and their cost to the company.

Social Class A group of people who have many of the same values and goals based on their income, occupation, housing, and residence area.

Software Equipment Aids that facilitate the programming of the computer. Paper punched cards, magnetic tape, and even the program itself are examples of computer software.

Span of Control The largest number of workers or subordinate managers that a superior can effectively and efficiently supervise.

Specialization of Labor Concentration by workers on single jobs, each job requiring that only a few tasks be performed.

Specialty Goods Merchandise of a distinctive quality in which price is not an important consideration.

SPIC Abbreviation for Securities Protection Insurance Corporation which insures a customer's cash or securities left with a brokerage firm up to $50,000.

Spread Difference between the selling and buying price of a new stock or bond issue handled by an investment banker. The profit comes out of this difference in price.

Standardization The development of uniform methods of operation within a plant.

Statement of Capital or Retained Earnings A financial statement to show changes in capital investments over a designated period of time. If the statement relates to a sole proprietorship or partnership, it is known as a statement of capital. If it relates to a corporation, it is known as a statement of retained earnings.

Subchapter S Corporation A domestic corporation with 10 or fewer stockholders which files its federal income tax return as a partnership to take advantage of lower tax rates when appropriate.

Syndication Similar to a joint venture organization except it is strictly involved with financial ventures.

Systems Analyst A specially trained engineer who works with a business to design the system most appropriate to the needs of that particular firm.

Target Marketing Directing the efforts of the firm to serving the segment of the market in which it has an advantage over potential competitors.

Tariff A tax on imports.

Test Market A geographical area in which a company introduces a new product.

Theory X The theory of management that states that work is distasteful and people do it only for economic survival. Therefore, the normal individual must be coerced and threatened to get the job done.

Theory Y The theory of management that states that work is as normal as play. The average worker can learn to accept and even seek responsibility if the rewards and recognitions are clear and worthwhile.

Thermal Pollution Heated water discharged from nuclear generators returned to lakes and streams that harms aquatic life.

Time Sharing An arrangement by which a firm may lease time for computer use from a computer leasing company. The leased time could be on-line or be based on a portion of time.

Top Management The level of management that makes or reviews all the most important decisions with regard to planning, organization, and control of the firm.

Transactional Analysis (TA) An approach to understanding human behavior based on how people relate to each other. TA is one area in the behavioral science aspect of management.

Transfer A shift from one position to another without an increase in duties, responsibilities, or pay.

Trend Analysis A statistical device (sometimes referred to as time series analysis) using historical data as it relates to identifiable time periods and attempts to forecast shifts in the economy.

Trustee A person and corporate body with the legal responsibility to represent the bondholders and enforce their rights under provisions of an indenture.

Trusts A combination of businesses controlled by one major firm and its board of directors.

Tying Contracts An agreement stating that the vendor requires the buyer of a certain commodity to agree to buy other products from the same vendor as a condition of the sale.

Underwriter An investment banker who buys a new security issue from a corporation and then sells it through syndication to the investing public.

Unemployed Persons The number of people 16 years of age or older who are registered with an employment office, but who are without jobs.

Unfavorable Balance of Payments Payments to foreign countries greater than receipts from foreign countries.

Unfavorable Balance of Trade Buying more from foreign countries than a country sells to them.

Union Shop Place of employment in which an employee does not have to be a member of the recognized union, but must either join it after a period of time on the job or pay union dues.

Universe Synonymous with "population." The area or total environment of data to be analyzed and interpreted in a statistical problem.

Unlimited Liability The legal obligation of investors to use personal assets when necessary to pay off the debt claims of business creditors. All sole proprietors and general partners are subject to unlimited liability.

Variable Costs Costs that change with the volume of production.

Vestibule Training Learning a job in a special type of classroom or vestibule which duplicates the work environment.

Walkout Strike Workers staying off the job to enforce their collective bargaining demands.

Want Something desired but less basic than a need to the existence of mankind.

Water Quality Act Law establishing guidelines for cleaning the navigable streams and lakes of the country.

Wildcat Strike Workers walking off the job without the sanction of their union leaders.

INDEX